THE LIBRARY OF
SOUTHERN CIVILIZATION

THE LIBRARY OF
SOUTHERN CIVILIZATION

Lewis P. Simpson, Editor

*Twelve Years a Slave,* by Solomon Northup
Edited by Sue Eakin and Joseph Logsdon

*Bricks Without Straw,* by Albion Tourgée
Edited by Otto H. Olsen

*Still Rebels, Still Yankees and Other Essays,*
by Donald Davidson

*The Diary of Edmund Ruffin*
Edited by William Kauffman Scarborough

# THE DIARY OF
# EDMUND RUFFIN

Edmund Ruffin in military array, April 19, 1861

# THE DIARY OF
# EDMUND RUFFIN

⤳

**VOLUME I**
## TOWARD INDEPENDENCE
### October, 1856–April, 1861

EDITED, WITH AN INTRODUCTION
AND NOTES, BY
## WILLIAM KAUFFMAN SCARBOROUGH

*With a Foreword by*
## *AVERY CRAVEN*

Louisiana State University Press
Baton Rouge
1972

ISBN 0–8071–0948–7
Library of Congress Catalog Card Number 75–165069
Copyright © 1972 by Louisiana State University Press
All rights reserved
Manufactured in the United States of America
Printed by The TJM Corporation, Baton Rouge, Louisiana
Designed by Jules B. McKee

FOR CATHY AND BRAD

"If Virginia remains in the Union, under the domination of this infamous, low, vulgar tyranny of Black Republicanism, and there is one other State in the Union that has bravely thrown off the yoke, I will seek my domicile in that State and abandon Virginia forever. If Virginia will not act as South Carolina, I have no longer a home, and I am a banished man."

Edmund Ruffin, November 16, 1860—Addressing a crowd in Charleston, South Carolina

# Contents

*Contents*

# Foreword

Edmund Ruffin has been called the father of soil chemistry in the United States. His *Farmers' Register* is still rated as one of the very best agricultural publications ever issued either in Europe or in this country. The agricultural revolution which cleared the wreckage left by tobacco as the single cash crop in colonial Virginia and Maryland was due in no small part to his teachings and practices. His *Essay on Calcareous Manures* is still considered something of a masterpiece and has been republished only recently by one of our university presses.

Edmund Ruffin's fame, however, rests primarily on the part which he played in bringing on the Civil War. He early became an ardent advocate of southern independence. He even saw his efforts to revive southern agriculture as a way of increasing and holding her population and making her independent of northern supplies. He defended slavery as good for both the Negro and the white man. In the end he became a kind of Peter the Hermit going about from one seceding convention to another to encourage action. As a reward for his efforts he was chosen to fire one of the first guns on Fort Sumter. And when the Confederacy came to an end he took his own life with a parting denunciation of all things Yankee.

Edmund Ruffin kept a diary of unusual quality. It provides a valuable insight into the psychology of an unusual man in an unusual situation. Perhaps it sheds some light on the psychology of a whole people on their course to revolution. It has great value for the agricultural historian and even for the practical agriculturist of our own day. To a nation now trying to bring its Civil War to a just conclusion it is filled with lessons. Its publication has long been overdue.

AVERY CRAVEN

# Introduction

It was a mild night, unseasonably warm for December and in marked contrast to the snow and ice which had impeded the old man's journey from his native Virginia a few days before. The outside atmosphere complemented the feeling of exultation which coursed through his body as he sat writing in his small room at the Charleston Hotel. When a gentle breeze wafted to his ears the martial air of a distant band, the solitary figure paused for a moment, then laid aside his pen and moved slowly to the window to gaze upon the scene below. Crowds of people wandered aimlessly through the streets, their joyful countenances revealed in the light cast by barrels of burning pine resin; some of the younger demonstrators set off firecrackers; military companies paraded in their splendid new uniforms; and periodic cheers rent the air as the bells of St. Philip's and St. Michael's tolled in the background. It was a fitting climax to the day, mused the venerable old Virginian, as he returned to his seat to contemplate the events which had engendered the celebration outside.

Little more than an hour before, Edmund Ruffin had been present in Secession Hall to witness the formal signing of the Ordinance of Secession. Tears of joy had welled in his eyes as General David F. Jamison, president of the convention, held aloft the parchment and proclaimed South Carolina to be a free and independent state. And so, on this twentieth day of December, 1860, the die had been cast. The movement for which he had labored so long and so zealously had at last begun. South Carolina had been the first. Mississippi, Florida, and Alabama would soon follow. He would go on to Tallahassee, and then to Montgomery if time permitted, to lend his support to the patriots and bolster the spirits of the faint-hearted. With the states of the Deep South securely bound together in a southern confederacy, the Upper South and border states would soon have no alternative but to join their sister states to the south. The "secession cannon" in front of the *Courier* office would boom again and again until—hopefully before Lincoln's inauguration—fourteen or possibly fifteen reports had sounded. Then, with all the slaveholding states presenting a united front, the abolition states would not dare to assume a hostile posture. Southern independence would be a reality!

I

Edmund Ruffin was one of the most significant figures in the Old South. Southern gentleman, farmer, writer, political commentator—he was all of these and more. His most enduring claim to fame derives from his contributions as the foremost agricultural reformer in the antebellum South. For ten years he edited the *Farmers' Register,* one of the most noted agricultural periodicals of his time. His famous *Essay on Calcareous Manures,* in which he expounded the gospel of marl, went through five editions and, as late as 1895, was hailed by a Department of Agriculture expert as "the most thorough piece of work on a special agricultural subject ever published in the English language." [1] He revitalized agriculture in the Upper South and conducted agricultural surveys of the two Carolinas. His Virginia plantations, Marlbourne and Beechwood, became models which others sought to emulate.

But, despite his universally acclaimed accomplishments in the field of agriculture, it was as a political extremist that Ruffin probably gained greatest notoriety. A militant defender of slavery, Ruffin, along with William Lowndes Yancey of Alabama and Robert Barnwell Rhett of South Carolina, is considered one of the foremost southern secessionists. Throughout the 1850's, in personal conversations and letters as well as by articles in various newspapers and periodicals—most notably in Rhett's Charleston *Mercury*—Ruffin sought to convince his fellow Southerners that their interests could not be protected while they remained in a Union increasingly dominated by northern abolitionists and radicals. When, in 1861, his labors were crowned with success, Ruffin was elevated to the status of a popular hero and was accorded the honor of firing the first shot in the Confederate bombardment of Fort Sumter. Following the war, his hopes and dreams shattered and his worldly goods scattered to the four winds, the despondent old Virginian took his own

---

[1] Avery O. Craven, *Edmund Ruffin, Southerner: A Study in Secession* (New York: D. Appleton and Company, 1932), 56.

life rather than endure the anticipated hardships of Yankee Reconstruction.

In his massive diary of twenty-five manuscript volumes, Ruffin has left an invaluable primary account of the crucial years from 1856 to 1865. Not only was Ruffin an intelligent and astute commentator on the events which occurred during the period of the journal, he was personally acquainted with most of the prominent southern political figures of his day. Moreover, his restless nature impelled him to "go where the action was." He was physically present as an observer or participant in the following events, all of which are covered in the first volume of the diary: the Southern Commercial Convention in Montgomery, Alabama (1858); the execution of John Brown; the Democratic Party conventions in Richmond and Baltimore (1860); the secession conventions of South Carolina, Florida, and Virginia; and the Fort Sumter engagement, in which he served as a private in the Palmetto Guard. He was constantly in either written or oral communication with governors, congressmen, state legislators, judges, and prominent private citizens. His own writings are voluminous. "Few men have written more," states his biographer. And the most comprehensive and informative of all his writings is this diary, which, it is hoped, will take its place with those of Gideon Welles, George Templeton Strong, and Mary Boykin Chesnut among the most significant diaries of the Civil War period.

## II

Born on January 5, 1794, Edmund was a seventh-generation descendant of William Ruffin, who immigrated to Virginia in 1666.[2] His father, George Ruffin, owned one of the great James River plantations, Evergreen, located on the south bank at Coggin's Point in Prince George County. Edmund received the usual upbringing accorded children of a tidewater aristocratic family and, at age sixteen, he matriculated at William and Mary College. However, his formal schooling was soon terminated by the untimely death of his father and by an amorous attachment with a Williamsburg girl, Susan Travis, whom he married in 1811. The following year his patriotic ardor induced him to enlist as a private in the militia after the outbreak of war with Great Britain. Though exposed to hard-

---

[2] Unless otherwise indicated, the following discussion is based upon Avery Craven's brilliant biography of Ruffin and upon the diary itself.

ships for which his previous background ill prepared him, he saw no action and was mustered out after six months of service to embark upon a career as a Virginia gentleman-farmer—a career destined to last forty-four years.

Ruffin's initial years as a tidewater Virginia agriculturist were not spectacularly successful, to say the least. Two centuries of soil exploitation under the one-crop system and poor agricultural practices had transformed the once-fertile region of eastern Virginia into a veritable wasteland. Undaunted, the young farmer began to experiment, at first without success. Finally, after reading Sir Humphry Davy's *Elements of Agricultural Chemistry*, he began to see a solution. The sterile soils of his neighborhood, Ruffin suspected, were afflicted with excessive vegetable acidity which had to be neutralized by some agent before the application of animal and vegetable manures could increase productivity. The solution was marl, a shell-like deposit consisting primarily of clay mixed with calcium carbonate, which was abundantly available in the desolated area. Early in 1818 Ruffin commenced marling operations on his Coggin's Point property, and that autumn he presented to his county agricultural society the first of his many provocative and enlightening papers on agricultural topics. His experiment proved an immediate success—within a few years his wheat crop had increased fourfold—and he soon set out to disseminate the gospel of marl to other farmers in his region and, indeed, throughout the South.

In the summer of 1829 Ruffin moved his residence to Shellbanks, a poor but healthy place situated about three miles from his Coggin's Point estate. During his six-year sojourn at Shellbanks he turned his attention to other activities and began to devote less time to the management of his farm.[3] From 1833 to 1842 Ruffin was engaged chiefly with the publication of his heralded agricultural journal, the *Farmers' Register*. In 1835 he moved with his family to the town of Petersburg, where he continued his editorial activities. Four years later, Ruffin's eldest son, Edmund, Jr., purchased a half-interest in the Coggin's Point property, now called Beechwood, and assumed full responsibility for its management. This arrangement continued until 1848, when the younger Ruffin procured the remainder of the

---

[3] Edmund Ruffin, "Incidents of My Life" (MS in Edmund Ruffin Papers and Books, Southern Historical Collection, University of North Carolina, Chapel Hill), II, 104.

farm from his father for a total consideration of $21,600.[4] By this time Edmund, Jr., had acquired a second plantation, Evelynton, located across the river about five miles from his domicile at Beechwood. The new tract, for which the younger Ruffin paid $10,000, contained 900 acres, of which 350 were cleared and the remainder in woodland.[5] Beechwood was considerably larger, with more than 700 acres of arable land and a six-field system of crop rotation in use.[6] Overseers were utilized on both places, and the combined slave force eventually numbered about 130.[7] Edmund, Jr., continued to operate both plantations until the summer of 1862, when farming operations were disrupted by the war.

Meanwhile, the elder Ruffin's increasingly controversial editorial pronouncements—particularly his tirades against banks and bankers—led to such a decline in subscriptions to the *Farmers' Register* that he was finally compelled in December, 1842, to abandon publication of the journal. That same month he accepted an invitation from Governor James H. Hammond to make an agricultural survey of South Carolina—a service which occupied him throughout most of the year 1843. Although many South Carolina planters greeted his enthusiasm for the benefits of marl with characteristic skepticism they were more receptive to his political views, now tending toward disunion. As he traversed the state, visiting one plantation after another, analyzing the soil and offering recommendations on the basis of his findings, Ruffin encountered some of the most prominent men in South Carolina and formed lasting associations with many of them.[8] Indeed, such was the empathy generated between him and his new-found friends that he ever afterwards looked upon South Carolina as his second home. He and Governor Hammond developed a close personal friendship and exchanged letters and visits frequently during the next two decades.

Having relinquished the personal management of both Beech-

---

[4] *Ibid.*, 139–41.

[5] Edmund Ruffin, Jr., to Edmund Ruffin, January 13, 1848, in Edmund Ruffin Papers and Books.

[6] Edmund Ruffin, Jr., Plantation Diary (MS in Southern Historical Collection, University of North Carolina, Chapel Hill), January 1, 1851.

[7] *Ibid.*, September 23, 1861, February 15, 1862.

[8] For a comprehensive account of Ruffin's experiences as agricultural surveyor of South Carolina, see his diary for the year 1843, listed as MS Volume 2 in the Edmund Ruffin Papers and Books.

wood and Shellbanks, Ruffin sought to acquire a new farm when he returned to Virginia in the fall of 1843. This was accomplished in October with the purchase of Marlbourne, a tract of 977 acres on the Pamunkey River in Hanover County. He moved from Petersburg to his new plantation on January 18, 1844, and during the next decade transformed the property into a model estate.[9] In 1849 he purchased two adjoining tracts containing 623 acres, thus raising the total acreage at Marlbourne to an even 1,600.[10] With a working force of only 25–30 hands, the veteran agriculturist produced an average of more than 4,000 bushels of wheat and some 3,700 bushels of corn per annum. He constructed an elaborate system of covered drains, applied large quantities of marl, and by these and other means increased the productivity of his property dramatically. Within eight years, the average corn yield per acre had more than doubled.[11] So impressive were his accomplishments that in 1849 Ruffin published in the *American Farmer* a detailed account of his operations during the five preceding years. The article, entitled "Farming Profits in Eastern Virginia: The Value of Marl," revealed that from a net loss of $74.23 in 1844, farm income from Marlbourne had risen to show a net profit of $5,810.06 in 1848.

Having demonstrated beyond doubt his success as an agricultural entrepreneur, Ruffin decided, at the end of 1854, to retire from the active management of his farm. He turned over the direction of Marlbourne to his second son, Julian, who, since 1843, had operated a modest 350-acre tract named Ruthven, situated just a few miles from Beechwood in Prince George County.[12] The agreement had scarcely been consummated, however, when Julian was obliged by family responsibilities to return to Ruthven. Thereupon, Ruffin decided to liquidate his estate, reckoned to be worth almost $150,000, and to divide his property—after reserving $25,000 for himself— among his six living children. The new joint owners appointed as resident superintendent of Marlbourne William Sayre, husband of Ruffin's second daughter, Elizabeth. The transfer of property was executed in 1856, and Edmund Ruffin, now sixty-two years of age, set out to conquer a new horizon—this one political rather than agricultural.

---

[9] Ruffin, "Incidents of My Life" (Ruffin Papers and Books), II, 161–62.
[10] *Ibid.,* 233.
[11] Statement of Marlbourne Grain Crop, 1844–53, *ibid.,* 253.
[12] Ruthven Farm Journal (MS in Ruffin Papers and Books), 1–2.

## III

Like others of his class in the Old South, Ruffin had displayed an early interest in politics and statecraft. In 1823 he was elected to a four-year term in the Virginia Senate, but after three years of service he was so disillusioned and disgusted with the game of politics that he tendered his resignation. Never again did Ruffin offer his name to the electorate for any public office. He was too much a man of principle, too candid, too much a party maverick, and too little disposed to compromise ever to achieve success in the political arena. Other shortcomings were even more deleterious. He was particularly aware of his deficiencies as a public speaker, a near-fatal obstacle to political success in the antebellum South. Moreover, as the years passed and he assumed more radical positions on the key issues of the day, he became so estranged from the majority of the Virginia electorate that it would have been sheer folly for him to stand for election to any important governmental post. In South Carolina it might have been different; but in the Old Dominion Ruffin was politically impotent until after the firing on Sumter. And so the crusty Virginian wisely eschewed active participation in politics to devote his talents to agriculture, and in that pursuit, as former President John Tyler once observed, did "more good to the country than all our political great men put together."

Perhaps the failure to achieve political popularity in his home state contributed to Ruffin's abhorrence of democracy and all its trappings—universal suffrage, party loyalties, and the machinery of popular conventions. He was thoroughly Hamiltonian in his distrust of the masses and belief in rule by the elite, albeit an intellectual rather than an economic elite. He had little confidence in a system which seemed to reward mediocrity and penalize merit, a system which facilitated the rise of popular demagogues who manipulated the ignorant masses in order to promote their own selfish interests. As an example of what might be achieved without recourse to popular elections and universal suffrage, he cited the selection by the Montgomery convention of 1861 of Jefferson Davis and Alexander H. Stephens, "who, for intellectual ability & moral worth, are superior to any President & Vice-President, elected together, of the United States since Madison's administration." So discouraged did Ruffin become with the evolution of the American experiment in democracy that in May, 1860, he predicted, "Our political condition will

*Introduction*

gradually grow worse—until, to save ourselves from the worst of political evils, the rule of demagogues sustained by the mass of the most ignorant & vicious of the people, we will gladly succumb to the usurpation of a wise & patriotic Cromwell, a military Napoleon, or even a Louis Napoleon, able, unprincipled, & infamous."

Never a regular party man, Ruffin experienced great difficulty in finding a partisan haven for his unorthodox political views. He disliked Jefferson and Madison, despised Clay and Webster, and detested Jackson. Technically, he regarded himself as a states' rights Republican. But when that party split in the 1820's he found the two alternatives almost equally unpalatable. Although adamantly opposed to both the tariff and the National Bank, he voted for the Whig ticket of Harrison and Tyler in 1840, primarily because of his personal friendship with the latter. He was overjoyed at Tyler's early accession to the presidency, viewing Harrison's sudden demise as the most important service he had ever rendered to the country.

In the 1840's personalities were subordinated to issues in Ruffin's mind, and, so far as he was concerned, the paramount issue was the maintenance of Negro slavery as the fundamental social and economic institution in the southern states. He had remained fairly open-minded on this subject until the onslaught of abolitionist propaganda in the 1830's. Then, along with most other Southerners, he moved to more extreme ground in defense of the "peculiar institution." He accepted the alleged inferiority of the Negro without question, though he "would not deny the possibility of one negro in a hundred thousand cases being capable of receiving a college education." He vigorously defended slavery on historical, scientific, and economic—but not Biblical—grounds. Deeming the Liberian experiment a failure of monumental proportions, he became a bitter opponent of the Colonization Society and sought to end both federal and state subsidies to that organization. He regarded the free Negro element as a menace to society and devised a scheme whereby that group would be gradually eliminated.[13] A thoroughgoing white supremacist, Ruffin enthusiastically supported white domination, not only in the South, but throughout the world. He applauded European imperial ventures in Asia and deplored the ascendancy of Negro elements in certain Latin American states, especially Haiti. In short, Ruffin believed that the future of civilization lay with the

[13] See Appendix C.

white race and that the only proper condition for members of the black race was slavery, an institution which he confidently expected to endure for centuries if only the white South manifested the will to defend and sustain it.

It is not surprising, therefore, that in the 1840's, when sectional strife was intensified by increased abolitionist pressure and by the dispute over spoils gained from Mexico, Edmund Ruffin should become a southern nationalist. He was particularly incensed by the Wilmot Proviso of 1846 and shortly thereafter became an avowed secessionist. His already-pronounced esteem for John C. Calhoun was heightened when the dying old warrior fought the Compromise of 1850 and pleaded for substantive constitutional guarantees to protect southern interests. When no other state would join South Carolina in secession during the crisis of 1850, Ruffin expressed bitter disappointment, but he remained hopeful that continued northern aggressions would eventually effect a change in southern sentiment. He did not misjudge the situation. Repeated violations of the new federal fugitive slave law, accelerated abolitionist agitation, the formation of a sectional political party, and open warfare in Kansas combined to propel the nation toward a new crisis in the mid-1850's. It was at this point that Ruffin, in conjunction with Rhett, Yancey, and others, decided to shift his disunion crusade into high gear and to utilize his pen—and even his gun, should that become necessary—in defense of southern rights.

## IV

Prior to 1856 Ruffin had never kept a regular diary. Following his retirement, however, the energetic Virginian decided to maintain such a journal to help occupy his leisure time and, more important, to keep up the habit of writing. Like many other authors, Ruffin found writing difficult when practiced only intermittently. Therefore, to fill the void between articles intended for publication, he began, in December, 1856, to make daily entries concerning his observations, experiences, and thoughts. He continued the practice, almost without interruption, until June 18, 1865, just moments before his death. At times, when his remarks seemed routine and unimportant, he faltered and nearly abandoned the project. But he persisted in his resolve because, as he explained in May, 1859, "I am anxious to keep employed, & writing is my only employment." The product was a massive work of 4,100 manuscript pages which, fortunately, survived the war and is now housed in the Manuscript Division of the Library of Congress.[14]

Ruffin's diary paints a vivid portrait of life in the South during one of the most exciting decades in American history. The utility of the diary extends far beyond its political significance, which is readily apparent. The diarist's inquisitive and versatile mind induced his pen to touch upon a variety of topics, ranging from descriptions of pine lands in the Carolinas and the artesian well system in Charleston to his impressions of a Jewish religious service and a concert by Thalberg and Vieuxtemps. The journal contains a wealth of information on travel conditions in the Old South, the reading habits and social customs of the planter aristocracy, activities of the Virginia State Agricultural Society, and various aspects of the plantation-slave system in the Virginia wheat belt. Indeed, through its pages, the reader is transported to another world—another civilization. And through the eyes of this perceptive, knowledgeable, articulate Virginia gentleman, he may gain a little better understanding of the society for which 250,000 Southerners gave their lives little more than a century ago.

Perhaps the most interesting facet of the diary is its characterization of a man and, to a degree, of a class—in some respects, one of the most remarkable in our history. This is not to imply that Ruffin was an altogether typical gentleman-planter. He was too much an individualist to be so neatly categorized. Nevertheless, he did exhibit many traits commonly encountered among members of the southern upper class. Certainly, his predilection for politics and agriculture was characteristic of that group. So also was the emphasis on family ties and his tendency to associate only with those of his own class. Ruffin was, in every sense of the word, a gentleman— courteous, honorable, generous, and conscious of the social amenities incumbent upon a man in his station. He was cultured and well read in almost every phase of human endeavor, from literature and the arts to scientific achievements and international developments. Few groups in American history have exhibited the intellectual

---

[14] Selected extracts from the Ruffin diary were published more than fifty years ago in the first series of the *William and Mary Quarterly*. See the *Quarterly*, XIV (January, 1906), 194–211, 215; XX (October, 1911), 69–101; XXI (April, 1913), 224–32; XXII (April, 1914), 258–62; XXIII (July, 1914), 31–45; (January, 1915), 154–71; (April, 1915), 240–58. So far as the editor is aware, no other extended selections from the journal have been published.

curiosity and versatility displayed by the large planters of the Old South, and Ruffin more than held his own in such company.

Like most of his peers, however, the venerable Virginian badly misjudged the aspirations and loyalties of southern Negroes. It is difficult to reconcile the paroxysm of fear and outrage which swept the South in the wake of John Brown's raid on Harpers Ferry with the oft-repeated contention of white Southerners that they felt no apprehension about dwelling among large numbers of blacks. Ruffin ridiculed Northerners for their belief that the slaves were dissatisfied and potentially rebellious and pointed with evident relish to the fact that he, along with many other white householders, slept behind unlocked doors and windows. Confident of the docility and loyalty of his Negroes, he felt perfectly secure. Yet, "we all know," he once observed, "that if our slaves so choose, they could kill every white person on any farm, or even through a neighborhood, in any night." When a rash of mysterious fires erupted on the Ruffin farms in the late 1850's, he was utterly at a loss to explain the motivation or identity of the incendiaries. When neighbors suggested that Marl-bourne Negroes might be the culprits in one such conflagration, Ruffin responded vehemently that he did "not believe a tittle of such deductions from premises which I know to be entirely false." Not until the fifth incident in as many years struck the properties of his children did he begin to suspect the true identity of the arsonists.

In his personal habits Ruffin was temperate and moralistic. He renounced the use of tobacco and alcohol in early manhood, though on rare occasions he indulged in a glass of spirits. Thus, upon receiving word of the secession of Virginia while dining with Judge Mitch-ell King in Charleston, he drank a glass of ale and another of wine by way of celebration. But such instances were exceptional, and he attributed his improved health in later years to his general absti-nence. Although he was a widower throughout the period covered by his diary, it contains not the slightest suggestion of scandalous be-havior with members of the fair sex. On the contrary, the journal indicates that its author was quite puritanical in his moral beliefs and practices. He was conscious of the disposition of some elderly men to "play the fool" with younger females and vowed to refrain from such temptations. He was even shocked by Montaigne's *Essays*, pronouncing much of that classic work "indecent to a dis-gusting degree." Though he abhorred New England Yankees, he shared their serious outlook on life. There is little humor in the diary, and most of what there is, is unintentional. One is moved to chuckle over his embarrassing habit of falling asleep during church services—a practice which caused him to forgo regular church attendance in the late 1850's—or the manner in which he rid the Beechwood household of an unwanted sponger who, Ruffin concluded, must have had "a touch either of insanity or idiotcy [*sic*]." But it is unlikely that the diarist himself found either incident very amusing. Perhaps his closest approach to intended levity occurred during the summer of 1860 when describing his visit to the Democratic convention in Baltimore. While standing among a group of ladies at that convocation, he wrote, "I . . . learned, by actual contact, more about hoops than I had known before."

One of Ruffin's most admirable traits was his intellectual integrity. Though sharply opinionated, he was able to recognize worth even in his bitterest adversaries and, in many instances, was capable of rendering an objective evaluation of the most controversial social and political issues. Thus, although he detested John Brown, he readily credited him with an abundance of raw physical courage. He regarded the noted South Carolina Unionist, James L. Petigru, as one of the "most distinguished men of Charleston." In his uncompromising defense of slavery, Ruffin refused to attribute the peculiar condition of the Negro to the curse of Ham, maintaining instead that there was no Biblical evidence to sustain the contention that the Negro descended from Ham. One might suppose that he would have been a vigorous advocate of the proslavery Lecompton Constitution in Kansas, but such was not the case. Perceiving clearly that the antislavery party was in the majority in that territory and that they could easily amend the constitution after statehood to prohibit slavery, he viewed the rejection of that tricky document with unaccustomed composure. Nor did Ruffin choose his friends on the basis of their political convictions. Although closely associated in the secession movement with Rhett and, to a lesser extent, with Yancey, he never developed a close personal friendship with either. Indeed, his most intimate acquaintance was probably Judge Thomas Ruffin, the distinguished North Carolina jurist and a political moderate.

It would be inaccurate to describe Ruffin as a connoisseur of the arts, but he did display an interest in painting, sculpture, and especially music. His pronounced dislike of pretension and self-glorification extended to the arts. A man of simple tastes, he decried the tendency of renowned musical performers to show off their skills in sophisticated pieces which not one in fifty of their auditors could really appreciate, though pretending to be greatly pleased. Thus, after attending an operatic spectacle featuring Caroline Richings, he paid tribute to her powerful, yet sweet, voice but found disagreeable the trills and cadences which were introduced merely to demonstrate her remarkable command of voice and which, of course, were wildly applauded by the audience. If the star had imitated perfectly the braying of an ass, he remarked disgustedly, her listeners would have applauded just as vociferously if only assured that all preceding audiences and persons of musical taste had similarly acclaimed her execution. In the quiet solitude of his room Ruffin would frequently take out his harmonicon and play some of the simple airs of which he was so fond. But, above all, he enjoyed the Sunday gatherings at Marlbourne where, accompanied by his daughter Mildred on the melodeon, he joined his other three unmarried daughters in a family choir to sing his favorite sacred songs and anthems. With the sudden deaths of his three choirmates in 1855, followed shortly thereafter by Mildred's marriage and subsequent departure for Kentucky, Ruffin was overwhelmed by a feeling of sadness that remained with him until the end of his life. Never again would these pleasant and deeply meaningful family sessions be repeated.

Ruffin's declining years were tragic ones, in a personal as well as a political sense. His wife Susan bore him eleven children, two of whom died in infancy. Her passing in 1846 was followed, during the next decade and a half, by the deaths of four daughters and a beloved daughter-in-law. Mildred, the old warrior's last surviving daughter, passed away during the autumn of 1863, and, several months later, his son Julian was killed in action at Drewry's Bluff near Richmond. Thus, only three of Ruffin's children outlived him, and, to add to his distress, he had long been estranged from two of these. After such a succession of personal misfortunes, it is little wonder that he elected to end his own life when the cherished dream of a southern confederacy was demolished in 1865.

Notwithstanding his contentious nature, Ruffin was a sensitive individual, capable of forming deep emotional attachments. He had warm relationships with most of his children and other near relatives. The two glaring exceptions were his eldest daughter, Agnes Beckwith, whose marriage to a spendthrift doctor her father termed "the greatest curse & trouble of my life," and his youngest son Charles, whose extravagance and indolence caused Ruffin much grief.

His favorites among those still living when the diary begins were Mildred, Julian, and Edmund. He was also sincerely devoted to the latter's first wife Mary. Shortly after her much-lamented passing in the summer of 1857, Ruffin assumed the role of matchmaker and began to promote a romance between Edmund and Jane M. Ruffin, one of Judge Ruffin's daughters and a particular favorite of the diarist. The two scarcely knew each other when the elder Ruffin launched his scheme, but friendship soon blossomed into love. Concerned about possible problems with Edmund's six children, Jane's family raised objections to the match, and the courtship progressed on a rather uncertain course for nearly a year. Finally, much to the gratification of the diarist, young Edmund's persistence overcame the reservations of the fair Carolinian, and the two were wed in April, 1861. Like most fathers, Ruffin took great pride in his grandchildren. He was especially affectionate toward Jane Ruffin Dupuy, the child of his nephew John J. Dupuy and his deceased daughter Jane. He always looked forward to little Jane's visits and on several occasions sought to persuade her father to place her in Mildred's care at Marlbourne, where he might see more of her. He got along famously with Edmund's children, especially Nanny, the oldest daughter. Nor were the younger children ignored. On one occasion he instructed young Thomas in making a fishnet; on another he had iron hoops made at the local blacksmith's shop for the youngsters at Beechwood and Ruthven and taught them how to roll their new hoops. Thus, despite the rather harsh image projected by his radical political views, Ruffin was after all a warmhearted, responsive human being.

Following his retirement Ruffin divided his time almost equally between Marlbourne and Beechwood unless absent at some distant spot for political, agricultural, or recreational reasons. But after Mildred's marriage to Burwell Sayre, a Kentucky schoolteacher, in the fall of 1859, he spent most of his time in Prince George County. Establishing his headquarters with Edmund at Beechwood, he made frequent visits to Julian and his family at nearby Ruthven and to the Glebe, the residence of the elder Ruffin's sister Dupuy. He delighted in the wild natural beauty of the woods near Beechwood and one spring embarked enthusiastically upon a project to trim the undergrowth and construct a network of walking paths through these woods. Though his hands were blistered painfully in the undertaking, he was gratified with the result of his labors and thereafter spent many a quiet hour reading or meditating in this favorite spot.

Shortly before the Sumter affair, Ruffin moved into more private quarters in an old house in the Beechwood yard. His books, bookcases, harmonicon, and other prized possessions were brought from Marlbourne, and the old man became comfortably situated. Unfortunately, military events soon brought an end to this pleasant existence.

Apart from his family, Ruffin formed lasting attachments with a number of individuals, some of them prominent in their own right. A complete list of his personal acquaintances reads like a *Who's Who* of the Old South, but of course only a few could be characterized as close friends. Next to Judge Ruffin, the venerable Virginian's most intimate friend was probably the Reverend John Bachman, Lutheran minister in Charleston, whom he once described as "one of the best of all the good men whom I have known." As noted earlier, another South Carolinian whose friendship he valued highly was James Henry Hammond. In Virginia, where political enemies far outnumbered allies, he especially enjoyed the conversation and company of men like Willoughby Newton, Elwood Fisher, William Boulwane, and Lewis E. Harvie. While serving as president of the State Agricultural Society, he was closely associated with Charles B. Williams, secretary of that organization and later editor of the *Southern Planter*. Among persons of high political rank in the Old Dominion, he was perhaps most warmly attracted to former President Tyler. Finally, he derived particular enjoyment from the company of Mrs. Mary Lorraine and Mrs. Mildred Campbell, two elderly widows whom he had known since childhood. The former had been a regular member of the household at Beechwood since 1845, and the latter, mother of the historian Charles Campbell, resided in Petersburg.

Never one to refrain from frank and bold expressions of opinion, Ruffin confided to his diary candid evaluations of a host of prominent persons, both past and present. As one might expect, the number receiving his condemnation far exceeded the number whose accomplishments he found praiseworthy. In the latter category were such early Virginia heroes as Patrick Henry, the "great orator & patriot" Richard Henry Lee, and Richand Bland, "truly one of the ablest founders of American liberty & independence." His evaluation of Washington was dispassionate and perceptive. While respecting the first President for his integrity, public virtue, patriotism, and administrative talents, he pronounced him only mediocre in military ability. Two contemporary Virginians with whom he was personally acquainted drew high praise from Ruffin. He lauded the famed oceanographer Matthew Fontaine Maury as "one of the most able men of this confederation" and similarly acclaimed the merits of Professor James P. Holcombe of the University of Virginia, an avid secessionist. Like most Southerners, he was an admirer of Sir Walter Scott, praising both his writings and his private character. Nor does his esteem for John C. Calhoun come as any surprise. Among contemporary foreigners, he reserved the highest approbation for one of the architects of Italian unification, Giuseppe Garibaldi, whom he described as "the noblest of modern patriots & heroes."

Heading the diarist's list of villains were such national figures as Andrew Jackson; Sam Houston, characterized by Ruffin as an "old scoundrel, & traitor to the South"; President James Buchanan, whom he considered imbecilic; and Stephen A. Douglas, who, though able, was "a great political scoundrel." He was an outspoken critic of Governor Henry Wise and similarly denounced such Virginia political moderates as William C. Rives and John Minor Botts. Nor did some of the earlier giants of his native state escape the venom of Ruffin's pen. He disliked Jefferson, primarily because the latter had never come to his senses on the subject of slavery, and he castigated Madison "for his political apostacies [*sic*] & infidelities to principle & to creed & to duty." Ruffin had mixed emotions concerning the celebrated filibusterer William Walker, whom he met in 1858 at the Southern Commercial Convention in Montgomery. While sympathizing with Walker's expeditions against the racially mixed peoples of Central America, he viewed the military chieftain personally as "a robber & murderer—a land-pirate." Of all mid-nineteenth–century European rulers, he held Napoleon III in highest disrepute. And three former kings of England received particularly rough treatment at the hands of the diarist. He denounced Henry VIII as the "vilest of all the kings of modern Europe," characterized James I as "the blackest & basest villain, by far, of all the English Stuarts," and pronounced George IV "the most infamous scoundrel . . . that has worn the crown of England since James I." Not even Biblical figures escaped his vilification. Thus, after reading several secondary accounts of the life of David in conjunction with the Biblical narrative, he concluded that the ancient prophet-king was a "villain of deep dye."

Such an interpretation of David differed considerably from the construction placed upon his acts by most theologians, but Ruffin was a strong contender for the right of private judgment. As unorthodox in his religious as in his political views, the fiery old Virginian had no intention of abdicating to others the function of interpreting scriptural passages when he was perfectly capable of forming his own conclusions on these matters. Theologians and preachers stood little higher in his estimation than they had in the eyes of Voltaire a century before. He once defined theology as "the science of misconstruction—to teach as the meaning of the scriptures ... what no unprejudiced reader, with mind previously unoccupied, would ever have inferred—& often *what is entirely opposed to the plain & obvious sense.*" Like Voltaire, he detested any form of persecution on account of one's religious beliefs. Ruffin recognized that religious history must be accepted on faith, rather than reason and evidence, and therefore speculated that it would be difficult for a historian not to be a skeptic. On the other hand, he saw no conflict between geology and the Mosaical account of the creation of the world.

Though nominally an Episcopalian, Ruffin's inquisitive nature induced him to sample the services of a broad spectrum of denominations—Baptist, Methodist, Presbyterian, Congregational, Catholic, and even Jewish. While attending a service at the Reformed Jewish Synagogue in Charleston he was amazed to see the Christian Bible in use. He concluded that the congregation was "on the middle passage from Judaism either to Christianity, or more generally to carelessness & disregard of both & all systems of religion." There is little evidence of anti-Semitism in Ruffin's writings, though on one occasion, he noted that Herodotus made no mention of the Jews and surmised that the Greek historian had found neither the people nor their history of any importance. One attempt to attend Catholic services in Washington ended in frustration because all the pews were private and the galleries were occupied almost exclusively by Negroes. Remarking that he did not mind being seated among decent Negro people, he nevertheless declined to take a place with them lest he be "mistaken for a rabid abolitionist." Although Ruffin occasionally attended the Presbyterian Church, he abhorred the harshness of orthodox Calvinism. "There is nothing of iniquity ascribed to Satan," he once wrote, "that is worse than the Calvinistic creed ascribes to the Almighty & all-merciful God." Well-versed and knowledgeable on the theological issues of his day, Ruffin displayed the same independence of thought and action in that area that he manifested in the political arena.

Perhaps Ruffin may be excused for his dogmatism, at least in part, if one reflects upon the vast and diverse store of knowledge which he accumulated through reading. In an age when conversation and reading constituted the principal channels of communication, he availed himself of both unceasingly. He once remarked that reading was the "greatest pleasure I ever enjoyed." And enjoy it he did, frequently rereading favorite books and periodicals for the second or third time in the absence of new material. Religious and historical works, biographies, economic treatises, travel accounts, commentaries on slavery, novels—he devoured them all and penned his impressions of many in his diary. Ironically, he preferred the fictional compositions of Melville and Hawthorne to those of Edgar Allen Poe, the preeminent southern writer of his generation. After a brief excursion into Poe, the disgusted diarist wrote, "Whatever of genius, or other talent, his strange writings may exhibit, they are as monstrous & abominable as his morals, & as absurd as his course of life." Like most southern gentlemen, he enjoyed the works of such English literary giants as Scott, Thackeray, Dickens, and Byron. He read Mill's *Political Economy* and Adam Smith's *Wealth of Nations*, which he pronounced "one of the greatest & most useful works ever written." On the lighter side, he waded through the *Diary of Samuel Pepys.* A few of the other works mentioned by Ruffin during the first five years of his journal include James Parton's biographies of Aaron Burr and Andrew Jackson, histories by Alphonse Lamartine and Louis Adolphe Thiers, David Livingstone's account of his missionary travels in Africa, the *Memoirs* of Sydney Smith, and Maury's *Physical Geography of the Sea.*

Not surprisingly, contemporary writings on slavery and the Negro held a special fascination for Ruffin. He considered Thomas R. Dew's *Essay on Slavery* the last word on that subject. While commending George Fitzhugh for his sound conclusions on slavery, particularly his emphasis upon the alleged wage slavery of northern factory operatives, he termed the author's opposition to interest and capital "absurd." Nor did he agree with the thesis propounded by his friend Dr. Bachman in *The Doctrine of the Unity of the Human Race.* Two influential works published on the eve of the Civil War evoked predictable responses from the militant secessionist. He denounced Hinton Rowan Helper's *The Impending Crisis* as "infamous & lying" and thereafter referred to the Republican Party as the "Brown-Helper party." On the other hand, he praised Thomas P. Kettell's *Southern Wealth and Northern Profits* for its "clear & strong argument."

Ruffin by no means confined his reading to books. He regularly perused the leading English reviews as well as such noted American periodicals as *De Bow's Review, Littell's Living Age,* and *Harper's,* though he continually referred to the latter as "trashy." In addition to *De Bow's,* he personally subscribed to *Russell's Magazine,* the *Southern Planter,* and, after 1860, the *Southern Literary Messenger* because of the strong southern position assumed by its new editor, Dr. George Bagby. To keep abreast of current events he took the leading Richmond papers, the Charleston *Mercury,* the New York *Tribune,* and the New York *Daily Herald.* Of all northern newspapers, he held the New York *Journal of Commerce* in highest esteem, terming it "the most truthful & honest paper I know." By the fall of 1860, as the sectional crisis approached its climax, Ruffin was so deluged with papers that it took him nearly the whole of every mail day to get through them when at Beechwood. If absent from home he would regularly visit the local newspaper office to pore over its copies of distant papers in his insatiable quest for news.

Next to reading, Ruffin probably derived his greatest pleasure from traveling. He was constantly on the move, utilizing railroads, steamers, and stagecoaches as his principal means of conveyance. Thanks to his fame as an agriculturist, he was accorded free passage on most of the rail lines in North and South Carolina. When rail executives in his home state declined to follow suit, the sensitive Ruffin could not conceal his disappointment. He ranged up and down the Atlantic seaboard from Washington to Charleston on a variety of missions; he journeyed to Alabama to attend the Southern Commercial Convention; he visited his daughter in Kentucky; he vacationed annually at the springs in western Virginia and, less frequently, at Old Point Comfort. And wherever he went he recorded for posterity his impressions of the lands through which he passed, the people whom he encountered, and the conditions of travel and public accommodation.

It is a tribute to Ruffin's fortitude that he enjoyed traveling so much despite the unsatisfactory nature of transportation facilities in the antebellum South. Public conveyances were notoriously tardy in meeting their schedules, and unexpected detentions were frequent. On a trip from White Sulphur Springs to Frankfort, Kentucky, Ruffin lost a total of thirty-eight hours by three delays, two caused by the failure of trains to connect and the other by the derailment of the Nashville-to-Louisville train when it struck some logs which "some villain" had placed across the track. In some areas changes in the traveler's itinerary were necessitated by the failure of railroads to operate on Sundays. Everywhere travel was slow. As the diary indicates, it required nearly thirty hours to traverse the 457 miles from Richmond to Charleston and nine and a half hours to go from Augusta to Atlanta, a distance of 171 miles. But these times were swift compared to those in more isolated areas where the terrain was difficult. When the diarist departed White Sulphur Springs for Kentucky in the autumn of 1860, he was obliged to ride for two full days in a mail coach before reaching Newbern, the nearest station on the Virginia and Tennessee Railroad and only about 80 miles from his starting point. En route to Gainesville, Florida, several months later, he rode from 10:00 A.M. until sunset to cover a distance of only 24 miles on a road of deep sand.

Water travel proved no more satisfactory than land travel. While outward bound from Charleston to Fernandina, Florida, the vessel on which Ruffin booked passage suffered a broken main shaft and was forced to return to port for repairs. Nearly two full days elapsed before he was able to embark once again for Florida. Less dangerous but almost as exasperating were the accommodations the Virginian encountered on a Selma-to-Montgomery steamer. Late as usual, the vessel was badly overcrowded, and he "passed a wretched night on a dirty & very bumpy mattress laid on a table." Even when one reached his destination lodgings were apt to be unsatisfactory, except in the largest cities. On a visit to Raleigh, North Carolina, in October, 1860, Ruffin found public accommodations at a premium because the state fair was in progress. Turned away by one of the principal hotels, he tried another and discovered that the guests were billeted three and four to a room and that there was a strong possibility that he might be forced to share his *bed* with a stranger. Fortunately, he was able to secure satisfactory lodging in a private residence. Although adequate quarters were usually available in Richmond, he was sometimes obliged to share a room with a stranger and on one such occasion was chagrined to learn that his roommate was a professional gambler. Notwithstanding the inconveniences and frustrations of travel in the Old South, Ruffin continued his excursions with undiminished zeal as long as his advanced years permitted.

In the course of his extensive journeys through the South, the veteran farmer took copious notes on the various soil formations and types of vegetation which he encountered. These observations furnished the basis for a number of valuable articles, which were published subsequently in the *Southern Planter* and other agricultural journals. He visited the fertile swamplands of eastern North Carolina and seemed particularly fascinated by the pine lands of the Carolinas and Georgia. He extended his trip to Alabama in order to examine at first hand the canebrake lands west of Montgomery. Not even the political crisis of late 1860 deterred him from making a foray into central Florida to see the orange groves, an excursion which provided the material for a series of three articles in the *Southern Planter*. While in Kentucky he visited the lush bluegrass region between Frankfort and Lexington and pronounced it "a beautiful & fertile country." Thus Ruffin's propensity for travel yielded rich dividends by enabling him to make additional contributions to the calling in which he achieved greatest distinction— agriculture.

Although increasingly preoccupied with political affairs in the 1850's, Ruffin did not lessen his efforts to promote agricultural reforms in his native state. In 1852 he was elected president of the rejuvenated Virginia State Agricultural Society and remained one of its most active leaders for the balance of the decade. He drafted a report providing for a representative Farmers' Assembly, which was implemented at the 1856 meeting of the society. In the same year he again was elected to the presidency, succeeding Colonel Philip St. George Cocke, and served in that capacity for three consecutive terms—1857 to 1859. Though elected by a unanimous vote on each occasion, his presidency was a stormy one. Always economy-minded, he sought to cut the expenses of the society, particularly those incurred during the annual fairs. When the host city, Richmond, refused to offer more favorable financial terms, he had the event transferred in 1858 to Petersburg. This removal spawned the development in Richmond of a rival group, known as the Central Agricultural Society of Virginia, and generated a good deal of personal animosity against Ruffin among influential members of the state society. Nevertheless, the years of his incumbency were generally prosperous and successful ones for the organization. As a result of the president's efficient and conscientious management, the autumn meetings and fairs were interesting, well attended, and profitable. In 1860, however, when the central and state societies formed a coalition and moved the united fair back to Richmond, the embittered outgoing president boycotted the entire affair and vowed to have nothing more to do with the state society. By that time, of course, Ruffin was engrossed in more important matters. His beloved South was finally moving toward independence.

V

Whatever its other merits—and they are many—the Ruffin diary is of supreme importance as a chronicle of political attitudes, moods, and motives in the South during the most critical period in its history. Through the eyes of an outspoken secessionist the reader is able to view the chain of events which drove the nation steadily and inexorably toward disunion and civil war. There are few surprises. To those who still doubt that slavery was the overriding cause of that conflict, this journal should prove unsettling, for that theme runs throughout the course of this first volume. The threat posed by the North was to Negro slavery, the cornerstone of southern civilization. Ruffin saw it clearly, and so did his contemporaries. The abolitionist crusade, attempts to restrict the spread of slavery, repeated violations of the federal fugitive slave law, John Brown's raid, the election of the "black Republican" Lincoln—these are the events which inflamed the South and drove her out of the Union.

With regard to Lincoln, we should remember that it is not so much what he thought or did but what the South feared he might do in 1861 that is important. It is all very well for the modern historian, basking in hindsight, to argue that Lincoln's election posed no real threat to slavery in the South. But Southerners had no firsthand knowledge of Lincoln. What they did know was that he had been nominated by a party pledged to contain slavery within its present boundaries, that he was backed by a vocal and growing minority of Northerners who were dedicated heart and soul to the complete eradication of slavery, and that he was almost certain to be elected by the vote of a section which, as a whole, counseled defiance of Supreme Court decisions and federal laws which it found unpalatable. It is little wonder then that Ruffin could write, on that fateful November morning in 1860, these words: "This is the day for the election of electors—the momentous election which, if showing the subsequent election of Lincoln to be certain, will serve to show whether these southern states are to remain free, or to be politically enslaved—*whether the institution of negro slavery, on which the social & political existence of the south rests,* is to be secured by our resistance, or to be abolished in a short time, as the certain result of our present submission to northern domination." [15] For Ruffin, it was a long and uncertain road to that day a month and a half later when South Carolina became the first state to sever the bonds of union. At times he despaired of ever reaching the goal of disunion. But, together with such other stalwarts as Rhett and Yancey, he persisted in his determination to arouse in fellow Southerners a spirit of resistance against alleged Yankee aggressions.

For those attracted to the conspiracy theory of secession, the diary affords ample evidence of cooperation among the three most celebrated fire-eaters—Ruffin, Rhett, and Yancey. They were all present at the Southern Commercial Convention in Montgomery in the spring of 1858; and immediately afterward, Ruffin and Yancey spearheaded the formation of a League of United Southerners to give unity and direction to southern opinion. Moreover, in August, 1858, Ruffin turned to Rhett's Charleston *Mercury* as the principal outlet for his political pieces. Previously, he had relied heavily upon *The South,* a Richmond paper edited by Roger Pryor, to convey his thoughts to the public. But he became disenchanted with Pryor when the latter denounced his scheme for a League of United Southerners. For the next two years Ruffin flooded the *Mercury* with a series of provocative communications—all designed to inspire southern resistance and, ultimately, secession. By the fall of 1860 the paper was even running editorials written by the militant Virginian. On the eve of Lincoln's election Ruffin wrote to Yancey, urging him to emulate Patrick Henry and use his eloquence as a public speaker to lead in the movement for secession.[16] Less than a month later Ruffin and Rhett journeyed to Milledgeville, where they conferred with Governor Joseph E. Brown and leaders of the Georgia legislature. They received a cordial welcome and were invited by both House and Senate to occupy seats in their respective halls. Thus, it is apparent from the diary that Ruffin, Rhett, and Yancy were in communication and actively cooperating in the drive for disunion for

---

[15] Italics added by editor.
[16] See Appendix E.

some three years prior to the realization of their common objective.

Despite their individual and concerted efforts, however, it was not these three who, in the end, achieved secession. True, they did much to create a climate of opinion receptive to disunion. But their most promising conspiratorial project, the League of United Southerners, never really got off the ground. Ironically, none of the three seems to have been closely tied to a genuine and successful conspiracy, the Association of 1860, a propaganda agency formed by a group of Charleston secessionists in September, 1860.[17] Yancey and Rhett did exercise considerable political influence in their respective states on the eve of secession, but Ruffin, pathetically, remained to the end a revolutionary who never quite wielded the power to accomplish his dream. Finally, it should be remembered that no individual or combination of individuals could have effected the goal of secession without the aid of external events over which Southerners had no control—in particular, Brown's raid on Harpers Ferry and the election of Lincoln.

By the middle of Buchanan's term, Ruffin was resigned to the fact that little could be done to rouse the South to action until the next presidential election. But he was hopeful that a Republican victory in 1860 would provide the needed spark. In the meantime, he became increasingly disgusted with the efforts of prominent southern politicians to preserve the unity of the national Democratic Party. Ruffin thought it sheer madness to entertain hopes for a southern president, but the politicians remained unconvinced. They softened their rhetoric and clung to the Democratic Party in the deluded expectation that it might serve as an avenue for their national political aspirations. So the old warrior bided his time, all the while fretting and fuming and sinking deeper into despair. So discouraged had he become by the autumn of 1859 that he was actually on the verge of suicide. "I have lived long enough—& a little more time of such unused & wearisome passage of time will make my life too long," he wrote on October 18. The following day, news of the bombshell at Harpers Ferry reached him, and immediately his flagging spirits revived. By late November he was on his "way to the 'seat of war,'"

---

[17] Headed by Robert N. Gourdin, the Association of 1860 disseminated nearly 200,000 pamphlets during the first two months of its existence and exerted great influence, not only in South Carolina but throughout the South. See Charles E. Cauthen, *South Carolina Goes to War, 1860–1865* (Chapel Hill: University of North Carolina Press, 1950), 34–43. Ruffin did join the organization in November, 1860 (see page 499), but apparently did little more than assist in the distribution of pamphlets.

hoping that abolitionist fanatics would attempt a rescue of Brown. After witnessing the latter's execution he returned home with renewed optimism, convinced that Brown's desperate foray had provided the South with the "best practical ground for dissolution" she had ever had.

Even before leaving Harpers Ferry, the exuberant Ruffin decided to dramatize the infamy of Brown's plot by dispatching one of the pikes seized from the conspirators to the governor of each slave state. He arranged with Colonel Alfred W. Barbour, superintendent of the Harpers Ferry arsenal, to have the requisite number of pikes conveyed to Washington in care of Senator Clement C. Clay of Alabama, who had agreed to assist in the scheme. Apparently Barbour did not share Ruffin's enthusiasm for the project, because the weapons were not delivered until mid-June of 1860. At that time, labels reading "Sample of the favors designed for us by our Northern Brethren" were affixed to the spears in the meeting room of Clay's Senate Commerce Committee, and Ruffin distributed the exhibits to members of Congress and delegates to the Democratic National Convention for transmission to the respective slave states. At the last minute, he decided to withhold the pike intended for Delaware because he "doubted whether the gift would be appreciated" and gave it instead to Senator Clay. Accompanying each of the other pikes was a letter to the governor, requesting that the weapon be displayed conspicuously and permanently in the state capitol "as abiding & impressive evidence of the fanatical hatred borne by the dominant northern party to the institutions & the people of the Southern States, and of the unscrupulous & atrocious means resorted to for the attainment of the objects sought by that party."

The Harpers Ferry episode also inspired Ruffin to undertake a new kind of literary venture, a political novel entitled *Anticipations of the Future*, which he commenced writing in late February, 1860. Using as his format a series of letters purportedly written to the London *Times* by an English visitor, the writer attempted to predict the possible consequences of continued submission by the South to the rule of a hostile northern majority. He focused upon the period 1864 to 1869, beginning with William Henry Seward's election to the presidency in the former year. As Ruffin envisioned it, the Republican Congress proceeded to abolish slavery by constitutional amendment, to enact a prohibitively high tariff, and to pass other legislation inimical to southern interests. In desperation the South finally seceded, with the border states serving as a protective barrier until the Confederacy was solidly established. Then, when the North initiated punitive action, these states joined their sisters to the south to form a united front. The ensuing war was ruinous to both sections, but the South, joined in the eleventh hour by the West, ultimately triumphed and went on to a glorious future. Ruffin had never before attempted an imaginative work of this type, but it caused him little difficulty and in fact afforded him considerable pleasure. In the midst of his labors he paused to remark that this "has been the most pleasant labor of the kind that I have ever performed." Within two months the 426-page work was completed, and the *Mercury* was already running the earlier chapters in serial form. But the author sought a wider circulation and soon concluded an agreement with J. W. Randolph of Richmond to publish the novel as a book. By early September Ruffin had the first two printed copies in hand, and he settled back to await the reaction. To his profound mortification, little was forthcoming. Although it was favorably reviewed in the *Southern Literary Messenger,* the book attracted little notice from other quarters and even fewer purchasers. Evidently, the writing of political novels was not Ruffin's forte.

Meanwhile, events were progressing far more rapidly than he had prophesied in his book. From the early months of 1860 Ruffin correctly divined that at least one state—South Carolina—would secede following the election of Lincoln. Though she might stand alone at first, he was confident that other states would soon follow her lead. Further, he anticipated that any attempt by the federal government to initiate coercive action against the seceded states would drive the remaining slave states from the Union and into a southern confederacy. Subsequent intelligence seemed to confirm Ruffin's estimate of the situation. Although disappointed in the general submissionist sentiment which seemed to prevail in Kentucky, the Virginia fire-eater was heartened by the attitude of Governor Beriah Magoffin, pronounced by Ruffin the most ardent Southerner he had encountered in the entire state. Magoffin vowed that if United States troops were dispatched through Kentucky against the seceded states he would do his utmost to make "every night's encampment . . . a graveyard." A month later, on October 17, 1860, Ruffin was apprised confidentially of a communication from Governor William H. Gist of South Carolina to Governor John W. Ellis of North Carolina in which the former asserted unequivocally that his state would secede

—alone, if necessary—should the expected election of Lincoln materialize. Thus, on the eve of the presidential election, one vital question appeared to be settled; but much doubt remained concerning another issue—whether or not secession would lead to war.

At first, Ruffin had thought that secession could be effected peacefully only if a sizable bloc of states left the Union simultaneously. But if only one, or a few, seceded ahead of the other slave states, he anticipated that the federal government would attempt coercion. When the latter occurred and no force was applied by the Buchanan administration, he concluded that there was nothing to fear from Washington until the inauguration of Lincoln, who would likely adopt a more forceful policy than his predecessor. In Ruffin's mind, the key was Virginia. If she seceded before March 4, carrying the other border states with her, the incoming President would be faced with a *fait accompli* and would probably not launch a military attack upon a united confederacy of fourteen or fifteen states. On the other hand, if Virginia delayed action, the probability of war would be increased. Thus on February 3 the diarist wrote that on the morrow the election of delegates to the Virginia convention would determine "whether there will be peace or war between the northern & southern sections of the former United States of America." Those elections proved disappointing to the impatient Ruffin. With moderates in control, the convention assembled but proceeded at a snail's pace (Ruffin complained that it took "as much time to elect door-keepers . . . as the Convention of S.C. used to dissolve the Union"), as delegates awaited results from the ill-fated Peace Congress in Washington. By the end of the month Ruffin was convinced that Lincoln intended to coerce the recalcitrant states and that war was almost inevitable. All doubts were erased by the President's inaugural address, which, averred the fiery Virginian, "settles the question that there must be war." The spotlight now shifted to Charleston Harbor, where Major Robert Anderson's beleaguered garrison still held Fort Sumter. But Ruffin was a step ahead of the march of events; he was already in Charleston.

Indeed, he was in Charleston for his third extended visit in the brief span of four months. This time he vowed to remain until his native state joined the Confederacy. He did not have long to wait. Events moved rapidly as the rival governments played their last cards in a grim game. In one of the highlights of this first volume, Ruffin provides the reader with a graphic account of the activities and changing moods in Charleston during the hectic months of March and April, 1861. He inspected the Confederate fortifications in Charleston Harbor on half a dozen occasions and penned detailed descriptions of these installations in his journal. He conversed daily with high civil and military officials and recorded their impressions and thoughts, their assumptions, and their reactions to the cavalcade of events. Above all, he captured in his diary the aura of excitement which enveloped all participants in this fateful drama.

On April 8, convinced that hostilities were imminent, the doughty old Confederate boarded an early steamer for the harbor forts in hopes that the vessel would draw the first fire from the Sumter batteries. "I greatly coveted the distinction & *eclat* which I might have acquired if the steamer had been fired upon, & we had refused to yield," he wrote on his return, "& I deemed the danger to be incurred as very trifling." The following day he embarked with his musket and other accoutrements for Morris Island, where he received an enthusiastic welcome from the troops. Three days later, as a private in the Palmetto Guard, he pulled the lanyard which sent the first shell from the Iron Battery on Cummings' Point arching over Fort Sumter. Ruffin's claim to the first shot appears strong. By order of General P. G. T. Beauregard, the Confederate batteries ringing Sumter were to fire in a definite sequence, with the Iron Battery accorded the honor of firing the first round. In all, Ruffin fired twenty-seven shots in the Sumter engagement, but he spent most of his time simply observing the bombardment. His vivid description of this first battle in the Civil War is unexcelled. Following Anderson's evacuation on the afternoon of April 14, Ruffin was one of the first to set foot in the still-burning fort, and again the reader receives a minutely detailed account of his observations. One can well imagine the exultation with which the weary old man surveyed the ruins and savored the fruits of victory. But this initial success was deceptive. Not a life had been lost in the actual bombardment; the Confederate batteries had emerged virtually unscathed; the enemy had been vanquished easily and painlessly. There was nothing to indicate the bitter adversities that lay ahead for Ruffin and his beloved Confederacy.

## VI

In editing the diary for publication, I have made every effort to follow the original exactly—even with regard to punctuation. Ruffin was not a bad writer, though he tended to be verbose and, on occasion, his constructions were awkward. Like most other nineteenth-century writers, he was guilty of excessive use of the comma. Infrequently, commas have been inserted or deleted to promote clarity, but, for the most part, they have been left as they appear in the original. Ruffin was careless about apostrophes, and these have been added where appropriate. I have retained the original paragraph structure, although in many instances very lengthy paragraphs result. It was the diarist's custom to separate major topics within an entry by dashes rather than by paragraphing. Obvious writing errors, the result of carelessness and haste, have been silently corrected. Although the diarist was an excellent speller, he did consistently misspell a few words, such as *niece, siege,* and *Breckinridge.* These errors have been noted at their first occurrence and thereafter have been silently corrected.

Since the manuscript version of this volume contained more than 1,300 pages, it was necessary to delete a considerable amount of inconsequential matter. Most of the material excluded concerned Ruffin's health (among other maladies, he was afflicted with cold feet, trembling hands, deafness in his left ear, and loss of memory), routine neighborhood visits, trivial family affairs, the weather, and foreign news which did not reflect the personal viewpoint of the diarist. Repetitious passages were also eliminated. Throughout the editorial process I have endeavored to retain all material which contributes significantly to an understanding of the political, social, and cultural history of the period and thus to make it unnecessary for scholars to consult the original manuscript diary. Where doubt has arisen concerning particular passages, I have invariably allowed the original to stand. Perhaps too much information of a purely personal nature has been included. But I have proceeded on the assumption that simply to retain the political commentaries, travel accounts, and other material of unquestionable value and to omit the remainder would dehumanize the volume and thus reduce its worth. Therefore, I have kept much of the family material, particularly that bearing on Ruffin's relations with his children.

Omissions within entries have been indicated by the customary use of ellipses. However, I have not utilized a full line of ellipsis marks to denote lengthy omissions. If the reader is concerned about the amount of excluded material, he may refer to the bracketed numbers within the text, which represent page numbers in the original manuscript diary. These numbers are consecutive except where they fall within a deleted portion and are omitted. Brief, inconsequential entries have been entirely eliminated. Since Ruffin wrote an entry for almost every date, the reader may infer that skipped days represent deletions by the editor. There are two places in this volume where some nineteenth-century insect with no appreciation for historical scholarship chewed a hole in the manuscript. One of these defaced portions extends for about seventy-five manuscript pages, and the other is much shorter. Wherever possible, the editor has reconstructed the torn passages to the best of his ability.

Ruffin appended to his diary numerous newspaper clippings, many of which consist of articles and communications which he had written for publication. Some are extremely important; others are frivolous squibs. The editor has summarized some of the former type in footnotes, and two of the most significant have been included as appendices. It has been assumed that most readers will have a basic knowledge of the period covered by the journal. Therefore, I have not thought it necessary to incorporate in the text a running editorial commentary on the events alluded to by the diarist. All editorial comment has been placed in footnotes, most of which simply identify persons referred to in the narrative. It is the editor's hope that these explanatory notes will suffice to render the Ruffin diary useful to scholar, student, and knowledgeable layman alike.

## VII

I am grateful to both the Manuscript Division and Photoduplication Service of the Library of Congress for the expeditious manner in which they handled my request for a microfilm copy of the entire Ruffin diary. Happily, my request coincided with the microfilming of the diary as part of the library's program for the preservation of historical rarities, and the copy was transmitted to me within five months of my initial inquiry. The possession of this copy has greatly facilitated editorial work on the project.

I wish to acknowledge particularly the assistance of Professor William W. Freehling of the University of Michigan, who read the entire manuscript and offered useful suggestions regarding the Introduction as well as the project as a whole. Above all, I wish to extend my deepest thanks to Professor Avery Craven, who, more than thirty-five years ago, wrote the definitive biography of Edmund

*Introduction*

Ruffin and who graciously consented to write the Foreword for this volume.

As usual, the editorial staff of the Louisiana State University Press has rendered the publication process as painless as possible. My special thanks go to Leslie E. Phillabaum, assistant director, and Mrs. Roberta Madden, editor. Finally, I owe a particular debt of gratitude to Mrs. Cynthia Van Devender, History Department secretary at the University of Southern Mississippi, who displayed her versatility by sketching the map of Charleston Harbor.

WILLIAM K. SCARBOROUGH

# The Ruffin Family

Edmund, Jr. (1814–?)—attended the University of Virginia; proprietor of Beechwood. First wife, Mary (1816–1857), died July 28, 1857. Married Jane M. Ruffin, daughter of Judge Thomas Ruffin of North Carolina, on April 25, 1861. Children:

> Edmund (1839–?)—died between 1850 and 1856.
>
> Nanny (1841–?)
>
> Thomas (1843–?)
>
> George (1845–?)
>
> Susan (1846–?)
>
> Mary S. (1848–?)
>
> John (1853–?)

Agnes (1817–?)—married Dr. Thomas Stanley Beckwith. Children:

> Julian (1839–1862)—attended William and Mary College for two years; killed in action at Seven Pines on May 31, 1862.
>
> Margaret S. (1842–?)
>
> Thomas Stanley, Jr. (1843–?)
>
> Edmund R. (1845–?)
>
> J.—male (1845–?)
>
> S. T.—female (1846–?)
>
> A.—female (1847–?)
>
> Lucy (1850–?)

---

All birth dates have been computed from the MS census returns of 1850 and 1860 from Hanover and Prince George counties, Virginia (MSS in National Archives). Because of the discrepancy between birthdays and the date of the census-taker's visit, a tolerance of one year should be allowed on all these figures.

Julian C. (1821–1864)—attended William and Mary College; proprietor of Ruthven. Married Charlotte Stockdell (Lotty) Meade on May 26, 1852. Killed in action at Drewry's Bluff on May 16, 1864. Children:

> Meade (1853–?)
>
> Jane (1857–?)
>
> Bessy C. (1859–?)
>
> Edmund Sumter (1861–?)—born one week after the bombardment of Fort Sumter.

Rebecca (1823–1855)

Elizabeth (1824–1860)—married William Sayre, who became resident manager of Marlbourne after Ruffin's retirement. Died December 4, 1860, after giving birth to a son. The infant also died within a few weeks.

Mildred (1827–1863)—resided at Marlbourne until her marriage to Burwell B. Sayre, a Kentucky schoolmaster and brother of William Sayre, on October 4, 1859. She gave birth to a daughter in July, 1860, but the infant lived only three weeks.

Jane (1829–1855)—married Ruffin's nephew, Dr. John J. Dupuy, of the Glebe. Children:

> Jane Ruffin (1855–?)

Ella (1833–1855)

Charles (ca. 1833–?)—a Prince George County farmer.

# THE DIARY OF
# EDMUND RUFFIN

"I will be out of Va before Lincoln's inauguration, & so will avoid being, as a Virginian, under his government even for an hour. I, at least, will become a citizen of the seceded Confederate States, & will not again reside in my native state ... until Va shall also secede, & become a member of the Southern Confederacy."

Edmund Ruffin, February 27, 1861

# 1856

INTRODUCTION ❧ VIRGINIA STATE AGRI-
CULTURAL SOCIETY ❧ OPINION OF COL-
ONEL PHILIP ST. GEORGE COCKE

Diary. Introduction to the attempt.

The heavy & repeated family afflictions with which I had been visited in 1855, had rendered me still less inclined to bear the labors & perplexities of conducting any regular business—for which indeed my interest had nearly ceased. Added to this unfitness to conduct my farm & business, my son Julian was required, by his own family affairs, to return to his own farm & home, in Prince George County.[1] The sudden death of his wife's father (John E. Meade,) in the early part of 1855, & the sale & distribution of his estate, made it necessary that Julian should reside at home to provide a home for his wife's mother & younger children. This would make it necessary for me to resume the charge of my farm, & either to take on myself again its immediate direction & supervision, or otherwise to submit to the annoyance of having an overseer. Rather than do either, I came to the conclusion to give up the bulk of my estate, in full property to my children. I had desired this long before, & had made vain efforts for the purpose, which were always discouraged by my children. But now I was determined. I arranged & wrote my plan of assignment & division of property, & submitted it to my children, & required of them the execution. After reserving a capital of $25,000 for myself, & $7,500 for the child of my deceased daughter

---

[1] Julian had assumed responsibility for the management of Marlbourne following his father's retirement at the end of 1854.

[5]

Jane Dupuy, (the property of the mother, not paid over in principal before her death,) I gave all the remaining property, in nearly equal proportions to my then living children. The Marlbourne farm, & the slaves thereupon, were sold to my children, Edmund, Julian, Charles, Mildred, & to William Sayre the husband of my daughter Elizabeth; & the proceeds of these & other sales, & of all the other of my property, were to be divided, as soon as the necessary writing could be drawn, among [2] the above-named, & Agnes Beckwith, my only other then remaining child. Her situation, as being married to a spendthrift & worthless husband, required other provisions. And this addition, like most of the property previously given to Agnes (& all that remains of it,) will be secured, by deed of trust, so as to prevent the capital being wasted.

The new joint-owners of Marlbourne appointed Mr. Sayre to be the resident superintendent. This was best in every respect—not only because of his great fitness for the trust & duty—though inexperienced in farming on a large scale—but also because the recent general bad health of Elizabeth rendered it improper for her to remove from all her friends to Westmoreland [County, Va.], where Mr. Sayre had lately purchased land & settled a farm. Though at much sacrifice in his previous arrangements, he was pleased to make this change—& Elizabeth's brothers & sister were glad to admit Mr. Sayre as a co-purchaser & partner, to return Elizabeth at Marlbourne. Mildred will then continue to make it her home also. It is also my home—though I may be generally elsewhere.

As soon as I had thus transferred the property, I assembled the slaves, & explained to them the general management & the change of their ownership. But I was sure that neither this explanation, nor any thing else I could do, if remaining at home, would serve. The negroes would continue to regard me as still their master, & their judge of appeals—& the new owners would not assume their full authority & will, but would continue to refer, & to defer, to me, as their father & head of the household. To prevent these consequences, & to compel the putting of things in their new train, I left Marlbourne, determined not to return for some months, & only for short visits, until my presence could no longer produce any ill effect such as I feared.

I first visited the homes of my children in Prince George, [3] making Beechwood, (my oldest son's residence,) my head quarters, & home for the time. The arrangements for the legal transfer of the property were commenced, & I hoped soon to have them concluded.

The health of Elizabeth especially, & also of Mildred in less degree, was impaired, & I thought would be benefited by visiting the Springs, to which I accompanied them as early as they could get off, the middle of August, & remained with them until late in September. Before, I had made an excursion for agricultural observations, to the county of Princess Anne, & the neighboring counties of N.C. on Albemarle Sound—& later, to eastern N.C. south of Pamlico Sound. Of the new facts observed, & deemed worthy of being mentioned, I wrote notes at much length, but without any care, or any plan of putting them before the public. They were written for amusement more than for any other object. And the writings served to fill pleasantly many an hour, & some entire days while I was in disagreeable & solitary places during my visit to lower N.C. Though I had deemed it necessary for me to be relieved of the harassing claims of my previous business engagements, I did not intend or desire to lead a life of indolence or inactivity. Occupation is necessary for me—& (as my children feared for me in this change,) if idle entirely, I should be miserable. Therefore I designed to visit distant friends & distant scenes, for which there had been no time in my previous busy life. Writing, & especially to describe or discuss agricultural subjects, was designed to be made one of the means of passing my time.

Mr. Sayre, & also my son Edmund & his wife, joined us at the Alleghany Springs, late in the season. After being with them all for a few days, being no longer needed as an escort, I left for upper N.C. where I had promised to go. Free tickets on the railways of N.C. had just been presented to me to induce & facilitate these excursions. No [4] such facility or compliment had ever been offered to me in my own state—though after this action in N.C. it was done in a few cases in Va. also. I did not directly ask for such favors—or perhaps they would have been granted.

In this visit, I was in Orange county, with Paul Cameron, & then went to Dr. Wm. R. Holt's in Davidson [County]—made a hasty trip to Charlotte, & afterwards passed on to Wilmington. Sundry places were visited in & near the routes of agricultural interest. Thus the time was occupied, until the time to attend the Fair of the State Agricultural Society at Raleigh, in October—after which I returned to stay with my children, until the time to attend the Annual Meeting & Fair of the Va. State Agril. Soc. at Richmond.

[7]

## Introduction to the attempt

Owing to the successive illness & deaths of my children in 1855,[2] I did not attend the Agricultural Fair of that year; nor any meeting of the Executive Committee, save one, for 18 months previous to this time. For my absence in the present year, I had another reason, besides my being generally far from home, if not out of Va. Col. Ph[ilip St. George] Cocke,[3] as president, & all others of us on the Executive Committee, had been re-elected, by one motion & vote, in the general meeting of Nov. 1854, because the society, in mass meeting, and the great number in the meeting, could not possibly indicate its preference, in any vote.—There had been so many difficulties between the President, & the Committee, & especially with myself & a few others of the more active members, that it was disagreeable for me to act with him—& I meant to be absent from the meeting, unless some important business had to come before it. There had been only one occasion of this kind, at which I attended. This was to act upon a long report which I had before drawn, as directed by the Committee in my absence, to put in operation the election of representatives by the Society, under the [5] lately changed constitution. To present this report, & explain it, (if needed) I attended the February [1856] meeting—when it was approved & adopted. Col. Cocke is an honorable, worthy & estimable gentleman —& a benevolent & good, though extremely narrow-minded man. But he is entirely deficient of the much higher requisites for the office he holds in the State Society. His being elevated to the high position which he is so ill-qualified to fill, has served to display his great vanity, which his diffidence & reserve had before concealed— while he is morbidly sensitive, & is frequently suffering from supposed slights to his dignity, when nothing of the kind was designed or thought of by the offender—as it was my misfortune to find as to myself in sundry cases. In every thing else, except in his office, & in our official relations, I would still hold Col. Cocke in very high esteem. It is to be hoped that he cannot retract his announced declining to serve again, & that we may get rid of the evil of his incumbency.

---

[2] Three of Ruffin's daughters, Jane, Rebecca, and Ella, had passed away unexpectedly during the summer of 1855.

[3] One of the largest planters in the South, with extensive holdings in Virginia and Mississippi, Philip St. George Cocke (1809–61) served as president of the Virginia State Agricultural Society from 1853 to 1856. A graduate of West Point, he served with distinction as a brigade commander at First Manassas. After eight months of active service, he returned in broken health to Belmead, his Powhatan County residence, and on December 26, 1861, committed suicide.

But though an absentee mostly from the meetings of the Ex. Com., I had still in another way rendered more labor for the society & the committee, than any other member. Besides the preparation of the long report just named, I wrote for newspapers several different articles to sustain our petition for the abrogation of the inspection system & laws—& also a series of three long articles, designed to explain the necessity for the new feature of representative government, & to recommend that amendment of the constitution, which had been adopted in the general meeting of 1855. This feature had many opposers—& many of our members, who approved of it, feared that the elections would not be effected, & that the attempt for a new system would be a total failure. On account of such opposition, & fears, I deemed it necessary to [6] argue the subject before the public, as stated. In my absence, I had been elected as one of the members from my county, Hanover, to the Farmers' Assembly.[4]

I went to Richmond, from Beechwood, a few days before the opening of the Fair, to be in place for the previous meeting of the Ex. Com., of which, owing to my absence from Marlbourne, I had missed the notice. In private conversations with other members, & particular friends, I endeavored to learn who ought to be put forward for Speaker of the Farmers' Assembly, & President of the Society. For the former office I proposed (in private) J. R. Edmunds of Halifax. But he positively refused to be nominated. We heard it rumored that W. C. Rives would be nominated either for speaker or president.[5] I felt very much opposed to any such honor being given to one who had done nothing to build up, & very little to help the society even after it reflected honor on the aider—who was no farmer, & whose only talents & claims were those of the politician &, as I believed, a most corrupt & unprincipled seeker of office & distinction. In other respects, the talents & reputation of R[ives], & the high positions he has occupied in public life, would make his appointment as speaker more creditable to the Assembly, abroad, than that of any other member, of less reputation, even though far more deserving of the honor.

---

[4] A representative body created by a constitutional amendment adopted at the annual meeting of the state society in 1855.

[5] A prominent figure in state and national politics for fifty years, William Cabell Rives (1792–1868) served four terms in the United States House, was elected to the United States Senate on three different occasions, and was twice appointed minister to France. Although too much of a submissionist to suit Ruffin, he was a delegate to the Confederate Provisional Congress in 1861 and was elected to the Second Confederate Congress.

For the next president of the society, I proposed to our friends, W[illoughby] Newton of Westmoreland.[6] He had been nominated the previous year, in the general meeting, by my son Edmund, but no vote, for a regular election, could be taken, & therefore the whole batch of old officers, (including President Cocke, although he had declined,) was re-instated by a single vote—& of which (& also others) it was very doubtful which way was the majority. However, the then chairman of the meeting, Vincent Witcher, with admirable skill & management, declared the majority to be whichever way he (& all reasonable men) thought it ought to be. And thus, by his legislative tactics, he declared the new constitution was adopted, [7] the whole Ex. Com. re-elected, & then that the meeting was adjourned *sine die,* so as to preclude the chance for a reconsideration & reversal of the hasty decisions just before made, on the very questionable acquiescence of the meeting. So we were indebted to Mr. Witcher for the *coup d'etat,* by which the new constitution was established. The main & great good was effected, of the government & the elections being placed in the hands of a representative body, instead of a great mob of individual members, incapable, from their numbers, of acting, or even of indicating their preferences. The defects of the new constitution may be hereafter remedied, by a proper deliberative body.

... As soon as Newton arrived he told me that he had written to me, some weeks before, a letter which my absence from Marlbourne had prevented my receiving, (& which reached me afterwards—) & he then proceeded to repeat its contents. He was not willing to be nominated as president & unable to serve properly, because of his distance from Richmond, & the want of speedy public conveyances on the north. He urged that I should be nominated for the office—& he, & Edmunds, & others of my most intimate associates or friends convened, & expressed their opinion that my election would be most acceptable to the Society. As I had served as President the first year of the Society, & had then declined a re-election, & on the ground of growing infirmities of age, I had no expectation of my name being again brought forward. But I was not insensible or regardless of the high honor & value of the station, nor unwilling to

---

[6] Newton (1802–74) was a noted agriculturist, lawyer, and political figure from northern Virginia. He pioneered in the introduction of Peruvian guano into Virginia in the 1840's and served as president of the State Agricultural Society in 1852. An intimate friend of the diarist, Newton was the only prominent Virginian who rivaled the latter in his commitment to secession.

accept the place, if I was really preferred. In consenting that my friends might thus use my name, if they chose, I entreated them not to do so unless sure of its being entirely acceptable. I had formerly been elected to the same office by a unanimous vote, expressed by private ballot. It would have been very mortifying then, not only to be rejected, but to have even [8] a respectable minority to vote against me. And that there would be such, I had reason to expect, if only because of the previous difficulties between the President & the Executive Committee—he & his friends deeming me to be the head of the *opposition* to his policy & opinions.

Before the day of meeting, we were gratified to learn that the primary elections [for the Farmers' Assembly] had been duly held, except in a few of the counties, & that nearly all the elected delegates would be present. So far the predictions of failure were falsified.

It had been arranged at the previous meeting of the Ex. Com., held a month before, & in my absence, that on every evening, meetings of the society should be held in two sections, for agricultural discussions. The President was to preside over the first, & I, as first Vice-President, over the second. The first meeting of my section was held on the evening of the 27th. Oct., before the beginning of the regular meeting of the Society. There were several other amusements, more attractive to most persons, every night—the Fair of the Mechanics' Institute, the theatre, other exhibitions & also public meetings with speeches of distinguished party men, by both political parties, who had taken advantage of this opportunity to obtain numerous auditors, on the eve of the very exciting election for President of the U.S. Notwithstanding all these different attractions, my section-meeting had good attendance every night it was held, & of persons deeply interested. I had to use much care & address to get a few farmers to be the first to state their facts & opinions. But in a very short time, the most diffident were ready enough to speak. The subject I elected was the "Culture & Management of the Wheat crop," with everything incidental thereto—& the subject was discussed for three nights, until 11 o'clock, without being exhausted, or the interest of the attendants flagging. I was much gratified with the success of this first trial, especially as an example for future farmers' meetings, either on these, or [9] on other occasions. The President, for his section, preferred to have regular addresses on two nights, & he had an agricultural discussion on one night only.

On the 28th. [the] Fair opened; &, at the appointed hour, the

[11]

members of the Farmers' Assembly met in the hall of the House of Delegates. About 100 members met—within some 20 of the whole number elected. The members were generally highly respectable, for ability, but there were not so many of our first-rate men, as might have been sent. Among the most distinguished men, formerly in public office, were Judge John Robertson, Wm. C. Rives, Willoughby Newton, T. Jefferson Randolph, & John R. Edmunds. The last one only is not now in private life.

By the time we had entered the hall, it was understood that Mr. Rives would be nominated for Speaker, & no opposition was expected. And such was the case. Nevertheless, three members present, of whom I was one, would not vote when their names were called. It mattered not, as to the small duty to be performed, who filled the Speaker's chair. But I was utterly opposed to voting for paying this honor to any mere politician, & much more to such a politician as Rives.

Our proceedings were conducted admirably well, & in perfect harmony. There was not the slightest disorder, or impropriety. And no one gave any evidence of being desirous to make speeches. When the officers of the Society for the next year ( 1857,) were elected, I was chosen president unanimously. All the others of the old officers were re-elected, except Judge [George W.] Summers, who had never attended, & three others who declined a re-election. Among these was Col. Cocke, who not only declined being voted for as President, but to remaining on the [Executive] Committee (as I had before done) as one of the Vice-Presidents. If he would have consented, he would have been thus retained on the [10] Executive Committee. Nevertheless his withdrawal will be very acceptable to most of us, & his occupying there an inferior position would be disagreeable to himself.

The Annual Message, or Address, of the President to the Farmers' Assembly, (which was entirely his own, & in which the Ex. Com. had no concern, or previous information about,) was very long, & very ridiculous, for the display of vanity & self-conceit, & for the recommendation in detail, of a system for agricultural education, so grand, that if carried out, it would have required 10 years time of every pupil, at full college expenses, to go through the course of study & preparation to make a farmer. But all this was covered over, & the President in addition covered himself with glory, by writing the next day to the Assembly, to offer a donation of $20,000, to the Society, to endow a professorship of agriculture at the University of Virginia. For this very generous & patriotic act, Col. Cocke received the enthusiastic thanks of the Assembly, & [*sic*] honor that he well deserved for his liberal public-spirit. On the previous day, he had in our private conversation, congratulated me on my election. On this day, when meeting him, I offered him my congratulations, first, for his having the ample means to exercise such liberality—&, having the means, that he also had the disposition. Before, & also after this time, all our intercourse was kind & respectful—indeed with some approach to cordiality. I tried, & did repress every appearance of any other than respectful & friendly feeling. But in the subsequent & latest meeting of the Ex. Com. for this year, this course was difficult, inasmuch as the president was in some of his conduct more arrogant & assuming & offensive than usual.

The Fair had as many attendants as on any previous occasion, & everything went off well. Still the receipts were less, & the expenses much increased. There are great & growing abuses, causing [11] both these results, which I fear it will be very difficult to prevent. The Farmers' Assembly worked in the best possible manner. Its proceedings embraced enough of the general superintendence of the interests of agriculture, to serve as precedents for future proper & full action—& not enough to excite jealousy & censure of this new power in the commonwealth, which, I trust, is destined to exert great influence on state policy, in regard to agricultural interests.

No voice has been heard to lament the change from the former purely democratic constitution of the Society, & the tumultuous & disorderly mass-meetings, in which nothing could be done, either in discussion, or in voting, to reach judicious ends, or even the objects preferred by the meetings.

The morning after the final adjournment of the Assembly & of the Society, there should have been a meeting of the Ex. Com., to attend which I remained. But so many members had left Richmond, or were otherwise engaged, that there was not a quorum present. The next day the Marlbourne carriage came for me, & I went there to spend the week intervening before the Fair of the Seaboard Agrl. Soc. at Norfolk, which I had promised to attend.

On Nov. [blank] I reached Norfolk, & attended the Fair through the three principal days. On two of the nights there were meetings for conversational discussions on agricultural subjects, in which I joined, by request; & thought that I was enabled to help in the pro-

[13]

ceeding, to good purpose. I had done the like at the Raleigh Fair—& also there delivered a long extemporaneous address to the meeting, on practical matters, & which was my first attempt to speak extemporaneously, at any length, & on previous notice.

After the close of the meeting at Norfolk, I accompanied Mr. Edw. Herbert to his residence in Princess Anne, & there made some [12] further investigation of the subject that I have been engaged upon for some time—the different kinds, & the differences of, the pines of this region.

Nov. [blank]th, went in the evening to Portsmouth, & the next morning, as before arranged, Capt. Cornick, President of the Dismal Swamp Canal Company, & Mr. Reardon, a Director, called for me, in a carriage, to visit the canal.[7] We pursued the stage road, which at Deep Creek crosses the canal, & then continues on the bank of the canal where it passes through the swamp. I had travelled this road, (in the mail coach) last spring, throughout, to Elizabeth N.C., mainly to see & be informed about the lands in view. But for want of any informed companion, I learned very little. To enable me to get the desired information, this trip had been planned. When visiting the interior of the swamp, & Lake Drummond, some weeks earlier, Capt. Cornick had offered to be my guide on this canal route, whenever it would be in my power to go with him. We rode far enough alongside of the canal for me to see every change of swamp soil, & of the small proportion of tilled, or formerly tilled lands—& to obtain from Capt. Cornick full information thereupon. We then returned to Portsmouth. The next day I proceeded to Richmond—& the next to Marlbourne.

Having obtained all the facts to be hoped for, though not all to be desired, on both the subjects on hand, I now proceeded, at my quiet home, to write the continuation of my views of the Dismal S[wam]p., as an addendum to the former long description, (written in 183[?];) & after this, an article on the pines of lower Va & N.C. It was, as always after an intermission, difficult to commence the writing. But after the beginning, I wrote with pleasure & industry. The two pieces made 40 pages of writing. The several pieces previously written, being notes or observations, of [13] what I had seen in my visits

---

[7] One of the most important artificial waterways in the South, the Dismal Swamp Canal connected Albemarle Sound with the port city of Norfolk and was an invaluable commercial artery for the inhabitants of northeastern North Carolina.

to N.C. this year, were the following: account of the new Albemarle & Chesapeake Canal. Description of the agricultural features of the low pine lands of Va & N.C. Theory &c. of the Drift Formation &c. —Notes on the lands of Mattamuskeet—Theory of the formation of the peat swamps of N.C. &c.—Visit to the "Open-Ground" prairie, near Beaufort—& a notice of the ocean beach, or islands, of N.C. All these agricultural writings of my first idle year, make 170 pages— besides the report drawn previously & early in the year, for the Ex. Com. & the sundry later argumentative pieces published anonymously in the newspapers. The latter pieces have been written as hastily, & with little premeditation, as is my usage—& remain in their first rough form, & perhaps may receive no further correction, unless any should hereafter be published. They were not written with any particular view, except for my then pleasure & profitable occupation of my mind. Nothing suits me so well in these respects, as writing. And when so engaged, on an interesting subject, there is no employment so pleasant & engrossing to me, or executed (in my always careless manner,) with more facility. When so employed, I can with pleasure write rapidly for 12 or more hours in the day & night—& until it is necessary to rest my cramped right hand. But, if, after finishing one piece, I allow even a few weeks to pass, without writing, I always find it very difficult to make a new beginning, & it is up-hill work, & badly done, until I can get enough into the subject to become fluent.

It will be necessary, for my killing of time, that I shall write, even if without any other definite object, or with any fixed intention of publication. But it is bad for me that I shall either be entirely & closely occupied in writing, for some weeks, & then requiring quiet & solitude, & then being idle, in this respect, for months together. And worst of all, is the great disinclination & difficulty of making any new beginning, after any such cessation of writing, for some weeks or months. For remedy, I propose hereafter to keep an irregular diary, which, without [14] requiring the least thought or labor of the writer, for better form, or matter, will serve to keep up the habit of writing, & prevent any difficulty in undertaking the more full treatment of any particular subject of observation. For this object I have undertaken this diary that will follow—& have written, as introduction & explanation of future concise entries, the preceding pages of more general statements. If the trial shall amuse & interest me, the writing will be continued—otherwise not. It is not my

purpose to enter minutely the trivial & useless incidents of every day
—nor even other important matters, which it would be improper to
mention even here. But entries will be made, even if unimportant,
often enough to keep up the habit of writing. Nor do I mean to
confine myself to mere incidents. I will allow my pen to run ever so
wildly, if my thoughts so wander, & will thus express anything that
occurs, & deserves noting, but not deserving more elaborate consideration. One good effect of such careless & irregular journalizing, I
expect to be this. Frequently some passing political or other events
induce reflections, or offer a proper subject of remark, but which is
too small or contracted a subject for treating as a substantive matter, or offering to public notice. Therefore, unless to a public speaker,
or to a newspaper paragraphist, all such little though useful thoughts
are unemployed & forgotten. It would often be interesting to the
thinker to have preserved some concise record of stray thoughts.
When my reflections on passing events, or anything else shall occur
to me, I will put them down, with no more consideration of the manner, than if in conversation with any of my intimate & confidential
friends, or of my own children.

I had however in design another writing, & for the public—& also
on other grounds, requiring much deliberation, & unusual care.—
[15] In my visit to the Springs, where of course I met with numerous
persons, (but nearly all of Va & other southern states,) & also where,
I used every suitable occasion to express my opinion, & the grounds
thereof, that the slave-holding states should speedily separate from
the others, & form a separate confederacy, as the only means of
warding off the continued & increasing assaults of the northern people to impair & finally destroy our institution of slavery, & thus ruin
the southern states. It was not so much to argue & convince, that I
thus uttered my strong & undisguised opinions, as to try the opinions
of the auditors. I was surprised to find how many concurred with
me, in the general proposition—though scarcely one of them would
have dared to utter the opinions, at first, & as openly as I did. My
zeal made me desirous to treat this subject before the public—
inasmuch as no one in Va had yet advocated such extreme measures.
I was willing to risk incurring the odium of opinions so unpopular
still with many. But I wished to be a worthy & efficient advocate of
the cause—& for its sake, & my own reputation, not to appear to disadvantage as a writer. And this I was (& am) much afraid of. Still I
was not deterred by this proper consideration of my fear of failure.

## Introduction to the attempt

First it was necessary for me to know, from [Roger A.] Pryor, the efficient editor of the Richmond Enquirer, whether he would admit pieces of the extreme character I designed.[8] This he readily agreed to do, & urged my action. I then began, & in [a] very short time, finished the first draft of my argument—& then proceeded to correct & copy, for the press, dividing the whole into separate short numbers, of less than a column each, when printed. This intended copying, became, as usual in all such attempts of mine, more of re-writing —& requiring much more time & trouble than the first draft.

While so employed, I saw in the newspaper the advertisement of the sale of Bellona Arsenal, belonging to the U.S. government, at public [16] auction in Richmond, on the 18th of Decbr. & I went there two days before, to understand the circumstances, & to bid, if useful. Years ago I had suggested, in conversation with the members of the Ex. Com. that this extensive structure (long useless to the government,) if to be obtained by the State Society, for nothing, or at a very low price, would be an excellent place for an agricultural school. (I now thought it would be still better for a military school, & state arsenal.) A sale had been twice made last year, but not ratified by the Secretary of War, & this next was to be the third sale of the property. I went to the agent & auctioneer to learn the facts, & to state my object, if able, to buy for the Agr. Soc. I there learned that Col. Cocke, for the same purpose, had been the buyer before, (through another bidder,) & would so bid again. This I was also informed more particularly, afterwards, & just before the sale, by Dr. J. Archer, who appeared to bid for Col. Cocke. I did not altogether like leaving the future direction of the matter to rest on so uncertain a footing, as on verbal statements of reported intentions. But, it could not be helped. Of course, I would not bid against Col. Cocke, both of us desiring the same object. But what I fear is that his offer of the property to the Society will be encumbered with the *condition*

---

[8] Roger Atkinson Pryor (1828–1919), lawyer, editor, diplomat, and politician, was at this time serving on the editorial staff of the Richmond *Enquirer,* probably the most important southern newspaper of the period. In 1857 he established his own journal, *The South,* and he later moved to the staff of the Washington *States.* Elected to a seat in Congress in 1859, he resigned two years later to join the Confederate Army, where he enjoyed a checkered career. Following the war he practiced law in New York City and in the 1890's served as an associate justice on the New York Supreme Court.

Although an ardent secessionist and eager to please Ruffin at this time, Pryor later incurred Ruffin's ire when he opposed the latter's efforts to promote a "League of United Southerners."

of its being made an agricultural school, under any circumstances, & under penalty of the forfeiture of any subsequent right to the property. Now if so fettered, the offer of the property, at its low cost, of $2,650, (as bid in for Col. Cocke,) cannot be safely accepted by the Society, as the failure of the school would cause a great pecuniary loss. But if the arsenal property is transferred, (as I designed for myself) to the Society, unconditionally, for its purchase money, the acquisition will be of much pecuniary value to the Society, even if eventually [17] there can be no school established there, & the place should be again sold, & the structures even demolished, for the materials. These buildings cost the government $175,000. It is understood that, if demolished, the materials would sell for $6000 at least.

I used the time of this stay in Richmond to look into the matters of the Exec. Com. & the Secretary's department, to be the more ready for performing my new duties, as President, after Jan 1. Placed Nos. 1, 2, 3 & 4 of my political series in the printer's hands. The title is "On the Consequences of Abolition Agitation, & of the Separation of the Union," & the argument is openly in favor of the separation, under present & all expected circumstances.

*December 19.* Left Richmond in the mail coach, at 3.30 A.M., & reached Marlbourne by sunrise. Find all well. Proceed with the copying & alteration of my series.

*Dec. 21.* Sunday. We went to church, through the beginning of a light snow—but found no minister, or congregation. Very cold. [18]

*Dec. 23.* Left Marlbourne, with Mildred, for Richmond, on our way to Beechwood. There was so much ice on the river that it was evident there would be no chance to go the next day, by steamer, as designed. So changed our route, & went over to Petersburg by the railway.... Intensely cold.

*Dec. 24.* Made an early move, in a hired carriage, & reached Beechwood by 10 A.M., & unexpectedly, as our appointment by way of the river had failed. Find all well, except my daughter-in-law, whose health is no better.[9] Hear that all others of my children in the neighborhood are well.

*Dec. 25.* The reports of negro plots of designed insurrection have in this neighborhood also induced proper measures of vigilance, though there are very few persons who feel any alarm. Patrols, composed of respectable men, have been out every night—& have found

---

[9] The reference is to Mary Ruffin, wife of Edmund, Jr., who remained in ill health until her death on July 28, 1857.

nothing whatever to give any indication of misconduct on the part of the slaves. And even where northern incendiaries, elsewhere, have instigated conspiracy, as usual, the evil consequences, & suffering, will all fall on the deluded victims of these abolition agents—& still worse, in many cases, on the innocent as well as the guilty. All that the whites may lose, or suffer, by these designs, will be well compensated, if they can detect & hang a dozen of these northern agents of mischief. Unluckily, where they have thus endeavored to excite insurrection, the prime movers usually flee & escape to the north, before their villainy is exposed.

Resume the writing (or copying in part,) of my series on Abolition Agitation &c. The Enquirer of yesterday brought up the publication to No 4, in as many daily issues.

My sister Dupuy's family, except herself & those now from home, came to dine with us, bringing to see us my little grand-daughter Jane.[10] Also came Julian & Lotty & Meade, to dinner. These two of my grand-children, & [19] John Ruffin, were as happy as they could be in meeting with each other, & in their other gratifications of Christmas. Milder weather, & bright.

*Dec. 26.* All the grown members of the household, except Mary, who was not well enough, went to dine with Julian & Lotty. The Dupuy family there, & another joyful meeting of the same young grand-children, of the three families. Returned to Beechwood at night.

*Dec. 27.* Finished copying, or rather the second writing of my series on abolition &c., which has stretched out to No XII. . . . I am much less pleased with the last than the prior numbers—& fear that I may already have indicated that it is time for me to stop writing for the public eye. . . .

*Dec. 28. Sunday.* With the family attended public worship at Merchant's Hope Church.—Heard nothing said, by any of the neighbors, of the rumors of negro plots, or of the late patrollings. As usual, all was unfounded & absurd rumor—except at the Tennessee Iron works. There was probably some plot, instigated by northern abolition agents—& whether justly or unjustly, & certainly illegally, many of the negroes have been put to death. The alarm there, & the removal of the laborers have caused the suspension of the operations of the Iron Works. Such are the only possible results of all such plots

---

[10] The child of Ruffin's deceased daughter, Jane Dupuy, this youngster was a particular favorite of the diarist.

of insurrection—the speedy punishment of the guilty, & also of many of innocent motives—& subsequently, as a necessary consequence, increased strictness of general discipline, & a withdrawal of much of the indulgences or freedom from restraint, which the negroes had before enjoyed. And these increased restrictions & sufferings of the slaves, & the severance of the [20] federal union, will be the first important effects of the abolition action of the northern people, to benefit & to free the slaves.—Sent my last Nos. 11 & 12, to the mail, for the Enquirer.

*Dec. 31.* . . . The melodeon, which I had aided the subscription of the neighbors to buy for the church, & which I had ordered, was brought here from Petersburg, & was tried & played by Mildred.

---

BLIZZARD OF 1857 ❧ IN THE NATION'S
CAPITAL ❧ AGRICULTURAL OBSERVATIONS
IN NORTH CAROLINA ❧ VISIT TO
CHARLESTON

*January 1.* Snow last night—covering the ground 4 to 5 inches deep.—Latterly I have slept badly—lying awake some hours of almost every night, & generally after having been asleep. . . . If I could use my thoughts for any purpose, of utility or amusement, when wakeful in the night, it would be some compensation. But I cannot. Even when I have been engaged in the day previous in writing some piece of much interest to me, & which is still in progress, I am unable, when lying awake, to plan a single passage for the next day's writing, or to arrange the substance, or to advance the argument at all. I have the defect of never being able to arrange my words in advance of my writing—& can scarcely think deliberately without having pen in hand, & noting my thoughts as they occur. In my most serious & careful writing, no more than in the most hastily penned note, do I ever attempt to frame a sentence before writing it. And when beginning to write, & for every sentence & passage of the writing, [21] I no more know, when beginning a sentence, how it is to be worded, or how it will end, than in the words of my ordinary conversation. . . . I have heard that some persons compose everything in their mind in advance of writing. Would that I had the faculty, even to the limited extent of thus using my hours of involuntary watchfulness in bed.

Notwithstanding this & some other symptoms of the increasing infirmities of my age, my general health has been unusually good for the last year, & is so indicated by my appearance.

Afternoon, Julian came. He & Edmund engaged until a late hour in arranging the details of the distribution of my estate among the heirs &c. The deed of trust to me, from them as purchasers of the Marlbourne estate, has been executed in part, but still requires the signatures &c. of the parties now absent.

*Jan.* 2. In the forenoon went to see Agnes, to inform her of, & explain her interest in the division of the estate. The subject of my communication led to others which have been generally avoided— the consequences reached & effected from Dr. Beckwith's conduct & management—which were painful & offensive to touch—but which were touched, I trust, to some future benefit—but not in his amendment, for that is hopeless. He will be wasteful & spendthrift, as long as he can find anything to spend—& lazy & heedless of the future, even if the next week his wife & children would be without bread, except to be furnished by the [22] attention & charity of their kindred.

*Jan.* 4. At church. Carried the melodeon, on which Mildred played, to the great improvement of the musical portion of the service. With Julian at night.

*Jan.* 5. On this day I am 63 years old—Went with Julian to Petersburg . . . . Remained in Petersburg until nearly 7 P.M. when the cars left for Richmond. The Executive Committee met, & as I was delayed beyond the time, I was glad to find that they had not waited for me, but were in session. On taking the chair, I stated what I deemed the powers of the President, & in how few points they exceeded those of every other member of the Ex. Com—& what were their different & their similar duties. I also stated that our business needed reform in almost every important particular, & urged that every member should strive to effect improvement—especially in retrenching excessive expenditures. We had a busy & useful session—& adjourned on the evening of the second day. We first provided for carrying into effect all the orders of the Farmers' Assembly—then for the speedy printing of the Transactions, (now two years in arrears,) appointed a committee to inquire into means for retrenchment, & all the other matters of routine, then ready for our action.

A letter received from Col. Cocke, in answer to mine, in reference to the purchase of Bellona Arsenal. He cannot meet the Ex. Com. now, but will do so hereafter, to confer on that subject.

*Jan.* 6. The committee in session both forenoon & afternoon. We were all invited to spend the evening with our fellow member Wm.

G. Crenshaw, who had company. But I had had so little sleep the previous night, that I could not go, but went to bed early.

*Jan. 7.* Start to attend to some business of my own, as well as some of my duties imposed by the Ex. Com. I was in doubt whether to go to Washington, or to return to Beechwood—when a conveyance to Marlbourne offering made me determine [23] to take that way.

*Jan. 8.* With Mr. Sam. Gresham, in his carriage, went to Marlbourne. . . . Found Mr. Sayre ready to go to Westmoreland for a week—& I easily induced Elizabeth, instead of remaining at home, alone, to set out, at the same time, with me, on her intended visit to Prince George. . . .

*Jan. 9.* Mr. & Mrs. Sayre & I to Richmond. Mr. S. will take the next train for Fredericksburg, & go thence to Westmoreland—and will come to Pr. Geo. some two weeks hence. Eliz. & I took the train for Petersburg. . . . We reached the station at Petersburg, at 4 P.M., & hiring a carriage immediately, we proceeded to Beechwood, before 7 o'clock. All as much surprised as pleased at our unexpected arrival. Besides the family, find Mildred, my son Charles, & my brother George.

*Jan. 10.* Last night, & still more the night before, I suffered more than of late, from cold, which is my constitutional & great infirmity. Yet on both of these nights I was at home, or where I could command every desired accommodation, or appliance, to protect me from cold. I suffer more, in this way, than any one I know, but more especially with cold feet, & when in bed. I need always at least about twice as much covering at night as would suffice for most other persons. . . . All my life I have suffered from this cause. But it has much increased with my age. A rainy day. Conversation, reading, & chess. With the latter, all except myself & Mrs. Lorraine much interested.[1] I have not yet been driven again to resort to this pleasant mode of killing [24] time. At three different times of my life, I was induced to play chess often enough to make it a habit with me, & in each case I became so fond of the amusement as to spend several hours of every day, or night, in playing. In all these cases, I found that I could not afford to lose so much time, & for that reason abandoned chess. Even if industry had not then required this sacrifice, or if, instead of

---

[1] Mrs. Lorraine, an intimate friend of the senior Ruffin for nearly half a century, had made her home at Beechwood with Edmund, Jr., and his family since 1845.

being busy, I had been idle, I would deem it wrong to give so much time to a mere amusement that is engrossing of time & attention, & which is entirely unproductive of any good effect, except of present amusement. I would rather read the lightest & most trashy tales, on the score of profit in intellectual improvement. When all other modes of killing time innocently fail, I will again resort to chess....

*Jan. 14.* ... A committee has been raised in the H. of R. to inquire into the charged & suspected bribery of members of the house, by individuals to obtain votes to pass laws for various measures of public plunder. I rejoice at it, & trust that some good may be produced. But there is not much to be expected of the exposure of villainy, by a committee selected by the present speaker,[2] the appointee of the corrupt & plundering northern party. As a body, the majority of the northern members of congress are as corrupt, & destitute of private integrity, as the majority of southern members are the reverse. This difference is admitted by some of the northern papers. And if such difference is permanent, & applies to constituencies as well as the representatives, this alone would be sufficient reason for separation of the northern & southern states. In Congress, we have not only to contend with a decided northern majority, & to be beaten in all questions in which that majority is interested, but in every question of private gain at public cost, bribery & corruption will be still more efficient than numbers.

*Jan. 18.* Sunday. Snow, with strong wind, & bitter cold. Violent & continued [27] north wind, fanning the snow in deep drifts. We could scarcely keep comfortably warm sitting by the fire. Temp. 7° at 9 A.M. & 3° at 4 P.M.

*Jan. 19.* The furious north wind but little abated. Snowing ceased in the night. The ways impassible [*sic*], by snow drifts, & other places barely covered. The thermometer blown down & broken, so cannot know the temperature this morning. I passed a wretched night, with cold feet. Yet I went to bed comfortable, with a good fire burning until it burnt out—& with as much covering as could do any good— 6 blankets, & 2 more over my feet, which were pulled up when needed, & also a doubled cloak over all, on my knees & feet. Woollen night socks, & over them a woollen wrapper, both well warmed, covered my feet. Yet, before the fire had quite burnt out, I was awakened by cold feet, & they continued to grow colder until I had fire & arose in the morning.... The snow lies so irregularly owing to the violent

---

[2] Nathaniel P. Banks, Republican from Massachusetts.

wind, that I cannot even guess the depth. Perhaps it may not average 10 inches. But while many places are scarcely covered, in others the drifts are from 3 to 7 feet deep. It is not only extremely laborious to walk, or even to ride in any direction, or pathway, but even dangerous, because of the snow drifts to be crossed. No work attempted today, by Edmund's order, except to feed the live-stock, & to put wood on the fires. Luckily a good stock of wood was on hand, & cut up, before the snow began. We hear that in the overseer's house, & all the negroes' houses, (the latter good framed & new buildings,) the entrance of the very fine snow, driven by the wind through the smallest crannies, covered all the floors & even the beds. Such a snowstorm I have never known before. Clear, & something milder. We needed the mail especially, but did not attempt to send to the Post Office, because of the difficulty & danger, & also under the belief that no mail could have been brought.

*Jan. 20.* By using still greater precautions, & especially by keeping the fire [28] burning in my room all night, & a servant sleeping there for the purpose, (neither of which did I ever have before,) I kept nearly warm & comfortable.... Clear & milder. My sons Edmund & Charles attempted to ride, & with great difficulty reached the Parsonage, on the public road, & but a mile from the farm buildings. The way was barely practicable, the riders having to dismount in several of the deepest snow-drifts, to enable their horses to scramble out. For even an empty wheel-carriage of any kind, the way was impracticable.... Every thing that has to be moved on this farm, except in the yard, has to be carried on horseback. The only firm walking is on the frozen river, over which the ice & snow extend everywhere. I walked out more than a quarter mile, & I believe that the ice is strong enough to allow walking across....

*Jan. 21.* Warmer. Edmund & Charles rode to the Glebe;[3] but Charles had to leave his horse there, & pick his way on foot through the fields to his farm. The public mail road, beyond the Glebe was impassable, & had not then been trodden by a foot. A physician attempted to ride farther, but was obliged to turn back, though in sight of his patient's house. Edmund heard the average depth of the snow estimated at 18 inches. He thinks it not much less. Having been confined to the house & yard, & seeing so much ground nearly bare, where the wind was most violent, I had supposed the average depth of the snow much less—perhaps 10 inches deep. But it is not the

---

[3] Residence of Ruffin's sister, Mrs. Jane Dupuy.

general depth, but the particular deep [29] drifts, that render walking & riding almost impracticable. I walked to Tarbay,[4] by favor of the frozen snow along the river shore, & the adjacent hillsides, on which the north wind did not allow much snow to remain. Of course, no mail has reached the Post Office since the snow began last Saturday night. Such obstruction to travelling, even for a day, I have never heard of before, in this region. According to present appearances & prospects, the roads will scarcely be practicable for carriages in a week. No one has attempted even to ride on horseback, except on compulsion. Those who have been compelled to send to the mill, for meal, have sent on horseback, & some on foot—& these have left the road so often to avoid the snow drifts, that the travel does not in the least prepare for the subsequent use of wheel-carriages.

*Jan. 22.* Colder last night, & a light snow. Clear & bright sunshine, but with a N.W. sharp wind & the weather colder (apparently) than at any time before. Confined to the house by the cold wind, & very tired of the confinement. Nothing heard from the outside of the farm. I have read everything I can find amusing in our late Reviews & other periodicals, & have been reduced to such poor stuff as the books of "Fanny Fenn."

*Jan. 23.* I walked across the river on the ice, to Berkley landing, from the beach nearest to this house. With the usual liberal measure allowed for distances on water, this broad part of the river is generally called 3 miles across. But it is certainly less, & from the time I made, I do not think the distance more than 2 miles. I walked over in 55 minutes, & returned in 60. . . . No doubt the passage was very safe. But we are so unaccustomed here to ice so solid, & still more to any one venturing to cross a wide & deep river, that my walking over was a very unusual performance. Except in the case of the sailors of a vessel frozen in, & who walked to the shore to obtain food &c. I did not hear of any walking across the river last winter, when it was hard frozen—nor in the many preceding milder winters, during my proprietorship & residence here. But though very few persons would now dare to walk across & still fewer except under strong necessity —& though certainly none ought to incur any apparent risk, without necessity—I am inclined to believe that a horse might have been supported on most of the ice over which I passed today, notwithstanding its numerous cracks. . . . Sent to the Post Office, only to hear that no mail had yet arrived—& that no wheel-carriage, or sleigh,

---

[4] Residence of Mrs. Martha Cocke.

had been on the main public & mail road. We have so little snow, that few persons, in the country, or for business, ever use a sleigh. But on this snow, because of its scarcity or absence in many spots, & the deep drifts in others, sleighing would be impracticable. We have now lost all three mails for the week—& have no prospect that the next mail can come. Yet this post office is but 16 miles from Petersburg & the main rail-road route, which must have been cleared of snow some days ago.

*Jan. 24.* Rode to the Glebe, & thence to Ruthven, to dinner. The road so deep in snow in many places that I had to leave it (following preceding tracks,) crossing fences into adjacent fields. Found, as expected, that Julian's thermometer also had been broken by the storm. . . .

*Jan. 25.* Sunday. No attempt to get to church—as it would certainly have been fruitless. Milder.

*Jan. 26.* Still no mail. Only one cart had passed along the main mail road, & that had been compelled to return, because unable to proceed.

*Jan. 27.* Very mild. Thawing—& no freezing by bed-time. Left Ruthven for Beechwood. A sale appointed for today had served to draw out sundry of the neighbors, to see other persons, & hear some news. I found some of these on my route, & heard something from abroad. Mr. Marks' thermometer showed 12° below zero, on the morning of the 23rd. This was 2° colder than I ever knew before. Mr. Dunn had been compelled to ride to Petersburg [32] on that day. Heard that the railway to Washington had not been then made practicable, & of course no northern mail, except from Richmond. 4 men in Petersburg & in the vicinity had been exposed to the weather of the night of the 18th. & 3 were frozen to death, & the fourth is expected to die. One of these was Dr. Cox, a physician, riding in a buggy from Petersburg to his farm in Chesterfield. He was unable to open the gate, or to reach the house on foot, & died close to it. His companion (Traylor) is alive, but is worse than dead. All these cases were probably the results of more or less of intemperance. But two negro men, supposed sober, were frozen to death, in different places of this county, in that dreadful Sunday night, in attempting to visit other houses but a few hundred yards distant. —The snow & snow ice over the hard ice on the river mostly thawed, & in soft wet sludge, or water, before night. . . .

*Jan. 28.* Thawing last night & all this day. Light drizzle. Julian

[27]

hearing yesterday that the mail had been brought as far as the Court House, sent there for his papers, & sent them to us this morning. We thus received the papers for 9 days at once—& scarcely any news, except the numerous accounts of the incidents of the snow storm, & of disasters therefrom. The roads were still blocked up & impassable everywhere heard from. The railways had been impassable for from 2 to 4 days—& no entire opening northward yet. Sundry more deaths reported, and others barely escaped, from freezing. The temperature correctly observed in Petersburg, on the morning of the 23rd. reported to be 14° below zero—& in Richmond 13°—& in different other places of the vicinity, still lower marks, & in one case as low as 20° below zero. I doubt these latter statements, but fully believe in the report from Petersburg. One of the negroes reported yesterday as frozen in Prince George, was in Hanover. And 4 whites, (one a small boy) in a wagon, were frozen to death in that county. In Richmond & Petersburg, (the only towns from which we [33] received papers,) there has been a general cessation of ordinary labor & business. No supplies or customers from the country. The passenger & mail train on the Central Railroad, (on which the great N. & S. mail is transported,) remained, with all its freight, blocked up within 6 miles of Richmond, for two days & nights, & could not be there reached, & the passengers relieved, by carriages, nor even by messengers on foot, sent with food. The mail to this office has not been brought yet—nor even attempted to be brought by the only means, that is, on horseback, & frequently through the fields, where the snow is too deep in the roads. It is not so strange that so many lives have been lost, as that there were so few. The great violence of the wind & intense cold, & the continued driving snow on the night of Sunday (18th) prevented the slaves visiting as is their usage. If the storm had abated, many more of sober negroes, as well as of drunken whites would have perished. The danger of the former was so great on this farm, that it was a mercy that all escaped. The negroes' houses were built in several different places, the better for health & comfort. If any one of the residents of one house had visited another, in that night, he might have sunk in a snow-drift, where no cry for help could have been heard, though within a few hundred yards of a dwelling.

*Jan. 29.* Mr. Sayre arrived, to the great joy of his wife, & of all of us for her sake especially.... The railroads from Richmond to Washington were only opened on yesterday. Got a late newspaper by [34] Mr. S., but with no important & definite news. Glad to learn that there had been no disaster, & no suffering, from the storm, at Marlbourne. The public roads there were at last made passable by the road laborers, called out by the surveyors of the roads. Here, no surveyor has moved, & perhaps has not thought of it—because working on the roads to remove or tread down snow was never heard of, or needed, heretofore. Unless it is done, no public road can be travelled by carriages for a week or more, & neither the church or the post-office will be accessible along the roads by carriages.

*Jan. 30.* . . . The mail reached the P.O., the first in 13 days. The little news had been mostly anticipated in our previous supplies obtained by private conveyances. The strong indications of war in Europe are dispelled. . . . But . . . England is like to have war with China—as Canton has already been bombarded by the British ships of war. If this leads to war, even if as unjustly provoked as was the late war with China by England,[5] it will be best for the people of China that extensive conquest shall be effected by England. The Chinese, & also the Japanese people, will be much benefited if their unimprovable despotic governments, & customs, are broken down, even if by conquest by civilized European powers.

. . . The late papers state the deaths of two Virginians of some note, William Maxwell & Andrew Stevenson, but whose claims for distinction were very different. Mr. Maxwell had great natural powers of mind, well cultivated by education, fine literary taste, was a good writer, & eminent as a conversational debater. Besides his general literary pursuits, through his long life, he had occupied (for the first year,) the post of editor of the Journal of Commerce in N.Y., & later the Presidency of Hampden Sidney College. His only service in political life was for one term in the State Senate of Va. in which, as elsewhere, his ready & pleasing elocution placed him in high rank. Still, with all his admitted abilities, and with unquestioned private integrity & worth, & a moral & religious life from his boyhood, he never succeeded in any effort, except in gaining the esteem of his friends; & his living has had as little effect on the public interest or action as in promoting his own private interests or objects. He was not wanting in industrious & proper effort, & yet lived & died poor. Stevenson was immeasurably inferior in natural faculties of the high-

---

[5] The First Anglo-Chinese War (1839–42), which erupted following an effort by the Chinese government to halt the importation of opium, a major item in British trade with China.

er order, & still more so in scholastic education. He was not a pattern of integrity in private life—& in public, was a corrupt & unprincipled politician, seeking [36] to advance his own interest in preference to all others. But his moderate abilities included perseverance & impudence, & were precisely suited to benefit himself. He succeeded in reaching eminence & wealth, as a lawyer—& high mark as a politician, in his long public life.[6] He occupied a high position in the legislature of Va—then in Congress, where he was Speaker, until (& indeed after,) he had received as pay for his corrupt devotion to Gen. Jackson's administration, the bribe of the appointment of Minister to Great Britain. This great honor, (if it had been honorably earned & deserved,) seemed however to have been deemed payment in full for all his political services—as he never could afterwards obtain anything more of political office from the government or people. Still he had empty compliments, flattering to his vanity. Thus, he was appointed a Visitor of the University [of Virginia], & Rector, or chairman of the board. He was little fitted by education for the government of an institution of learning. He had not even learned latin, though he was in the habit & very fond of using commonplace latin quotations in his speeches in Congress &c., which he obtained readily, with their meaning, from the "Dictionary of Quotations." I have had so bad an opinion of this distinguished Virginian, that I have avoided making his personal acquaintance—& (though I trust for different cause,) he seemed as little to desire my acquaintance, or to appreciate any worth in me. One reason may have been this: Among his undeserved honors, he used to be invited to deliver agricultural addresses (in other states,) & was President of the former State Agrl. Society of Va. (so-called,) until that abortion was merged in the present State Society, & when I was unanimously elected President, & not a vote was given to him, for that office.

It may well be doubted whether, in these degenerate times, the purest integrity & correct morals are any advantage to the man who is ambitious of popular support. I further believe, in many cases, that education of high order is rather an obstacle than an aid to an able & unscrupulous seeker of public honors. . . . A considerable amount

---

[6] Andrew Stevenson (1784–1857), lawyer, politician, and agriculturist, served seven terms in the United States House of Representatives, occupying the post of Speaker from 1827 to 1834. Following his service as minister to Great Britain, 1836–41, he retired to his Blenheim estate in Albemarle County, Virginia. His son, John White Stevenson, was a prominent figure in Kentucky politics, holding the positions of representative, senator, and governor.

of natural talent is necessary for the first rise of an uneducated man. But to continue to rise, more ability would be less important means than greedy ambition, great self-appreciation, & the boldness of impudence without limit. A man naturally so disposed will deem his earliest success as full proof of his ability & merit being superior to his rivals. Not being deterred or impeded by any sense of modesty, or shame of apprehended defeat, (the most discouraging impediment to a modest yet proud man,) he will be a candidate for every vacant higher office, even when so much higher than his then position, that success is hopeless even to himself. But in such cases he will offer himself, not with any present expectation of gaining the post, but to place himself conspicuously before the public eye, in connection with public office. If, while yet untried in legislative service, he is a candidate for Congress, or the State Senate, though defeated, it will induce many voters to think of him as very suitable for the lower station of the House of Delegates. . . . If such a man had been early & well educated, he would have thereby acquired modesty. However great his attainments in learning, he would also learn to see, at every [38] step of his upward progress, the greater & greater heights of knowledge above him, which he had not reached, & could never expect to reach. Thus the greatest measure of learning, by showing more strongly his still existing deficiencies, would nourish & increase his modesty. Not only would he think humbly of his own attainments, even if they were as great as those of a Newton, but, by knowing the labor of his own progress & success, he would look with toleration & compassion on his untaught fellows, who had not enjoyed his advantages, & he would not presume on his superiority over them. On the contrary, the uneducated or self-educated man, in public station, despises all learning, that he does not possess, as mere useless theory & pedantry. He knows many men who have had (as he supposes) all the advantages of schools, & colleges, & books, & who still are greatly his inferiors in ability & useful knowledge—& thence he infers that the learning which he has not [had] is useless, & that he knows every thing that is really worth learning, at least for his own advancement & service in public stations. Such a man perhaps is continually acquiring new knowledge, & he is not insensible of the value of every such new acquisition. But while each new step compels him to admit that he was mistaken before, in supposing he had reached the height of useful knowledge, he is then sure that he is now at the top, because his ignorance & self-conceit prevent his seeing, or even suspecting, the value of the knowledge he does not possess. Therefore, it is not only that he is urged by his ambition, & supported by his impudence, but he is encouraged by the confident belief that he is the best qualified to fill every high station that ambition or self-interest may invite him to aspire to.

*February 2.* . . . It is reported in the Norfolk paper that a man walked across Hampton Roads, from Old Point Comfort to Willoughby's Point, & thence, on the ice, to Norfolk. Though the ferry steamers were kept running, (by breaking the ice ahead) still most of the persons who passed between Norfolk & Portsmouth walked across on the ice. Persons also walked across the Chesapeake bay, at Annapolis, where 12 miles wide—& from Edenton to Plymouth, 20 miles, across Albemarle Sound.

*Feb. 5.* Warm enough for April. The ice on the river began to break, & some floated down with the tide, so as to leave much clear water. My daughters went in the carriage to Woodland, & also Julian & family came to Beechwood. Both passages made with great difficulty, owing to the miry & soft condition of the earth everywhere. In this respect, & for the depth of this soft texture, the roads are worse than I ever knew of them. It is now more difficult to travel than when the snow was deepest. Then the snow drifts might be passed around, by driving over the adjacent fields. But now the fields are even more miry, & less trustworthy, than the roads.

*Feb. 9.* Went to Ruthven to stay the night, (my daughters there also,) to go thence to Petersburg. I was afraid to wait for the steamboat's first trip.

*Feb. 10.* Julian had to send Miss Meade[7] to Petersburg, & I availed myself of the conveyance. . . . at 6 P.M. took the mail train to Richmond, to attend the meeting of the Executive Committee. Eight members present. All friends, & all very glad to see each other, & all would prefer to converse at their first meeting. Under such circumstances, together with my own unfitness to act as a chairman, it is very difficult to keep order, & attention to business. However—we got through a great deal before our adjournment at midnight.

*Feb. 11.* Again in session from 10 to 3 o'clock. By agreement, we held a farmers' meeting at night, for conversation & discussion on matters of practical farming. As it was a first experiment, & there might be failure, we made no notification, except, on that afternoon,

---

[7] Julian's sister-in-law.

to invite verbally any farmers we met with to join the meeting. Some 20 met, & we had a pleasant session of 3 hours. We design to hold such meetings regularly hereafter, at the future meetings of the Executive Committee—which hereafter will be quarterly.

*Feb. 12.* Remained in Richmond to attend to the business of the Society, belonging to my duty as President, or specially entrusted to me, with others, by the Ex. Com., & especially in view of correcting the former abuses & wasteful management of the Fairs.

*Feb. 13.* Went to Washington, by the Fredericksburg line—rail road & steamer. The Potomac much obstructed by ice still . . . . But the steamer is well constructed for breaking ice—& as the passage had been broken through, & travelled twice a day, we made better way than expected. To Brown's Hotel. Found there Mr. Wm Boulwane, & Thos. Ruffin, (M.C.) of N.Ca.[8] [41]

*Feb. 14.* In the course of the day, saw most of my former acquaintances, (members of Congress,) & was introduced to others—& saw some other & distinguished or great men, whom, humble as I may be, I would not be introduced to, or hold any communication with. Among these is Sam Houston, the "hero of San Jacinto," former President of Texas, & now senator of Texas. The position of this man, in regard to his merits, is marvellous. When long ago in Congress, he was only notable for his want of integrity, his being a tool & a pet of President Jackson, & his conduct as a bully & a western rowdy. Afterwards, when Governor of Tennessee, his conduct to his newly married wife was so monstrous & unaccountable, that he was obliged (by public indignation) to resign his office, & leave the state. Subsequently *that* wife obtained a divorce. He took refuge among the Indians, & became as one of them, & took an Indian wife, whom he basely abandoned when he found it convenient to return to more civilized associates. Next he turned up in Texas, & in that new community of desperadoes, of the worst habits & morals in general, it may be that Houston's vices were recommendations. He rose to the command of the army, & led in its seemingly hopeless retreat before the Mexican army, & in the signal victory afterwards achieved at San Jacinto. Yet many of the most respectable of the men who fought there pronounce that Houston showed total incompetency, & even

---

[8] Thomas Ruffin (1820–63) was a member of the United States House of Representatives, 1853–61, and a delegate to the Confederate Provisional Congress at Richmond. Later, he served as a colonel in the First North Carolina Cavalry until he fell mortally wounded at Bristoe Station, Virginia, in 1863.

want of personal courage—that his men forced him to stand at bay, or rather that the army fought without his will, or his direction—& the victory was gained without any aid from the nominal commander. Still the glory so acquired raised him to be President of independent Texas. During [42] all this time, in conduct & habits, he was a low black-guard & common drunkard. After the annexation of Texas, (which he tried all he could do to prevent,) he was elected one of the U.S. senators of the new state. He has since aspired to the presidency of the U.S., & has abstained latterly from his former drunken & other low habits. In the hope of obtaining northern support for his ambitious views, he has assumed northern ground as to slavery. But in this last corrupt movement he has overreached himself. It is understood that he will not be again elected to his present post—& he will have lost his previous popular support, & become as despicable as he deserves to be, without gaining anything from the north. He has married again, & thus has or had three wives alive at once—his divorced wife, his deserted Indian wife, & the last & legal wife. It is one of the foulest disgraces of this country, that this despicable wretch should have reached, & so long maintained, a high position in popular favor, & that he should have been even thought of as one who might be elected President of the United States. For though other as base men have stood as high, most of these (as [Thomas Hart] Benton) had great ability as well as villany [*sic*]. But Houston never has exhibited any evidence of uncommon talent. And his deviations from the course of discretion & good sense, as well as of moral rules, have been accounted for by some persons as the results of supposed partial insanity.

I sought & had introductions to Elwood Fisher & A. Dudley Mann.[9] The latter is full of confidence in the success of his scheme of a line of enormous steamers like the "Great Eastern" now building near London. These vessels will be 700 feet in length, of 30,000 or more tons weight, are expected to cross the Atlantic in 7 days, & can so economise fuel, & cheapen freights, as to command the monopoly of transportation. And these vessels will draw so much water, that the Chesapeake Bay & Norfolk harbor only will afford admittance. If half of [43] Mr. Mann's anticipations can be realized, they

---

[9] Ambrose Dudley Mann (1801–89), an ardent advocate of southern rights and southern economic independence, was at this time championing the establishment of a direct steamship line between the South and Europe. His schemes often lacked the substance of reality. Later, as a Confederate diplomat, he was particularly noted for his credulity and general stupidity.

promise a great improvement & a glorious future for southern & especially Virginian commerce. I called on him, & was much gratified to hear his views more fully detailed than in his publication on the subject.—I had long known, by his writings, Elwood Fisher, as the able & instructive advocate for the southern states & their institution of slavery, & was rejoiced to make his personal acquaintance, & to converse freely with him.—

*Feb. 15.* . . . Boulwane & Fisher came to my apartment, & we conversed for two hours—F. the main talker. I referred, with due & high commendation to his celebrated lecture on the "North & South," [10] & our conversation was on its subject, & that of my own former Address on the social results of slavery & of its absence. . . . Fisher's conversation is lively, amusing, & instructive. He was raised a Quaker—& his grandfather & father had emancipated their slaves & made every other incidental sacrifice to perform what they deemed their moral & religious duty in that respect. [44]

*Feb. 16.* Soon after breakfast Senator [Robert M. T.] Hunter called to see me. I did not recollect him, until he announced his name. When I had before called to see my old friend [William O.] Goode,[11] where Hunter lives also, I asked for the latter, but he was out—& I left no card, or message for him, so as not to make any claim on his attention. Long ago, when he had attained no higher place than a seat in the House of Representatives, there was personal acquaintance & some correspondence between us. I have in almost everything approved his political conduct, & wished for his success & higher elevation. But it is now 20 years since I had met with him, & nearly as long since any letters had been exchanged. His visit was [at] an unusually early hour, & otherwise without ceremony, & his manner cordial, kind, & as plain, as might be expected in country life. He offered to take me into the Senate Chamber, & some other attentions which I know would have been a tax on his much occupied time. I gladly, & only, accepted his invitation to the Senate chamber, at the proper hour. Since Hunter has been deemed a prominent aspirant to the presidency, & with much prospect of future success, he is said to have become in his manner reserved, cold, & very cautious of his words. I saw that he was (& properly in his

---

[10] Published in 1849.

[11] After a distinguished career in the state legislature, William Osborne Goode (1798–1859) represented Virginia in Congress from 1841 to 1843, and again from 1853 to 1859.

[35]

position,) cautious in his words, & very different from my own open & unweighed expressions on political matters—but nothing of coldness, or reserve otherwise, and no assumption of dignity, more than when we had met formerly. At the Senate Chamber, afterwards, & at my request, Mr. Hunter introduced me to Senator Toombs of Ga. I referred to his published letters to the late "Southern Convention," in which he assumed the position that the legislatures of the Southern States had the legal & constitutional right to tax the commodities of the north, after their introduction—& which power, if exercised, may be used effectually to defend & aid the southern states, & to retaliate the injuries of the North. I [45] told him that if he was sure of being correct in his views, he owed to our cause, & also to himself, to sustain his propositions, in detail, & to have their truth established. He answered that he was perfectly sure of the soundness of his positions, & that he had been collecting materials, & considering all the many published objections to his letters, & would, as soon as at leisure, present the subject, fully elucidated, to the public. I earnestly hope that he may be able to do so—& that the Southern States may fully avail themselves of this potent means for defence, & retaliation. But I doubt it. I have no legal knowledge on this or other subjects, & cannot present legal objections. But it seems to me that if the several states fully possess the power of taxing, (& of course prohibiting,) the sale of the commodities of other states, that it may be so exercised as to obstruct entirely the free commerce designed by the federal constitution, & to break the union itself. And though these results are exactly such as I would value the power for, I cannot believe that any such destructive power was ever designed to be admitted into the constitution.

With Mr. Boulwane rode to the Observatory to visit Lieut. [Matthew Fontaine] Maury.[12] I had known him before, & found him now, as formerly, cordial, affable & agreeable, in our conversations on ordinary topics, in addition to his far more exalted merits as a man of science. He is one of the most able men of this confederation —& perhaps has the most extended reputation in Europe of any living citizen of America. . . . [46]

---

[12] Maury, a fellow Virginian, celebrated oceanographer, and father of the United States Weather Bureau, was in charge of the Naval Observatory in Washington at this time. He enjoyed an international reputation and received an impressive array of foreign awards and decorations—more than any other American prior to Herbert Hoover.

*Feb. 17.* Attending to the two houses of congress. Went to dine, on invitation of Mr. Hunter, with his "mess," which consists of himself, Senator Mason of Va, Senator Butler of S.Ca., & Messrs. Goode & Garnett, members of the H. of R. from Va. I had previously been well acquainted with all, except Senator Mason. Mr. Boulwane the only other guest. We had a very pleasant sitting of several hours. There was nothing said seriously on political matters—but enough in other ways to make me think that Buchanan, the incoming president, has very little of the respect or the confidence of the men from the south, by whose support alone he was sustained & elected. I anticipate for him a reign that will bring to him but little of either pleasure or honor. The victory in the election of president, such as it was, was gained by the southern states & the democratic party, as I inferred, only because Buchanan was a Pennsylvanian, & had the votes of his state because of favor, & not because of their approval. But I heard from Fisher, & it was repeated today, that enormous sums of money were sent from the city of New York, & a good deal also from the democrats of New England, to buy votes in Pennsylvania—& which turned the vote of that state. The victory over Fremont & abolitionism, if thus gained by bribery, is worth even less than I had before estimated it.

*Feb. 18.* As proposed yesterday by Mr. Hunter, he called for me this morning soon after breakfast, & carried me to the public Botanic Garden, which is rather a collection of exotic & mostly tropical plants, in several green or hot-houses.... There were many curious [47] plants, which would have interested me for hours. But I would not detain Mr. Hunter long, as I knew his time was precious.... Saw [James D. B.] De Bow, editor of the Southern Review, & had some conversation in regard to it, & connected matters.

*Feb. 19.* An exciting scene in the House of Representatives, for which I had been watching two days previous. The report of the "corruption committee" was submitted. Four members, all abolitionists & northern men (3 of N.Y., & 1 of Con.,) are proved guilty of receiving enormous bribes, for their acts to enrich private interests, & their expulsion from the house is recommended by the committee, by 4 to 1. The committee, selected by the abolition speaker, consists of two democrats, two abolitionists, & one "know-nothing" whig. The reading, & then the reception of the report was opposed by every effort, by some of the abolitionists, in long speeches. But two others of that party denounced this attempt to produce delay, & thus ward off the trial—by which delay alone the rascals would escape punishment, as the session is so near at an end. After a long & animated & disorderly debate, the report was received, & ordered, with the testimony, to be printed. The discussion is postponed to next week.[13] We have enough of immoral men in the south, & enough of such representatives in Congress. Nevertheless, not a member from any slave-holding state has been suspected of sharing in this base conduct, of receiving bribes, which, though only now proved, has existed for a long time. So it had come to be understood that very few large private claims could be passed without bribery—& that few such were rejected, if enough money was used to forward them. Still, this was but suspicion, & the facts were known only to those who either paid or received the bribes. . . .

Who were to compose the cabinet of the new president has been a mystery until yesterday, when it was announced (though on no certain authority,) & the members are now believed to be understood. Cass is to be Secretary of State, Howel[l] Cobb of Ga., Sec. of War, & Floyd, of Va., Sec. of the Navy.[14] All these I deem bad appointments, & there is nothing to compensate these deficiencies in the other heads of inferior departments. In addition to objections to Cass's political views, (he being a representative of northern democracy,) he has seemed to have a monomania for war with England. Besides he is so old, that his mind is probably failing, & it was never of very high order. Cobb was an advocate for the "compromise" measures of 1850, by which the rights of the southern states were sacrificed. In Ex-Gov. Floyd's integrity, public or private, I have no confidence. Pickens of S.C. is the only member of the new cabinet who (I suppose) goes fully for the south.[15] But his own state could supply many men as true as he can be, & of greater ability. Yet all the democratic newspapers are pronouncing the appointments to be admirable.

*Feb. 20.* Called on Mr. Wheeler our minister to Nicaragua, with whom I had been slightly acquainted formerly. Had much informa-

---

[13] The report received by the House on this date related specifically to the case of Congressman William A. Gilbert of New York, who resigned his seat on February 28, thus forestalling his expulsion.

[14] This early report proved to be partially erroneous. Cobb was named Secretary of the Treasury and John B. Floyd Secretary of War.

[15] Francis W. Pickens, in actuality, did not receive a cabinet post; instead, he was appointed minister to Russia in 1858 and two years later was elected governor of South Carolina.

tion from him concerning that country & its inhabitants. He thinks that, according to his latest news, Walker's situation is good. He has nearly 1200 men from the U.S., which number Wheeler thinks can maintain their ground against all the forces that the allies of Central America can bring against them.[16] Nearly the whole population is of mixed blood, & no distinction made between, or repugnance of any one color to another. The [49] only inhabitants of pure blood are the aborigines. These are also the best of the population, in morals & habits—but they are few in number. Taken altogether, & throughout Central America, the people are worthless, & afford no hope of their improvement. They must give way to the Anglo-Saxon race—& their extinction will be a benefit to America. . . . This morning completed an arrangement with De Bow. I am to furnish to him any of my writings on general agricultural subjects, which, if approving & publishing them, he will pay for at the rate of $3 the page of his Review. I proposed for this purpose most of the several articles I have written (without correcting or altering as yet,) in the course of 1856. And this is the only proper channel for them—as they are too general, & not enough practical, & also too long, for communications to the State Agricultural Society, & unsuited to any other publication, even if the agricultural periodical papers were not all of too low character to receive my pieces. In addition, probably neither they nor the political or commercial papers would choose to publish such long & general or speculative articles, although furnished to them gratuitously. Of course none of them (in the south) would pay anything for communications of this or any other kind. De Bow also agreed to republish my recent articles advocating a dissolution of the Union—[50] & I was surprised that he should so consent. I had placed the series in his hands for his scrutiny—but I believe he read but little of them, before agreeing to insert them. Spent the evening in reading & correcting & making some change of form of the pieces, suitable to its place in a Review. At De Bow's request, it is to appear with my name as the author. If there is no other reason for its attracting notice, the boldness of the propositions, in a work of such character as this Review, will both attract attention, & bring on the acknowledged author plenty of censure & abuse.

---

[16] The flamboyant filibusterer William Walker (1824–60) had exploited a civil conflict in Nicaragua and set himself up as dictator in 1855. However, a coalition of Central American republics engineered by Cornelius Vanderbilt soon put him under severe military pressure, and he was forced to capitulate on May 1, 1857.

Gen. Cass has long been noted for the exhibition of hatred for England, & a seeming wish to get into war with that country. Fears seem to be entertained by many, that he may bring this about. Lord Palmerston, the prime minister of England, is about as old as Cass, with a general propensity for war, & probably hates this country as much as Cass hates England. It would be remarkable, though not a very improbable event, if these two old fellows, who ought to be pushed off the stage of action, should bring about so great a calamity as a war between their countries.

*Feb. 21.* Dined by invitation with A. Dudley Mann, at his boarding house. The few other persons expected were all engaged, & so he & I dined *tete-a-tete.* Mr. Mann is a strong southerner. We agreed not only in that but other things—one of which is opposition to all duties on imported commodities, (or indirect taxes) or advocating perfectly free trade, & direct taxation. I knew that Mr. Buchanan (like other Pennsylvania democrats,) advocated high protecting duties on coal & iron, the great products of Pa. But I did not know, until now (from Mr. M.) that he had voted for the high tariff enacted in 1842. In this act of support to the protection system, & also of the basest breach of faith to the south in thus violating [51] the noted compromise act [of 1833], Wm. C. Rives shared the infamy. It is understood here that the hungry office-seekers who were most active in supporting Mr. Buchanan, expect him to make room for them by dismissing the present office holders, though they also are of the same party, & as good Buchanan men—& no matter if they have discharged their official duties ever so well. It is thought that this will be done. If so, it will present a new phase of the proscription system, which was first established by President Jackson, & adopted by every succeeding administration. This course has been, when a party victory was gained in a presidential election, for the new incumbent to turn out every office-holder of the opposite party, no matter how meritorious, & to give their places to reward his supporters. This was sufficiently infamous. But when no change of party power is made, as at present, the partisans who have done all the dirty work of the election will lose their pay, if respect is paid to the occupancy or merit of office-holders. Therefore, as reported, there is to be a general sweep. And in rewarding his expectant friends, the president will convert as many other friends to enemies, by unjustly depriving them of office. Truly, Mr. B. will have an uneasy time.

*Feb. 22.* The city is filling with visitors, & no doubt office-seekers for much the greater number. And nearly all are suspected of it, even when innocent. If my being an outlaw as to party rule does not secure me from this suspicion, the charge will scarcely withstand the facts that I have neither seen nor had communication with either the out-going or the in-coming president—or any other of the expected dispensers of patronage or favor. I have always avoided & declined being introduced to presidents—& never saw one (while president,) or had any intercourse with any, except the least powerful one of all, Tyler, with whom I had [52] been long before acquainted, & on a footing of friendly intimacy.—Paid my hotel bill, to be ready for an early move homeward tomorrow morning.

*Feb. 23.* Left the wharf at Washington at 6½ A.M. & by steamer & railway reached Richmond at 2½ P.M. . . .

*Feb. 24.* At 3½ A.M. left in the mail-coach, & reached Marlbourne to breakfast. Found my daughters Elizabeth & Mildred as well as usual—& Mr. Sayre had gone this morning, in the carriage, to Richmond, to bring my old friend Mrs. Mildred Campbell—who arrived at night.

*Feb. 25.* Began to copy my writing of last summer on the "Drift Formation." As in general, the copying of my own writing is much slower, laborious, & less agreeable, than the first composition. . . . Alterations suggest themselves to my mind, & they are written, & I soon am no longer copying but re-writing the same matter in different form—& often find that the new form is no improvement. . . . Afternoon & evening, to 10 or later, pleasantly spent in conversation.

*Feb. 26 & 27.* Finished the writing, in 37 pages—&, before beginning to read & give last corrections, I am less satisfied with the copy than with the original, & doubt whether the changes of form are not defects. Mail day. No news. The corruption cases before Congress. I expect that the rascals & their party will prevent a decision by using every quibble for delay, until the short remnant of the session is exhausted. [53] The death of Dr. [Elisha] Kane, the Arctic explorer, confirmed—greatly to be deplored.[17] Renewed the reading of Pepys' Diary, which had been interrupted so long (since at the Springs last autumn) that I could not remember what portion I had

---

[17] Elisha Kent Kane (1820–57), naval officer, physician, and Arctic explorer, commanded the Second Grinnell Expedition (1853–55) in search of Sir John Franklin, who had disappeared in 1845. After a series of harrowing adventures, he returned to the United States and wrote *Arctic Explorations*, which became one of the most widely read books of the 1850's. Kane died in Havana, Cuba, on February 16, 1857.

read. Curious as it is, & interesting in many particulars, I find this book generally tedious—& I only labor through or glance over the dull parts, to reach the scattered notices of interesting matters.

*March 1.* Sunday. With the family went to church .... At night Mrs. Campbell & I talked of the incidents of our early acquaintance when I was but a youth of 17, & she a wife & mother, of 23. She referred to the then poverty of her husband, who had just commenced business as a bookseller on a small scale—& the consequent labor, hardships, & privations, she had to undergo. ... I said that in my opinion young people of "gentle blood," or used to early comforts, [54] but also of well-ordered minds, could undergo necessary hardships with more contentment & cheerfulness than other persons of lower origin, & less accustomed to the indulgences & the training that wealth & high position afford. I thought that both I & Mr. Sayre, as well as Mrs. Campbell were examples of the truth of my proposition .... Mr. Sayre's hard life was as a common sailor in merchantmen, & later as petty officer in a New Bedford whale ship, on a voyage in the Pacific. Mine was much lighter—even a time of care & comfort in comparison—in my six months service near Norfolk, as a private volunteer in the militia.[18]

*March 2.* After reading & correcting ahead, the first draught of my writing on the "Peat Formation," began to copy it. Determined to make no new alterations, in copying, except where, in the last reading, I had marked places needing alterations or additions. Copied 7 pages by 12.30 P.M., when set off, with the others, to dine with Dr. Wormeley's family, by previous appointment. ... After returning, reading Pepys.

*March 5.* Finished copying & in part ( as usual) changing & adding to my piece on the "Peat Formation," which extended to 42 pages. None of this copying yet read for correction, & cutting down. But these pieces are mainly of geological speculations—a subject which is very interesting to me, & on which I have made many practical observations—& some of which have been quoted [55] by distinguished geologists, & some stolen without being acknowledged ( especially by W. B. Rogers,)[19] & yet I have never learned the first elements of geology & cannot. Of course, when attempting to reason

---

[18] During the War of 1812.

[19] William Barton Rogers was at this time a professor at the University of Virginia, where he earned an international reputation as a geologist. He was later selected to be the first president of the Massachusetts Institute of Technology.

on a subject on which I am so imperfectly informed, I cannot avoid making great mistakes—& I shall try to have these views examined by some book-geologist, before I risk their being published. I am satisfied that my observations on these two subjects, are useful, & my deductions in the main correct. Still, by any variation from received geological terms, & technicalities, or showing my want of acquaintance with scientific rules, I may be made ridiculous. Began to read and correct.

*March 6.* Finished the corrections. For some days I have had an increasing bad cold, & today am much indisposed, with that most stupifying & disagreeable of all ordinary kinds of sickness. Cough frequent & troublesome, as well as running from the nose, headache, &c. After dinner, I went to bed for two hours—which I have not done for any sickness that I can remember, for some years. . . . The President's inaugural speech today in the papers. It gives no better hope of his course than I expected. . . .

*March 7.* Feeling better (as I thought,) in the morning, I rode to the Clerk's Office, 12 miles, to carry deeds to be recorded, & for which my personal appearance was required—in the carriage. Felt worse before getting home. Very cold.

*March 8.* Sunday. Much worse—every symptom I have formerly had in influenza—aching head & eyes, burning eye-lids, cold chills, frequent hollow cough which has made my chest sore, & continual running of limpid mucous from the nostrils—with feverishness. Took mild cathartic last night & this morning. Yesterday, made a very light dinner, & have eaten nothing since. . . . Today felt too badly even to read for amusement. . . .

*March 9.* Fast snowing nearly all day. Felt much better. Wrote something on business, & brought up these entries, omitted for the two previous days. Reading "Two Years before the Mast," an admirable book, not only for its graphic descriptions of sea life, but also because of the author being a well educated gentleman, as unused as any one could be to such a hard & wretched life, as that of a common sailor, in a vessel commanded by a tyrannical captain. . . .

*March 10.* In the morning, not so well as last evening. . . . Since recording the deeds on the 7th. (which completed the legal transfer of my estate,) & also the previous recording of the deed of trust to settle on & secure her portion to Agnes—& which arrangements had been dragging on for 8 months, & delayed by various impediments— I am at last enabled to write a new will, which is needed to fix for the future, the portions for Elizabeth & Charles, (they having been already receiving the annual income thereof,)—& then to dispose, after my death, of the fund [59] received for my own use. In the last few days, I had written the rough draft of my designed will—& today, I copied, & completed the execution. I have not yet destroyed my previous voluminous will, encumbered with numerous codicils—but have distinctly annulled it in the beginning words of the new will. In the former & recent distributions, I have given to all my children, in their portions of *capital*, about $16,800, to every one of the six now living, in the values of the property at the times it was transferred. For special reasons, after the early division, & sharing out among the four oldest children, of $9000 capital, both the shares of Agnes & Julian were further increased, (in sundry items,) about $1000, or more, for each. And to my since deceased daughters, I had given for Rebecca, in fee simple right $9000, & to Jane & her husband, $2500. To Ella, nothing of capital, (or as her portion in part,) had been given before her death. The last division gave the equal sum of $7,300 in bonds, & 8 shares of Petersburg Rail-Road stock, (then worth in market $500,) to each of my now six living children, Agnes included, & her recent share I have increased by $2000 more than any others, because of her necessities. Thus, upon estimate & recollection, as to sundry of the earlier advances, I think that I have in all given to Agnes, or for her *designed* benefit, some $3000 more than to any other of my children except Julian, & $2000 more than his increased share. Except what was early wasted by her husband's extravagance, I have recently had all the remainder settled on Agnes & her children, by deed of trust. And even after all the spendthrift economy & waste, & the laziness & worthlessness [60] of Dr. Beckwith . . . the property still remaining, at present valuation, would probably amount to nearly $16,000, or within less than $1000 of the full share just now transferred as to my other children. With even this amount, & though with a large family of children, an industrious & frugal man, & especially one who is really a capable physician, might support his family in comfort. Yet throughout her married life, or since the short time in which the first $2500 was lavishly squandered, Agnes & her children have been suffering great privations—& will so continue—although greatly aided by the affectionate generosity of her brothers & sisters who had the means to give. Her marriage to such a man has been the greatest curse & trouble of my life, in the same time. After making the distribution stated, recently, there re-

[44]

mained the reservation of $25,000 to myself, & $7,500, (with its accruing interest, not required for her annual support,) for the portion of the infant & only child of my deceased daughter Jane. The whole amount of what I have distributed to all my children, & my granddaughter Jane Ruffin Dupuy, exclusive of my own late reservation of $25,000, by estimate, is about $115,000—which has been distributed equally (with the two exceptions named,) among my living children, & to the dead, so far as distribution had then been made, & the party being of age to require the capital. Having done so much for *equal* distribution, I shall hold myself at liberty to do as I may please, with my own special residue, & its annual income. . . .

*March 11.* After writing some letters for the mail, walked upwards of a mile, for exercise, & was much fatigued, for a short time. Had not walked before since sick. . . . This morning finished "Two Years before the Mast"—which with all of De Quincy's "Confessions of an Opium Eater," the readable parts of the three last Nos of De Bow's Review & of the newspapers—& snatches of Pepys' Diary, & some other matters, have made up my reading for amusement, since I returned home. . . .

*March 13.* . . . By previous appointment, the carriage sent early to Richmond for our relations, who arrived here about 4 P.M.—my neice [*sic*] [20] Rebecca Dupuy, & nephew Dr. John J. Dupuy, with his child, & my grandchild, our beloved little Jane. All well—& the latter knowing me & Mildred, & seeming much pleased to be here—as we are delighted to have her.—I have felt worse today, & had continued bad head-ache. Am decidedly bilious, & took milder medicine early, & then a pill of blue-mass at bed-time. Snowing fast.

*March 14.* Earth covered with snow, 4 to 5 inches deep, which afterwards thawed fast. My head aching badly, & until late in afternoon. . . . Finished reading slightly Bishop Watson's "Apology [63] for Christianity," in letters to Gibbon—which I had long wished to see, & had never met with before. I think it a poor & very unsatisfactory argument—& did not quite finish it. . . .

*March 15.* My cold still very bad—& the pain in the head & eye returned worse than before, & continued throughout the day, until about sunset. Because of these regular & daily returns of head-ache, J. Dupuy thought it might be neuralgic, & advised a dose of quinine

---

[20] One of the few words consistently misspelled by the diarist. I will silently correct the spelling hereafter.

—of which I took 10 grains at night. Lying down most of the day, unfit to read or converse. Before bed-time wrote a few pages.

*March 17.* Walked for exercise, which I have neglected too much, & will try hereafter to do every morning. Felt better, & able to write until dinner. . . . At night took 10 more grains of sul. quinine.

*March 18.* No head-ache, except in morning, & that probably caused by the quinine. Walked a mile & then wrote until 2 P.M., & finished the copying & rewriting of the whole article—42 pages—on the agricultural character &c. of the low land region, between the Chesapeake & Albemarle Sound. Read for correction the [64] first part. Rested, & read Pepys & chatted with the ladies. Dr. Dupuy left us this morning. My cold in the head still very bad. My cough, though not latterly painful, or bad, is still frequent & troublesome. I never before had a bad cold of such long continuance. . . .

*March 19.* Read & corrected my piece. Read over, for reference, all my articles in the Farmers' Register, on the Dismal Swamp, & the other great swamps of N.Ca. I had the design of selecting passages from them to precede & introduce my later observations on the same general subject. But the necessary extracts would be too long—& I must abridge & re-write, if using the substance of them at all. Pepys, & conversation.

*March 20.* . . . Finished second reading & correcting the last finished writing . . . ("Notes on the Agricultural Features of the Lowlands, between Albemarle Sound & Chesapeake Bay,") so that now I have one article, of 43 pages, ready for the press. . . .

*March 21.* Felt so much better that I was sorry that I had put off my designed trip to N.Ca. for another week. Sent my article by mail to De Bow's Review. Two other pieces ready. Am at a loss what next to prepare, from my rough drafts—& did nothing. . . . Read in De Bow's Review & Pepys.—Mildred has been regularly reading Macaulay's History of England, 4 vols—2 hours every morning, & Mrs. Campbell listening to the reading aloud. They have got through the two first volumes—& have not been able to find out, & would not have suspected from his words, of what religion (or sect) the author was. As Mrs. C. is a zealous Presbyterian, & Mildred as zealous an Episcopalian, [65] this is pretty good evidence of the author's impartiality & fair dealing. For my part, I doubt whether he has any good claim to be either a sectarian or a Christian. I believe that there is, from the nature & manner of their studies, & habits of investigation, a tendency of the most profound historians to skepticism.

I do not speak of mere compilers & abridgers of voluminous annals & other materials—but of the historians who closely scrutinize, & weigh the probability of every recorded fact, & admit or reject them according to the rules of evidence, & upon sound reasoning. They thus learn to judge of sacred or religious history by the same rules of evidence by which they would test the alleged incidents of profane history. Of course no sacred or religious history can stand this test. Its reception must be upon faith, & not upon ordinary reasoning & evidence. Whether I suppose the right cause or not, it is certain that a large majority of the greatest English historians have been supposed skeptics, or total & avowed unbelievers. Such were Robertson, (though a Christian divine & preacher,) Hume and Gibbon. And even Prescott, raised & continuing in New-England, the land of puritanical or hypocritical observance—(where every decent man, if not a Christian, pretends to be one, for his reputation's sake—) I suspect that even Prescott is a skeptic—judging from some passages & opinions, slightly touched upon in some of his historical works— which I noticed when reading them, but cannot now remember. Voltaire's infidelity was as notorious as it was offensive. I know nothing of the opinions on religion of other distinguished French historians— (except Guizot,) who is understood to be a Christian.

*March 22.* Began to copy, or re-write an article on the Land-Reef & Land-locked navigable waters of N.Ca., which required [66] much alteration, transposition & abridgement from several different writings. Finished 12 pages. . . .

*March 23.* At Mr. Sayre's request, directing the laying off & digging ditches, to substitute some of my old covered-draining that has failed. Wrote 15 pages, & corrected & inserted of first draft 10 more. . . .

*March 24.* Read over & corrected my last piece, of 37 pages—& wrote heads of sections for same. Wrote letters. Saw to Mr. Sayre's ditch. . . .

*March 25.* Began to copy & mainly to re-write another piece, of observations on the swamps—& finished 10 pages.

*March 27.* . . . Wrote 10 pages, which concluded my last piece. Since my return from Washington I have copied, & much altered, & re-written to considerable extent, 198 pages—except 17 pages, which corrected & transferred from the rough drafts. The same afternoon finished Pepys' Diary—skipping & merely [67] glancing over a good deal. I had read very amusing reviews of this work with many extracts, & therefore had long desired to read the work, when Mildred saw & bought an English Edition last summer. It is the best work in the world to furnish amusing extracts & abridgements, for a review. But taken all together, most of it is uninteresting & tedious. Yet its notices supply many incidents which are excellent materials for the historian of Charles II, & his reign. Without Pepys, it would be difficult to conceive how unprincipled, dishonest, & mean was the man, & how utterly despicable the king. Yet by his good humor & wit, his apparent (or perhaps real) kindness of feeling, & his great courtesy, he was even popular with many who ought to have despised him; & on the merit of these qualities, Walter Scott has so disguised him as to make him appear quite amiable & interesting, & has glossed over & kept out of sight all his greatest acts of scoundrelism & meanness. This same great writer has in like manner indulged his toryism, & prostituted his great abilities, to white-wash, & present as amiable, James I, the blackest & basest villain, by far, of all the English Stuarts, if not of all the English kings.

*March 28.* Read over & corrected the rough draft (written last Autumn,) of my article on Pines—& then was without employment, & felt the want of it before night. . . . Began Boswell's [68] Life of Johnson, which I read first many years ago.

*March 29.* Sunday. To church. By passing over most of the notes, & nearly all the letters & long extracts quoted read the remainder of more than a volume & a half of Boswell, since yesterday noon. —My arrangements are made to leave home tomorrow morning, early, for Richmond, & to return to North Carolina, to resume my agricultural observations. My sickness, & other causes, have prevented my going much sooner.

*March 30.* Left Marlbourne very early for Richmond. . . . Saw Mr. [Charles B.] Williams (Sec. of S[tate] Agr Soc.) & arranged some business with him. Found that Pryor's new paper, "The South," was out, & paid for two copies. Found nothing to engage or interest me longer than Noon—& so, instead of staying in Rd., as designed, all night, I proceeded by Rail-road to Petersburg, after dinner, & reached by 4½ P.M. . . .

*March 31.* At 7½ A.M. left Petersburg on the railway, & reached Weldon where a letter from Mr. Th[omas] P. Devereux[21] awaited

---

[21] Next to the Hairstons, Devereux was probably the largest slaveholder in North Carolina at this time. The census of 1850 credits him with a total of 580 slaves on his extensive properties in adjoining Halifax and Northampton counties.

me, in answer to mine. At the Halifax station, his carriage was waiting for me, in which I rode 14 miles to his residence, on the Roanoke, below. This visit had been invited & promised some years ago, & last [70] year attempted, when Mr. D. was from home. Hearing from him that Halifax was his post-office, I took it for granted that he lived within a few miles of it. If I had known the distance was so great, I would have been unwilling to put the trouble of two such trips on my host, to have a short visit from me. However, he does not seem to regard the trouble, & sends 2 or 3 times a week if only for the mail. It was near 3 P.M. when I arrived. Mr. Van Cortlandt, of New York, & wife (Mrs. Devereux's sister,) here, & young Dunlop, of Petersburg, their nephew, who is also my "faraway" cousin.—After dinner, Mr. Devereux & I took a walk of nearly 4 miles, & mostly along his dykes raised to keep the high freshes of the Roanoke from overflowing his whole arable land. At night, conversation mostly on general political subjects—in which I was very cautious to avoid my usual free manner of speech on such subjects, & to utter nothing that could offend or annoy any northern hearer.

*April 1.* After breakfast Mr. D. & I rode out to see the Roanoke lands, on several of his neighboring plantations. But light showers of drizzle soon began to fall at intervals, & compelled us, before 12, to turn back. We had before rode some miles down the river, (left bank,) & got within the border, & in full view of Polenta, Mr. D.'s best plantation. All these lands, & also the neighboring plantations of three other large proprietors, are dyked to protect the lands from the floods of the river. These are enormous works, for their magnitude & expense—& this being deemed necessary by the most considerate proprietors, indicates how hazardous must be the general tillage on the like river lands, without the like protection. On Mr. D.'s residence, Connucanard, the mansion, & every spot of the arable land, (except two or three acres,) require & have the protection of a dyke, 26 feet above [71] the height of low water in the river. The highest known fresh was 22 feet above low water. That swept over all the land, & even washed away part of the brick foundation pillars on which the mansion stands. Of the first, or lowest terrace, which only needs dyking—but which makes most & the best of every river farm —the river side (as it is of every higher terrace,) is considerably the highest in elevation—& of course the embankments, when built

[49]

thereon, need less height. On this account, much of the length of the dyke is less than four feet in height. But as much more is double that height—not a little is much more. A portion which seemed near half a mile, was throughout 14 feet of perpendicular height. For every foot of height, there is 5 feet width of base. Besides the main & lower terrace, of the bottom lands, there are usually two more, & sometimes three higher, before reaching the table, or poor pine lands—& these are but slightly elevated above the highest low ground—though very different in quality. . . . The lowgrounds of the Roanoke are the richest of any river emptying to the Atlantic coast —& also the most liable to inundation, & the most unhealthy.—Designed to leave tomorrow. But as the drizzle today has cut short our ride, I will stay another day.—Find Mr. Van Cortlandt a pleasant gentleman, & of course, not too northern to be agreeable.

*April 2.* A strong & piercing cold wind from the north. Resumed our ride—& I suffered much with cold before returning. [72] Went down on one side of the river about 5 miles, & crossed & returned on the other. All the land protected by dykes, from the river freshes. One part of the dyke, at Polenta, is 17 feet high, & more than 100 wide at the base. This great size does not extend more than 200 or 250 yards. And the banks are not all the expense. There are culverts, with valves, to pass the water from the inside to the river. There are seven of these largest culverts, which cost each about $2000, on five adjacent farms, (three of them on one farm) besides more smaller & cheaper culverts. These are constructed entirely of wood, & of course must rot & require renewal. The largest culverts, of course, are required where the land is lowest, & through the bottoms of the highest parts of the dyke. All these farms are composed either wholly or mainly of "first lowgrounds," or land of the lowest terrace. The higher terraces are of worse soil. The first low-grounds vary between light & stiff alluvial loam. All originally very fertile soil. Three years ago, a fresh rose two feet higher than had ever before been known, & covered, in the night every foot of Polenta, except less than a quarter acre, near the river bank, & houses, on which all the slaves had to assemble, to keep out of the still rising flood. All the dykes were then broken. Since they have been raised to 26 feet above low water, which is two feet higher than that highest known flood. . . . Since leaving home, have been reading Stockhardt's Field Lectures (on Agrl. Chemistry,)—& today the newspapers. [73]

The soil of the "first lowgrounds," (alluvial formation, & liable to be covered by freshes, if not dyked,) has not generally so rich an appearance as it doubtless is entitled to. Except the lowest basins, it is not black or even dark colored, like most alluvial soils, but yellowish gray or hazel loam, either sandy or clayey. The time of year prevented my seeing any growth—except some clover of Mr. Devereux's, & a field of Wheat on Mr. J. C. Johnston's farm.[22] Both of these were very luxuriant, & both had been aided by guano. Not much of either wheat or clover raised. Corn is the great crop, & cotton next. Peas always a secondary crop with corn—but not much raised separately. The floods cover more of the lowgrounds on this river, & do greater damage (where unprotected by dykes) than any where else—& the Roanoke lowgrounds are richer, taken throughout, than those of any other river on the Atlantic coast. The lowgrounds are not generally high enough for cultivation more than 20 miles lower down the river. After that, it is only the highest parts cultivated, & these are rare. . . .

*April 3.* Ice on the pools in the road. Left for Halifax, to take the rail-road for Wilmington. The road, in gradually diverging from the river, passes a considerable distance through or along the first, second & third terrace, & then the highest table land. The latter is but slightly elevated above the highest terrace. In some places there are four terraces below the table land—each successive rise presenting different & poorer [74] soil from the next below. The second lowground, though much worse than the first, is generally good soil. The third terrace, which I rode through, is quite poor, & also a stiff yellowish clay soil & sub-soil. The table land mostly sandy.—For the 4 miles along which I rode alongside of the Roanoke, it had a rare uniformity of width, direction, height of banks, &c. It is said to be about 120 yards wide, 8 to 10 feet deep generally—but with a much shallower rapid below.—Left Halifax, on the train, after 12, & reached Wilmington at 8, where I went to the Carolina Hotel. . . .

*April 4.* Last night my cough worse, &, for a time, soreness in the breast, when coughing. Now, when too late, as usual, sensible of my imprudent exposure on the Roanoke, & even in leaving home before being well, & after so long being out of all exposure. I heartily wish I was now at home. . . .

*April 5.* . . . Sunday, & a rainy morning. Clear after noon. Rode with Dr. Anderson, to the new Cemetery, which will be a beautiful

---

[22] Another large slaveholder, James C. Johnston listed 272 Negroes on his Halifax County farms in 1850.

place, when the embellishments are enough advanced. Called to see two ladies, with whom I was acquainted before, Miss Lillington & Miss Waters—& took tea with Mr. & Mrs. Anderson.—Heard of much recent destruction of the long-leaf pine trees, "boxed" to collect turpentine, in this neighborhood, by firing the woods. Indeed, I saw it in progress, as passing on the rail-road, after dark, on the 3rd. The pine woods are set on fire every spring, by persons who have nothing to lose, merely to make the early grazing better, for their few cows—& great destruction is thus made of the partly worked turpentine trees, which, where covered with turpentine, burn like a torch. It is thought that much of this destruction is also committed by the negroes who would have to attend the trees, to collect turpentine, which labor they dislike very much, because it is solitary. The work is light & healthy, & the task easily performed. But each laborer is alone on his separate allotment of 10,000 trees. A negro cannot abide being alone—& will prefer work of much exposure & severe toil, in company, to any lighter work, without any company. Hence their aversion to the turpentine business.

*April 6.* A rainy morning, & a showery day. Last evening had been invited by Dr. Frederick Hill to go to see a great exposure of marl. At 10 A.M. we went in his carriage, & returned (in renewed rain,) by 2. The marl is the hard eocene like that at Rocky [76] Point, which I have visited before. The lower layer is as indurated as limestone—& has been quarried (by blasting) to supply stone for government work of construction. This has exposed a very large surface, in which I hoped to find many fine specimens of fossils—but found none perfect. Mr. Davis, the proprietor (on East Branch of Cape Fear river) has latterly made some use of the softer marl as manure. I advised him, in addition, to burn the marl & stone for lime. If judiciously managed, any amount of good lime may be cheaply burned here, & at sundry other places along the river. Yet it has never been done—& nearly all the lime for cement is brought from Maine, that is used in Wilmington—as well as most of the hay, from the northern states.—My cough again frequent & troublesome. The bad weather & other causes have frustrated the main objects of my visit, & I shall leave this place tomorrow morning. . . . [77]

*April 7.* Left Wilmington for New bern, where I had ordered my letters, & indeed appointed with another person to be. But before reaching Goldsborough, (where I waited 6 hours,) I determined, because of my continued bad cough & cold, to abandon, or postpone my designed visit & explorations, which could not be made without much exposure. . . . I had before intended to go, at a later time, to visit Judge Thomas Ruffin,[23] my distant relative & very near friend—in which latter relation most of my family stand to his. On account of my sickness, I will now make my visit, & be *at home* with these friends until I am well. At Goldsborough, saw & renewed a former acquaintance with Dr. Atkinson, Bishop of North Carolina, who is a very agreeable gentleman, as well as an estimable man & minister. Left in the Raleigh, or western train, at 4 P.M. & reached Hillsborough before 9, where I stopped, intending to give two days to my friends there (three of the children, & Paul Cameron, son-in-law of Judge Ruffin,) before proceeding. But, on inquiring, I learned that Mr. Cameron's daughter was very sick, & his family (on that account) all at Mrs. Roulhac's, & not yet removed to his own house. Therefore, I merely stopped the night at Brown Ruffin's, & deemed it best to proceed next morning, leaving my apologies for the other friends, whom the circumstances compelled me thus to pass without seeing. . . .

*April 8.* Before 7 A.M. again started, & stopped & took breakfast at Haw River—whence by a third buggy I went, (by 10 A.M.) to Alamance. Found all the family at home, except Jane . . . . I could not be more kindly or affectionately received, or more joy evidenced at my unexpected arrival. Especially did my sweet Patty welcome me with kisses & her bright smiles of joy, as if she had been my own daughter. Indeed, she & Jane have been so much with my family, & my daughters here with them, that we feel as if our relationship was the nearest, instead of being almost too far off to be traced. The day mostly spent in conversation . . . . I announced that I came to be *at home*, & that Judge R. must attend to his business just as if I were not his guest—which he will do. His vigorous & healthy old age, physically, is almost as remarkable as his great powers of intellect. In the latter respect, he has few if any living superiors in this country. Yet,

---

[23] Judge Thomas Ruffin (1787–1870), scientific agriculturist and one of the most eminent jurists in nineteenth-century America, had been at the head of the legal profession in North Carolina for more than a generation. He served on the state supreme court for twenty-four years, occupying the post of chief justice from 1833 to 1852. In addition, he was president of the North Carolina Agricultural Society, 1854–60, and was a trustee of the University of North Carolina, 1813–31 and 1842–68. Though an ardent Unionist, he was an intimate friend of the diarist, and the latter displayed toward Judge Ruffin's entire family— especially daughters Jane and Patty—the same high affection that he felt for most of his own children.

with all his great & acknowledged superiority of mind & ability, in his manners he is as plain, as unpretending, & as simple, as any ordinary farmer—& as industrious, & as active, & as devoted to his farming labors, as if he were 40 years younger, & yet had his fortune to acquire. Those who associate with him on terms of friendly intimacy almost forget to regard him as the man of great ability, & of highest mark as a jurist, in the absence of all appearance of the assumption of high position, & in the continual evidences of his kindly & amiable feelings, his good humor & agreeable manners, & his domestic virtues & attractions. There is no man in this country who [79] commands more high & universal respect—& no man so deserving to be respected, who less repels familiar approach, or more attracts the intimacy & confidence of even the humblest of all who associate [with] him. . . .

*April 9.* The finest spring weather. Warm. Near to midday walked with Judge R. to see his graduated hill-side ditches. I am a good walker for my age, & feebleness, & do not mind 4 miles when I am well. But Judge R. who is between 6 & 7 years my senior, can break me down ( even if well,) & also most others who are much younger. So I begged to return, long before he would have thought of it. . . . The newspaper today seems to confirm the most unexpected & remarkable reverse of condition of Walker's force in Nicaragua—of a signal victory over the Costa Rican troops, after his being [80] by the preceding accounts, at the verge of defeat & destruction. Looking to the good ends to be effected by the establishment of the Anglo-Saxon race & power in that country, I heartily wish success to Walker. But also viewing him as a robber & murderer—a land-pirate—if he was to be defeated, I hoped he would be captured & put to death, as the deserved reward of his crimes. Nothing can be hoped from the degenerate, mongrel, & mostly feeble people of that fine country. . . . My little reading, besides the newspapers, in Harper's trashy Magazine, & in Trench's "English, Past & Present" —an interesting & good work.

*April 10.* . . . Again contradictory reports ( by the same vessel) as to Walker's late battle, & his position afterwards. There is no reliance to be placed on them—as on both sides, they lie for policy—& we must wait for the result. Clear in after part of the day. Walked with Judge R. on some of his farm—& later, with the ladies.

*April 11.* Judge & Mrs. R. went to Hillsborough, to attend religious services tomorrow ( Easter) as well as to see their sick granddaughter, Rebecca Cameron. . . . Reading in (& glancing over) parts of Johnston's "Chemistry of Common Life." In a marginal note, (in the part on "Soils") I found he had paid a compliment to me, by name, that I should [81] not have looked for. But, formerly, & indirectly, he had paid to me a much greater compliment (as some think,) in borrowing, & using, without any acknowledgement, in his lecture (Geology & Chemistry applied to agriculture) on the use of lime, much of the propositions first asserted & argued by me in the "Essay on Calcareous Manures.". . .[24]

The newspaper contains the report of the death of my valued friend, Professor M[ichael] Tuomey of Alabama. His death is a great loss to his friends (the few who knew his great worth,) to his family, & to the public. He was most estimable for his integrity & private worth—& as remarkable for his scientific attainments, as for the modesty & diffidence which made his acquisitions almost unknown formerly. It is to me a subject of much gratification, that circumstances enabled me to learn something of his abilities & worth, when he was a stranger to nearly all—& that it was in my power to assist him in obtaining employment, & finally, the honorable distinction to which he was entitled. On my recommendation, while still he was an obscure & unknown teacher of a school in Petersburg, (& to which place & position I had brought him previously,) he was appointed geological Surveyor of South Carolina—& also, after that employment was closed, professor of Agricultural Chemistry, in the University of Alabama. Subsequently, in connection with this professorship, he was appointed to conduct the geological survey of Alabama.[25] By the notice of his death in the newspaper, I am glad to see that his eminent abilities & services were recognized. . . .

*April 12.* Drizzly nearly all day. Reading (& in part but glancing over) Lockhart's [82] Life of Walter Scott. Skip over most of the early letters, & many details of his early life, before his literary labors began. Afterwards, everything referring to his writings is interesting.

*April 14.* Judge & Mrs. R. . . . returned this morning. Finished 2nd. vol. of Scott.

*April 15.* Slightly frozen earth this morning. My appointed time

---

[24] Probably Ruffin's most prestigious agricultural writing, this essay was first published in 1832.

[25] Tuomey (1805–57), the first professor of agricultural chemistry at the University of Alabama and the first state geologist in Alabama, assumed both duties in 1847.

has arrived for leaving, & I feel well enough to proceed on my excursions, by using more care than before. I never more reluctantly closed so long a visit, & I & my kind hosts parted with much regret. . . . Reached Weldon at 11 P.M.—Very strong wind all day.

*April 16.* Earth again slightly crusted, but less than it was (here) yesterday. Had to wait for the train (Seaboard R.R.) to go to Edenton & Lake Scuppernong. Wrote letters home. Walked, & for the first time, saw well the beautiful water scenery & great water-power at Weldon. Saw & renewed acquaintance with Prof. Stuart, of Randolph Macon College. Past 2 P.M. the train set off, & after 4, reached & stopped at the Blackwater station. Walked about for an hour, & then went to the "House of Entertainment," Mr. Barrett's, where my trunk had been sent. Talked with him mostly about draining, which his land & all his neighborhood greatly [83] needs, & of which there is an entire want of knowledge, both of theory & practice. From all I heard, as well as the little I saw, all the land hereabouts is suffering from underlying water, & cannot produce half a crop for want of *deep* drains, which would tap the water-glutted quicksand beneath. Here my self-conceit had a good set-down. My land-lord is a man of some property & ordinary intelligence & knowledge of the world. I had long ago[26] represented in the Senate of Va. the then district of six counties of which Southampton (this county) was one. Yet when I incidentally mentioned this to Mr. Barrett, as well as my name, it was evident that he was totally a stranger to me, as an agriculturist, as in every other respect. He did not say so, but I felt sure that he had never heard of me before. This, so near to the scene of my labors was rather worse than what I found at Mattamuskeet. When I returned from that neighborhood, after a week's stay & examination of the farms, some person observed to me that he supposed my presence had been very gratifying to the farmers whom I saw. I answered that I had seen & conversed with many of them, & all were very civil & courteous in our slight intercourse. But, so far as I could judge, that, except my host, on whose kind invitation I had gone, I did not see a man who appeared ever to have heard of me before, or who cared whether he ever heard of me again. Of course, I did not obtrude my opinions or advice on farmers who seemed to desire to have neither.—

*April 17.* Left Mr. Barrett's plain but neat & excellent house of entertainment after breakfast. . . . The steamer started, at 9.45 A.M.

---

[26] 1823–26.

down the Blackwater, in which I reached Edenton by 4.30 P.M. After taking my lodgings & fixing my baggage at the hotel, walked, with Col. Payne [*sic*], (M.C.)[27] to call on Mr. James C. Johnston. Found him in better health than I had expected. He asked me to stay at his house. But I thought that it might be inconvenient to both him & me, & so excused myself—& returned before night to my lodgings. After tea, Col. Payne & Dr. Warren called on me, & arranged for an excursion for tomorrow. The latter urged my going to his house forthwith—which I declined, but promised to move there tomorrow.

*April 18.* Slow rain, or drizzle, all day. Went to Dr. Th[omas] Warren's house after breakfast.[28] Spent the day & evening mostly in conversation with him & Col. Paine, on agriculture, the peculiar features &c. of this low country, & something of politics. Two other gentlemen with us. All of them whigs, & of course all opposed to my disunion views.

*April 19.* Sunday. Steady slow rain, or otherwise drizzling, all day —still confining me to the house, as my cold has somewhat increased. Col. Paine again with us. He served in the Mexican war. He is a close observer, & especially of subjects of natural history, which come under his personal observation. I had much agreeable conversation with him on such subjects. Also I learned some interesting facts going to sustain my previous opinion of extensive subsidence of this low country, or portions of it. The bottom of Albemarle sound, & the deeper rivers & large creeks emptying therein hereabout, are full of stumps of trees, even to the depth of 20 feet below the present surface of the water—which can be accounted for only, as I thought, by the subsidence of the former swamp surface on which the trees grew. [85]

*April 20.* Strong & cold wind from north-west. Went with Dr. Warren & Col. Paine, in a carriage to see the neighboring lands in Chowan [County]—some 3 to 4 miles in the interior & as far as 12 miles distant, & thence returning through the farms on Albemarle sound to Edenton. The general elevation of the land 11 to 14 feet— the level more uniform than any before seen in the lowlands—soils

[27] Robert Treat Paine (1812–72), a shipping entrepreneur from Edenton, served in the Mexican War as colonel of a North Carolina regiment and was later elected to the Thirty-fourth Congress (1855–57) on the American Party ticket.

[28] Thomas C. Warren was another of the largest North Carolina slaveholders. According to the census of 1850, he had 353 hands on his Chowan County estate above Edenton.

moderately stiff, & good for wheat. Before clearing & ditching, most of the surface subject to be covered often by rain-water. The system of draining similar to that of Perquimons [County]—but the small parallel (or tap) ditches wider apart—about 180 feet. Saw some of the best lands, under culture. These seemed to approach swamp in their appearance, but were of the highest surface in the neighborhood. Their original growth, gum, ash, maple, poplar & some oak & pine—& a general undergrowth of reeds. For miles scarcely a change of level was manifest to the eye, & the general descent could only be told by the direction of the flow of water in the larger ditches. When returning near to the sound, there were some narrow depressions of a few feet in depth, serving to interrupt the otherwise general level. At 12 miles from Edenton, we reached the shore of Albemarle sound, at one of the great fisheries. The seine was out, & the hauling in by mules at capstans going on. But as it would have required waiting two hours longer than my limit of time, we had to return without seeing the landing of the fish. Everything was conducted here precisely as I have described formerly. I was more forcibly struck with the enormous waste of manuring value of the fish offal, & the dirty salt & oily pickle—all of which would make such excellent materials for compost, with additions of bog-earth, mild lime &c. The proprietor, Mr. Wood, invited us to an excellent fish dinner, which we eat [*sic*] with good appetite. Returned by 4.15 P.M. just in time for me to embark in the steamer [86] passing to Plymouth, 8 miles up the Roanoke, which I reached before 6 P.M. At Brown's hotel. . . .

*April 21.* Left Plymouth in the mail-coach, at 8 A.M. for Belgrade. The road, until near the end, along, & within a mile or less, first of the Roanoke, & afterwards of Albemarle Sound. Soil, first, stiff; then in some small spaces very sandy—mostly afterwards medium sandy. For about 12 or 14 miles, surface a little undulating—after, flat & much of it wet. Got out at Belgrade (28 miles), the residence of William Pettigrew, & found he was away. Borrowed a horse, & rode on to Magnolia, his swamp farm, where I found him. Thence, at my request, he carried me to his brother's, Charles Pettigrew, whose mansion is on the border of Lake Scuppernong.[29] This place I had visited, about 1845, when I staid a week at the close adjacent resi-

---

[29] William and Charles were the sons of Ebenezer Pettigrew, whose planting activities are detailed in Bennett H. Wall's excellent unpublished doctoral dissertation, "Ebenezer Pettigrew, An Economic Study of an Ante-Bellum Planter" (University of North Carolina, 1946).

dence of Mr. Josiah Collins, & wrote & published, in Farmers' Register, an account of these remarkable lands, reclaimed of the former swamp. The main object of my present visit is to note the changes in this time, & especially to ascertain the facts in regard to the sinking, or decomposition & rotting away of the soil . . . .

*April 22.* Frequent light showers of rain throughout the day, which did not prevent our long excursion to view the farms & their canals. Mr. Collins joined us after some hours. Though we had Mr. Pettigrew's open carriage along, & rode in it whenever the way permitted, to our riding was added 10 miles of walking—which I bore without much fatigue, much to my surprise. By invitation we all went to take tea with Mrs. Collins, & staid until 11, before returning. I found from Mrs. C. & her husband, the kindest welcome, & renewal of their most hospitable & agreeable entertainment which I experienced so long ago. . . . In our walk today, I was much surprised to find the general & large pine growth of the wild swampland (formerly burnt & naked savanna land, & the pines, the second forest growth,) to be all of the *pinus serotina,* which I had never seen before except near Lake Mattamuskeet, & had looked for elsewhere in vain. These trees were larger than I had ever heard of—many of 18 inches diameter, & tall in proportion, & making the general forest growth of large spaces of land, on which no other pine was seen.

*April 23.* . . . Accompanied Mr. Collins in a ride over the cultivated lands, & walking into the remaining wood-lands. Returned to Mr. Pettigrew's to dinner, where I found Mr. William P. waiting for me. After dinner, took [88] leave of my host & the ladies, & accompanied Mr. W. P. to his Magnolia farm. We walked about 2½ miles around his fields, (of the same former swamp) & viewed his spacious & well-fitted barn by lamp light. Went to bed, sleepy, by a little after 9. . . .

*April 24.* Still cold. After early breakfast, rode with Mr. Pettigrew to Belgrade, his other farm & residence, over which we walked until the stage coach called for me.—Much conversation with Mr. P. in reference to the swamp lands of the neighborhood, & as to drainage & other agricultural subjects. His father was a man of remarkable character & ability. His labors, in draining the swamp lands, & in combating & controlling the waters of the lake, as well as the other labors & habits of a life of most energetic & successful effort & toil, would be well worth recording—&, with the incidental description of the great swamp, & its later improvements, would make a most interesting agricultural memoir.—Reached Plymouth by 2 P.M. During the ride, nearly read through Franklin's "Present State of Hayti," [89] an English work, borrowed from C. Pettigrew. ... Shall stay here until Monday's steamer, to visit some of the swamp lands.

*April 25.* By previous appointment, rode with Mr. McRae (who is a large swamp proprietor & shingle-getter,) to see his canal & the bordering swamp lands. The canal is 4 miles in length, & 20 feet wide at the lower part, narrowing to 12 at the upper end, & 3 feet deep. The lower end passes through a rim of higher sandy & firm ground, such as is usual at the outsides of the great swamps—& next, towards the interior, for 2 miles or more, it passes through a swamp soil of about 15 inches deep, underlaid by fine clay. The general forest growth on this part is pond pine (*p. serotina*) of large sizes, many 18 inches through & 80 feet high. Still higher, & for half a mile of the farther extremity, the growth is gum, maple, poplar, &c. & the soil much deeper—& no subsoil reached in the canal. The whole fall in the canal said to be about 15 feet. ... An impression seems general here, that the *pine* lands of Mr. McRae are of very inferior quality. But this perhaps was owing to the also general opinion that the pines were of the "old-field" or loblolly species, which generally indicate poor land. Neither Mr. McRae nor any one else had suspected that the pines were of a different species, & which I have never seen grown except on very wet swamp, & rich soil. ...

*April 26.* Afternoon, rode out with Gen. Spruill to see Dr. Armistead's swamp farm, which I had seen many years ago, when newly ditched. It [90] never has been well drained, & is therefore in bad order. But still it gave me more confidence in the permanency & value of swamp-soils.

*April 27.* Rode with Mr. [T. B.] Nichols, & two others, along the public road to Pungo river, to see part of the Roulhac swamp land, which will soon be sold. The road through the swamp is scarcely passable by horses, & therefore we walked. It passes through but a small space of the Roulhac land, & all that part had been "deaded," or the trees killed many years ago, so that the growth & the land could not be judged of. The swamp was impassable, even for 10 yards, because of the thick growth of reeds & shrubs—& in addition water stood as high as the surface of the land, & generally within a foot (often less) of the surface of the road, though that had been laid with wood, & that covered by the earth furnished by a large ditch on each side. There can be no separate or small draining of the margin lands of the great swamps, for want of outlets of sufficient depth for the water. And for any extensive drainage, it is necessary, at first, to dig a canal of 20 to 25 feet width, from the outlet into the nearest river, as many miles as will reach & pass through the land to be drained. This tract, of 4600 acres, will require such a canal for 4 miles outside of its own border, besides through its extent, say 2½ or 3 miles more. I felt a strong temptation to buy this tract, which is said to be of the richest swamp, of abundant elevation, & great value —& which is expected to sell for less than $10,000. But even if so, it will require an outlay of equal amount, to begin to make it of any value for agricultural uses. It is said, however, with the canal made, & fit to use for navigation, that the cypress timber could be sold, standing, for enough to repay the whole outlay.—I had waited to my latest day to see this land, & after all the delay have had no fair view of even a small part. [91] I have to attend the meeting of the Ex. Com. tomorrow night—& so left Plymouth in the steamer for Blackwater, at 8 P.M.

*April 28.* Reached the Blackwater Bridge on the Seaboard R.R. by 8.30 A.M. The train passed in an hour, by which I arrived at Weldon by noon—& after 2 P.M. left for Richmond which I reached just before our hour of meeting, 7½ P.M. A good body of working members of the Ex. Com. present. Remained in session until 11.30 —& went to bed at 12.

*April 29.* In session from 10 A.M. to nearly 5 P.M. with a recess of an hour for dinner. . . . At night, we met & adjourned—& then held a meeting for agricultural conversation & discussion—& next in social conversation to 11. My son Charles had arrived, to join me here, in the afternoon.

*April 30.* Arranged for more definite & strict procedure of the sub-committee on accounts, & of the Treasurer & Secretary, by which I trust some abuses may be corrected, & part of our wasteful expenditure saved. I have required that *no* accounts or bills shall be paid by the Treasurer before they are passed by the Committee of accounts (instead of *all,* as has been the latter usage,) & that the sub. com. shall regularly meet & judge all accounts on the day preceding each quarterly meeting of the Ex. Com.—The carriage came for me (by previous appointment,) & in it Mr. Sayre & his wife—& after dinner Charles & I returned with them to Marlbourne. . . .

*May 1.* Continuing my article on the several improvements of [92] swamp lands, on the Scuppernong lands &c., using the materials obtained in my late visit. . . . Glanced over the newspapers, & the April No. of De Bow's Review. A letter from Edmund to Mildred. He proposes, as soon as weather is warm enough, to take Mary to New York, for travel, & to consult her uncle Dr. J. Aug. Smith—& next winter for her to stay in Aiken, S.C. which place is supposed to be very favorable to consumptive invalids. May God grant her relief, & health! But I have almost no hope.

*May 2.* Warmer, & rain. Finished writing & inserting the materials obtained in my recent trip. Making additions to & corrections of the different pieces written before. Reading last No. of Harper's Magazine—mostly pure trash—& conversation this, as every other evening—& music by Elizabeth on the piano, & Mildred on the melodeon. . . .

*May 3.* Sunday. Attended church. A damp & cloudy forenoon & but a small congregation. Steady rain all the afternoon & into night. Charles had met me at my request, to do for me some surveying & levelling here, necessary to complete my survey & memoir of the drainage of Marlbourne. We passed over the first day after our arrival, & that was the only one which was fit for our work. . . . Finished last No. of Harper (or the portion readable,) & resumed Boswell's Johnson.

*May 4.* We attempted the surveying & levelling, after breakfast, in cloudy & threatening weather, had scarcely begun, before we were [93] driven in by the recommencement of rain. Afternoon, made another effort, & but little more progress. Reading & adding to my recent writings—& nearly finished what I had in view. Steady rain at night.

*May 5.* . . . De Bow's Review for May received, containing the first part of my agricultural article, with numerous typographical errors. The editor had before written to close our arrangement with this first article. This he had a right to do, under my own proposed condition. But he has caused me to take much trouble, uselessly, so far as suitable to fulfil my engagement. However, it was a pleasant labor, & I do not regret it, even if for nothing else than the pleasure.

*May 6.* Mr. Sayre & I worked hard for some hours in boring at the proper stations of our levelled line, to find & note the under-strata, & especially the *water* bed, if within the length of the auger (11½ feet). In the lowest black land we failed, & suspended the attempt, because the recent rains had so filled the soil with water, which immediately filled the auger-hole, that nothing could be done. Must resume the continuation hereafter, of this still unfinished job. . . . [94]

*May 7.* . . . Mildred & I left after breakfast, with Charles, in the carriage for Richmond, where we left C. to proceed to his home, & M. & I, after stopping some hours in Richmond, rode on to Summer Hill, the residence of our friend & distant kinsman F. G. Ruffin, 3 miles beyond Manchester. . . . Reached Summer Hill to dinner, & found Mr. & Mrs. Ruffin at home—& a warm welcome. After dinner, the ladies rode with us on the farm, mainly for M. to see the then high fresh in James river. Then Mr. R. & I walked to see his wheat-crop, & the great effect of his improvements by surface draining, & sloping the sides & margin of his rain-ditches. He is pleased to ascribe much of the benefit he has obtained in these respects to my particular advice, & general instruction afforded in my publications on draining.—We spent the evening to a late hour in earnest & interesting conversation. . . .

*May 8.* Mr. R. & I again walked for some hours, talking of agriculture, as subjects were suggested by what we saw. Returning, we had an early dinner, & thence went to the nearest station on the rail-road, (close by,) where, after 3 P.M. we took the cars. At Petersburg, M[ildred] stopped . . . & I proceeded on the cars, southward, designing to lose no more time by delay. Supped at Weldon N.C. & found the night in the coach on its way.

*May 9.* At Wilmington to breakfast—where we stopped 2 hours. . . . At 8 A.M. left, on the Wilmington & Manchester rail-road, via Kingsville in Sumpter [*sic*] S. Ca. for Charleston. This W. & M. rail-road is the only one in North & South Ca. which had not previously sent to me a free ticket—so that on it I paid my passage ($6) which I might as well have saved by going the other route, by Raleigh & Charlotte, & without loss of time. The surface of the country, on this route extremely level generally, until after crossing the Great Peedee [River]—then less or more undulating until passing through Orangeburgh. The river swamps all overflowed—for 2 miles breadth of the Pedee [*sic*], & 4 of the Wateree. The native forest growth mostly long-leaf pine, & the proportion increasing as going southward, & through Marion, S.C. But still, the loblolly pine was the general second-growth—& also the proportion of (*pinus variabilis*) short-leaf pine, was much greater than usual through lower N.C. both as first & second growth. But in either case, its growth seemed to indicate a somewhat clayey soil, or subsoil. On the red soils of Orangeburgh, (silicified eocene beds below,) the land left untilled for some years had a very sparse sprinkling of young short-leaf pines—& no other kinds observed. Darkness there put a stop to my observations. Reached the Charleston Depot at 2 A.M. & thence to the Charleston Hotel, & to bed by 3 A.M.

*May 10. . . .* Went to the Lutheran Church, of which my valued & [96] revered friend, Dr. John Bachman is the minister, & heard his services & sermon.[30] Afterwards met him & his daughters, before leaving the church—& promised to visit them tomorrow early. The newspapers until dinner. Afterwards called on Professor F. S. Holmes.[31] We had an animated conversation for 3 hours, mostly in regard to our common friend Tuomey, & some geological observations, which we had respectively made. I proposed to Mr. H. that he should write a sketch of Mr. Tuomey's character, abilities, & public services—to which he agreed, & I promised to furnish him with some materials, of the time prior to that of Mr. Holmes' first acquaintance. . . . The Charleston Hotel, with its crowd of visitors is to me a solitude—as I do not know a single inmate, & have had no conversation with any one. Prof. Holmes, who next to Dr. Bachman, I should be most pleased to see much of, is to leave home tomorrow morning for Tuscaloosa. There are sundry other persons whom I desire to see & converse with here—but none with whom I have been very intimate.

*May 11.* Saw the operations of excavating for a culvert along Calhoun Street, which were very interesting, because offering an example & proof of my views of draining. This drain is dug to a level, which is 14 feet below the surface where deepest. The lower part, for several feet, is through quicksand, becoming more & more fluid towards the bottom. This has to be kept out by plank piles driven down on both sides, & supported by studing framing. Already some of the shallow wells in the neighborhood have become dry, & no doubt this evidence of draining effect will increase with time for [97] months to come. At 10 A.M. (by yesterday's appointment)

---

[30] Dr. John Bachman (1790–1874), renowned naturalist and clergyman, was born in New York but moved to Charleston in 1815. There, among other accomplishments, he organized the Lutheran Synod of South Carolina and in 1833 founded the State Horticultural Society. He is perhaps best known for his collaboration with John James Audubon on the three-volume work, *The Viviparous Quadrupeds of North America.*

[31] Francis S. Holmes, professor of geology and paleontology at the College of Charleston, was a close associate of Michael Tuomey. Holmes was the first man to explore the possibility of utilizing artesian well water in Charleston, and he was the first curator of the Museum of Natural History, which opened in Charleston in 1852.

called on Dr. Bachman & family. Mrs. Bachman has been very sick, & for a long time, but is now enough improved to ride out. Dr. B. took me in his buggy to see the Artesian well—but the superintendent being sick, I will go again. Then to see ["Lord John"] Russell the bookseller, & subscribed for his new Magazine, which I hope will be worthy of southern support & will obtain it.[32] Afterwards called on the editors of the Mercury, & conversed with them for an hour on the great question & the prospect of secession of the southern states. I urged the impossibility of Virginia moving first, or among the first. But if 5 or 6 of the more southern states would secede, then, as a necessity, Virginia & even Maryland, as well as all the intervening slave-holding states, would be *forced* to join their southern brethren. . . . Before going to bed, wrote a short secession article, designed for the Mercury.

*May 12.* Soon after breakfast Dr. Bachman called, bringing Dr. [William] Hume to introduce to me.[33] Dr. Hume is one entrusted, & also best-informed as to both the city draining, & the Artesian boring. We went together to make further examinations of both. Saw the excavations &c. for the drains in several different places. The digging usually reaches water at 3 feet—sometimes less. Thence wet sand, & after, quick-sand to bottom. The facts are practical examples & proofs of my views of draining the glutted under-lying sand-bed. The bottom of all these main drains (for culverts) are level, & 20 inches above low tide mark. A brick culvert is laid, [98] which is 3½ feet wide, & 4½ feet high, inside. Water from the sand-bed is received therein everywhere, & more & more as the digging descends —the upper sand being left dry, & becoming firm, when the digging has sunk much below. The plan now in the course of execution is for the upper part of the city only—& the culverts for this only (placed under the middle of streets, & covered over,) will be 20 miles in length, & the surface of the bottom of the culverts will make 3½ acres. The drainage effect will be excellent. But how far it may serve to remove soluble filth, or act as sanitary means, I cannot pretend to judge. There has been much controversy as to this scheme, & much opposition to it. Dr. Wragg & Dr. Hume, its chief advocates, & who are of the committee of direction, were as much gratified with my

---

[32] Ruffin's hope proved futile, as *Russell's Magazine* lasted only until the spring of 1860.

[33] Dr. William Hume, a native of Charleston, was professor of experimental science at the Citadel Academy, 1844–65.

approval of & confidence in the draining operation of the work, as I was in its serving to exemplify & sustain my theoretical views. For, as there was neither necessity, nor means, for digging so deep into the quick-sand in any of my operations for agricultural drainage, I had never before seen such perfect & extensive putting of my theory into practice. . . .

*May 13.* The Mercury of this morning contains my little article. . . . R. B. Rhett esq. called on me, & we had a long conversation on the secession question. No one has been more ardent for the measure than he was, & is—as he evinced in his various public services, of which the last was in the U.S. Senate. But he despairs of any early or efficient action by any of the southern states—and [100] mainly because there are no proper leaders—men who have the will & the ability, & also the necessary influence with their people. Some of the strongest men are seekers of high federal offices, & aspirants for higher, & therefore are self-bribed to a course of inactivity, or submission. Many others, formerly among the most earnest & zealous for resistance or secession, have abandoned the struggle in sullen despondency or despair.—In obedience to our agreement, I wrote a letter to Prof. Holmes stating what I knew of our friend Tuomey, to serve as materials for him to prepare a sketch of his labors, & qualities, for publication. My letter extended to 9 pages.—Most of the day spent in my apartment, writing, or in light reading. At dark, received a letter from Dr. Wragg requesting me to state in writing (as I did in words yesterday) my opinion of the city drains, in reference to my views of drainage—which he wants to sustain the action of his committee. I have answered, in a letter of 5 pages . . . .

*May 14.* Carried my answer to Dr. Wragg, & conversed with him some time on the subject—by which I missed Dr. Bachman, who was looking for me in vain. Spent the evening with him. I heard from him much about the early career of [John C.] Fremont, in Charleston, & his swindling of creditors, & other rascally acts. These acts were far exceeded in his subsequent swindlings of the government, when an officer in trust—& by his duplicity & lying. What a character does it give of his supporters, that, notwithstanding the exposure of all these acts, this man barely missed being elected President of the United States! [101]

*May 15.* Dr. Bachman called for me, & we rode out. Went to the Orphan House, a noble charitable institution of the city. Here more than 200 destitute orphan children are maintained & educated. Went up to the top of the building, which affords a fine view of the city, & neighboring waters & country.—Saw in the "South," of Va. (R. Pryor's new paper,) a strong editorial article recommending the legalizing the renewal of the African slave trade. This is the first publication to this effect that I have seen made in Va. though many persons there coincide in the opinion. And here, so far as I have gathered from conversation since my arrival, it is the general, if not unanimous, opinion. And so it is reported to be throughout all the more southern states. But the renewal of the trade by law, or even against law, to bring slaves to this country, is obviously impossible, so long as the present union with the northern states lasts. But if the policy is as extensively approved in the south, as it is asserted, that fact will operate strongly to promote secession, & separation of the union, because all men's self-interest will be deeply concerned in the result. All the southern states suffer greatly from the scarcity & high price of labor. They can obtain no supply from abroad, because the only available & useful supply, of negroes, is prohibited by law. In the meantime the northern states are receiving any amount of labor, in the hordes of destitute whites from Europe.—Long after I had learned to deem our system of negro slavery a benefit & a blessing, to both the slaves & their masters, I still retained my objections to the African slave-trade—& at a former time, I would have as soon expected that I should become the approver of piracy & murder, as of the slave-trade in any possible form. As to the existing *prohibited* slave-trade, my opinion & objections, & abhorrence, remain unchanged. Nothing can [102] exceed its horrors, & the amount of suffering it inflicts, unless it is its modern substitute, the transportation of so-called *free* men, in the coolie trade. But the sufferings & cruelties of the existing slave-trade are caused by its prohibition, & the dangers of capture, & severe punishment. To lessen this danger, the transportation of the slaves is effected in small & swift sailing vessels, in which the slaves are packed so closely that they can scarcely live through the speedy voyage. But if the business was legal, it would be the interest of the owners to take care of the lives, the health, & therefore of the comfort of their slaves. This alone would go far to remove all the present sufferings. But farther, governments ought to prescribe all humane & needful regulations for the slave-ships, which could be as operative as for passengers in emigrant ships. Under such operation of self-interest & of legal regulations, there is no reason why the African slaves, even on the

"Middle Passage" should not be even more comfortable, ( physically,) than their lives were before under their barbarous & inhuman African masters and rulers. And there cannot be any doubt that in the general, the subsequent condition of Africans, as slaves in these southern states, would be much more safe, comfortable, & happy than when slaves, or captives in Africa—& probably of even the few who might not have been previously slaves. It is true, there would be exceptional cases, in which individuals would be sufferers by the change. But such exceptions must be found in every great movement of portions of mankind, & even in the most beneficial of general & great changes. Probably in every emigrant ship that comes from Europe to America, & of which the adult male passengers at least are free agents, & chose to emigrate, . . . there are as many cases of suffering & unhappiness, . . . [103] owing to the removal . . . as would be among the like number of the ignorant & brutal savages of Africa in a slave ship, if under legal & proper regulation. And yet, because of the many cases of individual grief & suffering thereby produced—& which never can be compensated to the suffering individuals—who would stop emigration from Europe, as required by humanity for the would-be emigrants[?] Even our glorious revolutionary war, if judged by this rule, ought to be condemned as an evil, & a horrible infliction on humanity. For in that struggle, thousands lost their lives, or suffered worse than the loss of life— other thousands were impoverished—& every individual of the country probably lost or suffered more than could have been counted as his actual gain. And the cases of greater unhappiness of individual African slaves, when brought to this country, by a legalized trade, however much to be deplored, as of all other undeserved human suffering, would be as nothing in comparison to the greater benefits thereby produced in all other cases, to the first slaves & to their posterity.

My acquaintance in this hotel is increasing by the arrival of gentlemen whom I knew formerly, & also by introduction to others. Among the former, are the Ex-governors [John P.] Richardson & [John L.] Manning. . . .[34]

I had waited to see the superintendent of the Artesian borings,

---

[34] Richardson served as governor of South Carolina from 1840 to 1842; Manning, from 1852 to 1854. The latter was also one of the largest slaveholders in the South, with extensive planting interests in Clarendon District, South Carolina, and Ascension Parish, Louisiana.

Mr. Welton, before stating anything on the subject. He was sick at home, & I had to seek him there. The former boring was 1248 feet deep. At that depth, it passed through [104] a hard rock, & the water bursted up, which rose over the surface, & has continued to flow out, as it now does some 15 feet above the surface, in as large a stream as the pipe admits. But that is only three inches in diameter, & the supply of water is altogether inadequate. But as the fact of the supply, & the force of the ascending water has been ascertained, the city authorities proceeded immediately to bore another well, of which the pipes will be 11 inches in diameter, inside measure, within 20 feet of the other well, & which of course will pass through the like strata. The new boring is now but little more than 800 feet deep. It is in daily progress, with the power of a steam-engine. But still it does not increase in depth usually more than a few feet a day. . . . This water[35] is . . . a prodigious improvement on the former supplies of water. Numerous wells have since been sunk by individuals, in various parts of the city, & this water is always reached & drawn up at from 57 to 60 feet. These are known by the [105] designation of the "Sixty-feet" wells. Under this layer of sand & water is next reached the great bed of eocene marl, which I formerly designated as the "Great Carolinian Bed," & then ascertained that it was more than 300 feet deep, under Charleston. It has now been ascertained, as stated by Mr. Welton, to [be] 780 feet thick. . . . Below this was reached & bored through 25 feet of hard blue sand-stone, under which was reached loose sand, so surcharged with water, that it rose quickly above the surface, & with such force as to bring up, at first, sand in immense quantity—perhaps 50 tons, before the water had made its passage clear, & ceased to bring up sand. Sand so lifted perpendicularly for 1248 feet speaks strongly of the previous confinement of the water, & the force with which it escapes therefrom. The water is 87° of temperature, & would be excellent for tepid baths. It contains both carbonate & muriate of soda, so as to be unpalatable for drinking, but serves admirably for every other domestic use. It is soft, & excellent for washing.

The benefit of these supplies of water to Charleston cannot be appreciated except by one who knows what abominable filthy water was necessarily in general use before, & who yet has not been a resident long enough to become accustomed, by use, to the abomination. [106] The drinking water is supplied by rain, & kept in cis-

---

[35] In the second water bed, reached at a depth of about sixty feet.

terns. That *may* be clean—but is to be suspected, especially in a city in which the roofs are the regular resting places of hundreds of buzzards. But cistern water is too scarce to be used for cooking & washing purposes—for which, before the new supplies were obtained by boring, (either the 60 feet wells or the deep artesian well,) was obtained from the shallow wells sunk only to the first water-yielding sand, or 10 or 12 feet deep. Now to judge of the impurity of this water, it is enough to know the source of supply. But besides that, in summer, I have found it offensive to the smell, when washing my face. Charleston stands on a nearly level surface, located at most but about 10 feet above high water mark. The upper layer of earth, called dry, of clay & sand, varies from 1 to 4 feet deep, & under that lies sand always wet, if not drained. The sand becomes more pure & more *quick,* or fluid, as descending to 14 feet below the surface .... The water that pervades every portion of this universal bed of sand, (whether of the upper & merely wet, or the lower quick-sand,) has as free passage throughout as the texture of the sand will allow. It fills all the shallow wells; & the water supplying these wells must previously have dissolved, & carried with it, everything of soluble filth & organic matter which it had been anywhere in contact with. All the soluble organic matter on the surface of the soil, that is not floated off to the drains by rain water, must sink into the [107] sandy soil, down to the water bed—& in the water, slowly percolate into the shallow wells. But all this supply, abundant, & loathsome to the imagination as it is, is nothing to the buried filth, & its contaminating effect. The contents of every privy in Charleston descends in pits, of greater or less depth, into the earth, & to the bed of water-glutted sand. All this filth, or so much as is soluble, gradually, & sooner or later, must be dissolved in the water, & thus find its way to the nearest lower lateral out-lets, & these are the numerous shallow wells. Even this is not all. All the numerous dead bodies buried in the city grave-yards, in sufficient time, must go through the same process of being dissolved, & the products draining into the well-water which is used for every purpose except for drinking alone. It is to be hoped that the full supply of water to be afforded by the completion of the new artesian well, & the numerous sixty-feet wells, (of which there may be one on every lot of ground,) will relieve Charleston of this horrible nuisance of using filthy water. But there is another means of prevention now in progress, which will compel abstinence, if no other inducement will. The deep drains, now in progress, being deeper than the shallow wells, will drain them by cutting off their supplies, & so compel the disuse of their filthy water.

*May 16.* To Dr. Bachman's (study) soon after breakfast. An interesting conversation, & an account from him of his early & self-education. I knew that he was a man of various & great attainments; but had no idea before that he had alone, & without any aid but of books, acquired his knowledge of Latin, Greek, & elementary Mathematics, & so fitted himself to enter college. Also, & even without books or instruction he had made extensive acquisitions in Botany & Zoology, by collecting & preserving specimens, & observing the habits of the living subjects. And in his later life, even [108] after his removal to a city, & his having access to libraries & other aids, it is surprising how much labor of study & learning, & writing, he has continued to perform, superadded to care of his large family, & his ministry as a pastor, & his pastoral attention to many besides those of his own congregation. For, as I have long known, the love & veneration for him, & his own attentions of benevolence & piety, are not confined to his own congregation, nor by sectarian limits. I deem him among the best of Christians & of pastors, because his works prove it, & his uniform cheerfulness further confirms it.

Attended the Synagogue & worship of the "Reformed Jews" this being their sabbath. This is a noble & beautiful edifice, & the congregation is composed principally of Jews born in Charleston—about 200 adult males, & perhaps 500 counting the families & children. There are two other synagogues, the members of which are mostly foreigners, & more of the ignorant class. In these (which claim the name of "orthodox Jews") the Hebrew language is mostly used, & the old forms strictly maintained. The "reformed" congregation have altered or dispensed with old & unsuitable forms, & use the English language for the greater part of their services—& also have introduced the organ, & have very fine sacred music. I went in a little after the reading had begun (in Hebrew). With some later comers, there were but 9 men of the congregation, including myself, besides the priest & his assistant—& perhaps 25 women & children. The services were impressive & solemn—except for the usage of every one wearing his hat—even the priest. A portion of the service was in a kind of chanting, something midway in sound between speaking & singing, uttered mostly by the priest, but sometimes responded to by the men of the congregation. The sound was singular, & musical, but not generally melodious. The hymns, accompanied by the organ, were very fine. I was surprised to see, among [109] the books in the pew in which I sat, an ordinary English Bible, with the New Testament included. And this was not a solitary instance, as, in the pew before me, a young man held in his hand throughout, & frequently read in a small & handsome copy of the like Christian bible, which I examined. The other copy was a common edition published by the American Bible Society. From all the indications, I infer that the persons who compose this congregation are in a transition state, or on the middle passage from Judaism either to Christianity, or more generally to carelessness & disregard of both & all systems of religion. The obstinacy with which the Jews of the old world have clung to their religion, has in great measure been caused by their being persecuted or despised for it. In this country, they are entirely free from persecution, both direct & indirect—& are as much respected as other people, if their conduct deserves respect. The first emigrants from Europe generally remain strict & bigoted Jews. Their children grow up among & like the children of other people—& if they are educated & wealthy, generally neglect or cast aside their Jewish observances, & are more deists than Jews. In the next generation, the Jewish faith & prejudices are generally at an end—& the young people, as much as all others, are open to receive impressions of the christian religion. While the Jews of the second generation will generally lose their ancient religion, it will be rare that any earlier than of the third or fourth generation will become true converts to Christianity.

Dined by invitation with Wm. M. Lawton esq., a prominent & wealthy & very intelligent merchant, to whom I have before been indebted for much attention. Ten guests were there—intelligent & agreeable gentlemen—the most so were Richard Yeadon, editor of the Courier, & Isaac Hayne, Attorney General. We remained together from 4 to 9½ P.M. Much of our conversation on the subjects of [110] slavery, & of secession of the southern states—though the latter, as well as all references to party politics, were treated in jocular manner. Also the subjects of mesmerism & spiritualism, or rather the physical phenomena (as table-moving, &c.) were discussed. Mr. Yeadon is a believer in both—& stated some remarkable examples of apparent miracles in both . . . . Mr. Yeadon is a rare character. He is a distinguished lawyer & able editor & controversialist—& though a whig (& was the only one in the legislature,) was elected, & the foremost, by the city of Charleston, almost unanimously democratic & secessionist.

*May 17.* Sunday. Attended St. Philip's church. For the first time heard a chime of bells, & on them performed church music. The effect very good, at the church; but at a distance, where it would be better, if alone heard, it is spoiled by the tolling of three or four other discordant bells of other churches. When I before attended the services of this church, my daughter Jane was with me, bright & joyful & happy, in youth, health, & loveliness. The remembrance was forcibly & solemnly impressed on me, & the sense of my subsequent afflictions. . . . [111]

*May 18.* Raining slowly until 4 P.M. Went by invitation to dine with Mr. Yeadon. 20 at dinner, all told. . . . The ex-governors Richardson & Manning were there, Judge Wardlaw, & sundry other intelligent country gentlemen, then visiting Charleston. I sat between our very agreeable host & Mr. Cutler of the city of New York, a very intelligent gentleman. He has lately spent some time in Cuba. He told me that the greater part of the native Cuban population, or "creoles," are more or less of mixed blood, African or Indian, or both. This I was not aware of—& it will be a serious objection to our receiving Cuba as a sister state, & its highest class as fellow-citizens & equals. If correctly stated, this state of things would be worse than that of Central America, where the mixture with African blood is so general & great, that there would be no difficulty in a conquering white race keeping above & apart from the natives, & avoiding more extended intermixture of blood & races.—Went to take leave of the Bachmans, & paid my bill, ready to set out in the morning, for Augusta, & to call on Gov. [James Henry] Hammond. . . .[36]

*May 19.* Left Charleston by 7 A.M. on the railway to Augusta. The land low & flat & often wet, for 15 or 20 miles—& low & flat, though a little higher to Blackville, 90 miles from Charleston. The loblolly pine & the short-leaf (*p. variabilis*) the general growth—unless the rapid motion deceived my eyes as to the quantity of the latter kind. . . . Beyond Blackville, the surface more & more undulating & higher, & soon *all* the pines were long-leaf, to [112] past Aiken, the summit, when descending to low-land again, this pine was mostly re-

---

[36] Hammond (1807–64), prominent South Carolina statesman, agriculturist, and defender of slavery, was one of Ruffin's closest friends. He succeeded John P. Richardson as governor in 1842 and later served in the United States Senate, 1857–60.

placed by the two other kinds. The long-leaf has exclusive possession of the dry sandy & very poor land from Blackville to Aiken—& also of the spaces about Aiken where the subsoil is all of deep & very compact red clay. Reached Augusta Ga. (137 miles) before 3 P.M. Gov. Hammond's carriage was ready for me, & rode 6 miles (recrossing the Savannah into South Ca.) to his residence at Redcliff. Found Gen. H. & Mrs. H. well. He & I had plenty to talk about, of his new agricultural schemes, & politics &c. to near midnight.

*May 20.* . . . Gen. Hammond is full of two new schemes, superadded to his general & large cropping & improvements of regular agriculture on his other & much larger properties. One is vineculture, & to make wine when prepared on a large scale, as he has already begun. He has a large vineyard planted out, & in good progress & promise of success. The other scheme is the culture of the Chinese sugar *sorghum,* or rather, as now substituted, the African *imphee,* a superior plant of like kind. His success in expressing syrup, last year, from his Chinese sorghum has been published, & has conduced much [to] create the extended interest on that subject. He had pla[n]ted 52 acres of that variety, this year, when Mr. Leonard Wray arrived here, from England, bringing a few bushels of the African imphee seed, grown in the south of France. And such were the representations he made of the superiority of this variety, with other considerations of most interest to himself, that he induced Gen. Hammond to go extensively into the culture. It was then too late to prepare other land for this purpose, & so he ploughed up 50 acres of the Chinese sorghum, & 50 acres of his corn-crop, & planted the whole in the *imphee.* Mr. Wray [113] is an Englishman, long a sugar planter in Jamaica, from which he was at last driven by the ruin of its agriculture by the legal emancipation of the slaves. He then travelled & resided in Hindostan, & at Natal, in South Africa, where he found & tried this *imphee,* & its sugar-producing qualities. He has extensive knowledge on sugar culture & all its incidents; & is the author of an octavo volume on the subject. He is a man of general information & intelligence. But I want faith in the permanent value of this new plant, to the extent he anticipat s.[37]
—Rode out in the neighborhood from breakfast to dinner. The land

[37] Ruffin's assessment proved to be correct. Although the imphee sorghum cane soon generally replaced the Chinese variety, neither kind led to the production of sugar for commercial purposes. This was not the first time—nor the last—that the gullible Hammond was taken in by such an agricultural craze.

high, & rolling surface. Extensive views. Augusta in full view from the house at Redcliff. . . . Visited the Kaolin clay bed, & the new factory of earthen ware made of this material. The clay in an underbed (lying under a pure & loose white sand,) of perfectly white color, & in texture also such as could not be distinguished from English chalk. It was called "chalk," & supposed to be such. But it has not a particle of lime. Mr. Tuomey first ascertained what was its true character & value, & that it is Kaolin, of remarkable purity. A northern company has recently established works to make earthen ware of superior quality, & have brought workmen from England. The ware made is very beautiful, & the results promise to be of great public utility.—Gen. Hammond has been one of the ablest men in S.C.; & now, though he has been rusting in solitude so long, he has unquestionably the most powerful mind in the southern states. Pity that he is not in our public councils. But his former chance for great usefulness has been lost—& I fear [114] that it will never be recovered—or even desired by himself or the public. . . . Heard much from Mr. Wray of the decline of Jamaica, in consequence of emancipation, even farther than I had heard of, or conceived. He says that even the black population has decreased greatly, & he thinks by more than one-third of the former number, when slaves. He gave a very favorable account of the Chinese as laborers, when imported to the tropical colonies, (under the general, but incorrect, name of "Coolies,")—but admitted that they had been injudiciously & cruelly treated, & that their provocations & vengeance had produced many disastrous & even bloody results.

*May 21.* Rode with Gen. Hammond & Mr. Wray to the plantation of the former near Silver Bluff on the Savannah—where I had been before. Saw the hundreds of acres of rich swamp land, well-drained & under corn & cotton—& the 100 acres in "imphee." We dined at the old mansion, where I had staid some 10 days when conducting the agricultural survey, in 1843. Gen. Hammond's sons now reside there. Returned by night. The newspapers—& very animated & interesting conversation to a late hour. Arranged to leave early next morning. So cold this morning that I fear there was frost to damage the wheat in Virginia. [115]

*May 22.* Left Gen. Hammond's, in his carriage, little after 4 A.M. for Augusta. . . . Left there on the railway at 6, & reached Atlanta, Ga, 171 miles, by 3.30 P.M. I had once before travelled this road, but remembered very little, except generally of the rolling & much gullied fields, & evidence of exhausting tillage. It seemed to look less badly now. There is extensive use of hill-side ditches, to prevent washing—but they are mostly of very imperfect operation, because both too small, & inaccurately planned. The lands below Augusta, & in the neighborhood of Gen. Hammond's (in S.C.) are high, rolling, & generally of good quality. Very fine wheat was on the Ga side near Augusta. The railroad crosses the line of the falls of the rivers, & the upper boundary of the drift, at a very acute angle. For some 55 to 60 miles, the natural forest growth mostly pine, & all these the long-leaf. The second growth, mixed loblolly & short-leaf. As the soil became red, the long-leaf pine ceased—& then the loblolly diminished more & more. . . . Saw again, with much interest, the remarkable "Stone Mountain," 16 miles from Atlanta. This is an isolated & steep mountain of considerable height, rising up alone in the midst of a comparatively level surface. . . . The mountain is one solid mass of granite—& almost naked of all vegetation. There is but a little sprinkling of shrubbery on some parts, where I suppose the granite is partially disintegrated & rifted. Went to Thompson's hotel. At night, called to see Mr. Richard Peters,[38] whom I had met formerly, & who is a remarkable & valuable man, as an enterprising improver, for the public benefit in many [116] things, & in the general results—but who, in thus benefiting the public, especially aims first to benefit himself. And he has done so, to a very uncommon extent. He came here, from Pennsylvania, a young engineer, without funds or friends. By his speculations in various ways, & with the aid of his good judgment, in a few years he has acquired a large fortune. Not finding him at home, he soon followed me to my lodgings, & arranged with me an excursion for tomorrow.

*May 23.* Rode with Mr. Peters & Dr. Harden to their farm, recently bought & put under improvement. It is designed in part for a nursery of fruit trees. Viewed their hill-side ditching, which is well executed & effective. Mr. Peters' larger farming business is more distant. There he has his large planting of "Chinese" *sorghum saccharatum,* (some 50 acres,) from which, besides what the seed may bring, he counts upon making at least 300 gallons of syrup to the acre, worth as much as molasses, which now is at 70 cents. And yet even if this sanguine expectation shall be realized, it will be less

---

[38] A noted agricultural reformer in the lower South, Peters was a major advocate of pure-bred livestock and was the first to import and develop the Angora goat in this country.

than he got from 4 acres planted last year, & of which he sold nearly all the seed at $1 for a 6 oz. package. Out of the crop, after planting, he has but about 10 of these packages left. Probably he sold 70 bushels at that rate. What his gross receipts were he did not say, & of course I did not ask any such questions. But he mentioned that in Cincinnati, alone, his agent had sold seed to the amount of $3000. He had agents & made sales probably in every state in the Union. And besides his supply, there were hundreds of bushels furnished by the Patent Office, & all the seed raised by individuals from the Patent Office seed supplied for & grown in 1856. There will be ample means this year to test the value of this plant, for making grain & forage, syrup, & sugar. Dined with Mr. Peters, & had some hours of very pleasant conversation.

. . . At 6 P.M. left Atlanta, for Augusta—where I arrived (at the hotel) at daybreak.

*May 24.* Sunday. . . . Left, at 9.½, & reached Columbia at 6 P.M. From Branchville, at first the pines mostly long-leaf—young or second growth mostly loblolly—as red land of Orangeburgh began, the short-leaf became prevalent—afterwards as before on gray & more sandy land, the long-leaf & loblolly—& when near Columbia, & elsewhere on clay soil, the short-leaf almost alone of the pine growth. At Congaree Hotel.

*May 25.* Left Columbia for N.C. at 9 A.M. At Charlotte by 4 P.M. Again left on the N.C.R.R. & reached Haw river station at 1 A.M. From Columbia, the long-leaf & loblolly pines diminish, & the short-leaf pines increase, as the land becomes more red, until there are none on the forest, or of original growth, on the reddest soil, from Catawba river to near Salisbury. In these places, the second growth is still partly or principally, of short-leaf pine, & that kind only. On the remarkable "black-jack land" of Chester, S.C. there is no pine of any kind, even as second growth. That land, very level for its high locality, gray & very close clay. If drained, (which is much needed everywhere,) the land would be very productive. Even as it is, this land is highly valued, though extremely laborious to till, & the product precarious. A soft rock is general at a few feet below the surface, which would very much impede the digging of deep ditches. Still, this rock can be dug with picks—& when laid bare, soon disintegrates. After stopping, slept at the hotel at Haw river.

*May 26.* . . . This [118] morning, soon after daybreak . . . I started, & walked the 5 miles to Alamance, where I arrived before most of the family [of Judge Thomas Ruffin] had left their chambers. . . . A most kind & friendly welcome from all. . . . The Judge, as always, hard at work—& now busily attending to the planting of some seeds, & preparing for leaving here to attend the Episcopal Convention, now in session at Salisbury. I had learned this intention from Bishop Atkinson, whom I travelled with yesterday from Charlotte to Salisbury. The bishop & I had much interesting conversation— part of it concerning the colonization of Liberia, & the alleged success of the emancipation of slaves, there colonized—about which, as might be expected, the bishop & I were of entirely different opinions. He is a very pleasant & agreeable gentleman.

*May 28.* . . . The mail brought me a letter from Julian stating Mary's continued declining health, & that she is to leave home for New York (I fear to die from home,) on the [119] 30th—the very day I had fixed to reach Prince George. I determined immediately to set out this day, instead of tomorrow, as appointed, so as to reach Beechwood tomorrow morning. . . . I deplore this leaving home—though it is to be done in obedience to Mary's medical advisers. I know by experience, in my Ella's case, the doubled griefs & horrors of dying & death occurring far from home, & among strangers, however kind they may be. . . . At 1 P.M. set out on the railway & reached Goldsborough at 7—took the train from Wilmington after 9, to return northward—

*May 29.* At daybreak, reached Petersburg, 250 miles in all, of railway. Hired a vehicle, & before 8 A.M. reached Beechwood. Found Mary better, as she had been for a few days—& I trust well enough not to be made worse by the necessary fatigue. Mildred here, & also Mr. Sayre & Elizabeth, who had come from Marlbourne to see Mary before she left home. . . .

*May 30.* Early in the morning, Mary, with Edmund, Nanny & Mildred, left in the carriage for City Point, there to take the steam-ship for New York. Heard that Mary bore the travel to City Point without fatigue, & that all embarked [120] safely. . . . She goes, to travel, on the earnest recommendation of her physician—& the direction to New York is her own wish, that she may visit her near relatives there. In two or three weeks she will probably return, because unwilling to stay longer from her children & from home. She could not have the very necessary attendance of a servant of her own, because of the certain action of the abolitionists, who, if unable to entice a slave to leave the owner, would raise a mob, & force her away. My daughter Mildred goes to nurse Mary . . . . By appointment, Julian's carriage came for Elizabeth & Mr. Sayre, & they & I went to Ruthven to dine, ( & I to stay longer.) . . .

*May 31.* Sunday. Went with Julian's family to church, & returned to dinner. Rain in sudden showers. Afternoon, we rode to see Agnes. Her despicable husband some time back went to Petersburg to practice medicine, his family still residing at their home. If he was gone so far that he never would be heard from, it would be the next best thing to his death. But, so near as this, his different [121] residence is but a new cause of discomfort to his wife. She spends half her time in travelling to & from Petersburg, & in providing at home for his comfortable accommodation abroad. I shall hereafter, if ever again meeting him, pass him as a stranger. Regard for my daughter's feelings has induced me to maintain with him to this time the outward show of courtesy in our cold & slight intercourse. But I will no longer make this pretence of respect, when its' [*sic*] hollowness is manifest to all.

*June 1.* Came, with Julian, from his home to Beechwood. He proceeded thence to Petersburg, with Mr. Sayre & Elizabeth, on their way to Marlbourne. . . . Reading late numbers of Living Age. The house seems strange & desolate with Mary & Edmund absent—& the more melancholy for the cause of their absence. . . .

*June 5.* At daybreak, set out in the carriage, (which is to be there repaired,) for Petersburg. Thence, at 9 A.M. on the railway to Richmond—where, by previous appointment Mr. Sayre's carriage afterwards came for me. Raining & cold. Saw & conversed with Mr. Williams, (Secry. of S.A.S.) about the affairs of the Society—had a tooth plugged by the dentist—left & returned to Marlbourne. All well. E. & Mr. Sayre alone. Newspapers & De Bow's Review. In the latter is begun the republication of my letters in favor of disunion— prefaced by an editorial puff of myself. Gen. Walker, after having held out in Central America until his situation was hopeless, has abandoned his predatory enterprise & returned to the U.S. I heartily wished him success, in consideration of the general benefit that would result—but never viewed him otherwise than as an able villain, a robber & murderer on a large scale. As his plan has failed, I wish that he had been captured & hanged. The recent bloody election riot in Washington, & their more bloody suppression by the

U.S. marines, is a serious matter.[39] I wish that every forcible disturber of the election had been shot down. The ready authority given by the President for this effectual mode of suppression, is almost the only thing he has done that commands my applause, since the commencement of his administration. And I as heartily condemn his appointment of that political & unprincipled adventurer [Robert J.] Walker, as Governor of Kansas, whose proclamations show that he must be authorized & instructed by the President to use his official [123] influence to make Kansas a non-slavery state. The purpose is manifested in his conduct as well as his words.—The state government of Ohio is arrayed against the lawful jurisdiction & constitutional power of the Federal government, & I earnestly hope may push the opposition to the extent of treason & rebellion.[40] N. York, Massachusetts, & some other of the northern states, have also made like enactments, to nullify the fugitive slave law. I trust that all, like Ohio, may have an opportunity, & that they will also put their theory of opposition into practice. It would be a capital move, if one or more of these fanatical northern states would begin the operation of secession from, or resistance to the Union. . . .

*June 6.* Went with Mr. Sayre to see the wheat & other crops. Six weeks ago, the wheat had scarcely begun to grow, or to show recovery from the unprecedented bad weather of Winter & Spring. Now, the crop promises well, & shows wonderful improvement generally. . . . Looked over & corrected writings, & finished last No. of De Bow's Review. This No., besides my article, which is stronger than any that ever appeared in Va., is almost wholly of southern articles —& part even advocating the general principle of the African slave-trade, &, consequentially, the expediency of its renewal.

*June 8.* Continued correcting my written account of my drainage of Marlbourne, & inserting on the maps the recent levellings. . . . When marking the measures of elevation on the map, in very small characters, I could not write them decently, because of the trembling of my hand. This infirmity has greatly increased in late years, &

---

[39] On June 1 some fifty "Plug-Uglies" or Know-Nothings from Baltimore descended on the nation's capital and attempted to prevent the Irish from voting in a municipal election. Two companies of United States Marines were ordered out by the President, and, in the ensuing melee, six to eight persons were killed and some thirty were injured.

[40] The reference here is to a confrontation between a United States deputy marshal and three Ohio sheriffs following an unsuccessful attempt by the former to seize a fugitive slave in Mechanicsburg, Ohio.

has become a permanent affection. If I drank intoxicating liquors at all, & even so moderately, my trembling hands, & red face, would cause many strangers to suppose I was a drunkard. . . .

*June 11.* . . . Continue correcting my account of my drainage of Marlbourne. The extent to which this writing has grown, makes me doubtful as to what to do with it. It was at first designed mainly for instruction & information to my children who would succeed me as possessors of the farm. Then, as the plan & work were extended, I designed to make it [a] communication to the State Agrl. Society. I fear it may be too long & elaborate for that purpose—& I am hesitating between that, & the former alternative—or whether I shall not publish it, as a substantive work. I have always found agricultural memoirs of this general character—descriptive & narrative of actual labors, & their effects—as more interesting than any others. But it is most likely that the public would treat this with even more neglect than I have been accustomed to have shown to my publications, so as to subject me to mortification of my pride, as well as pecuniary loss. I shall proceed to copy, & put the article in shape, & determine hereafter on its destination. . . .

*June 12.* The carriage sent to Richmond for Julian. Received letters from Mildred of 9th & Edmund of 10th at New York. Mary's disease had taken a bad turn, & I fear a speedy & fatal termination. They were about to leave, if possible. I trust that they did so—& that she may have reached her home (this day) if it be to die there. . . . Julian arrived late—& had not heard of Mary's increased illness & danger before being here.—Today finished Boswell's Johnson.

*June 13.* . . . Read in Bishop [John H.] Hopkins' new book "The American Citizen" the several chapters in which he discusses the whole subject of slavery in the U.S.[41] I was curious to see how, in these times of heated discussion [127] & fanatical thought & action, a New England clergyman, of distinguished ability, & undoubted piety, would treat this question. In regard to the bible & religious question, & the moral, political, & constitutional questions, his views are sensible, enlarged, correct, & in all important points, such as an equally intelligent southerner might have written. But when he comes to consider the question of expediency, & matters connected,

---

[41] John Henry Hopkins (1792–1868) was the first Protestant Episcopal bishop of Vermont. Although opposed to slavery, he did not regard it as a sin and hoped that abolition could be effected amicably through mutual agreement between the sections.

the author is as much in the dark as most northerners are on the other questions in regard to slavery. While deeming, & fully conceding, that African slavery in the U.S. has been, & is, a blessing to the slaves, & their posterity, he deems the institution injurious to the masters, in an economical point of view as well as otherwise. Considering then that slavery is an evil, he proposes to remove it, by action of the U.S. government, & at the cost of all the U.S. by purchasing the slaves, & gradually ( 40,000 a year) transporting & establishing them in Africa, in & next to Liberia. This the good bishop estimates might be done for 1000 millions of dollars, & supposes that it would be easy for the people to agree to, & to bear, that burden of expence, for so great & good an object. Doubtless the writer would be willing to bear his share—& in believing that, I respect the patriotism, benevolence, & piety which are his masters, as much as I dissent from these particular doctrines, & would oppose the ends he proposes. But, what can be more absurd than to suppose that any people, even if having like general interests & views, would voluntarily incur an expence of 1000 millions, for any work of mere benevolence—much less of doubtful & disputed expediency. And much more absurd is it to suppose that the people of the north— even if generally as disinterested, & as friendly to the south, as they are the reverse—would incur half this great burden of taxation, merely to relieve & benefit the people of the south—or that the latter would pay the other half, to take away all of their now very inadequate supplies of labor, & produce privations [128] which would ruin the present generation, if not future generations, of the southern people!

*June 14.* Sunday. Julian & I set out, in a buggy, from Marlbourne, before 1 o'clock A.M. soon after the moon rose. We reached Evelynton by 7; & obtaining there a boat & hands reached Beechwood before 9. We were afraid to hear the answer to our first question—& were greatly relieved to hear that Mary was at home. Still more were we surprised & rejoiced to find her sitting up, & cheerful. She is greatly emaciated, & weak. The recent affection ( diarrhaea) which her physicians supposed to be the last & rapid stage of her general disease, has been nearly relieved, & therefore was probably a transient effect of some other cause.... As soon as she set out for home, she began to improve, for the time, & she is now much better, & as cheerful as could be, under her disease, & the knowledge of its danger....

*June 15.* . . . Reading parts of Burnett's "History of his own times" —& Littell's Living Age. The last No. contains two long articles for the service of abolition. One of them, by Elihu Burritt is an argument addressed "To Southern Statesmen," arguing for the same general plan of removing slavery with Bishop Hopkins, by purchasing the slaves by government—but with the important change of letting the emancipated slaves remain, to supply the needed labor to the southern states as hirelings. Bishop Hopkins' plan (of deportation & settlement in Africa,) is founded on the feelings of a good man, a philanthropist & a patriot. Burritt's are the narrow views of all thorough & practical abolitionists, varied only by his proposal to purchase the slaves, (though at but about half their present market value,) instead, which would effect the freedom of the slaves by inciting discontent, insubordination, & bloody insurrection. But, viewed as practical measures, working for the professed objects, it is difficult to say which of the two would be most absurd, inefficient, & disastrous. . . .

*June 17–18.* Continue to correct, alter, & copy the account of Marlbourne draining, when not otherwise occupied or amused. Have tried, & cannot read Burnett's History. Yet 25 years ago, when I first saw some odd volumes of the work, I read them with much interest. Resort to the [130] tales & other lightest articles of "Living Age."

*June 22.* Edmund began to reap wheat—the latest beginning known here for many years. A promise of a fine crop here, as well as at Marlbourne. Walked to see the operation of the reaping machine. Continue my copying & re-writing. . . . The newspapers give more full particulars of the recent fighting between the separate police forces of the city & the state of New York.[42] It seems very much like the beginning of a civil war, which the Federal government may have to interfere [with] to quell. I wish that the city would secede & form a separate state, with the consent of the federal government. The southern states would be benefitted, because the city as a state, & its two senators, would now be with the south. And if against us, a few years hence, it will be no worse for us, as there will be then a

---

[42] The trouble stemmed from a legislative act of April, 1857, which created a Metropolitan Police District governed by a seven-man Board of Police, which was controlled by the governor. Led by New York Mayor Fernando Wood, the old board declined to abdicate its authority to the new agency. The affair reached a climax on June 16, when rioting occurred and Mayor Wood was arrested by the metropolitan police.

majority of the Senate against the South, whether with or without [131] the City of New York as a separate state.

*June 24.* Left Beechwood early & went to Ruthven, with the expectation of proceeding in Julian's carriage to Petersburg, where it was to go to bring his family home. But here I found that one of the river steamers in which I designed to take passage tomorrow, is stopped —& also something else made it inconvenient to send the carriage, so I shall wait for tomorrow. . . . With Julian, & his harvest work in the fore noon, & in afternoon resumed my copying.

*June 25.* Went to Petersburg. . . . Read the papers at the office of the South Side Democrat, & had some conversation with the editor on southern politics. Saw J. R. Jones of Brunswick, at the hotel. Still, a tedious day. At night, wrote an hour in my room, & went to bed early.

*June 26.* Took the rail-way to City Point, & there the steamer for Old Point, where I arrived at 3 P.M. Only one person on board the steamer with whom I was acquainted, or with whom I had any conversation, a wealthy tobacco merchant, & extremely tiresome. Took lodgings at the hotel at Old Point Comfort—to stay as long as I may find agreeable. Saw Mr. Moncure, of Culpeper, & J. Darcey of N.C. the only farmers of my acquaintance. This being harvest, I shall see none, of the nearest wheat country, or of my intimate [132] acquaintance. More than 100 boarders here—mostly from cities—& the officers of Fortress Monroe.

*June 28.* Sunday. My writing is done—or as much as can now be done—& I brought no books with me, & can get none here. So already I am wearied, for want of employment or amusement.—In afternoon walked around the Fortress, on the ramparts. It is a beautiful place, independent of its military strength, & imposing appearance as a fortress.

*June 29.* . . . Had resolved to go to Richmond tomorrow morning— but in the afternoon I borrowed some books from Mr. Segar, the proprietor of the hotel, & also A. Dudley Mann, & Roger Pryor, (editor of "The South,") arrived, which made me agree to stay longer. Reading Ferris' "Utah & the Mormons." Conversed with Mr. Mann on his scheme of getting [133] the "Great Eastern" steamer to ply between Milford Haven & Norfolk—& with Pryor on political topics of the day.

*June 30.* . . . Finished "Utah & the Mormons"—a very poor description of either, such as might be expected from a traveller & sojourner—but a sufficiently full exposure of the villainy of the leaders. The growth & success of this bare-faced imposture is one of the greatest wonders of this enlightened age. An illiterate & ignorant man, poor & without friends or influence at first—a man of vicious & dishonest life, to establish a new religion, & to have 100,000 followers within 20 years! And after his death, & the suspension and banishment of his followers, & their taking refuge 1000 miles beyond the borders of civilized life, within 8 years to resist the laws & dare the power of the federal government, & require an army to check their rebellion! Major Reynolds U.S.A. one of the officers of this garrison, was in Col. Steptac's corps, which remained 8 months in Utah. He gave me some interesting details of what he learned among the Mormons. He thinks that very few of the leaders have any faith in their pretended religion—that many of the followers are disaffected, & kept in obedience only by fear of the despot—& that they can offer no armed resistance to the government forces.

# July–December

❦

# 1857

TRAVELING IN WESTERN VIRGINIA ❦ VISIT
WITH SENATOR HAMMOND ❦ NORTH CAR-
OLINA STATE FAIR ❦ VIRGINIA STATE
AGRICULTURAL SOCIETY MEETING AND FAIR
❦ AT SHERWOOD FOREST WITH FORMER
PRESIDENT TYLER

*July 1.* The weather unpleasantly cold. The Minnesota steam frigate started today, from her anchorage off this place, for China— carrying the American minister for China.

*July 2.* Left Old Point in the James river steamer, for Richmond, & arrived at 4 P.M. Saw Mr. Williams, & F. G. Ruffin. Went to the Exchange Hotel—& after reading the late newspapers, to bed early.

*July 3.* In the mail stage set off by 4 A.M. & reached Marlbourne by [134] 7½ A.M. Found all well. The harvest operations well advanced, considering the difficulties. Mr. Sayre had to buy a third reaping machine. All this week, rain every day since Monday, & heavy rains .... Found a letter from Franklin Minor of Albemarle, writing me to attend the joint meeting of the Farmers' Clubs, in that county, & at his house on the 18th inst., which I wrote in answer to assent to. ...

*July 4.* Two reaping machines again started at 10, for which operation the earth is still barely firm enough, owing to the thorough saturation by the late rains. Walked in the forenoon, until much fatigued, & again, with Mildred, in the afternoon, to see the reaping. I have been much amused to hear, from Mr. Sayre, of some of the remarks of Jem. Sykes, the foreman, (& my former overseer,) about the crops & the land. He is full of glorification & boasting, & exaggerates the truly great prospect of products enormously—& while he admits that Mr. Sayre's tillage & preparatory labors have, for the great part, been more carefully performed than mine were usually, still he gives the great credit of the present increase of production to the improvements made by "old master." I confess that I am especially gratified by these compliments from Jem, for though I am sure of the truth of the opinion, I did not expect a negro, even of superior intelligence as he is, to look back to causes so remote, & of such slow & gradual action. The different [135] fertilizing applications which were applied some years back had not earlier shown such great effect as now. But, more especially, the operation of deep draining, on my principle of operation, by tapping the low under-bed of water-glutted sand, is still progressing in its beneficial effect, & perhaps may not reach the maximum of benefit for some years to come, even though there should be no extension of the draining operations, as indeed there have been but very little in the last two years. I have latterly seen striking proofs of this increasing effect. There are now, in different places, heavy growths on ground in fine condition, where, for want of sufficient draining, I had never made half so much, & had to contend with the effects of wetness in winter & spring, & with hard land & clods in summer & autumn. . . .

*July 6.* . . . Walked to see the harvest operations, & through the cornfield, both morning & afternoon. Began to read [William H.] Prescott's Philip II, which Mildred has lately added to her small library.

*July 7.* The first entirely bright & clear sun & sky for the last 8 days. The prospect of the lowground, as now gilded & brightened by the sun-light, is more beautiful than I ever saw it before. The colors of the different fields & crops are regular, distinct, & vivid—the deep & uniform green of the corn, the yellow stubble of the wheat, as yellow & as uniform as the wheat appeared before being reaped, & thickly dotted with the shocks of wheat. The young peas only are a poor crop, owing to the cold & wet weather & the field is more covered by young grass & weeds than peas. But even these add beauty & variety, in the hue of pale pea-green color, so different from the color of the cornfield. I view this scene in the whole, & wander over & examine the details with great pleasure. The improvements of fertility & productiveness are now more fully in [137] operation, & more obvious to the eye, than in any earlier time, when they were newer. To see their growing extent causes to me feelings of high gratification & pride, & also of thankfulness for this reward of my labors. Nor is the gratification diminished in the least because the property is now no longer my own, but my children's. They are drawing on the resources of stored fertility more heavily than I had done, by more extended tillage & time. But independent of the increased production to be gained from a broader surface, the production from the same ground is better this year than I ever obtained. And still, & especially from the growing effect of my system of deep drainage, I expect the productive power of much of the farm to increase for years to come. I earnestly hope that, into whoseever hands the farm may pass hereafter, that its acquired fertility may never be lost. And then, if the original condition of the land could be known, as I found it in 1844, the contrast of the two conditions will serve as the proudest monument to my memory.

*July 8.* Attempted to draw some rough diagrams, to illustrate my memoir on the draining of Marlbourne, & found the now usual trembling of my hand so bad that I could not draw a line straight, making all designed for straight wavering, so that it would mislead an engraver of such drawing. This late increase of my usual or habitual trembling hands would seem to indicate worse health. Yet, in other respects & excepting the infirmities of age, I never felt better. ... The last mail, besides the usual supply of newspapers, brought Russell's Magazine, & De Bow's Review for July. The latter contained the conclusion of my article on the Agricultural features &c. of the Lowlands. The readable pieces of both publications, & the newspapers, got through in the same day.

*July 9.* Mr. Sayre finished the wheat harvest. ... Finished rough draft of an agricultural communication (for S.A.A.), begun yesterday, on ploughing upon my new plan—& corrected another, written some time back, on the Pegged Roller. Finished vol I of Philip II....

*July 10.* Rode to see the corn crop more fully. During harvest it was necessary that both Mr. Sayre & his overseer should be almost continually on horse-back, & I would not permit him to spare for my use one of his only two saddles. ... Another rain, which made the corn land too wet for ploughing immediately after.

*July 12.* Sunday. No church service in this neighborhood. ... Finished the two volumes of Philip II, which only are yet published. It will take four more, I guess, to finish the reign, at the same rate. ... Began to read Dickens' last work, "Little Dorrit."

*July 14.* A letter from Edmund. Mary's condition not much altered, but she is more feeble—& I infer she is gradually sinking. ... Elizabeth & Mildred determine to go to Beechwood next week (21st)

& I will also on the 23rd. My engagements will detain me until then.... [141]

*July 15.* ... Finished reading "Little Dorrit." Much of it, & especially in the first volume, is interesting. But like most of Dickens' novels, there is a great deal of wretched poor stuff—& even of the interesting parts, the incidents, & the final clearing up of the mysteries, are produced so unnaturally, that at the close the reading seemed a loss of time. The best thing in the book is an admirable picture drawn in the Dorrit family of the combination of pauperism & pride ( or rather self-esteem & conceit,) of abject meanness & ridiculous pretension, & with utter worthlessness, which I have seen in one real family—there being some exceptions to the general character in [142] the real & the fictitious family. Still more strikingly has the same author unconsciously drawn a portrait of the most remarkable individual of this family, (in his David Copperfield,) in the characteristics of Mr. Micawber. If my worthless son-in-law Dr. Beckwith had been known to Dickens, all who knew of the acquaintance would have been certain that he was the original of the admirable picture. In the Dorrits, there are no such true portraitures of individuals. But take the whole together, & the family characteristics are those most displayed by the more unworthy members of the Beckwith family.

*July 16.* According to my appointment with Franklin Minor, set off this morning early, & at Hanover C[ourt] H[ouse] took the railroad for Charlottesville, which reached, by noon. Found Mr. Minor & his carriage waiting for me, & reached his house to dinner.... Much interesting conversation with Minor, who is a very sensible & well educated, & also an estimable & worthy man.

*July 17.* Rode with Mr. Minor to see his & some of the neighboring farms on the Rivanna river. The alluvial bottom richer & more valued land than I had conceived. Cropped without any intermission, generally in corn, & without any known exhaustion. The high freshes of the river occur but rarely. It was formerly the calculation that one year in seven there would be a fresh high enough to nearly or quite destroy a crop. But in modern times the freshes have been less frequently destructive. Whenever they occur, they leave a deposit of enough rich mud to maintain perpetual fertility—& therefore these floods, however disastrous in each particular case, on the whole [143] are beneficial. The uplands are of the South West Mountain lands, & of the valuable though various soils of that range.—In the afternoon my friend Wm. W. Gilmer arrived, & also Lieut. M. F. Maury—both of whom are relatives of our host. We sat up, engaged in interesting conversation, to 11 o'clock.

*July 18.* This the day for the meeting of the two Farmers' Clubs, the members of which began to arrive about 10. All the members & some of the visitors rode over the farm, & on returning the session was begun. Another visitor of distinction arrived from Charlottesville—the Hon. Wm. C. Preston of S.C. the former senator, & great orator[1]—Now bowed down by disease & infirmity, & probably his once powerful mind as much impaired as his body. But there was no exhibition, or exposure, of such decay, & he appeared in all respects the intelligent & agreeable gentleman, as I knew him formerly. Including the guests & the members of the family, there were 25 gentlemen present. B. Johnson Barbour of Orange, & my friend R. W. Noland were present. An interesting discussion was held on the preparation for & seeding of the wheat crop. When called on, I described the construction & operation of my pegged roller—which was the only new information I had to offer that could be advantageous here. . . . The whole meeting & session were interesting, & protracted to late in the afternoon. Maury, Gilmer, Barbour, Noland, & some others remained through the night.

*July 20.* W. Gilmer left us. It is arranged for me to go on tomorrow to the Blue Ridge, & to the tunnel, & he will join me on the route. Ex-Governor [George R.] Gilmer of Ga. with his wife arrived to dinner.[2] He is a kinsman of F. Minor's. Mrs. G. a very intelligent & agreeable lady. Much conversation with Gov. Gilmer, on various subjects, & especially in regard to the characters & habits of sundry distinguished men with whom he had served in Congress—I objected to Prof. [Albert T.] Bledsoe's book in defence of slavery, because it defends the indefensible passage in the Declaration of Independence, that asserts that "all men are born free & equal," instead of admitting it to be both false & foolish. . . .

*July 21.* Went to Charlottesville & took the train for the top of the Blue Ridge to visit the tunnel. [William] Gilmer & Noland joined us

---

[1] William Campbell Preston (1794–1860), a Calhoun Nullifier, served in the United States Senate from 1833 to 1842. In 1845 he became president of South Carolina College and continued in this office for six years until obliged to retire because of ill health.

[2] George Rockingham Gilmer (1790–1859), author, historian, and politician, served three terms in Congress and was twice governor of Georgia—1829 to 1831, and again from 1837 to 1839.

on the Rail Road, near their houses. The present passage, by the temporary track over the mountain, offers the most beautiful scenery, of mountain & the valley—& the scene is made much more striking by the climbing of the railway trains over the steep & crooked ascent. The train was separated at the foot of the mountain, & to each portion was attached a heavy & powerful engine, used only for the passage of the mountain. The three smaller tunnels are completed, & passed through by the train. After passing them, the mountain ridge is ascended, which route will soon be superseded by the great tunnel, which is nearly opened to its full size, & will be passable by the trains in a few months. I came to use the only opportunity when the summit railroad is in use, & the tunnel open, & not yet in use. We stopped at the tavern at the Rockfish Gap, & proceeded immediately to explore the tunnel. We entered at the eastern & lower end. Nearly all the opening is done—some deepening only being now to do, & in progress, by blasting [145] the very hard rock. The whole passage has been opened through extremely hard stone. A temporary rail track had been laid, on which mule-carts were bringing out the excavated stone. Much of the tunnel has been lined & arched with thick brick walls, where there is danger of masses of the rock falling. The passage is 16 feet wide & 20 high. We carried a lamp, which went out once, & the laborers & the carts carried lamps. Still when our own light was out, there was little aid from the day light through the two openings, & we had to feel our foot-way, on the rail, or in mud & water. Our party had F. Minor & Mr. L[eroy] Broun (late Professor in the University of Ga.)[3] besides W. Gilmer, Noland & myself. Took supper & lodged at the Mountain House tavern.

*July 22.* Before sunrise we set out on our return on foot, the better to view the scenery, & the completed smaller tunnels. From the summit, the sight takes in the North Mountains, 40 miles distant to the northwest, & at 100 yards farther on we saw the South-west Mountains in Orange county, about 35 miles eastward.—The great tunnel is 4000 feet long. The three finished are 400 & 600 feet, & one perhaps less than 60. We walked 4 miles, & then waited for the train.

---

[3] William Leroy Broun was allied with the Le Conte brothers in a reform movement at the University of Georgia in the mid-1850's. He, along with others who ran afoul of President Alonzo Church, resigned in 1856. Following the war Broun returned to Georgia to teach natural philosophy, and, some years later, he served as president of Alabama Polytechnic Institute.

Went to Gilmer's to breakfast, & to Noland's to dinner, & saw the fine lands & crops of both, on Jay Creek. All of us, except Mr. Broun, staid the night with Noland.

*July 23.* Had waited to this day to return, because designing to stop at Hanover C.H. to vote for Willoughby Newton for judge—which I did, & afterwards took the freight train, & reached Richmond at 5.30 P.M. Saw Mr. Williams & conferred about the business of the Ag. Society.—This visit to Albemarle has been very agreeable to me, & I trust also to most of the farmers who met me. The residents of that county are of superior grade of intellect, owing, first to the advanced state of agricultural improvement, & its rewards, & still more to the neighborhood of the University. Good schools have been one of the fruits [146] of this institution, most abundant in the near vicinity. Every farmer who has reached a moderate income has his sons well educated, & in numerous cases, & always with the more wealthy, closing with the higher or highest studies of the University —which in the value of the course of instruction, as well in the number of students, this institution excels all others in the United States. As usual, lodged at the Exchange Hotel, & alone—reading in my room.

*July 24.* Early to the steamer, & reached Berkley wharf by 9 A.M., whence Edmund's boat carried me to Beechwood. A mournful, though gratifying visit. Found Mary much more reduced, by weakness & emaciation—but feeling better today than usual. She seemed delighted to meet with me. Though her voice was rarely raised above a whisper, & I had to lie by her on her bed, to be near enough to hear her, she talked much to me, & cheerfully, until I withdrew, fearful of her tasking herself too heavily, to return to her whenever, & only, when she should desire it, & summon me. She is sinking gradually, but certainly to the grave—whether her death may be at the end of months, or days, or but a few hours, none can foresee. She is perfectly aware of her condition, & resigned to it. We have all feared it for a year back, & latterly without hope. There could be no greater loss to a husband & children. In all my family, into which she was adopted by her marriage, she has always been loved as a daughter & a sister, & has herself fully reciprocated our love to her.—This, the enforced & unchosen day of my return to Beechwood, is the second anniversary of the death, (in this house,) of my first dying & well-beloved daughter Jane. Still more vividly than before did the present circumstances, & the place, bring back to my mind all the incidents of her death—soon followed by the deaths of two other of my daughters—& now another is soon to follow. . . .

*July 26.* Sunday. At church. Afternoon, Julian & Lotty rode to Beechwood, & I went home with them in their carriage.

On this afternoon, by previous appointment, the clergyman of the parish, Mr. Johnson, attended to administer to Mary the sacrament of "the Lord's Supper," & also he read the appointed prayers for those who are apparently near to the close of life. Her husband & children, & his sisters then at Beechwood, Julian & his wife, myself & Mrs. Lorraine, were all that were present. The occasion, the hopeless condition of illness of the beloved sufferer, as known to all, rendered the solemn services deeply affecting to all the attendants. . . . As soon as the services were ended, I went out, as did all except those nearest & dearest of all to her. But in a short time she sent for me, & I found her not only not depressed but her countenance radiant with a sweet though faint smile. She accosted me, in a scarcely audible whisper, in words of love, & endearing tenderness, & as I kissed her, she caressingly pressed my face between her feeble hands. . . .

*July 27.* Julian brought me to Beechwood. At 11, Mr. Sayre & I left for Berkley, & there took the steamer for Richmond, where we arrived at 4 P.M. I left Beechwood very reluctantly, to attend the meeting of the Ex. Com. tomorrow night, & to attend to preliminary business tonight, with Capt. Dimmock, the Marshal, which I am unable to do because of his absence. Fear that the meeting of the Ex. Com. will be a failure, as I already learn that four of the important members cannot attend.

*July 28.* . . . Called on Governor [Henry A.] Wise, at his office in the Capitol. After his delivering (to me alone) a very good speech on the defects of the trade between Brazil & Virginia,[4] & the remedies, I took the first chance to name for his consideration the abortive law on the statute book (of 1851) which authorized the appointment of an Agricultural Commissioner, & gave $4000 a year in aid of agricultural improvement & instruction, & which law has never been executed. I suggested that, defective as the law was, it must be supposed at least to indicate the *designed* policy of the government to give the annuity named for the improvement [148] of agriculture —& if so, the grant ought to be made effective, or otherwise the law

---

[4] Having served as United States minister to Brazil, 1844–47, Wise presumably fancied himself as an authority on this particular subject.

should be repealed. The governor did not know of the existence of the law—& I hope that my notifying him of it may furnish him some material to use in his next message to the legislature, in behalf of aid to agriculture. Wm. Ballard Preston[5] came in, & then Governor Wise delivered to us another speech, giving his views of the reformation of the governmental action in aid of education in Va. He is a remarkable man, & blamable for many things, as governor, & as a public man. He does not converse, but makes speeches to every auditor, & on every subject.—The meeting of Ex. Com. was held—& the business on hand completed, by a little before midnight, when we adjourned. This unexpected dispatch will enable me to return to Beechwood tomorrow morning.

*July 29.* Took my passage in a small steamer of a new line, by which I was put on shore at the end of Coggin's Point. Before reaching the house, I learned that Mary had died yesterday morning, about 8 o'clock. This event we had long known was certainly to occur—& latterly, that it might take place in any day. But when I left her, there was no reason to expect so speedy an end—& I felt much regret that I should have been absent, even for so short a time. . . . Her death was peaceful, calm, & painless. She had long been as fully aware as all others of our family, of the certain approaching end—& she was as much resigned to it as possible for one having such endearing & strong ties to life. All of her husband's [149] family, from her marriage, had learned to love her as if she stood in the same relation of blood to us as her husband. I loved her as a daughter—my children as a sister. Her husband was perfectly devoted to her—& no husband, for himself & for his children, could have lost more in the death of a wife. Yet so long & so surely has the end been foreseen, & deemed approaching with certainty in every thing but the time of fulfilment, that we all bear the last stroke with calmness, that might seem to some a want of sensibility, or love, or due appreciation of the virtues & worth of the deceased, & of the measure of loss to her family. . . .

*July 30.* The burial & connected religious services this forenoon. Such ceremonies, of a private individual, & among a country population, have rarely drawn together so many & deeply interested at-

---

[5] William Ballard Preston (1805–62), a first cousin of former South Carolina Senator William C. Preston, was elected as a Whig to the Thirtieth Congress, was secretary of the navy in the cabinet of Zachary Taylor, and later served in the Confederate Congress.

tendants. Notices of the time of the funeral, & with the usual general invitation had been sent throughout the neighborhood to all, within the circle of either visitors to the family, or ordinary attendants at the church. And nearly every family, & every one acquainted with the deceased, within these bounds, were here. Besides gentlemen on horse-back, there followed the hearse to the grave (on Coggin's Point) 18 coaches, 8 buggies, & a cart, in which came a poor family of the neighborhood, & whose attendance was the more welcome because of their humble equipage. These outward evidences of general & high respect for the virtues of our beloved connection, was [*sic*] highly gratifying to our family. All the adult negroes, who [150] were not too infirm, were present, both at the services at the mansion, & then at the grave.

*July 31.* Returned to writing. Deeming my memoir of the drainage of Marlbourne farm entirely too long for a communication to the Agr. Soc. I proceeded to make an abridgement of it to serve the latter purpose. . . .

*August 1.* . . . My daughters went to Petersburg to purchase mourning for the family. They brought back the melancholy news of the death of Mrs. F. G. Ruffin, whom, not long since we had visited, & seen well & cheerful. To her husband, children, & acquaintance, her death will be no less a loss than in the case of our similar affliction. She died on the 28th.—the same day!

*Aug. 3.* . . . Writing—& reading late numbers of "Living Age." This publication is a *moderate,* as Putnam's is a *violent* abolition tool.

*Aug. 4.* Finished rough draft of the new form of my report on the drainage of Marlbourne—& which also is much too long. I am destitute of the power of condensing or abridging my own writing.

*Aug. 5.* Began first draught of the annual address of President & Executive Committee to the Farmers' Assembly.—Reading [Washington] Irving's Life [151] of Washington. This I dipped into at the beginning of the blockade of Boston, & have continued to read thenceforward. Heavy rain.

*Aug. 9.* Sunday. To church—and I am almost disposed to make it the last time, under ordinary circumstances, because of my inability to keep awake during the service. I am very unwilling to treat the minister & the services with such apparent disrespect, or to render myself ridiculous to observers. My snatches of sleep are but momentary—but are repeated, & cannot be prevented by all my efforts. Under such circumstances my attending public worship does no good either to myself, or to others to whom I have heretofore aimed in this respect to set a good example. . . .

*Aug. 10.* Writing a little, in additions & corrections—reading Irving's Washington—with the periodicals & newspapers received by mail. There is a general lull or cessation of political news—& yet great events have not long since occurred, & are unfinished, & which must lead to others of not less importance. Gen. Walker has been driven out of Nicaragua, by the crusade against him of the adjacent states. But already such differences & animosities have there arisen, that Walker is called for by some of his former enemies. If he, or other freebooters, do not take possession, I think it will be necessary, & also justifiable for the U.S. to seize & hold all Central America & the Isthmus of Panama, opening the routes across to the free passage of the commerce of the world. I would wish this measure delayed, if possible, until the southern United States had seceded, & made a separate political community. [154] But the route across the isthmus of Panama ought to be taken possession of forthwith, as the only means of settling the just claims of this government against New Granada. The conquest of any of these mongrel & semi-barbarous communities, by any civilized power, would be a benefit to the conquered, & to the world. In this view, I heartily wish the most complete success to the British arms in the present war with China— which, after sharp & bloody action at first, has now, for months, been quiet as a truce. And since, another event has occurred, of awful threatening to the power of England. The native soldiers of the East India Company, which, under English officers, made nearly the whole great army of Hindostan, have generally mutinied, & in sundry cases killed their officers, & all the English in their power.[6] The revolted troops have possession of Delhi—& almost everywhere the native regiments have either mutinied, or elsewhere have been disarmed & disbanded by the English authorities, to prevent revolt. So far, except in seizing & holding Delhi, there seems to be nothing like concerted action by the revolters. But if that is brought about, under a competent leader, the native soldiers, well trained to arms by England, will themselves make a force that all England's power cannot put down. The probable consequences are most awful to England, &

---

[6] On May 10, 1857, three native regiments at Meerut murdered their white officers and marched on Delhi, forty miles away. Thus began the great Sepoy Mutiny, which for six months represented a formidable threat to British authority in India.

will be greatly injurious to the progress of improvement & civilization in Hindostan, & to the commerce & well-being of the civilized world. Unjust, cruel, & altogether unjustifiable, as has been the British rule & dominion in Hindostan, that government [155] has been far better than the previous, or would be any future government of native despots, or of their Asiatic conquerors. Except in Southern America, where our safety or progress would be endangered, I wish success to the British arms & policy throughout the uncivilized world.

*Aug. 13.* I had looked into Irving's Life of Washington at the beginning of the 2nd vol. & the interest excited made me continue to read ... to the end of the 4th, which I have just finished. I have never rated Washington highly as a military commander in the fighting of battles—& this work does not raise him higher, in that respect. But it has increased my high estimation of him in other & more important requisites for those times of trial & of peril. His patriotism, prudence, forbearance to his enemies & those working to undermine & supplant him, & his magnanimity even to these enemies after they had been crushed by their own errors—his disinterestedness & entire devotion to his country & his duty, will never be exceeded by any man. And his general policy of facing & restraining the more powerful British army, & yet avoiding battles, was what was indispensable for the safety of the country & its cause. Yet to pursue this policy, for years together, was what no other general, brave & daring as Washington certainly was, could have done, under the discontent of friends, & the sneers & taunts of the enemies of himself & the country. Irving's work is especially superior to the preceding histories of the revolutionary war in its portraiture of individual & different character in the prominent military leaders. . . . Irving enables the reader to know each man—& with this knowledge, their military & public acts are much more intelligible, & the narrative far more interesting. After all, the military events of the war were directed much more by the incapacity than the ability of the commanders, & especially of all the successive British generals in chief. Not one even of their commanders of separate armies had military talent, except Cornwallis, & he was rendered incapable by the inaction of the commander in chief, [Sir Henry] Clinton. And of the American generals, of higher grade, & who held separate & large commands, the greater number were incapable. [Richard] Montgomery's career was too short to afford any ground for censure, & not enough for correct judgment of his capacity. Of all others, [Nathanael] Greene & [Benedict] Arnold only seem to me to have had high talent as military leaders. And, even as to Greene, exalted as he deserves to stand, his great merit, & his peculiar characteristics, & also deficiencies, were like those of Washington. He did not do so much in gaining victories, as in rendering victories useless to the enemy—in making head while refusing battle—& with the most scant means of money, equipment, arms & soldiers, & almost continually retreating before more powerful armies, still in the end to be able to make good defense, & to secure more in adversity & defeat, than the enemy could by repeated victories. Arnold—the traitor—unprincipled as he always was, showed, & exercised, so far as his different commands afforded opportunity, more of military genius & talent, (with all other requisites of a [157] soldier & officer, except moral worth,) than any other officer of high grade in the American Army. . . . Began to read Dr. Antonio, by [Giovanni] Ruffini, & was so interested in it that I read nearly half the volume without stopping except for dinner . . . .

*Aug. 16.* Sunday. All the household except myself went to church. Very early I finished "Doctor Antonio." The latter part is mostly historical & political—& if authentic, exhibits more tyranny, perfidy, injustice & cruelty in the government of Naples than I had before supposed, badly as I thought of the government & its actions.[7] I trust that this picture may help to hasten the downfall of this horrible despotism. Afterwards read, in Living Age, abridged reports from [David] Livingstone's missionary travels in South Africa. . . .

*Aug. 19.* . . . We are to go tomorrow to Marlbourne. My grandchildren, Nanny, Sue, Mary & John Ruffin, & Jane R. Dupuy are to go with us to stay some weeks, & Jane still longer. She is sallow, & looks badly, though otherwise well—& I trust the change of air will be of service to her health. Mildred & I especially rejoice to have with us this child of our beloved Jane, & hope thereby to attach her more to us. . . .

*Aug. 20.* A steady rain seemed to make our departure hopeless. But just in time, it stopped, so that we got on board the steamboat at 12. . . . When reaching the wharf at Richmond, the carriage & a cart were awaiting our arrival—& we reached Marlbourne soon after dark.

---

[7] Written by an Italian exile and former member of Young Italy, *Dr. Antonio* detailed the infamous trials of political prisoners in Naples in 1850.

*Aug. 21.* Rode out to see the crops. The unprecedented frequency of rains, ever since harvest has very much impeded the thrashing, & kept all the wheat in bad order. This is universal throughout lower Va—but worse in this neighborhood than anywhere else I have seen. Not more than one-third of this large crop is thrashed, & even that is not dry enough to be safe. The great remainder, still in shocks, is in great peril, without a speedy & entire change [159] of weather. Resumed my writing & corrections. Afternoon, a long walk with Mildred & Nanny. Very cool.

*Aug. 25.* The last news from England is that the great experiment of laying the magnetic telegraph wire across the Atlantic has been commenced, & that 300 miles had been safely laid by the 10th inst. If successful, it was expected that in 20 days it would reach Newfoundland—so that in a few more days we may expect to hear either of the failure or the success of the most interesting & important scientific operation that was ever attempted upon design.—The mutiny of the native troops in India is still unchecked, & Delhi remains in the possession of the mutineers. To put down this dangerous insurrection every effort of England is now directed—& the war on China remains dormant, until the other is ended. . . . [160]

*Aug. 26.* Finished my report for the Ag. Soc. on the draining of Marlbourne—35 pages, besides the maps, diagrams, & explanations.

*Aug. 28.* . . . The mail brought the news of the breaking of the Atlantic telegraph wire, at between 300 & 400 miles out at sea, & in 2000 fathom depth. The enormous strain of so much suspended length of wire, the roughness of the sea & rise & fall of the ship, a strong lateral under-current, & especially the improper action of the engineer in checking the too fast running out of the cable, all are stated as the causes. But all these, except the last error, must be met in every attempt—& I fear the difficulties will be found to be impossible. . . . Got ready three communications for the State Agr. Society, to be delivered to the Secretary.

*Aug. 29.* Mildred being obliged to go to Richmond, to make purchases, I went with her, & also to confer with the Secretary & the Chief Marshal about the preparations for the Fair—but could see neither. I gave to a newspaper, to be published, a notice to the members of the Society in Hanover, declining to be a candidate for the Farmers' Assembly, at the next election. I had thought much on the question, & had come to the conclusion that the President of the society ought not to sit as a member of the Assembly, & therefore I use the first occasion to set the precedent of such abnegation. The president cannot have time to fulfil both duties. And in addition, his presence, as a member of the Assembly may in many cases be inconvenient, by imposing restraint on the freedom of discussion, & expression of opinion concerning the acts of the President. . . .

*Aug. 31.* . . . Began to assort all the old letters that have been retained of my correspondents. I regret that so few were kept, & none on system. And my whole collection of letters received during the 10 years of my publication of the Farmers' Register, (& most of which were filed & kept,) were left in Petersburg with all the printed papers, for years before I sold the house, & were lost. I shall [162] arrange what are left in different sets, & stitch & cover them for preservation & convenient reference. The greater number are letters of my children, & many of these when they were at school. These of course would be unfit for the eyes of strangers, but may be interesting as family letters, to my descendants. The interest of such memorials increase with time—& I now greatly regret the loss of many letters which long ago were destroyed as not worth being preserved. . . .

*September 1.* Continued to arrange such of the letters of my family, & other correspondents, as remain on hand, or have been preserved to this time, & to stitch, & hereafter bind them in strong paper covers. . . . All from members of my family are marked, on the covers, "Family & Private Letters," & should be seen by none except my own children & others standing as such. These are arranged either by the subjects & writers, or by dates. The letters of other persons are generally arranged in separate *brochures*, each embracing one or more years—Except the letters of Gov. Hammond, of which enough have been kept to bind together.[8]

*Sept. 2.* At 5 P.M. finished my job, & was weary enough with the labor. All done, except the covering, which must be delayed to another [163] time. . . . Mildred had to pack my trunk for me at night, & I to conclude some other preparations, for our designed departure tomorrow morning for a long visit (for Mildred) to Judge Ruffins, N.C. We will thus have to leave my grandchildren here, & much regret to leave them before their visit is ended—especially little Jane

[8] Many of the letters apparently referred to in this passage are located in the Southern Historical Collection, University of North Carolina, Chapel Hill. Included in the Edmund Ruffin Papers and Books is a series of fifty letters from Governor Hammond, covering the period 1842–57 and relating primarily to agricultural affairs.

who has yet scarcely learned to know or to love me.... Edmund will come about the 10th, & after accompanying his son Thomas to fix him at school in Albemarle, will take his other children home.

*Sept. 3.* Mildred & I left home after breakfast. In Richmond had not time to get through my business. Conferred with our Secretary— & also with the millers in regard to Mr. Sayre's wheat, which he is now shipping. Bad chance for sale—the price has continued to come down, until now 130 cents for the best red wheat. Further scarcely any crop that is not either damp or at least "tough," owing to the general dampness of the atmosphere, producing a condition of wheat never known before. Mr. Sayre has used unusual care & caution—& has omitted so much time that other farmers used, that he is not yet much more than half done thrashing. Yet his wheat is tough, & his first shipment was rejected, & had to be stored.... Left Richmond in the train at 3 P.M. Reached Weldon N.C. at 8, & left there at 11.

*Sept. 4.* Travelling all night, we reached Haw River to breakfast, & Graham station at 8 A.M. where Judge Ruffin's carriage was waiting for us, & soon carried us the few miles to Alamance.... Duncan McRae, late consul at Paris here on a visit. He was a foster child of Mrs. R. & is as one of the family....

*Sept. 5.* Resumed Lockhart's Life of Walter Scott, which I had left abruptly when here last—& now, from my bad memory, I could not guess, within half a volume's space, where I had before read to. This biography, though very interesting, has a great deal of what is uninteresting to me, & much that I merely glance over, & some (in letters) that I entirely skip. In addition to all the admiration of Scott, as a writer, no one can read his life, & his letters to his friends, without learning to love him as a benevolent, kind-hearted, & good man, as well as for his cheerfulness & good temper. But with these excellent qualities there is as manifest a *natural taste* for idolizing the high in worldly rank, ( of "boot-licking" or "flunkeyism") that is astonishing in so great & good a man as Scott. And this he was by feeling, & taste, & certainly not for any mercenary or base motive. He could not see the vices of a lord or a chief minister, who was of his own politics, & still less of a prince or king, even when as despicable as James I, when treated by his pen, or as detestable as George IV, when spoken of as his contemporary.—Walked, & also rode to see the crops. [165]

*Sept. 6.* Sunday. As there was no episcopal church service in the neighborhood, Judge Ruffin, according to his usage, read the morning service & a sermon, to the family.—After the newspapers (which we get every day,) I continued Scott's Life. . . .

*Sept. 7.* Seeing Edgar [Allan] Poe's works, I read a few of his shorter tales. I had heartily disliked his writings before he rose to celebrity of reputation—& I thought to see whether I would now view them with more favor. But the same impression was produced. Whatever of genius, or other talent, his strange writings may exhibit, they are as monstrous & abominable as his morals, & as absurd as his course of life.

*Sept. 9.* At 8 A.M. set out on the railway to visit Gov. Hammond, as I had written to inform him, & had in vain expected his answer at Alamance. Reached Charlotte after 3 P.M. where the train waited to 7 P.M. Then, on the road to Columbia all night.

*Sept. 10.* To Kingsville to breakfast, & Branchville 10 A.M. & Augusta, Ga. by 3 P.M. After dinner, hired a conveyance & rode to Redcliff. Found Gov. H. & family at home. My arrival seemed to be as gratifying as unexpected—for my letter of notice had not been received. Find that the operations to make syrup & sugar from his sorghum have not been yet begun, but will be next Monday. So instead of seeing the best operation, I fear that I will not see through the difficulties & blunders of a new beginning. This was the main business object of my visit at this time. The season has so cut short the crop of grapes, that instead of the older vines [166] yielding enough grapes for wine-making, there are scarcely any for eating.— Read in the newspaper that a famine is impending in Liberia, which (it is now confessed) has been more & more threatened for three years—& mainly owing to the indolence & improvidence of the residents. This is a result altogether suitable to the negro race—but which is surprising even to me, in this case. So, after more than 40 years of nursing & supporting this pet colony, by the Colonization Society & the bounty of its benevolent dupes—after millions have been spent to feed, protect, & to support the colonists, on a fertile soil, they will not do enough work to find themselves in bread. Besides, the settlers were mostly of such as were deemed the best subjects, & many of them having partly the blood & therefore the qualities of a white ancestor. But with all these advantages, & with a continued flow of aid from this country, this long continued experiment is a failure, & more than even I had before supposed, affords the clearest evidence that the negro will not work, nor take care for his support, unless when compelled by a master of the white race. If after relieving the Liberians of their present famine, they were then left to themselves, in 20 years, half their numbers would be lost by desertion, (where possible,) deaths from privation, & the remnant would soon become as barbarous as their African ancestors.—At night, Mr. Wray returned, who has continued here generally, to supervise the crop of "imphie" [*sic*] & to attend to his interests connected therewith.

*Sept. 12.* Very early arrived Judge [Pierre A.] Rost, of Louisiana, who, passing by, [167] called to see the sugar operations.[9] He staid the day, with us, but had to go back to Augusta at night, to continue his journey homeward early tomorrow morning. He is an extensive sugar planter, & a very intelligent & pleasing gentleman, well educated & well informed, & of best manners—but whose English still has a strong foreign accent, which I cannot identify, but which seems more German than any other. After breakfast we went to the plantation, 7 miles off, & saw the magnificent growth of the "Sweet Reed" or African "Imphee," which here & at the Silverton plantation, covers 110 acres of land—here, all of richest drained swamp soil. There is already much waste in the crop, by the stalks having fallen, & heads lying on the ground—& all greatly exposed, if a spell of rain should occur. This risk seems to me the great objection to the crop, in reference to the grain, which otherwise would promise a great product for feeding stock, independent of the saccharine sap of the stalks. It is much to be regretted that the pressing & bailing operations were not in operation, as Mr. Rost's experience & intelligence would have been a great aid to Gov. H., who, strange to say, has been able to derive scarcely any instruction from Mr. Wray, an experienced sugar planter & manufacturer in Jamaica & elsewhere, & an educated man of very extended observation, in Hindostan & Natal, in regard to this subject. He seems to have an "Imphee" monomania, but no common sense, or the least knowledge of how to promote his own interest in this planting, from which he expected to acquire an immense fortune by sale of the seed, & the patent right

---

[9] Born and educated in France, Pierre Adolph Rost (*ca.* 1797–1868) went to Natchez in 1816 and studied law with Joseph E. Davis. He then moved to Louisiana, where in 1846 he was elevated to a seat on the state supreme court. In the 1850's he became one of the largest sugar planters in the state, annually producing in excess of one thousand hogsheads of sugar on his two St. Charles Parish plantations, Destréhan and Hermitage. At the beginning of the Civil War he was dispatched to Europe on a diplomatic mission for the Confederacy, and he remained abroad for the duration of the conflict.

of his method. It is now a month since the cane was ripe enough for him to have tested its value, & at least to settle the great question as to whether the syrup would crystalize & make good sugar—& he has not begun to grind—& all that has been done, provided, or suggested, has been by H., & with scarcely any aid from Wray's instruction [168] or advice. W.'s profit in this contract was to be in the sale of the seed, which was to be exclusively in his hands. Yet now, when most of the seeds are ripe, & like soon to rot on the field, he has not even fixed a price for them, or made any arrangements for the sale— & he is not ready to sell a bushel, or a head, to any one who would come to him & offer to purchase. Obvious defects in the setting up of the press & furnace &c. were suggested by Judge Rost, which Mr. Wray had never mentioned. From the existence of these defects, & others, I fear the operations will be very imperfect.—After dinner, interesting conversation on various subjects, & especially on general politics, & southern political questions.—On the Silver Bluff plantation, which we went on today, there are 1400 acres of drained swamp under tillage, very rich, & the oldest of which is now under its tenth crop in succession, of either corn or cotton, & this crop (of corn) better than any that has preceded. The "imphie" crop is on part of this land principally. 300 acres more drained, but not cleared.

*Sept. 14.* After breakfast we rode to Silver Bluff, & staid the remainder of the day at the sugar works. We found the grinding of the cane in progress, & soon the boiling of the juice was begun. Numerous difficulties had been expected, & more were found. The machinery of the steam engine & the mill, because of their newness, did not work smoothly, or well—& the power of the engine was not adapted to the requirements of the mill. Stoppages occurred, & the operations were very slow. Before we left, only one boiler of syrup had been emptied to cool—& it was so manifest that that would [169] not "grain," or make sugar, that it was not designed to attempt it, but the syrup was to be given out to the slaves, as part of their provisions. We carried home a bottle, of which I ate part for my supper. It was too thin, because not boiled long enough, but of very pleasant flavor. There was some foreign flavor, of vegetable matter, but not strong or unpleasant. I do not doubt that good syrup may be made, & cheaply enough to serve for home use. This alone will be a great benefit to the country. But I do not now believe that sugar can be made of either the African or the Chinese cane, by ordinary & known processes, or by any other, that will make the product profitable for sale in this region, or farther northward—or preferable to that of the sugar cane where the climate will admit its culture. . . .

*Sept. 15.* We went again to the sugar boiling. The operations better, & though still very slow, improved in speed. A negro slave, who had been lent to Gov. Hammond by a friend in Florida, and who was an experienced sugar boiler in the rude & simple method of that country, today had the entire direction, as Mr. Wray had withdrawn for the present. The juice was boiled without any previous addition of lime, & made lighter-colored & better syrup than before. . . . I am now tired of witnessing the operation—but must again attend tomorrow, as it is agreed upon that a trial will then be made of the products of different kinds of cane—& also [170] of Mr. Wray's method & ability for making sugar. I have no faith in his success. And if, as I now believe, it cannot be done by him, what could have induced him to assert it, when exposure was so certain to follow, is past my comprehension.

*Sept. 16.* Went to the sugar house—where also came some of Gov. H.'s friends & neighbors by invitation, & sundry others uninvited to witness the trial. After all, none could be made, of the comparative products of different kinds of cane, because of the still worse performance of the mill, & other new difficulties. Not one half, if so much, of the juice was expressed, owing to the imperfection of the mill. The interruptions & delay were disadvantages to the later operations. Mr. Wray directed & superintended the management of the juice, & the boiling. The first portion was poured out to cool quite late. It was good syrup, & had the indications of "graining" after standing longer. But that could not be then known. We had to leave—& night soon overtook us, so that we rode more than an hour in the dark, before reaching Redcliff.

*Sept. 17.* We remained at the mansion. . . . Excessively hot, as it has been for some days, & dry. No report from the plantation, & therefore it is understood that the syrup had not grained, up to 1 P.M. . . . At 4 P.M. I took my leave & departure, & went in Gov. Hammond's carriage to Augusta. I had been invited the day before by Mr. William Eve,[10] & accordingly spent the evening & night at his house, to remain to the time of starting on the railway tomorrow

---

[10] Like Ruffin, William J. Eve of Augusta was a progressive agriculturist interested in promoting scientific farming techniques in the South. He contributed to agricultural periodicals, especially the *Southern Cultivator,* which was published in his home town.

morning. On Gov. Hammond's offer, concurred in previously by Mr. Wray, I had been supplied with three heads of each of 9 or 10 of the most esteemed kinds of "Imphee"—one of each of which I am to exhibit at our agricultural fair, & the other two to distribute among any [171] persons, with the larger share for myself. This will enable me to know the like kinds, to buy, when any shall be offered for sale.

*Sept. 18.* At 9 A.M. left on the railway. Reached Columbia before dark, & continued through the night.

*Sept. 19.* Reached Charlotte about day-break—& Graham at 1 P.M. where I hired a carriage & proceeded to Alamance. . . . Yesterday, on the journey, finished reading the 5th vol. of Life of Walter Scott—skipping much of the extracts of others' writings. . . .

*Sept. 20.* Sunday. . . . Religious services in the family, as usual on the Sundays when there is no preaching at Graham.—Continue reading Scott's Life. Surely Scott was one of the kindliest & best of men—& also one of the most fortunate & happiest, until he reached the beginning of old age. But after that his misfortunes & causes of grief & suffering were heavy indeed! His private diary, embracing the time of his severest trials & afflictions, is especially interesting, & seems perfectly descriptive of the writer.

*Sept. 21.* . . . In late papers the electioneering letter of that Bobadil braggart, Gen. Gid[eon J.] Pillow, who by Pres. Polk's favor was raised to such undeserved rank in the Mexican war, & to such conspicuous notoriety by his own self-praise & false boasting.[11] Still he *may* tell some truth—& if he does so in this case, it will bring dark transactions to light. He charges that Gen. [Winfield] Scott had bribed Santa Anna with $10,000 paid in advance, & $1,000,000 to follow, for the surrender of the City of Mexico—& that this understanding existed between them before the Armistice was made, & before the succeeding & last bloody battle was fought. In conversing on this matter, & Scott's merits & demerits in other respects, Judge R. mentioned that he & Scott were fellow law-students in the same [174] office in Petersburg. They were then very intimate & he still has kind feelings for him, & a better opinion of his mental & moral

---

[11] Ruffin's harsh evaluation of Pillow is not unjustified. After rising, through Polk's favor, to the rank of major general in the Mexican War, Pillow did little, fifteen years later, to justify such extraordinary confidence in his military capacity. As second-in-command at Fort Donelson, he bore much of the blame for that disgraceful Confederate defeat and never received another important command.

qualities than I have. He said at that time he was remarkable for his vanity. In writing a short note to a young lady, he would spend hours, & re-write it sundry times, to make it as perfect and as striking as possible. It is within my own remembrance that Scott's first name was "Wingfield," the name of many & obscure people in Va. It was after his great successes & victories, (so called, but for which I think he ought to have been cashiered for misconduct, & useless waste of blood—) in Canada, that he dropped the g, so as to spell his name "Winfield," by which he aimed to make a retrospective augury of his great character & ability as a conqueror. Until the Mexican war, I did not believe he had even military talent. I have since awarded to him that claim to high distinction. But I do not think he has any other talent, or, as a public man, any great merit whatsoever.—Found lately that I weigh 150 lbs. This is 5 lbs. more than my greatest known former weight—& I did not exceed 130 before I was 40 years old. I am rather ashamed of becoming fatter, & that it should be generally observed, within the last years, when so many things have occurred to cause me grief & distress. My general health was never so good as it has been since I gave up the direction of my farm & the possession & management of my estate. The labors & exposure of my previous time could not in themselves have been hurtful to my health. Could it have been the connected harassing cares & perplexities which had become more & more burdensome, until thrown off as intolerable?

*Sept. 22.* At 12 o'clock left Alamance for the station & by 1, on the [175] railway for Hillsborough. . . . At Hillsborough after 2. Left my trunk at the tavern, & went first to Mrs. Roulhac's (Judge Ruffin's widowed daughter) & afterwards to call on the Rev. M[oses] A[shley] Curtis, & first make his personal acquaintance. He is the ablest botanist in the south, & the resident episcopal minister here.[12] Next called by to see Mary Cain, (Judge R's niece,) who had made a long visit to Marlbourne. . . . Next to Mr. John Kirkland's (a little out of the town,) where I staid the night. He is the brother of Judge R.'s wife. Mr. K. had been engaged in making syrup of his Chinese sugar cane, with very imperfect means, & in a very small way. Yet he is as

---

[12] A native of Stockbridge, Massachusetts, and graduate of Williams College, Curtis (1808–72) first came to North Carolina in 1830 as a tutor in the family of Governor Edward B. Dudley. Five years later, he was ordained in the Episcopal Church. During his long ministry, all of it in North Carolina except for a pastorate of nine years, 1847–56, in Society Hill, South Carolina, he published several books and numerous papers on botanical subjects.

much gratified with his success, as Gov. Hammond is disappointed with his operations & their poor results. [176]

*Sept. 23.* After breakfast, Mr. K. went with me to pay other visits, some of which were in return of calls, & kinder attentions in invitations, made to me last year, when I was here, & my time too much occupied to return such civilities. Among those, visited Col. Jones & family, who lives a little out of the town—& called merely to notify P. B. Ruffin (the Judge's son, & who married Col. Jones' daughter) that I will take tea with them this evening. As he is a merchant, & now especially busy, he is at home only at night & at meals. . . . At night, at P. B. Ruffin's, where also was Col. James H. Ruffin, now staying in Hillsborough. He was my companion & fellow-lodger at school—is a worthy man, & not deficient in information (for himself,) but somehow, I have never found anything interesting in his conversation or companionship. . . . And so, in a day & a half, I have paid my debts of courtesy, in return of all attentions & civilities, & to urgent & repeated invitations. My intimacy with & very great regard for Judge Ruffin & some few of his children, makes me both levy & pay a burdensome tax, as to most others of his numerous family & their connections by marriage. All such, in their kindness, seem to think that they owe to my family attentions because of their being as near in blood, or as married to such, as the very distant blood relationship of my daughters to Jud[g]e Ruffin's. Every connection by marriage is emulous to do as much. And [177] thus they tax me, & compel me to tax them. I would have given offence to all these kind people if I had again passed without calling on them. Yet excepting Mrs. Roulhac, with whom only I may call myself an *acquaintance*, & good & kind & hearty John Kirkland, there was not another to whom I believe my visit gave any pleasure, except as a paying or returning of courteous attention. Yet this is much better than most of the visiting & receiving visits, & social intercourse, which takes up so much of our time & life. At 9 P.M. went to the tavern to bed.

*Sept. 24.* Was waked up to dress before 1 A.M., & rode to the station, to take the cars, at 2. Reached Raleigh before 11, where we had to stay until 2 P.M. . . . Reached Petersburg after 5 P.M. Julian's carriage not waiting for me—by which I knew my letter to him had not been received. Could not hire a conveyance so late, & so had to stay the night—at the Bollingbrook Hotel. . . .

*Sept. 25.* Early, took the railway to City Point, & there the steamboat, to Maycox—where I got a boat to take me across the water to the end of Coggin's Point, where I left my baggage in care of the hands picking peas there, & walked to Beechwood. . . . Though the household is so little changed in other respects, yet the absence of its former head, & light, gives an air of desolation to everything. My son was one of the most fortunate & blessed of human beings before his recent heavy affliction, & the preceding long expectation & even certainty of its consummation.

*Sept. 26.* Resumed writing the annual report of the President & Executive [178] Committee to the Farmers' Assembly. I have chosen not to follow the example of my predecessor in offering a separate report, or address, as president—&, by direction of the Committee, I shall prepare a joint report from both, submitting the concurrent views & harmonious action of both. . . . Heard by Charles that, notwithstanding my declining to be a candidate, & stating sufficient reasons why I should not serve, I have been re-elected a member of the Farmers' Assembly, by the members of the Society in Hanover. This is as unexpected as it is uncommon. But as my county fellow members so honor me, & insist on my serving as their representative, notwithstanding my stated objections, I must act, to such extent as may not be rendered improper, or impossible, by my other duties & position as President of the Society. . . .

In conversation in reference to my improved health in latter years, & my habits, Gen. Hammond told me that he would ensure my life to 80 years of age, for a very small premium. I answered that if [179] his insurance could extend my life certainly to 80 years, I would not have it—preferring the uncertainty of my actual life, & its probable much earlier, though unknown time of termination. I do not pretend to be desirous, or resigned, to meet death knowingly— though I have earnestly wished & prayed for immediate & unexpected death—& probably may not be more ready to die at any future time. But, if at my choice to live to 80, far as it is beyond my expectation, I would hesitate to accept the boon, even with the chance of uncertain life still longer. And I would reject the offer to live to 80 or 100, if then certainly to die. Even if on the former terms, of living certainly to 80 years, how many things would probably occur before that time, that would be worse for me than my own death! Within a few months, I lost three grown daughters by deaths anticipated or threatened but for very short times before. Within two years thereafter, another has been removed who was a daughter to me & a sister to my children, in love & by marriage, though not in kindred. . . .

How many more of beloved children or grandchildren might I not lose by death in the next 17 years, if my life were so extended! And perhaps the misconduct and consequent misfortunes of others, might be more grievous to me than the deaths of deserving & beloved members of my family. Already, & more & more with the passage of time, I have found, in one case, nothing to afford to me pleasure or comfort, & in another nothing but subjects for grief, condemnation, & growing alienation.[13]

*Sept. 28. . . .* The mail brought letters to me & Julian from Marlbourne, with Mr. Sayre's urgent request that some one of us would go there immediately to advise him, under his difficulties, especially in regard to ploughing under the pea-vines, with the ranker growth of tall weeds intermixed. As it will be most convenient for me to go, I will set out tomorrow, by the steamboat, which is now the earliest available conveyance. . . .

*Sept. 29.* Finished the *general* matter of the Report to F[armers'] A[ssembly]. At 11 rowed to Berkley wharf & there embarked on the Steamer for Richmond. Arrived before 5 P.M. & found Mr. Sayre's carriage waiting for me. Reached Marlbourne at 9 P.M. Found Elizabeth, Mr. Sayre & my little granddaughter Jane well. . . . Mr. Sayre is all this week on the jury, which doubles his difficulties, his overseer being good for nothing, except for good intentions—too ignorant to direct anything. Heard & discussed all about the work & difficulties.

*Sept. 30.* Mr. Sayre had to return to court early. After breakfast, I viewed [181] the state of things, & changed the ploughs to the pea-land, from which work Mr. S. had taken them away, because he deemed the execution of the ploughing to be so bad as to be intolerable. He had told me that Zack, the head ploughman, had told him that "Old master would have thought the work *good*"—& so I did, or at least good enough to put up with. . . . Changed the other work from cutting down & shocking corn, to gathering, shucking & housing it, as I deem it dry enough for safety. Mr. Sayre is an excellent manager of business, & will be an excellent farmer in all respects, (as he is already in the main parts—) but his want of experience, as might be expected, has led him into some bad mistakes, & especially in ploughing for & sowing the peas too early—& he is therefore the more fearful of the difficulties produced by these errors. It will be a

---

[13] The references are to son Charles and daughter Agnes Beckwith, respectively.

bad job any way—but all that can be done is to choose the least objectionable mode of preparing the land for wheat. . . . Finished 7th & last volume of Life of Walter Scott.

*October 1.* White frost last night. This will, I fear, cut off all hope of enough peas ripening to be worth gathering. . . . The banks began to stop payment (avowedly) some days ago in the north, & all may be expected to follow, unless the existence & operation of [182] the independent treasury system shall prevent. . . .[14]

*Oct. 3.* . . . Nearly all the banks of the U.S. already have stopped payment, so far as news heard. Those in the city of N.York, in the three principal towns of Va. & in Charleston S.C. still stand & profess to pay. All the small fry of banks in Va have stopped payment. They did not pay before—nor the principal Va banks, that still pretend to pay—& it is not difficult to pretend to pay now as they have only done since 1844. . . .

*Oct. 5.* By previous appointment, carried my little granddaughter Jane to Richmond, where we met her father to take her home. . . . We have all become so much more attached to her, & she to us, that we give her up with much regret. . . .

*Oct. 6.* A great calamity. In the night (about 2 or 3 hours before [183] break of day,) I was awakened by the cry of fire. On rising I saw it was at the barn-yard. Before I could get there, it had progressed so far that it was impossible to save the barn, as had been hoped & attempted by Mr. Sayre, who having ridden, got there before me. The barn, new stable & old, three corn-cribs, all soon were on fire & rapidly consumed. All hands were there, & worked zealously—but so great was the heat that but little could be saved. Fortunately, the last delivery of wheat had been in progress for the preceding two days, by which nearly 3000 bushels have been saved that otherwise would all have been lost. All the seed wheat, & as much left of the sale wheat as would make about 1000 bushels has been burnt. Also about 100 bbls of old corn & 2½ days hauling & shucking of new. All the grain is less loss than all the straw & chaff, securely stacked, which made all the long forage for the next year, & from this hour. The moveable implements & machines were saved, mainly, except 2 of the 8 good reaping machines. All the mules in the stable, & the oxen in the pen, were saved, that a little more delay in relieving would have lost. In this, & in the delivery of wheat, we

---

[14] The failure of the Ohio Life Insurance and Trust Company on August 24 touched off the short-lived Panic of 1857.

have reason to be thankful. . . . By very rough estimate, I suppose the actual value of the articles burnt, & mainly in the buildings, grain, straw & chaff, & machines & implements, to be between $5000 & $6000. But whatever it may be, there will be an additional loss of full $2000 in the great inconvenience & future consequent losses, because of the [184] sudden & entire deprivation of what cannot be dispensed with, & cannot be supplied. The entire want of barn, grain houses, & stable until they can be slowly replaced—the total destruction of all the straw & chaff, (relied on for provender) & with little more left of other long forage, in the fields—are evils beyond estimate on a large farm like this. . . . Finished copying (or re-writing) a communication on "The Peg-Roller & its use"—& with another article, sent to the Secretary of the Society. . . .

*Oct. 9.* . . . A pamphlet from Charleston, the final Report of the Commissioners entrusted with the construction of the draining culverts of the city, in which is embraced my answer to [185] their inquiries. My letter has been put to good use by them. . . . Wrote, & afterwards copied, a piece on the "Colonization Society & Emancipation." Reading Congressional Document on the introduction of camels into this country, last year, by government—which contains a great deal of curious information concerning that animal.

*Oct. 10.* Read & corrected my article, & sent it by mail to the newspaper. Also letters to Mildred, Gov. Hammond, & others.

*Oct. 11.* Sunday. Began & at night finished rough draft (12 pages) of a piece on "The Great Error of Southern Agriculture." Went to the Presbyterian church, where a young stranger preached. All the talk there about our loss by the fire, & speculations as to the cause. We have nothing to induce suspicion. It may have been accidental, by the dropping of fire from a passing & careless negro's pipe—or it may have been the incendiary act of a secret enemy. . . .

*Oct. 12.* Aiding Mr. Sayre in directing his wheat-sowing operations, as his attentions are greatly divided, (owing to the sundry difficulties caused by the fire,) & his overseer, though meaning well, is such a fool that he does more harm than good by his very slight directing action. Prepared to leave home tomorrow morning.

*Oct. 13.* Went to Richmond—also Mr. Sayre had to go, to arrange [186] for disposing of his last cargo of wheat. It cannot be sold, except at a very reduced rate. The money crisis is still worse. Nine of the N.Y. city banks have suspended payment, & the state bank of S.Ca. . . . . No doubt all will follow before long. Numerous bankrupt-

cies among merchants & other men of business, depending on credit.
—Went with Mr. Williams to see the Fair Ground, & the recent
repairs thereon. . . .

*Oct. 14.* Left Richmond by daybreak, in the steamer, & landed on
the end of Coggin's Point, in a drizzle—had a wet & fatiguing walk
to Beechwood. All well of the now diminished family. Nanny &
Thomas away at school.

*Oct. 16.* I went in the carriage to Petersburg, whence, at 5 P.M.,
set [187] out, on the railroad—reached Weldon, at 8.30, where I had
to wait to 11 P.M. for the starting of the train for Raleigh. A
wretched supper, of which I could swallow but a few mouthfuls.
Here I am waiting, without any resource of conversation, or reading, or other occupation, except to bring up these notes.—As I had
expected all the banks in Va. & I suppose in the U.S. have stopped
payment. And this in a time of the greatest general prosperity, for
some years back, that the southern states have ever enjoyed.

*Oct. 17.* At 11 P.M. last night the train for Raleigh set out, & arrived before daybreak, & changed to the train going westward. I
have never before seen, among people who, by their positions are
esteemed, & consider themselves as gentlemen, such strong evidences of the selfishness & want of politeness which are common in
passengers. The only passenger car, on each of these roads, was
crowded. The greater number of passengers, (about 20 of them)
were of one party, delegates who were returning from a Presbyterian
synod in Virginia, & who were from the interior of South Carolina
mostly. I was one of the latest to enter the car at Weldon, & found
every double seat occupied by two persons, except a few in which
there was a vacant half. On one of these, I seated myself, evidently
to the discomposure of the previous occupant of the other half. However, he showed no more of incivility than mere coldness of manner.
In public conveyances I always meet all attempts of my neighbors to
begin conversation, & often, as on this occasion, I make the beginning. But after my companion merely replied to my first remarks or
inquiries, I followed his example of silence. Being on the seat next
[to] the passage-way, I had not even a place to lean my head against
&, though I can sleep well when travelling, I could get but little
sleep, & passed a very uncomfortable night. In the next train, I was
situated in the like manner. I suppose that I was unknown [188] to
every other passenger, as all were unknown to me. I was the oldest
man in the car—& but few others seemed to approach my age. At the

station near to the University (Chapel Hill) three other passengers entered, of whom one was an emaciated youth, 18 or 19 years old, borne in the arms of a negro man, accompanied by an elderly lady, who seemed to be the young man's mother. The party advanced along the passage. No one moved, or offered any accommodation, until they reached nearly to my place, when I rose, & offered my seat to the young man. My companion then followed my example, so that the mother also was seated by her son. The only vacant places then in my sight were the seats on each side of the stove, which I & others had before been driven from by the heat of the fire being too great to be borne. But now, having no other place, I returned, & found that the fire had so abated, that the seat was quite comfortable. We next reached Hillsborough, after sunrise. There was waiting a new supply of passengers, some 8 or 10 in one large party, mostly of ladies, children, & their servants. They entered the end of the car most remote from my place. Amidst the stir produced, the seating of some & the still remaining standing of others, I saw that P. B. Ruffin, of Hillsborough, was one of the escorts of the party, & I called out to him (as we were some 8 seats distance apart,) that if he had not seated all the ladies, I could give up my seat, & invited him to bring them. Those who had not obtained seats were still slowly advancing —& as the mistresses were previously seated, I suppose that they told their servants to go & take the offered seats. So it was, while I was still standing & offering the seat, two black maid servants, one of them carrying her mistress' infant, came up, & quietly took the seat which I had offered. Theirs was not the color of the ladies to whom my invitation had been [189] given, but I said nothing. . . . I then continued standing, until the father of the infant came up, who took off the nurse to the servants' car. As this vacated a seat, I took it, by the side of the other negro woman. This probably afforded amusement to most of the young men—& would have shocked a northerner, by my occupying such close neighborhood to a negro. . . . Stopped at Graham, & proceeded to Judge Ruffin's. . . .

*Oct. 18.* Wrote a letter to my son Charles, announcing my reasons & determination, for restricting his income, & restraining his means for indulgence. Before my recent settlement was completed, by which I had at first designed to make him an equal sharer with my older children, & in full [192] property, I learned such indications of his former extravagance & heedlessness, as to induce me to retain the legal right to the larger part of the new capital. Since, his waste of time & money have become more obvious in proportion to his increased income, & his expectation of increased capital. He has disregarded recently as he had done formerly, all warning, admonition, advice, or threats. Nothing is left for me but to stint him to a bare competency . . . . At bed-time, Judge Ruffin left us to take the night train for Raleigh, to begin tomorrow morning the duties required of him as President of the N.C. State Agrl. Society.

*Oct. 19.* Looking over & reading the interesting parts of Wharton's Law Treatise on Mental Unsoundness. I have always found much gratification in reading of cases of medical jurisprudence, such as this work offers in numbers. Yet I know nothing of, & care nothing for medical or legal subjects, separately. It is wonderful how far insanity extends, & how much it is concealed as monomania. It would seem from this treatise, that a large portion of mankind are mad, & that many of the most atrocious criminals were the involuntary agents of insanity. . . .

*Oct. 20.* At noon left Alamance for the train, with Mildred & Patty, both of whom stopped at Hillsborough to pay a visit, & I proceeded to Raleigh to attend the Fair. Arrived there at 5 P.M. . . . Attended the meeting of the Society at night. Not much of interest in the discussion. A long (extempore) speech from the moderately sensible, & supereminently voluble & [193] fluent Abraham Venable,[15] which was, in purport, scattered broad-cast over everything. To bed a little before 12.

*Oct. 21.* At the fairground. A thin attendance of people & of subjects of exhibition. The Petersburg Fair being held on the same days with this, has operated to prevent attendance here. . . . At night again at the meeting of the Society—where there was nothing done of interest, except of the business of the Society. Judge Ruffin, notwithstanding all his continued & strenuous efforts to withdraw, compelled to serve again as President for next year.

*Oct. 22.* Attended the Fair Ground & heard the address. In the afternoon, went to the station to receive Mildred coming from Hillsborough. A great crowd, & great pressure & difficulty. At 5 P.M. we proceeded in the train for Weldon, where we had to wait to 1 o'clock.

*Oct. 23.* Then proceeded, & reach Richmond, Exchange Hotel, by

---

[15] A native of Prince Edward County, Virginia, Abraham Watkins Venable (1799–1876) moved to North Carolina in 1829 and represented that state in Congress from 1847 to 1853. During the Civil War he was a member of the Confederate House of Representatives.

7 A.M. where we both retired to our rooms & beds, to a late breakfast. Mr. Sayre & Elizabeth arrived at 12, & Mildred returned to Marlbourne. I attended to business of the Society with the Secretary & Marshal. At 7.30 P.M. a meeting of the Ex. Com. which remained in session to after 11 P.M. My annual report approved & adopted by the Committee. Also my plan for the night meetings during the Fair week. A new feature I propose is, in addition to the agricultural discussions, in meetings of sections, to have, on two nights general meetings of the Society, for the discussing of any subjects of the important & general interests of agriculture. This will enable every one to speak, & argue, who feels disposed, on any such subject [194] of his own choice. This will afford pleasure to many, either as speakers or hearers—& such debates & arguments will do good. And they can do no harm, because these mass meetings cannot act, or decide upon any question. If the thing shall work as I hope, while the Farmers' Assembly only can legislate, or decide upon any action, the members generally, in mass meetings, may say & argue anything, & have the freest expression of opinion.

*Oct. 24.* Resumed our session at 9 A.M. & continued to near 1 P.M. The report of the sub-committee of which Edmund is chairman, & drawn by him, on the fence law, adopted—& everything else done that was ready for our action. The reports put in the printer's hands. Numerous arrivals of visitors to the Fair, & my meeting with many old & making new acquaintance. . . .

*Oct. 25.* Sunday. A letter from Edmund stating that he cannot come. I am sorry for it—but feared as much. Drizzle yesterday, & cloudy today, & threatening, which I fear will keep many persons away. . . .

*Oct. 26.* Still cloudy, & some light showers. Many of my friends arriving—& among them, F. Minor & R. Noland. Col. P. Cocke has been here some days. [Willoughby] Newton at night. The committee met & had no more preparations to make. According to the published *programme*, a general meeting of the society called at African Church, at night, to fill vacancies in the numerous committees of awards—& afterwards a conversational discussion on "Meadows, Grass, Cattle-feeding & fattening," in which our plain western members joined & almost exclusively [195] carried on, well, & with spirit. This plan is working well. F. Minor, in private consultations, pushing his scheme for agricultural education. . . .

*Oct. 27.* The first day of the Fair. Cloudy, rain, & a strong & keen wind. The attendance on the Fair Ground unusually small. By aid of our last night's arrangement, we got the committees of awards to work much earlier than heretofore. I had to see the printer, & wait for the engraver, (who has blundered on my map of the drainage of Marlbourne,) & at the Fair Ground by 9 A.M. to superintend generally. At 4 P.M. the Farmers' Assembly met. [William C.] Rives again made speaker, without dissent. He & I very courteous & kindly in manner, & he quite cordial & familiar. I read my report—& as it & the accompanying documents were printed in advance, they were distributed among the members. The portions on agricultural education, & the fence law, were made special subjects of reference to committees. A report made of the progress of Cocke's former donation, & its obstruction, & also he offered (he is a member) the purchase of the Bellona Arsenal, at the price he bought it, but, as I expected coupled with conditions, which will render it too hazardous for the offer to be accepted. At night a section meeting on tobacco culture, at African Church, over which I placed J. R. Edmunds to preside. The other section, at Bosher's Hall did not attend.

*Oct. 28.* A bright day, though cool & airy, & a large attendance on the Fair Ground. The Assembly sat at night, which prevented the meeting of a section at African Church, & the other at Bosher's Hall also failed. Animated discussion on the *conditions* of Cocke's donation [196] of $20,000 for a professorship of agriculture at the University—his having the appointment. This the Board of Visitors objected to both as contrary to the law, (which requires the visitors to appoint to all professorships,) & also to good policy. I voted in a minority of 25, to sustain the visitors' opinion, against 36 who went for a petition to the legislature to modify the law, & to instruct the visitors to admit Cocke's appointing power. Much dissatisfaction with this decision, & several of the majority afterwards would have voted differently. The measure will stand no chance before the legislature—& it is very bad that the first & most prominent petition of the Farmers' Assembly should be without strength, & such as ought to be rejected.

*Oct. 29.* Another good forenoon, though lowering soon after—& a large crowd at the Fair. Afternoon session of the F.A. I was gratified to learn that I had misunderstood the *extent* & strictness of the *condition* affixed to the offer of Bellona Arsenal. I sought & had a conversation with Col. Cocke on this subject, & found that nothing more is required by him than that the *bona fide* attempt shall be made to establish a school there, to afford agricultural instruction in part, & to make it as perfect as possible without much expense or risk. But if the effort, after sufficient trial shall fail, & the scheme has to be abandoned, the property is not therefore to be forfeited, but will remain in the Society, & may be disposed of at the will of the Society & for its sole benefit. [197] In purport, it is precisely what I designed to offer to the Ex. Com. if I had been the purchaser, except that I would have not even required a *trial* of a school, unless such was preferred by the Society. When thus explained, I voted for the acceptance being referred to the Ex. Com. The officers elected. Nearly all the old ones re-elected, & without opposition to any. A few declined, & two who never come left out. F. Minor, & other new appointments all good. At night, the general meeting for the regular address to be delivered—which however was not done, as the chosen speaker, A. Holliday was unwell. Therefore I called for a discussion on agricultural education, & afterwards on practical agriculture. But though I called out good speeches from several, the whole hung heavily, & the meeting adjourned before 10. As usual, some 4 or 5 of my friends sitting in my room until late, in interesting conversation.

*Oct. 30.* The last day of the Fair. Large attendance, though smaller than for the previous day. I trust that the falling off, caused by both the preceding bad weather & the money pressure & difficulties will not be so great as expected. The premiums awarded, & the list read at the stand. Four were awarded to me. Of these the two for "Written Communications" I announced that I relinquished them to the Society. Another, for my pegged roller, exhibited by model, $20, I shall give to John Haw, who made the model for me, by my directions. The fourth, $50, is for "The best drained farm," & my report of the drainage of Marlbourne. This only I will myself receive the money for.—At night, a general meeting called, but only a thin attendance, at African Church, for leave-taking off-hand addresses. After some few of these, & all seeming done, before 9, I was putting the question of adjournment to the vote, when a member announced [198] to me that Gov. Wise had entered the hall. I suspended the vote, & requested his excellency to address the meeting. He did so, in his own remarkable & peculiar manner, in support of his grand scheme of general education for the state, & in reply to the strictures thereon made by Newton the night before. His first speech was upwards of an hour & a half, to which Newton replied for about half an hour, & Gov. Wise rejoined at the length of an hour—thus himself consuming full 2½ hours, & keeping us until a little after midnight. The audience became very thin, & I wondered at the patience, or extent of courtesy, of all that remained to the end. Notwithstanding the lateness of the hour, & the gradual withdrawal of the wearied audience, he continued to speak, & to make long pauses, according to his artificial manner, just as if he had the largest & most attentive audience. He can speak for 6 hours as easily as any less time, on any subject, & whether he is acquainted with it or not, & without the least regard for the scoffing & disapproving opinions of his hearers. He is an actor in his oratory, & a bad actor—though the very faults of ranting & thundering, seem to attract hearers & admirers, in proportion to his departure from correctness & good taste. He is certainly a man of great powers of mind. But I believe that the greatest powers by which he has succeeded are, not his superiority of intellect, but his unbounded ambition, which impels him forward to seek his own personal advancement—& his unbounded assurance & effrontery, which leave nothing untried that can push on his claims on popular favor. He is not in the least held back from any thing that can help him, by either sense of propriety, moderation, or shame. [End of MS Volume 1—p. 199]

*Oct. 31.* This day had been appointed for Julian's family to go to Marlbourne. . . . I joined them, & we proceeded to Marlbourne. Found all well. . . . I felt relieved & rejoiced to get home, & to rest, in quiet. Found a letter from Gov. Hammond, which with a previous one received a few days ago, states the entire failure of his, & also Mr. Wray's attempts to make sugar from the Imphee, or African Sugar Millet. He authorizes my publishing extracts from these letters, which I shall do.

*November 2.* Finished & enclosed to De Bow, for his Review, a concluding addition to my argument in favor of secession of the southern states, which he has been so long republishing. It is to be completed in his Dec. No. . . . Reading the Nov. No. of De Bow's Review. Besides the part of my piece, there is a strong & eloquent article in favor of separation of the union, from a Whig & until a late visit to the north, always a Union man. I should like to know who is the writer.

*Nov. 4.* Began & read some 50 pages of "Consuelo," [16] & found it, so far, much more innocent, absurd & dull than I had expected. I

---

[16] A romantic novel by George Sand which tells the life story of a great singer in an eighteenth-century setting.

was induced to buy it by seeing that it was read by Charlotte Bronte, & mentioned by her without censure. I have before read notices of other novels of the noted "George Sand," & opinions of their general immoral tendency—but had never read any one of them. . . . Began to write a communication to the "Southern Planter," & found it up-hill work.

*Nov. 6.* Julian & I came to Richmond. . . . Saw Mr. Williams. Hear that the gate-money received at the Fair was nearly $2800 (including premium on the specie received & sold,) & that the expenses will be reduced. Better, on the whole, than expected. Had to direct the correction of more errors of the engraver of my maps, besides sundry previous corrections. Also gave directions to the printer in regard to my communications to the Society, & added some notes, made necessary by the [201] errors of the engraver of the maps. This required my remaining in Richmond, even if there had been an earlier time to go to Beechwood than by steamer tomorrow.—No companion, & no amusement at night, at the hotel, except to look over my papers—& went to bed by 9.

*Nov. 7.* To the steamer & left the wharf at 6.30 A.M. But few passengers, & no acquaintance of mine, except Ro. Douthat of Wyanoke. We had a conversation respecting the noted conduct & characters of two of his countymen, of distinction in other respects, & whom we heartily agreed in condemning as infamous for their shameful disregard of their marriage relations. . . . It is such revolting cases of vice in high positions, (in connexion with our institution of slavery,) which give color to the general libels of such writers as Mrs. [Harriet Beecher] Stowe—& it is the too great toleration of such criminals in society, even by many who abhor their vices, & despise the actors, that give any force to these general libellers & denouncers of slavery. —Landed at the end of Coggin's Point (which [202] formerly was known as Merchants' Hope Point,) on my son's land, & finding a neighbor's carriage there, rode to the Beechwood house. All from home, at Brandon church, except the 4 youngest children. . . . It was the occasion of the Bishop's annual visitation. Nanny had come from her school at Richmond, to be confirmed, which was done yesterday, at Merchants' Hope Church. Bishop [William] Meade[17] had staid at Beechwood, & had gone this morning, with the family, to conduct

---

[17] The third Protestant Episcopal bishop of Virginia, Meade served in that position from 1841 until his death in 1862. Bishop Meade was active in the American Colonization Society and in the establishment of Liberia.

the services at Brandon Church. I am sorry that I was not here soon enough to meet with this good & brave old man, for whom I entertain high respect & even veneration, for his virtue & piety—although his intellect is not more than ordinary. . . .

*Nov. 8.* Sunday. Went to Merchants' Hope Church. Mr. Johnson at Brandon, & his place supplied by a Mr. Tizzard who preached in a regular & most disagreeable tune, which would have destroyed the interest of the most excellent or eloquent words. What was the manner or merit of his sermon I had no idea, for I could not attend to anything but his regular tune, which I could arrange in musical notation, & sing, or play [203] on an instrument. . . . Agnes removed to her new residence in Petersburg a week ago. This move, with the necessary accompaniments of the sale of her land, &c. was against the urgent advice of her brothers & trustees. But as things were— the previous removal of her husband, & her entire alienation in feeling from all of her own family—her conduct in these respects, & the many painful circumstances that necessarily occurred—I think it better that she should have taken this last step—bad as it would be, & must be, in other respects. . . . It is a most deplorable state of things for a father—but as it is so, I prefer entire separation from Agnes & her family, to such intercourse as could only exist. For such of her children as show promise, I would willingly do something for their proper & suitable education & training to earn a livelihood by honest & meritorious industry. But it is impossible, while they are under the control & influence of such a father. . . . All along, even for the many years that I tried to make the best of this wretched marriage, (which I in vain opposed,) & to try to feel as a father & a grandfather ought, I could not feel *love* for the children of Dr. Beckwith—& still less in later years, when it was certain & evident that they were taught to entertain the father's hostile feelings towards me, & to all their mother's family—the mother also entirely the same feelings. I have latterly had little means of knowing them, as formerly when some of the children staid for months in my house. But I feel confident that one of them, Thomas, the second son, is a fine boy, & I would be glad to take charge of him entirely, if it were possible. But it would not be acceded to, I am sure, by either parent—& even if permitted, the still continuing parental influence would spoil the attempt to raise the boy as would be desired, to make a good, industrious man, & worthy member of society.

*Nov. 9.* . . . I corrected & copied a piece of 8 pages (on the advan-

tages of drilling peas, in partial substitution of the general broad-cast
sowing,) & [205] sent it to the "Southern Planter."... The mail of
today brings accounts of awful omen, in the city of New York. Thousands of destitute men, who are demanding work & bread, have assembled & marched in procession, threatening to take by force
what they need for subsistence, if it is not accorded to them for their
offered labor, or by consent. They are instigated & led by foreigners.
This before winter begins. What will it reach to hereafter! They
promise to continue their threatening marches through the city as
long as their numbers increase, & they expect to recruit 30,000. Half
that number of desperate villains can sack & burn the city, & murder
its best inhabitants. This fate I predicted for New York, whenever
the dissolution of the union shall remove the conservative influence
of the south & of its institution of slavery. But the fulfilment seems
impending, or openly threatened, sooner than I expected.

*Nov. 11.* After breakfast rowed across the river to Berkley & took
passage on the steamer to Kennon's wharf, landed, & with my very
light carpet bag, walked 3½ miles to Sherwood Forest, the residence
of Ex-President Tyler. Found him at home—& had a most cordial &
kind reception & welcome. Mrs. Tyler appeared as young & blooming as when I saw her here two years ago, & enough so for 20 years
only, though now the mother of 6 children. We had her company &
agreeable joining in our conversation, from before dinner to nearly
our late separation for going to [206] bed. With the exception of her
portion of the conversation, & the time taken to read a few newspapers, Mr. Tyler & I talked from 1 to 10 o'clock, upon various matters of politics, measures & men, in all which we, as to all important
things, agreed in the main. I was much interested in hearing from
him many pieces of the secret history of his administration, & anec-
dotes of the distinguished public men with whom he has acted in his
long public life. With regard to Jackson's administration, we agreed
in strong condemnation—as to the gigantic intellect & argumentative
power of [Littleton W.] Tazewell,[18] the wonderful mind of [John]
Randolph, as profound as it was brilliant, & as to other able men. Mr.
Tyler thinks much more favoribly [*sic*] of Webster & of Wise (both
acting with him & aiding his administration) than I do—except as to
the intellectual power of Webster—which I hold as high as I place

---

[18] Littleton Waller Tazewell (1774–1860) was elected to the United States
House of Representatives in 1800 to fill the unexpired term of John Marshall. He
later served eight years in the Senate and was governor of Virginia from 1834 to
1836.

his morals low. I do not think we differ much as to the expediency of a separation of the union. He had formerly told me that he had the engraving of my portrait framed & hung as a companion to that of Webster—"the one" as he said "the first among American statesmen, & the other the first of American Agriculturists." I now saw the exhibition of this flattering compliment to me. The two portraits are of like size, & were framed alike in neat embroidered frames, designed & worked by Mrs. Tyler's lately deceased sister. Each portrait stands within the circumference of a shield, (as represented in coats of arms,) of which Webster's is surmounted by stars, & mine by a plough. These hang on the opposite [207] sides over the fire-place of the small (or family) sitting room, which is in ordinary use. Between them, & higher, is a much larger oil painting of Patrick Henry. The other pictures which are around on the walls of this apartment (besides some large family portraits) are the engraved portraits of Mr. Tyler's most valued personal friends, & members of his cabinet. [Abel P.] Upshur & [Thomas W.] Gilmer,[19] & his supporter & friend Henry A. Wise. . . . I asked Mr. T. why he had omitted the greatest of all his former cabinet ministers, Calhoun, when placing here the others most deserving remembrance. He said he had Calhoun's portrait elsewhere, & showed in the dining room, an oil painting of the size of life, & the most conspicuous object. Upshur was another man of great & remarkable power of intellect. But he was placed in high station, where his eminent ability could be put to use, too late, & his deplorable death occurred so soon after, that his true measure of worth & greatness is not known to the world, & only to the few, of whom I was one, who had the opportunity to know & appreciate him in his private as well as his public life.

Among the many subjects touched upon in our conversation, & some of the lightest & most trivial character, when some reference was made to my own age, in connection with my improved health, Mrs. T. told me I ought to follow Mr. [Theodore] Frelinghuysen's recent example—who, at 72 or 3 years of age, has married a young wife.[20] I could have readily stated, in half a dozen different strong &

---

[19] Upshur was secretary of the navy and later secretary of state in the Tyler cabinet. Gilmer, a former governor of Virginia, was appointed secretary of the navy on February 15, 1844. Two weeks later, he and Upshur were killed in an ordnance mishap aboard the USS *Princeton* while cruising on the Potomac River near Washington.

[20] Actually, Frelinghuysen, former senator from New Jersey and at this time president of Rutgers College, was only seventy when he took as his second wife Harriet Pumpelly of Oswego, New York, on October 14, 1857.

bitter modes of expression, my opinions in opposition to old men marrying young wives. But the circumstances here restrained every such answer. But I must do Mrs. Tyler the [208] justice to say that she, & her marriage to an old man, seem to offer an exception to the rule I have thought to be universal, that such marriages could produce nothing but unhappiness to both parties—if not disgust on one side, & hatred on one or both. When she a young, beautiful, & much admired belle, of the city of New York—of a high position in family & fortune—accomplished, travelled, & of excellent mind—married a widower of nearly 60, with a family of grown children, doubtless she was blinded by ambition, which led her to marry the then President of the United States. But even if so, it was a noble & generous sentiment, compared to the ordinary inducement in such cases of avarice, or to obtain wealth. And when, leaving public life, Mr. Tyler retired to this seclusion, & they were (for some time) deprived of almost all social pleasures, Mrs. Tyler has never seemed to miss or regret the world of fashion & pleasure in which she formerly lived exclusively, & had every means to enjoy. If ever a young wife truly loved an old husband, (which I have deemed impossible) she does. And it is not exhibited in any displays of fondness which would be to me evidences of acting & deceit. Her manner in this respect is unexceptionable. But she listens, in silence, to every remark he makes, & seems to admire in silence every expression, as if the words of wisdom.

*Nov. 12.* Rode with Mr. Tyler over his farm. Learned accidentally in conversation, what I did not know before, that with Mrs. Tyler, then Miss [Julia] Gardiner, her father [David Gardiner] was on board the Princeton frigate on the pleasure excursion, & was one of the persons killed by the explosion of the great cannon—Judge Upshur & Gov. Gilmer, two [209] of the cabinet ministers being also victims to the horrible accident.—The news, by yesterday's mail, of the state of things in New York, still more alarming. Matters look very much like the incidents of the beginnings in Paris of the first French revolution. The mayor has to be protected by a guard of 50 police-men—& U.S. troops have been sent from the neighboring fort to guard the public treasury in the custom-house. The mayor, [Fernando] Wood, had at first encouraged the kindling of this flame by his own jacobin declarations.

Mr. Tyler is about 4 years my senior. He is now (as he told me) in his 68th year, & I in my 64th. He is even more thin, or gaunt, than formerly, but still is ruddy, & seems hale & hearty. . . . We have talked almost incessantly. It is to me no subject for surprise, but it would be to every stranger, to see the man who once occupied the station & wielded the power of a constitutional king—as truly does a President of the United States—to be since, the plain & unassuming country gentleman & farmer, pretending not in the least to anything in position or appearance, because of his former place & power. I knew him slightly from my boyhood—& I may say well, from the year 1824, when I was first associated with him in public life. For a long time I perhaps underrated him—thought lightly of his abilities, differed with him in his views of men for public office, & especially opposed by my votes & expressed opinions his own advancement, when he was first a candidate for the place of U.S. Senator, & of Governor of Va. For the former, I zealously aided to defeat him, voting first for [William B.] Giles,[21] & next for Randolph & Tazewell. In his election as Governor, soon after, though there was no opposing candidate, I [210] voted against him, together with a few other malcontents in the legislature, for the older Floyd.[22] This opposition would have irritated many a man, & by his showing resentment, would have converted my slighting opinion & opposition to fixed dislike or hostility. But not so with John Tyler. He never showed any consciousness of my want of high appreciation of him, or of his objects—& it has never been referred to between us, in our long personal intercourse, until by myself, in jocular allusion & remark, addressed to Mrs. Tyler, during my present visit. On the contrary, whenever we have come together, his manner to me has been courteous, cordial & kind—& such as seemed to recognize fully my right to act in opposition to him, & to evince that he respected the integrity of my purposes, & grounds for preferring others to him. And this manner of conduct has been his to all, & it has been the great secret & means of his remarkable success as a candidate & a representative of the people. In our free conversation last night, I said to Mrs. T. that her husband had been the greatest "electioneer" I had ever known—but desired that that term, usually used in reproach, should be taken from me as also complimentary. It indeed mainly was

---

[21] A member of the First Congress of the United States, William Branch Giles (1762–1830) occupied a Senate seat from 1804 to 1815 and was governor of Virginia from 1827 to 1830.

[22] John Floyd (1783–1837), who succeeded Giles as governor. Tyler was governor from 1825 to 1827, when he was elected to the United States Senate, where he served for nine years.

owing to his real kindliness of feeling, his want of rancor & revenge-
ful disposition, & his courtesy to actual enemies (or opponents,) & his
readiness to overlook & forgive enmity, that had retained to him
numerous friends, & converted enemies to friends. This conciliatory
manner is as evident now, as it ever was when it could help to sustain or elevate him—& this proves that it is natural to him. His political career ended with the close of his presidential office. Since he has
had nothing to hope for in the game of politics. Almost any other
man would have been soured by the disregard shown of his abilities,
& ingratitude for his really great services, [211] & would have sunk
into misanthropy & seclusion, to all who either exhibited towards
him evidences of dislike, or slighting conduct. But he acted more
wisely & benevolently, & much has he profited by it. When he returned to his native county, to his present residence, to spend the
remainder of his days among neighbors whom he had known from
his or their childhood, & with all of whom there had formerly existed
kind relations, he found almost universal evidences of reserve & distance, if not hostility & dislike. Nearly every neighbor, & most of his
countymen were whigs & followers of Clay, & who had learned to
hate Tyler as a traitor, a renegade, & everything that was esteemed
bad in their party creed. Old friends & neighbors generally refrained from visiting him—which, even if he had been a stranger,
was due to him as a new resident & a gentleman. But very few ladies
even called on Mrs. Tyler, who for the first time had come to her
new home, & who also was a stranger to Virginia. Even more positive manifestations of dislike & censure were not wanting. One was,
that the late president of the U.S. was appointed by the county court
overseer of the public road which crossed his farm. The clerk of the
court called specially on him to deliver the order of court for this
appointment, not for respect, but doubtless to enjoy the mortification
that Mr. Tyler would exhibit, when receiving the civil insult, &
scornfully rejecting it, by paying the legal fine for failing to perform
the service. On the contrary, Mr. Tyler professed to receive the appointment as an evidence of favor, & said he would endeavor faithfully to discharge the duties, as he had done of all the much higher
offices which he had been formerly placed in by his country—& that
he felt honored by any trust so reposed in his hands. By acting generally upon this rule of conduct—never improperly seeking the favor
or support of any, & never repelling returning kindness by coldness,
he [212] has successfully outlived & conquered all this general &

strong inimical feeling, & now stands among his neighbors as if no such feelings had ever existed. I had myself evidences of this, when I saw him some two years ago at his county court, when called upon to act with & among his countymen. I had not then heard of any change of the earlier state of things; & I felt much gratified to see, instead of distance & aversion, evidences of general kind & cordial intimacy of intercourse between him & his countymen of every grade, & who were generally of the same political opinions still, & as much opposed to his presidential policy as formerly.

*Nov. 13.* . . . The mail brought information that the riotous indications in New York had been put down, partly by forcible repression, but mainly by the corporation providing public work for a great number of laborers. This takes away the pretext for mob demonstrations.—Mr. Tyler produced from his papers the letter which I wrote to him soon after his accession to presidential power.[23] Some how the copy I had kept has been misplaced or destroyed, & I was glad to be thus permitted to make another, as I did today, from the original. I felt flattered by the care taken of this letter of mine, & the several endorsements on it—as follows: In the hand writing of Mr. Tyler— "E. Ruffin—Private" & seemingly, from the ink, at another time, "Important"—& also in pencil "Mr. Ruffin voted for Gen. Harrison." In the writing of his private secretary & son, was "Edmund Ruffin, June 29/41, On [213] the President's delicate position, & the Policy to be followed." . . .

*Nov. 14.* The same kindliness of feeling which is one of Mr. Tyler's most remarkable characteristics, (as stated above,) & which is so much to be approved in many respects, also in others led to his most serious errors of government. While always so ready to forgive offences, & to receive as a friend a repentant enemy, he always remembered with gratitude the attachment & support of his undeviating friends, & deemed & rewarded such devotion to him as the first of merits, & the most deserving of office & public trust. This was the cause of many bad appointments by him—not that he would have bestowed office on any one he deemed unfit or unworthy, but he was content with a low degree of capacity & of worthiness in an applicant who was his steady personal friend, & would appoint him in preference to others who did not bear that relation to him, but possessed far superior qualifications for office, & far better claims on the country. Neither were all such appointments by Mr. Tyler made to

[23] See Appendix A for the text of this letter.

retain or to gain political support or aid for himself. For in some cases of offices of mere pecuniary value, I know that the recipients of his favor never had possessed, or ever could exert, any political influence—& their appointment operated to do harm to the popularity of the administration. In the references, in our conversation, to numerous public characters, he always spoke as kindly as the [214] case admitted of every man who had in any way been his friend. And of opponents, & even of some of whom I spoke in terms of strongest reprobation, for their political offences & base conduct, he rarely said any thing reproachful, or strongly in denunciation. He only evinced bitterness of feeling in regard to two of his revilers, [Thomas] Ewing & [John M.] Botts, whose baseness & malignity he deemed such that (as he said) he would not mention their names when he could avoid it.[24] And this slight & passing notice was as much as he bestowed on them in our free conversations. This grateful sense of benefit & support to him causes him to think much more kindly of Webster than I think is his due, even on this score. For though, as Mr. T. says, W. served his administration both ably & faithfully as chief cabinet minister, still I doubt not it was to serve his own purposes, & that he would as gladly have overthrown Tyler & his policy as would Clay or Ewing. On these grounds, Mr. Tyler is greatly attached to Wise, & would now vote for him for the Senate of U.S. in place of Hunter. And when stating to me as sufficient reason for this, the warm support of the one, & the coldness of the other, in his own former great difficulties, & his equivocal position in the early part of his administration, he seems entirely blind to the fact (as I see it) that he is for rewarding, as a virtue, personal friendship & political support to himself, & as a higher claim to public office, than superior qualifications & better public services, in another who had not been his personal friend or political supporter. But with all his faults, Tyler acted nobly & admirably for his country & our common political principles, in the main, & in all after the very beginning of his administration [215]—or while he was still wishing & striving (& very naturally) to please & retain the favor of the whig party, to whose favor he owed his election as Vice-President, & the succession to the Pres-

---

[24] Tyler inherited Ewing (1789–1871), a former senator from Ohio, from the Harrison cabinet. The two became estranged when Tyler twice vetoed bank recharter bills drafted by Ewing, and the latter resigned his post as secretary of the treasury. John Minor Botts (1802–69), a native Virginian, was elected to Congress in 1839 as a Henry Clay Whig and served three terms in that body before retiring from public life.

idency, caused by the speedy death of President Harrison. He went as far to please this party, as he could without violating the constitution & his oath, & the great principles he had before professed to maintain. When he found that nothing short of such violation would suffice for that party, he, after too long waiting, cut loose from them. Still he did not thereby gain the confidence & support of the opposite democratic party. And he struggled through his term, & performed important services, without the support of any party, & with no more supporters than the few personal friends, or interested partizans, who, for their small number, were in derision then called "the Corporal's guard." There is no other political opponent, or former friend, whom the Whig party (the followers of Clay,) so much hated & vilified as their own chosen candidate John Tyler. The Whig party, when in opposition, & having the one common object of opposition to the usurpations of Jackson, & the abuses of his administration & of its sequel, Van Buren's, had no common principles or political creed, or object, except to expel the ruling powers. Previous to its success in 1840, under the common name of *whig*, there were embraced men of all grades of political opinion, from monarchists to agrarians. Jackson's famous proclamation (written by [Edward] Livingston,)[25] had driven from his support & into opposition nearly all of the purest & most worthy & talented of the state-rights men. And though Mr. Calhoun with many others of these, (he seeing fully the selfish designs of his whig cooperators,) drew off from the other & main body of the whigs, still many others, & of as sincere republicans remained to vote for Harrison, & to [216] thus aid in driving Van Buren & his partizans from power. Among these, in our very different positions, & also in different modes of action, were John Tyler & myself. I, in private life, & without political aspirations, & always disdaining party rule, while voting with the whigs in the presidential election (& also generally,) denounced their bad measures, or men, whenever they were exposed to me. I had no confidence in either the principles or the ability of Harrison, before he was elected, & had a much worse opinion soon afterwards—& when his death occurred, in a month after his accession to the presidency, I publickly expressed my gratification at hearing the news, & pronounced that "his dying then was the only important service he had ever rendered to his country in all his long career of public life." This was in view of the succession of

---

[25] The reference is to Jackson's Nullification Proclamation of December, 1832, which was written by Secretary of State Edward Livingston of New York.

Tyler (the Vice President,) whom however I still viewed with some dislike & more suspicion, but from whom still something was to be hoped in maintaining state-rights principles & the checks of the constitution. While still thus doubting & fearing, I immediately wrote the comments which appeared in the "Summary of News" in the "Farmers' Register," vol. IX, p. 253. This, & also my private letter, written later, & which was referred to above, expressed much stronger hopes than I felt. But I aimed, in both, to appeal to his professed principles, & nobler motives of action, & also to flatter him through his vanity, in the hope of possibly inclining the balance on the proper side. Ultimately, he entirely & boldly took the course I advised, (though I do not mean that my advice had any agency in directing him,) in time to save the country, but not in time to save himself. He tried to hold to the [217] whigs, & to have whig cabinet ministers, long enough to forfeit all support from the democratic party—& by sustaining state-rights policy (as far as he could,) & finally rejecting whig counsellors, he not only lost all the support of the whig party, but gained their greatest detestation. He was, & still is, accused by them of being guilty of the blackest treachery, inasmuch as, having been elected Vice-President by the whig party, he, as President, opposed the policy, & all the great measures of the real whig dictator Clay, & whose word was law to the party, & supplied them with principles & measures to contend for. But never was charge more groundless. The whig leaders had selected Tyler as the candidate for Vice-President, not because they supposed he concurred, or was believed by the public to concur, in their then concealed & denied desire to re-establish a U.S. Bank, a high protective tariff &c.—but they chose him precisely because he had always & only been known by the public as the staunch opponent of these measures, & all others of doubtful federal power. He was chosen on this very ground, for the purpose of cheating & betraying the southern states & the state-rights men, by offering to them a candidate unexceptionable, in his known principles, to both. They counted safely on managing the President—& they did so entirely—& the Vice-President is a nullity in the government. But by the death of the President, the Vice-President became President. This contingency, strangely enough, had never been thought of. By its occurrence, the whig leaders were caught in their own trap. They first tried to coax Tyler to act as their tool. It is natural that he should have desired, & tried, to please & conciliate the party which had placed him in power, by every sacrifice which his good [218] & too facile disposition prompted & induced. But he could not be brought (except when deceived,) to sacrifice principle on great questions of policy, or to violate his oath of office to promote party objects. When they saw that he could neither be coaxed nor bullied into obedience, & that, under necessity, he even no longer relied on whig ministers & counsels, the party gave up all hope of using him for their purposes, & denounced him as a traitor to their principles, a deserter, & an apostate, & violator of his *implied* pledges of fidelity—& have since visited him with general & unmitigated hatred. And in these feelings have followed thousands of honest men who were formerly true state-rights republicans, but who, after acting for years, in opposition, with the real whigs, reading whig newspapers, & supporting whig candidates, became so identified with them as to entirely forget their old principles—& they denounce & vilify Tyler because he did not forget them in like manner, & as completely.

John Tyler's intellectual powers have always been more showy than solid, or deep. He is not eminent either as an original thinker, or strong reasoner; nor has he by industrious labor much cultivated his natural quick mental powers. But though without the higher qualities of a debater, or controversialist, he is a very ready & fluent & pleasing speaker & writer—& by his smooth & flowery language, has, with most auditors, more reputation & success, than many far more able & solid reasoners, who have less command of words & figures of speech. He commenced the game of politics, (which is generally but personal partizanship,) & to court popular favor, almost from his boyhood. He began to practice law at 19 years of age—& at [219] 21 he was elected to the legislature of Va—& successively afterwards sent to the House of Representatives, to the State Convention, made Governor of Va, & then Senator of the U.S. & next Vice-President & President—though the last & greatest honor & service were obtained by *chance.* This remarkable success & rapid ascent to eminence was enough to convince a less vain man that he owed his unprecedented success mainly to his own merit—& to his solid, & not to his showy qualities of mind. Mr. Tyler has always been a vain man. But under the circumstances, I think he is less to be condemned for the vanity he exhibits, than to be admired for his plainness, & general absence of all pretension. The cultivation & growth of this foible is the result of his political life—& also some other defects, & especially the blunting of his natural moral sense in cases when stern integrity would forbid the bestowing of favor & reward (in offices) to friends & political partizans. If Mr. Tyler had never been out of private life, & had gone through none of the corrupting temptations of political service & successful ambition, he would have been in every respect as estimable as the good & rare qualities of his kind heart & benevolent disposition have always prompted, & have effected, when not opposing his ambitious views. I, who always opposed him, & thought lightly of him, in all of his early positions, readily award to him the praise of having acquitted himself better in his last & highest office, than in any of the previous & inferior places. And one of his great merits was the absence of envy or jealousy of superior minds, which is so often seen exhibited in men of inferior ability when raised to stations far above their capacity. Mr. Tyler, when unexpectedly raised to the presidency, found in the place of Secretary of State, Daniel Webster, who had been placed there by the leading Whigs [220] to direct & govern the feeble Harrison. There were radical differences of opinion between the new President & his Premier, & probably also something of personal aversion. Policy also, (at least I so thought,) required his speedy discharge. Yet, while Mr. Tyler soon refused to be governed by Webster's views of policy, he retained him in the cabinet as long as he would consent to remain, & used his great intellect to accomplish most important negociations [sic], including the Ashburton treaty with England. Tyler then called to the same post Judge Upshur, another man of powerful intellect, who was scarcely known to the public, but whose superior abilities were well known by Mr. Tyler, as by all his other intimate acquaintances. Upshur only, of those who occupied this high place, was also the former & private friend of Tyler. After his early & deplorable death, by the terrible calamity on board the Princeton war steamer, Mr. Tyler, without any consultation with Calhoun, & without any communication for a long previous time of party alienation, nominated that great statesman, & the appointment was confirmed unanimously by the Senate, before Mr. Tyler wrote to him to inform him of the appointment, & to appeal to his patriotism to assume the duties of Secretary of State. This he did, as nobly as it was offered, & continued & conducted the before commenced negotiation for the annexation of Texas. Yet, from the time of separation of Calhoun & Tyler before the presidential campaign of 1840, there had been not only political but also something of personal alienation, (the consequence of the former) &

the President knew that the great intellect & reputation of Calhoun would serve to award to him the merit of whatever great measures he acted in. Yet he was thus invited to office, & to take charge of & carry through the acquisition of Texas, when the President could have as well effected it (as there was indeed no difficulty as to the government of Texas,) through some minister so obscure as to leave to the President all the honor of this important political event.[26] [221]

Mr. Tyler took me in his carriage to the steam-boat wharf, & remained until I embarked, after 12, M. Reached Beechwood by 3. . . .

*Nov. 16.* A rainy day. Conversing—writing, & reading. Began "Omoo," by Herman Melville.

*Nov. 17. . . .* Finished reading "Omoo." It is an amusing, &, no doubt, a much embellished narrative & description of scenes & incidents in the Pacific, both at sea & on the islands. The author shows great talent. But it is always unsatisfactory to me to read such a mixture of fiction with facts, without any means of knowing the limits of either. Also finished Consuelo. Interesting, though unnatural & absurd in many of the incidents. While (contrary to what I expected from the authoress & her reputation,) the book inculcates the virtue of chastity, still it throughout places the heroine in circumstances in which it was impossible the character, & almost the reality, of that virtue should exist. . . .

*Nov. 18. . . .* The mail brought news of Gen. Walker having again sailed for Central America, to recommence his attempt to conquer & occupy the country. The British forces have retaken Delhi—& the Mormons have taken the initiative in their approaching war of rebellion, by attacking & destroying a government convoy of 78 wagons. . . .[27]

*Nov. 21. . . .* Began to read a collection of Essays from the London Times—admirable articles. One of them a biographical sketch of Lady Hamilton. . . . Another of Ro[bert] Southey.[28] How admirable

---

[26] See Appendix B for additional fragments from Ruffin's conversation with Tyler during this visit.

[27] Conflict between Governor Brigham Young and three federal judges in the Utah Territory caused President Buchanan in May, 1857, to order Colonel Albert Sidney Johnston with 2,500 troops to proceed to Utah and enforce federal authority over the Mormons. The latter responded with guerrilla warfare against Johnston's approaching army.

[28] Eminent British poet and historian. In 1813 Southey (1774–1843) was named poet laureate, preceding Wordsworth and Tennyson in that distinguished position.

he is! Not only for his great talents, & his unexampled literary labors, but still more for his benevolence. According to his means, & his economical habits in regard to his expenditures, few have bestowed more on the wants of others than Southey. Nothing that I hear or read brings to my mind so forcibly my own deficiencies [223] & short-comings in charity, & acts of benevolence, as to learn & consider the immeasurably superior merits, in this respect, of others.

*Nov. 24.* Read & made last corrections to my article on Pines. All 5 now ready for the press (214 pages) if there was any demand for them—which there is not. Began to read Lamartine's History of the French Revolution of 1848. It is truly French, in its manner—melodramatic & romantic—& as unsatisfactory as it ought to be the reverse, as the work of one of the most prominent & ablest actors & leaders in the remarkable events of that exciting epoch. . . .

*Nov. 25.* Set out, in the carriage . . . before 6 o'clock. Took the train at 9, for Richmond. Saw no other members of the Executive Committee until nearly night. At our meeting, at night, only F. G. Ruffin, Knight & Tate, besides myself. There being no quorum, we could not decide on any thing, but discussed & prepared much business. . . .

*Nov. 26.* Part of the day conferring with others about the business in hand, & drawing different papers. Find that the measures of retrenchment which I adopted for the Fair have served to cut off $1500 of the previous amount of [224] expenses. We must now use strong & sustained efforts to induce the city of Richmond to furnish a sufficient Fair Ground—or money to enable the Society to obtain proper accommodations. For this end, we are now working several schemes in private, as well as doing what is designed to appear in our proceedings, to go before the public eye. At night held another meeting, & by the coming of Lewis Harvie & J. B. Newman, had a quorum & went through our business. We unanimously approved the report of the Sub-committee on the Bellona Arsenal property, to reject the offer of sale, on the ground of the dilapidated condition of the buildings, the great expense of necessary repairs, & the other cause of unfitness of the site &c. for an agricultural school. We adopted a preamble & resolutions of my offering, asking of the City Council to refer to the citizens the question of an annual grant from the city treasury to enable the Society to purchase Fair Grounds, & aid to defray the annual expenses of the Fair. Also adopted a petition of my writing, to the legislature, renewing the former petitions, for pecuniary aid, & for relief from the inspection laws, &, in addition, asking relief from the operation of the law of enclosures. After getting through these & also other matters of routine, adjourned. The members present continued in our usual manner of family & friendly conversation, gradually dropping off, until the last of us retired, at a late hour.

*Nov. 27.* At daybreak left the hotel for the steamer—& reached Berkley wharf at 11, where the boat was waiting to convey me to Beechwood. Found there my daughters Elizabeth & Mildred .... [225]

*Nov. 29. Sunday*—At church. Reading Dr. [Elisha] Kane's "Arctic Explorations," at such times as it is not in the hands of my son, who had begun it earlier. In such intervals, read one of Hans Andersen's Story Books, for children.

*Nov. 30.* Began to write an article on the institution of slavery—to furnish me with occupation. . . .

*December 2.* Edmund delivered the remnant of his wheat crop. In all for this farm, 6018 bushels, of which 100 grew on an adjoining piece of rented land. This the largest crop of wheat ever grown on this farm.[29] A wonderful change from my largest crop, which I think did not exceed 2400 bushels—& still more my earliest crops, of 627 average.

*Dec. 3.* . . . At night Edmund returned from Petersburg with Miss Breeden, a young lady who comes to begin service as teacher to his two younger girls. As a stranger, she has made an agreeable impression on us all.

*Dec. 4.* Reading Dr. Kane, & finished, except omitting most of the appendix of accompanying documents, at close of 2nd vol. It is an account of the most painful privations, the longest & most bravely endured, & with the strongest efforts for relief, that I have ever read. If the commander [226] & his crew had been placed in their terrible situation by shipwreck, & by accidental misfortune or disaster had been required to undergo their sufferings & to make their struggles, my commiseration & admiration would have been far greater. But I confess that my mind has not sufficient elevation, or power, to appreciate & to approve the encountering such great dangers & sufferings for such objects either as extending geographical discoveries farther to the north, which never could be of any utility—or searching for Sir John Franklin's crew, in the feeble hope of their being then

---

[29] The average annual wheat crop at Beechwood during the decade 1851–61 was 4,424 bushels. Computed by editor from Edmund Ruffin, Jr., Plantation Diary (Southern Historical Collection).

alive. If that expedition of two ships & 135 men, with four years' provision, & every other necessary supply, & commanded & directed by one of the most experienced & able arctic navigators, had failed, what hope was there for the relief of that expedition, if the men were still living, by a crew of 20 men, scantily provided even for their own wants? The hopes were so feeble, & the risks of thus attempting to find Franklin & to offer relief, were so great, & more especially to one of Dr. Kane's previous experience of Arctic navigation & its difficulties, that his attempt was braving destruction, & was inexcusable for himself, & still more in reference to his drawing to the same sufferings & dangers the sailors who were much less informed of their inevitable sufferings.

*Dec. 5.* Found "The South Vindicated from the Treason & Fanaticism of the Northern Abolitionists," [30] which I read when it first appeared in 1836, & which I again read today—& wonder that so able & admirable a work should have been so little noticed. It is one of the best books, & arguments, of all the able works on slavery that have [227] appeared in this country since the first, [Thomas R.] Dew's Essay on Slavery, which had more effect than any argument I ever knew in changing & giving a new direction to public opinion.

*Dec. 9. . . .* The newspapers brought the first *three* Messages of Gov. Wise to the General Assembly—& the President's Message to Congress. Continue light reading, the second time, in Living Age.

*Dec. 10.* Went with Edmund to Prince George court. My object to get the signed copies of the petition for a legal sanction to a common enclosure, so as to get relief from the general fence law, so far as contiguous landowners may choose. I started this practice, by voluntary arrangement 30 years ago. It has extended, still upon voluntary agreement only, until three large neighborhoods are severally under common & single surrounding fences, & all their & nearly all other residents in favor of the general law of enclosures being repealed, at least as to them. I felt great interest in aiding this reform here, believing that it would best lead to as general extension of the relief as would be wanted & desirable. Therefore I urged the residents to act—I wrote the petition last summer, & lately a form of the bill for the consideration of the legislature—& went this day to close the business to be done here, & to send the papers to the representa-

---

[30] Written by William Drayton (1776-1846), a former four-term congressman from South Carolina. A strong unionist, Drayton opposed nullification and in 1833 moved to Philadelphia, where he later published this proslavery tract.

tive of the county. But though almost every person is anxious for the measure, & two copies of the petition had been out for months, not half the names were down of even the persons in the space to be first embraced. Upon finding this dilatory & careless neglect, I stopped my action, & will wait for those immediately & personally interested to take some trouble & do their part in this matter. . . . Read the pamphlet publication of the recent travels & discoveries of Livingstone, [229] the bold & adventurous & successful traveller, & devoted Christian missionary, in Southern Africa. Though he found the natives in a very low state of savage barbarism & ignorance, they seemed generally to be remarkable for their good & kind disposition, & for hospitable & benevolent conduct to him. He was generally received with welcome, & by numerous persons with hospitality, love & veneration. Yet in the years of his extensive travels, & missionary labors so far as then practicable, he does not report the making of a single convert to Christianity! If any such benefit was effected, it is not mentioned—& therefore it may be inferred that there was none. If so, & in regard to such subjects & opportunities, does it not offer the strongest proof yet presented of the truth that through slavery by Christian masters only can Christianity be taught to African savages —or rather that the children of such slaves, as other children in Christian communities, will have an equal chance to grow up under Christian belief & improvement in morals?

*Dec. 13.* Reading light articles in the last volumes of Living Age. Wrote the bill for the desired change of fence law.

*Dec. 15.* Went to a sale at High Peak, & there obtained more signatures to the petition—& hastened to City Point, & took the steamer for Richmond. Went to the Exchange Hotel. Saw & conversed with sundry members of the legislature, on the petition from Prince George—& also the petition of the Ex. Com. which had before been presented, & a bill is in progress. However, for the latter, I entertain but little hope.

*Dec. 16.* Saw the delegate & senator from Prince George, & placed the petition & bill in their hands. Endeavoring to push on the objects & business of the Ag. Society, both with the legislature & the city council. Met with some old friends who are members of the legislature.

*Dec. 17.* A discussion arose in the House of Delegates about the election of state printer, which I hope will lead to an examination & exposure of the abuses of the system, & the imposition on the public

—& that it will result in reducing the exorbitant pay of the incumbent, Wm. Ritchie, & perhaps result in displacing him. The election, which had been appointed for this day, is postponed, & a committee of investigation will be called for. . . . Saw the Dec. No. of De Bow's Review, containing the [231] conclusion of my article on the dissolution of the union.

*Dec. 18.* John Seddon obtained the committee of investigation. By my knowledge of the business & of the tricks of the trade, I am able to give him useful information of the impostory heretofore practised in the public printing. The expense may certainly be reduced by 25 percent, if not considerably more. I have hopes of having some influence on this business. . . . In the room of John Seddon (next to mine) met with his elder brother James,[31] Lewis Harvie, Fred. Coleman, & others—a pleasant conversation on matters before the legislature. General condemnation of Gov. Wise. It is believed that he has gone far to destroy his popularity by his recent course, directed by his unscrupulous ambition & inordinate vanity & self-conceit.

*Dec. 19.* At 10 A.M. Left Richmond . . . to Marlbourne. . . . Just before leaving Richmond, I had received, by Express, a pamphlet reprint of my disunion views, as they had appeared in De Bow's Review—together with the postscript addition, in which the *manner* of secession was pointed out, & urged. Read it over, to see that no mistakes had been made in the reprint.

*Dec. 21.* Returned to Richmond. Mailed a number of copies [232] of my pamphlet, to sundry public men of the slave-holding states, including all the governors.—I had returned here today, by appointment to meet (with our sub-committee,) the City Council, on the affairs of the Society—where we attended at 4 P.M. But it was raining, & no meeting was held.—Conversing with members of the legislature, & others—& afterwards writing & correcting until past 11, before going to bed.

*Dec. 22.* . . . Appeared before a committee of the Senate, to which had been referred the petition from Prince George, & the bill, & got the latter reported, without any objection. At 7 P.M. again went before the City Council, which held a meeting, & Crenshaw & I stated the case for the Society—but the subject was postponed to the next meeting of the Council in January.

---

[31] The better known of the two brothers, James Alexander Seddon (1815–80) served two terms in Congress before his retirement in 1851. During the Civil War he was Confederate secretary of war from 1862 to 1865.

*Dec. 23.* Left Richmond with my granddaughter Nanny. In Petersburg, the carriage, with Mildred met us—where some business in shopping, & more the pleasure of the driver, detained us more than three hours. . . . Left before 3 P.M., & reached Beechwood after dark. Of course, a joyful return of Nanny, & meeting with her family. All regret the absence of Thomas who is at school in Albemarle, & had no vacation.

*Dec. 24.* Read the long minority report to the legislature of South Carolina, adverse to the re-opening of the African slave trade. It is by J. J. Pettigrew,[32] who alone, in a committee of seven, dissented from the approval & recommendation of reopening the trade. The resolutions of the committee however were not adopted by [233] the legislature, probably because it would have been but a barren expression of approval of what cannot pos[s]ibly be effected. Mr. Pettigrew's report is an able argument—& impresses on me sundry great evils of the renewal, to which before I had not given due weight. Continue my copying & making additions to my writing. Reading for the second, & in part the third time, particular articles of Sydney Smith's miscellaneous writings, which first appeared in the Edinburgh Review.[33]

*Dec. 25.* The younger children found their Christmas presents on their early rising, & were delighted, & noisy. Snowing & raining, & dismal weather—of course none of us could go to church. Writing & copying, & Sydney Smith. The weather last night & this forenoon prevented our man Titus, who has a wife here, arriving from Marlbourne until this afternoon. He brought, from Elizabeth, more Christmas presents for all the young children, & letters. . . .

*Dec. 27.* Sunday. At church. The roads bad & sloppy, & but a small congregation. Afternoon, Mr. Johnson came & preached to the negroes at Beechwood, & afterwards staid until 8 P.M.—Reading some parts of Sydney Smith's miscellaneous writings, & articles in Living Age—old numbers.

---

[32] James Johnston Pettigrew ( 1828–63 ) was a brother of William and Charles Pettigrew, whom the diarist had visited in North Carolina the previous spring. After occupying a position at the United States Naval Observatory in Washington for three years, Pettigrew moved to Charleston in 1850 and entered the practice of law. During the war he rose to the rank of brigadier general in the Confederate army and was mortally wounded in the retreat from Gettysburg.

[33] Sydney Smith ( 1771–1845 ), canon of St. Paul's, was instrumental in establishing the *Edinburgh Review* in 1802 and, during the next twenty-five years, contributed eighty articles to that periodical.

*Dec. 30....* The mail brought the important news that the commander of the U.S. vessel of war Wabash, acting in concert with two English vessels of war, had compelled Walker to surrender his forces & his munitions &c. & that Walker has reached New York, as a prisoner on parole. This act of our government (or naval officer) in attacking Walker on foreign soil, & especially in cooperation with a British force, I think will raise a burst of indignation through the southern states. This is certainly going far beyond all the obligations of neutrality.... The United States troops sent to put down Brigham Young's rebellion have got within 113 miles of the Mormon capital; & there I fear they will remain until their animals are all destroyed by cold, & then will be too weak to attack. In November the mules were dying with the excessive cold. From the encampment to Salt Lake city the approach is only through a narrow defile, which may be defended by a few men against a host of invaders.—

*Dec. 31.* Added 7 more pages to my writing, & which I think will complete it—making 64 pages in all.—Reading last Nos. of Living Age—looking over (the second reading) of Bledsoe's "Liberty & Slavery." With all its reputation I think this defence of slavery much inferior to some of the earlier works of much less pretension.

# January–June

ॐ

# 1858

*January 2.* . . . The President has disavowed the capture of Walker
& his troops. I think that still he will be in a tight place. It will be a
difficult job to repair the wrong & injury now confessed to have been
done in this case, in violating the neutral rights of the territory of
Nicaragua. Walker may justly claim either to be replaced in his position by this government—which would be another invasion of the
territorial rights of Nicaragua—or pecuniary damages so great, that
the payment will enable him to make another attempt with better
means than before.

*Jan. 4.* Set out, with Mildred & Nanny for Richmond, by Petersburg. We reached the latter by 1 P.M. & had to stay to 6, when the
train started. . . . When we got to Richmond, took a hack to Mr.
Minnegerode's, where Nanny boards, & then returned to the
Exchange Hotel. . . .

*Jan. 5.* . . . As I counted on, Walker's arrest has created a great sensation, & general condemnation. Resolutions of condemnation have
been presented in both branches of the Va. legislature. I am sorry
for it—as the discussion will consume more time than can be spared.
If a mere vote could be taken, without a single speech, it would be
well—as there is no doubt of the large majority being for disapproving. It seems that the dissatisfaction of southern men with Buchanan's administration is extending & deepening, & the pretence of

approval is but a thin disguise which will soon be thrown off. The Kansas affairs [237] make the greatest difficulty. The anti-slavery party there, doubtless much the strongest, in their strange procedure, generally refused to vote, either in electing the convention to form a state constitution, or on the pro-slavery feature adopted by the convention, & submitted for rejection or ratification, to the people. Consequently, a pro-slavery constitution has been made—& formally, application will be made to Congress to admit Kansas as a slave-holding state.[1] Even if the northern members allow this to pass, it will be an apparent gain & victory to the south, but in a bad cause, & the slavery feature will be certainly struck out of the constitution within a year after Kansas is a state. Besides, by adhering to & sustaining the slave-constitution of Kansas, which is universally admitted not to express the will of the people, the south will appear to support what is wrong, for selfish ends. Already civil war seems beginning in Kansas, & some men have been killed in a fight between the government force & anti-slave resisters of law.—The carriage, with Mr. Sayre, came up early . . . but his business detained us to 2.30 P.M. before we (with Mildred) set out for Marlbourne, where we arrived before night.—Learned in Richmond that my fence bill had passed the Senate, without any opposition. I think it will also pass the House of Delegates.—I am 64 years old this day.

*Jan. 6.* . . . Began to read "Hansford," but after 70 pages, gave it up. This is the fourth new Virginia novel that I have attempted to read within the last few years, & neither of which I could finish. Yet all have been greatly praised. The others were "Alone," "The [238] Hidden Path," and "The Virginia Connections." It is said that of "Alone" several editions, & even one or more translations, have been published in Europe. If so, it shows that there is more bad taste there than here—as there is no patriotic illusion to prevent Europeans seeing the faults of an American book. Began to read [William M.] Thackeray's "Newcomes."

*Jan. 8.* Went to Richmond, with Mildred, who will make a visit for a few days . . . & attend Thalberg's concert.[2] I attended the annual meeting of the Richmond & York river Railroad, in which I have a

---

[1] The diarist, of course, refers here to the controversial Lecompton Constitution. Ruffin's attitude toward that tricky document is contrary to what one might expect from a southern fire-eater.

[2] The world-famous Austrian pianist and composer Sigismond Thalberg was touring the United States at this time in company with the Belgian violinist Henri Vieuxtemps.

dead investment of $500 subscription. Endeavored to stop one of the abuses & useless expenses, but in vain. I shall take no more trouble about this hopeless concern. . . . I went to the concert, to hear Thalberg on the piano, & Vieuxtemps on the violin, both renowned performers. Their *execution* was indeed wonderful—exceeding my expectations. But great as was their ability to perform the best, there was no *music* (or but little,) to my ear. The performance of these celebrated musicians was all in flourishes to show off their wonderful skill, or perhaps in pieces which none but highly cultivated musical taste could appreciate. Though I am very fond [239] of music, & probably understand more of it than one in a hundred of men in this country, I would have found more pleasure in hearing simple airs correctly & plainly played or a band, or harmonised songs, by a few good voices, than to hear this scientific music (if it is such) even if of the highest order, & executed by any number of Thalbergs & Vieuxtemps. I do not think that I will ever attend another performance of first rate & world-renowned musicians. And with the great majority of the crowded audience, even though most of them would affect to be greatly pleased, the thing was worse than with me. One half of those who were present would have more enjoyed the hearing an ordinary fiddler playing common reels, & Yankee Doodle, to the performance of this night. It is as strange as it is annoying to persons who, like myself, love good music, but without much knowledge, that good musicians will confine their performances to pieces, which not one in fifty of their hearers can appreciate, & can derive no pleasure from. I would by no means have them pander to bad taste, & ignorance, by playing Yankee Doodle & other bad music, because popular. But there are thousands of beautiful & simple airs, & simple parts of other music, which would give pleasure to the least cultivated taste, & by hearing which natural music taste would be gradually taught to understand & appreciate the compositions which at first are like Greek read to the multitude.

*Jan. 9*. . . . Got a copy of Dew's "Essay on Slavery," & read [240] it for the third time—though I have not read it before for some 20 years. This, the earliest modern work that justified & defended the institution of slavery, is also the best that has yet appeared. Yet there have been many & able followers & supporters of the same views.

*Jan. 10*. Sunday. Glanced over & partly read the last year's numbers of the "African Repository," which is the organ of the Colonization Society—my object to find statements that would show, by statistics, the true condition of the colony of Liberia. . . .

*Jan. 11.* . . . Afternoon, attended the meeting of the City Council, & heard the application of the Ag. Society discussed & refused. The council not only has refused to do anything more for the accommodation of the Society's Fairs, but refuses to take the vote of the city on the question. We will now have no other resource but to move the Fair, if any other suitable place will do more for the object.—A letter from the prolific pen of Gov. Wise to the New York Tammany Society appeared in this morning's papers. In it he recommends the adoption by Congress of the lately enacted Kansas constitution, (which allows slavery,) & the admission of Kansas as a state, on the condition that the constitution shall first be submitted to the people for ratification. This is one of his excellency's nets set to catch northern favor & votes, to elect him to the Presidency. This letter put in a flame [241] all his democratic & silent opponents in the legislature, & assumed ground that not one of [his] most devoted friends would dare to maintain. A meeting (or caucus) of the democratic members of the legislature (who constitute an overwhelming majority) was called, & met at 7 P.M. Sundry resolutions were offered, of which the only difference was that some were supposed to reflect on the governor's recent action, while others merely expressed the approval of the contrary course. One set of the latter description was adopted, almost unanimously. This, I hope, will prevent Wise appearing to speak the sentiments of Virginia, & so giving ground & strength to the abolition party of the north.

*Jan. 12.* . . . Gen. Walker the great *flibustier* & *soi-disant* President of Nicaragua, arrived yesterday, on his way southward from Washington, & stopped in Richmond. Today he visited the Capitol, & (as I hear) was stared at, & introductions to him sought, by great numbers. I did not see him—but heard that he appeared diffident, & even embarrassed.—All four of the political papers today out on Gov. Wise's letter—even his own dirty tool, the Enquirer, condemning it, though with an accompaniment of panegyric on other grounds. The resolutions which were adopted last night in caucus, were today passed in the House of Delegates, on ayes & Nays, with only two dissenting votes. They were laid on the table in the Senate, to be acted on tomorrow. [242]

*Jan. 13.* The resolutions passed the Senate by a very large majority, & the opposers did not vote. This unanimity in both houses will show that the governor has not spoken the opinion of the State. This rebuke, from his heretofore friends & followers, will be a strong blow to him.—At night again attended the Committee on Printing, at Seddon's request, to answer two questions of his as to my opinion of the present prices. I had said that the work could be contracted for, & be as well done, at prices reduced by 25 percent, & that if necessary, I would bid that price, & take it, & undertake the work, if permitted. It would be one of the last things I would wish to go into such business at that (though a sufficient) price. But I knew I would incur no risk of keeping it, because three competent printers had severally offered to take it as low. But Seddon wished me to make the statement that I would take it at that price, because he thought my name & position would settle the question. But when I was called to testify, & had been sworn, one of the several devoted friends of the incumbent (& who act on the committee as if they were his hired attorneys or agents,) objected to my evidence, on the ground that I was a candidate for the office. This objection was sustained by the majority, & I had no opportunity to say a word to explain, or even deny the ground assumed. After leaving, I wrote such answers as I should have given under oath to the two questions, [243] & also a separate protest against the reasons of the Committee, for excluding my evidence, & denying that I was in any sense a candidate for the office of Public Printer, or that I wanted the work, if to be given in contract —but stating also that I would be willing to bid for it, at the reduction of price stated. These papers were begun so late, that it was nearly 1 o'clock before they were done, & left with Seddon, to use at his discretion. . . .

*Jan. 14.* At 6.45 A.M. left, on the train for Washington, & partly by steamer. Arrived at Brown's Hotel by 3 P.M. In the afternoon, & among the crowd in the hall of the hotel, saw sundry of my acquaintance—among them, [M. R. H.] Garnett, Wm. Smith,[3] [Charles J.] Faulkner, members of Congress from Va, Th. Ruffin, member from N.C. & Elwood Fisher. Also heard that Gov. Hammond was here, with his family, & called on them, & at a later time was with him & other gentlemen his visitors, (among them Mr. Wray,) until I retired to my room. . . . The (so-called) "United States Agricultural Society" is in session here, & will meet again tomorrow—discussing *sorgho sucré* &c. I will attend as a spectator & auditor only.

---

[3] In addition to his service in Congress, Smith also occupied the office of governor of Virginia on two occasions—from 1846 to 1849, and again in 1864.

*Jan. 15.* Attended the meeting of the U.S. Agr. Soc. I was immediately introduced by the new president Gen. Tilghman of Md. to the late president, M. P. Wilder, & Mr. French, & Mr. Brooks of Massachusetts, & welcomed by them so cordially & in so complimentary a manner, that I felt a little conscience-struck [244] for my general dislike to all Yankees. The business was mainly a long speech from Mr. Wray, on his "imphee." I left at 2 P.M. & heard afterwards that the Society adjourned *sine die.* I was invited by the President to deliver the valedictory address—but excused myself. . . . Visited Thos. Ruffin (of N.C.) & again Gov. Hammond. Indeed, by the kind invitation of the latter, I drop in at any time, as if at home, to read his newspapers, & converse, if he is disengaged.

*Jan. 16.* Called on acquaintances, but found none at home, except W. O. Goode, & J. D. B. De Bow. By accident, I have met with Gov. [William] Smith, M. R. H. Garnett & J[ohn] Letcher[4] of Va., [Lawrence O.] Branch & [Thomas L.] Clingman[5] of N.C. & Lieut. Maury.

*Jan. 18.* Called on De Bow by appointment, & at last had a settlement of his debt to me. Thence visited & saw A. Dudley Mann. He is as hopeful as ever of the great steamer, Leviathan, though the many ineffectual attempts to launch it made me fearful of failure. Thence to the Capitol. In the gallery of the House of Representatives (the new chamber) I could hear but badly, & the business was of no interest. The Senate gallery full & impossible to enter. I wish that Gov. Hammond, or R. M. T. Hunter, (who returned my call today, & left his card,) had thought to offer me entrance into the Senate Chamber.—In the office of the Librarian of Congress, I saw & was introduced to Mr. Stevens, a[n] agent to collect & buy books in America for the British Museum. I was surprised to learn [245] the extent of the collections, embracing every pamphlet, & not only every book, but every edition of each book. Mr. S. had a thick octavo volume, which was merely a descriptive catalogue of the American publications already in the library of the British Museum. He looked for my name, & found under it the "Essay on Calcareous Manures." But on my remarking that it was an early edition, & that five had been published, he expressed a wish to buy all, & took such directions as I gave to obtain them, & the Farmers' Register. I gave him some pam-

---

[4] At this time a member of the House of Representatives, Letcher succeeded Wise as governor of Virginia in 1860.

[5] Clingman (1812–97), currently serving his seventh term in the House, was soon after elected to the United States Senate.

phlets of mine, & furnished the names of some of the best books of Virginia, which were not on his list.

*Jan. 19.* Called on Gov. Hammond at his private house, which he occupied yesterday. . . . Went to the Capitol. Nothing of interest before either house. Learned that more stringent regulations had been adopted, since my last visit here, to prevent private persons being admitted to both houses, by invitation of members—which is very well, as great abuses had thereby crept in.—At night, attended an annual meeting of the Colonization Society. The report had been read before my entrance—but I heard most of the speech of the General Agent, & addresses from Bowen, the Missionary in Africa, & the Revd. Mr. Seys, a recent agent in Liberia. In the speech of the latter there was much that (though it might be literally true,) was calculated to delude—& seemed especially designed for the hearing of negroes, & to persuade them of the great advantages [246] of emigrating to Liberia. No doubt there had been especial anxiety to have an audience of the very large class of free negroes, that this city contains. But, in the gallery, where they sat, I only could see two negro men, & about a dozen women.

*Jan. 20.* This morning I accidentally met the Rev. Philip Slaughter, the General Agent of the Va. Colonization Society, & had a long conversation with him.[6] I have long known him slightly—& we both spoke much more freely than could have been expected from our slight acquaintance. But though we are entirely opposed as to the utility of the Col. Soc., he & I are alike in being frank, out-spoken, & earnest men. We went through our arguments in perfect good temper. He expressed surprise at seeing me at the meeting last night. I answered that I went to get information, & that I wished to learn the whole truth about the colony of Liberia. He agreed with me in several of my views & objections. He deems the highest value of the colony is as a means for establishing & spreading the Christian religion in Africa. I asked him if I heard rightly the Rev. Seys last night, (a recent missionary & agent in Liberia,) state that the mortality of all the colored colonists had been only 5 percent. This was also Mr. Slaughter's understanding of Mr. Seys' statement. And yet the colored emigrants, in 40 years, have been between 8 & 9,000, & they & their descendants now are less than 10,000—having scarcely in-

---

[6] A native of Culpeper County, Slaughter (1808–90) was an Episcopal clergyman and, during the period 1850–55, edited the *Virginia Colonizationist* in Richmond.

creased at all. If they had all remained in lower Virginia, & as slaves, they [247] would certainly have been tripled in number in this time —the emigration having been going on for 40 years.—Called on Lieut. Maury, & conversed with him for an hour. He is one of the most pleasant companions, & full of general information, even apart from his especial scientific pursuits.—Thence to the Capitol, where I could not hear anything in the Senate, & in the other House, there was nothing worth hearing. Went to see Mr. Mann, & there saw Mr. Austin, the Collector of Boston, who is a rare case of a pro-slavery man in New England. After tea, at Gov. Hammond's. . . .

*Jan. 21.* Wrote a letter, containing a number of queries addressed to Mr. Slaughter, on his invitation, & his promise to answer any that I would ask of him. . . . At the capitol, & for the first time was able to squeeze into the Senate gallery, & had a good opportunity to see & hear. But there was nothing of interest—& Mr. [James R.] Doolittle[7] delivered a long speech which finally drove me away, & had previously emptied half the chairs of the Senators. Then to the House gallery until the adjournment. Our senator Hunter, seeing me in the gallery, sent a note to me stating that he had called twice at my lodgings, & [248] inviting me to dine with him on Saturday—which I promised.—Afternoon & at night, visited A. Dudley Mann, Gov. Hammond, & others.—Had bought & have read a new & much praised volume on Slavery, "Modern Reform Examined," by the Rev. J[oseph] C. Stiles. I am disappointed in it as a general view of the subject, though it may be a very good & conclusive admonition, or series of sermons, addressed, as it seems to be, to the author's northern Presbyterian brethren.

*Jan. 22.* At the capitol, & still nothing of interest in the proceedings. The recently adopted constitution of Kansas has been expected daily, & when it arrives & is under consideration, on the question of admitting Kansas as a state, there will be a violent struggle. And yet there is nothing in this corrupt & rotten issue to excite zeal. By the secret connivance of both Pierce & Buchanan, (as I believe,) & with the combined action of the northern abolitionists (in sending in emigrants & aid,) there is a decided anti-slavery majority—& yet, by rascality of both parties, a constitution admitting slavery has been adopted. The stronger abolition party permitted this (by refusing to vote at the polls,) for the purpose of keeping up the general agita-

---

[7] Republican senator from Wisconsin, 1857–69.

tion, & by it hoping to influence the next presidential election. By this course of the abolitionists, & with the further aid of illegal votes, & great fraud, the weaker pro-slavery party have made the constitution, & it will come before Congress with the forms of law & outward appearance of right. The southern men will all vote for the admission of Kansas under this constitution, (unless Gov. Wise [249] will have any followers,) as ought to be done. For if there has been even so much fraudulent voting, Congress is not the power to settle that difficulty. But the northern democrats will use these alleged frauds as excuse to vote against the admission of the state. And whether now admitted under this pro-slavery constitution, or refused, another convention will be speedily called, & another constitution enacted which will prohibit slavery. So that even if the south conquers in Congress, it will be defeated soon after.—Visited A[lexander] H. Stephens of Ga, & at his room saw Senator Toombs, & had a pleasant conversation with both. At Gov. Hammond's saw our Senator [James M.] Mason—& afterwards, at the room of Mr. Letcher, found Senator Hunter, & with the two commenced on political affairs. Both Mason & Hunter (different from nearly all of the other southern members,) fear that there will be danger of being defeated on the admission of Kansas, by the northern democrats generally voting against it. It seems generally believed here that by the late remarkable moves of Douglas & Wise, that these two distinguished demagogues, of immeasurable & unscrupulous ambition, have over-reached their objects, & effectually destroyed themselves for their hopes of the presidency. Heard from Mr. Hunter some interesting statements in regard to the population & condition of Dominica, or the larger former Spanish portion of the island of Hispaniola. The inhabitants, (as I knew,) are generally of mixed blood, but few as the [250] pure whites are, they are at the head of public affairs, & either directly, or by influence govern the whole community. And this community (or republic) by virtue of this direction of white rulers, & the population generally being nearly white, has been able to resist & repel the hostility of the much more numerous black population of Hayti. Mr. Hunter told me that when Mr. Calhoun was Secretary of State, & the Dominicans were in great danger from the Haytiens, he used the secret service fund to supply arms to the former, & enabled them to repel their more barbarous invaders. This government may easily avail itself of the permanent hostility of the two populations, & the weakness of the Dominicans, to aid the latter, get footing on their territory, & ultimately annex that larger portion of the island. But in that case, there would be great difficulty in fixing the condition of the mixed population. They are too near to being white to be denied the equal rights of citizens—& yet it would not do to contaminate the purity of blood of Caucasian settlers, by intermarrying with the mixed blood. If they could be kept from mixing, the great accession of new white settlers would almost obliterate the mixed race—& it would gradually diminish, or be absorbed, & disappear. This acquisition would soon & necessarily lead to the conquest of Hayti. And all the mass of the population, perfectly destitute of property, & ignorant, & virtually slaves to government, would be improved in condition by being reduced [251] to their former condition of individual slavery, to white masters. All the blacks & mulattoes, of higher grade, in property, position, or education, might be allowed to emigrate. I should state that these are *my* views & speculations.—Have seen in a Richmond paper that fence bill has passed both houses, & is now the law of the land. This will be the commencement of a reform & revolution in this heretofore fixed policy of Va, & which, by other means, I have been laboring to produce, for 20 years. Though this is but, so far, a small operation, yet the law is so framed as to permit its indefinite extension, even if radiating but from the first point in Prince George. But what I have obtained for those who desire the benefit of the change of law, in that locality, cannot be denied to any future petitioners from any other locality. And soon there will be many other such beginning associations, which will spread until they will meet each other, & embrace more than half of lower & middle Virginia. In effecting this first measure, silently & quietly, & without exciting the least opposition, I have effected almost as great a benefit for the agricultural interests of Virginia, as I had before rendered in any other way.

*Jan. 23.* Called on Mrs. Senator [Clement C.] Clay (of Ala.); & on Goode, where I found Garnett, & had a conversation on political affairs. Dined by invitation with Senator Hunter & his colleague Mason, & [Thomas S.] Bocock of the H. of Rep. Much conversation on public matters of present interest. Afterwards saw Gov. & Mrs. Hammond, & Letcher.—The bronze equestrian statue of Washington has been raised & fixed on the [252] pedestal in Richmond. So by my visit here, I have missed witnessing the difficult & interesting operation of raising the statue to its place.

*Jan. 24.* Returned to Richmond, to the Exchange Hotel. . . . Called on Gov. [David S.] Reid, U.S. Senator from N.C.[8] who has been ill here, but now better.... Could not see Seddon until late—& after receiving my papers (which I had before written) & also information from him, I was reading, correcting & copying them until nearly 1 o'clock, before I went to bed. The Committee on Public Printing is to report tomorrow, & my papers will be made use of by Seddon in his minority report, & speech....

*Jan. 25.* Dropped in at the Agrl. Office, & saw sundry friends either there or elsewhere. At the Capitol, for a short time, & heard nothing of interest. For the last few days the most interesting subject [253] with everybody, is the fight which took place between the son of Gov. Wise,[9] & [Robert] Ridgway, the editor of the Whig, & the subsequent reports of the parties, published in the newspapers.... Went to the Capitol square, where there were many persons looking at the equestrian statue, & among them I saw Gov. Wise, whom I saluted, & had some conversation concerning the monument, which I criticized as severely as I think the plan deserves....

*Jan. 26.* ... By dinner, my fellow-members of the Executive Committee [254] began to arrive, to attend the meeting, for which I was waiting. At 8 P.M. our session began, & continued to past 11. Went to bed a little before 12.

*Jan. 27.* ... The weather warm enough for the early part of May, today. The whole winter has been remarkably warm. In November, there was some severely cold weather. But since, there has been scarcely any freezing, & generally the weather very warm for the season, & unprecedented in continuing warm so long.—At 10 A.M. the Committee in session again, to afternoon, when it adjourned. The main business done is the resolution to hold the next Fair at some other town, if any will offer us any greater inducement than Richmond does—or its Common Council—which is almost nothing. A sub-committee, to which I was added, is instructed to communicate with Petersburg, Norfolk, & Alexandria....

*Jan. 28.* Mr. Sayre's carriage came for me, by previous appointment, but waiting for some of his business to be done, I did not leave

---

[8] After serving two terms in the House of Representatives, David Settle Reid (1813–91) was elected governor of North Carolina in 1850 and again in 1852. Two years later, he won a seat in the United States Senate, where he remained until 1859.

[9] The governor's eldest son, O. Jennings Wise, at this time on the staff of the Richmond *Enquirer*.

until 3 P.M. Had before begun, & continue to read H[enry] C. Carey's book on "The Slave Trade &c.," which is, in the beginning at least, of very different tone & purport from what I would have anticipated from the author.[10] On reaching home found my daughters & Mr. Sayre well. Owing to the great difficulties & delays caused by the want of houses, the waiting on & assisting sawyers & carpenters, & also the very large crop, the corn is not yet housed, by more than a [255] week's work. Mr. Sayre now thinks it will exceed his earlier estimate of 10,000 bushels, considerably. . . .

While in Richmond, I wrote a hasty piece of suggestions & hints to the Legislature on some of the existing evils, requiring new legislation, in regard to emancipation of slaves by bequest, the Colonization Society, & its aid by the state, & the nuisance of vicious & idle free negroes. It appeared in today's paper. While in Washington, (as well as previously by mail,) I made a large distribution of my pamphlet "Consequences of Abolition Agitation," urging the separation of the Union, & recommending a manner of procedure. I had directed Mr. De Bow to have reprinted, at my own expense, 500 copies of this article in separate pamphlet form, for my gratuitous distribution. By his forgetting, this was first reduced to an impression of 250 copies—& next half of these were rendered useless by the Appendix being omitted by mistake. So I obtained only about 125 perfect copies, which, by the high charges caused or permitted by De Bow's carelessness, cost me very nearly 25 cents per copy, & for gratuitous distribution.

*Jan. 30.* Except taking a walk, nearly all day reading Carey's "Slave Trade, Domestic & Foreign," which I finished at night. . . . The work is not what its title would indicate, & what I desired to read as the opinions of an intelligent northerner, [257] whom I only knew as a thorough disciple of the protection school, & whom I supposed to be also as thorough in his hostility to negro slavery, & that this would be the subject of his book. On the contrary, it is but slightly & incidentally treated. The greater part of the book is a collection of numerous facts & proofs of the iniquity of the commercial & colonial policy of England, & the misery thereby produced generally, & especially on her own poor, & more on Ireland & Scotland, & the evils to her former & present colonies. I never saw or heard of

---

[10] Henry Charles Carey (1793–1879) was a well-known Philadelphia publisher and economist. In this book, published in 1853, he advocated manufactures for the South.

this work, ( published in 1853,) until I accidentally saw it in the State Library a few days ago. Opposed as I am to Mr. Carey in his views of negro slavery, & of the protective system & free trade, there are points in which we agree, as premises, but would use to lead to opposite conclusions. He extends his definition of slavery as far as I have done, & would cover all that I call class-slavery, or the bondage of labor to capital. He furnishes numerous proofs of the cruel & horrible effects of England in producing & maintaining the worst kinds of slavery, & especially in India, while government & people hypocritically are crying out aloud against the comparatively humane & beneficial negro slavery. Mr. Carey's great argument for protecting manufactures in the United States, is the gain to be thereby produced in establishing a "home market" for agriculture, in bringing the manufacturer to be the neighbor & customer of the farmer. He denounces the English policy for forbidding this result in all her dependencies, & striving effectually to make England one & the only great work-shop, to supply with manufactures all her colonies [258] & dependencies, & to permit them only to produce agricultural commodities, to be sent to England in exchange for her manufactures. This denunciation is just, because England forcibly prevents the establishment of beneficial manufactories, which would otherwise grow & sustain themselves. Even Lord Chatham (the great friend of America, to whom the gratitude of the then colony of South Carolina erected a statue,) declared that he would not permit the colonies to "manufacture even a hobnail." But, because it would be beneficial for manufacturing industry naturally to grow up by the side of agricultural, for their mutual benefit, & it was & is monstrous tyranny in England to forbid it, it is far from being a legitimate consequence that the U.S. government should *compel* the establishment of manufactures that cannot sustain themselves, by the artificial encouragement of indirect legal bounties, given by taxing agriculture. If southern agriculture could have in its midst established factories, & villages & cities, & all the benefits of this neighborhood, it would at least vary the question. But no matter how high the protection afforded by laws, the northern states are so much better suited for manufactures, that nearly all would be established there, & while the southern states would pay nearly all their cost, they would derive no more benefit from the home market in the northern states, than if in England. If the argument is good for anything, it will prove that Virginia, & every other state should thus protect its own manufactures, against the competition of the northern states, as much as against [259] England. As it has been, & is, the southern states are taxed by protecting duties to build up factories in the north, & to provide a home market beneficial (by vicinity) to northern agriculture only. No such legal protection can be given to southern manufactures, while under the same general government with the northern states. If the argument for protecting manufactures, & establishing a home market is sound, it is another & a very strong argument for a dissolution of the union—as then only can the southern states protect their own manufactures by discriminating duties on northern as well as European fabrics.—Began to read the recently published large work of Livingstone the missionary, "Travels & Researches in South Africa."

*February 3.* . . . Finished reading Livingstone's "Missionary Travels & Researches in Africa," 728 pages 8 vo. The author must have been a most pious & devoted Christian, & a brave man, who willingly incurred the greatest risks & sufferings, to forward his great objects. And yet, his want of success is the most striking evidence known, of the inutility of attempting to [260] make Christians of savage & free heathens. The dispositions & manners of these savages in all the interior of Africa seem to be mild, amiable, & affectionate. The missionary gained their respect, admiration, & love. He had every facility, & he lost no opportunity to offer to them religious instruction. He was heard at least respectfully, always, & with ready acquiescence in his doctrines. Though very superstitious, they had no previous system of religion that would obstruct their reception of Christianity. Yet in his four years of travel & of effort, it does not appear that the missionary made a single convert, or even made any durable & useful impressions on the mind of any one heathen hearer. . . . At night, dipped into, & looked through "The Christian Doctrine of Slavery," by the Rev. Geo[rge D.] Armstrong, a northern man, who has for 20 years resided in Virginia. This little book, (published in 1857) I have no doubt is a good one for its object—but as I had no doubt on that point, I found nothing interesting in the argument. Glanced over the latest Agricultural Report, from the Patent Office (all of them worthless—) & after my daughters had gone to bed, returned to reading "The Newcomes," which I had begun some months ago, & had to suspend when leaving home. . . .

*Feb. 5.* . . . Finished "The Newcomes." Very interesting—but it is not a romance—& scarcely a narrative (until near to the end—) but is a series of most biting satires. The satire is excellent, & well expressed—but it is too much of it to be continued through nearly an octavo volume of small print. But the latter part is very different—it is narrative of much interest, & with very pathetic scenes, which I did not expect to be presented by Thackeray. . . . Mr. Sayre returned from Westmoreland this afternoon. He has succeeded in selling the remainder of his land & property there, but has not been able to collect any of all the money before due to him there.

*Feb. 8.* . . . Finished reading Russell's "Polynesia." It is a general account, but more especially & fully a history of missionary efforts & action. Though the effects of these have been greatly exaggerated by preceding writers, & are probably too favorably viewed by this one compiler & reviewer, & though, in numerous cases, the converts are worse than when heathens—still much has been done for producing civilization, & the breaking down heathen superstition & a bloody worship, & for making at least nominal Christians. This is very different, & much greater effects, than has been approached on any negro tribe in Africa, showing great difference of the races, in docility. But after all, the Polynesians are much less thriving & populous, far less happy, & perhaps not generally more virtuous, than were they before knowing civilized men. The communication with the vicious white visitors, & their evil habits, perhaps alone might have produced all the harm to the simple & ignorant islanders, & that the evils of narrow-minded bigotry, & a gloomy religion, established by the missionary preachers, have been [266] much more than countervailed by the purer doctrines of religion, & pure, though overstraned [*sic*], moral & religious conduct which they have more or less induced. . . .

*Feb. 9.* . . . The Kansas discussion has produced much excitement in Congress—& a fight between [Laurence M.] Keitt of S.C. & [Galusha A.] Grow (abolitionist) of Pa, in which a dozen other members joined, & there had like to have been a very general engagement of the two parties in the House of Representatives, & during the session. All such brawls are disgraceful to the body. But it seems to be as probable a manner of the beginning of a separation of the states as any other. The Kansas constitution has been, by a majority of 3 only, referred to a select committee—by which all definitive action on it will be suspended, & the agitation maintained as the abolitionists desire. . . . Began to read Porte Crayon's Virginia Illustrated.

*Feb. 10.* . . . Finished Porte Crayon's book. The author is a Virginian, [David H.] Strother of Martinsburg.[11] His sketches & delineations, both with pen & pencil, are admirable. In this department, the author stands alone in Virginia, [268] and exalted far above all others in the United States.

*Feb. 12.* . . . Reading & arranging my manuscripts, which *I* deem worth notice by the public, or of the care & regard of my family—but which the public does not want, & perhaps my posterity will not value, & which therefore will be destroyed as waste paper, after my death—as has often occurred in cases of writings more valuable than mine. . . .

*Feb. 13.* . . . Covering & trimming my previously stitched letters & other writings, not designed for publication. Mildred assisting me, in securing with paste & patches of thin paper, some of the oldest & worn letters, which were given to me by different persons, & most of which were from the letters addressed to Col. Theodorick Bland,[12] & which have been published with his other papers, by Charles Campbell, as the "Bland Papers." Among these old papers, I have letters either written or signed by Richard Bland, Richard Henry Lee, Gen. Washington (of whose there are 6 family & private letters,) Jefferson, Edmund Randolph, Alex. Hamilton, Count Pulaski, Gov. [John] Page,[13] Gov. Reid, Baron Reidesel, Gen. Henry Lee, with sundry others from correspondents of less note. . . . Resumed reading "Count Julian," an historical romance by [William Gilmore] Sims [*sic*].

*Feb. 14.* Sunday—a cloudy & gloomy day. Finished Sims' romance, which is not worthy of its author. Reading [Robert] Burns' Life, with portions of his intermixed writings. What a noble being he was, by nature, in intellect & feelings! How deplorable it is that among his even early admirers, there was no one desirous & able to relieve Burns from a life of crushing bodily labor, to earn his bread, & afterwards to remove him from the temptations accompanying poverty & low company!—Conversation, & Mildred's sacred music on her Melodeon, as usual. [271]

---

[11] Under the pen name "Porte Crayon," David Hunter Strother (1816–88) became one of the top illustrators of the 1850's, contributing numerous sketches to *Harper's New Monthly Magazine*. Although a Virginian, Strother fought for the Union during the Civil War and was brevetted a brigadier general before its close.

[12] A nephew of Richard Bland, Theodorick Bland (1742–90) served as a colonel in the Revolutionary War, was a member of the Continental Congress from 1780 to 1783, and died a year after his election to the First Congress of the United States.

[13] Governor of Virginia, 1802–1805.

*Feb. 16.* The mail. The House of Delegates, 89 to 33 votes, have resolved to reduce the pay of public printer 25 percent. In bringing about this result, I think that I have done good service. I trust that the Senate will concur, & so alter the law. For 40 years, the Ritchies, father & son, have held this office, & have been receiving annually thousands of dollars more than a full price & fair profit. And yet the Ritchies & the Enquirer, their newspaper, have done more than any other men & paper to betray & sacrifice southern rights & interests (in the "compromise" acts of 1850,) & so acted for the purpose of subserving their own base pecuniary & private interests.... Several towns, Norfolk, Petersburg & Wheeling, are considering the expediency of paying for our next Fair, to obtain the benefits.

*Feb. 17.* Arranged to go to Richmond on the business of the Ag. Society.... Set out in the mail coach for Richmond, from the Post-Office, & owing to a kicking & balking horse, a heavy load & bad road, did not reach Rd. until nearly dark. The Exchange Hotel nearly full—many persons already come to the great festival & pageant which is to take place on the 22nd. Saw many of my acquaintance. Among them, John Seddon, who gave me a narration of what had been done on the public printing. He, & also others, compliment my small share in the matter as having been of important influence in inducing the House of Delegates to vote for reducing the pay of the public printer 25 percent. It is not doubted that the Senate will concur.... I had written & placed in Seddon's hands, to be read in the house, a protest to correct the false position in which the committee had placed me. But he has failed to make it known—& I suppose it is now too late for me to publish it. I cannot help feeling somewhat sore & mortified at being supposed to be, in any way, a seeker of office, or a government contract. [272]

*Feb. 18.*... Saw Mr. Williams & Mr. Crenshaw about our committee business. Learned that the conference in Petersburg had been postponed to the 20th. A letter from Wheeling has been received, offering [273] everything we could ask, if we would hold the Fair there. But the remoteness of the locality, & the difficulty of access for nearly all the present members of the Society, will make it impossible to choose that place.—At night attended the session of a caucus of the legislature, which resulted in nothing.—This hotel already completely filled with visitors, waiting for the 22nd, when the statue of Washington is to be unveiled, with great pomp & ceremony. The President of the U.S. was expected as an invited guest, but has declined coming. I am glad of it—as it will prevent much "boot-licking." I hear that Gen. Winfield Scott has arrived.

*Feb. 19.* Held consultation with Mr. Crenshaw, my fellow member of the sub-committee, & agreed upon our course. Afternoon, I went to Petersburg, & there hastened to see the mayor, & learned that the meeting was fixed for tomorrow. . . .

*Feb. 20.* Col. Knight, the member of our sub-committee to whom this business had been especially entrusted, arrived very early, & [274] we held our consultation. At 10, we met a sub-committee of the Union Agr. Soc. & the City Council. We stated our demands, & conditions for holding our General Meeting & Fair here, & nothing was objected to—but nothing was agreed upon, as on our side we have to wait to hear what Norfolk will do. Drove out to see the Fair-Ground. On returning, found my son Edmund & grandson George, on their way to Richmond—where we all went by the train at night. Was lucky enough to get a bed at the Exchange Hotel. This great establishment full, & I suppose all the other hotels. The city full of visitors already, who have arrived from two to four days before the beginning of the pageant. Saw several acquaintances among the last arrivals, & among them, my friend Wm. Gilmer of Albemarle, Senators Hunter & Mason arrived today. In Petersburg, I met Dr. Beckwith, but, as I had before determined to do, I passed him without speaking to him.

*Feb. 21.* Sunday. I had been placed in a double-bedded room, on the highest floor, with a stranger. He did not come in until nearly daybreak this morning—& I hear from a friend who occupies the next room, that such has been his habit since he has been here, about a week—& that he infers he is a professional gambler. So I will take care to avoid the usual intimacy of compulsory room-mates. . . . Saw Senator Hunter. Hear that some of the abolition governors of northern states have arrived, as invited guests. None such ought to have been included in the invitations, however general. . . . Visited Ex. Gov. Reid, as I have done several times before. He has been long lying here, under severe illness, from which he is now slowly recovering. He is U.S. Senator from N.Ca. His wife is with him—a lady of pleasant & attractive manners & conversation.—Col. Knight & I, in my room at night, prepared a form of contract for the signature of the two parties, if we can arrange a plan for holding our next Fair in Petersburg.—The great iron ship, Leviathan, (formerly called the Great Eastern,) has at last been launched—after months of delay & failure, & immense cost for additional means.

*Feb. 22.* This, the day for the great pageant, & the unveiling of the equestrian statue of Washington, & his birth-day, opened with fine snow, which continued through most of the day. Nevertheless, all the designed ceremonies were performed, as fully as if in the brightest weather. The procession was very great—mainly of uniformed military companies, & also of m[an]y other associations, in their peculiar dresses. The march continued perhaps an hour & a half, snow falling all the time, & but few persons protected by over-coats. I viewed the procession passing from the door of the Agricultural Office—& afterwards walked to the Capitol Square. There, nearly two hours were consumed by the foolish mountebank ceremonies, & addresses, & as much mountebank prayers, of the masonic fraternity. I was tired & disgusted with their foolery, & left at 2 o'clock. Then followed the Address [276] by Senator Hunter, & several others. Then the enveloping covering was taken off, & the statue exposed to view. The crowd of spectators, as well as the numbers in the procession, were very great. It is thought that the city was never so full. . . . A public dinner, to the invited guests, & to which the members of the legislature invited themselves—& a subscription ball at night. The legislature appropriated $5000 to entertain guests, & the city also provided refreshments for other visitors. By both these facilities, there were perhaps thousands made drunk. . . . I went to the hotel before 2 P.M., & heard nothing of Hunter's oration. But I had been annoyed & fretted by more than an hour of the previous time having been consumed by the stupid ceremonies & fooleries, & speeches & long prayers, of the free-masons in their mountebank dresses. It is absurd & disgraceful that such mummery should be permitted on any such occasion.

*Feb. 23.* The crowd not lessened. By invitation of some members of the legislature, I attended at their parlour a reception of Gen. Scott & Mr. Hunter. I left very soon, to make room for some [277] new visitors. [Edward] Everett's Eulogy on Washington ( so often spoken before, 70 times— ) was again delivered today at the Theatre —which could not hold the people who had purchased tickets at $1 & 1.50.[14] I did not attempt to attend. . . .

---

[14] The proceeds from Everett's oration on Washington were donated to the Mount Vernon Ladies' Association, an organization formed in 1853 by Ann Pamela Cunningham to purchase and preserve Mount Vernon as a national monument. In all, the Massachusetts orator delivered this address 129 times prior to the Civil War and turned over to the Mount Vernon Association a total of $69,064. The purchase was finally consummated on February 22, 1859, much to the disgust of Ruffin, who viewed the project as a great fraud.

*Feb. 25.* .... At the Capitol conversed with Pryor (editor of "The South,") about the Mount Vernon humbug, & I urged him to advocate the placing the remains of Washington in the interior of the monument. I wrote a short piece, immediately, before leaving the Capitol, & carried it to his printing office for tomorrow's paper. Immediately after early dinner Mr. & Mrs. Sayre & I set out for home .... Arrived at dark. ... Among the invited guests who appeared at the celebration of the 22nd, were the governors of New Jersey, Connecticut, [278] & Michigan. I am glad that, under the general invitation, none personally offensive did come—as [Salmon P.] Chase of Ohio, & [Nathaniel P.] Banks of Massachusetts. There were also present, & in the procession, Gen. Persifer [*sic*] Smith,[15] Gen. [William S.] Harney,[16] & some other officers of the U.S. Army. Among these was Capt. Van Vliet, who had been sent on a mission to Brigham Young, at his capital, a short time before the arrival of our army invaded the territory. Capt. V. told me that the position of the Mormons is very strong, & the approaches very difficult. He inferred that the people were very generally sincere fanatics, & that those acting hypocritically under duress were but a small proportion of the great body. If so, this will make their being completely suppressed a very difficult business. ...

Every spectator has been criticizing the monument, & generally with unmeasured praise of the principal object, the equestrian statue. For my part, I pretend to no artistic taste—& would not have to judge of the form & proportions & execution of any one figure. But even if each figure were perfect, in itself, I think the design of the whole monument, & the mingling together the different figures, is in very bad taste, or rather is very absurd. In the first place, I object to all equestrian statues of men. If a horse alone were represented, noble & beautiful in appearance, as nature made him, it would be a grand subject for the sculptor, &, on this huge scale, & at such elevation, perhaps nothing else would be more noble or beautiful to the spectator. But a horse under bridle & saddle, & a rider, is compara-

---

[15] Shortly after leaving Richmond, General Persifor Frazer Smith (1798–1858), who had previously served with distinction in the Mexican War, was assigned to command the Department of Utah. However, he died in Fort Leavenworth, Kansas, on May 17, 1858, while still organizing his expedition.

[16] Notwithstanding some serious difficulties with General Winfield Scott, Harney had a brilliant military record during the Mexican War. But, apparently because he was a native of Tennessee and suspected of southern sympathies, he was given no active command during the Civil War.

tively [279] degraded by subjection, & deformed by artificial equipment. And yet, the horse will be considered by all as the principal & great object, even though the rider is Washington. An equestrian figure is truly the statue of a horse, with a man attached. . . . Another & greater error I think is the assembling around the monument, & as parts of the whole, the statues of six other of the illustrious men of Virginia, of which two only (Henry & Jefferson) are as yet completed & in place. If these stood each isolated, & complete in itself, each one would be at least a worthy subject for the gratitude of the commonwealth & they *may be* for any thing I know, admirable works of art. But the grouping all these personages around & beneath the fiery horse of Washington, each in a different action, neither one having reference to another, & yet all forming one connected whole, seems to me to be an offensive & ludicrous absurdity. . . .

There is another unpardonable error in the plan, which is not the fault of the artist, but of the persons in Richmond who have been [280] entrusted with the direction of the work, & who have thus shown themselves unworthy of the trust. Richard Henry Lee, one among the first & greatest of the movers of the revolution, & of the founders of the liberties of Virginia—the delegate to whom was especially confided by Virginia the great duty & action of first proposing in the Congress of the United Colonies the Declaration of Independence—this great orator & patriot is omitted from the six chosen as the most illustrious, & John Marshall is put in the place that Lee ought to occupy. Now though objecting strongly to Marshall's political opinions & course, I hold him in the highest veneration as a jurist, a patriot, & especially as a man. But it was proper in the subjects for these honors to present contemporary worthies of the revolutionary period & action only. Great and well-deserved as is Judge Marshall's fame, it has been of subsequent growth. It is true that he acted in the revolutionary war—but only in an inferior military command & service. . . . His great worth, as evinced in his later life, deserves our high respect & veneration. And to few, if any, could a statue more worthily & appropriately be erected, separately & alone, than to the wise, virtuous, & yet modest & simple-mannered Marshall. But among the sages, patriots & heroes of the revolution he had no distinguished place, & neither should his statue make [281] one of this group around the Washington monument.

There is no objection to the selection of either of the three other Virginia worthies whose statues are to occupy the vacant places—

George Mason, Gen. [Andrew] Lewis, & Gov. [Thomas] Nelson.[17] But there is still another for whom it is much to be regretted that there is no place. Gen. George Rogers Clark, commanding Virginian forces only, (militia or volunteers,) and the whole enterprise being strictly Virginian, conquered the British garrisons in Detroit & other places of the north-west, & thus subjected to Virginia, by conquest, the great north-western [282] region to which she had before been entitled by charter from the mother country. The difficulties of the long march, by which Gen. Clark completely surprised & conquered the British posts, made this one of the most remarkable military exploits in history. John Randolph of Roanoke compared the three-days passage of the flooded borders & morasses & the Wabash river, by the Virginian troops under Clark, as equal to Hannibal's passage of the Thrasymene marshes. Yet this great enterprise is scarcely known to the present generation. And the only monument or memorial of the great deed & valuable conquest made by Clark, for Virginia, is in the subsequent sacrifice of the whole conquered territory by the unwise counsels of those who guided Virginia in later times. If we have with reckless prodigality thrown away this great possession & conquest, & made it the stronghold of our enemies, at least due honor should be rendered to the conduct, endurance, & sufferings of the brave men & the able leader, who achieved the conquest.

*Feb. 26.* The mail. Read the latest newspapers. Finished a pamphlet address by Richard Yeadon of Charleston, (sent by him,) on the action of the Federal government on slavery. . . . Began to read the 1st vol. of Irving's Life of Washington, of which I read the three last volumes previously. . . .

*Feb. 28.* Sunday. . . . Finished first vol. of Irving's Washington. Began the "Scarlet Letter." . . . [283]

*March 1.* . . . Finished the "Scarlet Letter"—a strange book, by a powerful writer. I earnestly wish that Hawthorne would undertake some work in which he would fully describe the grim & sour "pilgrim fathers" of New England, with all their good & all their detestable traits, as Scott has done in "Old Mortality" for the Covenanters. His sketches in the "Scarlet Letter" show how well Hawthorne could perform this task. And I infer that he would not be disinclined to

---

[17] Lewis was closely associated with Washington during the French and Indian War and won a decisive victory over the Indians in Lord Dunmore's War on the eve of the Revolution. Thomas Nelson (1738–89), a signer of the Declaration of Independence, succeeded Jefferson as governor of Virginia in 1781.

expose these hard, & ferocious bigots, who, (whether sincerely & correctly were true followers of the hell-flavored doctrines of Calvin, or, as compulsory hypocrites, served a cruel & hateful deity by intolerant & bloody worship,) were the leaders & rulers of these times in New England. Besides the main feature of such a work, the characteristics of these peculiar men, there would be matters of deep interest in the curious political condition of the people. While appearing to have the only free, & the purest republican government in the world, the civil government was in fact completely subordinate to & ruled by the priesthood, who, by religious influence alone, maintained a despotic hierocracy, or pretended theocracy, more rigid, tyrannical, persecuting, & bloody, than any other government of the English race. But Hawthorne would be afraid to depict the forefathers of New England in their true colors—these men who are falsely held up as asserters of freedom, and the most illustrious of patriots & self-sacrificers for the good of their fellows. If he were thus to strip from his countrymen their great claim to distinguished merit, he could no longer live among them—[284] & would be deemed not less a traitor than Benedict Arnold.—Read a sketch of the life of Isaac Newton, in the Edinburgh Review. Began the "Blithedale Romance" of Hawthorne, which also I bought when last in Richmond. . . .

*March 2.* . . . The mail. Read the newspapers, & some of the articles of De Bow's Review. The recent unsuccessful attempt to assassinate the Emperor of France, by Italian refugees, conspiring in England, has caused much exasperation in France because of the asylum thus afforded in England to such political enemies of or traitors (so called) to the governments of the continent. Sharp & insulting expressions have been uttered in the French government paper, & recriminations in speeches in parliament, & otherwise in England. This villain, who has reached supreme power in France, by perjury, treason, usurpation & murderous bloodshed, will scarcely escape finally from the many seekers of his life. And though I have no belief in France being bettered by his being killed, so much do I detest him for his crimes, that I earnestly wish for his overthrow, & the heaviest punishment to him, whether in his assassination or a longer punishment. . . .

*March 3.* Finished reading the Blithedale Romance, & now have no more *new* books. Hawthorne is a powerful & beautiful writer—& his books, while very interesting, have great defects & deformities.

His "House of Seven Gables," which I read first, I liked best as a whole. But there is one long & tiresome part (which follows immediately after the sudden death of a principal character,) which is an unnecessary & disagreeable digression or excrescence. The description & painting of characters are there especially to be admired. The Blithedale Romance is very interesting—but there are left in the narrative & plot as great gaps, without explanation, as if each of several entire chapters had in separate places been cut out. If he had given a full picture of the physical, economical & moral difficulties & absurdities of a socialist community, such as he barely touches upon, he would have had excellent materials left unused.—Glancing over parts of Bishop [John H.] Hopkins' "American Citizen," & re-reading all the portions on slavery in America. His general views, on the religious & moral questions, are excellent, & wonderful in a Northern clergyman. But when he comes to discuss the alleged evils of slavery, & to propose remedies, he shows his entire want of practical knowledge. If so good & fair a man could reside a year in the slaveholding states, he would gain all the [286] light from facts, & of truth, to which he is, by his situation, a stranger.

*March 5.* Extremely cold. Temp. 10° at sunrise. It has been a strange winter. In November there was cold winter weather, & so far in March, with the last week in February, there has been cold weather—remarkably cold for spring. But all the months of Dec., Jany. & nearly all of Feb. (to near the close) was warm, & unprecedentedly warm for so much of winter.—The mail. My last piece[18] comes in the "South"—& a pro-slavery address, delivered in Cincinnati! ! ! by my late acquaintance Mr. Quinn of that city. There is reported from N[ew] O[rleans] papers, some notable facts, or statements, of which there had been before slighter intimations. A long editorial of the N.O. "Delta" announces (& approvingly,) that the introduction of African slaves into Mississippi, in violation of the U.S. laws, has already been begun successfully, & it is presumed will be maintained & continued. Another kindred fact, & of more serious importance, is that the House of Representatives of La. "has passed a bill authorizing a company (already organized,) to [transport] 2500 free negroes from the coast of Africa, indentured for not less than 15 years." Now it is very obvious that these "free negroes" could only be obtained in slaves purchased in Africa. But if imported as free ap-

---

[18] On the Washington monument in Richmond.

prentices, under precisely such forms as have been already used by Britain & France, I do not see how such traffic can be opposed as the *slave trade* by either of these powers—nor by the U.S. under the existing laws. And if "apprentices" can be [287] so indentured for "not less than 15 years," the term may be extended to 50 years, and, for males, be made equivalent to complete slavery. Besides—if such indentured "free negroes" can be imported legally & safely, what is to prevent *mixed* cargoes, of slaves & (so-called) apprentices, which could not be distinguished. To visiting cruisers, all the passengers would be reported as "indentured free negroes"—& as soon as landed & distributed, all might be slaves—as indeed such pretended "apprentices" will be under any circumstances, & much worse off than avowed slaves. If this last movement is carried through, it will be attended with important consequences—of which one of the first will be, for all practical purposes, the renewal of the African slave trade. [288].

*March 8.* Snowing fast until 4 P.M., & a violent wind from N.E. Of course very cold. I had designed to go to Richmond today, in the Glocester mail coach, to attend the adjourned meeting of the sub-committee on the Fair business, which I hoped then to arrange with the Petersburg committee—but this dreadful weather made it impossible. If I had attempted it, it would have been with great exposure, & even risk of the coach not being able to reach Richmond. So I wrote my views, & order for another meeting, to the Secretary, & sent it by the mail, if that should go. Snow 4 inches deep, where on a level, but generally much drifted by the wind. A dull day, with all the aid of conversation & reading.

*March 9.* The mail. No letter to inform me about the Society business, & so I determined to go tomorrow, by the next mail coach, to learn. . . .

*March 10.* Set out in the mail coach at 2 P.M. for Richmond. Saw Mr. Williams. There was no meeting on the 8th. Another appointed for the 15th. Met W. Gilmer & sundry other acquaintances at the hotel. Read the newspapers in my room, & glanced over [John] Fletcher's Studies on Slavery.[19]

*March 11.* With all the resources of newspapers, books, & conversation, passed a dull day, because I had nothing to do. . . . At night, went with Gilmer to a musical entertainment of Yankee performers disguised as negroes. Heard some good music, intermixed with much

[19] Published in Natchez, 1852.

more of miserable low buffoonery. I left the place long before the close, wearied & disgusted. Yet this is the most popular performance. The house was completely filled, & mostly with people who seemed to be respectable. This is an indication of a low standard of taste of the people of Richmond. [290a]

*March 12.* After very early breakfast, left Richmond, on the Central Railroad, designing to pay a visit, long intended, in the interval of spare time. Reached Hanover C.H. station by 8 A.M. & . . . I walked to North Wales, the residence of Mr. Williams Carter—nearly 3 miles. Found Mr. C. at home, & alone. We spent a pleasant day, to late at night, in conversation, & partly, when tired of talking, in reading. . . .

*March 13.* After breakfast, I left, in Mr. Carter's carriage to Hanover C.H. where I counted upon being able to hire a conveyance to Marlbourne. But neither horse, servant, or carriage of any kind could be had. I should have walked on to Dr. Nelson's but that my neighbor & friend, B. W. Talley, the deputy sheriff, had his horse ready to go on his official business on my route. He pressed me to ride his horse, & let him walk. That I would not agree to—but consented to "ride & tie," & share with him both the walking & riding—which we did. As there was time enough, we kept together, in a walk, until we separated. Found Dr. Nelson at home &, as always, alone. Spent some hours with him, in continued & pleasant conversation, including dinner. In the afternoon, he sent me to Marlbourne, in his buggy. . . . It is strange to me that the two gentlemen whom I visited should live as they do, almost entirely alone. . . . They are both able to live as they please, & yet each lives almost in solitude, & harassed by their property & business matters, which neither needs. I would not live as they do for all the wealth of both together. Yet I am far from being entirely satisfied with the different course that I have chosen. I am still as well pleased as ever to be rid of my property (transferred to my children,) & of the trouble, labor & perplexity of its management. But I find my regular occupation of labor has ceased—& already my time is hanging heavy on my hands. My various jobs of writing are completed—& I have no subject to offer regular & continued occupation for my mind & labor. I cannot do without such occupation. This I foresaw—& my children foresaw it —& [290c] therefore some of them strongly opposed my proposal to give up my labors & property. To guard against it, I resorted to travel & to writing—which, with my duties to the State Agrl. Society, have kept me employed until recently. But I have latterly been out of employment, & have felt the expected evils. I must find something to do.

*March 14.* Sunday.... Reading, or rather skimming over Montaigne's Essays, which I had borrowed from Dr. Nelson. I had never before had an opportunity to read this celebrated book, & expected much entertainment from it. But except as a literary curiosity, for its antiquity, the author's excentricity [*sic*], egotism, & free communicativeness, I found it generally tiresome, & soon I read only the heads of subjects (conveniently printed on the margins of the pages,) & such of the body as those headings, or glances over the pages, indicated to be curious or amusing. Much of the matter is indecent to a disgusting degree, & so unnecessarily, that it is strange that a man of the author's ability, & high appreciation of his own character, should have so written.—Conversation, a walk with my daughters & Mr. Sayre, & Mildred's sacred music on the melodeon, filled up for me the day.

*March 15.* ... [291] Went at 11 A.M. to the Post Office to take the mail coach. It arrived full, & I could only go by taking a seat on the top, which I did, & so rode, very uneasily, to Richmond. Went immediately to the Agr. Office—& soon after recd a telegraphic dispatch from Petersburg saying that the notice, mailed here on the 11th. had just been received, & too late for their members to come tonight. Our sub-committee held its meeting at night—& deputed me to go to Petersburg tomorrow morning, & either to close a contract, if the other party is ready, or otherwise to appoint another time of meeting. Telegraphed my intended going, to Petersburg, to Major Lyon. —Met & conversed very pleasantly with 4 or 5 members in reference to subjects before the legislature. The Mount Vernon bill has been discussed, & rejected (the appropriation of $200,000, to advance for the purchase,) by a large majority.... [292]

*March 16.* Left Richmond at 5 A.M. & to Petersburg, soon after 6. By my appointment, Major Lyon came immediately after breakfast ... & together we went, in a carriage, to the residence of Mr. Charles Friend, the chairman of their committee....[20] The delay which had occurred by the necessity for our waiting to hear from other towns

---

[20] Friend (1817–71) was the proprietor of White Hill, a small plantation located two miles east of Petersburg on the City Point road. For details of his farming operations, see the White Hill Plantation Books (microfilm copy in Southern Historical Collection, University of North Carolina, Chapel Hill).

(in courtesy,) had served to remove every chance for a competition for the fair, except Petersburg. And as no *distinct offer* had been made for the latter, the committee took advantage of the present state of the matter to reduce the terms which they had been before ready to accede to, & had so given me to understand. So I was placed in the condition of either taking terms lower than expected, & which reduction my authority did not cover, or to break off the negotiation, which would make things much worse for our side. So I thought it best to "take the responsibility" of violating the letter of my instructions, & to contract for medium terms, something, though not very much below what I had counted on, but still very good for our society, & better than our sub-committee had been authorised to accept by the resolution of the Executive Committee. By the contract now made, Petersburg, through the Union Agricultural Society, will provide & pay all the outfit & expenses of the Fair, including the awards of premiums [293] not exceeding the limit of $4000. And the only loss that our Society can meet with, will be if the premiums to be paid shall exceed $4000, for such excess, & which is very improbable. This is very far better than such use of grounds & all other benefits that Richmond has ever afforded to us, or even the annual grant of $3000 which we would have been willing to accept in lieu of all accommodations, & which was refused. This arrangement with Petersburg is, substantially, putting us on the footing that I trust will be maintained hereafter—that is, that the city or community that has the benefit of the Fair, shall pay all the expenses thereof.

After dinner, having borrowed a horse of Mr. Friend, I rode to Beechwood, 12 miles. Found all well. Learned (more fully than before,) that the perversity & foolish obstinacy of J. B. Cocke, whose land extends across the whole section, will partially defeat the operation of the new fence law . . . . I do not think that his power extends so far. I must try to counteract him.

*March 17.* Read & walked through forenoon. Reading in [James] Parton's "Life of Aaron Burr," (a new work,) the account of the violent political contest of 1800. . . . The newspapers report heated [294] discussions & proceedings in Congress, on the admission of Kansas. The change of ministry in England, & still more the cause of the parliamentary censure of Lord Palmerston's ministry, (being too crouching to the French emperor,) seem to me, with the previous & inducing circumstances, to be ominous of variance between the two governments, & a breaking down of the recent cordial alliance & friendship. . . .

*March 20.* Finished reading Parton's "Life of Aaron Burr," except the first part, preceding the adoption of the Federal Constitution. Very interesting, & especially as to the alleged treason & trial of Burr—which were among the earliest historical events which I remember to have read with interest in the newspapers when they occurred.

At night a messenger arrived from Marlbourne with a letter of very bad news. Last night (3 A.M.) the new stable & granary was burnt, with all the 20 mules, & all the corn housed therein, except 4700 bushels, which had been just delivered. This second burning, with circumstances so nearly like that of the barn in October, make it certain that not only the last, but both, were by a malicious incendiary. But who it can be, or what motives can prompt any one to such extent of enmity & crime, none of us can conceive. In addition to the heavy pecuniary loss sustained, it is even still worse to be continually exposed to a secret enemy, against whom it is impossible to guard. Mr. Sayre has sent a carriage to Evelynton for my sons. . . .

*March 21.* Sunday. . . . Edmund & I crossed the river (in the rain) to Berkley, where we found the carriage had been, & had gone back to Evelynton—where we sent for it, & walked on until we met it. Reached Marlbourne at 5 P.M. . . . The incidents of the fire the general subject of conversation. The delivery of corn was still in progress, & in a few days more, all would have been taken out of this house. 4700 bushels had been delivered, & about 2250 remained & was burnt. . . . The 20 mules (all on the farm) were all young & good, & in excellent condition. Two had been bought only 4 days before, for $304. The value of the 20 was not less than $3000—& Mr. Sayre thinks the entire loss $6000, in pecuniary value, besides the great [297] inconvenience, which will be certainly very great in addition. . . . There is a general suspicion in the neighborhood that the incendiary is a certain near neighbor of bad habits, & character, who is one of a large family, with all [of] whom the intercourse of my family has been friendly & kind, & to whom we have done many small favors. Mr. Sayre had offered a reward of $1000 for the discovery & conviction of the incendiary.

*March 22.* We have reason to be gratified with the sympathy & concern expressed by our neighbors. Today there was a meeting held at Old Church for conference on the subject. It is a serious matter to all, even on selfish considerations, that there should be among us a secret enemy so malignant & unscrupulous.—Several neighbors have offered to lend such mules as they can spare—& Edmund's wagon, with 4 good mules, arrived this afternoon, to remain as long as needed. Except the axes, there were scarcely any hand utensils which were not burnt—& for want of these, very little work can be done of the many kinds wanting.

*March 24.* . . . Edmund & I walked over the wheat land—& selected places to build a brick granary, & to make bricks. He & Mr. Sayre have determined to attempt these operations, to be completed, if possible before Harvest. Near bed-time Mr. Sayre returned from a long ride, having engaged 10 more mules, which will be here tomorrow morning. He has been enabled to make these purchases of mules broke to work, only by the circumstance of rail-road contractors having lately closed their operations on the York-River rail-road.

*March 26.* . . . I attended throughout the day to some of Mr. Sayre's work. The last purchased mules at work, & all those lent sent home, except Edmund's four.—The mail. The legislature has appropriated $2,500,000 to different rail-roads, & some of them useless & some even injurious to state interests. Probably in consequence of this increase to the very large state debt, & the fear of "repudiation," the state bonds sold yesterday at 90; & my son who had designed to purchase, was afraid to invest even at that price. The finances of the commonwealth have been woefully managed.—The bill which had passed one branch of the La. legislature, to authorise the importation of African "apprentices," has been rejected in the other. The statement of African slaves having been recently imported into Mississippi, was a "hoax," or perhaps put out as a "feeler" to try public opinion on the subject.—The recent change of the British ministry, Lord Palmerston's going out, & Lord Derby's coming in, does not seem to indicate any change (as at first supposed,) of the friendly relations with France.

*March 27.* A public meeting of the neighbors at the Post Office, to consult upon measures in regard to the late incendiary acts. Nothing was done, except offering a further reward for the discovery, of $500, made up by subscription of the neighbors, in addition to that of $1000 before offered by [300] the proprietors of Marlbourne. . . .

*March 28.* Sunday. No service in the neighborhood. The Presbyterian church, which my family has regularly attended on every other Sunday, when there was no service at the Episcopal church, has been without a minister for more than half a year. . . . Finished reading through (with some skipping & much skimming,) Montaigne's Travels in Italy &c. I was curious to know what such a writer, nearly 300 years ago, had observed & said of the scenes & customs he witnessed. [301] There is much that is interesting, but more that is tiresome.—Looking over many old numbers of the African Repository, the official journal of the Colonization Society, for statistics & other facts respecting the colony of Liberia.

*March 30.* . . . Read Senator [Judah P.] Benjamin's able speech on the Slavery question, or nominally on the admission of Kansas. A still abler speech on the same subject was delivered by Senator Hammond, and which has been much applauded. [302]

*March 31.* . . . Having finished clearing out the important & necessary parts of the upper branches in South Field, commenced, at the north outlet, the great annual job of clearing out the main ditch of the farm.—Went to examine the present discharge of water from the marl pits where I formerly worked on Newcastle farm. I am satisfied, of what I suspected in advance, that the amount of water thus discharged, & also that from the adjacent open ditch, is not now as much as one-tenth, perhaps not one-twentieth, of what passed regularly, & even in summer & autumn, 7 or 8 years ago, when I worked there regularly for years, & since which time I have not before examined the water. The difference must be caused by my draining operations on Marlbourne having cut of[f] most of the former supply of water, which had passed underground through all the other land to the river. The deepening of my main ditch, into the water-glutted sand-bed, though a mile distant, has cut of[f] the former supply of water to this marl digging & upper ditch, which have not been drained in any other manner. Doubtless the whole of Newcastle farm, (lying [303] between Marlbourne & the river,) & also other adjoining farms, have been partially drained by my operations cutting off or draining off the supplies of injurious water. But the effect has been so gradually & slowly produced, & the proprietors are so ignorant on this subject, & so little observant, that, though they may know that their ground is now much dryer than formerly, they would probably all ascribe the beneficial change to their own better draining, by open shallow ditches—the old plan which never had before served, & cannot serve, but very imperfectly, & insufficiently.

*April 2.* . . . Reading the newspapers, which were especially welcome, though containing no news—& continuing a foolish Irish novel

"O'Halloran" by [William H.] Maxwell.[21] The writers of Irish novels seem to consider [304] that it is the universal & perfect character of a young gentleman, & especially of a young officer, to drink as much liquor at every dinner as he can carry off soberly (*Hibernice*) & to get beastly drunk on every temptation. If the descriptions of Maxwell & [Charles J.] Lever &c. have any resemblance to truth, the Irish gentlemen (boys & men) & English officers, almost universally are regular deep drinkers, & unmeasured prodigals, & more often drunk than sober after dinner of every day. . . .

*April 3*. . . . Read the sketches of the lives of Shakespeare & Byron prefixed to their works. Out of all reading—reduced to the necessity of again reading some of my own manuscripts—which productions it seems will not soon (if ever) have any other reader. . . .

*April 5*. . . . Today glancing over the last reports of the Smithsonian Institution, & of the Patent Office (Agricultural.) The last is less worthless than of former years, inasmuch as it contains *one* article that is worth reading for instruction.—Before, read the long report of the committee of the legislature of S.Ca. approving of the reopening of the African slave-trade. I had before read the counter minority report. Both able papers.

*April 6*. . . . The mail.—The bill for admission of Kansas as a state rejected by the H. of R. after having passed the Senate. I am not sorry for it. We shall gain nothing by the admission, as Kansas will certainly & speedily alter the present constitution, & forbid slavery. Consistency required that southern men should vote for the admission—as all have done, except 6 "Americans" or "Know-Nothings" —but I am perfectly satisfied to be defeated.—I fear that the system of under-drains of the farm is requiring much repair, or renewal in [306] particular places, & the defect has not been observed until now too late to repair it for the benefit of the present crops. With all Mr. Sayre's great merit as an industrious & capable conductor of business, he is not acquainted with draining, or my system of draining, & has not looked out for such necessary failures, & the repairs frequently required.—The two principal conspirators who failed in the late attempt to kill the Emperor of France, have been executed. It is reported that he has since been shot at. I trust that the perjured

---

[21] The Irish novelist William Hamilton Maxwell (1792–1850) developed a rollicking fictional style which reached full flower in Charles James Lever's *Harry Lorrequer*, the first installment of which was published in 1837 in the Dublin University Magazine.

villain & murderer is suffering a living death, & that he will yet pay the full penalty of his crimes, by which he sought & reached his eminence.

*April 7.* . . . Continued to attend to the opening & deepening old ditches.—Began to read Pepys' Diary, the second time, for so long as it may afford enough interest, or until I get something that is newer. . . .

*April 9.* The carriage went to Richmond for Julian's family, & brought him & Lotty. They had brought their children as far on the way as Petersburg, but learning there of the measles being here,[22] they were afraid to bring them farther.—Clearing out the main ditch.

*April 13.* Julian & Lotty, & Charles had appointed to return home today; & I went with them as far as Richmond. . . . The mail brought the news of [309] the death of Thomas H. Benton. He was an able & bad man, who has long occupied a prominent position in American politics. It is an astonishing & disgraceful fact, that he was 30 years a U.S. senator, & latterly a hopeful aspirant for the presidency, in spite of the known stealing of money which he had been detected in when a youth at the University of N.Ca. And base as was that conduct, he was guilty of less venial violations of integrity in his after life & dignified stations—though of course avoiding larceny or felony in law.—The Va. legislature has adjourned, after doing almost nothing for the public good. Among the many subjects before it which were neglected or rejected, was the proposition to compel the Board of Visitors of the University to receive Col. Cocke's donation of $20,000, to endow an Agricultural Professorship, on the conditions he affixed. The Committee of Schools reported unfavorably, & no further notice was taken of it—& no one in the legislature advocated the adoption. The intended donor must be greatly mortified, though I have heard nothing since on the subject.

*April 14.* Left Richmond early for Washington, where I go merely in search of amusement, having no business object. . . . Reached Washington at 3½ P.M. Saw no one that I cared to meet, but Mr. Thomas Ruffin, of H. of R. from N.C. who is a lodger here (Brown's Hotel,) & who has been very attentive to me in many respects, connected with his position as a member of congress. Passed an hour in his room. Read a newspaper, wrote a little, . . . & went to bed early.

---

[22] Ruffin's son-in-law, William Sayre, broke out with the measles on April 2.

*April 15.* Had last night very uncomfortable lodging, on the hard lumps of an old mattress, which were disagreeably perceptible through a very thin & soft feather-bed spread above. This is a new addition to the regular & usual discomforts of the table, at this "first-class hotel," for which wretched accommodations I pay $2.50 a day, or $3 if there is the least fire kindled. For my mere animal comfort, a lunch on cheese & crackers would be preferable to any meal I have had here. This is the only hotel at which I have ever put up in Washington, brought by its character & its company. If I only knew the town, & how to choose, I would go to some private lodging or boarding house.—Made some calls, & found no one I sought. To the galleries of both Houses of Congress, and found nothing of any interest. But, by accident, [saw] sundry [311] of my acquaintances—among them Elwood Fisher, Senator Hunter, & old Richard Randolph.

*April 16.* Left the hotel immediately after breakfast, & went to a private boarding house, to lodge & board. . . . Nearly all the forenoon, & before dinner, in the library of Congress, looking over books, & reading here & there. Looked into the galleries of both houses of congress. Nothing of interest in either. Afternoon went to see Lieut. Maury, at his house adjoining the Observatory. Had [312] a pleasant conversation with him, as always. Walked with him on the beautiful grounds in the rear of the buildings. The place offers the finest view that I have seen of or in the city.—After tea, went to Gov. Hammond's, & remained until 9.

*April 17.* Called on my friend Wm. O. Goode, partly in reference to a matter on which he had before written to me his views. He had asked to retain & read my MS. on the "Political Economy of Slavery," which he did—& urged on me its publication, & extensive distribution by aid of some of the members of congress. This I agreed to he might try, taking care to maintain my position as the much largest contributor to a public service, & not a solicitor for the money of others, for my own gain. I offered to pay one half of the expense of printing 5000 copies, provided enough of the southern members would contribute the other half, & also would distribute the pamphlet under their franking privilege. Goode soon obtained enough subscriptions to cover the half of the expense, & I immediately arranged for the printing. This has given me some pleasant employment. I forthwith proceeded to read the article, for the last corrections.—At night, again with Gov. Hammond. Interesting political conversation & discussions. His late strong & able speech on the

Kansas bill, gave great offence to the northern members, by his comparing what he called the "white slaves" of the north with the black slaves of the south—& claiming for the latter, & for our slavery system, the preference. It is both strange & amusing that this speech has been more circulated & noticed at the north than perhaps all other of the southern speeches put together. First, there were several indignatious [313] replies to it in the Senate, the speakers of which took care to spread widely among their constituents. Next, the more to excite indignation, northern members sent also some thousands of copies of Hammond's entire speech to the north, & several northern newspapers republished it in their columns. And since, he has received hundreds of particular applications, by private letters, & such are now daily coming in, requesting to be furnished with a copy of his speech—& as may be inferred, either from their commendation expressed, or their silence, because of approval. To all these applicants, copies were sent. In addition, a little 50 cent newspaper has been started in Lowell, Mass. the "Spindle City Idea," for readers among the operatives, founded on Hammond's declaration of white slavery. For however this charge, whether treated as true or false, is to all northern men, it falls in with the complaints of the operatives that they are made bondsmen by the avarice of their employers, & especially by the great manufacturers & capitalists. As they have been complaining of this before, & wish to establish the position against the[ir] employers, Hammond's speech serves for them a good purpose, though his views are warped by them from their designed direction.

*April 18.* Sunday. Went to the Catholic church, but on inquiry found that there was no place free for strangers, all the pews being private property. The galleries were used by negroes only. I would not have objected to taking a seat among decent negroes, but did not choose to be alone in that position, lest I should have been mistaken for a rabid abolitionist. I was told that I could [314] easily obtain a seat, by asking for any one in a vacant place. But as I did not choose to *beg* my way among strangers, I declined entering the church. I have often before thought, but was never so forcibly impressed with the truth, that city churches, instead of being designed to invite the attendance of all, are planned to exclude all who have not bought pews, or otherwise are not assigned a humiliating & disgraceful position. . . . At night, at Hammond's, with Elwood Fisher. Much interesting conversation on past political events, & the prominent actors therein.—Yesterday the bill to construct a railroad to the Pacific ocean was postponed in the Senate—which its movers say is equivalent to its defeat. I trust it is so. Rather than this enormous work, of incalculable expense & difficulties should be undertaken—& especially on the northern route, (which would be the one adopted, by force of northern votes)—it would be better that all the Pacific slope should separate from the Union.—A high functionary of the government of New Grenada, in a recent official report to his government, has made a strong argument in favor of annexing New Grenada to the United States. This is a strong sign. The five states of what has since been called Central America, when first independent, more than 40 years ago, sent commissioners to Washington to offer the incorporation of their country with ours. That proposition was then refused, as I presume a like one from New Grenada, or Mexico, now would be rejected—or ought to be, on the same ground for all, the mixed blood & degraded character of the great mass of the population. This is known to be the case with Central America & Mexico, & I presume is so with New Grenada, of which [315] I have but little information. Dominica, the Spanish & larger portion of the island of St. Domingo or Hayti, would be glad to come to us in the same way—but the objection of mixed blood is there still more strong. The populations of all these countries are too numerous to be absorbed in ours, or to be excluded from intermixture. If the mixed class of either was comparatively small, it could be kept separate, until it would die out & disappear—as happens with the *lowest* class, if not personal slaves, in every country.

*April 19.* . . . The Emperor of Russia has declared in favor of the general emancipation of the serfs of Russia, & the measure is in progress. It will probably be followed by bad consequences—to the serfs & their present masters, & perhaps to the government & the whole country.—Lounging, as usual, for some hours of the forenoon, in the Library of Congress, looking over books, or their pictures, & in the galleries of the two houses. . . . An official Russian document, in favor of the emancipation of the serfs, says that there are 25 millions of them—or nearly half the population of the empire. There must be awful results from the compulsory & speedy emancipation of so many ignorant beings, who though capable of improvement, are now almost as ignorant, destitute, & improvident as would be our negroes, [316] if emancipated. The most humane as well as safe course would be to let time, & general improvement, bring about the gradual emancipation of serfs generally, as has been done in England; & in the mean time to offer means for every suitable individual case, for the serfs to obtain their freedom, by self purchase, or otherwise.

*April 20.* Another dismal day of slow rain & drizzle. . . . Sought an introduction to Gen. [William L.] Cazneau, of Texas, (the only one I have sought) & called on him at his hotel, to obtain from him information about St. Domingo, the former Spanish part of the whole island. He was there as political agent of our government, & made a very advantageous treaty[23] with the President [Pedro] Santana, which the English & French consuls (under instructions,) prevented, by threats, the ratification of by the Dominican congress, & our government tamely submitted to the insult. I made many inquiries concerning the condition of the people &c. & was fully answered. When the general negro insurrection occurred, & the negro government of Hayti was established over the Spanish portion of the island, in these long continued disorders, all the whites were either killed, or fled the country. At a much later time, their children, who were mostly in the neighboring island of Curaçao, were invited back, by the resident mulattoes, & returned, & were received very kindly & permitted to resume possession of their fathers' lands. But [317] this Dominican republic, after having thrown off the negro yoke, (of Hayti,)[24] has been continually harassed by war, or threats of it, with Hayti, & civil war, the whites & mulattoes, & also many negroes, against the Haytian or negro party. [Buenaventura] Báez, a dark mulatto, was made president by the last party, & Santana (mostly white, but part Indian blood,) who had been the lawful president, was expelled, & his seat occupied by Báez. The party of the former is again in the ascendant —& the last accounts were that all the country had gone to the support of Santana, who was besieging Báez, in the capital, & would compel him to surrender. The territory embraces two thirds of the island, & its most fertile & healthy portion. Indeed the interior of the island is generally healthy, though the sea-ports are pestilential. In the Dominican republic, there is political equality of the different

---

[23] The treaty provided for cession to the United States of the port of Samaná Bay. For some years, Cazneau continued his agitation for the acquisition of a naval base and even establishment of a United States protectorate over the Dominican Republic. His efforts nearly bore fruit during the Grant administration when a treaty of annexation was rejected by a tie vote of 28–28 in the Senate.

[24] After more than two decades of brutal Haitian rule, the Dominicans finally won their independence in 1844.

races—& also social equality. The pure whites are very few—not more than one to fifteen or twenty of the black & mixed races. But (very different from what I would have supposed,) the numerous black & mulatto population respect the superiority of the whites, & choose them to fill all the civil offices. (I presume the "whites" include those like Gen. Santana, slightly touched with Indian, or perhaps negro blood.) Some blacks & mulattoes are military officers—but none (except when the Haytian power & Báez had supremacy,) were in high civil offices—as members of congress, or judges. There is no jealousy felt by the inferior race—but on the contrary every disposition to respect, favor, & obey the whites. As elsewhere, [318] in the Spanish tropical colonies, the people are indolent, & wanting in energy, & efforts to thrive. There are only 200,000 inhabitants. No doubt the whites, & even the colored population, would be very glad to have Americans to settle there, or even to be annexed to this country, for protection against the Haytian blacks.[25] And but for the great objection to a black or mixed *free* population, this fine country would be a valuable acquisition. But what could be done in regard to this difficulty? Amalgamation with this black & mongrel race is out of the question. They could not be deprived of their present position of social equality—& yet the claim could not be admitted. But degraded & indolent as is this population in general, it is either brave & determined, or their Haytian neighbors must be as cowardly, as they are ignorant & ferocious. There has been either active war, or merely uncertain truces, or suspensions of operations, since the Dominicans threw off the Haytian yoke. The Haytians are very far more numerous, & are under a military & despotic government. Yet every invasion of the Dominican territory has been driven back, & the negro troops have been defeated by one-tenth their number of Dominicans. In addition, the British & French governments have systematically & shamefully aided the Black power by their influence, & as much as possible, worked to produce internal dissentions among the Dominicans, to promote the negro ascendancy.

These glorious portions of the earth cannot always remain as they are under negro population & power. While our federal union continues, with northern votes & abolition influence predominant in our

---

[25] The diarist's supposition is correct. After Santana had engineered a brief and ill-fated reunion with Spain during the period 1861–65, Báez, who seized the presidency for the fourth time in 1868, championed a movement for annexation to the United States.

public councils, nothing but evil consequences [319] can result from any extensive arrangements with the Haytian power, whether by war, or peaceful negotiation. But if our union is dissolved, & the southern confederacy & power well established, it would not be difficult to extend our power, & our race, as masters, over Hayti. There would be no difficulty in determining what to do with the subjugated blacks. All having property, or other means for the purpose, might be permitted to leave the island—& all of the destitute, who are in fact now slaves to their rulers, might be made slaves to individuals. There is no question of the benefit of such a change—& not only for the black community of Hayti, but for Jamaica & all the other emancipated British Islands. Yet any measure of this reenslavement policy would be denounced, with holy horror for its iniquity, by hypocritical England, that is even now putting to the sword every rebel conquered in Hindostan, giving no quarter to any prisoner, & will not cease until 100,000 shall have been slain, of men of whom the greater number have committed no greater offence than did our fathers & the Swiss under Tell, in asserting & defending their country's independence against wrongful & oppressive rulers—& of whom the outrages & injuries were as nothing, compared to those committed by England on Hindostan. It is true that horrible atrocities were perpetrated by many of the insurgents—which ought to be properly punished. But this would not require the killing of 100,000, most of whom must have been innocent of these crimes. It is also true, & ought to be desired by every friend of civilization, [320] & of the well-being of the world, that the European & superior race shall be dominant in Hindostan, as well as elsewhere—& therefore that the British rule shall be re-established & maintained. But this might be done without the enormous & numerous acts of injustice & cruelty which have attended the establishing the British rule, & which will probably continue so long as the conquering & conquered races shall remain distinct.

*April 21.* Correcting proofsheets in the morning & evening. At the capitol as usual for some hours. Climbed to the top of the present structure, & saw the fine view of the city. The new dome, now in the course of construction, will be very much higher than the old one—& this addition alone will cost more than a million of dollars. Met with Jer[emiah] Morton of Culpeper, who requested me to make him acquainted with Gov. Hammond. I went with him, at night, & we conversed with H. until a late hour, much to M.'s gratification. He is, though a whig, a strong asserter of southern injuries & rights, & earnest for the independence of the southern states.[26]

*April 23.* The Kansas question again brought before both houses of Congress, in the unexpected agreement to a report by the joint committee of conference.[27] Great excitement in the H. of R. in the opposite efforts to produce & prevent delay of the consideration. But as usual in such cases, little done, except multiplied counting of the votes, by calling for *yeas* & *nays.* The bill is now in *rather* a more tolerable shape than that passed by the Senate, & supported by all the southern votes. But still it is objectionable—& I care nothing whether it is enacted or not. If passed, it will admit Kansas *nominally* under a pro-slavery constitution, which will be changed for anti-slavery in 6 months. If the bill is rejected, Kansas must wait for admission, the numerous land speculators will be foiled, the prices of land will fall, & numerous poor northern settlers, (sent there for political purposes, by a northern association,) will leave, for want of support.

*April 24.* Another day of disorderly proceedings in the H. of R. & nothing done, except to prevent action. Obtained 500 copies of my pamphlet, & had (through friends who are members) a copy laid on the desk of every member from the slave-holding states, & some others. Began to cover & direct to names for the mail—Mr. Th. Ruffin of N.Ca. franking them. Goode & Senator Mason's franks will also be affixed to as many as I may choose to send. This business occupied most of my time.

*April 25.* Sunday. Another day of drizzle (some snow,) & there have been several other rains lately, besides such as I have mentioned.... At night, sat an hour with [323] Elwood Fisher at his house, with a Mr. Pratt, who has been lately engaged on the preparation of the wagon road across the isthmus of Tehuantepec, Mexico. He states that the route is very healthy—&, contrary to my supposition, that the residents are industrious, especially the Indians, and plenty of laborers to be employed at 35 to 40 cents the day. All are of mixed blood, except the Indians, who are mostly unmixed, &

---

[26] Elected as a Whig to the Thirty-first Congress (1849–51), Morton later served as a member of the Virginia Secession Convention.

[27] Reference is to the English bill, providing for a popular referendum on the Lecompton Constitution. After a bitter debate, the bill passed both houses of Congress on May 4. Unimpressed by the apparent sentiment in Washington, Kansas voters proceeded to reject the Lecompton Constitution by a margin of six to one, and Kansas remained a territory until 1861.

speak their own language. The taint of hereditary *syphilis* is very general, as in Central America. But it was said not to be so general now as it was 20 years ago. Fisher's remarks, as always, original & interesting. He is much disposed to maintain paradoxes—& always argues well, if not convincingly; & is the more ready to advance his own opinions when he knows they are most opposed to those of his auditors. Thus his striking & then entirely novel views stated in his celebrated argument on the "North & South," in which he maintained the superior profit of slave labor, & greater wealth of the southern states, was delivered as a public lecture in Cincinnati. I well remember, when first reading the lecture, with this source stated on the title-page, & when knowing nothing else of the author, I did not believe that it could have been addressed to, or would have been tolerated by a Cincinnati audience. He told me tonight, that he had also lectured there on the *common school* system of Ohio, which (as of the northern states generally,) he maintained was worthless. We discussed this subject, with entire agreement of his with my views, taken up without any knowledge of the practical working of the [324] system, but merely from reasoning *opinion.*— At Hammond's. I was sorry to learn that Jonathan Doolittle, of Lowell, who had started the "Spindle City Idea," (to prove & protest against the *slavery* of northern operatives,) had been compelled to stop the publication, after two numbers only, for want of sufficient support.

*April 26.* Early finished, what I had been doing in the two preceding days, folding & covering copies of my pamphlet for the mail— franked by Hammond & Ruffin of N.C. About 300 have been so distributed, & 450 in all. Today the remainder of the impression of 5000 (including the half which are at my cost of printing, $60,) will be delivered to the members who subscribed for them. The remainder of my 2500 will be mostly left with Goode, to be distributed by him through the mail, under his frank & Senator Mason's.—The last mail brought the news of the conquest of Lucknow by the British army—the last rallying point of the embodied insurgent Seapoys [*sic*]. This completes the triumph of the British government in this atrocious war. But it will be long before peace & security are restored, as before the breaking out of the insurrection. The civilized nations of the earth are now all at peace—but there are various threatenings of approaching war. Many of the semi-civilized countries are torn to pieces by civil war—China, (though the great rebellion there is now seemingly quiet—) Mexico, & Dominica. Venezuela has just had another revolution—Central America is without government or union—& New Grenada almost asking to be annexed to the United States. Each of these American states is ready for a [325] new master, & unable to resist any invader. It is strange that no foreign power should think them worth being conquered.—Both Houses of Congress engaged in discussing preliminary matters to the Kansas conference adjustment, merely to cause or prevent delay. For three entire days the House of Rep. has done nothing but squabble about whether the bill shall be taken up in a few days, or two weeks hence. Settled my business & bill with the printer, & ordered some 800 copies of my pamphlet to be sent to me at Richmond, for my own gratuitous distribution, by mail, or in person.

*April 27.* Left Washington early, & reached Richmond by 2½ P.M. Immediately after dinner to the Office of Agr. So. Heard from Mr. Williams the particulars of a recent procedure, of which something had been seen in the Richmond newspapers. An effort is making to get up a new local agricultural society in Richmond to hold a fair next fall, in place of & in opposition to the state fair. If the scheme is carried through, there will be the remarkable & absurd result produced, of the people of Richmond, after refusing to give $3000 (or anything) to aid & retain the great state fair, paying not less than double that sum to obtain a fair that will be of much less importance, attraction, or respectability. If even so successful, this scheme will not cause any pecuniary loss to the State Society—but perhaps may injure Petersburg, by detracting from the attendance there.—At night, the meeting of the Executive Committee. We sat late. [326]

*April 28.* The committee concluded all the business, & adjourned by noon. . . . Returned to Marlbourne before night. . . .

*April 30.* Put in envelopes (franked for this purpose by Mr. Thomas Ruffin,) a number of my pamphlets, & sent some of them to the mail.—Began to read a new book of Mildred's, which I thought, from its beautiful appearance, [327] to be good for nothing else—but which I find very amusing. It is the "Court of Napoleon." It gives a very black picture of the morals of the characters, & especially in reference to the almost universal absence of female chastity. . . .

*May 1.* Finished the "Court of Napoleon." Selecting & copying passages, & writing others, for additional notes to my article on slavery, to be used in case another edition is demanded for even gratuitous circulation. Received my credentials as being elected at last court a delegate from this county to the Southern Commercial Convention, to meet in Montgomery Ala. on the 10th. Before, preparing to go. Though these Conventions have been of no *direct* use, they may be of indirect benefit. I shall go to meet & exchange views with men of the south, & for the possible chance of forwarding the union & welfare of the southern states, & in my private capacity, instigating secession from the northern states.

*May 2.* (Sunday) At church. . . . Finished my additions to the Essay on Slavery, for a second edition, if it should be required.

*May 3.* . . . Reading, or looking over, the Document published formerly by Congress, embracing every paper that could help to bolster up the Colonization Society. This is a large 8 vo volume—probably printed & distributed in great number. This was one of the many heavy expenses caused by that society to the country.

*May 4.* Having been left by the stage yesterday, I went to Richmond in the carriage. Attended to business for some hours, & at 3 P.M. set out on the train for Charleston, S.C. Travelled all night.

*May 5.* Reached Wilmington by 5.30 A.M. A new road, made since I was here last, diverges at Florence, & shortens the distance to Charleston very considerably. At the Florence station had the pleasure of meeting my old acquaintance & friend of 1843, Dr. Thomas Smith, of Society Hill.[28] He was on his way to Columbia, so we soon parted. But we will meet at Montgomery. Reached Charleston at 6.30 P.M.—457 miles in 27½ hours. Stopped at Charleston Hotel. . . . The conference bill for the admission of Kansas to the union, as a state, has passed both houses of Congress. I would have cared very little if it had been defeated, if by abolition votes. It is admitted under a pro-slavery constitution. But the constitution will be speedily altered, & made to forbid the holding of slaves. So while it is a nominal victory for the South, it is no gain, & will be soon converted to a defeat & a loss.—Had on the cars some discussion on the southern & disunion questions. The only opponent was William Wickham, my countyman, who deems the union a

---

[28] A native of Yorkshire, England, Dr. Smith emigrated to South Carolina in 1803. After graduating from South Carolina College, he studied medicine in Philadelphia and established a practice in Society Hill. He eventually acquired large land and slave holdings and, in 1861, was elected to the South Carolina Secession Convention as a replacement for a deceased member.

greater blessing of itself than all the benefits it was made to secure, & who is one of those who will submit to every possible wrong from the north, before resisting to the extent of secession or separation.[29] Had opportunities of giving into good hands several copies of my slavery & disunion pamphlets, to be carried to distant localities.

*May 6.* After breakfast to Dr. Bachman's. He was delighted to see me, & at our meeting seemed as cheerful as he is noted for. But I soon learned that he was in much trouble. His daughter, Mrs. Haskell, had been very sick for some time back, & had this morning been delivered of an infant, that was expected to die. The mother, considering her previous & great illness, was doing well, as it appeared. Under these distressing circumstances, of course I cut short my visit. Saw & conversed with Mr. Russell, proprietor & joint editor (with Paul Hayne) of Russell's Magazine. Then [330] I met with my valued former acquaintance, Edmund Rhett of Beaufort.[30] Next called on Mr. Richard Yeadon, principal editor of the Courier, & Messrs. [John] Heart & [Robert Barnwell] Rhett [Jr.], editors of the Mercury, & had interesting conversations with both, on political subjects. Also saw Gov. Richardson, & his brother Col. Richardson of Sumpter [*sic*]. After dinner called to see the Artesian Well. The depth reached is only something over 900 feet. The work has continued in progress, & is still proceeding. Saw Prof. Holmes at the museum of Charleston College. At night wrote some sketches of matters for the Southern Convention, should further consideration confirm to me their value.

*May 7.* Left Charleston at 7 A.M. & reached Augusta at 2 P.M. Thence, at 4, proceeded, by Atlanta, & by West Point R.R.

*May 8.* Reached West Point to breakfast—& with many stoppages, reached Montgomery, Ala. at 4 P.M., & took quarters at the Exchange—together with Lewis E. Harvie, Roger A Pryor, Wm. B. Preston, also delegates from Va. & R. B. Rhett of Charleston. Harvie, Pryor & myself in one small room. While I was dressing, Dr. [Noah B.] Cloud, editor of the [American] Cotton Planter, whom I had known by correspondince [*sic*] only, waited on me with a kind in-

---

[29] Notwithstanding his opposition to secession, William Carter Wickham (1820–88) served honorably in the Civil War, rising to the rank of brigadier general. He participated in most of the major campaigns of the Army of Northern Virginia and twice incurred serious wounds. Immediately after the war he joined the Republican Party—a step which reduced his popularity in Virginia dramatically.

[30] A brother of Robert Barnwell Rhett.

vitation from Mr. [Charles T.] Pollard,[31] to take up my quarters at his house—& soon after he came himself, was introduced to me & renewed his invitation. But I declined it, preferring to be with my old friends & at a public house. Several other men of position called & were introduced to me, & we held conversation on southern affairs. Major [David] Hubbard[32] & Mr. [William L.] Yancey of Ala. & Judge S Jones of Ga.[33] [331] were among these. Yesterday made sundry new acquaintances, all of whom stated they knew me well long before by report, & were rejoiced to know me personally. Found on the train ex-Governor Gilmer & his wife, whom I had been with last year at Franklin Minor's house. I have never had from any persons a more cordial recognition & reception. They were going home, in Oglethorpe, & begged me to go with them—& as that was impossible, to go there on my return. . . .

I was never before farther south than Atlanta & Macon. After the light of morning permitted seeing, the appearance of the country had much improved, approaching the border, & in Alabama, passing by West Point. The surface broken, & not rich. Afterwards, when approaching Montgomery, the surface was level as are broad river flats, & seemed to indicate, by the improved richness, & appearance of soil, the beginning of the impregnation of lime.

*May 9.* Sunday. Continue to be introduced or otherwise to become personally acquainted with sundry persons, nearly all of whom refer in most kind & flattering terms to their previous estimation of my labors & usefulness—& with many holding conversations, or exchanging sentiments as to the interests of the Southern States. There seems in many a strong feeling of disunion. At Church. Saw there & spoke to Mrs. Cobbs, the wife of Bishop [Nicholas H.] Cobbs,[34]

---

[31] A native of Fredericksburg, Virginia, Pollard was a prominent Alabama railroad contractor and president. He built and managed the Atlanta and West Point, Montgomery to Selma, and Alabama and Florida lines.

[32] Major Hubbard (1792–1874), a former congressman from Alabama, was elected to the Confederate House of Representatives in 1861. He was a pioneer railroad builder, having constructed the line from Tuscumbia to Decatur, Alabama—one of the first railroads in the United States.

[33] Probably Seaborn Jones (1788–1864), a native of Augusta, who was named solicitor general of Georgia in 1823 and later served two terms in the United States House of Representatives.

[34] Originally from Virginia, Nicholas Hamner Cobbs (1796–1861) moved to Alabama in 1844 when he was appointed the first Protestant Episcopal bishop of the diocese of Alabama. It is probably fortunate that Bishop Cobbs was absent during Ruffin's visit, for he was the most noted opponent of secession in Alabama.

whom I formerly knew in Va. The Bishop resides here, & this is his church—but he is now abroad. Dined by invitation with Mr. Pollard, President of the Railroad, & a leading citizen—with Mr. Rhett, Harvie, & a Major Chase. Saw [332] & was made acquainted with at different times, several planters (formerly Virginians,) who cultivate in the neighboring prairie lands, & invited to visit them. I will do so, & see something of this remarkable region, of which I have studied & written so much, & yet never saw a true prairie, or was in any western state. Not many arrivals as yet, & this day there can be none, as the railroad cars do not run on Sunday. In the night, both the trains & the two Steamers will arrive. Walked in the afternoon, with Dr. Cloud (editor of the Cotton Planter,) to see something of the town. It is well built, containing many handsome edifices, public & private, & withal is so new, that it is one of the best looking towns I ever saw.

*May 10.* The Southern Convention met. The Delegation from Virginia only 19 or 20, & except five of them, a poor set, & mostly very young men. However they will follow the lead of the others. Harvie, Preston, & Pryor chosen by us as our members on the general or business committee. I was chosen chairman of our delegation. A very long report, & resolutions, in favor of reopening the African Slave Trade was presented by a member (the only acting one) appointed at last session. On this an earnest debate was commenced. Many persons, & embracing some who would approve of this policy if it were practicable, strongly opposed to the introduction of this subject for discussion, because no effect can be produced, except to divide the southern people. All our delegation will act on this opinion.— Gen. Walker the noted "flibustier" is here. He is a man of very common, & even vulgar countenance. I did not choose to be introduced to him.—James W. Cook of Greenville, Va, who has estates here, joined our delegation. [333] He is a very intelligent & agreeable gentleman. I lately had him elected on our Executive Committee of the State Agr. Society.—A[ndrew] P[ickens] Calhoun, son of John C. Calhoun, was elected President of the Southern Convention. He is a worthy gentleman, & of good intellect; but he owed his nomination entirely to the influence of his father's name—which gratified me so much the more in his election.

*May 11.* The Convention met at 9. I read a report & resolutions which I had written since leaving home, from the committee (appointed last session,) to suggest business, & which was referred to the present business committee. The whole day, except a recess for dinner, consumed in three speeches—Pryor's, against the opening of the Slave Trade, Yancey's for, & a Yankee preacher residing in Georgia, for the opening. Pryor spoke very well. Yancey is a very eloquent & powerful speaker. But he is so fluent that he does not know when to stop. He is too wordy, & too long. When near to night, this debate was adjourned to tomorrow morning, & then a flood of resolutions, & some very improper or very foolish, poured in, from different members, which were all, as a matter of course, referred to the business committee. The sentiments expressed in debate, & especially by Yancey & the preacher, were strongly in favor of disunion. And in conversation, out of the Convention, I have not yet heard a dissenting voice to the measure. I had myself to attempt a short speech, in reply to a censure improperly cast upon Virginia by Yancey.—Dined, by invitation, [334] with Col. Jones—& took tea with Mr. [Edmund] Harrison.[35] I am almost oppressed with invitations, & to various places. I think I shall be tempted to visit the prairie lands in this neighborhood, & also farther south.—This day, by motion, & vote of the Convention, the two noted individuals, Gen. Walker & John Mitchell, the Irish patriot & refugee convict (from Australia,)[36] were admitted to the honors of the session. I was much tempted to vote against the invitation—but as it would have had no good effect, I remained silent.

*May 12.* Long speeches from R[obert] G[omain] Scott (lately of Va. & now of Ala.)[37] & Mr. [Henry W.] Hilliard [38] of this place—an

---

[35] Harrison, a native of Petersburg, Virginia, moved to Alabama and entered the mercantile business while still a young man. Later he became a large planter in Lowndes County and an ardent secessionist. His Montgomery residence was utilized as the first "White House of the Confederacy" following Jefferson Davis' inauguration as President in February, 1861.

[36] Banished from Ireland in 1848 for a period of fourteen years, Mitchell (1815–75) came to the United States in the mid-1850's and continued his agitation for Irish independence. He also became a strong proslavery advocate—a posture which doubtless facilitated his admission to the Southern Commercial Convention. At this time Mitchell was publishing the *Southern Citizen* in Knoxville, Tennessee.

[37] Scott, a lawyer by profession, was an ardent states' righter and Confederate sympathizer who, in 1864 at the age of seventy-three, volunteered to defend Mobile.

[38] Henry Washington Hilliard (1808–92) was the first professor of English literature at the University of Alabama, receiving his appointment in 1831. He later won a seat in Congress and in 1861 was appointed Confederate commissioner to Tennessee.

eloquent & graceful speaker. . . . Spent the evening with Dr. [George] Rives.[39]

*May 13.* . . . At the Convention, W. B. Preston of Va. made a good speech. Afterwards Yancey occupied the whole remainder of the day, for some 4 hours (omitting the recess for dining,) & in all the after dinner part he was under the influence of strong drink, & his speech suitable to his condition.—A ball at night, given to the delegates, to which I shall not go.

*May 14.* Received a letter from Dr. Bachman containing the sad [335] news of the death of his daughter, following that of her infant. Wrote to him a letter of friendly sympathy.—The debate on the question of re-opening of the slave-trade was closed at noon, & the vote presented most unexpected unanimity. The subject was laid on the table, & ordered to be printed, (which procedure does not indicate any opinion,) by a unanimous vote. We have thus, fortunately, avoided exhibiting to our northern enemies the division of the south. Afterwards followed the passage of resolutions approving the Walker-Nicaragua procedures & policy, & denouncing the interference by Com. [Hiram] Paulding.[40] This, on a vote by states, also passed unanimously. In the Va. delegation, (then reduced to 5) it was carried by one vote only, against my vote in the minority— Harvie & Pryor taking the other side. This was the only question on which there was any division of opinion in our delegation—& our opposition has served to prevent indiscreet & perhaps violent action by the body. It is a singular state of things, & not a little amusing, that Harvie, Pryor, & I, who, at home are regarded as extreme disunionists, & disorganizers, should here be acting (in appearance) as conservatives & union men. After more of unimportant business, & with some disorder & confusion, the Convention adjourned at night. —By invitation, at night attended a party of gentlemen at the home of Mr. Yancey, where there was a superb cold collation. It was an

---

[39] A native of Bedford County, Virginia, and a cousin of William C. Rives, John Y. Mason, and Winfield Scott, Rives earned his medical degree at the University of Pennsylvania and in 1818 migrated to Elmore County, Alabama. At the time of the sectional crisis he was a member of the Alabama Secession Convention.

[40] Walker's second expedition to Nicaragua was broken up by Capt. Paulding in November, 1857, after Walker had landed with 150 men at Greytown, near the mouth of the San Juan River. Paulding's unauthorized action resulted in his censure and removal from command of the Home Squadron by President Buchanan.

agreeable meeting of a number of the delegates, & also some ladies, which latter I did not expect. Among the company was Gen. Walker, to whom I was introduced, & as I was the last in the circle, he took his seat by me. Though I had before avoided an introduction to him, yet as here I could [336] not avoid it, I entered into conversation with him, respecting Nicaragua. I was amused at his coolness in pronouncing the pure Indian race there, (who are much the greater number,) as being proper to be made slaves, in case of Americans becoming conquerors & masters there—& he supposed the mixed & mongrel population would emigrate to South America, or die out gradually. The piercing "gray eye" of Walker has often been spoken of. To my view, his eyes are not gray. They are remarkable, but of a light greenish blue color. He is continually shifting their direction, & this gives to him an appearance of suspicion & uneasiness. His manner is reserved, retiring & modest—& his voice & manner of speaking, in conversation, very quiet & mild. I learned subsequently from a great partizan of Walker & his schemes, that 700 men were now engaged, a steamer bought, & money was now being subscribed, (or loaned on bonds, whose ultimate value will depend on success,) for another invasion of Nicaragua, but as immigrants & settlers. It is expected that by August or September the invasion will be made. This was told me, in a casual conversation, as *confidential* indeed, but by a person to whom I had just been introduced, & who did not even know, or ask, my opinions on the subject—though of course he inferred them to be favorable—& as indeed they are, to the success & ends of the scheme. I left the party as soon as I had eaten supper & even then it was 1 o'clock before I reached my lodgings. Most of the others remained much longer, & had toasts & speeches over their wine. Mitchell was there, & spoke. But I had not seen him. [337]

*May 15.* I had before been invited by Charles Pollard, esq. President of the R.R. to go out to see the neighboring prairie lands of Lowndes along the route of the R.R. so far as finished, 25 miles. He offered to me the accommodation of a special train, to run slow, & stop at will. This morning we set out. All the Va. Delegation (remaining,) were invited, & as many more as made some 25 gentlemen. ... This my first view of the celebrated calcareous or "prairie" lands, was to me very gratifying. It would have been far more so 20 years ago, when I devoted so much inquiry, & labor of writing, to the investigation of the peculiar qualities of these lands, & the cause of the formation of naked prairies, or of the absence of trees on such or other lands. What I then wrote, before having ever seen a prairie, was in general correct, even as to the particular features which I could only learn from the loose & imperfect descriptions of residents. But in some minor points, I was mistaken, though in no way affecting my reasoning & theory. Most of these lands (of Lowndes county,) were of what was called "timbered prairie," because set with trees. But the calcareous quality of soil, the marl or "rotten lime-stone" under beds, & the peculiar agricultural features of the soil, were alike. The [338] "bald" or naked (of trees) prairie grounds were generally of small extent. These differ from the others in having the lime-rock to be nearer the surface, & therefore the soil still more highly calcareous. All these prairie lands were under crop, cotton or corn, except a few small spots of original bald prairie, & these spots were closely grazed—so that I could see nothing of the original condition & natural appearance of such land.—We returned to Montgomery by 4 P.M. to take the steamer at 6, but found the departure postponed until tomorrow morning. I had had another invitation from Major [James L.] Price, President of another railroad from Selma to Woodville,[41] to go over it, & to visit him, to see the more remarkable & valuable prairie lands of his neighborhood. This is now my design.—At night, I was invited by Mr. Shepherd of Mobile, (Walker's friend, & a gentleman of high standing, & good ability,) & pressed by Pryor, to go into the reading room to hear an address from Gen. Walker on Nicaraguan matters. I went in with some 20 others. But Mr. Shepherd's introductory remarks seemed to assume that all present were friends to the enterprise, & if not so, were requested not to report what might be said, to the disadvantage of the enterprise. Conceiving that if I remained I might be considered as participating in a secret conclave, I deemed it proper to withdraw, & did so immediately. . . . [339]

*May 16.* Left Montgomery, in the steamer, on the Alabama river, at 8 A.M. The river was moderately low, serving to offer the best navigation combined with the best view of the banks. This is a beautiful river—narrow for its great length, seeming to my eyes in some parts not more than 80 yards, & rarely 150. After some miles, the lime rock, or marl, showed above water at every steep bluff, & rose higher as we descended the river. It is generally bluish—sometimes a hard

[41] Born in Richmond, Virginia, Price moved to Perry County, Alabama, in the mid-1830's and engaged in legal, planting, and business pursuits. He was the first president of the Selma and Meridian Railroad.

clay marl, separated or marked by numerous small fissures—more generally hard as stone. No shells seen for a long time. At Rock Bluff the steamer stopped—& I found in the very hard rock some of the shells which I had seen no where else, except in the eocene of Rocky Point, on Cape Fear river N.C. Higher up, in Lowndes, the bed is wholly of the cretaceous formation, & so I had supposed it was here. Lower down, the lime rock was often perpendicular at the river's edge, & with stratification so regular as to look like a wall of artificial masonry, built in regular & parallel courses. The scenery, & especially the trees & their varied foliage, were beautiful. There were sundry agreeable gentlemen on board, of visitors to the Convention—among them, Major Chase, recently of the U.S. Army—Mr. Calhoun, & Gen. Walker & his zealous aid Mr. Shepherd. The latter told me that he had obtained for Walker's service $13,000 at Montgomery. [340] We reached & landed at Selma ( 100 miles from Montgomery,) after sunset, all the last named persons except Major Chase. Mr. Calhoun is going to his plantation in Marengo, & invites me earnestly to go with or after him—& Walker & Shepherd I suspect are seeking to raise contributions from friends to their objects. We all stopped at Gee's hotel for the night. Had a long conversation with Calhoun before retiring to my room to write. We agreed in opinion that, ( despite, as I think, the many incidents, & much of the procedure, calculated to discourage & even disgust the judicious members,) that the effect of this meeting will be important & influential abroad. In the conclusions, there was great unanimity, so as to seem to indicate union of sentiment & of action. And though there was no direct expression of opinion, by vote, on disunion, all present saw that every expression favorable to that result was applauded strongly. I sought to learn opinions on this subject—& outside of our delegation from Va. I only heard two individuals express themselves favorable to the continuance of the present union with the northern states.—However much I was dissatisfied with the proceedings of the Convention, I had every reason to be gratified by the kind & respectful manner of my own reception, by the many persons who sought my acquaintance, & offered me attentions.

*May 17.* After breakfast Mr. Calhoun & I left, on the new & unfinished railroad for Woodville, & Gen. Walker & Mr. Shepherd took another direction. I had inquired of Walker as to the capabilities & difficulties, [341] so far as he had learned, of constructing a ship canal, or passage from the Atlantic to the Pacific, through the river

San Juan & Lake Nicaragua. At present, obstructions in the river forbid any but small steamers; & from Lake Managua (?) there is land passage ... to the port on the Pacific. He knew of no insuperable obstructions to the great work of a deep ship canal. When this can be done, so that the largest sea vessels can pass without any transshipment of the cargoes, this will be the greatest improvement for transportation in the world. Mr. Shepherd is a very intelligent & agreeable gentleman. He has been the possessor of a large fortune, but lost all in cotton speculations. He is again recovering in fortune. His conduct in all respects, but more conspicuously when surrendering everything to his creditors, has shown him (as Mr. Calhoun says) to be entirely honorable, & he is universally & highly respected & esteemed. He is ardent & impulsive, & engaged with all his heart in aiding Walker's scheme by his influence, for the benefit that he fully believes will be produced to these southern states, in the establishing Central America, as an American conquest & colony, & a slave-holding community. He told me that he had obtained $13,000 at Montgomery during the Convention, in advances by individuals, who receive bonds for their loans, the payment of which will depend on the conquest & retaining peaceable possession of the country, & will be of no worth or validity otherwise. This success indicates great interest & sanguine expect[at]ions.—[342] The finished part of this railroad is some 28 miles from Selma, nearly all of which is through the calcareous lands. Mr. Calhoun, who is still a planter & was long a resident in this region, gave to me every information of the lands we passed over. We stopped at the end of the finished road, where Major Price's carriage & himself awaited my arrival. ... We drove through the village of Woodville to Major Price's family residence, on his plantation. ...

*May 18.* We rode to the village, where I bought some muriatic acid, for testing soils, & read the latest newspapers. Saw there several of the neighboring planters, & we talked of the usual subject, the proceedings of the recent convention. Soon after we had returned, six of the neighbors came to dine with me, having been invited the previous day. A pleasant conversation, on the peculiar soils & culture of this calcareous region, & on southern politics & interests. Three invitations to dine pressed on me, & two accepted. ... [343]

*May 19.* Rode out, first on horseback, & afterwards in a carriage, about the neighborhood, to see & test sundry soils, as to their contents of carbonate of lime. It is the general opinion here that *all* of their soils are highly calcareous. Such is the case with all of the "prairie" or black land, except the "slue" land, of which latter I tried one place—& found that, & all of the yellow ( or "post-oak") lands, to be non-calcareous, or not effervesing [*sic*] with acid. . . . In the afternoon, according to previous invitation & arrangement, I went home (with my luggage,) with Mr. Richard Adams, who resides in Marengo, in the midst of the best body of the "cane-brake" lands. On our way, called to see Mr. Calhoun at his plantation, where I saw 80 acres of well-set & fine clover. . . . Mr. Adams & his wife both Virginians, & they & I well known to each other by report. In all such cases, & in others where there was no previous acquaintance of any kind, I am received & welcomed as if an old friend.—The sight of this new country is to me very interesting, but I will postpone any comments until I have completed my observations. . . . On the route of the railway from Selma, I had seen a few pines, without having an opportunity to examine any, or to determine the species. On inquiring, I heard that there was only one pine tree known in the neighborhood—which I rode some miles to see. It is *pinus variabilis*, as fixed by the small size of the cones, & still more certainly, by most of the leaves growing in twos, but a few in threes. But the leaves were longer than any I had seen in Va. of this species, which if alone observed, would have caused doubt, whether this was not a different species. The longest of the leaves of this tree were 5⅓ inches. In Va. they rarely exceed 3 inches. Of the many scattering pines that I had before imperfectly seen along the railroads in Ala. before reaching this calcareous region, I believe that all were either the *p. variabilis* or *p. toeda*, the older trees of the former, & the saplings doubtful. But not one seen of the *p. australis*, or long-leaf pine of the Carolinas.

*May 20.* Drove some 6 or 8 miles distant in the neighborhood, to see plantations & different soils. Continued to test different varieties of the "post oak" lands, & found every one non-calcareous. [345] Again a dinner party to meet me, of 12 guests, at Mr. Adams', all his near neighbors & all Virginians, or sons of Virginia immigrants, except one, a Tennesseean, who had married in Va. This is almost a Virginian colony. Found some good specimens to two kinds of shells (cretaceous) on the "bald prairies." Also 5 young pine trees, together, & like the one seen yesterday, on "post-oak" land. All of them *p. variabilis*. Have agreed to accompany Mr. Adams to his plantation in Dallas county, 25 miles distant. This will prevent my going to

Mobile, as I had proposed—but which I was before getting out of the notion of. . . .

*May 21.* Set out in a buggy with Mr. Adams, & travelled 25 miles to his plantation in Dallas county. The road passed through a continuation of the same lime lands, but in the latter part becoming more hilly, or approaching to hilly surface. We reached the place about 1 P.M. [346] The calcareous land ends, & the sandy surface begins in this tract. The first pines were seen in the last two miles— of both the *p. variabilis* & *p. toeda*—& one young *p. criops*, the only one I have ever seen south of Va. But the overseer here told me that they are plenty from here to the Alabama river, which is 10 miles distant, & the land poor & sandy. The dwelling house on this plantation is like all those of the first settlers. Two square rooms were built of hewed oak logs, about 12 or 16 feet apart, & this interval covered in by the same roof. This gave two closed apartments, & an open one between, which served as the common sitting & eating place in warm & good weather. As the size or wants of the family increased, one or perhaps two sheds were attached. The whole structure was rough & plain. In such dwellings the wealthiest settlers lived for years, until they found it convenient to erect new & handsome mansions, & to leave the old houses for their overseers or servants. . . .

*May 22.* Rode on horseback with Mr. Adams, to see the plantation & some of the neighboring lands—partly of the usual intermixed calcareous lands, & partly of the adjacent (& overlying) sandy lands. We passed over a broad & fertile bottom, bordering on the Chehatchee creek, (now & generally dry,) which sometimes overflows but a little of the lowest of this flat of some miles width. . . . Part of this land is cleared (or the trees killed,) & under cotton. The field is not ditched, & does not need it, though so level a bottom. The forest trees on this land are of great size & height, & magnificent appearance. . . .

*May 23.* Sunday. Returned, with Mr. Adams, to Joseph Selden's, by his invitation. He is the son of John A. Selden of Westover, Va.[42] who has married the only daughter of George Minge of Marengo, a wealthy planter also from Va. We reached Selden's house by 10½ A.M., early enough to attend church in Union Town, the village

---

[42] In 1829 John Armistead Selden purchased Westover, the famous colonial estate of the Byrd family on James River. He prospered as a wheat planter until obliged by wartime exigencies to dispose of his plantation in 1862.

close by, but the minister was absent. After dinner, rode to Mr. Price's, which is within two miles, where Mr. Adams left me—& at night I came back to Selden's, which is to be my quarters, until taking the train for Selma tomorrow. Heard this evening, for the first time, that I have some relations, as near as second cousins, in this neighborhood, whom I will try to see tomorrow morning, before leaving. . . .

*May 24.* Finding there was not enough time for my visit & to take the train, I deferred my departure, & went, with Mrs. Selden . . . to see my newly heard of cousin, Mrs. [Sarah] Fitts. . . . Mrs. F. is an intelligent & agreeable woman of 36, & with a very attractive countenance. We soon became as intimate as if long acquainted, & old friends. I have never had a more friendly & kind reception from strangers. We conversed late, before retiring. . . . [349]

*May 25.* After sitting with my hosts as long as there was time to spare after breakfast, I took my leave, & all sorry to part—& Mr. Fitts went with me in his carriage to the rail road Depot. At noon, the train started, & we reached Selma to dinner. There I will wait for the first steamer going up the river, which will not arrive before tomorrow morning, & it may be much later. . . . An intelligent old gentleman, Dr. Bowman of Ga. who is the brother in law of my much esteemed old friend Dr. W. S. Morton of Va. is my fellow traveller, & awaiter, in this wretchedly dull town & bad hotel, of the uncertain arrival of the next steamer.

*May 26.* The steamer, which was due early, did not arrive until 2 P.M. when I embarked. The low state of the water had rendered it necessary to substitute smaller steamers, & this was crowded with passengers & loaded with freight. Grounded [350] several times, but luckily got off. Passed a wretched night on a dirty & very bumpy mattress laid on a table—the earlier passengers, or ladies, having engrossed all the staterooms & berths.

*May 27.* Reached Montgomery at 6 P.M. At the Exchange Hotel. . . . I saw & conversed with Yancey, which was a main object of my stay today. He is strenuously for secession—& he has great power of eloquence—& even by his faults as a public speaker, has remarkable power over popular assemblies. I suggested to him my schemes for operating on the public mind of the south—by an organized association, & operating by discussion, publications & public speeches. In the last I deemed him capable of the greatest power & utility. After inquiring whether he supposed that he could venture (safely for both himself & the cause,) to deliver a public speech urging seces-sion, & his answering affirmatively, I proposed that there should be a large gathering got up for the 4th of July, when he should deliver a stirring speech on the occasion, directed to southern independence —& making use of the examples of the disunionists who declared independence of our mother country, to show that there was then much less cause for separation, in wrongs suffered & threatened, than now in the wrongs of our northern brethren. He seemed to take readily & heartily to the plan—& I also conversed with F. B. Shepherd, (Walker's zealous & efficient aid,) & who is equally zealous for separation, & has ability & opportunities to render the cause much service. I understand that he is very popular & much esteemed. He is certainly intelligent & agreeable, [351] & zealous & ardent in what he undertakes. I had before written a concise "Declaration & League" which would be suitable for all friends of the cause to sign, when we are strong enough to make a beginning. This I showed to Yancey, Shepherd, & Judge [George W.] Stone,[43] who agrees with us in sentiment—& all seemed to approve the plan. . . . Called on the Governor of Ala. ([Andrew B.] Moore) at his office at the State House.—Afternoon, at 5.30, left on the cars on my way homeward, & travelled all night.

*May 28.* When light enough to see, we were within 40 miles of Atlanta. In that distance, the pines were not many, & nearly all of *p. variabilis.* The very few others, *p. toeda.* . . . But in all Ala. & Ga. until getting within 50 miles of Augusta, I did not see a single long-leaf pine, *p. australis.* There I saw the first—& thence they increased along the road. Very hot, & dusty. Supped in Augusta, & then proceeded.

*May 29.* Reached Kingsville at daybreak. . . . Proceeded through Columbia—& reached Charlotte at 4 P.M. where I must wait to take the Express Train at 1 o'clock. Three gentlemen on the train, with their families—most of the ladies from Ala—& one family from Wis-consin. We got into conversation, without introduction to the ladies, (those ladies from the south beginning) & I found them pleasant companions. . . .

*May 30.* Sunday. We left in the train at 1 A.M. & at 6 reached Haw

---

[43] Judge Stone (1811–94) was an associate justice of the Alabama Supreme Court at this time. Born in Bedford County, Virginia, he served a total of twenty-five years on the Alabama high court before his retirement in 1892.

River station, where we had breakfast. There I hired a buggy & driver to carry me to Alamance. Found all the residents of the [Judge Thomas Ruffin] family at home & well . . . . The Rev. Moses A. Curtis (the botanist) also there. I was received, as always, most kindly and affectionately by all, & by Jane & Patty as if they were my daughters—& I returning their caresses as if they were more than daughters to me. I should even fear that my attraction was allied to *love*—& the most foolish & reprehensible of all, that of an old man for a young woman—if there was only one of them. But as there are two, & together, & I so equally & greatly love them both, & equally enjoy the caresses of both, I trust that I am safe from that greatest of follies, which in my case, will be only the effect & indication of dotage. If I were to consult merely my own selfish feelings & inclinations, without considering propriety, or looking to future consequences, I might be as great a fool as most other old men, & seek to marry a blooming young girl. But I trust that I shall never be (as I never yet have been) so deficient in discretion as to have any such desire.—The family went to Graham to Church, where Mr. Curtis is to preach this forenoon—Judge Ruffin making an excuse for me to remain, because of my two last nights & days on the rail-road—& of which I was very willing to avail myself of, though not to sleep, but to write & read. Mr. Curtis returned with the family, to leave tomorrow morning. He is a very agreeable talker, as well as distinguished botanist, & a highly esteemed preacher. . . . [354]

*May 31.* . . . Judge Ruffin had to attend the county court at Graham, on which he condescends to serve as senior magistrate, & faithfully performs the duties. I copied & corrected two papers written before, for a "Declaration & League" for the South, & a "Constitution for the Association of Southerners." . . . I tried, but in vain, to obtain the concurrence, & name of Judge Ruffin to my scheme of an association to agitate & maintain the rights of the Southern States. He is too cautious—perhaps too wise—to go with me. Moreover he would adhere to the Union much longer, as a greater good than all to be gained by separation. He does not admit the doctrine of the right of secession (except as a revolutionary right,) & believes that its exercise never can be peaceful.

*June 1.* . . . I spent the day in reading, conversation with the ladies &c. until Judge Ruffin's return from court. Afterwards some free & confidential conversation with him in relation to my own domestic & family matters. We both have been accustomed to expose freely to the other, some of our family distresses, & the causes, which are the most afflicting, & also hopeless.

*June 2.* Today Mrs. Ruffin taken sick, with symptoms which seem to indicate typhoid fever, which her son John has had for three weeks, though but slightly. This produces much uneasiness in the family. It will cause me to anticipate the designed time of departing. Took leave at bed-time, to set out before sunrise tomorrow morning. [End of MS Volume 2—p. 355] [44]

*June 3.* Left Alamance before sunrise, & reached the breakfast house, 5 miles off, at Haw River before 6. The Express train soon arrived, in which [I left before] 7, & reached Richmond before 7 P.M. . . . Read the last newspapers. It is reported, & believed, that Brigham Young has determined not to resist the approaching attack of the U.S. troops, but to yield & retreat. If so, it will save some risk, & a great deal of trouble & additional expense to the government. An enormous cost has foolishly & uselessly been already incurred, in sending an army just too late in the season for it to do anything for the next six months, except to starve & suffer with the terrible cold of the climate. After waiting for the return of warm weather, of supplies of animals (to replace the thousands that had perished,) & of provisions, & reinforcements of men, & also for the grass to grow enough to sustain the animals, the army was about to march to the attack, & the Mormon leader deems it best not to resist by force. I heartily wish that he had resisted, so that he & his chief followers might have been put to death.—The newspapers of late, have a most exciting topic in the conduct, habitual latterly, of British war steamers stopping & examining American merchant vessels on the coast of Cuba, by firing on them, & by force. [356] This lawless conduct seems to be a settled policy—under pretence of preventing the African slave trade. More than 20 vessels have already thus been boarded—& [strange to s]ay, though slave-traders are sufficiently numerous, [not one of] the vessels visited was even suspicious. . . . If the British [torn] their pretensions, this course of insult . . . may suddenly produce war between En[gland &] the U.S. This would be the most deplorable & injurious for both countries—& the Southern States would have to bear most of the evils on our side. Our prosperity would be entirely repressed, our interests greatly

---

[44] Beginning on this page and continuing for the next twelve MS pages, a hole in the upper half of the diary pages makes it difficult to sustain a legible narrative. Wherever possible, the defaced portion will be deleted.

damaged & more endangered—& we would come out of the struggle weakened & prostrate, & no longer able to resist the aggressions of the Northern States, which would gain in influence, strength, & perhaps in wealth, by the war.

*June 4.* Corrected two connected pieces, written while at Alamance, & copied one of them for the "South" newspaper. Wrote answer to the President of the U.S. Agr. Soc. giving my full consent that he may arrange with the new "Central" Society here, to hold their next Fair in Richmond—for which negotiations are going on, & two letters have been written by Prest. Tilghman, to consult with me. Conversed with Daniel London, a well-informed merchant, about the probable results of a war with England. He thinks that the effects would be much [357] less disastrous on the southern than on the northern states. I am ready to be convinced of this. . . . [England wo]uld be almost ruined[45]—even if her present [friend F]rance, & her late foe, Russia, did not make use of the opportunity so afforded to destroy their ancient foe & rival. . . .

*June 5.* Left Richmond early, in the steamer, for Beechwood, where I landed at 10.30 A.M.—Mr. [John] Tyler & Professor [Benjamin S.] Ewell (of Wm. & Mary)[46] on the steamer. The latter a pleasant & well-informed gentleman, whom I saw for the first time. Much agreeable conversation with them both—& argument on the policy of reopening the slave-trade. Mr. Tyler opposed, & Mr. E. seemed favorable. Though I have strong reasons against the measure, as well as others for, I here met Mr. Tyler's objections, as I am much accustomed to do, & thus support or oppose particular arguments for or against either side, without as yet having determined in favor of either policy, if considered as a practical question.—Found all well at Beechwood . . . . [Several letters] forwarded here for me, & among them a long one [from my] friend Willoughby Newton, on my slavery pamphlet, & giving his views as to the policy for the south. Like myself, he deems separation from the northern & oppressing states as the only remedy, & which should be no longer delayed. I

---

[45] As a consequence of loss of trade, destruction of her merchant marine, and the vulnerability to attack of her seaport towns.

[46] Benjamin Stoddert Ewell (1810–94) was president of William and Mary College. Although a strong Unionist, Ewell served throughout the Civil War as chief of staff to General Joseph E. Johnston. Ewell and former President Tyler were returning from a meeting in Richmond of the board of visitors of William and Mary when Ruffin encountered them on the steamer.

proceeded immediately to answer him, at length, & enclosed to him a copy of the form of a "Declaration & League" for the south, which I had lately prepared. Also wrote to W. L. Yancey, on the same subjects, & offering suggestions, & sending the same paper. . . .

*June 8.* Julian & Lotty came to dine. A day pleasantly spent. Began to copy & correct my notes on the "cane brake" lands, for publishing. Began to read "The White Slaves of England."

*June 9.* . . . The "South'" of the 8th contained the two pieces which I sent for publication[47] . . . . Read the June number of Russell's Magazine, & continue the "White Slaves of England.". . .

*June 13.* Sunday. . . . Yesterday I finished reading the "White Slaves of England." It is a poor book. Yet its subject & design are so good that it is very interesting generally, notwithstanding that the plan is badly executed. It describes the actual slavery, of the worst kind, of the poor laboring classes of England—& it presents a picture of wide-spread & general misery, severe labor & great privation & suffering, degradation, ignorance, indecency & vice—& all these still increasing—worse than could be supposed possible of human beings called *free*, & under the most free government & enlightened policy of the old world. The condition of our negro slaves is immeasurably superior & preferable, in care & comfort, extent of labor & of privations, & even in means for instruction in moral & religious duties, & certainly in their attainment. Yet with all this general condition of horrible suffering, excessive toil & misery, ignorance & horrible depravity & vice among all the English population truly & strictly enslaved by want, all the efforts of English philanthropy are directed to enlighten & convert the heathens of foreign countries, & to [368] destroy African slavery throughout America! There never was more unblushing hypocrisy than in this pretence.—Began to read [Lord Henry Peter] Brougham's Miscellanies.

*June 14.* . . . Important news from Utah. Brigham Young, & all his Mormon subjects with him, have determined to make no resistance to the U.S. power, civil or military, & to leave the country. The retreat had been begun, & they are moving southward (as is reported) to settle in Sonora, in Mexico. I wish it was northward to the British

---

[47] The two articles, under the general heading of Suggestions to the Southern States, were entitled "Southern Conventions—Their Objects and Uses" and "Proposed Plan of Association for Defence of the Rights and Interests of the Southern States—Form of Constitution." In the latter Ruffin unveiled his plan for an Association of United Southerners, a project which he labored zealously to bring to fruition during the next several years.

dominion—& still more it is to be regretted that the head & principal followers of this villainous set had not continued their act of treason & rebellion so as to be hanged for it. . . .

*June 15.* . . . Edmund began to reap wheat this afternoon. The crop everywhere greatly injured by disease—& the [369] appearance of great loss, not less than one-third, in quantity, weight, & quality of the grain already incurred.

*June 17.* Raining at intervals, & slowly, & heavier at night. Used Julian's apparatus to analyze 3 specimens of marl & soil from Marengo, Ala. Wrote letters to R. H. Adams on this subject—& to Hugh B. Grigsby, at his earnest request, to give him some information about the life of my grandfather, which he wants as materials for his proposed history of the Va. Convention.[48] I furnished such as I have—but stated, first & last, that there was nothing worth using for the publication. Reading [James] Stuart's "Three Years in America." [49]

*June 19.* Writing & reading as before. The wheat is worse than had been suspected. A letter from Mr. Sayre by last mail gives a still more deplorable account of the prospect there. Yet but a short time back, the crops were luxuriant, & promised a large product.—The complaints of the recent stopping & boarding of our vessels by British cruisers in the Gulf of Mexico, have made much sensation in England. Both in Parliament & in the leading newspapers much regret is expressed, & great disinclination to offend the United States. Also a readiness to stop the acts complained of. But still there is great difficulty [370] how they can satisfy us, without renouncing their *right* of search. This the British government will not do, (as yet,) & we will be satisfied with nothing less than the abandonment of the *practice*, as to our vessels. This, no doubt they will abandon, as they have already abandoned the right of impressing seamen, (pretended to be English, & generally so, but often American born,) & the practical acknowledgment in the late war with Russia, that "free ships make free goods." I am very glad however that we escape, honorably, the great calamity of a war with England. The Senate of the U.S. have passed strong yet temperately expressed resolu-

---

[48] Hugh Blair Grigsby (1806–81), the leading Virginia historian of his day, had recently published histories of the Virginia conventions of 1829–30 and 1776, and was now collecting data for his study of the Virginia Federal Convention of 1788.

[49] The controversial Scottish journalist and politician penned this account after visiting the United States from 1828 to 1831. The work is strongly biased in favor of America.

tions, declaring that this recent practice of visitation & search of our vessels, in time of peace, will not be submitted to. The present tone & temper, on this general subject, both in England & this country, are in remarkable contrast with what was inflicted by England & endured by the U.S. so long before we declared war in 1812. . . . After having resorted to war, much too late, peace was made without any settlement [371] or mention of the rights claimed by Britain to search our vessels, & impress seamen (alleged to be of English birth). But our growth & strength has served better than any treaty stipulations. England knows that the first renewal of impressment, or of capture, would cause war to be declared by the U.S.—& that even the claim of right of "visitation," as recently exerted, though more defensible, will not be long submitted to.—Finished reading Stuart's "Three Years in America." A fair enough view, for a Briton, & even too favorable to the people of the Northern states. But the writer's unmeasured hostility to African slavery perverts his judgment in regard to southern people & their condition. He has exposed, & I am glad of it, some detestible [*sic*] cruelty of particular southern slaveholders—especially of the late Gen. Wade Hampton. But he was in search for such horrors, & of course his inquiries elicited reports of many which doubtless were false. Besides, every hardship necessarily incident to the general condition of slavery, every strong act of repression of disobedience of slaves, mutiny, or of amalgamation of the black & white races, the author treats as gratuitous cruelties. If he had looked at home, & merely to the single atrocity of the ordinary impressment of men, by force, to serve in the navy, he might have found, a hundred for one, acts of greater injustice, hardship, and unmerited & deepest distress thus produced to free men, & their wives & children, of minds & feelings capable of receiving pain from such injuries, as much exceeding our negroes, as negroes are in this respect superior to horses & oxen. [372]

*June 20.* Sunday. Finished Brougham's "Miscellanies." I especially enjoyed the excoriating delineation of George IV—the most infamous scoundrel, as I think, that has worn the crown of England since James I. . . . Began to read Simms' "Life of Marion.". . . Also read the chapters in [William] Paley's Moral & Political Philosophy on the institution of private property—of civil government—civil liberty—& the subjection to government. I cannot get exactly to what I want, or adopt the proper train of argument for my purpose. But it seems to me that the moral authority & expediency of the institution of individual slavery, or the subjection of the individual slave to an individual owner, & the rights of the owner & the obligations of obedience of the slave, have the same general foundations, & the like reasons in support of, with the rights of private property, & of government, & the corresponding duties of the destitute & the powerless to respect & obey the possession by others of all the property & all the political power of the world, & from both of which most of the men living are not only deprived, but are hopeless of ever being able to become possessors, to the smallest extent.

*June 21.* . . . A letter from Willoughby Newton to me (in answer to mine,) informs me that he is to deliver the annual address to the Cadets of the Military [374] Institute, at Lexington, & that he will use that occasion to speak plainly on the great question of the south & north. He proposes to dine with me at Marlbourne, on his way to Lexington. I do not think that I can then be at home conveniently, (or without going home merely for that purpose). I rather think that I may join him on the way, & accompany him to Lexington. Having received this letter, I will not wait longer for the others expected, & will go to Richmond tomorrow. During harvest, every farmer is so continually & laboriously engaged in his field, (or ought to be,) that I can have but little pleasure in then visiting any, & would fear that my presence would be an inconvenience to any friend except my own children. I do not wish even to visit Marlbourne during harvest, & especially in the existing very bad & sorrowful condition of the crop of wheat, & indeed of everything else. But I shall be compelled to go there for a hasty visit, to obtain papers &c.—Reading the 2nd vol. of [Henry S.] Randall's History of Thomas Jefferson.[50]

*June 22.* At 11, left Beechwood for the Berkley wharf. Reading the Life of Jefferson, until the arrival of the Steamer, past 1 P.M. on which I embarked. . . . Reached Richmond past 5. Saw L. E. Harvie, & afterwards, at the Exchange Hotel, Wm. O. Goode. Talked with both on political affairs. Went to see my sweet & dear granddaughter Nanny, after tea. [375] Read the last newspapers to bed time.

*June 23.* . . . One of my objects in being here was to converse with Judge [John] Robertson[51] on political matters—but he is at his

---

[50] Randall's three-volume work, *The Life of Thomas Jefferson*, was published in 1858. The author was a prominent New York agriculturist and educator.

[51] After five years in Congress, Robertson (1787–1873) became judge of the circuit court of chancery for Henrico County, in which post he served for a number of years.

country property, & I shall be a second time disappointed. Went to the Agricultural Office, & conversed with Mr. Williams about the matters of our Society, & also the progress & prospects of the new "Central Agricultural Society of Virginia." Went to the Land Office, & copied a list of the various Patents issued to all the Ruffins. This I had done before, as to the older patents, to assist me in making out my family chart. The time heavy on my hands. . . .

*June 25.* Called up & dressed at 3 A.M. to take the stage coach at 4, but which did not set out until 5, for Marlbourne [376]—where I arrived before 8. All well, except that the measles passing through the younger negroes, & some so lost to Harvest work. Mr. Sayre in full progress, & getting on well, except for the great discouragement of the recent great loss in the wheat. The present prospect is of a loss of one half, in quantity & quality, & a low price even for good wheat. . . . Read the newspapers of today—the small amount of new & readable matter in the last No. of De Bow's Review, & "A Northern Presbyter's Second Letter to Ministers of the Gospel, on Slavery," by Nathan Lord, President of Dartmouth [377] College. A well written & able argument in defence of the institution of slavery—& wonderful as coming from a northern minister of the Gospel.[52]

*June 26.* Rode to see the crops, & the harvest work. Returned soon & began to perform a service which I had promised at the request of N[athaniel] F. Cabell.[53] This was to write a list of all the writers of the communications to the Farmers' Register, (designating for each article,) by copying from my own set, to which I had written the writer's name to each piece. I spent full 6 hours at the job, & got through only the first two volumes. . . .

*June 28.* Took the stage coach & reached Richmond at 3.30 P.M. . . . At the Hotel saw J. W. Cook, of Greenville, whom I left in Alabama. Had with him, in my room, a long & interesting conversation on the calcareous lands of Ala., & also on southern politics.—From the newspapers—the second attempt to lay the Atlantic telegraph cable is again in progress. In a short time we may hear of the suc-

---

[52] Lord's proslavery views, when published in detail in his treatise entitled *A True Picture of Abolition* (1863), led to his resignation as president of Dartmouth College after a term of thirty-five years in that office.

[53] Proprietor of Liberty Hall, an estate in Nelson County, Virginia, Nathaniel Francis Cabell (1807–91) was a frequent contributor to agricultural and religious periodicals.

cessful issue. But I much more expect, & greatly fear, another failure, more complete & hopeless than the first. It is stated (though not as yet officially,) that the English government has acquiesced in the claims & protest of ours as to their [378] claim of the right of search or visitation, & in the position of denial asserted by our government. Not only is the practice abandoned, but the principle yielded. If so it is a wonderful degree of submission to be made by England. . . .

*June 29.* . . . Read the newspapers, & talked, & wrote the rough sketch of an article on the removal of free negroes, of 8 pages. Saw Pryor in the street, who told me of the annexed article,[54] & gave me the Montgomery paper in which it appeared together with my plan of a Constitution for Southern Associations. No doubt it was written by Yancey. Conversed with Pryor on Southern politics. He is fettered by his position—& dares not express in his paper sentiments as strong as he would wish. As yet, in Virginia, any public man would destroy his political prospects by advocating the separation of the Union. I, & others [379] who have no political connexions or aspirations, can do so, because not to be injured by denunciation or disapprobation. There are plenty who think as I do, if they dared to avow their sentiments. But as yet, there is no candidate for office who does not think he would be ruined by such avowal, & so would every publisher & press in Va, dependent (as all are) on popular favor for support. Received an answer, on same subject, from Judge John Robertson. As I expected, he declines taking any prominent or active part to stir up the South for preparation, or future action.

---

[54] "To the Southern Rights Men in Alabama," from the Montgomery *Advertiser and Gazette*. The article lauds Ruffin.

# July–December

ew

# 1858

---

TWO VISITS TO THE NORFOLK AREA ew
LEAGUE OF UNITED SOUTHERNERS ew VA-
CATIONING AT THE SPRINGS ew VIRGINIA
STATE AGRICULTURAL SOCIETY MEETING
AND FAIR ew STATE DEMOCRATIC CONVEN-
TION ew VISIT TO WASHINGTON, D.C.

*July 1.* On the impulse of articles which appeared in the "South" of this morning, I wrote another article in condemnation of the Enquirer, & carried it to the editor—who promised it shall appear tomorrow, though the time was very short. . . .

*July 2.* At 4 A.M. went in a hack for Nanny, & thence to the steamboat. She stopped at the Berkley wharf, where the Beechwood boat was waiting for her, & I proceeded to Norfolk. My main object was to see Mr. [Hugh B.] Grigsby—who, as I learned from Mildred was at home, & not in Charlotte where I had written to him. He expressed to Mildred so much desire to see me, that I thought I would go to meet with him. . . . Reached Norfolk at 6 P.M. Went to the National hotel. After tea, called on Mr. Grigsby, & sat until nearly 10. He is a man of high order of mind & education, & of very extensive reading & research. He has the misfortune to be very deaf, which I feared would cause conversation with him to be difficult & disagreeable. But I soon got over the awkwardness & novelty of the impediment. We sat close together on a sofa, & as he always inclined his ear to receive my words, & I spoke loudly, we conversed conveniently. He has directed particular attention to the private memoirs of our past political history & men. I heard from him many minor but very interesting circumstances of the great men of the revolution. He informed me that he had evidences in private letters & other writings of there having been numerous bitter feuds among

[206]

our great men—& much vilification of each other. Mr. Grigsby is singular (in this country,) for his admiration of statuary & painting. In his house he has all of [Alexander] Galt's best pieces of sculpture, five in number, as well as others, & some fine paintings, which he liberally permits to be seen by all who desire it.[1] As my view by lamplight was imperfect, he requested me to return tomorrow, at 9, to have a better view. . . . The "South" of today contained the first of my late articles.[2]

*July 3.* Went again to see Mr. Grigsby's pictures & statuary by daylight. I am no judge of either—but I was especially pleased with two female heads, copies from celebrated old paintings—one a Mary Magdalen & the other of an angel. A full figure (though of small size,) of Eve, soon after her creation, pleased me much more than usual with sculpture.—Called on Marshall Parks, President of the Albemarle & Chesapeake Canal. Learned that this important work is far advanced, & is expected to be open for navigation throughout by the close of the year. Mr. Parks expects to pass along the line soon, & invited my company—kindly offering to extend the trip to different parts of the sea beach that I may wish to stop at. I am much tempted to go—& will have to the 5th to determine.—Called to see Governor Tazewell, whom I had not seen for more than 30 years. Instead of being met by a servant at the door, as I expected, & to send by him my card, Governor Tazewell himself was sitting in the passage near the front & open door. It made my entrance very awkward, & disagreeable to me. He was so much changed in appearance, & yet looked so florid & fleshy, & so healthy, that I did not know him—& of course he could have no recollection of me. . . . However, as soon as I could make myself known, he welcomed me with cordiality. I hoped to hear him speak of political affairs, & to hear his opinions—which even after 25 years of disuse & rusting of his great intellect, I would attach much value to. But though I several times made remarks to draw him to such subjects, he did not continue to speak of them more than a few sentences. I soon saw it was in vain, & ceased my attempt. Among his incidental observations were the following expressions of opinion: That the government of the U.S. was now the most corrupt in the world: that the

---

[1] Galt, a native of Norfolk, studied in Florence, Italy, during the 1850's. In 1860 he opened a studio in Richmond, but died three years later of smallpox.

[2] See Appendix C for the text of this article, entitled "The Free Negro Nuisance and How to Abate It."

most astonishing thing now exhibited was this government borrowing money to pay its ordinary expenses in time of peace—(& as I added, within a year after there had been so much surplus revenue in the treasury, that it was deemed an evil, necessary to abate). . . . The only remark that he made on public affairs, that was not called forth, was in reference to the approaching removal of the remains of President Monroe, from New York to Richmond. "They are about to make a great parade with removing the body of my old friend Monroe." "Yes," I answered, [387] "& very foolishly." "Yes" he rejoined, "it had better be let alone. Where the tree falls, there let it lie." He paused a moment & then added, with much appearance of deep feeling—"A good man!—A good man!" These few words, & the manner of their utterance conveyed to my mind more in favor of Monroe's worth than all that I had ever heard in his favor. For Tazewell knew him well, & was well able to appreciate him—& I would have supposed would have thought very slightingly of Monroe, both as to mental ability & moral worth. Such has been my estimate of him. Fearing to be intrusive, I took my leave after half an hour's conversation. I could not but grieve to witness such a wreck of one of the greatest minds that has ever been in Virginia. Yet with all his ability & power, & the readiness of the people & the government to recognize & to use his services, he has been of scarcely any use to the public. He was pressed by Jackson (as Mr. Tyler told me) to take any place in the cabinet, or to be ambassador to England. He refused all—& has only served, & then not zealously, as U.S. Senator of Va, as a member of the Convention of 1828, & as Governor, which last post he resigned before completing his service. He has had no ambition. For 25 years he has lived almost a recluse, scarcely going out of his doors, & seeing no one but his family & the few of his old friends who call on him as a matter of respect. In public life, he made some brilliant displays of the most incontrovertible argument—without seeming to care much for the object, or to be conscious that he had done anything to deserve notice or applause. . . . At 4 P.M. left Norfolk in the steam boat for Old Point Comfort. Found there but few of my acquaintance, & none that I cared for. . . .

*July 4.* Sunday. Among the guests who are here I saw [Robert] Ridgway, the editor of the Richmond Whig, who introduced himself to me on the steamer when we were coming from Richmond. He is a pleasant companion, [390] & seems to be what is called a "good fellow." Also [James D. B.] De Bow is here, & J. W. Cook, [William

L.] Goggin,[3] [John H.] Wheeler (late minister to Nicaragua,) all of whom I knew before. The notorious [Henry S.] Foote, formerly governor & then U.S. Senator of Mississippi also is here, whom I never saw before, & do not choose to be introduced to.—At 5 P.M. as arranged & expected, the steamship from New York passed, conveying the remains of President Monroe. Several other steamers met & escorted the ship. Minute guns were fired from Fortress Monroe as long as the steam ship was in sight. A great number of the guests & of the garrison were on the ramparts—& two steamboats full of people from Norfolk came to witness the scene. Conversation until 9 P.M. when, not having left any interesting company, I retired to bed. . . . Wrote & mailed a letter, enclosing my "Plan of Association" & "Declaration & League" to a committee in Louisiana, which had drawn up a somewhat similar plan, & which had been adopted by a public meeting at Clinton.—A drunken & noisy man in the next room disturbed me until midnight.

*July 5.* The celebration of Independence—which is usually a great day at this place. Many sailing vessels & boats arrived, & 8 steamer trips with many passengers from Norfolk. [391] At night a brilliant display of fire-works in the Fortress, to see which most of the visitors staid—& many had to remain through the night, for want of conveyance to Norfolk.—Mr. Parks came, & I have arranged to start with him on his trip on the 7th.—Today I wrote a letter to Gov. Tazewell asking him to give his opinion on the great southern question—but apologizing at the same time for taking this liberty, & saying that I shall not take it amiss should he fail to answer my letter. I have scarcely any hope that he will answer it. . . .

*July 6.* Pryor arrived—& with him, Cook, De Bow, & Goggin (about California) I had interesting conversation. Still much of the day hung heavy on my hands, & I shall be glad to leave the place so soon. I have nothing to read or to write—& I take no part in the various amusements in some of which nearly all others join, for pleasure, or to kill time, as fishing, billiards, ten-pins, smoking & drinking, card-playing, or for a few, faro bank.—At night, Dr. R[obert] W. Gibbes of S.C.[4] arrived, with whom I had a conversation about the soils of Ala, which he formerly analyzed. [392]

---

[3] After serving four terms in Congress, Goggin (1807–70) was an unsuccessful candidate for governor of Virginia on the Whig ticket in 1859.

[4] Twice mayor of Charleston and formerly on the faculty of South Carolina College, Gibbes (1809–66) was at this time editing two Democratic newspapers. During the Civil War he served as surgeon general of South Carolina.

*July* 7. At 5.30 A.M. went on board the Baltimore steamer for Norfolk. Left Norfolk, in a carriage with Mr. Marshall Parks, (President of the Albemarle & Chesapeake Navigation Company,) & Lieut. Murdaugh, U.S.N. & rode 17 miles to North Landing, the southern terminus of the main section of the new canal, where I went in 1856, to see the operation of the excavating machine. The work here is now ready for use, as soon as the remainder shall be done, which is less than a mile here, & less on the smaller section. But there will be no passing until these remnants are removed—which it is expected will be by the end of the year. The excavating machines are now kept at work night as well as day. There have been unforeseen & great difficulties—but all seem now to have been surmounted, & the completion will be certainly reached. At the landing, the little steamer Calypso, belonging to the Company, was waiting for us, & ready to move as soon as we had taken a short walk along the margin of the canal. The steamer is 50 feet long, with an engine of about 6 to 8 horse-power—& neatly fitted up for such excursions as this. When deeply laden with coal, (which we stopped afterwards to take in at a landing in Currituck,) the vessel draws two feet water. The North River has a namesake close by in N.C. as well as several more elsewhere—on which account I proposed & it was agreed to, to use instead the name of Cohonk. This river is like all others in this low region, deep & still, with water colored deeply by the vegetable matter of the swamps [393] from which the only supplies of water flow. Mr. Bisbee, a literary man, & formerly an editor, was at the landing & made one of our party, as well as a young son of Mr. Parks'. I found pleasant conversation & companionship. Lieut. Murdaugh has more than the usual stock of information & resources for pleasant conversation of our intelligent navy officers. He has been to Brazil, was one of the expedition to explore & examine the almost unknown upper waters of the great rivers Parana & Paraguay, & was in the Advance (under [Edwin J.] De Haven,) the first American ship that went to the Arctic region in search of Sr. John Franklin. . . . Before sunset we reached to near Crow Island, which we had designed then to visit. But we got on the shoal, & frequently touched the sandy bottom, as the steamer slowly moved on. After more than two hours waste of time, we found deeper waters, & cast anchor. . . .

Mr. Murdaugh describes the people of the great regions along the Parana & Paraguay as of the same worthless [394] & unimprovable kind as are all others of Spanish America. These too are nearly all a mongrel race of mixed blood. But, different from those of Mexico, to Brazil, these of the southern hemisphere are mostly free from any mixture of negro blood, though generally mixed with Indian. This is not so bad, & will not be an insuperable objection to the Anglo-Saxon race amalgamating with these, as would be with any tainted with negro blood.

*July 8.* Our anchorage was within a mile of Crow Island, & after breakfast four of us set out in the small boat to see that place, as well as for Mr. Parks to get some information about the navigation. . . . Crow Island is a very interesting spot. It has only 40 acres of firm land, the highest about 8 feet above the level of the water, & on one side, a larger quantity of the usual firm marsh land. A former sea captain, Hatfield, bought & built a comfortable dwelling house on this island. The house is within a few feet of the water's edge. It is a beautiful spot—& I was so much taken with its Robinson Crusoe loneliness, that I should like to be the owner of the island. The surrounding scenery is beautiful—of the broad water, interspersed with other islands of firm marsh, covered by luxuriant & tall grass only & sundry high sand hills on the ocean beach, in view. Cattle live well on the grazing afforded by these marshes, & pass from one to another across half a mile width of water, by wading & partly [395] swiming. . . . On returning to the steamer, the approach of rain, & the difficulties of the shoals, determined Mr. Parks to run back to Currituck C.H. which we had passed [several] miles back. There he engaged a pilot, who promised to join us on the way, but who did not. The rain stopped after we had stopped for some hours, & we again started. . . . In the afternoon we again got in to very shoal water, & had to go very slowly, & frequently touched bottom, & had to change the course. No pilot or information could be obtained, [396] & indeed we only saw one boat. After making scarcely any way for two hours before night, we cast anchor. Yesterday we only made 35 miles from North Landing—& today, of our onward progress, but about 24 miles from Crow Island. The marshes, & these mostly forming islands, had become more frequent. They are usually of heights varying from a foot above the water to even with its surface. The soil is a rich & partly vegetable formation, but with enough earth to be firm. This I could be sure of by seeing the cattle running rapidly & with ease, when alarmed by the whistle of the steamer. The distant sand-hills, standing separately & far apart along the line of ocean beach, added much to the interest of the scene. There were 8 in sight off Crow Island—& the number increased with our advance, to nearly 20 before night. They are mostly naked, & of the dingy whitish color of sea sand—but some are partly covered with stunted shrubbery. But for their color, the naked sand hills would seem like high mountains when first coming into distant view of a traveller approaching them. The water, though still colored, is very clear, & as slowly feeling our way, we can see every deposit or lump of the oyster shells, which make the worst difficulties of the shoal bottom. The water is generally full of water grass, which grows at all depths less than 8 or 9 feet—& except in the channels or where the water is least sluggish. In many places it grows as thickly [397] as tall grass on dry land, & is a serious obstruction to the passage of small boats, & even of our steamer.

... One part of the passage this afternoon was through "The Narrows," which is a very narrow & also crooked water-way, not exceeding 200 yards wide, between high marshes—& this is the only channel in the whole width of the sound, which is there from 3 to 4 miles wide. Much of this breadth is occupied by marshes, & the open water is too shallow for continuous navigation of even 1½ feet.

*July 9.* Very early Mr. Parks rowed ashore, & up a creek, some 4 miles to engage & did obtain a pilot for the remainder of Coratoke sound. Even before he came on board, (at a lower point,) we had found no more shallow water, or difficulty. Reached & entered Ginguy creek, which is a deep & good harbor, entering a broad part off the sand reef, & running up several miles diagonally. The land separated from the main reef by this broad creek is a peninsula of considerable size, on which is one of the plantations & the residence of Mr. Gallop, who, from his wealth & high position, is a sort of king of the sand beach. Though his land at his residence, is of the same general character, & same wind-sand-drift formation with the older & back lands of the sand-reef, & in part is being blown away by the winds, he raises there crops of 400 to 500 bbls. of corn, & in great perfection, potatoes & garden vegetables. Mr. Gallop's wealth, & extent of cultivation & production, are as great as all others put together on the N. Ca. reef, south [398] of Knott's island. He owns 10 or 12 sea-going vessels, of which two were then lying off his wharf. Mr. Parks was well acquainted with him, & he gave us a very kind & hospitable reception. We dined & supped with him, being detained by wind too high, & weather too threatening, to go with our little steamer into Albemarle sound. As soon as we stopped at the wharf, our party crossed the creek in the small boat, & went to the ocean, a mile distant. . . . The naked sand-hills here are high, perhaps 60 feet—but others must be 100 feet above the level of the ocean. Though the sea was smooth farther out, a fine surf was breaking near the shore. I took advantage of the opportunity to take an ocean or surf bath, for the second time in my life. This is a delightful bottom for bathing, but some parts, & near the shore, (within an outer sand shoal,) are rather deep for persons who cannot swim. A heavy shower fell before we took our bathing, [399] & after dinner, Mr. Parks thought it most prudent to stay for morning. . . .

*July 10.* By sunrise the steamer set off. Though the wind had much abated, the water was rough for the little steamer, in crossing part of Albemarle sound. The water there was muddy from the Roanoke—& as soon as we neared the mouth of the Pasquotank river, we crossed again into the dark yet very clear water of that river, across a precise line where it joined the muddy water from the Roanoke. We had intended going as low as Nagshead & Roanoke [400] island. But so much time had been lost that we concluded to omit these places. We entered the broad Pasquotank & reached Elizabeth City by 12.30 P.M. where we had to wait 3 hours—after which we proceeded up the river, 25 miles to the Dismal Swamp canal. The river above the town is growing narrow, & after some 13 miles becomes very narrow & crooked, so as to obstruct navigation. The water is 8 feet deep or more, with a channel from shore to shore. The bordering land, with a few exceptions of low dry ground, is low swamp on both sides, covered by forest growth. The river, so bordered, is beautiful. We entered the canal about dark, & reached Deep Creek, near the northern end, after midnight—where we stopped & slept.

*July 11.* Sunday. Set out very early, & reached Portsmouth at 7 A.M. where I landed. Took breakfast at the Macon Hotel, and at 8.30 A.M. set out in another steamboat for Old Point Comfort. Found a great increase of company—over 700 in all. Of my acquaintance but a few left, but more arrived. Among the new-comers, I found Col. P[hilip] S[t. George] Cocke, (who soon accosted me & we had a long conversation on general topics—) Boulware, S. Gresham, & several others whom I knew but slightly. A conversation begun with Boulware on African character & the slave trade, attracted others, [401] & among them an intelligent gentleman of

Louisiana, whom I afterwards learned was named Hayden. . . .

*July 12.* Begin to be tired of this place, & feel lonely in the great crowd. If I had not appointed the 15th for my departure, I would set out tomorrow. . . . Nothing to employ or amuse me but conversation—& nothing to read. . . .

*July 13.* Went to Norfolk this morning, & returned to dinner. . . . Saw Mr. Devereux on his way to the Springs. Had several interesting conversations with different visitors on southern politics. [402]

*July 14.* . . . A government steamer (revenue cutter) arrived this morning, with a party of dignitaries from Washington, who cannot get quarters, the rooms being all occupied. [Among] them are Howell Cobb, Secretary of the Treasury (I believe) & a great political scoundrel—the French ambassador, Compte de Sartiges, Sir [William] Gore Ouseley, the British *extra* minister,[5] the President's niece, Miss [Harriet] Lane.[6] Their not being able to obtain rooms is good proof that the house is quite full. . . . The Washington party after going to visit the Navy Yard, at Portsmouth, returned here to late dinner, & went into the ball-room at night—where I suppose most of the guests went to see a real French count, & an English baronet. I did not. Made this afternoon acquaintance with Wm. R. Cox of N.C. a very intelligent & agreeable talker, whom I regret I did not know earlier. He is a distant relative of mine, & a strong disunionist.[7] I have been endeavoring to arrange with [J. W.] Cook & [Josiah] Deans for the forming of the first club of the "Association of United Southerners." I think Gloucester county would be a good place to begin. [403]

*July 15.* Early left Old Point in the James river steamer. Gen. [John S.] Millson, the member of congress for the 1st district on board.[8] Find he is much more hopeful & conservative than I had supposed, & less apprehensive of the future for the southern states.

---

[5] Ouseley had just returned from a special mission to Central America, where he had been sent by the British government in 1857.

[6] With Miss Lane presiding over social functions at the White House, the Buchanan administration was one of the most successful socially—if not in other respects—in the nation's history.

[7] At this time an Edgecombe County, North Carolina, planter, William Ruffin Cox (1832–1919) later earned a distinguished military record with the Army of Northern Virginia. Wounded eleven times during the war—five times at Chancellorsville—Cox commanded the brigade which fired the last shots of Lee's army.

[8] Millson, a resident of Norfolk, served six consecutive terms in the United States House of Representatives, 1849–61.

At the Berkley wharf found the Beechwood boat waiting for me, & my grandsons Thomas & George. . . . Found a short note from the son of Gov. Tazewell stating that his father had been too sick to answer my letter. This is as much as I expected. Newton's address is in "The South." It is short, but good, & fully to the point in the position in which he recommends the separation of the present union of these states. And this, except my pamphlet, is the first plain out-spoken opinion put in print in Virginia to this effect. . . .

*July 16.* Looking over my papers, & began to copy one of my N.C. pieces. M. Dupuy went to the Glebe, & at night returned, bringing with him his sister Juliana, & my grandaughter [sic] Jane, at my re-quest, to stay a while here with me. She is a very interesting & at-tractive child—but I greatly fear she will be damaged both in health & conduct by the improper indulgence of my sister especially, & of all the family. She soon became very [404] free & cordial with me.

*July 19.* After breakfast, sent home my granddaughter Jane, who returned with great reluctance, overcome only by the pleasure of the drive, & other inducements. How I would rejoice if permitted to take her home with me, to remain, under Mildred's care. It would give delight to all at Marlbourne. . . . At 11.30 I left to row to Berk-ley, where the steamer took me up at 1.30 P.M. . . . Reached Rich-mond, & the Exchange Hotel at 5.30. Saw Mr. Williams at the Agri-cultural Office. . . .

*July 20.* Left Richmond in the stage coach by day break, & reached Marlbourne to breakfast. . . . The new [406] fire-proof gran-ary is completed—which I had not supposed possible, after all the many delays caused by bad weather & other causes, to the making of the bricks, & the building the house. The measles have made many sick here, & in addition, dysentary [sic]. There have never been so many cases of sickness altogether, since my ownership began, as in the last year here—mainly of these two diseases, & previously vario-loid, of which there were some 30 cases, but all mild except one, which was of a valuable young man, that brought on lingering dis-ease & death. . . .

*July 21.* . . . Mr. Sayre's brother, Col. Burwell Sayre, of Kentucky unexpectedly arrived before dinner, with his young daughter.—I had yesterday begun to read for the second time Fitzhugh's "So-ciology for the South," & finished it this evening. . . . The author is a profound thinker, though a careless writer—sometimes altogether wrong, [407] but his views often novel, & generally correct, as well as striking & convincing. Many of the positions which he has assumed, I have also entertained & presented, in regard to slavery. I think he has fully established his main proposition, the "failure of free society"—or what is miscalled *free society*, in contradistinction to what is usually & only understood as *slavery*—but which condition for the destitute laboring class is truly the most grievous & wretched slavery. It is a pity that Fitzhugh should present his argument in so careless a manner. He is so deficient in method, that sound & forcible [as] are many of his positions, & conclusive as reasoning, yet he jumbles together his major & minor, his premises & conclusions, without regard to priority or separation.

*July 24.* Reading & correcting my last writings, (on the sand-reef & sounds,) & arranging the whole piece. . . . This the anniversary of the death of my beloved daughter Jane. Some hours engaged in reading the writings on her illness & death, & Ella's, with other services connected with these mournful recollections.

*July 25.* Sunday. No preaching in the neighborhood—& all remained at home. Dr. Brockenbrough made his daily visit to the sick negroes. Several of them still very sick, with measles, dysentery, or both together. . . . Finished a list of the writers of anonymous articles in the 10 vols. of Farmers' Register, referring to each article, for N. F. Cabell—& directed the paper to him, together with a letter of queries about the statistics of Liberia & the Colonization Society.

*July 26.* Left Marlbourne for the stage coach, & in it to Richmond. Arrived at the hotel at 2 P.M. Saw sundry of my acquaintance on their way to the Springs. . . . At night went to the preliminary meeting of the Ex. Com. but had only three other members—no quorum —& adjourned (as before arranged) to meet tomorrow in Albemarle, at Franklin Minor's house. [409] Read the newspapers.

*July 27.* Set out on the Central R.R. Reached Charlottesville at 12, & Minor's before 2 P.M. Col. Knight, Mr. Scott of the Executive Committee, & Mr. Williams went with me. A company of between 40 & 50 farmers met us & dined at Minor's. Also Professors [James P.] Holcombe & [James L.] Cabell.[9] With the former had some inter-

---

[9] Holcombe, at this time professor of law and bellelettres at the University of Virginia, later served as a member of the Virginia Secession Convention and sat in the Confederate Congress from 1862 to 1864. A leader in the early public health movement in America, James Lawrence Cabell (1813–89) was a professor of anatomy, surgery, and physiology at the University of Virginia from 1837 until the time of his death.

esting political conversation. After dinner, the session of the Farmers' Club, & a discussion on the economy of the use of guano, at the present price, & also the reduced price of wheat. Every experienced farmer thought that the use could still be afforded. After tea, we held a meeting of the Ex. Com. & had nothing to do. Sat up late conversing. . . .

*July 28.* Went to the University—heard the oration to the Society of Alumni, & sundry other of the ceremonies of the different Societies. Dined with a number of the Professors & distant alumni, at Professor Cabell's. None of the Board of Visitors present except Col. T[homas] J[efferson] Randolph.[10] He invited the members of the Executive Committee to occupy the lodgings prepared for his absent colleagues—where we sat in pleasant conversation before going to bed. Gen. J[ohn] H]artwell] Cocke dined with us.—On my proposition, the Ex. Com. by resolution requested of Prof. Holcombe an address at our next fair "On the grounds of the right of society to maintain the institution of African slavery & its obligations." He has accepted the invitation, & I have no doubt will make an able argument.

*July 29.* This is the great day of the University, when the degrees [410] will be conferred, & orations delivered, preceding the vacation. But, though I should like to meet many of the persons who will be present, I have no fancy for the ceremonies. So after taking breakfast with Col. Randolph, our party returned by rail-road, & reached Richmond at 2½ P.M. At the Hotel, met Wm. H. Harrison of Amelia, & Wm. Kirkland, of the Navy, & just from his home in N.C. . . .[11]

*July 30.* On the steamer, for Beechwood. Wm. Harrison & his wife on board, John Selden &c. Stopped at Westover, & Mr. Selden sent me across the river in his boat, to Beechwood—where I arrived by 11 A.M. I found all well . . . . I had come in the hope of being able to get my granddaughter Jane to go with me to Marlbourne, & immediately wrote to her father, & soon received his answer & consent—which I did not much expect, as several obstacles & difficulties oppose. Shall see him tomorrow, to make arrangements. . . .

---

[10] Randolph, Thomas Jefferson's favorite grandson, was president of the Farmers' Bank of Charlottesville and had been a member of the Board of Visitors for thirty years.

[11] William W. Kirkland switched to the army during the Civil War. He participated in numerous battles on the eastern front, from First Manassas to Bentonville, and rose to the rank of brigadier general by war's end.

*July 31.* Resumed the "Life of Jefferson." Immediately after breakfast, rode to the Glebe, & arranged with Dr. Dupuy the carrying my granddaughter Jane to Marlbourne, next Saturday, with Edmund's three youngest children. Went thence to Ruthven, & found Julian closely engaged with his thrashing of wheat. . . .

*Aug. 2.* . . . The mail. The [412] Atlantic Telegraph cable is again to be attempted to be laid. The steam-frigates having it on board have again set out for the purpose—& only, as I am confident to fail again. I have no doubt of the success of this great scheme at some future time, & by other means—even if it should [be] by crossing the continents of Europe & Asia, & over Bhering's [*sic*] strait, across North America. But I have not the slightest faith in the means now used. A letter from Elizabeth to Edmund. One from R. B. Rhett jr. editor of Charleston Mercury to me, on political matters, which I answered.

*Aug. 3.* Nearly all the day in the house, reading the "Life of Jefferson." Wrote some notes of contents for the next Annual Report to the U.S.A.S. Late, took a walk with Nanny—who is very neglectful of using proper exercise, & whose health I fear will suffer because of that neglect.

*Aug. 4.* Wrote the rough sketch of an article—12 pages—recommending the taxing northern commodities under license laws.—The mail. Reading the newspapers, & Jefferson. . . .

*Aug. 5.* Copying & correcting my writing, & as usual, copied more slowly than I had written at first. My grandchildren begged me to read to them some tales in Irish brogue, in which I indulged them both in the forenoon & at night, to their great amusement. . . .

*Aug. 6.* My copying & additions extended to 18 pages. Lotty & Meade dined at Beechwood. Julian too closely engaged with his wheat-thrashing to leave [413] home, or even to be from his work an hour together. In afternoon, I rode with Lotty to the Glebe, & afterwards with her home, to stay the night. . . . The papers today bring the report that the western end of the Atlantic Telegraph cable has actually been landed on Newfoundland, & that the eastern end was within 100 miles of Ireland, & the communication throughout maintained. This is a most wonderful event, of which I was incredulous before. Still I dread some accident that may cause total defeat in the short distance remaining to lay the cable.

*Aug. 7.* Returned to Beechwood, after breakfast, where I found my granddaughter Jane . . . already arrived, & impatient to set out for Marlbourne. John well today, but his father very properly deems his sickness for the two previous days make it unsafe for him to go, as designed, with the other children to Marlbourne today. After 11, we set out, Sue, Mary, & Jane with me, & crossed the river to the Berkley wharf, & waited for the steamer until it passed at 1 P.M. Reached Richmond after 4, & found no carriage waiting for us, as ordered. . . . Had to go to the hotel & leave the children until I could hire a carriage, which luckily was done quickly. A little before 6 P.M. we had again started—& after a slow journey, we reached Marlbourne at 9. Found our arrival unlooked for, [414] as Mildred had written to me not to bring the children so soon, & had expected me to be thus warned in good time, but which letter had not been received. The cause of the notice, of the fear of danger to the children, is that the dysentery has continued since my departure to extend to new cases, (& some of the old still very low,) & at last reached the white family. Elizabeth & Mildred have been taken, & have not yet recovered, though both much better. . . .

*Aug. 8.* Sunday. Last night, Col. Sayre & his old servant Elinor both taken with the dysentery, & his daughter's maid, (a white woman,) also taken sick, & as is feared, with the measles. . . . Col. Sayre was to go to Richmond tomorrow, on his journey to Kentucky —& nearly at the last moment, three out of four of his family party are suddenly taken sick. Finished writing my article—extended to 21 pages. Read the attractive parts of the last numbers of De Bow's Review & Russell's Magazine. . . .

*Aug. 9.* Answered letters to Senator Hammond, Professor Holcombe, Willoughby Newton, & wrote letters to R. B. Rhett jr. & W. L. Yancey—which occupied me the greater part of the day. Another case of measles, unexpected, which I fear will cause the disease to be communicated to my grandchildren. The other cases of sickness improving.

*Aug. 10.* The mail. No news. The Atlantic telegraph reported to be connected at both ends with the land lines, & the communication across the ocean perfect—but still not ready for use, or transmitting messages. The managers say that it will be some days, or it may be some weeks, before all will be fixed. I fear that there is something wrong, or imperfect. A letter from the editor of the Montgomery Advertiser, respecting the "League of United Southerners," which I answered at considerable length. Began & finished the reading of Prof. [Raleigh E.] Colston's pamphlet, "The Problem of

Free Society." [12] There is not a view presented in this that was entirely new to me—& most of them I had discussed, or glanced at, in my late pamphlet on the "Political Economy of Slavery." But Mr. C. is much more full on the evils, & sufferings, of what is miscalled "free society," & has given a clear & forcible account, & a valuable treatise. Still, he does not offer a solution of the problem, & no remedy, but only feeble palliations, of the great & always growing evils of "free society"—and no remedy has been or seems likely to be pointed out, by any one. The institution of African slavery, where general, & maintained in its purity, not only excludes the existence & the evils & sufferings of general free labor, [416] but must, for a long time, postpone the inevitable change of personal slavery to class slavery, or slavery to hunger, which is miscalled "free labor." As long as there is an outlet for the excess of population, as now in this country, African slavery may continue to exist, & all the evils of the corruption of "free labor" be avoided. But without such outlet, the change, however long postponed, must come in the end. . . .

*Aug. 11.* Wrote to Edmund & to Dr. Bachman, & Dr. Cloud. A *private* letter for publication in the Montgomery Advertiser, in reference to the "League of United Southerners." Also wrote my request to be received as a member. Reading parts of Chambers' "Encyclopedia of English Literature." . . .

I will here insert several recent editorial pieces of Pryor's, which caused to me no less surprise than displeasure & disgust.[13] At first, I could not conceive a motive for charges so unfounded & absurd. But his later comments, together with others, indicate that he is fearful that the movement for a "League of United Southerners," which I first proposed, & which Yancey has started in operation, will endanger the national democratic party, & the chance for retaining northern votes to support southern candidates. He doubtless loves the cause of the South much—but he still more cherishes the hope of making Hunter president, by aid of northern votes—[417] which,

---

[12] Born in France, Raleigh Edward Colston (1825–96) moved to the United States and graduated from the Virginia Military Institute. He then taught French at V.M.I. until the Civil War, when he offered his services to the Confederacy and saw extensive action as a brigadier general in the Army of Northern Virginia.

[13] The editorials referred to, "Conspiracy Against the Democratic Party—'League of United Southerners'" and "A New School of Southern Statesmanship," are critical of Ruffin's pet scheme for a League of United Southerners. Pryor apparently took particular exception to a letter of June 15, 1858, from William L. Yancey to James S. Slaughter in which the fiery Alabamian evaluated border-state sentiment in most disparaging terms.

whether for Hunter, or any other southern man, is as vain & foolish a hope as can be entertained by any one. My "Suggestions for the Southern States," Nos. 1 & 2, which set forth the reasons for such a means for combining the south, & presented the form of a Constitution for the "Association of United Southerners" were first printed in "The South," with Pryor's concurrence, & as I thought his full approval. He certainly expressed to me not the slightest objection, either to the publication or the contents—& readily forwarded my wishes to have both these Nos. printed in two consecutive daily issues, so as to appear in the same semi-weekly paper, & of which he sent many extra copies to different southern men & newspapers. Of course, I do not understand that by publishing a communication, without objection or comment, an editor indicates concurrence with its views. But, surely, if my scheme was so "mischievous" & reprehensible, the time for Pryor to oppose or denounce it was when it first appeared in his own paper, & had extra circulation by his own aid. Though, in terms, denouncing Yancey, & certain "Knownothing" auxiliaries & supporters of the scheme, (of whose concurrence, identity, or existence, I remain utterly ignorant, & also incredulous,) Pryor knew that the scheme, of association, & the general policy recommended were *mine.* In my pamphlet published nearly a year ago, I had first recommended the secession of a portion only of the more southern states, & leaving Virginia & other border states at first, to serve as a barrier of protection & safeguard of peace, but to follow soon after. No one could ascribe to *me* (as he has done to Yancey,) the wish to exclude Va. from the Southern Confederacy, finally & entirely. [423]

*Aug. 12.* . . . Wrote a little, but did not feel like undertaking any new job, as I shall leave tomorrow, to visit my friend Willoughby Newton in Westmoreland.

*Aug. 13.* Left early, & took breakfast at the old Church hotel, when the stage coach arrived. 12 passengers, of whom 4 were outside, & 2 on the top. A weak team, with a heavy load, made it 1½ hours before we reached Tappahannock. There I waited nearly 2 hours, while the ferry boat was delayed by high wind. At last, I hired a boat & hands of a vessel, lying at the wharf, & crossed the Rappahannock river, nearly to sunset. There found Mr. Newton's carriage waiting for me, & a letter from Mr. Thomas Jones, inviting me to stop for the night at his house, at Warsaw, 6 miles on my route. As it was now so late, I was the more ready to accept his invitation. Reached his house (in the village,) about dark. . . . Talked southern politics & the crops with Mr. Jones. . . .

*Aug. 14.* Immediately after breakfast proceeded on my way, & in 12 miles more, reached Linden, in Westmoreland, the residence of Willoughby Newton. Found him awaiting my arrival. [424] We were soon engaged in earnest discussion on the great Southern question, & in regard to our respective recent actions therein—his disunion address, on July 4th, before the Va. Military Institute, & my published scheme of association of "United Southerners." For his part, he has been strongly assailed in the newspapers—& I have, for my share, only escaped with less denunciation because of the greater obscurity of myself & my scheme. Newton & I have exchanged several long letters on these particular points, & the whole general subject. But much was left untouched for our expected personal meeting & free conversation. We agree entirely as to the necessity for, & the advantages of a separation & independent confederacy of the slave-holding states. Also we agree that nearly all the leading & prominent men of the south, even when agreeing with us in general opinion, are rendered timid, & silent, & unwilling to make any *public* avowal of disunion sentiments, because they are fearful they are on the much weaker side, & that such avowals would destroy all their political hopes, & favor, from the majority. The aspirants to the presidency, of whom nearly every very prominent southern politician is one, are bribed by their entirely vain hopes, either to openly & actively go into the service of our enemies, to buy northern votes, (as Douglas, Wise, & Jeff. Davis have done,) or otherwise, like Hunter & others to remain silent & inactive, for fear of offending the North, in cases where justice to the South requires their active defence. While it is, to my view, a vain hope that any southern man can ever be again elected President [425] of the present United States, yet scores of political leaders, & their thousands of the most active & influential several partizans, are, either actively or passively, working to further the supremacy of the North & the submission of the South, as the means of attaining their own selfish & base objects. So now, & it will increase with the nearer approach of the presidential election in 1860, every man who hopes to gain anything from the continuance of the Union, will be loud & active in shouting for its integrity & permanence. The many & zealous recent defenders of the Union, & denouncers of its enemies, have been stimulated by the fear that . . . upholding the southern party will operate to overthrow the *national* democratic party, by driving off the smaller northern wing of that party. If the success of this party is to be best effected by injuring (& still more if by destroying) the supporters of southern rights, then I shall more anxiously wish for the speedy overthrow of the national democratic party, & its being beaten by the "Black Republican" or abolition party, in the next presidential election. This is wanting to unite southern men under the banner of the south, disentangled from all northern alliances. Newton has convinced me, (& I readily yield to his better judgment,) that in this view of prospects, it will be bad policy for me to endeavor to establish associations of "United Southerners," or in any such manner to separate & identify our true & boldest men. For, under present circumstances, not one in 100 of those [426] who think with us, will dare to avow their opinions, & to commit themselves by such open action. And the very few who would so move, would be by our opposers counted as being *all* of the disunionists—& we would be powerless, & sink in our apparent weakness. I admit fully the force of these views, & I will desist from any further effort for the present time—hoping that the events of 1860 will change circumstances, so that the dishonest & the timid southern men may then be as strongly *bribed* by their selfish views to stand up for the South, as now to stoop & truckle to the North.—Walked out with Newton, to see from the nearest edge of the high table land, the magnificent view thence of the broad lowgrounds, of the Potomac, with the broad water of that river, & of Mechadack creek, seen in various detached places, as if of islands filling the larger surface of an extensive lake. Conversation on various subjects, but mostly of southern politics, to bed-time.

*Aug. 16.* After breakfast, Mr. Newton took me in his light carriage to drive over some of the neighboring country, so as to see fair samples of the peculiar lands of this long & narrow peninsula between the lower Potomac [427] & Rappahannock, known as the Northern Neck. It is a beautiful & valuable agricultural region, with many advantages, & especially in regard to the contiguity of deep navigable waters on one or the other side. . . . Afternoon, several gentlemen came in—& among them Jos. Mayo jr. of this neighborhood, but now assistant editor, in Petersburg, of the South-Side Democrat.—The last number of "The South" contained another editorial . . . more contemptuous & offensive in manner than the preceding. [James L.] Orr & Keitt of S.C. have both lately delivered what are called "conservative" speeches, in public meetings, & Jefferson Davis, a candidate for the Presidency, in a speech delivered at the North, has vied with Wise in fishing for northern votes, by lauding the Union. Hammond's late speech is reported to be in the same "conservative" tone—though in his letter to me he denied the correctness of all the newspaper reports. All these demonstrations, together with Pryor's strange change of attitude, seem to indicate a concerted purpose, & arranged plan, to sustain the "national democratic party," by courting & submitting to the northern & small portion of it, by silencing & postponing, if not sacrificing the just claims of the south. If the northern members of the democratic party should not be retained, there will be no possible chance to elect the next president—& still less that he will be a *southern* man. It is to effect the latter impossible object, & each [428] one favoring his own selfish ends, that all our southern aspirants have become such good union men. And all their respective partisans & followers obey the commands of their leaders, & follow their course. Scarcely a dozen men in Va. (& not one of them aspirants to political station,) who will now even speak openly, much less act, in defence of the south to the extent that was avowed very generally a year or two ago. Under these circumstances, there is no use in attempting to collect auxiliaries, or to make any arrangement for action. Nearly all, even of those who think with me, are either under this corrupt influence, for themselves or their leaders, or otherwise intimidated by the prevailing outcry, so that all fear to act to sustain the South. All that these few of us can do, will be, from time to time, to continue to proclaim resistance through the newspapers, & to show that all have not submitted. There have been sundry attacks in the newspapers on Newton's disunion Address on the 4th of July. He will use them merely as an excuse to defend his views, & set them forth at length & elaborately, in another publication. I hope this argument in support of the political necessity, and also the many & great prospective benefits to the South, of seceding from the Northern States, will attract notice, & have good ef[f]ects in future time, even though now no voice shall be raised in concurrence or approval. When the issue of the next presidential election shall be known, in 1860, & all southern candidates defeated & their hopes shown to be baseless, & their aspirations desperate, they may come to their senses, & to their former southern [429] support. Still better if this "national" democratic party shall then be defeated & ruptured, & an abolitionist elected. Then perhaps the South may act for its defence & only salvation. If not, then submission to northern oppression will be the fixed course of the South, & its fate sealed.

*Aug. 17.* . . . Immediately after dinner, I set out in Mr. Newton's carriage on my return. Reached the ferry, & crossed to Tappahannock at sunset. Spent the night at the wretched tavern. Nothing decent for supper—& I could only drink a cup of poor tea. The only wheaten bread too sour to eat. . . .

*Aug. 18.* Left in the stage coach soon after 4 A.M. & after a slow passage, with a heavy load, reached home to dinner. . . . Found letters—from Mr. Williams, R. B. Rhett jr, Ch. F. Osborne, & Prof. Gilham. Rhett invites me to send any writings to the Charleston Mercury—which I shall do, as I will no longer insert my pieces in "The South," & hold the two other democratic papers of Richmond in detestation. One, the Enquirer, is the mouth-piece of Gov. Wise, & edited by his son, & the Examiner is the mere tool of [John B.] Floyd, as great a private scoundrel, as Wise is a public evil, & now [430] unfaithful to the South. Wrote first sketch of an article.—The Atlantic Telegraph is not yet at work, for public use, & the delay is suspicious. I very much fear that a sufficient current of the electrical fluid cannot be preserved, because of the waste, or escape, for so long a passage, & the success after all will not be of practical use. . . .

*Aug. 19.* Prepared my writing (done before my late journey,) & also some before printed matters in relation to southern politics, & enclosed them to Rhett, for the Charleston Mercury. This I shall make my channel of communication on such subjects. Wrote also to Newton.

*Aug. 20.* Went to Richmond in the carriage, with Mildred & Mr. Sayre. . . . Saw Mr. Williams, & arranged Society business with him. Saw Harvie at his office, & had a long conversation with him on political affairs, & on Pryor's late course. Different from myself, H. thinks that there is a good prospect to elect a southern man as the next president. I deem it impossible, & as long as the Union lasts, unless as a betrayer of the South. I think that, in the difficulty of reconciling the views of northern & southern men [431] of the democratic party, that the selection of a candidate will again fall on Buchanan.

*Aug. 21.* Read again & answered Prof. Gilham's last letters. He has found & reported the proportions of organic matter in sundry peaty soils (of the N.C. swamps,) & more particularly reported the valuable recent discovery he has made, that the olive earth over the marl of Marlbourne (& others, as inferred) contains from 5 to more than 7 percent of phosphate of lime. Read Rev. P. Slaughter's History of the Va. Colonization Society—a poor affair. . . .

*Aug. 25.* . . . Another letter from Prof. Gilham received yesterday announces that he had just analysed the black gravel of the "olive earth" which I had given to him in 1853, recommending him to examine them, because I suspected they contained phosphate of lime. He has just done so, & found that they contain 56 percent of Phosphate of lime, & the residue mostly carbonate of lime! This is a very interesting fact. But there is too little of the gravel for it to be worth separating & grinding—& it is too hard to be worth much as manure when put out in the olive earth or marl. . . .

*Aug. 27.* The mail. The first news by the Atlantic Telegraph—that peace has been made with China by the English & French, China to pay indemnities. But the use of the telegraph is not yet open for the public use, &, by the delay, I fear there are great difficulties. Wrote letters. Disappointed in obtaining J[ohn] B. Baldwin[14] to deliver the valedictory address at our next Fair, & wrote to Ex-president Tyler to request his doing it. It is arranged that Nanny will go with Mildred & myself to the mountains. Nanny had a slight bilious attack at home, & she has a delicate frame & constitution. Mildred is thin, though well. I go merely to accompany her, & for recreation. My health was never so good as it has been in the last 18 months—& I continue in better flesh, or heavier than ever in my life before. We will leave home next Tuesday.

*Aug. 28.* . . . I do not believe that anything can be done at present to rouse the South. All the prominent politicians are either aspirants to the presidency, or seeking other high offices, & know they can only reach their objects by support of northern votes. Hence they desire especially to conciliate the north, & particularly now, for the nomination of a candidate for the presidency in 1860. All the newspapers are in the service of one or other of these aspirants, & obey their bidding. The great mass merely follow the directions given by [434] their leaders through the newspapers—and as the *cue* is now to laud the union, it is vain to say anything against it. Nothing can be done until after the nomination & election of 1860. Then these

---

[14] A Staunton, Virginia, lawyer, John Brown Baldwin (1820–73) later served as a member of the state secession convention, where he voted against secession, and as a member of the Confederate Congress.

southern leaders, blinded now by their ambition, will all be disappointed, & may understand the truth that no southern man can be made president, or as a candidate, receive the support of the northern democrats. To obtain their support, everything must be yielded to their wishes, prejudices, & interests—& by so doing, the South may *rule*, as it is called. This disappointment, or some new outrage, or the entire separation (as I hope may occur) between the Southern & northern democrats, may dispose the South again to resist. At present everything that can be said to that purpose, is addressed to deaf ears. I will trouble myself no more about it, until a suitable time shall come.—With the children, I was weighed today—made 152 lbs.—which is 2 lbs more than last year, & 12 lbs. more than I ever weighed before the last two years. Earlier in life, 135 lbs was my best usual weight.

*Aug. 31.* The mail. The people of Kansas have voted, by a large majority, [not] to be admitted to the Union under the pro-slavery constitution[15]—& so the whole matter is at sea again. If they apply to be admitted, under an anti-slavery constitution, the conditions affixed by the last Congress will be disregarded by that body, & the new state will be admitted—enough northern democrats (if not all) voting with the abolitionists (or "Republicans," as they call their political party,) to effect the purpose.—Thomas had a chill & fever yesterday, & Nanny & George sick in like manner today. . . . This will delay our designed departure for the Springs tomorrow, as it would be very unsafe to have Nanny there sick, or in danger of sickness. . . . [437]

*Sept. 1.* All the three invalids taking physic today, & no chill or fever. But we fear it may return on Nanny, & deem it too hazardous for her to risk being sick on the road, or at the Springs, which would be but little better. So after full deliberation, it is decided that Mildred & I will go tomorrow, leaving Nanny behind, to our great regret. . . .

*Sept. 2.* . . . Mildred & I set out for Richmond immediately after breakfast. . . . Saw Mr. Williams, & finished all my other business, & had some weary hours on my hands before night. At night saw President Tyler, who had just arrived. Though he had not yet deter-

---

[15] On August 2, Kansas voters rejected the Lecompton Constitution by a vote of 11,812 to 1,926. Thus, under the terms of the English bill, the territory could not be admitted to statehood until its population reached about 90,000, the number required for a congressional representative.

mined, I think he will consent to deliver our [438] valedictory. The Enquirer of today publishes a long letter from Yancey to Pryor, (which P. had refused to publish,) in which he ably opposes his attacks on the "League of United Southerners." . . .

*Sept. 3.* We set out on the Central Railroad, & reached Jackson's river about sunset. Passed through 6 tunnels on the route, one of which was the long one through the Blue Ridge mountain, which I walked through last year, before it was quite finished. From the present end of the railway, we went in stage coaches, & got to Callaghan's past 11, & to bed a little before 12.

*Sept. 4.* Set out after breakast, & reached the White Sulphur Springs at 12. After having our rooms assigned to us, & dining, I looked about to find what friends we had here. There are W. H. Ray & his wife & younger children—Wm. B. Harrison of Prince George, (who is avowedly seeking for a second wife,) Dr. Charles Cocke & family,[16] Jer. Morton, Mr. [William] Sayre of Mobile,[17] Mr. James C. Johnston & Wm. S. Pettigrew of N.C., Williams Carter & many others of whom I know less. At night, in the great parlor, made the acquaintance of J. Johnston Pettigrew of Charleston, the younger brother of William. Old Mr. Johnston & the Pettigrews took a long sitting with Mildred & myself.

*Sept. 5.* Sunday. . . . Made acquaintance with Judge [John] Perkins of La.[18] & had a long conversation with him on southern politics. He is a man of ability, & a disunionist. His wife, before the widow of Judge [Thomas H.] Bayly[19] whom I had a slight acquaintance with previously, is a very intelligent & agreeable woman in conversation.

---

[16] Son of John Hartwell Cocke and a younger brother of Philip St. George Cocke, Cary Charles Cocke was a physician and planter in Fluvanna County, Virginia. He served as a captain in the Confederate Army during the war.

[17] Sayre (1791–1861), a native of New Jersey but resident in Alabama since 1818, was a wholesale grocer and cotton commission merchant. Formerly mayor of Mobile, he was a Whig in political viewpoint.

[18] John Perkins, Jr., born in Natchez and educated at Yale and Harvard, was a prominent north Louisiana cotton planter with extensive holdings in Madison and Tensas parishes. After serving two years as a circuit court judge, he was elected in 1853 to the United States House of Representatives for a single term. Later he presided over the Louisiana Secession Convention and sat in the Confederate Senate from 1862 to 1865.

[19] After two years on the superior court of law and chancery, Thomas Henry Bayly was elected to Congress from Virginia in 1844 and served until his death on June 22, 1856. He was also the commanding brigadier general of the state militia.

*Sept. 7.* . . . Finished correcting & copying an article "Treachery to the South—active or passive," & mailed it for the Charleston Mercury.

*Sept. 8.* The most interesting events reported in the last few days by the newspapers, is [*sic*] the bringing into Charleston a captured American slave ship, with more than 300 Africans on board—& the burning, by a mob, of all the quarantine buildings of Staten Island. The latter occurrence shows a disregard to law which is ominous of much worse results in New-York.—Most of the persons whose company we most prized have left this place, & we have become weary of it. Shall leave tomorrow morning. Judge Perkins & his wife earnestly invited me & Mildred to visit them in Louisiana, should I attend the Southern Convention in Vicksburg. [444]

*Sept. 9.* At 6 A.M. left the White Sulphur Springs in the stage coach, for the Red Sweet Springs, 16 miles distant, which we reached & stopped. Found a moderate company of quiet people, as is usual here—the more gay preferring the Old Sweet, close by. . . .

*Sept. 10.* After breakfast walked to the Old Sweet Springs. Saw Isaac Hayne of Charleston,[20] & several other acquaintances. . . . I have no writing on hand, & feel no disposition to begin any, . . . [445] & find my time pass rather heavily. . . .

*Sept. 11.* Yesterday & today read the greater part of the full report (a bulky pamphlet) of the proceedings & speeches of the "Free Convention" held at Rutland, Vt. The resolutions & speeches were on all sorts of subjects, & by the most different characters, but all in opposition to generally received opinions, except the violent & unmeasured denunciations of negro slavery, which of course are approved by the most of the northern people. There was a minister of the gospel & a Shaker elder, women advocating "women's rights" & "free love," spiritualists, & all uttering the wildest & most offensive doctrines. Nowhere in the world except in New England could such an assembly have met, or persons to utter such doctrines. But I am glad [446] that the convention was held, & I hope more such will be held, & the freest utterance given to the most outrageous opinions. It seems that the most ultra abolitionists, finding that the bible & the constitution are both opposed to them, or support the institution of slavery, are becoming denouncers of the constitution, & also of the

---

[20] Isaac William Hayne (1809–80) was attorney general of South Carolina from 1848 to 1868. A strong supporter of southern rights, he was one of the most active members of the South Carolina Secession Convention.

bible. This must array against them the power of the Christian Church—& that power is enough to put down any opposing doctrine. . . .

*Sept. 12.* Sunday. Attended the sermon preached by the son of Gov. Wise. He promises to be as eloquent as his father, & to have much better taste. Saw in the Mercury No 5 of my series of "Suggestions &c." which I had actually forgot having written—& by so forgetting it, I have in the later piece, "Treachery to the South &c." used some of the same positions, & even nearly the same language. I am ashamed of this evidence of my failure of memory. But I trust to the general carelessness & want of observation of readers to save me from detection.—Nothing beyond a few short messages have yet been sent through the Atlantic Telegraph—& it is now reported that for 10 days there has been no transmission of communication. More & more I fear a total failure of this attempt. [447]

*Sept. 13.* I am getting tired of this lounging life, with no amusement but conversation & very little reading. . . . Walked over to the Old Sweet Springs, & saw there Judge [Arthur F.] Hopkins of Mobile,[21] & Judge [Thomas J.] Withers of S.C.[22] Dr. C. C. Cocke & family arrived today at the R.S.S., & they are nearly all our *old* acquaintance left here.

*Sept. 14.* Letters received from Elizabeth & Edmund. All well at Marlbourne—& Edmund & Nanny were to leave Richmond this morning, to join us here tomorrow. . . . Mildred has sought & made the acquaintance of two families of ladies from S. Ca. both of them in deep mourning—the Pringles & Thompsons—& found her attentions bestowed on very agreeable persons, & received with welcome. It has been my usage ever since I served in S.C. to seek the acquaintance of any persons from that state whom I found as strangers at the Springs, & Mildred also, as to ladies, & especially of those who were (as in these cases) suffering under sickness or grief. . . . [448]

*Sept. 15.* The coach arrived without Edmund, or any account of

---

[21] Born in Pittsylvania County, Virginia, Judge Hopkins (1794–1865) moved to Alabama in 1816 and soon became active in public life, serving as a member of the first Alabama Constitutional Convention and, in the 1830's, as chief justice of the state supreme court. He was the leader of the Whig Party in Alabama and, at this time, was president of the Mobile and Ohio Railroad.

[22] Thomas Jefferson Withers (1804–65) was elected common law judge in 1846 and served in this post until his death. Although opposed to separate state action, he was a member of the South Carolina Secession Convention and was a delegate from his state to the Confederate Convention at Montgomery in 1861.

him. Afterwards the mail brought a letter from him stating the bad news that prevented his coming. After he & Nanny reached Richmond, on their way here, a letter was sent to him from Mr. Sayre, informing that Elizabeth had been suddenly taken ill, & that her great danger was apprehended—& Mildred requested to return immediately. . . . We will take the earliest return passage home, early tomorrow morning. . . . Three years ago, after about as short a stay in the mountains, we left this same place with my dying daughter Ella, on our hurried return to home. May God grant that the two cases may not be alike in their termination! . . .

*Sept. 16.* Left early in the stage to the western terminus of the Rail-road, & thence on the train to Staunton, by 7 P.M. The principal hotel crowded with travellers from the Springs, & some stopping for a few days. . . . [449]

*Sept. 17.* Left Staunton at 7 A.M. & reached Richmond at 3 P.M. . . . At Richmond hired a carriage & set off as speedily as possible, but could not get off sooner than 4. . . . On our way from Richmond, met Dr. Wormeley, who told us that Elizabeth was much better—as we found her. She had miscarried, but has recovered as much as could be hoped for, considering her otherwise feeble condition of health. . . .

*Sept. 20.* Nothing to read, & much at a loss to kill time. . . . Before night, Elizabeth had a nervous chill, & in the night another—& previously bad pain in the head. The symptoms alarming. I fear for her life. And even if restored to her previous condition of health, there is no better prospect than of life-long disease, & if again becoming pregnant, of repetition of her recent & present danger.

*Sept. 21.* . . . The mail brought a very short letter from Dr. J. J. Dupuy requiring that Jane shall be carried to him in Richmond next Friday. This, of course, will be obeyed—greatly to our regret. Under existing circumstances, I am almost of opinion that we had better not seek or enjoy the gratification of having her here again—but to let absence & separation cause us to forget & cease to love her, as much as possible. She is a most interesting, attractive, & loveable child—indulged improperly by all the family at home, & so encouraged in her disposition to be wilful & capricious, as well as having her health endangered. Still, she is easy to be corrected in the effects of this improper system of indulgence. But this ungracious duty is required all of the little time she has been permitted to be with us, & then she is returned to the previous improper treatment.

*Sept. 24.* . . . After there had been no communication through the

Atlantic Telegraph cable for 20 days, & when the newspapers had broke their patient silence & began to pronounce the general belief of utter failure, it is suddenly announced today that the communication is renewed, & as good as ever. The cause of suspension, & its cessation, both without known cause. Still, even if the like cessation does not again occur, the use of the telegraphic communication seems as remote as when it was first made. [453]

*Sept. 25.* Though feeling but little inclined to write, & also still very deficient in authorities & documents, I determined to begin my designed attack on the Colonization Society. Wrote 16 pages, without getting fairly in train, & with the expectation of having to rewrite the whole, & remodel nearly all. Tired before sunset, & yet without amusement for the remainder of the evening.

*Sept. 26.* Sunday. A cloudy & drizzling day. Continued writing & consulting documents for authorities. 20 pages more. . . .

*Sept. 28.* . . . Left in the mail [454] coach for Aylett's, where soon Mr. Boulwane came for me, & we went on to his house, 5 miles farther. . . . We spent the day in conversation, mostly, & in part in reading late reviews &c.—The papers report that the late statement of communication through the Atlantic Telegraph having been renewed was false. It is now admitted that there has been no communication through the cable since Sept. 1st. There seems but little ground for hope of any hereafter, by this cable. . . . [455]

*Sept. 29.* . . . Mr. Boulwane had before sent to invite his neighbors & my friends, B. F. Dew & S. Gresham, to dine with me, who came, & remained through the afternoon. Our conversation mostly jocular, & embracing many subjects. Among others, I remarked how strange it was that men who made great figures in history were never correctly estimated in or soon after their own times—but were much better known a century or more later. For example, Cromwell is now understood much better than at any much earlier time, & by the greater number, as much lauded as heretofore he has been vilified. B. said Washington will in all future time stand higher than any other man that has lived. R. "Yes I believe so—& highly as I estimate him, & more for his virtues than his great qualities, I think he has always been over-rated, & will be more & more so." Jackson was mentioned, & his claims to greatness stated by B. & questioned by me. Dew mentioned the parallel drawn by [Joseph G.] Baldwin between Jackson & his great rival Clay, & the higher position awarded by the author, though a Whig, to Jackson.[23] R. "I have never read that parallel; but I have long thought that a competent writer might make a very interesting article, in a parallel between Henry VIII of England & Jackson."—Jackson's late religious profession was discussed. B. gave to him the credit of sincerity while he yet was president, which was earlier than others of us did. B. said he was present when Jackson was under the most trying infliction of his life, when his [456] nose was pulled, & he bore himself admirably, & his rage did not draw from him an oath. Having never heard the particulars of this incident from an eye-witness, I asked for the facts, which B. stated as follows: "I did not see the whole of the circumstances, but perhaps as many as any other person, & heard the others from Mrs. Thruston (wife of Judge [Buckner] Thruston)[24] who was sitting by Gen. Jackson, & conversing with him when the affair commenced. The President was going by invitation, in the steamer from Washington, to Fredericksburg, to assist in laying the corner-stone of the 'Mary Washington monument.' . . . When the boat stopped, as usual, for a few minutes at the Alexandria wharf, to put out & take in passengers, nearly all who were in the cabin went on deck, as is usual, to see what was to be seen. I was one of these. After a little time, I saw Lieut. [Robert] Randolph passing hastily on the deck, & near & approaching to the plank, placed as a gangway to the wharf, & old Beverley (his kinsman) following & pushing him forward. In meeting some obstacle in the returning crowd, Randolph's hat was knocked off (accidentally) & I heard him say 'Let me get my hat'— when Beverley answered 'Damn your hat' & continued to urge him forward, & both were instantly out on the wharf, & walked away rapidly. By this time the report & alarm had been received from below, & a perfect uproar had spread through the crowd both on the steamer & on the wharf. I hastened down into the cabin, with as many as could be squeezed in there. When I first [457] got in view of the President, he was striving, with uplifted cane, to pursue Ran-

---

[23] Better known for his humorous work, *Flush Times in Alabama and Mississippi,* Baldwin first drew the parallel between Jackson and Clay in an article prepared for the *Southern Literary Messenger* and later expanded it into a book entitled *Party Leaders,* which he published in 1855.

[24] After representing Kentucky in the United States Senate for five years, Thruston in 1809 was appointed to the United States Circuit Court for the District of Columbia, where he remained until his death in 1845.

dolph, & denouncing him loudly & violently as a scoundrel & a coward. A[ndrew] J. Donelson (his *protegé*) & Gen. Cass were opposing his movement, & endeavoring to calm his violence. Among other expressions J. said, 'I knew that he was a dishonest villain, who had robbed the widow & the orphan, but I had not supposed he was a coward, as he has shown himself in assaulting an old man, when approaching him in the guise of friendship.' . . . I afterwards was told by Mrs. Thruston of the earlier circumstances. She & Gen. Jackson were sitting on a moveable settee, without any back, in conversation, when, as before stated, nearly every other person went on deck. Immediately, a man hastily approached the President, & as approaching, was pulling off his right-hand glove. Gen. Jackson, supposing that it was some acquaintance, designing to accost, & preparing to shake hands with him, said 'Never mind your glove, Sir,' & began to rise from his seat as if to meet the expected salutation. The gentleman, as soon as getting close, said 'I am Lieutenant Robert Randolph,' & immediately seized Jackson's nose between his thumb & finger, & while wringing it, pushed him backward, so that he lost his balance & was near being pushed over his seat. Randolph [458] then turned & walked out of the cabin, & was gone before Gen. Jackson could fully recover his feet, or the few persons present were fully aware of what had occurred. After I entered the cabin, there was a perfect hubbub of confusion, & all sorts of suggestions offered. One man exclaimed to the President, that if he would grant him a pardon, he would pursue Randolph & shoot him. Jackson impatiently waved him away. Another met with the like contemptuous dismissal, who attempted to prove to Jackson that Randolph had not succeeded in subjecting him to the attempted insult, & had not even touched his face. Yet there had been left no possible place for doubt on this score. For, if as by design & for this purpose, Randolph's thumbnail had been allowed to grow long, & he had stuck it so deeply into one side of the nose, that the wound was bleeding, & a basin of water was brought & used by the President to wash off the blood."

Whether Randolph had previously been criminal or not, & whether a justly punished or a greatly wronged & outraged person—& how far he was or was not justifiable in thus outrageously avenging his personal wrongs, are still matters disputed. He had always been considered a brave & good officer, & a gentleman of undoubted honor & integrity. At sea, Timberlake, the purser died, & Lieut. Randolph was directed to take charge of his goods, & to discharge, to the end of the cruise, the duties of the office. Timberlake's widow (residing in Washington) afterwards the notorious Mrs. [Peggy] Eaton—whose influence served afterwards to break up the cabinet, & to make ruptures between the President & his previously chief supporters—in some manner [459] was able to acquire unbounded influence over Jackson. She was an unchaste & base woman—first the concubine (in secret) & next the wife (by his compulsion) of one of Gen. Jackson's basest favorites, Gen. [John H.] Eaton. I do not believe that it was sensual influence that she operated on Jackson. On the contrary, strange as it may be, he alone seemed to have faith in her virtue,[25] when she was assailed by imputations from every side. She, and her friends, claimed that Randolph had made way with her husband's property to a large amount. Whether there was any truth in this, or whether (as is generally believed) that R. was only careless in his accounts, & ignorant of such business, he could not entirely acquit himself, & yet there was not ground to convict him of any defalcation. Mrs. Timberlake's story & influence however were enough for Jackson. Without his being condemned (or even tried, as well as I remember,) by a naval or civil court, the President, by his own order, dismissed him from the naval service, thus vacating his commission, & turning him out to poverty & degradation. It would have been disgrace enough to be thus dismissed, without comment, or cause stated. But in the order, the President published that Randolph was unfit to associate with officers of the navy.

Attempts were made immediately by the Marshal of the District of Columbia to arrest Randolph for the assault. But he failed, for the several reasons that the Marshal (who was one of the passengers with the President,) had no legal warrant to make an arrest in Va, where R. had gone & was found, a few miles from Alexandria, & also that he was well armed, & refused to surrender without compulsory force. At a later time, he was arrested, for I visited him in jail in Richmond. But I believe that it was on a civil process, in [460] reference to the Timberlake business. At any rate, nothing could be done with him on either charge—& the matter of the assault on the President was quietly dropped.

*Sept. 30.* After breakfast we left, in Mr. Boulwane's baranche, &

---

[25] At a cabinet meeting on the subject, Jackson termed Mrs. Eaton "as chaste as a virgin."

reached Marlbourne before 12 m. . . . Resumed writing extracts, for proofs, from Colonization Society documents—& reading in "Living Age."

*October 1.* The mail brought 3 letters from Prince George—& others to me—one, with a book I had written for, "Liberia as I found it," just published by the author, the Rev. A. M. Cowan, of Ky, long an agent of the Ky. Col. Society—which I proceeded forthwith to read.

*Oct. 2.* Received delayed back Nos. of Charleston Mercury, containing the republication of two articles from the South, the proposition for & constitution of the "Southern League," & also the other 6 Nos on the License laws, & the piece sent from the White Sulphur Springs. Finished the book on Liberia. Though it is written by a warm advocate of the scheme, I find much in it to support my opposition to it. . . .

*Oct. 3.* Sunday. Attended church. Continued writing. Looking through a volume of [Robert R.] Howison's Hist. of Va. Wrote letters to Willoughby Newton, Robt. E. Scott, R. B. Rhett jr, & Lieut. M. Maury.

*Oct. 5.* . . . Mail brought me the promised communication from Prof. Gilham, for the A.S. on his discovery of phosphate of lime, in larger quantity than he supposed before, in our olive earth. Wrote some remarks, as an appendix to his piece, & shall put both in the Southern Planter, in advance. Began to correct & copy my writing on the Colonization Society, though the first writing is not done. . . .

*Oct. 7.* . . . Julian & I left, in the carriage, for Richmond. Arranged business of the Society with Mr. Williams. The Whig (at my request) has republished my last articles (written at the Springs) from the Charleston Mercury. Saw Lewis Harvie—& Col. J[ames] L. Price of Alabama. At 3, on the Railway train with Mrs. Lorraine, who, as had been arranged, took this opportunity, under Julian's escort, of returning home. . . . Edmund's carriage was waiting for us at the Petersburg Depot—in which we rode to Ruthven, to spend the night. All well there.—In Russell's Magazine there appears, at last, the first portion of my "Notes on the Pine Trees of Lower Va, & N.Ca.," of which I feared the M.S. had been lost. [463]

*Oct. 8.* After breakfast, with Mrs. Lorraine, went on to Beechwood. Edmund much indisposed still, (& lately quite sick,) with bad cold & cough. The two younger children have the whooping cough,

& Nanny & Sue have also bad coughs, & Nanny has been otherwise quite sick, & is still thin & pale, though well. . . .

*Oct. 9.* Had a fire made early in my chamber, & resumed copying my writing—though the first writing is not all done. As usual, making numerous alterations—which sometimes cause me to leave out portions of the first draught which I afterwards think were better than what substituted them. Wrote through the greater part of the day.—Began today to read a book recently published, "Sketch of the History of Slavery" by T[homas] R. R. Cobb, of Georgia, which I bought in Richmond.

*Oct. 12.* Corrected & sent to the Society an appendix to Prof. Gilham's late communication on his discovery of phosphate of lime [464] in our beds of "olive earth"—5 pages. Got to the end of my writing—to the extent of 75 pages—& nearly all copied or corrected —but there are still some parts to be written & inserted in different places.—Finished reading Cobb's "History of Slavery"—an interesting & able work, evincing much research. The author has a chapter on the colony of Liberia—of which he thinks as I do, but does not go quite as far in his opposition & denunciation.

*Oct. 13.* Wrote the rough draft of Annual Report of the President & Executive Committee for the next Annual Meeting of the Agr. Society. Returned to reading Jefferson's Life.

*Oct. 17.* Sunday. . . . Skimmed over Mrs. [Anna M.] Scott's "Day Dawn in Africa" a new publication—hoping to get some facts or statistics respecting Liberia, where she & her husband had lived, as missionaries—or at least some facts serving to give information as to the progress of the missions.[26] But there is scarcely a new idea, or any particular information in the foolish book. . . .

*Oct. 18.* Added, as insertions, some more pages to my M.S. & closed it, as finished. In all it is 95 pages.—Reading Jefferson's Life. Received by mail proof slips of Prof. Gilham's communication to the Society, & my appendix thereto which I corrected for returning.

*Oct. 20.* . . . Finished Randall's Life of Jefferson. It is an able work, which has served much to exalt Jefferson in my estimation, both for his talents & his virtues. Yet I have not got rid of my dislike to him. The author is also much raised in my estimation—by his work. Yet both he & Jefferson were abolitionists, covertly & cunningly. I suppose that one of the objects of his undertaking to write

---

[26] Mrs. Scott resided at the Protestant Episcopal mission at Cape Palmas, West Africa, during most of the decade of the 1850's.

this biography, was to use the influence of Jefferson's great name & popularity to aid the anti-slavery preferences of the author. I, who in the early [466] part of my life, was opposed to slavery, & a speculative abolitionist, have no claim to denounce other persons who retained these opinions later than I did. But I cannot but wonder that a man of Jefferson's gigantic intellect should have so remained in the wrong on this subject as long as he lived. Whether excusable or not, he has done great harm, by the countenance which his opinions on this subject, & even the words of the Declaration of Independence, have afforded to the anti-slavery fanatics of the present times.

*Oct. 21.* . . . At 11 A.M. left Beechwood, & got on the steam-boat for Richmond, which I reached after 3 P.M. At the Exchange Hotel. Saw Mr. Williams. Much talk, & much puffing in the newspapers about the Richmond (& U.S.) Fair, which is to begin here next Monday. Every effort has been made to promote its success, & also to claim & boast of success in advance. Much dissatisfaction has been produced by the rules but lately announced, of demanding 10 per cent of the offered amount of every money premium, as an entrance fee, to each competitor—& 50 cent[s] for admission to the Fair Grounds. The charges of the State Society have been 25 cents admission, & nothing for offering for premiums.—On board the steamer, reading (second time) "Cannibals All"—& at night, the newspapers, & looking over sundry reports of the Colonization Society, which Mr. Williams had borrowed for me. Col. S[amuel] McD[owell] Reid here, & sat with me an hour.[27] Saw Dr. C. C. [467] Cocke, & some other friends.

*Oct. 22.* Slept last night not more than 1½ hours—without any known cause for lying awake, before rising at 3 A.M. to take the stage, at 3.30. . . . Reached Marlbourne to breakfast. . . .

The biography of Jefferson states a habit of his which I doubt not is excellent for a politician, & a man who would gently bend other wills to his own, & to avoid arousing opposition, which might increase to hostility. This was, that when, in conversation with another person, whether friend or stranger, & no matter whether the subject was serious or trivial, if the person expressed a decided opinion & resolve, Mr. Jefferson never opposed it, or expressed dissent—but remained silent, & either permitted his companion to speak, without interruption, or reply, or, as soon as was proper, changed the

---

[27] Reid, a resident of Lexington, Virginia, was the proprietor of nearby Mulberry Hill plantation and clerk of Rockbridge County.

subject. On this account, many persons after full conference, as they severally supposed, parted with Mr. J. believing that he fully agreed with him [*sic*] [468] in the matter spoken of, & others that they had convinced Mr. J. of his previous error, when there was not the slightest foundation for either. But however good & successful may be this rule of conduct for a politician, I cannot bear it between *friends*. And I dislike it the more, because my universal course is directly the reverse, & that carried to an improper & blamable extent. It is a result of my warm feelings, & want of proper caution, to hasten, even unnecessarily, to express opposition, when the opinion is entertained, to any different view I hear from one conversing with me, no matter how much I may defer to him in general. I feel, at the moment, that if I were to remain silent, it might appear as tacitly assenting to the other opinion—& that candor & fairness required me to let my opposition be known, even though not saying anything more to maintain or argue for my different opinion. Upon reflection, I now recollect that Mr. Tyler pursues the same course as that ascribed to Jefferson. When we were talking together, for hours, & on various subjects, & as I then thought with no more reserve on his side than mine, I *now* know that in some cases he must have let me talk alone, & when I inferred his entire assent, & perhaps he was entirely opposed. I remember having thus talked in my freest usual manner in denouncing the Colonization Society & scheme—& do not remember any thing said by him. I had then forgotten, & have since been reminded, that he formerly was President of the Va. State Society, & a warm advocate for the policy. When I shall have an opportunity, I will tell him of this, and object to our unequal positions when we converse on [469] subjects on which we differ, & his opposition to my views remains unsuspected by me.

Heard from Mr. Williams that my countrymen have not re-elected me to the Farmers' Assembly, & have taken my neighbor G. W. Bassett in my place. He will be a very troublesome member, from his great fondness for speaking. Last year I had declined a reelection on the ground of the position being somewhat incompatible with that of President of the Society. But despite of my objections, my county members chose (in my absence) to reelect me. And as they thought fit to waive any unfitness on my part, & no one else had supposed it to exist, I was willing to continue to represent them in the Farmers' Assembly. From my being now left out, & replaced by one who has neither popularity or fitness, I suspect it is the result of some trickery, prompted by hostility to me for the alleged influence I exerted in the removal of the Fair from Richmond to Petersburg. Except Henrico, there is no county which has so many members who would prefer Richmond to Petersburg, as Hanover. And with the many misrepresentations that have been circulated of my having caused the removal, & of my motive being hostility to Richmond, & even partiality to Petersburg (!!) [470] it is very likely that such false charges have been used to effect. So few members care about attending the elections, that 4 or 5, combining for a particular vote, can usually decide an election. In Richmond, where 17 delegates were elected, there were only 7 votes cast.

*Oct. 23.* . . . Began to copy my draft of the Annual Address to the Farmers' Assembly. I very much fear that there may be no session, for want of a quorum present. There was scarcely one at first last year, even in Richmond—& never after the first day—so great is the carelessness of the members elected. . . .

*Oct. 25.* Reading Lord [John] Hervey's "Memoirs of the Reign of George II," [28] which I borrowed from Mr. Boulwane's library. Writing more extracts & notes, for my Colonization article, though I fear it is too long already. . . . Received a letter from Newton. He highly commends my piece "Treachery to the South &c" recently published in the Charleston Mercury. It was copied (at my own request) in the Richmond Whig, & the Montgomery Advertiser. But I have not seen any word of comment—nor heard one, before Newton's. Wrote an answer.

*Oct. 26.* The mail. Letter from Mr. Williams, & also the newspapers, indicate a poor exhibition of the U.S. & Central Agr. Societies in Richmond. . . . Finished "Cannibals All." This is the second time of reading since its publication in 1857. Yet so wretched is my memory, that there are important & interesting portions that I have not [472] the least recollection of having ever seen before. The author, Mr. [George] Fitzhugh is an original thinker, & many of whose thoughts have much value. But others, though put in a manner that seems plausible, must be false, & in some cases absurd. Nearly all that he says of slavery, & of what I have called class-slavery, & which he terms slavery of labor to capital, is true & forcible. But his opposition to interest or capital, which is in fact opposition to the accumulation of capital (as what inducement

---

[28] Baron Hervey of Ickworth (1696–1743) was a contemporary of George II, though publication of his *Memoirs* was delayed purposely until 1848.

would there be to accumulate, if it could yield no profit?) is foolish. I should be put to the trouble to reply to his arguments as he presents them. But it is sufficient for his refutation to suppose his doctrine to be acted upon, & accordingly, that a community existed, in which there was enough labor, & enough raw materials for production—but no accumulated capital in money, & no interest permitted on capital, either to draw it from abroad, or to induce future accumulations at home. It is manifest that under such circumstances, there could be no employment of laborers, & the only use for labor would be to produce indispensable necessaries for the immediate consumption of the laborer & his family. There might be the richest natural resources for agriculture, manufactures, trade & commerce— but none could be put to use. This entire extinction & prohibition of the uses of capital, would be far worse for the whole community, & nearly as much so even for the poorest class, than the complete ascendancy of capital, & its cruel domination over labor as exists in England. Still the former would be better for the poorest or laboring class alone, [473] inasmuch as the savage life they would then experience, with all its privations, inconveniences, & dangers, would be less wretched than the continued toil, hunger, & suffering, under the complete power & crushing oppression of capital.

*Oct. 28.* . . . Lord Hervey's Memoirs improve in interest, as the parts of public history & political movements decrease in the space occupied, & the private details of the family of George II increase. It is astounding how much of vice, meanness, the world, & the free English, have tolerated in royal personnages, & still reverenced them. It is a pity that for every reign of a base & despicable king, there is not a Hervey or a Pepys, to record what flatterers disguise, & contemporary history is ignorant of. Reached the middle of the 2nd. vol.

*Oct. 29.* Slow rain. Set out in the carriage, after breakfast, for Richmond, on my way to Petersburg. Went to the Agricultural Office, & saw some of the northern delegates to the Richmond or U.S. Fair. Heard that it was a failure, or more so, by far, than a success. At 3 P.M. set out, with sundry of our members, on the [474] railway. . . . The Executive Committee of the Petersburg (Union) Society were waiting for our arrival, & we forthwith went into an informal joint meeting, & arranged the order of proceedings for our fair. At 7 P.M. our Executive Committee went into session. I laid before them my draft of the Annual Report, which was referred to a sub-committee. As there will be nothing to do, except recast this draft, for which my presence is not necessary, I will go tomorrow morning home with Edmund, to return next Monday.—Our meetings of the Executive Committee are always very pleasant, in bringing together intimate friends & intelligent companions. In such relations most of the members have stood to each other, from the beginning of our service to this time. We had 9 to attend this evening, of which number, F. Minor, F. Ruffin, W. C. Knight & W. Tate, I especially value. The sub-committee in session very late.

*Oct. 30.* Immediately after breakfast the Ex. Com. again in session—& had the report of progress of the sub-committee. By 10 A.M. I left in Edmund's carriage . . . . [475]

*Oct. 31.* Sunday. Last night began at the beginning of Parton's "Life of Aaron Burr," which at first I had skipped over, & this morning read to join my former commencement. The details of his early life, & especially in the revolutionary war, different from what would be found of most of his contemporary patriots, were quite interesting. But I suspect that the biographer is not entirely to be trusted, & that he borrows from romance embellishments for history. Yet certainly Burr was a great man, & especially in the greatest power to raise men to distinction, that of bending the wills of other men to suit his own purposes. Nothing but Burr's vices, & the want of an equal theatre of action, prevented him rising as high as Jackson, Cromwell, or Julius Caesar. It is to me a striking & significant fact, that Burr, when acting as an aid to Washington, an intimate member of his military family, & holding a high place in his favor & esteem, should yet have formed a low estimate of Washington as a leader, & as a man of great reputation, & have gladly sought release from the connection. . . . I have no doubt that, as to Washington's ability as a military or political director, Burr judged much more correctly than the world has, with increasing unanimity & zeal, to this day. That Washington was the man, & the only man, & it would seem even designed by Providence, to be at the head of affairs, in war & in peace, to the end of his administration, I as much believe as do any of his idolizers. [476] His very defects, in some respects, made his success, & the results in the good of his country, the more certain & complete. His *not doing*, in numerous cases, was eminently beneficial, when the most brilliant *doings* of a brighter intellect & a more ardent temperament, would have led to failure. Neither would I detract a tittle from the integrity, public virtue, & patriotism of

Washington. Yet I do not believe that he ever exhibited a trait of the great military leader, in fighting battles, or planning military movements & campaigns—or that in politics, or government, he ever originated an important idea, or was the first, or even among the first, in any new & important political movement, or devised any policy conducing greatly to the welfare of the people or the government. Yet his fame has been growing continually—& taken all together, now stands higher, & less questioned, than that of any man who lives, or has lived. Will remote posterity hold it as high? . . .

*November 1.* At 11 A.M. Edmund & I left for Petersburg. Found the other members I had left at the Bollingbrook [Hotel]. They had, with my full permission in advance, changed the form & language of the early part of my draft of the Annual Report; & had retained nearly all the words of the latter & longer portion. Though very willing, I thought they had changed for the worse. Their object was to state the argument more strongly, in regard to the removal of the Fair from Richmond, & to avoid giving offence. At 4, a meeting of the Farmers' Assembly was attempted but failed, for want of a quorum. 25 members wanting, & I fear but little hope of that number being added. At 7 P.M. a meeting of members of the Society was held (in the appointed building, the Baptist Church,) to discuss subjects of practical agriculture. The subject, the experience of persons of different reaping machines, especially, & also of other machines used to harvest, prepare, or secure the wheat [481] crop. I presided, & we had an interesting conversational discussion. Newton arrived. Conversing until late with my many friends & acquaintance.

*Nov. 2.* After an early & short session of our Committee, we proceeded to the Fair Ground, which is spacious, & beautiful, with enough buildings & accommodations. There is already a fine collection of stock & other articles—& more yet to come. In this important respect, success is certain. But I fear that the number of visitors may be deficient, especially as this day is lowering, & the latter part steady drizzle. We give up all of the details, & management of the Fair, to the Ex. Com. of the Petersburg society, so that I have but little to do in that respect.—It is understood (as had been before surmised) that a movement is designed, if sufficient force can be found, to oust me from my office, if not all others of the Ex. Com. The opposition to me is made up of all enemies on all scores, & the alleged several grounds of my political (disunion) opinions, & my being charged with the cheif [*sic*] agency in removing the Fair from

Richmond. But I believe that the secret source of the movement is the old Cocke & Richardson feud with the remainder of the committee, & with me especially—& a desire to get the society into other hands, that will again bring forward & elect Richardson to the secretaryship. I earnestly hope that a quorum of the Farmers' Assembly may be obtained, & that they may try to make these changes. For my part, I am tired of the burdensome duties of my office, & will be glad when I can be honorably released from them. And even if now re-elected, for another [482] year's service, that, by the constitutional limit of three years, must be the last. I wish that term had now arrived. But, after my very honorable election, by a unanimous vote, when I had no right to expect that renewed favor, I cannot justifiably decline, or resign, so long as there is no apparent withdrawal of that favor. Therefore I will not decline, or yield to any clamor, or to anything but a dismissal by the vote of the Farmers' Assembly. But when succeeding, if there is much show of discontent, I may feel released from my obligation, & consult my own wishes to retire. It is the Hon. Wm. C. Rives that the plotters propose to vote for against me. For this purpose, he, though Speaker of the F.A. will not come, that he may be out of the way, & so, if defeated, have it appear that he had not authorized his being put in nomination.—At night, another failure to get a quorum of the F.A., & afterwards another & still more interesting agricultural discussion, in which many members & visitors participated. Among them Gen. Tilghman, President of the U.S. Agr. Soc. who, on our invitation, had come over from Richmond.—At night, Edmund & I went to see [William R.] Barbee's statue of the "Fisher Girl." [29] Besides the great beauty & perfection of the sculpture, it had to me another interest. It struck both of us that the face was very like to my deceased daughter Jane.

*Nov. 3.* A fine clear day. Good attendance on the Fair Ground. At night, another failure to get a quorum of the Farmers' Assembly— but considerable discussion. Some of my friends, injudiciously perhaps, alluded to & rebuked the plotting going on, which [483] called forth disclaimers from some of being concerned, & high eulogisms on me from some who defended me. I was not present, & had requested Edmunds to take the chair. In another department I conducted a

---

[29] Along with *The Coquette*, this statue is considered one of the principal works of the Virginia sculptor William Randolph Barbee (1818–68). Both pieces were exhibited in Richmond, Baltimore, and New York in 1858–59.

farmer's discussion—but so few attended that we soon adjourned. Afterwards we went into a joint mass meeting of the two societies, & resolutions were adopted recommending to their Ex. Committees to confer together & endeavor to devise some plan of uniting the two societies.

*Nov. 4.* The two committees met & discussed the question of uniting, but could come to no conclusion. Our committee has no power —that being in the F.A. of the meeting of which there now remains no prospect. Further, the other committee require, as an indispensable condition, that our society shall receive & keep up their "model farm," which has proved an utter failure, & which can be nothing else. This we would not attempt to maintain on any terms.... At night another general meeting, & the report of our Ex. Com. of the inability to offer a scheme of union.

*Nov. 5.* A steady slow rain all day & late into the night. At 11 A.M. Ex-President Tyler arrived. Last night was the Annual Address, delivered by Professor J. P. Holcombe, as requested on the subject of "The right of the state to establish slavery, considered as a question of natural law, with special reference to African slavery as it exists in the United States." It was an able argument, & a splendid composition, with [484] [which] all the hearers were delighted.— Dined with Thomas Gholson,[30] with Mr. Tyler, Mr. Holcombe, Mr. Bruce, Mr. Seddon, Wm. O. Goode, W. Newton, & some others. Wrote a short piece this morning in reference to the proposed amalgamation of the two societies, & sent it to the newspapers.—At night, the last meeting of the society, to hear Mr. Tyler's valedictory address—after which there were off-hand speeches from several other prominent members, & then an adjournment *sine die.* A full house, for such weather, & a pleasant session. When we returned to the hotel, Mr. Tyler, Edmund & I sat & talked some time before retiring. —Determined to go tomorrow to Norfolk, to attend the Fair there next week.

*Nov. 6.* . . . At 7 A.M. set out on the Norfolk & Petersburg railway. This road has just been completed & opened for use. It is straight nearly throughout, passing through a very level country. It will be a great facility to travellers between the two ends—but very worthless for other use. The country very poor, & uninteresting, until reaching

---

[30] Thomas Saunders Gholson ( 1808–68), a lawyer by profession and president of the Bank of Petersburg, was serving at this time as judge of the fifth judicial circuit of Virginia. He was later elected to the Second Confederate Congress.

Suffolk. Within a few miles after, entered the Dismal Swamp, through which the road passed for some miles. . . . On the train had some interesting conversation with a Connecticut machinist & inventor. He says he has invented an important simplification of steam engines—& designs to use steam power to draw carriages on common roads, & to drive ploughs. I suggested that the best possible application would be to peg-rollers, for getting in wheat—& he says he will fix for it. I will have a premium offered for a successful application of that kind.—Reached Norfolk at 11.30. Went to National Hotel. Before dinner, Mr. Charles Rowland a merchant was introduced to me & invited me so kindly & urgently to stay at his house, that at last I consented, as I could not have a separate apartment, or otherwise comfortable accommodations at the only first-class hotel. I however postponed my [486] going until after dinner. Met Mr. Granberry of N.C. my old acquaintance, & who is now the President of the Seaboard Agrl. Soc. We went to the office of Marshall Parks, President of the Albemarle & Chesapeake Canal Co. & had a conversation about that work. At dark, Mr. Rowland called for me, & I went with him to his house. . . . A pleasant & animated conversation on various subjects, before my retiring to my very comfortable apartment for lodging. . . .

*Nov. 7.* Sunday. Walked to the hotel & saw Mr. Granberry again. To church with Mr. & Mrs. Rowland. Very fine music, & some beautiful chants new to me, with a dull sermon. Afterwards walked about the town, both before & after dinner. Reading last Nos. of Harper's Magazine. I stopped taking this years ago, because of its abolition taint. It was always a very light & poor affair, recommended to its great circulation & sale by its pictures & its low price. But the collections of jokes & wit, regularly inserted under the head of the "Editor's Drawer," are the poorest that I ever saw. Perhaps I am deficient in perception & appreciation of wit. But in many of these incidents & sayings given as capital jokes, I cannot see any wit at all, nor any fun or merit, worth putting in print. . . .

*Nov. 8.* After breakfast walked to the reading room, & read the latest papers. Saw a speech lately delivered by Senator Hammond, which I [487] was much pleased to see clears him from all ground of suspicion of being unfaithful to the South. It is true that he is not in favor (now) of disunion, as he was at a former time. But he does not yield anything of the rights of the South. . . .

*Nov. 9.* After going to the Reading Room, & looking over the late papers, went to the Fair. This the first, & not a public day. Not many persons present, & not many of my acquaintance met with. At night, Pres. Tyler arrived at the hotel, where I saw him. . . .

*Nov. 10.* At the Fair again. Dined (or lunched) there with the officers of the Society. Saw many acquaintances. At night attended a conversation meeting (or so intended) of the Society—but which, in that respect, was a failure. Few know how to encourage farmers to address such meetings—as I think I do, when I have presided. Here, very improperly, the President called first upon *me.* I could not refuse to lead—& after I had spoken, (on my plan of drainage, for this region,) not another person followed, & this main business [488] of the meeting was at an end. Afterwards Mr. Tyler was called upon, & as requested spoke for a short time on the trade that Norfolk *ought* to have.—My kind hosts so press me to stay longer that it is difficult for me to abide by my intention to depart tomorrow. I would like to stay one day longer. But if not going tomorrow, I shall miss the stage coach from Richmond, & not have another for 4 days.

*Nov. 11.* . . . Not knowing the steamboat's time of departure exactly, I was at it too soon. It started at 6.30 A.M. On board saw no acquaintance, except Dr. Osborne & Wm. B. Harrison. Reached the Richmond wharf at 4.30 P.M. At the Exchange Hotel. . . . It is now certain that Pryor is about to move "The South" to Washington, to be there amalgamated with "The States" a Douglas newspaper. Pryor has already completed his apostacy from his earlier strong support of the south, by defending such traitors as Douglas & Jefferson Davis.

*Nov. 12.* Called up at 3 A.M. & at 4 left Richmond in the mail coach. Reached Marlbourne soon after sunrise. . . . Russell's [489] Magazine for Novr. contains the remainder of my "Notes on Pine Trees &c," with many typographical blunders.—By this time I can compare the results of the State Fair in Petersburg, & the Fair of the new Central Society & United States Society, gotten up in opposition to the former, in Richmond. The people concerned in the latter (which came on first in time,) & some of the Richmond newspapers, claim a signal success, because the receipts of the Fair rather more than paid the expenses incurred. But these receipts, (about $13,000) were swelled by double payment of members to the new Central Society, & a doubled admittance fee at the gate—& the expenses were reduced by services & things being supplied gratuitously by individuals & the city, for which our society had been heretofore compelled to pay extortionate charges, to as much as $2000 to 3000. All these high charges of receipts, & abatements of payments, were at the cost or loss of citizens of Richmond. Further—to increase the attraction, there were given to the foreign visitors, a splendid dinner & ball, on subscription. High as was the charge for both, there were so few subscribers that the hotel keeper lost $1000 by the ball—& perhaps made no profit by the dinner. The payments, on both these scores, were so much loss to the subscribers, & not counted in the stated expenses of the Fair. Altogether, these extra costs, which either would not have existed if it had been our Society, or would have been partly borne by the Society, must have amounted to full $8000—incurred because the city would not give $3000, nor anything, to retain our fair. By changing to Petersburg, the whole expenses of the Fair are taken from our Society & borne by the town— and [490] all the expenses incurred even by the town, & in every shape, will not exceed $5000, of which $3500 will be paid by the standing appropriation of the city for the Town fair merged in ours, & by the admittance fees, & members' annual payments, both at half the rates charged in Richmond. So that however the opposition in Richmond may boast of success, they have lost nearly thrice the amount that the State Society would have been content to receive & hold its Fair there. The gain to the Society, over holding the Fair in Richmond, on any terms to be obtained, will be at least $4000, & probably more. As an exhibition, the Fair in Richmond was inferior to that of the State Society, which was good, & in stock, better than any preceding. As to the visitors, the collection at Richmond was more of Northerners, & less Virginian than any preceding.

*Nov. 14.* Sunday.... Finished "John Halifax." [31] It is a well-written & interesting book. As of every other resident of England, the author is a thoroughgoing advocate for the abolition of negro-slavery. Yet there are statements of "free" laborers working at starvation prices, & [491] of consequent privations & sufferings tenfold exceeding all that necessarily or usually attend African slavery. It is strange that it never occurs to the European writers who so feelingly & powerfully describe such distresses & calamities—alike unavoidable by the sufferers & their employers—that these sufferers are as much slaves to want, & very far more wretched in their slavery, than are negro or other slaves to individual masters.

---

[31] *John Halifax, Gentleman* was a novel published in 1856 and written by the English novelist and poet Dinah Maria Mulock Craik (1826–87).

*Nov. 15.* . . . Looking over my remaining old writings (in manuscript) & making out a catalogue of all my writings, directed to the care of my sons Edmund & Julian. This may serve to indicate to any of my children, or later descendants, the authorship of some pieces which otherwise might be too trivial to be known, or to be valued, if proceeding from any other source. . . .

*Nov. 16.* . . . Mr. Buchanan's expedition sent to Paraguay will be probably as badly managed, & as much a loss without benefit as that to Utah.[32] The long delay, & open publicity of the former will enable the chief to fortify, or obstruct the passage of the Parana—so as not to be required to make the mere nominal & barren submission that Brigham Young did, without suffering any punishment. This merely apparent submission, to last no longer than an army is kept in Utah, has already cost this [492] government more in expense, than $5,000,000, & not the least restitution made, or suffering inflicted on the traitors & rebels. Deficient as the President has shown himself in most things, his warlike operations are especially worthless & contemptible.—Found the first published report of Mr. Tuomey's Geological Survey of Alabama, which he sent to me, & which I must have read, (at least on the calcareous formations,) but which I had entirely forgotten. It furnishes some information that I wanted—but in some other respects, I think that my observations would show the author was mistaken. I have been waiting impatiently for the latter part of his Report—promised to me, & which I see is at last printed.—Looking over Reports of the Am. Colonization Society.

*Nov. 19.* The mail—& no letters. Reading the 2nd. vol. of Howison's History of Virginia. . . .

*Nov. 20* . . . At night a long & late family conversation, on the fires, & all the painful & disagreeable subjects connected therewith. There has been no evidence elicited, nor (after the first general suspicion against a worthless white man of the neighborhood,) any strong ground to suspect any person as the incendiary. Therefore,

---

[32] The expedition was dispatched to exact reparations for several incidents in Paraguayan waters, most notably one involving the United States survey vessel *Water Witch,* which was fired upon on the Parana River in January, 1855. Notwithstanding the diarist's melancholy predictions, the United States did receive a $10,000 indemnity to compensate the family of a helmsman killed in the *Water Witch* affair, and on February 4, 1859, Paraguay signed a treaty of amity and commerce with the United States in which she conceded to American merchant vessels the right of free navigation on the Paraguay and Parana rivers.

being at a loss for other objects, our neighbors have latterly directed their suspicions generally to our own negroes—& to bolster up such general charges, there have been started & circulated various false reports concerning them. I do not believe a tittle of such deductions from premises [494] which I know to be entirely false. There are no slaves more carefully & properly treated, having better allowances of food & clothing, & proper indulgences, & as I believe better content- ed. Mr. Sayre is firm & strict in his government & discipline, but hu- mane & just—& better qualified to govern, & *therefore* & so far, a better master than I was, though perhaps not better than I desired to be, & failed of being only because not enough regular in ruling, & firm & consistent of purpose. But, still it was entirely within the power of any slave on the farm, safe from discovery or suspicion, to have caused the great fires. And the very idea that some one, whether on or off the farm, has twice so acted, & can again so act, is enough to cause bad & uneasy feelings in us all, & especially in the female members of our family. The evil results of the fires on farm & pecuniary interests, are still in operation. . . . However, if there are no more such heavy losses as by the two fires—& the general sick- ness of laborers this summer, we may expect hereafter a clear farm income of $8000 a year—after paying all farm expenses. . . .

*Nov. 21.* Sunday, & the day for preaching at church. Attended, with Mildred, Julian & Mr. Sayre. . . . A very thin congregation.— Finished Howesson's [*sic*] History. Though published only in 1848, it treats of slavery in Va as an evil, & the author looked forward with hope to its future extinction. There are now but few persons in Va east of the Alleghany mountains, who entertain these opinions, & still fewer who would affront public sentiment by avowing them. The change of opinion has been as great on this subject since 1832, as has ever occurred—& if reason governed, & not prejudice & fanaticism, the like change would extend over the Northern States & England, before many years. This writer also shows that he is a federalist in party politics, & a New School Presbyterian in religion. On the whole, his book was more interesting than I expected, & from it I learned some things, of later times, that I knew less perfectly before. But I cannot conceive what should have induced the author to suppose that he was qualified to write history, or that any such history was wanting.

*Nov. 24.* A daybreak start for Richmond . . . . I had attempted & [496] failed, to get my colonization article published, on suitable terms. I find the influence of the Col. Society operating against me, & two persons afraid to publish an attack on it. I could readily have it printed in a newspaper—but I want it also in pamphlet form—& cannot have it so, except at my own cost, & entire loss. Returned to Marlbourne. Began reading "New England's Chattels."

*Nov. 29.* Sunday. . . . Made some more insertions in my writing. Read part of the Rev. P. Slaughter's very dull & empty article in favor of the Colonization Society—made up mostly by cutting out by the scissors, of articles not worth copying. This was published in the Literary Messenger, and filled 116 of its large pages. And yet the editor declined inserting my much shorter argument on the other side, making the excuse (not required to be stated,) that if he admitted mine, he would be expected, & compelled to admit a reply "from Slaughter," & that he would find it difficult to limit the controversy.—Finished reading "The Chattels of New England." It is designed [497] to show & expose the inhumanity of the usual treatment of paupers in New England—& this is well effected. But there is too much of it, & on the whole, it is a tiresome job to read through the book.

*Nov. 30.* More clippings, as evidence, added to my piece. Mine will be almost as much as Mr. Slaughter's former publication, made up by aid of the scissors. But I trust my selected quotations, as well as the original writing will be the result of more research, & be of much more value.—Now entirely out of work, & also of amusement. . . .

*Nov. 30.* I find I am, & have been for a long time, a day ahead in my dates—for *this* day is the 30th & not yesterday. Strange that I cannot remember the day of the month from one day to the next! although making an entry, & dating it, every day. . . .

*December 1.* Went with Lotty & her children to Richmond, & placed them on the train for Petersburg. . . . Trying, & so far in vain, to get my colonization article published, at something less than the entire expense on [498] myself.—The hotels full of delegates to the democratic convention which is to meet at Petersburg tomorrow to nominate a candidate of the party for governor of the commonwealth. It will be an animated if not boisterous scene, & I will go over to see the tumult, as well as to meet friends & acquaintance from all parts of Va. At night, went to both the principal hotels, to find acquaintances in the crowd—but saw very few that I knew, & none whose company I cared for—& retired to my solitary apartment by 7 P.M.—Saw my late friend Pryor in the street. We exchanged polite bows at a distance. . . .

*Dec. 2.* At 9 A.M. went to Petersburg, on a special train, overflowing with delegates. . . . Met with Edmund, & many other acquaintances among the delegates. A very numerous assemblage—between 7 & 800 delegates—& the old theatre was filled with them & some interlopers like myself, spectators only. A most disorderly session, & especially in the afternoon, when many members were drunk. I left the place before 7; but the session continued until 10, & the organization only effected. . . .

*Dec. 3.* After breakfast, returned to the convention. The great contest, [499] (though there were sundry other persons proposed,) is for & against John Letcher for Governor—& the heat of the contest is caused by the question really being for or against the attempted dictation of Governor Wise & his son, the editor of the Enquirer. Both have exerted themselves in the most indecent manner to prevent the nomination of Letcher; & thus the present contest is more a trial of the influence of Gov. Wise & the Enquirer, than of the popularity of Letcher. I again left the scene at 6 P.M. when the debate was at its height . . . .

*Dec. 4.* Heard that the session had continued until 5 A.M. of this morning. Letcher nominated, by a majority of delegates representing 17,000 democratic voters, over all his competitors—& by 70,000 over the one having the highest vote. This is a signal rebuke of the Wises, which I heartily rejoice at. At 3 P.M. (leaving the remaining delegates still in session, to nominate a Lieutenant Governor,) Edmund & I left for Beechwood, where we arrived after dark.

*Dec. 6.* . . . The mail brought report of the close of the convention in Petersburg, after sitting until to 2.30 A.M. Sunday morning. The only other business done was to nominate [Robert L.] Montague, of Middlesex, as democratic candidate for Lieutenant Governor, & an attempt by young Wise (editor of the Enquirer) to endorse the course of Douglas of Illinois—which had nearly succeeded, but was defeated.—If there were not enough other & great objections to these conventions, & the usurped authority they exercise to act for the state, or its dominant party, there would be enough in the enormous expense required to bring together so many delegates from all [500] parts of the state. I have been rejoiced that Letcher was nominated, as a signal rebuke to the Wises, father & son, who have so indecently opposed him. But I would have been as well pleased, if the whole operation had been frustrated by the meeting being unable to work, & breaking up in ungovernable disorder, as at first seemed most probable. I would be glad to have thus clearly shown the worthlessness & real impracticality of this part of our present abominable state constitution, of electing a governor by the popular vote. It is not done in fact, & never can be done, by the people—but by a few office-seekers & demagogues, who first indicate the course, &, secretly operating, direct the event.

*Dec. 7.* . . . . Finished reading "My Lady Ludlow," by Mrs. [Elizabeth C.] Gaskell[33]—which I bought & began in Richmond. This, like "Cranfield" by the same author, is an interesting delineation of character, & of commonplace incidents, admirably told. Resumed [William F.] Lynch's "Jordan & Dead Sea" [34] which I began yesterday at Ruthven. The day wearisome, and hard to get through. . . .

*Dec. 8.* . . . . Finished Lynch. He had a novel & interesting subject, & might have made a very interesting book. I glanced at parts of his first large work some years ago—& then thought that it would be greatly improved by abridgement, & leaving out all of the writer's fine writing, sentimentals, & romantic descriptions. This work is an abridgement, reduced to less than half the original bulk, & by the author. Still, he has left too much by far. The really novel portion, describing the [501] course & banks of the Jordan, & the Dead Sea, does not occupy much space. The incidents & sketches of Arab manners, though nearly as repeated in many books, are always interesting to me. The long continued & unchanged characters of the Arab race—without any common government or bond of union— thousands of petty tribes always at war with each other—& yet all making the only people never subdued by any conqueror—altogether constitute the greatest & oldest marvel of the human race. The prophecy in regard to the future of the children of Ishmael, in Genesis, seems to me more completely fulfilled, & less obnoxious to objection, than any other claimed to be found in the bible. . . .

---

[33] Mrs. Gaskell (1810–65) was an English novelist noted for her depiction of English country life and her studies of industrial conflict in Victorian England.

[34] A native of Norfolk, Virginia, and a professional naval officer, William Francis Lynch (1801–65) is best known for his exploring expedition to the River Jordan and the Dead Sea in 1848. His account of this expedition, published the year after his return, went through several editions. During the Civil War, Lynch was a captain in the Confederate Navy.

*Dec. 12.* Sunday. Finished (with skipping reflections & remarks,) [John] Kitto's [Daily Bible] Illustrations[35]—& then, to conclude the subject read in the Bible the remainder of the life of David, & all of Solomon. This commentator, like most others, asserts, or insinuates, upon supposition (& often the most improbable,) many things that are not in the bible—& exerts such claim & manner of explaining away difficulties, that it would be hard to say what they [*sic*] cannot make [502] out, as the meaning, or may not deny when it seems to be plainly stated. So it is with the preachers throughout. Thus, the scripture narrative, for the greater part, has two entirely different & opposite constructions. One is the plain & obvious meaning, such as would appear to any intelligent & unprejudiced reader, who first read the portion carefully, but as he would read any other portion of the history of an ancient & strange people. The other is the construction forced by commentators or theologians, & stamped by prejudice on young minds—or on the older, even more strongly impressed, by the previously fixed & great law that it is schismatical, & damnable, to construe scriptural statements of facts or doctrine, contrary to the generally received views of what are termed "orthodox" christian churches. One of the fundamental doctrines is the verbal or literal inspiration of all the canonical books & passages of scripture. Therefore, nothing can be rejected as unworthy of being deemed the words of Almighty God, however evident it might be as such, to an unprejudiced mind. Next, not only, by this law, all of Judges, & Ruth, & Esther, & the Song of Solomon be thus received—though containing nothing religious, or elevated, & much the reverse of both—but these & all other portions of scripture must be construed in many respects contrary to the letter & obvious meaning, & to common sense.—All went to church, except myself. . . .

*Dec. 13.* . . . The mail. Nothing of interest, except a sensation at Washington on account of the apparent pretensions of the British naval force at Nicaragua. A steamer from the U.S. was visited by a British boat, & a report of the passengers *requested,* to learn whether they were Walker's men. It is understood that any such illegal immigrants will be arrested, whether on water or land—& it is rumored that the British & French government[s] will concur not only in preventing & defeating any such invasions unauthorized by the Amer-

---

[35] A book published during the years 1849–54 by John Kitto (1804–54), an English author of Biblical works. Ruffin read only that portion dealing with Saul and David.

ican government, but will maintain the continuance of the Clayton-Bulwer treaty, with the provisions as construed & claimed by the British government.[36] Walker has been attempting for some weeks to embark at Mobile a number of (so called) emigrants for Nicaragua—without arms or any military equipment—& the men have been refused passage, or the vessels refused a legal clearance from the custom-house, by order of the President of the U.S. One vessel however has got off, though fired upon by the Revenue Cutter, without papers, & with some 140 men. Many more have been stopped by the government order. There are indications of future trouble. A war with England, & with France also, if remaining so long the ally of England, is very likely to grow out of these Central American difficulties, if the causes are not soon removed by negotiation, & a treaty that both parties construe alike.

*Dec. 14.* Left for the Berkley wharf before 12, & the steamer reached in 2 hours. Nearly 7 P.M. before arriving at the hotel in Richmond. . . . [504]

*Dec. 15.* The chance for getting my colonization article published has disappeared. I will now go on to Washington, partly on that account, & partly to hear & witness the political passages of the time. Prof. Holcombe's Address is published in the Literary Messenger, & some copies separately for our Society in pamphlet form. I have had some No of these mailed to members of congress, & shall take on with me as many as the vacant space in my little trunk will hold.— Saw & conversed with T. T. Giles, Lewis Harvie, & Wyndham Robertson—the latter about his Pocahontas genealogy.[37]—At 7.30 P.M. set out on the Fredericksburg train for Washington.

*Dec. 16.* Last night at 12, reached Aquia creek, & embarked on the steamer. Reached the wharf at Washington [at] 3.30 A.M. . . . In the course of the day I saw sundry members of my acquaintance—

---

[36] The United States and Britain had been at odds in Nicaragua since the 1830's, as the feasibility of an isthmian canal became more apparent. In 1850 the two nations signed the Clayton-Bulwer Treaty, which, among other things, included a pledge not to occupy or exercise dominion over any part of Central America. The British insisted that the treaty did not apply to existing protectorates, such as that established by them in 1835 over the Mosquito Coast territory, but this interpretation was challenged repeatedly by the United States during the 1850's.

[37] Robertson, a former Whig governor of Virginia, had sought Ruffin's assistance in preparing a genealogical work listing the descendants of Pocahontas through her marriage to John Rolfe. The book was not published until 1887, just a year before Robertson's death.

by calling on them, Letcher, Goode, Hammond of S.C. & Ruffin of N.C.—& accidentally, Senator Hunter, Gen. [John] McQueen,[38] &c. &c.—Took steps to get my colonization article published for mail distribution—if necessary, half at my own expense & loss, as was done with my slavery pamphlet. Consulted Goode on the subject, who asked for the M.S. to examine.

*Dec. 17.* Moved from the Hotel to the same boarding house [505] at which I staid last spring—now in other hands. It is on the Pa. Avenue, & near the Capitol.—Put into the printer's hands the first sheets of my M.S., & proceeded again to read the remainder, for final consideration, & corrections. Went (as I did yesterday,) to the sittings of Congress, & to the Congress Library. . . . Nothing of interest before either House today, & I returned to my new lodgings, to write letters &c.—Bought the last No. of Edinburgh Review, to read a ferocious article against slavery in the U.S., & the Colonization Society. The especial charge against the authorities of Liberia is the participating in the Slave Trade. I have no doubt that most of these charges are either grossly exaggerated, or entirely false—but that there is much true foundation for some of them.—Read & made final corrections & alterations to the 76th page of my M.S.—The printers began to put it in type.

*Dec. 18.* Among the few of my fellow boarders, I this morning found & was introduced to the Rev. Mr. [Ralph R.] Gurley, the Corresponding Secretary of the Am. Colonization Society, & who also, as I first learned from himself, is the editor of the Society's journal, the "African Repository." [39] I found him very polite, & agreeable in conversation—& seems ready to afford any information concerning the Society. It would have been well if I could have had his acquaintance long before, when I relied on the voluntary & offered promise of Mr. Slaughter, to obtain for me information, & from which nothing was obtained. But as late as it is, any new information cannot be made use of, unless to correct errors.—As every day, was partly at the Congress library, & looked in at the sessions of both houses, & called to see members, Th. Ruffin of N.C. (who is confined by sickness,) Letcher, Goode, & Hammond.

---

[38] A native of North Carolina and graduate of the University of North Carolina, John McQueen (1804–67) was a member of Congress from South Carolina from 1849 to 1860. During the war he served in the First Confederate Congress.

[39] Ralph Randolph Gurley (1797–1872) was an important figure in the American Colonization Society for half a century and edited the *African Repository* for twenty-five years. He made a number of trips to Liberia and helped draft the Liberian constitution.

*Dec. 20.* On seeing the portion in type, found, by aid of the printer's calculation, that my M.S. will exceed the designed full sheet (32 pages) of small type . . . . This was very bad. Our contract, the cost, & also the design of having the publication suitable for mail conveyance, & to avoid the cost of stitching, all forbade extending the printing beyond one sheet . . . & so there was no course but to cut out as much as would make 20 pages out of 129. This I did, & unfortunately, having to take out entire subjects, in part, which could not be separated, I had to give up several of what I deemed the best sections & subjects, & thereby greatly to damage the general argument. This cutting down was as disagreeable to me as it was to Puff, in the "Critic," when he found that the players had retrenched sundry of the most highly valued parts of his new play.[40] —Nothing of interest before either house of Congress. I have visited, or called at the lodgings of only four members since I have been here—Ruffin, Letcher, Goode, & Hammond. . . . A rumor has prevailed for some time, which is now rendered certain. A slave vessel has landed in Georgia a cargo of Africans—about 400—of which 270 were brought up the Savannah in a steamer, & openly landed within 8 miles of Augusta.[41] The facts are notorious, & stated [508] fully in the newspapers. It would seem that the actors rely on general sympathy for impunity from the penalties of the law. If they are thus protected, the African slave-trade will soon be reopened fully in effect. It is to be hoped, however, that the law will not be so trampled underfoot—bad as the law is—& absurd, in its declaring the African slave trade to be piracy.

*Dec. 21.* . . . Read & corrected the printer's revised proof sheets of half my article.—In the Senate gallery, had an interesting conversation with Mr. [James C.] Welling, a very intelligent man, who is assistant (literary) editor of the National Intelligencer, & whom I have known slightly for some years.[42] . . . Reading [London] Quarterly Review—articles, among others, on the improvements in Eng-

---

[40] *The Critic* was a famous eighteenth-century comedy written by the Irishborn playwright Richard Brinsley Sheridan. One of the principal characters in this play, a satire on the contemporary stage, is Puff the promoter.

[41] The cargo was transported from Africa in the schooner *Wanderer*, which landed the Negroes on the Dubignon plantation at the south end of Jekyll Island on the night of November 28. Two weeks later the vessel was seized as it took on supplies in Brunswick, Georgia, but the Africans could not be traced.

[42] Welling, a native of New Jersey, became president of St. John's College in Annapolis, Maryland, after the Civil War and, from 1871 until his death in 1894, was president of Columbian College (now George Washington University).

lish Agriculture, & Life of Admiral [Robert] Blake.[43] There have been few greater men in English history [509]—& no great man who was also so patriotic, unselfish, & virtuous a man as Blake.

*Dec. 22.* As Congress will adjourn for 10 days on tomorrow, I can do nothing with my pamphlet by having it ready sooner than Jan 1st —so I hurried on the type-setting, & for aid, spent half the day in reading the proofs—both of which parts were finished by night. This will enable me to go home, instead of staying here longer.—In the forenoon, went to see Lieut. Maury . . . .

*Dec. 23.* Left Washington early, & reached Richmond at 2.30 P.M. Saw Mr. Williams & F. G. Ruffin, at the Agricultural Office—& Sam. Gresham, & several other acquaintances at the hotel.

*Dec. 24.* By 4 A.M. set out in the mail coach, & reached Marl-bourne to breakfast. . . . Glanced over the accumulated newspapers kept for me during my absence, & read my letters.—I had lately seen, with surprise, that Judge Ruffin had been again appointed to the place he had so long held, & had resigned some years ago, of Chief Justice of the Supreme Court of N.C. As I knew that, in re-signing, he had sought retirement from his arduous public labors, & from all public service, I could not conceive why [he] had sought to return to both, when over 74 years of age. But it is explained, & in a manner highly [510] honorable to himself, & also to the legislature that thus elected him. Ever since he left the Supreme Court, (whose decisions he had chiefly shaped & directed,) it has been losing in reputation, & public favor, in the hands of his successors. After the recent death of the latest Chief Justice, so great was the dissatisfac-tion with the Court, that it was desired by a large portion of the leg-islature to abolish the present Court, & re-organize the system. But, as a preferable alternative, it was suggested, & readily agreed upon, to endeavor to call again to the direction the man who had served so long & so well. Accordingly, not only without his seeking, or desiring it, but without his having any intimation of the design, the legisla-ture appointed Judge Ruffin by a unanimous vote. Thus honorably distinguished, I suppose he must consent to return to service—&, at his now advanced age, when so consenting, must expect to die in harness. . . .

*Dec. 25.* Christmas day. Service at church. . . . Read some col-

---

[43] Admiral Blake (1599–1657) was the naval counterpart of Oliver Cromwell, leading parliamentary naval forces against the royalists in the English civil war.

onization reports &c. given to me by Mr. Gurley—& in last Edinburgh Review & Russell's Magazine.

*Dec. 27.* Set in to make a full & correct copy of the genealogical chart of the Ruffin family. At the work from breakfast until too late to see, & did not complete it. It will show, as I believe correctly, every descent from the oldest known ancestor, William Ruffin, in 1666, to the present time—including 9 generations. There are two doubtful points, in the second & third generations, which, however, do not affect the accuracy of either of the branches which remained in Virginia, or have removed in my lifetime. There is a doubt of both the parentage & descendants of the first Edmund Ruffin, who was living in the time of the second generation, & I presume was one of it. There also is some doubt of the precise parentage . . . of Samuel, the oldest known ancestor of the branch that lived first in Edgecombe county, N.C. But this doubt can only affect that branch. The three main & more numerous branches—from which severally descended Judge Ruffin of N.C.—William E. B. Ruffin of Surry—& myself—are set down correctly & fully. Of the branch long settled in Bertie county, N.C.—& which I *guess* to be descended [512] from the first Edmund, (just referred to,) there is now no male, bearing the name of Ruffin, left alive. And as my chart does not include the descendants of females, after they, by marriage, have lost the family name, this deficiency, or error, is at an end, in the extinction of the name in that branch. Another doubt may arise hereafter, and a supposed omission & defect in my chart. The second John Ruffin (5th generation) left no legitimate child. But it is said that an illegitimate son, born in Dinwiddie, bore the father's name instead of his mother's & his legal name. From this person, who lived in a very humble & obscure position, there has descended a family of sundry members—of whom, some have risen to respectable positions. One such, now head of a respectable family, James Ruffin, lives in Petersburg. His brother, in the same place, is a low & mean character. Some Ruffins in Ohio, whose descent I have not been able to learn, may perhaps owe their name to this illegitimate source.

*Dec. 29.* . . . I resumed my work, &, in the whole day, completed the new copy of the chart for myself, & extended two others, made before, to the present time. These two I will give to Wm. E. B. Ruffin of Surry, & Thomas Ruffin, M.C., of Goldsborough N.C. . . .

*Dec. 31.* Steady slow rain all day. . . . I had planned to go to Washington, by tomorrow's stage—& now fear that if delayed longer, the road will be very bad, & perhaps no seat in the coach to be had. For the last 6 weeks, or more, there has been slow rain so frequently, that the intermissions of fair weather have not been one day in four. The earth is full of water. No farm labor can be done here, & half the crop of corn is yet in the field, & not a furrow yet ploughed.

# January–June

e~o

# 1859

---

AGAIN IN THE NATION'S CAPITAL e~o MORE
ON THE "WANDERER" INCIDENT e~o ATTACK-
ING THE COLONIZATION SOCIETY e~o POLIT-
ICAL AND PHILOSOPHICAL SPECULATIONS

*January 1*. Raining all last night, & continuing slowly today. . . .
After 3 P.M. I set out in the mail coach for Richmond. The roads so
bad, from the quantity of rain, that we did not arrive there until
after 7. I had designed to go on tonight to Washington—but there
was too little time. Stopped at the Exchange Hotel. . . .

*Jan. 2.* On to Washington—where arrived by 3 P.M. At Brown's
Hotel. Saw T. Ruffin, & Goode.

*Jan. 3.* Monday. Congress does not meet again until tomorrow.
It is a shameful neglect of public duty to take a recess of 10 working
days out of the short session, & the members abating nothing on
that account from their extravagant salary of $3000.—My pamphlet
went to press this morning—& by 1 P.M. I had enough copies for me
to direct more than 100—under the franked covers of Mr. Th. Ruffin.—Went to what is called a *private* boarding House. But this has
more than 25 boarders at table, male & female. I do not know one of
them—& probably shall not. . . . At night, went to T. Ruffin's room,
where I carried my written envelopes, [515] & fixed my pamphlets
to send by mail—& read the newspapers. . . . It seems to be now considered, by most persons, that the impunity & success attending the
landing of a cargo of Africans in Georgia, & distributing them
through several states, with the vain attempts of the U.S. authorities
to obtain any evidence, or to arrest the procedure, shows that public
opinion has so decidedly taken part against the law, (which foolishly

[261]

& absurdly makes the African slave trade to be *piracy*, & a capital offence,) that it cannot be enforced. These Africans have been sold at $250 (in stated cases) when the usual price is $1000 & more for like native negroes. This state of things will invite plenty of northern vessels & crews, & capital, to go into the trade, & practically, the slave trade will be re-opened.

*Jan. 4.* The Senate moved from the hall heretofore used [514][1] for its sessions to the magnificent new hall in the new building. The printer had caused to be placed a copy of my pamphlet on the desk of every senator. I did not get into the gallery until sometime after the senators were in their new places. Then I had a rebuff to my vanity, in seeing that not one, whether acquaintance or stranger, was taking any notice of the pamphlet, or seemed conscious that it was before their eyes.—Putting copies in covers franked by Th. Ruffin, & sending them to many persons, of whom I had made a list. . . .

*Jan. 5.* This day I reach the age of 65—which is older than any of my progenitors lived to be, since my great-grandfather, Edmund Ruffin. Having always been of weak constitution, & generally in delicate health, if not actually sick, as I was generally through the earlier 15 years of my manhood, I little expected to reach this age. But so much has my health improved in the later part of my life, & more especially in the last two years, that, it would now seem more probable that I should live any certain number of years, say 5 or even 10, than at earlier times. But I do not desire to attain extreme old age—nor any extension of years, if accompanied by great infirmity [515] of body, or much less of mind. And even without these evils, I do not deem the coming of death, without long delay, as to be dreaded or deplored, provided the death shall be sudden & unexpected, & without suffering. So far, since my change of occupation, I have been as contented & happy as my other circumstances permitted—& there has been as yet no decrease of my contentment & enjoyments. But I am sensible that nothing but employment will keep me contented, or moderately happy—& I fear that my principal latter employment of writing for the press must come to an end, not only for want of interesting subjects, but because of my growing mental inability. I am not able to know the progress of mental decay in anything but as to memory—which is to myself most evident, & rapidly increasing with time.—Senator Hammond has

---

[1] Misnumbered by the diarist. Should be page 516.

changed his residence, & gone to keeping house, so far from my lodgings that I did not go to see him until this evening. We had a long, & to me, an interesting conversation on political subjects of the day.... [516]

*Jan. 6.* By invitation of the Commissioner of the Patent Office, sanctioned by the Secretary of the Interior, on the 3rd inst. there was assembled here a "convocation" of agriculturists. The members were doubtless designated by D[aniel] J. Browne, the head of the Agricultural Department of the Patent Office. That I was not invited to this meeting seems surprising to all who speak of it—but it is not so to me. Browne knows that I hold him very low, & have freely expressed my contemptuous opinion of him, & the whole working of his department. He has selected as members more unfit persons, not deserving the name of farmers, who are his supporters or tools, than he has of good & distinguished farmers. The body, & its institution, have been denounced in "The States" by its editor, my *quondam* friend Pryor, & a sharp reply, & a sharper rejoinder have followed. I wrote a light article this afternoon, & sent it to "The States," designed to lash Browne & the whole system of his department. Since, I have heard that the question has been moved today, in the House of Rep. as to the authority to call together, & to pay this assemblage. The meeting is contemptible, & so must be its proceedings, whatever they may be. But the controversy, & the sparring, have given a degree of interest to the subject that would not be produced by its importance in any way.—Senator Douglas of Illinois is re-elected—& tonight he arrives here, met by great rejoicing by his partizans. He is a great political scoundrel, as well [517] as one of the ablest, & as likely as any to be the most successful of all the aspirants to the presidency.

*Jan. 7.*... Went to see Goode, (as I do every day) & think he cannot live long. Yet he is in his seat in Congress at least part of every day when the weather is not very bad, or he more sick than usual. He is dying of consumption. Yet he is here alone, without the company of one of his family—& seems entirely unconscious of his danger....

*Jan. 8.* Some days ago I made the acquaintance of John Mitchell, the Irishman, noted formerly as a bold & able writer & publisher, in Ireland, in opposition to British rule, & for his banishment, as a political felon (to Australia,) & his subsequent escape to the U.S. He has since been a strong southern & pro-slavery advocate, & has lately moved his paper [518] to this city. When I subscribed for it, & left my card for him, he called on me, & had a political conversation. I see that he is anxious to conciliate my favor. I gave him some of my pamphlets & a newspaper article. Today he has republished a long extract from the latter—& states that he will next notice my Colonization pamphlet.... This evening, my squib ... was printed in the "States"....[2] If Browne's incapacity (though he is a writer of agricultural books,) was his only defect, I should not have pushed him so hard. But I have heard enough to satisfy me that he is a scoundrel also, who uses the facilities afforded by his official trust, for his own selfish purposes, & especially to make dishonest gains, & to a very great extent. I hope to obtain proof of one act of this character.

*Jan. 10.* Had ordered, & received today, sent by Mr. Williams 10 copies of Holcombe's Address, for every member of Congress [521] from the slave-holding states, which I proceeded to have distributed. Afternoon visited Gen. Tilghman, & H[enry] K. Burgwyn of N. C. who are members of the "Advisory Board of Agriculture," & are so much opposed to Browne that I think he will have packed that body with sundry of his own tools in vain.... [Stephen A.] Douglas made his first appearance, this session, in the Senate chamber. His re-election to the body had just before been heard. And he had kept away, for fear of being drawn into some dangerous confessions, before he was safe in his place. It is now a matter of interest & doubt, how he will act towards the administration & his party— from which he had before partially separated—& how he will stand with his fellow members. Hammond thinks he will sulk. But I have more confidence in the strong vitality of his political scoundrelism, & of his ability as a demagogue.

*Jan. 12.* Long speeches in the Senate in advocacy of or opposition to different proposed routes for the Pacific rail-road—which I trust will never be constructed on any one of them, nor any that is not far enough south to go through part of Mexico. But such is the degree of carelessness of public interests, of members of congress generally—& of corruption of many—[522] & of even the desire to squander from the treasury of others, the better to promote the increasing the tariff duties—that there is no telling whether this most

---

[2] Ruffin's "squib" was a blistering attack on Superintendent of Agriculture Daniel J. Browne, delivered in the form of a purported speech by Major John Jones of Delaware, who consented to lend his name to the little hoax.

gigantic undertaking & flood of expense, will not be assumed, & in its worst shape.—Did not attend the House of Rep. Hear that there arose there a debate on Walker's "filibustering" in Central America —which resulted in the virtual adoption by a majority of a vote of approval & thanks to Com. Paulding, for his illegal & unjustifiable capture of Walker & his troops on the territory of Nicaragua.— Goode is better. Sat with him last evening & this, each some hours. His friends coming to see him. Among them, last night, our senators Mason & Hunter. Tonight came in Pryor—whom I met courteously, but with distance & reserve. I am sorry to learn of his great pecuniary embarrassments. It is ascribed to them, his recent political change, & the removal of his publishing from Richmond to [t]his place. His truly splendid abilities as a writer & journalist will not serve to save him, nor all friendly & political acts, (of which he has had much [*sic*],) so long as he is addicted to gaming, & especially at the faro table—at which, it is said, all his money has been sacrificed. . . .

*Jan. 13.* Last night attended a lecture, on Nitrogen, [523] at the Smithsonian Institute, by my old acquaintance [Thomas G.] Clemson.[3] The United States Agricultural Society is now in session. Though I am very friendly & cordial with its officers, & have been urgently invited by them, I will not attend the meetings. They are striving to gain patronage from the treasury—which I, & our State Society, do not approve—& I do not wish, by my presence, to appear to go with them. I had intended & desired, to meet the members, as intelligent farmers. But, from what I hear, I believe that there are very few such present. . . . Nearly all the time, attended the session of the Senate. The splendid cushions & carpets of the galleries to the new chamber will soon be made filthy, by the sitters spitting tobacco-juice on the carpets, & then, with soles so soiled, stepping, on the cushions, from one range of seats to vacated seats on others nearer the front. [524]

*Jan. 14.* Mitchell, in his "Southern Citizen" has published two columns of review & comment of my Colonization pamphlet—& told

---

[3] Thomas Green Clemson (1807–88), mining engineer, diplomat, and son-in-law of John C. Calhoun, was a founder of the Maryland Agricultural College and in 1859 was appointed United States superintendent of agriculture. During the Civil War he was superintendent of mines and metal works in the Trans-Mississippi Department of the Confederacy. He died at Fort Hill, South Carolina, and provided in his will for an endowment which led to the founding of Clemson Agricultural College at that site.

me that he designed to continue the remarks. It then occurred to me that I had better give to him, as materials, what I had written lately, & all the omitted parts of my earlier manuscript. This I afterwards offered to him, when he called on me, & he took charge of the papers with much apparent gratification. He is a very able & interesting writer—& his denunciations are very severe. I am glad to have his aid in lashing & exposing the great humbug, the Colonization Society. . . . Sent some specimen copies of the "Southern Citizen" to some of my friends. I wish it could be supported. Mitchell is an able editor & writer, goes fully for the rights of the South. I fear however that his having so boldly advocated the re-opening of the African slave-trade will prevent his paper being supported by the many southern men who still view that proposed policy as most objectionable & condemnable. [End of MS Volume 3—p. 525]

*Jan. 15.* At last effected the giving out to all the members of Congress from the slave-holding states, 10 copies of Holcombe's Address. Sent to [J. W.] Randolph of Richmond, to try to sell, a portion of the impression of my colonization pamphlet. I do not expect that enough will be sold to pay me for the trouble & cost of the attempt —much less to pay for the printing. But the advertisements may make it more extensively known & induce orders from persons who would not obtain them from the gratuitous distribution. I have myself already given away (& mostly through the mails, under members' franks,) 500 copies; & 2100 were bought by members, to distribute.— Report has given the authorship of Major Jones' speech to B[enjamin] Perley Poore, a newspaper writer of note, & especially for humorous description.[4] He was one of those to whom I had confided my action. Mr. Browne has been getting other blows from various quarters. But this he cares but little for, provided he can keep his office, & continue his peculations.—At dark, Gen. John Tyler called on me to consult on the condition of the south. His conversation soon grew into a vehement & loud speech, very suitable for a popular meeting. It is a pity that he will thus, by his grand air & artificial & [526] mock tragic acting, together with his glaring exhibition of vanity & self-conceit, operate to discredit the powers of

[4] A celebrated author, journalist, and editor, Poore became Washington correspondent for the Boston *Journal* in 1854 and during the next three decades gained acclaim for his famous column under the by-line "Perley." He was also secretary of the United States Society of Agriculture and edited its *Journal of Agriculture* from 1857 to 1862.

mind & reasoning which he really possesses in a high degree. After he left me, I went to Elwood Fisher's, & sat until past 9. . . . He told me some curious things connected with the late cruise of the yacht Wanderer—& promised more.

*Jan. 16.* Sunday. Soon after breakfast, I met Fisher near my door, & asked him into my room. Im[me]diately after, Gen. Tyler joined us, & fell into our political talk—& interesting as was the subject, & glad to exchange views, I was soon tired by his harangue, uttered as loudly, vehemently, & with as much of oratorical manner & trick, as if he was making a set speech to a crowd. He presented the strongest contrast to Fisher's very quiet & calm manner—but of whose good sense, & striking opinions, the other gave me but little opportunity to hear expressed. Our conversation, & for the much greater time, Tyler's speech, lasted for three hours.—Afterwards, in walking on the Pennsylvania Avenue, I met President Buchanan, also walking, & not distinguished from the crowd. As we first passed, he had one eye [527] shut, (as is his frequent habit,) & with the other stared at me as if he thought he knew me. But he did not. For though I have seen him several times before, I do not think that he ever saw me. I think so badly of him that I have no desire to have any personal acquaintance with him.—Saw Mr. Boulwane & Mr. Washington, (a very intelligent young man residing here—) in the public room of the National Hotel, & had a discussion on the policy of re-opening the African slave-trade—B. against, & W. & I stating the arguments in favor—but B. admitting some important political advantages, & I concurring with him as to some economical disadvantages; for example, in increasing the supply, & so lessening the price of cotton. At night, Fisher, by my previous invitation came to my room. I had requested Mitchel [*sic*] also to come—but something prevented. Fisher sat with me several hours. We conversed on various political matters, affecting southern interests—about starting (or strengthening Mitchel's) a southern paper, & the manner of proceeding, & the dangers of failure. Of the latter, had Fisher's experience in his conducting the "Southern Press," which so ably sustained southern rights, & which southern men allowed to go down, for want of support. We talked of the purchasing of votes (by the great Texas bribe of 10 millions,) to pass the compromise [528] measures in 1850—& of the co-working of Clay & old [Thomas] Ritchie—the former the briber & the latter the bribed—to produce the result. I did not know the particulars before. But I knew enough to be sure that Ritchie was bribed by the prospect of securing the $100,000 which he claimed on so false, iniquitous, & fraudulent pretences. And I have always since declared that the Ritchies, & their papers, the Union & Enquirer, had betrayed the South, for mercenary objects, & had done more harm to the South than any other men or publications— because professing to be friends, & being trusted as such. Talked of the purchase of Cuba, which was foolishly brought forward by the president in his annual message—& of which the proposal is now under consideration of both houses of Congress—& all the powers of Europe expressing indignation at these avowed designs, & France & England, in close alliance, threatening war, in this event, or any attempt to seize Cuba, by purchase or otherwise. They desire to Africanize Cuba, which would be the greatest evil to, & outrage upon the U.S. We talked of the slave trade, & the probable effects on the condition of the Africans. The adventurers in the yacht Wanderer were not such men as usually engage in the African slave-trade, whether in person, or as an investment. [529] Besides the stimulus of expected profit, there were inducements to test the ability to violate the law, & to test its constitutionality, if trials took place. Men of high standing in the south furnished the funds, & according to their shares, were to be repaid in negroes, if the adventure should be successful. A gentleman (in his position, & associations) named [William C.] Corrie, was captain of the apparent pleasure yacht.[5] Another adventurer, named [J. Egbert] Farnham, who had been a colonel in Walker's first invasion & war in Nicaragua, was another of the officers.[6] He is now in this city—is a fearless adventurer, a gentleman (unless his recent adventure is deemed exclusion from that character—) & a very intelligent man. Fisher has conversed with him, & heard much from him in regard to the adventure. Farnham has kept notes of all the incidents, & offered them to Fisher if he would write out the account. He is disposed to do so—& I urged him to do it. As this is, under the law, *piracy*, & the offenders liable to suffer death, the principals do not speak very openly. But the disguise is very thin—& Farnham has told Fisher

---

[5] Captain Corrie, from Charleston, was also the ostensible owner of the *Wanderer*. Efforts to remove him from South Carolina to Georgia for trial as a pirate under the federal act of 1820 proved futile.

[6] Farnham was the supercargo (or factor) of the *Wanderer*. He was indicted under the 1820 act and brought to trial in Savannah in May, 1860. However, the jury deadlocked and Farnham went free.

many of the facts, & his observations in Africa. There were about 400 negroes shipped in this vessel, which is so small that it has been supposed that it could not possibly have brought so many, & that there must have been another vessel in company. [530] Yet the loss, on ship-board (on the "middle passage,") was only 9 percent, which is less than usual on the white emigrant ships. Even this loss would have been much less, but for reaching the American coast in cold weather, & no blankets or clothing had been previously provided. It was a remarkable fact that no manacles, or other mode of confinement, was used, during all the voyage. The Africans were loose & at large—were tractable & obedient—never a case of resistance to command—& no punishment ever was required, except to administer some blows to make peace whenever a fight took place between some two of the negroes. They made no objection to any of the dispositions since made of them—show no sorrow or suffering —& as we learn from all the newspaper reports, have been taken in small parties by the different public conveyances through Georgia, & Alabama, without exhibiting any reluctance, or requiring restraint or confinement—seemingly good-humored & contented. As yet, no legal process has been operative, & no one has been arrested as *pirates*. The vessel has been seized by the officers of the law, for adjudication. But it cannot be condemned, until some offender has been found guilty.—Heard that yesterday the democratic members of the Senate held a caucus, & decided to support the bill for appropriating 30 [531] millions as a beginning for the purchase of Cuba. This seems to me worse than the president's recommendation. I cannot conceive any good, but much evil, to flow from thus proclaiming our wishes & designs. The indignation of Spain is already excited highly. That would, of itself, be of little moment. But with England & France ready to aid Spain, & united as allies to make war on this country would be an awful state of things. Yet, even in such a war, France could gain nothing (except perhaps glory,) & England would be an immense loser—&, on the other hand would gain greatly in commercial profits, by Cuba being transferred to the U.S.

*Jan. 17.* At night went to see Hammond. He thinks that neither the President, nor either of the movers in Congress, are sincere in their proposed measures to acquire Cuba—but that each only wants to cultivate popularity by pretending to be foremost in the move—that all of them would be horrified if the bill should, by possibility, be enacted. H. thinks that war would certainly be made on us by France & England, if we were to acquire Cuba, even by purchase. He ascribes this evil political move, & most others, to the aspirants to the Presidency, of whom [532] he enumerated & named 18 in the southern states, as understood by the public—(& among which he counted himself,) & of them 11 who were active in the pursuit. These were: Hunter, Wise of Va, Breckenridge [*sic*] & Crittenden of Ky, Orr of S.C. Bell & Johnson of Ten. Toombs of Ga, Houston of Texas, Davis of Mi, & Slidell of La. We had not been together half an hour before Elwood Fisher came with his friend recently from Africa, Col. Farnham. As soon as the latter was introduced to us, H. entered upon the subject of the African slave trade, stating his strong objections of expediency to it, & Fisher opposing his argument, until we left, at half after 8, as I knew that H. had then to go out. We others then came in Fisher's carriage to my room, where we continued to converse an hour longer. Farnham repeated what I had before heard of his experience through Fisher—& stated sundry other interesting facts about Africa & the natives. He avoided saying anything to the direct purport that he had been engaged in the African slave trade, or that the "Wanderer" had brought the recent supply of Africans to Georgia. [533] But he used very little care for this merely formal concealment. He stated that, in the Wanderer, he had been anchored for some days close to a British vessel of war, then engaged in preventing the slave trade, & that the officers of the two ships were quite intimate & cordial, & dined together every day on one or the other vessel. Of course, not the least suspicion was entertained by the British officers that the Wanderer was not merely a pleasure yacht, & the hospitable commander & his companions voyagers for pleasure. At the same time, a French ship of war lay close by, protecting a slaver, that then was receiving on board 1200 African "apprentices" for the French sugar islands. There was no difference in the manner of capture, or purchase, or bringing on board, of these "apprentices," & other slaves for Cuba. The only ground latterly remaining to me, on which I suppose that the existence of a legal & regulated trade in slaves would be hurtful to the Africans, as a general rule, is that wars would be incited, & kept up between the savage tribes, for the purpose, or in consequence, of making captives to sell as slaves. In answer to my inquiries on this point, Col. Farnham admitted his belief that such evils would [534] be so increased. But on the other hand he says that the wars of the tribes are almost bloodless, or exempt from slaying & deaths, compared to others. As an example, he cited a war that had been prosecuted for two years between the kings of two named tribes, in which not a man had been killed. Incredible as this statement may seem, it has much support from other unquestionable facts of the last war between the Liberian Colonists of Cape Palmas & the close adjacent native villages—as stated in the recent work of the Rev. Alex. Cowan, who learned the facts on the place, & who certainly was not disposed to underrate the dangers or the disasters of the war. It was caused by the unjustifiable wrongs perpetrated by the colonists in seizing the lands of the natives, whose villages were intermixed with those of the colonists. The events of the war were strongly & ludicrously in exemplification of the timidity, & inefficiency of the negro race for warlike operations. The war continued for some months. The opposite parties were close together, & indeed their previous settlements had been interspersed with each other. They had no fortifications, or [535] places of defence, secured against assault. The damage & loss by the war was very great to both sides. But the operations were not in fighting & killing, but in plundering & burning the villages & habitations. In the whole war, Mr. Cowan says that not one of the Liberians was killed —& it was not known to them that any one of the natives had been killed. The only known loss of life was in the drowning of 28 colonists, caused in the following manner. On a lake near Cape Palmas, they equipped a large canoe with a small cannon, to fire into the thickets on the borders, where the natives were supposed to be hidden, & where the colonists were afraid to approach by land. The first firing of the cannon, by its recoil, broke out the side of the canoe, & nearly all of its crew were drowned. Col. Farnham says that the natives are so cowardly, & ignorant, that one resolute white man, well armed, would drive hundreds of them. He described their condition as generally most abject & wretched, from which a change to captivity on ship-board, (such as he had seen, though that was a remarkable case, & rare exception to the usual treatment—) & subsequent bondage in this country would be a great benefit. The family ties among them he deemed but little better than those of brutes. He thought that few [536] fathers could be found, who would not sell a son or a daughter to a slave dealer—& few, if any of even the wives of the chiefs, or petty kings, that could not be bought of their royal husbands & masters for a sufficient, & not very high price.

*Jan. 18.* Every day I go to the gallery of one or both of the houses of congress, generally of the Senate, & remain as long as the debate is interesting—& that is not often. The late & still continuing subject is the Pacific rail-way. This is the most gigantic folly, & proposed expense, that ever a people were expected to undertake voluntarily, through its government. But though the President, & three-fourths of Congress profess to be zealous for it, & convinced of its utility, I cannot believe that it will be undertaken, north of all that is now eastern Mexico. Across Tehuantepec, I doubt not that a rail-road would be highly advantageous—& ought to be undertaken as soon as the route is under our control.—Continuing to read the English Reviews. In the Edinburgh, a long notice of [James A.] Froude's recent History of England, containing Henry 8th. This must be a curious work, inasmuch as the author endeavors to excuse, if not to justify, every one of the numerous & deep crimes charged [537] to this vilest of all the kings of modern Europe. From my own love of what is singular, odd, & paradoxical, I have been fond of reading ingenious arguments to prove historical characters different from what history set them up for. Thus I have been gratified to read vindications of Napoleon, though still believing in his guilt in general—was delighted to be convinced of Cromwell's worth & greatness—have even read with pleasure attempts to defend Robespierre, Marat, & Judas Iscariot. But I could not conceive how anything could be said to lighten the burden of infamy which has remained on the memory of Henry. Nor can I yet conceive it, from what the reviewer reports of this author & apologist, & often panegyrist of the bloody & all-selfish tyrant. Even his religious persecutions, which might be respected if executed by sincere persecutors, in him were but ready means to murder for selfish ends. Nothing can be more detestable & atrocious in homicide, than when religion, & duty to God, are made the pretexts. And such were the religious murders committed by Henry 8th, & aided by [Thomas] Cranmer, his fit tool for his infamous purposes. When Henry or Cranmer caused men to be hanged or burned for holding the same opinions which they respectively had held but a few years or months before, they could not but be conscious of sufficient reasons for excuse, & for mercy. Very different is the case with the consistent fanatic, who has never deviated from the same creed, & who cannot conceive any other, with even a shade of difference to be otherwise [538] than erroneous & damnable. With such sincere & honest fanatics, intolerance is a necessary principle & action, & persecution of heretics is not only right, but is a duty which it would be a sin & a crime against God to neglect to enforce. In these modern times, & among the most enlightened people, all religionists have become wiser, & in proportion, more moderate in their doctrines. They may still assert the old creeds in their former integrity & purity, & profess to believe them to as full extent. But they do not. . . .

At night, attended (unseen) the annual meeting of the American Colonization Society. There was nothing done, except a long speech, of the usual tone & purport, by the President.—Had a long conversation with Mitchel, as to the means for increasing the support & usefulness of his paper.

*Jan. 19.* Wrote a squib for the paper, which I carried [541] immediately to the editor, but was too late, for today's publication.—At night, [Dr. John H.] Van Evrie, the editor of the New York Day Book, a strong pro-slavery paper, called on me & we conversed for some two hours on the subject of slavery, & connected matters.[7] I infer from what he said that the anti-slavery fanaticism is not declining.

*Jan. 20.* . . . By accident, met with Senator Reid, of N.C., whom I had visited last winter when he was so long ill in Richmond. He seemed very glad to see me, & invited me to visit him—which I did the same evening. Also, went to see Letcher & Goode.—My squib appeared in "The States" this afternoon. I expect it will make northern members quite angry—whether they see fit to show it or not.[8]

*Jan. 21.* . . . Got more back numbers of Westminster Review, from the Congress Library, & spent most of the day in reading.—Mitchel's paper came out, with continued remarks on the Colonization [542] Society, & my pamphlet. I trust he will enable me to be heard of, & my views to be sought & read, far beyond my limits otherwise. —See in a Richmond paper that the millers have gained their suit, & near $2000 damages from the flour inspector, for his illegal drafts of flour, made a perquisite of the office.—This at least is one victory

---

[7] Dr. Van Evrie was a militant defender of slavery and white supremacy, as evidenced by the titles of his two major books—*Negroes and Negro 'Slavery': The First an Inferior Race, The Latter Its Normal Condition* (New York, 1861), and *White Supremacy and Negro Subordination; Or, Negroes a Subordinate Race and (So Called) Slavery Its Normal Condition* (New York, 1868).

[8] In his "squib," Ruffin humorously suggested that the British annex New England.

which has been the result of our paper war against the legal inspections, & the illegal acts of the inspectors of flour.

*Jan. 23.* Sunday. Went to the Congregational church, & heard a northern minister preach an abolition & incendiary anti-slavery sermon, or argument. It exceeded everything that I could have supposed possible in Washington, & was equal in folly, falsehood & malignity to any discourse that might be heard in Boston. Made my farewell visits to my most intimate acquaintances, & made my other arrangements for an early departure tomorrow, to attend the Ex. Com. next day. [543]

*Jan. 24.* Left Washington before daybreak, & the wharf at 7 A.M. & reached Richmond (Exchange Hotel) before 3 P.M. John Seddon & Bev[erly B.] Douglas,[9] whom I had seen in Washington, returned with me. . . . Read the newspapers, & looked through some periodical pamphlets—& for want of more amusement, or company, had to go to bed early. There seems, from the last European news, a strong probability of hostilities being begun between France & Austria—& also between Austria & Sardinia—& as a consequence of the latter, a general outbreak of the heavily oppressed Italian people.[10] I earnestly hope this may occur, for the chance of relief to the Italians— of ruin to the leaden despotism of Austria—& of danger to the iniquitous tyrant & usurper of France. And if, in any way, England shall get involved, & opposed to France, that will be excellent in reference to our self-interest. When these great powers, & our great though covert enemies, shall be entirely engaged in war with each other, than we shall be at liberty to settle our own little matters, with our near neighbors—or with our sister states.

*Jan. 25.* . . . At night our members met at the office of the Society. Much discussion as to the manner of offering terms, general or particular, to Richmond, as to the holding the next Fair—some members fearing, if not making any advances, to cause more hostile feeling, & a final separation from Richmond. Others unwilling to make any special advance to Richmond, lest our stooping should [544] not only again [be] treated with contempt, but that it will render any arrangement more improbable than if we preserved an in-

---

[9] Beverly Browne Douglas (1822–78) was at this time a member of the Virginia Senate. Following Reconstruction he was twice elected to the United States House of Representatives.

[10] The news reports were accurate. War erupted in late April, thus commencing the struggle for Italian unification.

dependent & more dignified position. Adjourned at 11 P.M. without reaching a vote.

*Jan. 26.* .... Our meeting resumed at 9 A.M. After many proposed alternatives & amendments, we concurred in the resolutions below.

1. Resolved, That now, as heretofore, repeatedly avowed, it is the unanimous opinion of the Executive Committee of the State Agricultural Society, that the city of Richmond is the place most suitable for the holding of the Annual Fairs, and that it is highly desirable that arrangements should be made by which this object can be obtained, and, if possible, placed on a permanent basis.

2. Resolved, That whilst it is thus desirable that the Fairs should be held at the city of Richmond, the constitution of the Society and imperative obligations of duty in the administration of the funds of the Society, require that wherever the Fair shall be held, it shall be done without loss to the Society; and upon this principle alone, therefore, can the permanent usefulness of the Society be secured.

3. Resolved, That a Committee of six ( any three of whom may act, ) be appointed to receive propositions from, and negotiate with any cities, towns, or Agricultural Societies of the State, in regard to holding the Fairs of the Society for 1859, with the power to decide as to the manner, terms, and locality—*provided,* that no such arrangement shall be made to the loss and detriment of the Virginia State Agricultural Society.

Committee.—Wm. G. Crenshaw, Franklin Minor, Frank G. Ruffin, Wm. C. Knight, John R. Garnett, and Chas. B. Williams.[11]

The third & chief one I proposed & carried, but after accepting as amendments the two to precede, which were offered by W. C. Knight. After this, & appointing the committee, but little more was done, & we adjourned at 1 P.M. I declined being made a member of the committee, & to appoint the members—preferring that the proceeding should not risk being weakened by the odium which I have incurred with many in Richmond, who ascribe to me the removal of the last year's Fair, & say that my feelings hostile to Richmond were the motives.... [546]

... Arrived at Marlbourne after dark....

---

[11] From clipping appended to MS page 545.

*Jan. 28.* . . . I think that my pamphlet is showing effect in congress. Opposition [547] has been made by Mr. [James F.] Dowdell[12] & Mr. [J. L. M.] Curry,[13] of Ala. to the appropriation of $75,000 for defraying the charges for the recaptured Africans, delivered in Liberia, under the President's contract with the Colonization Society—which contract however only was for $45,000—the remaining $30,000, I suppose are for extras. Wrote a long letter, suggesting other grounds of objection, to Messrs. Dowdell & Curry. . . .

*Jan. 29.* . . . Already, I have had more notice taken, or reported to me, in letters, both from members of my family & other friends, of my late pamphlet, than of anything I ever wrote before. Although all such persons have spoken highly of it, I do not ascribe its being thus remarked to its merit, but to the novelty of the argument, (all previous publications on the Colonization Society having been in its favor—) & to the tendency to produce controversy. But, if this greater notice is not evidence of merit, or of weighed approval, it may serve me otherwise in a matter that I have much desired, & could not have. I have long feared the effects of age on my mind, though not perceived by myself in anything except the rapid & great failure of memory, & the growing dulness [*sic*] of ability to learn new things that required much thought & close reasoning. . . . But in arousing such enmity as I shall by this attack on so strong an interest—& especially its clerical position—every means will be used to decry my argument & its author, without restraint from respect, or other grounds for forbearance. Therefore, if I have given any indications of growing dotage, however unsuspected by myself, & indulgently overlooked, or screened by my friends, it will be exultingly exposed, or the effects treated as they deserve, by angry or hostile opponents. Thus, if the fact exists, I may learn it from the tenor of antagonists' replies, even though it shall not be charged in direct words.

---

[12] A native of Georgia, Dowdell (1818–71) migrated to Alabama and in 1853 was elected to Congress as a State Rights Democrat. During the Civil War he was colonel of the Thirty-seventh Regiment, Alabama Volunteer Infantry.

[13] Jabez Lamar Monroe Curry (1825–1903), like Dowdell, was a State Rights Democratic congressman from Alabama. After the war, in which he served as a lieutenant colonel in the cavalry, Curry was successively president of Howard (Alabama) College, professor in Richmond (Virginia) College, agent for the Peabody Fund, and special minister to Spain.

My late writing to Jane & Patty Ruffin has been mainly to persuade them to come & see us soon . . . . I have ulterior views, on the grounds for which my daughters (Elizabeth & Mildred) & I have conferred, & earnestly concur. We think that my son Edmund ought to marry, if he can make a judicious choice—& of all we know, there is no one whom we would so much rejoice to be his choice, & he to be so fortunate to obtain her love, as Jane Ruffin. . . . He & Jane have not met for years—& I am very sure have not thought of each other in this aspect. But they have a high appreciation of each [551] other, & the mutual & well-founded esteem that would be the surest foundation for happiness in marriage. . . . Of course it would not do to hint my wishes to any one. But I am therefore the more anxious not to more relax the ties of friendship & intimacy between the two families, but to bring them still closer—& so to permit the fullest opportunities for growing & intimate acquaintance, & then trust to the future for the end I wish.

*Jan. 31.* Mailing more of my pamphlets (both on Colonization & Pine Trees,) to distant friends & others, as suitable names occur to me. . . .

*February 1. . . .* The mail. Letter from Newton. Applauds my Col. pamphlet. Also came two pamphlets, before published, sent to me to present opposing views of the capacity of the negro race—both from Benjamin Coates, an abolitionist of Philadelphia. One of these pamphlets, which I had read before, is an argument in favor of the feasibility of raising cotton in Africa, & thereby underselling & breaking up the cotton-planters of our southern states—& so, by destroying the profits, to destroy slavery itself. And so far as to the ability of producing cotton well in Africa, I concur with him—but *I* would require as a necessary condition, that the African cultivators should be slaves, & also have white masters & overseers. But as *free* laborers, which Mr. Coates' argument [556] requires, they will never make enough cotton for exportation to affect the prices of the world. The other pamphlet is an Address delivered in Monrovia by a negro gentleman, & a graduate of Cambridge—& to whom it is probable the diploma was given because he was a negro. However, I would not deny the possibility of one negro in a hundred thousand cases being capable of receiving a college education, & being competent to write a commonplace address, passably for both.—Received further report of the debate in Congress in reference to the expense of the recaptured Africans, & which I doubt not that my pamphlet suggested.[14] The objections caused the general appropriation to be rejected. If the resistance should cut down the designed & expected appropriation to the bare amount required by the President's contract & obligation, it will be a first great triumph of my argument, & much more than I had looked for so soon. I will attach an extract from the debate, which will show how strong are now the objections to Mr. Buchanan's malversation under the pretended authority of the law of 1819, slight and cheap as it is compared to those of Mr. Monroe &c. in former times, which did not attract a word of censure from any quarter—all then being either friends to the Col. Society, or careless & neutral. [557] Perhaps the *vote* of Congress may not now prevent this abuse. But if not, the *debate* will for the future, as is observed by one of the speakers. . . . [559]

*Feb. 2.* . . . The newspapers report that [John Esten] Cooke is engaged in writing another novel, the scene of which is to be Flower-de-Hundred, in Prince George. If it is no better than his "Virginia Comedians," which I could not finish, it will be a poor affair. Yet there were many materials in that neighborhood which if known, might be worth incorporating in a novel, as specimens [561] of manners of former times. Some of these, in reference to clerical affairs, I formerly wrote for Bishop Meade, & at his request, to aid his materials for his work on the Old Churches of Virginia. . . .

The minor incidents of the revolutionary war which occurred in the neighborhood of Merchants Hope, were well worthy [567] of being noted, & would have furnished good materials to a romance writer like Walter Scott. Some of these, in which my grandfather was the leader & chief actor, I have written in my sketch entitled "The Blackwater Guerilla." [15] At an earlier time, the great massacre

---

[14] The debate concerned a request by President Buchanan for $75,000 to provide for the return and support of Negroes captured by the United States Navy when the slaver *Echo* was intercepted. According to a federal law of March 3, 1819, the officers and crews of United States naval vessels were to receive a bounty of $25 per head for each Negro captured on a vessel engaged in the African slave trade and turned in to a United States marshal. The President sought $45,000 to compensate those instrumental in seizing the *Echo,* but, in addition, pursuant to an agreement with the Colonization Society, he requested an appropriation of $30,000 for the support and education of the Negroes after their return to Liberia. It was the latter request to which Ruffin and many southern congressmen objected.

[15] This forty-three-page manuscript, written in 1851, is Volume 3 in the Edmund Ruffin Papers and Books, Southern Historical Collection, University of North Carolina, Chapel Hill.

of the whites by the Indians extended over the then few settlements of this neighborhood. I remember the names of Macock, & West, among the heads of families, which names were the origin of the designations of the places on the river now known as Maycox, & Westover. The last was the subsequent princely mansion & residence of the first Col. William Byrd, whose talents add distinction to this neighborhood. Another & a much greater man, Richard Bland, was born, I believe, & lived & died at Jordan's, in the Merchants Hope parish. Richard Bland, who was one of the Delegates of Virginia to the old congress, though he died as early as 1776, was truly one of the ablest founders of American liberty & independence. He was a profound thinker & reasoner, & a man whose great wisdom was acknowledged & duly respected by all his contemporaries. But he did not embark on public & political life until he was an old man—he wrote but little, though with great ability—he was neither a public speaker nor a military character—& therefore his great merits & services are scarcely known, & his name almost forgotten, compared to others of his day, who were orators or soldiers, though greatly inferior to him in council & in wisdom. [568]

*Feb. 3.* Reading Canot's "Twenty Years of the Slave Trade," for the second or third time (for part). At night, Mr. Sayre returned from Richmond, bringing me two new books I had sent to buy. Began on one, Prof. [James L.] Cabell's "Unity of Mankind."

*Feb. 4.* The mail. Received the full report of the late debate of which I had before seen but fragmentary & few parts. It seems that my pamphlet had supplied abundant materials for speeches to several members, (who probably otherwise would not have known anything on the subject,) & that they used them well to oppose the passage of the appropriation for paying for the support & "education" of the restored African captives, to the Colonization Society. Their objections caused the whole appropriation bill to be rejected; & it was only reconsidered & passed by a few votes, by two northern members having changed their votes from negative to affirmative. Mr. Curry, of Ala, made a very good speech, & of considerable length, entirely out of the facts adduced in my pamphlet, & by pursuing references therein made by me to forgotten official documents. Yet neither he, nor any other of the debators, made the slightest reference to my labors, or to the recent source from which they had been indebted for all their light on the whole subject.—De Bow's Review, and Russell's Magazine. Finished a rather cursory reading of the

"Unity of Mankind," which I am disappointed in. It is not new (as I had supposed,) & neither [569] is it very clear or interesting. . . .

*Feb. 8.* The mail. . . . Answer from Messrs. Curry & Dowdell. They speak in complimentary manner of my pamphlet, & of its agency in exciting the recent debate in the House of Representatives. They say that my last statements (by letter to them) will induce further inquiry—& also that the whole subject will be further argued in the Senate. Hoping to supply additional & useful materials, I copied some of the more important parts of my manuscript which had been excluded from publication, & sent the extracts to these members of congress to be used if deemed useful.

*Feb. 9.* . . . Began the last Geological & Agricultural [571] Report of Prof. [Ebenezer] Emmons,[16] of the Eastern part of North Carolina, published last year, & sent me by last mail. He has gone over much of the swamp lands & others which I visited some two years earlier—& my notes, not published, will be of diminished novelty & interest, wherever he has examined & reported carefully & correctly. —Wrote a third letter to Messrs. Curry & Dowdell, to convey some additional matter, for opposition to the C. Soc. quoted from Canot— & also suggestions of inquiries to be made respecting the past connexion of the government of U.S. with the Society.

*Feb. 10.* Read all the portion of Emmons' Report on the soils, swamps &c. of Eastern North Carolina—& glanced over the remainder of the volume. I think it very defective, & as an agricultural report, of very little worth. By his chemical knowledge, he has supplied some few analyses of swamp soils that are interesting & useful—and by his great facilities in continued & long service as a salaried agent, he has extended his researches much farther than I had done. But even with these grounds of superiority, I think his observations on the swamp lands far inferior to mine, & the whole Report a marked example of Yankee book-making, & the pretension of what the author wanted either ability to perform, or of industry, & fidelity to his trust.—Arranged the letters received within the last two years, for stitching together & covering—left undone since my last operation. I regret that I did not preserve until of latter years, but very few of the letters written to me. With very few exceptions,

---

[16] Emmons (1799–1863), a native of Massachusetts who had previously held teaching positions at Williams College, Rensselaer Institute, and Albany Medical School, was appointed state geologist of North Carolina in 1851. He was also a professor at the University of North Carolina during this period.

[572] & for special reasons, I have never taken and preserved copies of my own letters, or even copied the first draft, for sending. If ever, after my death, my correspondence should be sought for, there will be almost none of my own letters to be supplied from my remaining papers—& probably very few from any other accidental sources.

*Feb. 11.* . . . . No news, except that which is greatly to be deplored, of the destruction by fire of William & Mary College. This great loss will probably complete the ruin of that institution of learning, in that location at least, which has been so long seemed approaching and sometimes impending, from other causes.

The greatest difficulty of the doctrine of the original unity of the human race, or of the common parentage, to me, is not in the existing great differences of varieties, or of these differences having existed as long as historical records give us any information. We know that many of the inferior animals have, by change of location & other circumstances, separated into varieties as different as the Caucasian man from the African negro, the Australian or the Basquesman or Laplander. And it is also certain that varieties, which seem to be so easily produced in animals by changes of conditions, are often as fixed in character as original differences. So I would by no means deny that man, if originally of one stock & kind, might not, by subsequent changes of conditions, in his posterity show [573] all the existing varieties of mankind, & also that the new characteristics might become fixed—as undoubtedly are the marked differences of the white & the negro families. Neither is it incredible, or difficult to conceive the possibility, that, after navigation was learned, that, by storms or other accidents, boats & their crews might have been driven from the eastern coast of the continent of Asia so as in the course of time to people all the islands of the Pacific ocean, & the continent of America, by such involuntary immigration. But, the great difficulty of mankind proceeding from common parentage & one locality, is the existing dispersion to regions, where settlers could not have been brought by accident, & to which none would ever have voluntarily gone—as the Arctic region, the residence of the Esquimaux tribes. We may suppose that destructive wars may have driven the vanquished survivors to places of refuge & security far less desirable than their previous residences. But if the earliest men all lived in one locality, as common origin would demand, it must have been in a warm, or a mild climate, & on a fruitful soil. If otherwise, it would require a perpetual miracle for their

preservation. Then admitting the race to be subsequently extended
to every similar climate & land, to which the winds & currents &
accidents of navigation could carry them, it would not serve to explain how the former inhabitants of productive lands & mild climes,
could be placed in the inhospitable arctic region, which the actual
present inhabitants prefer to [574] any other, where only other
varieties of mankind could exist.

There is, to me, another great difficulty in supposing America to
be the last peopled continent, from a common origin & location—as
all inferences would teach—& for which only would the supposition
serve, of accidental migration by winds & currents across the smooth
Pacific ocean. Though civilization was greatly advanced among the
ruling races in Mexico & Peru, when America was discovered, it was
a remarkable fact that neither there nor anywhere else in all America
was the use of iron known. And with slight exceptions, it may be
stated that the use of domestic animals was also unknown. In Peru
only, the llama was domesticated. Yet so far as history or even tra-
dition goes back, both these important improvements seem to have
been known in Asia. And it would seem that any people understanding enough of navigation to make long voyages (even by accident,) must have been otherwise enough civilized to have had the
use of iron, & of domesticated animals. Of course it is not to be supposed that in the boats of such accidental emigrants there would be
either a worker of iron, or domestic animals to serve as breeders. But
men who had before known & enjoyed these benefits, would never
have been content to be deprived of them. And iron ore would have
been sought, & put to use—& wild animals would have been domesticated—before the memory [575] of such advantages, formerly enjoyed, had been forgotten. And that this was not done, seems to be
a very strong indication that the first inhabitants of America did not
come from Asia, & from more civilized progenitors.

*Feb. 15.* The mail. . . . Letter from Hon. C. C. Clay, Senator from
Alabama, requesting me to draw up & send to him such resolution
for inquiries of the President, as I deem proper, for him to offer to
the Senate of U.S. Wrote to him at length, & also referred him to my
recent letters on the same general subject of the Colonization Society
& Liberia, which I had written to Messrs. Curry & Dowdell—which
I infer that Mr. Clay has already had access to. . . . I trust that there
will be important & also early good results from my late pamphlet on
this subject, in correcting the improper action of the government,

continued without any check since 1819, in connection with the Colonization Society.—Another & still worse outrage has been perpetrated by a British war steamer not only in visiting & searching, but in capturing and burning an American vessel, suspected by the British captain to be engaged in the African slave trade.[17] Nothing yet known of it except from the official report of the American commander of the Vincennes. I am surprised that I see no other notice, or comments on this affair, either in Congress, or by the newspapers. . . . The Examiner brings the following piece, which I had sent for publication.[18] Next Tuesday, Court day, there is to be a meeting to nominate a candidate, the last member having declined. These *caucuses* have dwindled until scarcely more than 30 citizens attend, & in them are found almost no men of high position. I will attend this one, to try to put down the usual *pledge*, & if so permitted to participate, to help the nomination of my young friend William B. Newton.

*Feb. 17.* Took up my writing on the cane-brake region of Alabama, & read it over, & made some corrections. Also, in connection, read the portions referring thereto of both the geological reports of Mr. Tuomey—which give me very little information in addition to what I gathered myself from observation—& which, in the relations to soils & agricultural qualities, are deficient, & in some things incorrect. . . .

*Feb. 18.* . . . All day reading newspapers & periodicals, which the mail brought . . . . Sundry colonization & anti-slavery papers & pamphlets sent to me, through Senator Hammond, by a rank abolitionist, Benjamin Coates, of Philadelphia—to whom I shall return the civility, by sending him others on the opposite side. We [579] had before exchanged some such missives.—By the Washington papers, I see further action in both houses of Congress, which was certainly prompted by my pamphlet, & by my letters—though my last letter to Senator Clay had not then been received. Mr. Dowdell moved an inquiry, all the points of which were suggested in my

---

[17] Vessels involved were the brig *Rufus Soule* and the steamer *Viper* of the British African Squadron.

[18] Ruffin's communication to the *Examiner* was addressed to the Democrats of Hanover County and concerned the upcoming caucus to nominate a candidate for the House of Delegates. In his letter the diarist attacked the usual practice of imposing a pledge which would bind every member of the meeting to the majority decision.

letters to him. As unanimous consent was required, & some objection was made, he could not then have the motion adopted—but I suppose it will be, at a later time, when in regular course. In the Senate, Mr. Clay opposed the appropriation for the Colonization Society—but did not succeed in striking it out. [580]

*Feb. 20.* Sunday . . . . Mr. C[arraway] preached in the afternoon to our negroes, & also christened 4 of the young children. Both these services are of rare occurrence—& the last one unheard of for many years back. Nearly all negroes who profess religion, are Baptists,[19] & are baptised when making the profession, & by immersion.—This morning, added the last corrections to my article on the cane-brake lands—& it is now complete, so far as my defective materials serve for. I had hoped to have been supplied with more—in specimens of soils &c.—or perhaps to have again visited that region, & made more full personal investigations. But neither seems now to be probable. Again without employment, or amusement. Having nothing preferable to read, resorted to [Henry C.] Carey's "History of the Slave Trade," which I have read before, & partly twice.

*Feb. 22.* Rode on horse-back to Court, & back, making 24 miles, & a fatiguing labor to me, so little accustomed as I have been in latter years to riding. Went for the purpose of attending a meeting of the people of the county, of the democratic party, (of which, in the usually accepted party meaning, I confess myself to be a very *unworthy* member,) called [591] [20] to nominate a candidate to represent the county in the House of Delegates. There was the largest & most respectable meeting that I had ever known in the county. No one proposed, as usually done, the pledge for every one to support the nomination of the majority, & there was no allusion to such an obligation. Therefore there was no occasion for me to object to it, protest against it, & to refuse to have it imposed—all of which I designed to do. The meeting was very harmonious in action. William B. Newton, the son of my friend Willoughby Newton, was nominated by a very large majority—& the choice readily concurred in by the few who had preferred another, C. W. Dabney. This is the first nomination for the county I ever would unite in acting with. And in thus withdrawing, I have done wrong. . . .

*Feb. 23.* . . . . Read the arguments of the opposing counsel, [Leoni-

---

[19] Mr. Carraway was an Episcopal minister.
[20] Misnumbered by the diarist. Should be page 581.

das W.] Spratt[21] & [Isaac W.] Hayne of Charleston, on the motion to discharge the crew of the captured slave-ship Echo—on the alleged ground of unconstitutionality of the U.S. law that declares the African slave-trade to be "piracy," even when between foreign countries, as between Africa & Cuba. The argument of Spratt, maintaining the law to be unconstitutional, seemed to me to be impregnable, until I read the answer, which then seemed the stronger. I fear that [592] [I] have a natural defect of judgment, or of decision, in regard to legal arguments—a too great facility to be convinced by either side, & by both separately—& an inability duly & correctly to compare & weigh them, & to appreciate their relative & proper values. But whether the newly advanced proposition, that the law is unconstitutional be sound or not, it is so plausible, & concurs so well with the feelings & passions of the people of the south, & with the interests of many also, that I have no doubt that it will be sustained in practice, by the juries acquitting every prisoner charged with this legal crime of piracy—made so by legal definition. In this case, the judges refused to admit the plea, & thereby to discharge the prisoners—& the jury were divided, & so did not convict them. They remain in jail, to be tried again—but never will a jury be found to give a unanimous verdict against them.—Finished reading Carey's "Slave Trade, Foreign & Domestic," in a cursory manner. It is a curious book, & very different from what would be inferred from the title. The author is a strong enemy of slavery in every form, & of African slavery as existing in these southern states. But he furnishes a strong array of testimony to prove the great evils which have been the consequence of emancipation of African slaves—& of the far worse sufferings & cruelties of the laboring classes in so-called free England, & other countries of Europe & Asia. Different from all other anti-negro slavery writers, [593] he (correctly, as I have maintained,) applies the term "slavery" to other & more extended cases— the subjection of labor to capital, through the operation of law, the supply of labor exceeding the demand, & under the cruel pressure of want, cold, & hunger. But he is a thorough supporter of the protective system for forcing manufactures in every country—& sees in the operation of this system the healthy & beneficial extinguishing of

---

[21] A first cousin of President James K. Polk, Spratt (1818–1903) was an ardent champion of the slave trade, having presented to the Montgomery Commercial Convention of 1858 a series of resolutions calling for a reopening of the African slave trade. He was at this time a member of the South Carolina House of Representatives and later served in the secession convention of his state.

slavery of every kind, & of universal good to every country & community. Carey's materials are good, & generally his premises—& after the earlier steps of his reasoning. But his conclusions are inconsequent, & false—& it was not always in my power even to follow his argument, or to trace the connection that he desired to show. Of course, his great object & specific remedy for this country not only to extinguish slavery, but for its greatest prosperity, is the establishment of a high protective tariff, as existed in 1828, & again in 1842, to protect manufactures against the competition of lower priced foreign products. There is much force & truth in Carey's positions as to the value of the "home market," produced by establishing workshops, mechanical employments, & manufactories near to cultivators of the soil, so as to lessen the costs of transportation of their exchanged productions—& for the artizans, & the towns they build up, to consume numerous agricultural productions, which could never reach a distant market, & so would be lost. This argument is sound, if addressed to the northern farmers, in whose neighborhood would be established nearly all the factories that any protective tariff can bring out. [594] For whatever may be the amount of indirect bounty thus given by government, the northern people have so much more facilities & inducements to resort to manufactures, that they will be as much in advance of the south in the number of such establishments, under the heaviest protecting duties, or under moderate, or without any. Mr. Carey has gone far to convince me of the good policy of government measures being used (properly & discreetly,) to establish such manufactures as a country is manifestly suited & ready for, & thus "bringing the mechanic & manufacturer to the neighborhood of the farmer," & so making them the best customers of each other. But to obtain this valuable result of establishing manufactures, for these southern states, a general protective tariff law, for the United States, would by no means serve. *That* would establish manufactures principally where the conditions are best for their profit—& nineteen-twentieths of them would be in the northern states. And these would not be "home-markets" for southern agriculturists, any more than if they were in England. The agriculturists of the southern states, as always, would pay much the larger share of the tax, & cost in higher prices of sustaining these establishments, & would derive none of the benefits of neighborhood & home-market. To do this, for the southern states, it would be necessary that there should be some other means, by which Virginia, for example, or

South Carolina, could, by paying [595] the costs, have the protected manufactures fabricated within their respective limits, & for the benefit of their people. And I would be glad to have this done, as I have advocated by means of taxing the commodities of other (northern) states through the license laws. In this, it is true, that the political object would be more sought than the economical. But there would be great benefit in the latter respect also, if the taxes & prohibitions were imposed judiciously, & by a disinterested government, not influenced by partiality for the manufacturing interest. Much as I have always approved of the free-trade doctrines, first set forth by Adam Smith, I have learned to distrust or to deny some of his minor positions or premises. And one of these is, that private individuals, or the members generally of every community, will always know best to direct their industry & capital, & will pursue the best course in that respect. We all know that this is not true in many cases, both as to individuals & communities. We know many things which we ought to do, for better economy & profit, & which we continue to neglect, because of want of industry or enterprise, & the inveteracy of old habits. In such cases, it would be well for a discreet & just government to compel the desired new production, by forbidding the importation. Thus, nothing but good could arise from an absolute prohibition of the great quantity of northern hay that is annually imported into Virginia, & all the southern states. But so prone are all governments to go wrong, from folly or corruption, or both, that it would be dangerous to authorise such proper & beneficial restrictions on the [596] freedom of trade & industry, because they would extend such policy to other subjects that would be altogether improper, & a damage to the community, for the gain of some minor interest. . . .

There is another false & dangerous doctrine of the free-trade school, & I believe of Adam Smith's, which has been almost universally admitted, or rarely opposed or questioned. This is the doctrine that the free laborer, working entirely for his own benefit & gain, is more powerfully stimulated to exertion & to produce industrial results than the slave by the coercion & fear of his master. This is the foundation of the further proposition, so generally admitted, that free-labor is cheaper to the employer, under nearly all circumstances, than slave-labor. This latter proposition I deem false as to most countries, & certainly as to this, even as to the employer's expense. But if looking to all expenses—including the government's

to govern & restrain the so-called free laboring class—in pauper support, legal, judicial, & penal expenses, & police & a standing army—
I do not think that in any country, unless for transient times, &
peculiar conditions, free labor is so cheap as slave labor. There is no
general rule as to individual free action. Many persons are disposed
to be industrious, provident, & economical—& such persons, if laborers, & still more if small proprietors, will be more stimulated to
labor by self-interest than slaves are usually by force & fear. But I
deem only those to be *free* laborers, who are free, for more or less of
their time, to be idle, if they so choose. The laborers who are driven
to daily & hourly labor, for wages so [597] low that many hours' hire
is necessary to secure bare subsistence, is [*sic*] not free, but has, in
want & hunger, the severest & most coercive of masters. The indispensable necessaries to sustain life, in the lowest condition of animal
comfort, are only food, clothing, shelter (from inclement weather),
& fire. If the day laborer can obtain these only by working diligently
every hour of every day, he will so labor. But he is not then free, but
truly a slave to his wants. Such are the laborious & cheap operatives
of England—& such are they becoming, & will be hereafter, in our
northern states. But if laborers can by two or three days' labor in a
week, obtain the necessaries of life (as in this state now,) though
some will work all their time, & accumulate, & become proprietors,
the greater number will work no longer than will be enough to provide necessaries for themselves & their families, & will be idle, if not
drunken also, the remainder of the week. It is only when men are
stimulated by artificial wants—the desire to secure luxuries as well
as necessaries—or the stronger desire to accumulate their earnings,
& so become capitalists or employers of laborers—that they regularly
& systematically labor more industriously & effectively than slaves to
individuals. The slave is rarely so laborious or effective a worker as
the industrious free laborer; but he is far more so, & in the general,
than the indolent & improvident free laborer. And these, in the few
countries & conditions in which labor really can be *free,* (as in these
new countries,) are so many compared to the industrious & provident, that on the whole, & in the great majority of cases, slave labor
(so-called, or such as of our negro slaves,) is much cheaper & more
effective [598] to the employers, than free labor, in the general, is to
either the employers or to the great majority of (idle) laborers. And
such must be the case, until, in the regular progress of events, the
price of labor becomes so low that the whole time of the laborer

is necessary for his bare support—when indeed he will work continually & most effectively. But then he will no longer be free, but a slave to want. The truly free laborers who work diligently & regularly, & truly perform more work than slaves to individuals, are those who are seeking, or have already acquired, more than the first necessaries of life. They are laboring to supply artificial wants —which are unlimited. The laborer may be urged to exertion by mere avarice—the love of accumulation merely for its own sake. Or he may desire to accumulate for better & laudable ends—to educate his children, & give them higher position in society. Or it may be the ambition of excelling in show & ostentation. But any of these motives operate more frequently to induce great exertion & continuous labor, than to satisfy natural or animal wants.

*Feb. 24.* . . . Read (second time) a pamphlet entitled "The South —or a letter from a friend in the North" or discussion in reference to slavery. The author, though claiming to be southern by birth, & in feeling, has been for 30 years a resident of the North, & views his subject as a northerner. Of course he is mistaken in many points, & prejudiced in all. But he still shows some strong reasons of danger to the South. That which I deem most fearful, is the interference of England & France, [599] if their close alliance should then continue —as both governments would rejoice to crush the political power of the United States, or their separated portions, & especially to crush negro slavery. This enmity, & its consequences, would be much more to be expected than war between the North & South. . . .

*Feb. 25.* A dismal day of slow rain, or hail or snow, at different times. . . . Last accounts from Europe state nothing positive as to any great events. But there are continued & great preparations for war making by France, & such military & naval efficiency already reached, as to indicate that war must be in prospect. Austria seems to be the threatened power. But so suspicious a character is the French Emperor, & so great his power for mischief, that even his now close ally, England, is afraid of his becoming suddenly her enemy. If he will use his power to free Italy, & drive the Austrian power out of that country, it will be a great benefit to Europe & to humanity. That is supposed to be the most probable design of the emperor of France. But such ends are not in accordance with the previous despotic policy of this great & vile man. England & France would not quarrel as to that policy & procedure of the latter—if such should be. But for *our* interest & safety, I earnestly hope that they may quarrel about some other cause. The hatred of the governments of both these countries to our institutions, & their present alliance, threaten great danger to us. . . .

*Feb. 28.* Reading Dr. Bachman's "Unity of the Human Race," for the second time—which I opened by accident, & found it so interesting that I proceeded to read regularly. . . .

*March 3.* . . . Finished reading Dr. Bachman's book. It is very interesting, in its many accounts of animal history. It is mostly on hybridity, & on varieties of animals. It is a very strong argument for the unity of the human race in its origin, & I think unanswerable as to the unity of species. . . .

*March 4.* . . . The mail—which brought no news—except the assurance that the bill to entrust the President with 30 millions, & power to negotiate for the purchase of Cuba, cannot possibly pass either house of Congress in this short session. I am heartily glad of it. Desirable as the annexation of Cuba seems to be to most men & parties—& as I would deem it, if to be effected without too great cost of money, & hazard of war—still there would be great evils, even if effected cheaply & peaceably. The slave population is nearly all of African birth & consequently of very low order. The treatment of the slaves generally is most cruel, & the system could not soon be changed to such as ours. The great number of free mulattoes, & many of them possessing education & wealth, & their having heretofore enjoying [*sic*] equal social position & privileges with the whites, would offer an unmanageable & dangerous element in the new member of our confederation, & of our federal system. Add to this the ignorant, & worthless character of the whites, so long enslaved & enervated by their colonial & despotic servitude, & their religion being the Catholic—would give even to that race but little fitness, or early capacity, for making part of a republican government & system. Yet, if Cuba remains much longer in the present state of unlimited subjection to Spain, & also by so uncertain a tenure, the policy of Spain, & also of England & France, will tend still more to "Africanizing" [603] the island. The free negro & mulatto class will more & more be increased, & general emancipation be more manifestly approached. And if there was any serious & important effort made, either from within, by revolt of the white inhabitants, or from without, by foreign invasion, to free Cuba from the Spanish yoke, doubtless Spain would do, as France did, (from different motives,) as to St. Domingo, & declare the freedom of the barbarous African slaves. These alone could effect nothing, by insurrection, against the whites. Weak & cowardly as these have been made by colonial subjection, they, if alone to act, could control, or conquer easily, ten times their own number of negroes. But it would not be a struggle between these parties only. Spain, & England, & France, & also the negrophilist fanaticism of all Europe & America, would be aiding the cause of negro insurrection & freedom. And the whites of Cuba, even if sustained directly by all the naval & military force of the United States, could not prevent their country being brought to the condition of either St. Domingo or Jamaica. As to our own policy, I am unable to conceive any proper course. To move, with effect, to acquire Cuba, in the present state of the world, & especially with the existing close alliance of England & France, & the certain enmity & jealousy of both their governments of this country, would merely hasten the evils feared, & also involve this country in a ruinous war. And if nothing is done, the progress of time alone will make Cuba a negro community & power, lying at our threshold. I trust that England & France cannot long keep allied, or even from being engaged in war with each other—in which case, Spain, as the tool of France, could [604] scarcely remain neutral. Or, even as now, if the Spanish army in Cuba should become dissatisfied & mutinous, & take part with the people, (as has been the beginning of revolutions in Europe, in so many cases,) in either case, the independence of Cuba & of the whole dominion might be declared & maintained. And if this could be, the real independence of Cuba would be better for this country than its annexation. But if the inhabitants preferred, after being independent, as doubtless they would prefer, they could then easily, & also safely, bring about their being included in this confederation—if it should then exist as now—or otherwise in the southern portion of it, if then standing separate & independent.... Began this morning to read [Charles] Kingsley's "Hypatia," lent to me by Mr. Boulwane.

*March 7.* ... Finished reading "Hypatia." It is a vivid & interesting picture of the remarkable & woful [*sic*] condition of society in the 5th or 6th century. But as a romance, for the plot, incidents, & individual characters, [605] it is a poor book.

*March 8.* Rain nearly through the day—&, in part, very heavy. This is the third very heavy rain that has fallen within some ten days. For four months, it has been the most rainy season ever known here.—The mail. Enough newspapers, with De Bow's Review, to occupy me nearly all the day—but nothing interesting. Congress adjourned without passing the bill so much needed, & to which both houses had agreed, to raise the postage, & to abolish the franking privilege of members. Also, & most happily, the bill to entrust the President with $30,000,000, to *begin* the negotiation for the purchase of Cuba, could not be carried. I begin to doubt whether the acquisition of Cuba, even on the most favorable terms, & by purchase, would not be injurious to the United States. The first time that we should have war with a much stronger naval power, as England or France, the island would be conquered by our enemy, and probably after enormous expenses had been incurred to defend the possession.— Had begun yesterday, & finished today, looking through parts of the translation of Herodotus, which I had formerly read, to decide whether an opinion I had before formed was correct. According to my remembrance, Herodotus makes no allusion to the Jewish people, their actions, government, or country. Yet he seems to have treated of every considerable people & country that had any connexion with those which were his chief subjects. According to the Jewish historians, there were very notable incidents of their nation connected with the Egyptians, Assyrians, & Persians, & some of which occurred within the times of these nations, of which Herodotus treated. There can be no explanation of this, so different from his usage, except that the historian had never [606] heard of the Jews, or anything that made him believe that the people, & their history, were of enough importance, or interest, to be worth his attention, or even the slightest notice.—The adjournment of Congress on the 4th (the termination of its time,) left unfinished, or prevented the execution of many important measures which would have been effected if there had been enough time. Among such, it is no wonder that the small matters induced by my late pamphlet could not be carried through. The grant to fulfil the President's illegal donation to the Colonization Society, thus escaped being annulled, because it could not be got rid of without rejecting the whole general appropriation bill, in which it had been engrafted. And the motion for inquiry made in the lower house failed, because requiring unanimous consent—& there was no opportunity in the few remaining days of the session, for Mr. Clay to move a similar resolution in the Senate— which he designed, & for which he asked of me, & I furnished to him, the subjects for inquiry.

*March 9.* Preaching at church (Ash Wednesday) & all except myself went. . . . Arranged to leave home tomorrow, with Mildred, Edmund & Nanny, for Beechwood.

*March 10.* We left home after breakfast—a cart to carry our trunks. The road, as expected very bad—& Edmund & I walked over all the worst parts. At the Exchange Hotel. Saw F. G. Ruffin & Mr. Williams, & went to see L. E. Harvie, but he was not in town. . . .

*March 11.* We left Richmond early, & landed at Maycox wharf after 10 A.M. where Edmund's boat awaited us. At Beechwood, all well—except Thomas, who appears perfectly well, but has suffered so much & so long with dyspepsia at school, that it was necessary lately to order him home. It was produced there by the badly cooked & indigestible food, & by his previously injured stomach, caused by improper indulgence in eating at home. . . .

*March 12.* . . . I rode to my sister's, to see my grandchild Jane. She was well, & seemed delighted to see me, & was very anxious to return with me to Beechwood. All will go there on Monday, [608] & leave Jane for a few days. She was so engaging & loveable, that I could not continue in my design of endeavoring to wean myself from her. . . .

*March 14.* . . . After the newspapers, reading [Charles] Ellet's[22] pamphlet Report of his plan for improving the navigation of the Kanawha & Ohio, by means of damming up artificial lakes on the higher headstreams, in the mountains, to be discharged gradually to supply the rivers [609] & increase their depths, during droughts & low water. And, further, as the water thus held back in such reservoirs, would be obstructed from the most abundant supplies of rain floods, the effect, as maintained, would be not only to supply enough water for the purposes of navigation when it would otherwise be deficient, but also to lessen the height of the great river floods, which would otherwise occur. When this plan was first presented to my notice, I thought it not only visionary, but even absurd. But the details & reasoning of the projector, Mr. Ellet, go far to satisfy me of the correctness of his views. But it is essential that the artificial lakes should be very high in the mountains, where there would be united the several advantages of a short dam, the land to be submerged of

---

[22] One of America's most prominent engineers, Charles Ellet (1810–62) was appointed chief engineer of the James River and Kanawha Canal in 1836 and, from 1853 to 1857, was engineer for the Virginia Central Railroad. In addition, among other projects, he designed and built wire suspension bridges across the Schuylkill River near Philadelphia and across the Niagara River near the falls.

low value, the watershed to the lake, steep, yet extensive. If the improvement could be carried out on an extensive scale of operations, I believe that eastern tributaries of the Mississippi might be rendered at all times navigable, & then floods, as well as those of the Mississippi, be materially lessened in height, & injury. But the *political* difficulty would be greater than any other. No one state (as Virginia) can effect these improvements for its own rivers & navigation, without rendering even greater service for the lower rivers beyond its territorial limits—& the other states, so benefited, would not pay for their share of the benefit. It could not be done, except by the federal government, & by its exercise of powers which strict constructionists deny to be granted by the constitution.

*March 21.* . . . Wrote to De Bow, & sent corrections & additions for his designed republication of my colonization pamphlet. The mail. . . . By the last European accounts, the government & papers of France still disclaiming & denying all intention or preparation for war—& all other powers more & more believing in both. Certainly it must soon break out, in Lombardy, between Sardinia & France on one side, & Austria, & probably the German confederation on the other. . . .

*March 23.* . . . The governor of Maryland has granted a *second* respite to four murderers, who had been condemned to be hanged, under the miserable canting pretence of allowing the criminals longer time to make their peace with God, & themselves fit to receive the reward of the joys of heaven! Baltimore has long been under the rule of law-breakers—of organized rioters, robbers, & murderers. Two of these condemned villains separately were the deliberate murderers of officers of justice, for doing simply their duty in apprehending & bringing to trial some of their confederate villains. Every effort of importunity & intimidation has been used on the Governor to obtain from him successive respites, & pardons. [613] And his yielding so far, it is feared, is an indication that the criminals are to be allowed, in some way or other, to escape the justice & vengeance of the law. The last fixed day for the executions is the 8th of next month. I look forward to the event with great interest. If the Governor of Maryland should finally pardon any or all of these criminals, he will be not much worse than our Governor Wise ought to be deemed. He has had no case of such horrible murder & unmitigated criminality to occur, & to extend mercy to. But for smaller offences, & yet many of deep die, & without any excuse, he has pardoned nearly 70 different convicted criminals, within two years. And this wholesale dispensing with the justice of the country in the due punishment of criminals I believe is but a part of his general & systematic pursuit of popular favor, & votes, to aid the ambitious views of this greatest of demagogues.

*March 25.* Nothing to do, & my time wearisome. Returned to look over & to read the more attractive articles (for the third time,) of the old volumes of the "Living Age." Took a long walk with Edmund.

*March 27.* Sunday. After breakfast, I walked alone in the beech woods & thought, as often before, how easily the ground might be made still more beautiful, by grubbing & clearing out the [614] small growth of bushes, & superfluous trees, & making paths intersecting each other, & leading to different outlets. I have never seen so small a space of ground that embraced so many objects of beautiful scenery, even now—& which could be so greatly improved in beauty at such small expense of labor.... [615]

*March 28.* ... The mail. No news but rumors, or unreliable reports. These, as to France, more indicative of peace. But no reliance can be placed on even the positive declarations of the great scoundrel who rules France. Of course it is his interest & object to mislead the public as to his intentions, until he is ready to put them into action—& he has neither shame or scruple to prevent his resorting to any means for deception, or to compass his ends.

*March 29.* ... Heard of the death of William F. R. Ruffin, by the report of his body being carried along the road to Surry. He was a pious & good man. He & I were nearly of the same age, & he was always the more healthy—so his death is a strong warning of the near approach of mine....

*April 1.* ... Yesterday, began, & this morning finished writing the rough draft of an article on the effect of the [616] high price of slaves on agricultural interests.

*April 4.* Another heavy rain last night. This continuation of rainy weather, since the beginning of November, is very strange, & now very alarming for the growing crop of wheat, & for the preparation for the crop of corn. In all this time, the land has very rarely, & for very short intervals been dry enough anywhere to plough, & scarcely to draw loaded carts upon. Very few farmers have yet finished their corn land—& some have not ploughed two-thirds, & even that when not dry enough. Finished copying my writing, 15 pages. Shall send it to De Bow's Review by next mail.

*April 5.* Began to write another article on a connected subject— The Effect of the high price of land on agricultural interests &c. . . . Wrote 10 pages, but not at all to my satisfaction.

*April 9.* Selected, & in part altered & copied, most of the parts of my writing which, for want of room, had been necessarily omitted in the printing of the Colonization pamphlet. These will be sent to De Bow, [617] for him to insert, or as many as he may have room for in the second edition which he proposes to print in his Review, & for which he has written to ask for these omitted parts. It is remarkable that, to this time, there has not yet appeared any answer to, or the slightest direct allusion to my attack, in any of the Colonization publications, or from any person or paper favorable to that scheme. I had expected to be opposed immediately, & from various quarters. For heretofore, the very few & slight charges made against the Society, or its colony, have always been met, & silenced, by the clamor of the defence, & by stout & unanimous denial, & vituperation of the assailant, in lieu of examination & argument founded on facts. I have taken care to place the publication (through the mail, by franked copies,) in the hands of every known & strong colonizationist, & publisher of that school—& also of numerous clergymen & some bishops that way inclined. It cannot be pretended that the universal silence is the result of contempt for the attack—or because my statements & views are not worth notice. Even if ever so worthless in themselves, they would have been raised to importance by the action they produced, & the effects very nearly consummated, in both houses of Congress. It must be that the colonizationists find that my argument cannot be met, or any of my important charges rebutted; & however much they feel & fear the effect of the attack, they deem it most politic to be silent, & not to make its existence more extensively known, by ineffectual attempts at defence. The only *even indirect* notice that has appeared, is (as I infer it was meant to be applied,) in the concluding paragraph of the last Annual Report of the [618] A.C. Society—which was made soon after the publication of my pamphlet. This paragraph is obviously a later addition to the Report, added after the financial statement & formal & customary conclusion, as at first designed. If induced, as I suppose, by way of general answer, it is precisely in the usual manner of Liberian defence. If evils of action, or false statements ar[e] charged against the colony, the established mode of reply has been to simply deny the charges, & to re-assert & double the magnitude of the falsehoods. . . .

April 14, 1859

*April 11.* . . . The mail—nothing in it, except that the four murderers, who had been condemned to death in Baltimore, & twice respited by the Governor, were actually hung on the 8th. inst. This is more than I had expected, from the existing triumphant condition of mob law & influence in Baltimore. . . . Continued writing—an endless flow of words, without my arriving at the designed point. Indeed, in the writing, I have so far deviated from my proposed main subject, that it will be necessary to change the title. I had designed to treat of "The effect of high price of land on agricultural interests" —but, while that subject is embraced as incidental, the main discussion is on the different kinds of slavery & slave-labor, & their different values in reference to agricultural & general interests. I never wrote more fluently & easily—& for so long an article, so little to my satisfaction. Came to an end, at 26 pages.

*April 13.* The mail brought a report, which seems well founded, that the Paraguay difficulty is ended—the despotic chief Lopez having made apologies & pecuniary compensation for the wrongs he had committed, to the amount of $35,000. The naval expedition to coerce him has cost in expenses more than a million of dollars—so that our triumph has been more costly than glorious. . . .

*April 14.* Began to trim & grub walking paths through the [620] woods between the high land & the river, near the house. I thought this would bring me amusing & healthy exercise & employment. Worked at it an hour after breakfast, & as long late in the afternoon, & was heartily tired both times. This small piece of ground, though not exceeding five acres, affords more beautiful natural scenery, & more variety, in itself, & in the immediate surroundings, than any as small space that I have seen. It has always been a favorite spot with me—together with the originally-like & wider extension which stretches below the yard & mansion. On this portion, when the buildings were begun 20 years ago, the forest was thinned out, leaving a thin covering of the finest & most beautiful trees, through which the view from the house takes in the river, partially veiled by the still remaining screen of large trees. Though these may be seen through, from the house & yard, the house, & all signs of a residence, are hidden by the trees from being seen from the vessels passing up & down the river. The irregular hill-side & other lower ground shaded by these trees, & extending to the river bank, & beach, is kept clear of undergrowth, & is covered by grass (of coarse kinds) & low weeds, allowing good walking every where that the steepness does not forbid. . . . Over much of this ground, & almost covering some parts, are thickly scattered the wild columbine—the beautiful & curious flowers of which, when growing thickest, on the marl knolls, give to the whole surface a sprinkling of bright scarlet. But beautiful as [is] this improved part of the ground, . . . it is not, considered alone, as pleasing to me as it was in its original [621] wild state—& as is the other portion first referred to. This remains nearly as Nature left it. None of the larger trees have been cut down for many years, & it has all the appearance of original forest growth, of various kinds of pine trees—some of great sizes, & venerable age, but mostly of young & luxuriant growth. The great variety of soil, caused by the manner of its formation, . . . encouraged the growth of various kinds of trees, that are rarely found together within such small bounds. Of these, the beech most abounds, many of them of large sizes & great age. . . .

If a very little aid of art was given, this now thickly wooded pass with its immediate surrounding margins, & all embraced within not more than 6 or 7 acres, would afford different walks, all beautiful, & various, & for a mile or more in length. . . .

*April 15.* Worked more than an hour in grubbing paths. Rode with Edmund to dine at Evergreen, the residence of Capt. H. H. Cocke. . . . I went to the kitchen to see Ritter, the former cook, who has for years been past work, though still looking well. She is the only one left there of my father's slaves who is older than myself. She seemed, & no doubt was, very much gratified with my attention in going to see & talk with her—more so probably than by receiving a half-dollar which I gave her, when shaking hands with her. . . . A long letter to me from a Mr. Asa P. Moore, of Maine, paying high compliments to my two pamphlets on Slavery & African Colonization. The writer is entirely opposed to the general fanaticism of his country—& views the different kinds of slavery much as I do. I wrote an answer, requesting leave to publish his letter.

*April 19.* . . . Afternoon, the ladies & children took their walk along the new paths in the woods, & even Mrs. Lorraine, dreading hills & rough ground as she does, chose to accompany us, to use the facilities of easy access, now first afforded, to see the beauties of the scenery. Afterwards, Thomas & I rowed the younger ladies & children out on the bay—Nanny & Sue also rowed for a short time, to learn, & performing very well.

*April 22.* Reading certain chapters of Smith's "Wealth of Nations," which was always deemed by me one of the greatest & most useful works ever written—but which I have not read for more than 40 years.—The mail—no news except that the crew of the slave ship Echo had been promptly cleared on their trial, in Charleston. I presume the ground of acquittal was that they were not guilty of "piracy" which the law of the U.S. declares the African slave-trade to be. This [626] acquittal, with the immunity of the crew of the Wanderer, will, probably, by showing the penalties will not be enforced, serve to re-open the African slave trade to considerable extent.

*April 23.* . . . The first hour of my recent working with the grubbing hoe had served to blister my hands—& in addition, in the palm of my left hand there is a deeper-seated bruise, which has induced some inflammation, & swelling, & seems inclined to fester. It had remained stationary until today, when it is getting worse.

*April 24.* Easter Sunday. . . . Judge John Robertson has declared himself a candidate for the Richmond congressional district, at which I greatly rejoice. I had before determined to cast my vote on him, & so told him. But I had no idea then that anything would induce him to be a candidate. Even as it is, & with all the superiority of his claims & ability, to serve the district & the south, I doubt whether the caucus system is not too powerful for any but the present drunken & inefficient nominee, [John S.] Caskie,[23] to be elected. Nevertheless, such a man as Robertson opposing that system will do much good, even if the greater good of his being elected is not obtained. . . .

*April 25.* . . . [627] It is surprising that sundry of the democratic papers, which had (as all of them) supported the election of Buchanan, now denounce in strongest terms the imbecility & corruption of his administration, & yet the most prominent of these papers (as the "States") & all the democratic party, profess still to sustain the administration of the president, & the democratic party as a unit. It is evidence of the supremacy of party rule over opinion & common sense. There never has been a president, when parties existed, who was so plainly denounced & spoken of so contemptuously, in almost every particular act, as Buchanan, & yet every public & general declaration of Congress, the party, & the party press, would seem to give entire support to the President & his administration. The "Southern Citizen" & the N.O. "True Delta" are exceptions—as they

---

[23] Caskie, a Richmond lawyer, had already served four terms in Congress—from 1851 to 1859.

mingle no general expressions of respect or approval with their particular denunciations. But this hollow truce cannot last—nor the outward seeming of respect for Buchanan by the southern democrats. I heartily desire its end—& for as complete a separation of the south from the northern democrats, as exists in opinion—& an open disruption of the "national" democratic party, & the arrangement of men according to their actual principles, into a southern & a northern (or abolition) party. In such new arrangement, the many submissionists in the south would be compelled to concur with the true men—& the still more numerous defenders of the constitutional rights of the south, & supporters of the institution of negro slavery, in the northern states, would also be compelled to be silent as to their preferences, & outwardly lend their support to the abolition party.

*April 26.* Went to Richmond, by steamboat, to attend the stated meeting of the Executive Committee. There was on board a Georgia [628] planter, from near Columbus, named Hurt, who introduced himself to me, on the ground of his long acquaintance with me through such of my writings as he had seen. I heard some interesting facts from him concerning the Africans brought in by the Wanderer, which had not been reported in the newspapers. Besides, sundry false statements have been published, as I believe designed to mislead & deceive the public. He said that they had been sold readily, & were scattered on many plantations in Georgia, Alabama & other southern states. About 30 had been sold near Columbus, Ga. at the average price of $850, notwithstanding the want of legal title. These were, except one young woman, all males, & boys or young men. They had in no case displayed any ferocity, or intractability—& were generally good-humored, gentle, & docile or obedient. No dissatisfaction seemed to be felt for their new condition—& when a return to Africa was intimated to them, all showed marked repugnance to it. The high prices at which these Africans have been sold, in opposition to both the Federal & state law, (of Ga,) the impunity of the owners & crew of the vessel, & also the prompt acquittal of the crew of the captured slave-ship, Echo, will all serve to make a practical re-opening of the African slave trade. The law of Congress making the trade "piracy," by that absurdity, has offered an excuse to juries to acquit all persons so charged. And the law prohibiting the African slave trade, for all slave vessels that can reach our shores without being captured by American ships of war, will be as completely nullified in the southern states as the fugitive slave law is nullified in the northern states.—The committee met at night. No offer had been made for the holding of our Fair—& it was decided that good policy [629] required we should still wait, & not on our part make any offers. Near midnight, adjourned.

*April 27.* Returned to Beechwood, by 11 A.M.—Yesterday received a letter from Mrs. Evelyn Perkins, of La, writing for her husband Judge [John] Perkins, repeating their former invitation to me, & Mildred, to go & see them, at the time for the Southern Convention.[24] Answered it, & stated my acceptance, if well enough to go so soon. The rising of my hand, & the pain thereof, continue to increase very slowly. I fear it will not be ripe, & discharged, soon enough for me to visit Judge P. in advance, even if to be at the Convention on the 9th. of May. . . .

*April 30.* Passed a bad night, both from pain & wakefulness. Did not sleep more than an hour & a half. Morning, found a small spot enough ripe to cut open, which I did—& the discharge of thick pussulent matter, though small, relieved me considerably for a time. Much the greater part not reached, & probably not ready. The swelling is extended to my fingers' ends—& the pain sometimes extends slightly above my elbow. . . .

*May 2.* . . . The opening of my risen hand now discharges a good deal, the swelling & pain continues so great, that I think there must be more sufferation in progress, & another place to break. Wrote to excuse myself to Judge Perkins of La.

*May 4.* The last night more than usually bad, with pain & wakefulness. Sent to the Examiner Mr. Asa P. Moore's letter, Mildred having written a copy for me.—De Bow's Review—& Harper's Magazine.—The newspapers of last mail report that *rust* has already appeared on the wheat in Ga. This I counted on here, from the unprecedented wetness of the whole winter, with parts of autumn & spring. But if seen anywhere as early as this, there will most probably be a general failure of the wheat crop.

*May 8.* Sunday. Yesterday (at noon) Dr. [John J.] Dupuy, having previously made full examination, & arrangements, administered sulphuric ether to me, & then cut open my hand. He inserted the knife three times—making an incision about an inch in length, & three-quarters deep, extending from the middle of the palm, between the two middle bones, [632] nearly to the junction of the mid-

---

[24] Site of the 1859 Southern Commercial Convention was Vicksburg, Mississippi.

dle & fourth finger. The cut was down to the bone, & still deeper, reaching the cavity (before discharging,) on the back of the hand. I asked the doctor to make me completely insensible, if possible, & it was effected. As I was told, I groaned loudly, & shrank from the entrance & passage of the knife. But if I felt pain, I was unconscious of it. For when I recovered, a few minutes after the cutting, I did not know that anything had been done—& supposed that the operation had yet to be performed. When the sponge saturated with ether was first held over my nose & mouth, there was too little of atmospheric air admitted, & the too strong fumes of the ether were almost choking & strangling. But when it was held farther off, & inhaled more gradually, it was not very disagreeable, even at the strongest. I was perfectly conscious of gradual coming over me of the stupifying & also soothing & grateful operation of the gas—& soon after, knew nothing more until I came to, in my clear senses, & with but little feeling of pain—& none whatsoever, except, when observed, of the sense of soreness of the newly cut wound. After a short time, I became very nervous, & needed the stimulus of a strong drink of toddy. Gradually, the pain (of the recent cut,) increased, & after the dressing (with emollient poultices) had been finished, & I was on the bed, it seemed to me that this pain might have then become such as would have been if no ether had been used, & after some hours rest. Before 2, I got to sleep—& soon awaked much refreshed, & then perfectly free from pain. I ate & enjoyed a good dinner, propped up on my bed, so as to avoid moving my hand [633] from its position of rest & quiet. Later in the afternoon, I walked down stairs, & took my customary reclining position on the couch, to see & talk with our friends. . . .

*May 10.* Slept well last night. Dr. Dupuy came again to see my hand. He deems it in as good, if not better condition—but he alarms me by the probability, even if nothing worse occurs in the rising, that it may be long before easing. This is owing to my advanced age. He recommends to me more indulgence in generous food, & to take tonics to stimulate my usually feeble appetite. . . .

*May 12.* My hand is much better, though some threatening of new risings still continue—& in other respects I feel well. It [636] no longer causes me pain to walk. Went to complete the commenced paths through the beech woods, by making bridges across the stream & deeper part of the Dark Dell, & good crossing places over the fence, for ladies. But of course I did not attempt to work, with even my one hand, but directed a servant. The improvements have added much to the facility of access, & the inducements to walk on the ground, without detracting from the wildness of the natural features. All the younger people, with myself, walked through the paths this afternoon, & sat on the seats placed in some of the most beautiful & secluded spots. . . .

*May 15.* Sunday. . . . The last mail brought such European reports as to indicate that the war must have already commenced between Austria & Sardinia, [637] & in which, France & all Italy will next be involved, & next Russia, & perhaps England. It will be a gigantic conflict. . . .

*May 18.* A steady slow rain continuing, since yesterday at noon. As all arrangements had been made for Mildred, Nanny & Edmund . . . to set out this morning for Norfolk, to attend the Episcopal Convention, they went—but in the carriage to Maycox to take the steamer, instead of going by water. . . . [638]

*May 20.* Rain at intervals in every day of the last four, & this morning very heavy. Undoubtedly this is the "Long season" in May —& very bad for the numerous attendants of the religious frolic, in Norfolk. Such are all these conventions & great meetings with the pretext of religious service. However, I do not condemn them as assemblages for recreation & innocent social enjoyment—but only for religion being made the pretext. However, as the priests of all the religious denominations have now shut out their members as much as possible from all cheerful enjoyments, it is well that they have provided this new substitute, & resource for social pleasures.—Was much gratified to receive notice from Julian that Lotty had given birth to a daughter, & that both mother & child were doing well. . . . Finished reading Alton Locke—a remarkable book.[25] It is a powerfully drawn picture of the sufferings of the laboring poor in England, or their subjection to the worst evils of what I call hunger-slavery —[639] or the slavery of labor to capital. The earlier & main portion very interesting—but the latter part very tedious, so that I glanced over it very hastily. Began to read "Two Years Ago," a novel by the same author.

*May 22.* Sunday. Finished the book. Like "Alton Locke," the first half is interesting, & the remainder the reverse. Except in the draw-

---

[25] A novel written in 1850 by Charles Kingsley. Inspired by the Chartist movement, it was one of the first English novels to portray critically the conditions of industry in that country.

ing of two characters, it has nothing—& a large portion is superfluous to the main story, & had better have been omitted. Among the many faults, one of the greatest, & also the most remarkable for this author, who had so powerfully delineated the hunger-slavery of England, he has introduced a most absurd & impossible angelic quadroon, & fugitive slave from Georgia, as the vehicle of his anti-negro-slavery doctrines & denunciations. There never was a conception of a romance more untrue to nature & to facts, nor deductions thence drawn more absurd & ridiculous. . . .

*May 27.* . . . The Mail. De Bow [641] in the April No. of his Review, had begun the republication of "African Colonization Unveiled," & inserted the first 8 pages. But instead of continuing it thereafter regularly, the May & June Nos. will contain nothing of it, & it will only be resumed with the July No. These delays & long intermissions are vexatious.—I am weary of keeping this diary, which has become a mere series of entries of the most common-place & uninteresting incidents of my daily life. It has been so for a long time—& I should long ago have abandoned it from being weary of the uninviting task, but for one reason, which was the original motive to begin, & still operates, though very feebly, to persist longer in the practice. I am anxious to keep employed, & writing is my only employment. I cannot be always so engaged—& whenever there is a cessation of some weeks or longer after one job has been completed, I have great difficulty & reluctance to resume such labor—& the longer the cessation, the more unwilling & unable I feel to begin again. The *compelling* myself to the habit of making these usually daily entries, however worthless they may generally be, offers at all times an opportunity & inducement to insert any occurrence or thought, that may seem to deserve being noted, but which otherwise would be too unimportant to be put in writing, or to be thought of again. When there is any such impulse, I am glad to let my pen run to the full extent. And such writing, without premeditation or effort, serves to keep up something of the habit of writing, which would otherwise be lost in long & complete [642] cessations of labor, & inaction of mind.

*May 28.* The Southern Convention, which met at Vicksburg, on the 9th, was thinly attended, & I fear indicated less than former interest in these meetings. Members from but 8 states were present—& not one from Virginia. Resolutions were adopted approving the repeal of the existing prohibition of the African slave-trade, &

nothing else was done, except to appoint the time & place of meeting in 1860.—From the reports of the elections,[26] so far as heard, there is an unexpected & surprising change in favor of the combination ticket of whigs & Americans ( or "Know-nothings,") & some possibility even of the election of [William L.] Goggin over [John] Letcher, for Governor. . . .

*May 30.* At 11, we got on board the steamer—Mrs. Campbell, Mildred, Jane & I, for Marlbourne . . . . On the wharf at Richmond, Mr. Sayre's carriage waiting for us, & a cart for the luggage. We stopped awhile for the ladies to do some shopping, & reached Marlbourne before dark. The reports of the election, so far as heard from, made it most probable that Goggin is elected governor, & the whigs are already uproarious in their triumph. Whether such is the case, or not, it is certain that there have been great changes in many counties & districts, evinced in the turning out of the old democratic members, having the heretofore great strength of a caucus nomination, & these being substituted either by anti-caucus democratic nominees, or whigs. Such reverses are well deserved, both because of the unfitness or vices of the excluded persons, or the abuse of power of the democratic party—& I am [644] not sorry that a severe rebuke should be thus given—though I trust it will not extend so far as to exclude Letcher from the governor's place. I would have been glad to have been able to go to the election to vote for him—& still more so to give my vote against the regular nominees (& previous incumbents) of the places of member of congress & of the senate for this district —though I should not have voted for the opponent of either, but have "thrown away" my vote on a worthy person. I am glad that both these persons have been turned out.—Saw F. G. Ruffin & Mr. Williams in Richmond. Heard that a proposal will be made to our Ex. Com. from the Central Agr. Society, for an arrangement in regard to the Fair, & that there is ground to expect an agreement.

*May 31.* Today, my hand is entirely healed, & no indication of any new festers or pustules. Still, there is considerable swelling remaining, & I cannot open or close my fingers, or make any use of them. . . . The reports by this morning's mail indicate that the great gains of the whigs, for Goggin, were exaggerated—& that he was behind, so far as the returns had been received. . . .

*June 1.* Took another long walk. Remainder of the day, reading, &

---

[26] The state gubernatorial election, held on May 26.

partly conversing. Mrs. Campbell, as always, affording excellent companionship. Notwithstanding her [645] strong sectarianism, & bigotry, she is remarkable for the liberality & charity of her manner, if not opinions, for differences of views of the heterodox. There is no other Christian with whom I have always conversed so freely, & who would hear as patiently my heterodox opinions of the construction of the Scriptures. This toleration & patience on her part, & the ardor of controversy, have seduced me to committing an error which I had latterly, & successfully been striving to avoid—& which I again will renew my efforts to avoid. This was the uttering of my opinions of the construction of various portions of the bible, differing from & in some cases entirely opposed to the received opinions among those called orthodox Christians. Whoever presumes to judge for himself of the true meaning of the bible, instead of receiving the interpretation of theologians & sects & their preachers, is immediately suspected, & charged, with opposing the doctrines of the bible, & of the Christian religion. This denunciation is the certain punishment of every individual who may dare to exercise, even in a single important particular, the *right of private judgment,* which was one of the great ends sought & contended for by Luther in the Reformation. Yet his professed followers, & all Protestants, no more dare to exercise that right, (except on pain of excommunication from every sect & shade of Christianity) than did the former, or now do, the still adhering papists. Theology is the science of misconstruction—to teach as the meaning of the scriptures, or of numerous important passages thereof, what no unprejudiced reader, with mind previously unoccupied, would ever have inferred—& often *what is entirely opposed to the plain & obvious sense. . . .* Not only is false (& often absurd) construction thus made to take the place of the plain meaning of passages of scripture, but, by all those who thus submit their understanding to the dictates of others, any who presume to judge for themselves, & of course to construe the meaning differently, are at once pronounced to be unbelievers in the bible, & enemies of religion. I would care nothing for such denunciations of my opinions, or myself, by all outside of my own family. But my children, like all other Christians, hold to the erroneous constructions of the theologians & preachers, & submit their judgment & understanding entirely to their dictates—& all their respect for me would not prevent their confounding my opposing the false or unsupported constructions of the bible, with opposition to the bible itself, & to the religion it teaches. Therefore, to avoid giving pain to my [647] children, or affronting their "orthodox" doctrines, I have tried, & will still more try, to be silent on the points of construction on which we differ—as well as on all other matters of difference of religious opinions & the subject of religious doctrine altogether. Even where such differences are unimportant (as I conceive) to Christian belief & conduct, I would not wish to change an opinion of my children to conform with mine. Far more would I avoid leading to such change in important doctrines.—Afternoon, the ladies & Mr. Sayre went to visit some friends who are staying with Mrs. Carraway—& there met with Bishop [John] Johns,[27] who is to preach tomorrow, & will dine here. Mrs. Campbell, for my daughters as well as herself, has given me my instructions, that I must not utter my opinions before the bishop of the Colonization or Foreign Missionary operations, or any other of my views which he would deem heterodox. I trust, however, that, even if not so reminded, I should not have so offended against the rules of hospitality & good manners.

*June 2.* All of us at church—where I met with most of our neighbors. The bishop preached, & came to dine with us, . . . & Mr. Sayre afterwards drove the bishop to Richmond in the smaller carriage. Reading two negrophilist pamphlets, (written by negroes, as alleged,) sent me by my abolitionist quaker correspondent of Phila., Benjamin Coates. One, from the title of which I expected much of interest, "A Vindication of the African Race," in reference to the alleged mental inferiority, I found a very poor pretence of either facts or argument. Some of the passages, which I read to [648] Mrs. Campbell brought on a discussion between us on the curse of Noah on Ham, & seduced me into a violation of my resolution made on yesterday, to avoid all discussion of theological opinions, on questions of bible construction. Nearly all pro-slavery Christians are quite ready to admit, & even to claim & insist upon, that the color, & other negro characteristics, & slavery, of Africans, are the obvious fulfilment of the prophecy, which was indicated in the terms of the curse of Noah, on Ham, or Ham's son Canaan & his posterity. It is

---

[27] A native of Delaware and graduate of Princeton University, Johns had served as assistant bishop of the Protestant Episcopal Church in Virginia since 1842. In addition to his clerical duties, he served as president and professor of moral and intellectual philosophy at William & Mary College during the early 1850's. Elevated to the office of bishop of the Episcopal Diocese of Virginia in 1862, Johns functioned in that capacity until his death in 1876.

usually assumed that the Africans, or certainly the negro Africans are the descendants of Ham, & that their peculiar characters, & degraded condition is most striking evidence of the fulfilment of Noah's curse & prophecy—&, with many, that the enslaving of Ham's posterity is but conforming to the law of God. On the contrary, I deny that there is any evidence in Genesis, or elsewhere in the bible, so far as I know of, that either the Africans generally, or the negroes particularly, are descended from Ham. And the Assyrians, who were among his descendants, were certainly not a black race—nor the Canaanites, (if we may rely on negative evidence,) who were descendants of Canaan. Further—I would utterly reject the belief that the just & merciful God would sanction & consummate the curse of Noah, by which, for an act of unfilial conduct, which, however condemnable & shameful, was not worse than almost every parent has had to bear from some child, not the truly guilty son, but his innocent posterity, through all subsequent time, & for perhaps a third of all the human family, were doomed to live in degradation & misery!

*June 3.* Letcher is certainly elected governor. No [649] other news. . . .

*June 8.* Reading in [John Stuart] Mill's Political Economy, which I borrowed yesterday from Wm. Newton—the parts on Communism, Wages, population, profits. The author is a disciple of Adam Smith & of Malthus—his views, & especially in regard to circumstances which have arisen since these writers put forth their then new systems, are interesting & instructive. On Slavery, he is as much in the dark as all other English authors. I have from him learned much in opposition to my previous one-sided information as to the results of the minute division of land in France. There certainly are many evils caused by the system—but also many benefits, which perhaps are of equal weight. Probably the greatest voluntary division of farms & landed properties bring less of their evils than does the general system of very large landed properties, such as follow the institution of primogeniture & entails. . . .

*June 11.* . . . Mill, in his Political Economy, presents some views which at first would seem as revolutionary, & destructive, as novel. But there is much reason to advocate them. One is denying the right, or good policy, of property of deceased & intestate persons, being inherited by any but their descendants, or wife, or living ancestor, where there are no descendants. Another is to [655] deny the right of bequest, by will, to any other than the foregoing relatives, more than a limited amount of property. The prohibition of collateral inheritance would exclude no one as an heir who had any just claim. The prohibition of bequeathing more than a moderate competency to any one collateral relative, or other person not a relative, could not lessen even the happiness of such heir by bequest, as a competency is as likely to be beneficial to the unexpected receiver, as an overgrown fortune—& the remainder might make several other competencies for other individuals, or otherwise aid public objects. Perhaps it would be good policy to go further, & forbid the bequeathing even to children, more than an amount ample for comfort & happiness. The surplus amounts thus prohibited either as inheritance or bequest, if not directed to other uses by the owner, by gift or testament, would go to the state.

*June 13.* This morning finished reading through a volume on "Farm Drainage," by Judge French of New Hampshire, which he had sent me by mail. In it he notices my communications on the subject to the U.S.A. Society, which I had given to him. His book is sensible & interesting, & sets forth in strong colors the great value of thorough draining by the use of tile-pipes. I will send to him my volume of "Essays & Notes &c," containing my earlier publication on draining. . . .

*June 14.* The mail. . . . Later news still favorable to the allies. Indications of Germany taking part in the contest—& if so war will become general. I think Russia will use the opportunity to seize Constantinople, & all European Turkey. In England, all voices seem to be for neutrality. Yet I doubt its continuance, if more of the continental powers are engaged, & the greatly enlarged dominion & strength of France becomes probable. After the newspapers, reading the last Quarterly Review, which came by the mail. Determined to go tomorrow, by the stage coach, to Richmond, & thence proceed to Washington, to see about the publication of my last writing. It is too long for a newspaper—as it would require to be cut up into sundry parts, & separated issues, & the only proper magazine, De Bow's Review, would take several months to bring it out in different numbers. . . .

*June 15.* Set out in the stage coach from the Post Office & reached Richmond at 5 P.M. Obtained a copy of De Bow's June No, & read therein my article "On the Effects of the high price of slaves, considered in reference to the interests of Va." Also saw a notice of the editor that the continuation of my Colonization pamphlet, which he began to print in his April No. will not be resumed until after some months of suspense. These long interruptions & delays are very vexatious—& I shall not furnish the remaining M.S. to De Bow, without strong assurance of its being more speedily attended to. Saw Mr. Williams, & heard that nothing had yet been done [658] in the negotiation with the Central Agr. Soc. about the holding of the Fair. . . .

*June 16.* Saw Wm. Old jr. the new editor of the Examiner, who will reprint the article from De Bow's Review. . . . Saw Harvie & F. Ruffin—with whom & Old, had a pleasant conversation on political affairs, & Gov. Wise's mis-doings.—After I had arranged to set out for Washington in the afternoon, I happened to see in a Charleston paper that De Bow was there, instead of being in Washington. As the main object of my going was to see him, I gave up my intention. . . .

*June 17.* Left Richmond at 5 A.M. in the Norfolk steamer, & landed at Maycox wharf. This was not the day for the little steamer Schultz, which only will put passengers on shore at Coggin's Point. Hired a sturgeoning boat & hands, & was rowed to the Beechwood house landing. . . . Edmund at his harvest labors. Repeated heavy showers—& very bad weather for reaping & securing wheat. Read June No. of De Bow's Review—& the newspapers. . . .

*June 20.* . . . Later & very important news from the European war—though only the chief points are as yet stated, & probably these very incorrectly. It is the French account only that has yet reached us. It reports a great battle in Lombardy, gained by the French & Sardinian armies—the Austrian loss very great—one rumor stating 25,000 killed & wounded, & 5000 prisoners. The loss of the allies stated to be comparatively small. Milan evacuated by the Austrians, & the inhabitants in a [666] state of insurrection against the Austrian government. It is also reported that the Pope is a prisoner to the French, who have so long garrisoned Rome, to protect him from his own subjects. This is incredible, as the French government would draw upon itself odium in every part of Catholic Europe.

*June 22.* . . . The mail. Later accounts confirm the main points of the last reported successes of the allied army of France & Sardinia —though serving to lessen the disproportion of the respective losses of that and the Austrian army. Milan is occupied by the allies, & the Austrian force has withdrawn from Pavia. The partisan chief Garibaldi is reported to have gained another victory, & to be moving on successfully through Lombardy, gaining strength from the population, & sowing the seeds of insurrection in every part of enslaved Italy. I have more respect for him, & am more interested in his success, than in either France or Piedmont, the rulers of which are impelled solely by their own selfish objects. Garibaldi is alone directed by patriotic & pure views for the destruction of the Austrian supremacy, & the liberation & independence of Italy. His last noble effort, in the general outbreak & temporary revolution of 1848 & 9, was in fighting, as long as there was the last hope even of his [667] own escape, against the French army sent by this very villain, the Emperor of France, (who now professes to fight for the freedom of Italy,) to quell & extinguish the evanescent free government of Rome. If any large portion of the people of Italy really desire freedom from the iron despotism, or as intolerable indirect control, of Austria, the successes of France & Piedmont will incite them to taking sides with Garibaldi, & the breaking out in extensive if not general insurrection. This may make them too strong to be dictated to by the allied crowned heads, & secure equitable terms of adjustment. The Italians are totally unfit for republican government. The best result will be the independence of all Italy, & the formation, including Sardinia & Sicily, of a constitutional federal monarchy, under the king of Sardinia. Under a limited monarchy, with representative legislature, there would be as much of freedom as the people could enjoy or preserve—& enough to obtain more in future, should it be expedient & desired.—My last article, reprinted from De Bow's Review, on the effects of high prices of slaves, appeared in the last issue of the Richmond Examiner.

*June 23-24.* . . . Some days ago I began to write, and today extended it to 7 pages—on Northern aggressions—but with the want of interest, & difficulty of composing, which is customary with me after having ceased to write for some weeks. It is an up-hill undertaking —& the little that is written, under such circumstances, is never satisfactory to myself.

*June 27.* In extracts from a "Naturalist's Note Book," (in Living Age,) it is stated that in the territory of Pisa, Italy, only of all Europe, camels have long been introduced, & still remain—but that the young animals are defective in strength, or power to suck without being held up, & the stock degenerate. The Moors brought camels into Spain—but as none remained, there must have been an unfitness of the soil or climate to sustain these animals. Everything in regard to the [670] camel is strange. According to the above account, it seems incapable of continuing its existence in Europe—& yet has been naturalized, & made useful to man, in almost every region & climate of Asia & Africa occupied or traversed by any partially civilized tribes. A few years ago, camels were brought to this country, by the government, & have since been used to good purpose, for transporting the baggage &c. of the Army, in crossing the territory from Texas to California—& found preferable to any other beasts of burden. The success of this government experiment, has since encouraged a contractor who had procured the first supply of camels, to import others on private speculation. Very recently, they have been placed on some plantations in Alabama, & used, advantageously, it is reported, to transport bales of cotton &c. instead of by wheel-carriages. They have not yet been tried as draught animals. This no doubt will be done, & with success in this country of new improvements—though never before, in 4000 years of its Asiatic & African servitude to man, does it appear that the camel has ever drawn either carriage or plough. It is said that so far the camels in this country have been healthy, & seemed to thrive as well as in their native lands. Should this be true, we may expect that this more powerful, & yet cheaper animal will extensively substitute the horse & mule, both for road & farm uses, through all the southern states. . . . The tory ministry (Lord Derby's) of England has been compelled to resign, & the whigs, with Lord [671] Palmerston at the head, are reinstated. The leaning of the late ministers to the side of Austria was the chief cause of their defeat—showing that the House of Commons & the people favor the allies. I am sorry for this change, because I wish that England & France may be less united, if not hostile. Palmerston is devoted to the French alliance, & to the French emperor. Moreover he is especially inimical to this country, & to its progress to greater power. I would wish England to maintain her neutrality, but with great jealousy & distrust of France. And if she goes to war, I hope that may be against & not on the side of France. . . . I have determined to go to pay a visit to Judge Ruffin's family, as he is now at home, in the vacation of his court. Edmund has to go to Petersburg on business next Saturday, & I will go with him, on my way to N.Ca.

# July–December

❧

# 1859

VISITING IN NORTH CAROLINA ❧ WARN-
INGS BY CASSANDRA ❧ VACATIONING AT
THE VIRGINIA SPRINGS ❧ EXCITEMENT AT
HARPERS FERRY ❧ WITNESS TO THE EXE-
CUTION OF JOHN BROWN ❧ THE CONTEST
OVER HOUSE SPEAKER

*July 2.* Edmund & I made an early start, in the carriage, [672] for Petersburg, where we arrived by 8.30. Found that I had to wait to near 5 P.M. to take the train for Weldon, & that there would be no direct connection thence with Raleigh. So, instead of being able to reach Graham & Alamance very early tomorrow morning, there will be no train on the Raleigh & Gaston road from Weldon until tomorrow at 11 A.M. This will compel me to go on to Goldsborough. In the long stay I had to make in Petersburg, I visited Mrs. Campbell, & her son Charles. Conversed with the latter about his new history of Virginia which is now being printed in Philadelphia, & about the difficulties to any southern writer in publishing a book, in the south, without certain pecuniary loss. A few great publishing houses in the northern cities have a virtual monopoly of the business, & they only can sell a book to any profit. . . . Before reaching Weldon, I found that there would be still longer delays, & greater difficulties of my travel, after reaching Goldsborough—which I did after 12 at night. Went immediately to bed. . . .

*July 3.* Sunday. But for the disappointment caused by the Express train not going last night over the Raleigh & Gaston road, I had hoped to be at Judge Ruffin's early this forenoon.—Saw & spent some hours with Mr. Thomas Ruffin, (M.C.) who resides at Goldsborough, & to meet with whom was one of the inducements for me to come here, instead of spending the interval at Weldon. At 1 P.M. set out in the Express train—& reached the "Company's Shops," the new station & only stopping place of the Express train, two miles above Graham, at 6.30 P.M. . . . Did not reach Graham, & the house of Thomas Ruffin jr. (the Judge's son,) until after 8. I had been anxious to go on, because hearing that Judge R. was at home, but would leave again tomorrow morning early, for his court in Raleigh. But I unexpectedly found Jane at her brother's house, & also heard that her father would remain at home through tomorrow, it being the 4th—& so I abandoned my first intention, & request of Th. R. to be sent on immediately, & staid with him through the night. Jane & I were greatly rejoiced to meet. Mrs. Th. R. is in Hillsborough, where she was recently confined, & is not yet strong enough to return home. Jane or Patty stay here in turn, to keep the house, especially on account of their oldest brother William's unfortunate condition, & for his greater comfort & better attendance. He broke his leg some months [ago] [674] & which, after long procrastination (in hope of saving it,) was at last amputated, half way or more up the thigh. His accident occurred in Graham, & he was carried to, & has since continued in his brother's office, across the street from his mansion. He was gradually improving—but very lately, & temporarily as supposed, there is increased inflammation. . . .

*July 4.* Immediately after breakfast, I went on to Alamance, & of course my unexpected appearance was a very agreeable surprise. . . . Of course, I had much pleasant conversation with my old friends, & especially with Jane & Patty, who are acquainted with so many of our neighbors in Va. & are therefore interested in inquiring & hearing about numerous things that would not be worth mentioning to strangers. I am sorry that the condition of things at Graham requires one of them to be always there, so that they are apart, & I cannot be with both together. But as there are ready facilities for passing between the places, I shall often use them. Judge Ruffin had to go this evening to stay at Thomas' in Graham, to see William, & to take the train early in the morning, to return to his court in Raleigh. Mrs. Ruffin went with him—& I, to have the last of his company at night. I was permitted to go to see William, who was then at ease, & better, & seemed very glad to see me. . . . The Italian proverb says that "there is a skeleton in every house." The "skeleton" of this large & otherwise happy family is & long has been this the oldest son— whose opening life promised as much happiness to his parents, & to himself, & every advantage & reward of high talent, character, & good position, as ever occurred in any other case—or as there has been, in measure, the reverse of these bright early prospects. His natural abilities were of very high order—indeed many persons have said that he might have even surpassed his father in his exercise & application of intellect—with a first-rate education—& every facility for achieving success in his profession (of the law,) which his talents, education, & social & family position offered. All was speedily blighted by an early addiction to intemperance. The indulgence was not habitual, & was entirely avoided in his father's house, & for the longer intervals of time. But the irregular & temporary outbreaks were frequent enough to destroy every chance for useful application & effort, & every hope of reformation. So it has continued—& will continue to his end. This recent & most painful & dangerous calamity, its cause, & its long continued effects of pain, abstinence, & danger, I had hoped might be more operative than all other preceding motives & reasons to produce future reformation. But from what I have heard from his physician, I already have lost all of that faint hope. . . .

*July 6.* Began yesterday to read & finished this morning a small volume "A defence of Slavery," by Matthew Estes, of Columbus Miss. published in 1846. I found it in the library of T.R. jr—& before had never heard of either the book or its author. Yet it is a very good plain compilation & statement of sound doctrine & facts. It did not indeed present to me a single new fact, view, or argument. But it is a clear exposition of the question. It presents some views which I have used much more fully in my latest writing, (especially,) & which have been scarcely touched on by others. These are, the practical extensive existence of slavery, even more rigid than our negro slavery, in England & other so called free countries. . . .

*July 8.* . . . Formerly it was a very general belief that the doctrines of geology were in such plain contradiction to the Mosaical account of the creation of the world, in the 1st. chapter of Genesis, that the truth of either being established would as effectively show the falsehood of the other. This would have been unfortunate—for if it were so, the great doctrines of geology would certainly stand firm, & the bible, or rather the ignorant or bigoted priests & unfair reasoners who assume to be its only expositors, would have to give way. Such was the case in earlier times, when theologians denounced geographers as opposing religion & scripture, in asserting that the earth was spherical instead of a flat surface—& astronomers, in like manner when they discovered & declared that the earth revolved around the sun. In time, both these strongly denounced truths of science came to be universally admitted, and neither the bible nor Christianity are supposed to have been weakened in authority thereby. So will it be as to geology—& indeed that end has been [678] nearly reached already. Ministers of religion & theologians of the most undoubted piety & learning already have admitted that the six *days* of the creation were not (as formerly believed) natural days—but geological periods, which might have been each of millions of years of duration. For my own part, (if I, ignorant as I am of both theology & geology, may presume to offer an opinion,) I have thought that the geological truths exhibited & established by the fossil remains of successive & extinct races, if not entirely & literally agreeing with the scriptural account, is far more in conformation thereof than contradictory. Indeed, the accordance of the order of the successive creations, as already declared, or indicated more obscurely, by the bible, & as proved by geology, is so remarkable, that it is difficult to believe that the account given in the bible, even if it were fabulous, & a work of mere imagination, could have been dictated altogether by chance. I find confirmation of my views in Hugh Miller's "Testimony of the Rocks," & evidences & illustrations formulated by his knowledge, which my want of scientific knowledge prevented my reaching, or approaching nearer than in general & superficial opinions. But still I think that he might have extended his evidences, to advantage, farther than he has done . . . .[1]

Miller's speculations on the Noahian deluge are very unsatisfactory. He denies its being general, over the whole earth—& conclusively establishes that position. He also maintains the impossibility of some of all the animals existing in the world, being so long preserved in the Ark, whether of the usually estimated, or of any assignable dimensions. But to support his own doctrine—of the submersion of but a small portion of the earth's surface, & the confining in the ark of but the animals peculiar to that portion, his reasoning is as open to objection, as that which advocates the literal interpretation of Genesis, & the universality of the deluge. For his supposed partial & limited overflow, he has recourse to the gradual subsidence, [685] in 40 days of the small portion of the earth supposed to

---

[1] Hugh Miller (1802–56) was an English geologist and writer, whose principal works were *Footprints of the Creator* (1847), *My Schools and Schoolmasters* (1852), and *The Testimony of the Rocks* (1857).

be then inhabited by man, to the depth of 16,000 feet—& afterwards, its being as gradually upheaved to its first elevation. Thus two great miracles, (though of geological operation,) without any authority of scripture language, or indication, have to be supposed, instead of the one great miracle, taken as a whole, of the preservation of some of all kinds of living beings. I was surprised to learn from another part of this work, that what I held as true & certain, that there is no scriptural authority, nor Christian injunction (of the bible,) for keeping the Christian sabbath, has actually been publickly preached in England, by a clergyman of the established church of high reputation, the Rev. Baden Powell.[2] He has also maintained "that it is in vain to attempt to reconcile the Mosaic writings with the geologic discoveries"—& therefore he "virtually sets aside the Mosaic cosmogony." He assumes that the "introduction (in Genesis) is but mere picturesque myth, or parable, as little scientifically true, as the parables of our Savior, or of Nathan the seer, are historically so."

If, as it appears, a learned clergyman can preach & publish this doctrine, that there is no scripture (of the New Testament) or Christian authority, to keep holy the ancient Jewish, or the modern Christian sabbath, without being degraded or censured for opinions opposed to almost the whole Christian world, it seems to indicate the dawn, in England & this country, of a new condition of things, when men may truly exercise the "right of private judgment," (claimed to be allowed by the Protestant Reformation, but always practically withheld—) in interpreting the scriptures, without being therefore denounced as unbelievers [686] of the bible, & enemies to the Christian religion. Such would now be the case in this region, & in the opinions of all the so-called orthodox preachers, & their blind & obedient followers, as to any one who would presume to construe the scriptures according to his own understanding, & not by the glasses of theologians.

Though parts of this book "The Testimony of the Rocks," are very interesting, on the whole, or rather for the portions I have read, I think it very inferior to the author's "Old Red Sandstone" & Foot Prints of the Creator, & so unworthy of his great mind & reasoning powers, that I suspect that the overthrow of his intellect had already

---

[2] Savilian professor of geometry at Oxford University, 1827–60, the Reverend Baden Powell was as noted for his work on optics and radiation as for his latitudinarian theological principles.

begun, which soon after closed in confirmed insanity & suicide of this truly great man.

*July 13. . . .* Took leave for my final departure, & went to Graham, to visit Mr. & Mrs. Thomas Ruffin jr. both being now at home. Spent the day there, & in part sitting with William R. Excessively hot weather. After sunset, I walked to the "Shops" station hotel, to be ready for the express train early tomorrow morning. My trunk had been sent on before, with a letter to the landlord, & with every precaution on my part for his keeping it safely until my arrival. But, by total neglect & carelessness, he had suffered it to be carried off, by mistake, on the train to the west. This puts me to great inconvenience, in the delay, even if the trunk should be returned. Saw Messrs. Cameron, Kirkland, & Brown Ruffin, there on rail-road business. Was introduced to a few others—but found little inducement, or opportunity, for conversation, & a dull evening.

*July 14.* I had some hope that the early (express) train might bring back my trunk, from Charlotte, after the mistake had been discovered. But it did not come. The gentlemen of my acquaintance used every effort to recover the trunk, by sending inquiries to different stations. They went to Greensborough, to attend the meeting of the R.R. Company, & there, I suppose, found the trunk had been put out, as it came back to me by the noon train, to my great relief. So I was enabled to proceed, on that train, as I had [689] designed in the morning, on my way to Beaufort. But this did not prevent my losing 24 hours of time, from the Shops station to Beaufort. Reached Goldsborough at 6 P.M. where I was before aware that I would have to wait until 3 P.M. tomorrow, for the earliest train on the Atlantic R.R. to Beaufort. But I was induced to come & wait here, expecting to have the company of Mr. Thos. Ruffin (M.C.) & the reading of his newspapers. But he is away—& my time is like to be spent as heavily here as at the Shops this forenoon. A country or village tavern, without acquaintance, books, or employment, is the most disagreeable of all places to me. . . .

*July 15.* Went to the office of the newspaper published here, & was politely permitted to see the exchange papers from Va. In one, there is the correspondence between the sub-committee of the Va. S.A. Soc. & James Lyons, Prest. of the Central A. Soc. negotiating for an arrangement between the Societies, to hold the State Fair in Richmond—which resulted in failure. The exorbitancy of the demands, & the lofty & supercilious & even contemptuous tone of Mr.

President Lyons are remarkable, but characteristic.—Mr. L. C. Desmond, a planter of Lenoir, whom I had known before, & Mr. C. Wooten, & Mr. Bryan, all directors of the Atlantic & N.C. R.R.[3] arrived to go on the train to their homes—with whom & others I had some interesting conversation for some hours before our setting [690] out, at 3 P.M. These gentlemen offered to me a free ticket for my trip to Beaufort & back—placing their offer on the complimentary ground of the important services I had rendered to the agriculture of the country. The general freedom of passage on the Raleigh & Gaston, Wilmington, & N.C. railroads, as well as most of those in S.Ca., had been formerly given to me on the same ground, probably with the expectation added, of my future like services, facilitated or enabled by this permission. And I think that I have already rendered these services, & a hundred-fold more, in the writings & publications I have already made in regard to North & South Ca., besides the larger amount of writing still unpublished.... After many & long stoppages, which might well be avoided, if time were of any value on this route, we reached the wharf of Morehead, at 9, & crossed over the water to Beaufort. By the time we had eaten supper it was 10.30 o'clock. In the train, from Newbern, I had met with Mr. P. G. Evans, whom I knew here before, & have seen since. He is a newcomer to this low country, a man of much intelligence & energy—& informs me that he has already profited much by following my instruction as to draining his land near Newbern, on my theory of tapping the under water-glutted sand bed.

*July 16.* Found not a person here among the visitors whom I knew before—but was introduced to some 6 or 8 gentlemen, who are pleasant companions. Finished the copying (which I began at Goldsborough,) of my last writing, on the danger of the South, [691] & headed "Cassandra—warnings," & mailed it to the Charleston Mercury.—The new hotel (Pender's) at which I am, has been built on piles in the water, so as to be most exposed to the sea breeze. My apartment fronts the open view of the ocean. The situation is pleasant—& the table fare excellent, in abundance & variety of all that salt water supplies, in fish, oysters, & soft crabs. But except the fine air, sea bathing (in a new & very poor bath house,) & the good fish &c. there is little to recommend the place, & I fear that I shall soon tire of it.—Mr. Humphry, of Onslow, & a member of the legis-

---

[3] This railroad, which ran ninety-six miles from Goldsboro through New Bern to Beaufort, was chartered in 1854 and completed four years later.

lature, solicits me strongly to accompany him home, to examine a very extensive body of swamp land in his neighborhood—which I am inclined to do, if I can remain long enough.

*July 17.* Sunday. Last night, as usual, a fresh breeze from the ocean, & the regular dashing of the high waves against the foundation of the house, & immediately below my window, gave a pleasant & soothing sound, as I lay awake. . . . Mr. Evans came over the water from Moorhead, to visit me.—There are two rival new cities, in name & law, Moorhead at the termination of the railroad, & Carolina City two miles above. Both adjoin deep navigable water—17 feet deep—but so far the facts, & the prospects seem to show, as I had predicted, that mere deep water to the ocean, & a railroad to reach it, will not divert trade from its old channels & marts, to a new seaport where there is neither existing business, capital, nor merchants. [692]

*July 18.* . . . After 9.30, there arrived in the train from Newbern, Mr. C. [693] Wood, who was introduced to me, & stated that he was deputed by the Craven county Agr. Soc. to invite me to meet with & address the Society, at Newbern, at such time, during my visit as would suit my convenience. I agreed to do so, & will meet the society next Friday night, as I return homeward. Mr. Wood came specially for this purpose, & will return early tomorrow morning. I regard this invitation, among so lethargic & unenergetic a people, as a high compliment—& I am glad of the opportunity to endeavor to offer to them some general views & instructions as to the improvements most needed, & for which there exist great facilities, for the greatly neglected agriculture of this region.

*July 19.* Went with a party of 16 or 18 persons in a sailing "flat," the term here for the ordinary undecked & flat-bottomed vessels, to witness the "horse-penning" on the sand-reef, 25 miles from this on Cane Sound—expecting to return that night—but could not get back until 4 P.M. on 20th. This trip has been more a complete waste of time, of comfort, & more filled with petty but serious annoyances & disagreeable occurrences than any within my experience. The vessel was a fast sailer. We carried our own provisions. The vessel grounded on the shallow shoals & knobs several times on our outward passage, so as to make our arrival late. But it was soon enough, as I soon saw enough of the business of penning, catching, & selling the beach ponies. I have before described this business, on report of others. I found the reality to fall far short of the reported description

& accounts. Our setting out to return was delayed by the putting on board 9 of the marsh ponies, from 2 to 4 years old, caught that day, & sold to different persons in our party. These, by their weight, & otherwise, added much to the difficulties of our return voyage. We had sailed [694] but a few miles, before a storm which had been threatening, came with great violence—rain, at one time very heavy, strong wind, & thunder & lightning. Before that, we had grounded, & could do nothing, but attempt to shelter ourselves during its worst continuance. Afterwards, it rained, but more gently, & with intermissions, through half the night. . . . Repeated attempts were made to get the vessel off the ground, & to proceed, in the intermissions of the storm. But after several new departures, & soon again grounding, the anchor was cast before sunset, & so remained through the night. . . . I passed a wretched night—wet, cold, under a strong & cold wind blowing on my wet clothes. I did not sleep more than a quarter of an hour, if as much. . . . When we grounded last yesterday, the negro captain was so bewildered that he did not know where we were, nor in which direction to steer. Therefore of necessity we would have [696] remained still. But when we floated, with the rising tide, (some of the passengers, with all the crew, getting out into the water to shove off the vessel,) the locality was recognized, & we proceeded—but continued frequently to ground. . . . In addition to all the other discomforts of last night, there was neither fire nor light on the vessel & the night very dark, as well [as] the wind very cold to those who were wet—as nearly all were.

*July 21*. . . . Read over my account of a new principle of drainage, & made notes thereof, to speak from tomorrow, should I be able to meet my appointment in Newbern. Heard that notice had been published there that I am to make a public address in the theatre, & of course all the public invited. I should not do this, if ever so well—& am glad that my feet afford abundant excuse for declining.[4] I at first told the envoy of the Society that he must not speak of an "address" or speech from me—that I was incapable, & should not attempt any such thing. But I was willing to meet the Society, or any farmers, at their wish & request, & to talk with them plainly & without form, & to say what I could for their information on their particular condition. If ever so competent & accustomed to speak in public, I would avoid speaking on agriculture to a mixed audience, including ladies,

---

[4] On his memorable outing of the previous day Ruffin had shed his wet shoes and socks, only to have his tender feet blistered by the hot sun.

of whom not one person in five would either know or care anything about my subject, & would very soon be weary of listening to me. . . .

*July 22.* Left Beaufort before 6 A.M. & reached Newbern before 9. Took lodgings at the Gaston House. Found in the town paper an editorial complimentary notice of my expected speech at the theatre. Took immediate steps to let it be known that I would be unable to attend—but stated with my excuse, that if any farmers desired it, & will come to the Gaston House this evening, I will hold with them a farmers' talk, & say everything that I could say in any other way. . . . Heard that the large tract of Judge [William] Gaston's,[5] 5000 acres of land, which I had visited & examined in 1840, & made a report upon in the Farmer's Register, was sold, some time after the death of the owner, at about 50 cents the acre—a plantation under culture, drained (though insufficiently) & with farm buildings! Subsequently, it was bought by Mr. Evans, some few years back, at $1.20 the acre; & since he has found in deeper ditching, & boring, rich marl near the surface everywhere it is wanting. Even with the late advance of prices of lands, I still deem this region the best known place for the settlement of an improving farmer.

Mr. Wadsworth, the President of the Agr. Society, did not arrive from his home (in the neighborhood,) until nearly 6 o'clock, when I informed him of the state of things. He proceeded to make the necessary arrangements, & afterwards to have verbal notice given to such persons as would be interested in the subject. We met in the sitting room of the Hotel—& so late had notice been given, that the attendants did not begin to come in until after 8, & had not all arrived at 9—a little before [699] which time I began. My remarks were confined to the one branch of draining or the principle of tapping the underlying sand-bed, & subjects incidental. I had a blackboard, & drew diagrams thereon to illustrate my views. After speaking an hour, & forgetting perhaps half of all the points I had intended to present, I closed. But the company did not immediately begin to move, & another hour was spent in my answering questions which some of the most intelligent farmers asked, in further explanation of draining, or other connected subjects of improvement. There were, as I guess, 50 to 60 persons present—& I never saw an audi-

---

[5] A distinguished North Carolina jurist, William Gaston (1778-1844) served two terms in Congress and was chief justice of the North Carolina Supreme Court from 1833 to 1844.

ence so entirely attentive, & apparently interested. Among them were Gov. [John M.] Morehead,[6] Judge [John R.] Donnell,[7] & most of the intelligent farmers here.

*July 23.* Conversation with farmers who are directors of the Railroad, & now in session here. Left before 9. Gov. Morehead, (who was also with me yesterday on the train,) sat by me, & we had much interesting talk about the swamplands of the state. Reached Goldsborough after 12, where I had to wait until night for the next train, which will take me to Richmond in 10 hours. Had I known that the passage was so quick, I would have accepted the urgent invitation of several farmers in Lenoir, to stay longer & visit them. I shall now stay an unnecessary & tiresome three days in Richmond, before the meeting of the Executive Committee, which I return now to attend. Saw Thomas Ruffin, M.C. & looked over his newspapers, as well as others. By the last news, an armistice, which was proposed by France, has been agreed to by Austria, & has been declared. No one seems to expect this to lead to peace. Both the contending parties have been greatly exhausted by the many bloody battles so rapidly succeeding [700] each other, & both needed a time to recruit strength for the next conflicts. In addition, the politic villain who rules France probably also thinks that his proposing a cessation of arms, which would indicate a desire for peace, in the uninterrupted flow of his victorious course, would give him some claim to the character of moderation. He needs this—for his recent friend & ally, England, (as well as other powers,) is growing very suspicious of his ulterior designs. In a late & long debate in the House of Lords, the venerable Lord Lyndhurst spoke at much length, to state his suspicions & apprehensions of the enmity of the French Emperor, & urged the arming the nation to the extent necessary for defence. This speech, which was concurred in by other Peers, must have a strong & not a conciliatory effect on France & especially on the Emperor.—Left Goldsborough a few minutes after 8 P.M., and

*July 24.* (Sunday) reached Richmond at 5.45 A.M. Went to the Exchange. . . . After a late breakfast, read, or looked over, all the late

---

[6] John Motley Morehead was governor of North Carolina from 1841 to 1845 and during the following decade was active as a railroad president and promoter in the state.

[7] A native of Ireland, Donnell came to North Carolina and settled in Craven County, where he was judge of superior court, 1819-36. His son, Richard Spaight Donnell, was a Whig member of the Thirtieth Congress and sat in the North Carolina Secession Convention.

& interesting newspapers I could find. . . . Read a No (for this month) of "Colonization Herald" of Phila. which contains the last annual speech of [John H. B.] Latrobe, President of A.C. Soc.[8] & also an article, of a column in length, taken from the N.Y. "Colonizationist," commenting on my pamphlet, "African Colonization Unveiled." This is the first notice, even of a word of reference, that has been published of my attack, by any one of the Colonization Society or its friends—so far as I have heard. Of course I read this eagerly. It applies only to my charges of the wretched condition of Liberian agriculture & commerce in 1843 (& generally,) & this reply does not attempt to invalidate my statements, but only to offer reasons in mitigation of the facts. The writer promises that he will hereafter consider & remark upon "other points in this pamphlet"—which I hope may come to my view. Any reply or strictures so weak as this, I shall not notice. . . .

*July 25.* The telegraph brings most unexpected & astounding news. The armistice has been immediately followed by peace. Austria cedes Lombardy, (not the Venetian territory,) to France, & France transfers it to Piedmont. All the remainder of Italy is to be embraced in a confederation, under the nominal authority of the Pope. Though [702] nothing yet has been said, I have no doubt that Savoy & the adjacent other Piedmontese Trans-Alpine territory will be ceded to France. Though France will gain but little (even then) directly, for her enormous expenditure of blood & treasure, the indirect gains will be great. The kingdom of Sardinia will be virtually, in submission, a province of France. At the next outbreak, France will be able to extend her conquests much more easily. But will the fermentation of Italy be as easily cooled & hushed? Will Garibaldi, so far triumphant, lay down his arms, or Kossuth stop suddenly in his effort to excite the insurrection of Hungary? Will the papal states be ready to return to their before compulsory submission, when the Austrian power, their compeller, is crushed? And will the Italian states, either including or excluding Naples, submit to come even un[der] the nominal government of the Pope, the government heretofore the worst in Europe? Louis Napoleon has broken his announced pledge to free Italy. His peace will place him in the worst position with the

---

[8] Son of the celebrated architect who reconstructed the Capitol and White House following the War of 1812, John Hazlehurst Boneval Latrobe ( 1803–91 ) was president of the American Colonization Society from 1853 until 1890.

deceived Italians, & especially with those who have accepted the invitation to take arms. There has also been suspicion felt & expressed by England, of treacherous breach of faith, & of enmity, from the Emperor of France, & his desire for revenge for Waterloo which he doubtless designs at a convenient time, may be exasperated & quickened by the suspicions & insults of prominent English peers in parliament, as well as many others. I heartily wish that their cordial alliance may be broken up, & substituted by mutual suspicion & fear. That will put an end to their combined efforts to impede the progress of, & to injure the United States—& leave us free to settle our own business, whether foreign or internal, [703] without the interference of always hostile England, or France. . . .

*July 26.* The members of the Executive Committee coming in. At night, our meeting, 10 members present. A committee from the Union Society (of Petersburg) arrived, & in conference & negotiation with our sub-committee. After considerable discussion in our body, & new instructions given to the sub-committee, an arrangement was made, by which the Fair & General Meeting of the State Agrl. Society will be held again at the Petersburg Fair Ground. The conditions are not quite so favorable for us as last year—but very far preferable to those offered by the Central Society (for Richmond,) which were so extortionate as to be absurd, as well as altogether inadmissible. Adjourned after 11 P.M. to meet at 8½ tomorrow. . . .

*July 27.* The committee arranged the premium list, & appointed the judges of awards—& other necessary business, & adjourned at 2 P.M. to the next stated meeting. . . .

*July 28.* . . . Took a place in the mail stage for tomorrow morning —but Mr. Boulwane afterwards arrived, & offered me a seat in his carriage to Marlbourne, which I will wait for a little longer, to have his company. Afternoon, saw at the Exchange Wm. B. Harrison, Ro. Douthat, & Gov. J. L. Manning of S.C., & had a conversation with them & Mr. Boulwane. Gov. Manning is strongly opposed to the reopening of the African slave-trade—but thinks that the advocates of that measure are gaining strength in S.C.

*July 29.* Went with Mr. Boulwane to Marlbourne, where he staid until evening, & proceeded home. Found all well—Elizabeth much improved in appearance of health & strength. Mr. Burwell Sayre here on a visit, which was just about to end, & he left after dinner. . . . Among my papers received during my absence, found, in

Charleston Mercury of 21st inst. . . . my article sent from Beaufort.[9]

*July 30.* Looking over the newspapers received & accumulated during my absence, & some letters. One from the editor of the New York Day Book, offering, (in accordance with my previous proposition,) to republish my recent article on "Slavery & Free Labor &c." Began to correct the printed *errata*, for this purpose—& to write additions to be inserted in this second edition.—My daughter Mildred made to me an important private communication, of what I had not the least suspicion before—her conditional engagement to marry Mr. Burwell B. Sayre—which we discussed in a long conversation. She is so dear to me, that it would be a great source of grief for me to part with her—& my opinion of her merits is so exalted, that perhaps I should not think any suitor worthy of her. But I would not suffer my selfish wishes to interfere with her happiness, which is my supreme object. In this case, there are obvious objections, and one of the chief is that we know so little of this gentleman. But my daughter is old enough to judge for herself, & her discretion & sound judgment may be relied upon as much as in any like case. I had long determined, in such case, not to oppose any objection of mine, unless of very serious character, such as affecting morals, manners, or very objectionable & near family relations. So far as we know, there is [709] no such ground of objection, (and as to relations, of none now alive) & before frankly stating my opinions & objections in some minor respects, I gave my full consent, should Mildred determine to make her conditional engagement absolute. Still the occurrence causes me to feel much uneasiness & sorrow—which I must try to conceal. . . .

*August 1.* Finished correcting & copying another section, to conclude my long article & the additions to it—to be sent by next mail to the Day Book. I have written to know the cost of a pamphlet edition. . . .

*Aug. 2.* . . . Read half of [Samuel] Nott's pamphlet on "Slavery & its Remedy," & gave it up. He seems to have just general views—most uncommon in a northerner—but so enveloped in diffuse verbiage, that I could gather but a glimmering of his meaning.—Looked through & read parts of the "Abstract of the Census of 1850." This I had examined formerly—but did not know until now that [710] this

---

[9] See Appendix D for the full text of this article, entitled "Cassandra—Warnings."

little abstract had supplied to Mr. [Thornton] Stringfellow[10] all his census statistics bearing on slavery, which he presented in his little book—& which I have made use of, (with due acknowledgment of his previous labor,) in my writing sent this morning to the "Day Book." I read his book "Scriptural & Statistical Views of Slavery" for the second time, when in Richmond on 25th—& was so impressed with the value of his numerical facts, quoted from the census, that I was induced to arrange, & condense, & publish them in a much more concise & also clear form. His statement was long, & the quantities (the most important items,) rendered obscure, & scarcely intelligible to cursory readers, by being expressed in words instead of numerical figures. By substituting the latter, & arranging the figures in a table, I have made the view clear, & also reduced the space occupied to a very small proportion. Also, by thus using, & making more clear his matter, as well as my commendation, I think that I shall bring the author & his little book, into much more notice than before.—Looking over & reading attractive articles of Blackwood's Magazine, & British Reviews received since I left Marlbourne. [711]

*Aug. 3.* . . . . Reading in late Reviews & Blackwood's Magazine. But though this is to me the most attractive of reading, & there is now much that is new, (as Mr. Sayre receives four Reviews & Blackwood's Magazine,) I cannot find pleasure, as formerly, in reading—& can read for nothing but mere present amusement, & that so slightly & skippingly, that I forget almost as fast as I read. . . . Writing only, on some subject of interest to me, affords to me undiminished pleasure, & as long as the particular labor lasts. I wish that I could undertake some long & laborious & engrossing writing, which, though promising completion, would not be finished during my life. Yet I have no inclination to attempt any such extensive work—but only articles, which though too long for newspapers, are too short to occupy me more than a few days, or, at most, a few weeks.—Read a pamphlet on "Free-negroism" in Maryland, by C. W. Jacobs, of Worcester Md., a sensible & good argument, in favor of banishing, or, as the alternative, enslaving the free negroes [712] of that State. Bad as this nuisance is in Virginia, it is far worse in Maryland. Yet emancipation doctrines have so far gained influence there, that there is as little prospect there as here of the nuisance being abated by

---

[10] The Reverend Thornton Stringfellow was a Baptist minister in Culpeper County, Virginia, whose scriptural defense of slavery enjoyed a wide circulation in the 1850's.

proper & stringent legislation. . . . Determined to force myself to begin some piece of writing, for occupation—& decided to undertake the more full treatment of the free negro population & nuisance of Virginia—& made a beginning. In this, I will not pretend to restrain my pen, nor to attempt to be correct in plan or expression—as is more or less the case usually in my writing, designed for publication. Whatever thoughts pertinent to the subject may occur to my mind will be put down, without care of selection, or pruning of superfluities. Nor will I read over & correct the earlier portions, as usual, to keep my subsequent writing strictly confined to the argument, & to avoid repetition, and irregularity of [713] discussion. Wrote a few pages with effort & disinclination.—Reading Lady Blessington's "Conversations with Lord Byron."

*Aug. 6.* Finished Lady Blessington's "Conversations with Lord Byron." There is too much of this book—& I skipped over much of the latter part. It does not serve to raise the reader's estimation of Byron. [714] Dipped into his works—& read his drama "Werner," which I had not read before, & parts of "Sardanapalus" & "Cain" which I had not seen since soon after they were first published. . . . Received from Mr. Williams the last "African Repository," containing a "Review" of, or answer to my attack on the Colonization Society, which I was glad to see, whatever may be its character. . . .

*Aug. 7.* Sunday. Read the Review. It is long, but tame, & contains nothing that I need complain of, or answer. Of course there will be no rejoinder. . . .

*Aug. 9.* . . . The mail. Further details of the disfavor of all Europe, except Austria & her friends, with the Emperor of France & his peace. The publication of the "Southern Citizen" closed, & the editor John Mitchel going to Europe. Sorry for it. . . .

*Aug. 10.* Finished reading "Sardanapalus."—The Whig of yesterday contained the annexed private letter [from Henry A. Wise appealing for support for the 1860 presidential nomination] to one of his political friends in New York, & which, by the simple or treacherous conduct of his correspondent, has got into the newspapers. I was induced to write a comment thereupon, & on the Wises, father & son, this morning, which I sent to the Charleston Mercury for publication.—Read 1st Canto of Don Juan[11]—the second time. But neither that, nor half so much of any poetry have I read in 30 years, before the last few days. [716]

---

[11] Another work by Lord Byron.

*Aug. 13.* . . . Finished reading all that was attractive to me in Westminster Review, & resumed Don Juan. Cannot go on with my writing on hand, for want of inclination. . . . I find that my plan of keeping on hand some article to write in whenever a thought on the subject strikes me, or when not otherwise occupied by business or amusement, will not do for *me*. When I have begun, & am interested in writing any argument, I must keep on—or the interest is lost, & even my remembrance of the last portion, & the general train of thought & reasoning. If I were to write this way, at snatches of spare time, there would be neither method nor force in my words—&, unless, at every resuming of the labor after two or three days intermission, I were to read over what had preceded, I should write twice many parts of the same matter, because forgetting that it had been treated already. On the plan I have lately attempted, & without reading over what had been written, my writing would be little more than roughly noting copious materials, to be subsequently put in shape.

*Aug. 15.* . . . Continued to read Don Juan, though find the latter cantos rather tiresome. Finished the 14th, & gave it up before reading the 15th & last. I read the whole some 30 years ago, when first published. The author ought to have stopped at the end of the 8th Canto. Then all would have been, however objectionable in regard to decency & morality, [718] very interesting, & showing great talent. —Our preparations making for our start tomorrow—though we shall remain in doubt as to our course, until tomorrow's mail.

*Aug. 16.* The mail brought no letter from Alamance, & so we had no course left for us, but to abandon our intention of going there— & so left home to go to the Springs. . . .[12] We reached Richmond at 11 . . . . Saw Mr. Williams, & F. G. Ruffin. Was much concerned to hear from the latter, confidentially, that a duel is impending between young Wise, the editor of the Enquirer, & Wm. Old, the editor of the Examiner, for their writings growing out of the letter of Gov. Wise, lately exposed. The former, as well as his father, is a professional duelist, & a bravo, bully, & designed murderer upon system, & calculation. I hope that the son may yet meet the bloody doom, which he has so well deserved long ago, & the father suffer the remorse that will follow the using his son as his partisan & bravo, & by both

---

[12] The diarist was accompanied on this excursion by his daughter Mildred and granddaughter Nanny.

precept & example, to make him a professional bully for political gain, & a murderer in intention, if not yet in deed.

*Aug. 17.* Left Richmond, on the Central Railroad, at 7 A.M. & reached its present end, at Jackson's River, at 6 P.M. Thence in stages 16 miles [719] to Callaghan's tavern, which we did not arrive at until 10.30. Remained there to sup & lodge.

*Aug. 18.* Left Callaghan's after Breakfast, & reached the White Sulphur Springs before noon. Got better rooms than I had expected, though not as good as we had last summer. About 1200 visitors here now—& the number smaller than some days earlier. Found many acquaintances—among them, Mr. Boulwane, Judge Perkins of La. & his wife, Judge John Robertson of Richmond, Mr. L. Branch of N.C. & lady, our especially valued friend William W. Gilmer of Albemarle—J. D. B. De Bow, Wm. B. Harrison & lady of Prince George —& sundry others. Mildred & Nanny also are meeting with many of their acquaintances—& continually finding others, in the parlor, & afterwards the ballroom—which apartments, enormous as they are, were crowded at different times.

*Aug. 19.* Other of my former acquaintance either first met with, or new arrivals today—among them, Gov. Manning of S.C. Judge [Benjamin F.] Dunkin,[13] Mr. [Henry W.] Conner,[14] of Charleston, Mr. [Francis S.] Lyon[15] of Ala. & my former friends, Mr. Fr. Nixon & J[osiah] T. Granberry, of Perquimans N.C. . . . My whole time pleasurably enough occupied in conversation with the many different acquaintances. But there is so much bustle, & such crowds in the parlor & ballroom, that there has been no opportunity for even quiet conversation, & discussion of any serious topics. Nanny does not join in the dancing, & has no inclination to participate in the whirl of

---

[13] A native of Massachusetts, Dunkin moved to Charleston following his graduation from Harvard in 1811. He soon became one of Charleston's leading lawyers and in 1837 was elected chancellor of the court of equity, a post he held until the Civil War. A strong advocate of states' rights, Judge Dunkin was an active member of the South Carolina Secession Convention. Immediately after the war he served for three years as chief justice of the state supreme court before being ousted by the Radicals.

[14] Henry Workman Conner (1797–1862) was a prominent Charleston banker and railroad executive. An intimate friend of John C. Calhoun, Conner was later elected to the South Carolina Secession Convention where, as the last public act of his life, he signed the Ordinance of Secession.

[15] A former congressman from Alabama, Lyon later served as a delegate to the Charleston Democratic convention of 1860 and was elected to the First and Second Confederate congresses.

fashion & dress. But she is, with all the freshness of youth, delighted to be a spectator, & with her many agreeable old & new acquaintances. The first night I had remained with her & Mildred in the ballroom until 10.30, when the company began to disperse. But this night, as I was tired & sleepy, I left them there at 9, to take care of themselves.—A letter from [John H.] Van Evrie, editor of N.Y. Day Book, informing me that the beginning of my long article had appeared in that paper, & that it would be regularly continued, embracing the two new sections. This will extend its circulation to some 20,000 new readers, north & south. The "Southern Citizen" of John Mitchel, has been merged in the Day Book.

*Aug. 20.* The mail brought . . . the Charleston Mercury of 16th, with my late letter.[16] [721] Among other persons met with, of former acquaintance, were several farmers from N.C., & Dr. [William S.] Plumer, my old friend, though also the great dignitary of the Presbyterian church.[17] I had not before seen him for years. He is now a professor in a Theological Seminary in Allegheny City Pa. He sat at our table, & at once renewed his old familiar acquaintance with Mildred [722] as well as myself. Among new introductions made at different times, are Gen. [Milledge L.] Bonham (M.C.) of South Carolina[18]—Mr. [Jacob] Thompson, Secretary of the Interior Department, & his very agreeable lady. He is very ordinary, in respect to talent. Banks, formerly an editor in Petersburg, & now of the Cincinnati Enquirer, is strongly in favor of Douglas for President, & I doubt not is here as his partizan & secret agent, as well as in the conducting of his paper in Cincinnati.

*Aug. 21.* Sunday. . . . Found a very intelligent & agreeable new acquaintance in Judge Wm. Robertson of Albemarle.[19] Had a long

---

[16] In his communication to the *Mercury,* Ruffin ridiculed the presidential aspirations of Governor Wise.

[17] Doubtless the diarist had known the outstanding Old School leader, William Swan Plumer (1802–80), during the latter's tenure as pastor of the First Presbyterian Church of Richmond, 1834–46. At this time a professor at Western Theological Seminary in Allegheny City, Pennsylvania, Dr. Swan moved to the Columbia Theological Seminary in South Carolina after the Civil War.

[18] Bonham, a veteran of the Seminole and Mexican wars, was elected to Congress in 1857 as a States' Rights Democrat and served until South Carolina seceded from the Union. During the war he was successively commander of the Army of South Carolina, a brigadier general in the Confederate Army, and governor of South Carolina.

[19] A native of Culpeper County, Virginia, William Joseph Robertson (1817–98) was judge of the Supreme Court of Appeals of Virginia from 1859 to 1865. Following the war he was active as a corporation lawyer.

conversation with Gov. Manning of S.C. on political matters, & especially on the policy of re-opening the African slave trade, to which he is strongly opposed, & stated strong reasons of objection, in reference to southern interests. Mr. Boulwane introduced me to Mr. [Charles M.] Conrad of La. formerly U.S. Senator from that state, & afterwards one of Pres. Fillmore's cabinet.[20] He & Boulwane were discussing Gov. Wise, & I joined in very warmly. Boulwane is a personal friend of Wise, & is always very cautious & temperate in his expressions. He defends his motives, & apologizes for some of the results in action, but does not excuse the worst of them. Mr. Conrad & I very nearly agreed in opinion as to the monstrous egotism, self-conceit, & immeasurable ambition, assurance & impudence of Wise. . . .

*Aug. 22.* I learned last night that there was here a returned Liberian colonist, & today I went to see & converse with him. He is acting as bath keeper & attendant. He is a mulatto named Joseph Mackintosh, was born free, & lived in Culpeper county, whence he was induced to go to Liberia. He had before accumulated, & carried with him $1600, of which he brought but little back. He would not be sent out by the Colonization Society, but went at his own cost, so as to be under no obligation or duress. He lived with Roberts, the then President of Liberia, of whom he speaks in kind terms—& must have stood high in the President's [724] favor, as he was appointed by him a judge, & acted as such. He can read, but, of course, was entirely ignorant of law. But he does not appear to doubt his competency to be a good enough judge for the administration of justice in Liberia. But even in this position, he could not remain, & suffer all the disagreeable conditions of residence. He gives a much worse account of the country, & the condition of the colonists, than I had inferred & stated in my pamphlet on Liberia—as to the prevalence of disease—the extortion of the older & richer settlers on the new colonists—& the general discomforts & discontent. He returned, & before coming to Virginia, spent some weeks in Canada —where he also found the condition of the free blacks & fugitive slaves very deplorable. When he came to his old home, those gentle-

---

[20] Born in Winchester, Virginia, Conrad (1804–78) moved to Louisiana at an early age and represented that state in both houses of Congress before assuming the post of secretary of war under President Fillmore. Later, he was a member of the Provisional Confederate Congress at Montgomery and served in both the First and Second Confederate congresses.

men who knew him before, & respected him for his good conduct, obtained for him the legal privilege, & exception of the general prohibition to remain in Virginia. He greatly prefers his present menial employment, or any other service of labor, to his judgeship in Liberia. Moreover, he told me that if the threatened measure should ever be enacted, of banishing all the free negroes, or otherwise allowing them to enslave themselves, he will go to Mr. Jeremiah Morton & ask him to make him his body servant—& of course his slave. One of our party, to hear Mackintosh's statement, was Mr. Alexr. Little, editor of the Fredericksburg "News," who designs to publish the substance.—Nothing yet heard of the issue of the designed duel, between Old & Wise, & general anxiety felt thereupon. This result of Gov. Wise's exposed letter is the great subject of interest here, [725] & throughout Virginia—as is the letter itself, in other states. Nothing, of so little intrinsic importance, has made more noise, or drawn forth from the newspaper press in general so many comments, & nearly all of condemnation, stern rebuke, or ridicule. It is to be hoped that, if he stood any chance before (which I do not believe) for even a respectable support for the presidential nomination, that this letter will effectually destroy his prospects. But that, & all his worse offences of writing, are nothing in comparison to the using his son as his daily advocate, as editor of a newspaper, & as the bravo to bully, or if he cannot put down by bullying, to fight, & aim to kill, every man who strongly opposes his father's course & efforts.... [726]

*Aug. 23.* News of the duel, but very meager in details. The parties met at Bladensburg, fired twice, without hitting, & then left the ground—as reported, not making any adjustment of the quarrel. Col. J[ames S.] Deas[21] of Mobile arrived today—& all the [Virginia] Board of Public Works, Gen. Clay, Dr. [Zedekiah] Kidwell,[22] & Alex[ander R.] Holladay.[23] Many other arrivals, & more persons now here than at any time before.—Many persons are calling to see Mackintosh, to hear his Liberian experiences. My report of him has made him quite a "lion." If he was in Yankee land, under the like

---

[21] Formerly a militia colonel in South Carolina, James Sutherland Deas moved to Mobile in 1835 and in the late 1850's was elected to the Alabama Senate.

[22] Following two terms in the United States House of Representatives, Dr. Kidwell was appointed in 1857 to the board of public works. He was a graduate of Jefferson Medical College in Philadelphia and a resident of Fairmont, Virginia.

[23] Also a former two-term congressman, Holladay was president of the board of public works from 1857 to 1861.

circumstances, he would go straight to delivering public addresses, or a course of lectures on Liberia.

*Aug. 24.* Col. J. Ferguson, my former acquaintance in S.Ca., with his family, arrived yesterday.—Had a long conversation, in my room, with Col. J. Deas, on the calcareous soils of Ala. & incidental matters.—A "Fancy Ball" is to come off tonight, & all the ladies who are to figure in it are busy preparing their costumes, & others, who are not, assisting to prepare their friends. Mildred & Nanny are among these assistants. According to the advertised terms, which admitted young ladies only in some fancy costume, they were excluded from the ballroom, as spectators—& I should not have cared to go except to allow them to be there. But an exception was made in our favor, & I bought a ticket, & carried my daughter & granddaughter to look upon the gay scene & fantastic dresses of the men, & the beautiful & tasteful dresses of many of the young ladies, until we were tired, & then retired before 11 o'clock. The[re] was no pretension to acting the assumed characters, except partially in a few cases. Generally there was the absurdity of the mingling in the dances of characters the most unsuitable for that amusement—& of partners who represented characters who never [727] possibly could have come together. Among other arrivals, & to whom I have been introduced, are Judge Guyanne of La., & Judge [Charles P.] Daly of N.Y.[24] My old acquaintance John Baldwin of Staunton arrived tonight. I am sorry to hear from him that he cannot comply with the request of our Executive Committee, to deliver the next annual address. I must immediately write to Gov. Hammond, the second choice.

*Aug. 25.* . . . This day was the designed limit of our stay, & we prepared, with regret, to leave so many pleasant acquaintances. At 3 P.M. we left, with 4 coaches, of which nearly all of the passengers went to the Old Sweet Springs. We stopped at the Red Sweet Springs, which we prefer in every respect, & especially as the more quiet place. This however is nearly full, having nearly 300 visitors. The register shows no names, among late arrivals, of any of our distant friends—and but a few families of late acquaintance arrived before us from the White Sulphur Springs. I fear we shall not find many agreeable companions. . . .

*Aug. 26.* Walked over to the Old Sweet Springs, where I found

---

[24] Judge Daly, a member of the New York constitutional conventions of 1846 and 1867, was one of the foremost members of the New York bar and the author of a judicial history of his state.

sundry acquaintances, & made some pleasant new ones. Among the former, Mr. Boulwane (who came with us yesterday) Thos. Ruffin (M.C.) of N.Ca. Engaged with some South Carolinians & others in a disunion discussion. When returned, saw Mr. & Mrs. Branch, who are the only agreeable people I have yet found here, except Prof. Cabell & his wife. More letters by the mail today for Mildred & Nanny, [728] & some to me, forwarded from Old Church. One from Gov. Hammond, in which he intimates an intention to resign his seat in the Senate of U.S. before the next session. . . . So far, I find this place dull, & it is worse for Nanny. There are but few young girls here, & but one of them of her acquaintance. . . .

*Aug. 27.* Received a letter from Willoughby Newton. He & Hammond both oppose my argument that the high price of slaves is injurious to agricultural interests—& on different grounds.—Mr. Boulwane & Mr. Ruffin came over from the Sweet Springs, to call on my ladies.—Among the new arrivals some of my acquaintance—but none whose company I desire. . . . Had bought in Richmond, & today finished the reading of the latest volume of travels of an Englishman in the United States—Charles Mackay's "Life & Liberty in America." [25] He shows a more liberal feeling to the government & people, on the whole, than most of his predecessors, but on the subject of negro slavery, he is scarcely less blind [729] than most others. Yet he admits the greater hardships & misery of the laborers of his own country, (slaves of competition & hunger,) & that our negroes have more physical & sensual enjoyment than his own poor countrymen. He is so far carried by his bigotry, that after assuming an existing inferiority of the southern to the northern states in the production of literary works, & especially of poetry & other writings of imagination, he ascribes the deficiency to the presence of slavery! and pronounces that high literary pursuits & productions are incompatible with the existence of slavery. Even if his premises were true, it is strange that he entirely forgot the examples of Greece & Rome, & their poets, & orators. But in truth, he set out with a wrong estimate & comparison, which he learned, like all his other prepossessions in the northern cities, before he entered the southern states. It is true

---

[25] While editor of *Illustrated London News*, the Scottish song writer and journalist Charles Mackay (1814–89) had visited the United States and Canada in 1857 on a lecture tour. During the Civil War he had another opportunity to observe American society while living in New York as a correspondent for the London *Times*.

that the north has been much more productive than the south in poetry & light literature of high order of merit—& still more in works of fiction of low order & character, & in all literary productions written for pay & support of the writer. Writing for gain is a business not yet begun in the southern states. But even without that incentive or reward, our productions on the far higher subjects of government, philosophical argument, & politics, are as far above any of the north, as are southern statesmen superior to those of the north.—Began to read "White Lies," a new novel by Charles Reade.[26]

*Aug. 28.* Sunday. A drizzly & dull day. J[ohn] R[euben] Thompson, the *literateur* [sic] & editor of the Literary Messenger is here.... This bad weather has cut off [730] the pleasant interchange of visits, & the walking, between this place & the Sweet Springs, which are less than a mile apart. I had avoided going to the forenoon preaching, because of my unconquerable bad habit of sleeping at snatches during the service. At night I went, trusting that the dim light would conceal my offence. As usual, there was occasion for such concealment.

*Aug. 29.* Rode over to the Sweet Springs. Saw some of my acquaintances, & was introduced to others. As usual when talking with men of the states south of N.C. the conversation with some of these turned upon the secession of the southern states—I advocating my plan of the secession of but a portion, say 4 to 8 of the more southern states, & thus forcing the more northern of the south to follow, after they have served as a protecting barrier to the others, & so prevented all chance of collision & bloodshed.—Finished reading "White Lies." It is said on the title-page to be by Charles Reade—& no suggestion of any other source. But I would be willing to swear that it was written by a Frenchman, & in France. No English or American author could conceive, or describe, such characters & incidents. It is stated in such manner as to be interesting, though the plot is foolish, & the morality (as designed in good faith,) is very French.

*Aug. 30.* Mildred ... left this morning [731] for Richmond & Marlbourne. She went with Mr. Wynne, formerly tutor in my son's family, & a valued acquaintance & friend of us all. The parting with my

---

[26] The English novelist and dramatist Charles Reade (1814–84) is perhaps best remembered for his work *The Cloister and the Hearth* (1861), which appeared four years after *White Lies* was serialized in the London *Journal*. In his novels Reade attacked the social abuses of his time.

most beloved & always loving daughter was especially painful to me, inasmuch as she is about to marry, & I shall never again see her in the same intimate & exclusive relation to me that has heretofore subsisted. I cannot help feeling, with grief, that she will be separated from me, even if remaining in the same locality—& that seeds of alienation are already sown (in previously existing as well as new circumstances,) between her own family, & that of her intended husband.

*Aug. 31.* Among my interesting new acquaintances, are Mr. [Lucius Q. C.] De Yampert & Mr. [John] Walthall, planters of Alabama.[27] Of old acquaintances among the late arrivals, Dr. S. W. Barker of South Carolina, & Dr. Whitten of Ga. Some of these are at the Sweet Springs—but we walk from one place to the other every fair day. Nanny received a letter from her father stating that he will be here, as we had before expected, tomorrow. Col. [J. J.] Williams of Florida arrived, an old acquaintance of mine.

*September 1.* Edmund arrived at 1 P.M., bringing his son George, for his health. . . . We awaited Edmund's arrival for him to decide where it would be best for Nanny to go. It is decided that they will go to the White Sulphur Springs tomorrow, & I will go with them. The former crowd there has been reduced to about one-third of the number. . . . [732]

*Sept. 2.* We left the Red Springs at 7 A.M. & reached the White Sulphur at 11. About 500 visitors remaining. . . . Found among the guests Henry K. Burgwynn [Burgwyn of N.C.], & was introduced [733] to the latest ex-governor of Alabama, [John A.] Winston,[28] who agrees with me entirely as to the policy of the secession of the southern states.

*Sept. 4.* Sunday. Heard last night that the celebrated Whig editor, & "fighting preacher" [William G.] Brownlow, of Knoxville, was here. I made his acquaintance this morning. His conversation is very entertaining, & his language forcible. . . .

*Sept. 5.* Mr. Brownlow gave me a copy of the volume containing

---

[27] De Yampert, a Methodist minister as well as planter, resided at his country estate, Montevallo, in Hale County, Alabama. Walthall was born in Amelia County, Virginia, but moved to Alabama in 1820 and acquired large tracts of land.

[28] After some years as a leader of the states' rights faction in the Alabama Senate, John Anthony Winston (1812–71), a planter and cotton factor, was elected governor in 1853 and reelected to that high office two years later.

the public discussion on slavery, carried on by him & the abolitionist preacher [Abraham] Pryne, in Philadelphia.[29] I am reading it with great interest. He has also aided me, by his [734] acquaintance with & communication of facts in regard to the history & division of the Methodist church, by which I am much furthered in a work on foot. The company of proprietors of the White Sulphur Springs had publickly offered to give deeds for lots of ground for either of five named protestant denominations, & among them the "Methodist Church." Now since the great separation of that former one Church, into the present two churches "North" & "South" upon the question of slavery, the Baltimore Conference adhered to the North, & within its bounds was embraced all northern Virginia including this part of the country. So the "Methodist Church North" took possession of the lot of ground, have begun to build the church edifice, & the agent has begged & obtained several thousand dollars from contributors. Among those so giving their money liberally, were sundry visitors here from lower Va. who neither heard nor suspected that they were aiding to strengthen an abolitionist religious association, & that too to the exclusion of the "Methodist Church South." My old friend Williams Carter thus had promised $50, but luckily had not paid it. I worked hard with him to persuade him not to comply with an engagement obtained by false pretences, or concealment of facts. He has so agreed, & requested me to write a letter stating his declining, which I have done, & which he will copy & send from himself. In the mean time, the facts have been talked about, are making a noise here. Judge Perkins & Col. Wm. Whitehead had protested against the proceeding to the principal proprietors, & they are now alarmed, thinking that we will [735] denounce the matter through the press, & that the place will be injured in public estimation. I have tried to excite & to keep up this ferment—& have allowed them to expect ( as others have intimated to them,) that I, as well as Brownlow, if not others, will expose the facts in the newspapers. Brownlow I hope will. *I* have no such intention, though willing they shall expect it.

---

[29] In his celebrated debate with Pryne, a Congregational minister and abolitionist editor, "Parson" Brownlow vociferously defended the institution of slavery as it existed in the South. The subject "Ought American Slavery to be Perpetuated?" was discussed by the two men before numerous auditors at the Philadelphia National Guard Hall on five consecutive evenings in September, 1858. Though a warm advocate of slavery, Brownlow was the leading Tennessee Unionist during the war and served as governor and later as United States senator during Reconstruction.

They cannot take back their promise to give the lot, & its privileges. But as it was offered & promised to the "Methodist Church" without distinction of its separated factions, I have suggested to some of them that the deed shall be so worded as to give equal rights to both the churches, "North" & "South," & also require the approval of the Directory of every preacher sent to occupy the pulpit. This will comply with their general engagement, & as far (as to right of property) as they ever had designed or thought of at first, & yet will prevent the abolition branch having exclusive possession. But the whole matter about this particular church building is of but small account —& I am using it not so much for itself, as to draw more attention to the strange & great abuse, in a religious association, avowedly hostile to negro slavery, having sway over a large portion of the territory of Virginia.—A steady rainy day, after two preceding of intermitting rains—making the place & company much less gay than usual.

*Sept. 7.* Every day there are new arrivals, but less in number than the departures by more than half. I am getting very weary of this place. . . . Finished reading "Ought Slavery in America to be perpetuated &c.," the volume of controversial speeches of Parsons Brownlow & Pryne. It is entertaining—& also instructive, especially to display the usual manner of argument, & what they deem their strongest grounds, of the northern abolitionists. But it is obvious that the two disputants had previously prepared their arguments, & that neither troubled himself much to answer his opponent. Both deal much more in loose declaration than in close & strict reasoning & evidence. Brownlow declaims with great force, & originality of expression—& Pryne with much eloquence in depicting, as he believes them to be, the horrors & iniquities of slavery in the South.—Among the latter arrivals here, are old Mr. De Yampert, of Ala, & his son & daughters. I made his acquaintance at the Red Sweet, as a good & large planter of Ala, & an intelligent & estimable gentleman. I now learn, what I did not suspect before, that he is a methodist preacher of long standing.

*Sept. 8.* Col. Charles Haskell of S.C. & his lady, whom I had visited at their home in Abbeville district, arrived, [737] with his brother, who had married the daughter of Dr. Bachman, & who died when I was last in the South. I hastened to renew my acquaintance with them—& afterwards introduced them to others. Mrs. Haskell is a daughter of Langdon Cheves.—The company reduced, as said, to 200—& they seem not half so many. I was so much at a loss for

[339]

amusement, that this morning I began to copy & correct my last written piece, on Free Negroes &c.

*Sept. 10.* We left at 6 A.M. & were nearly to sunset, including stoppages, reaching the Healing Springs. Found there some 10 or 12 of my acquaintance—including Messrs. Wm. P. & John Taylor, & George Minge, & their wives, Messrs. Granberry & J. C. Johns[t]on of N.C., Judge Robertson of Albemarle.

*Sept. 12.* Made the acquaintance of, & had a long conversation with Barney Reybold, a visitor from Delaware, on the economical condition of his state, especially in regard to their numerous free negroes, who are 18,000, to only 2000 slaves. He deems them a bad population, & their faults & vices very much as they are here. [738] But at the same time, they supply so much of the present amount of labor, that this class could not be dispensed with.

*Sept. 13.* Finished the alterations & copying of my writing, & now I am impatient to have it printed, & before the public, & especially the members of the Virginia legislature, & of the other southern legislatures. My plan for removing the nuisance of free negroes has grown on my favor with the progress of my writing—& especially the entirely novel consequence of the main measure, the compelling the northern states to forbid the entrance of our negroes, & so to make the abolition states the effectual police force to execute the federal fugitive slave law, & to secure our property in slaves, & to maintain the integrity of the institution of negro slavery. I have mentioned this idea to sundry intelligent gentlemen of those whom I have met with since my leaving home—and there was not one to whom it was not entirely novel, & who did not also admit that the remedy for restraining the practical operations of abolitionists did not seem likely to be effective.—We have determined to leave tomorrow, & I may perhaps proceed at once to Richmond rather than pass a dull day in stopping, as Edmund intends, at the Warm Springs.

*Sept. 14.* Left the Healing Springs in stage coach—passing by Hot & Warm & Bath Alum Springs to Millborough station on Rail Road, & thence to Staunton, where we slept. . . .

*Sept. 15.* Reached Richmond at 2.30 P.M., & went to the Exchange [739] Hotel. . . . Began to negotiate to obtain the publication of my last writing. I wish to secure a pamphlet edition, from the same type-setting, as well as a newspaper publication. The latter alone would be easy enough to obtain.

*Sept. 16.* A steady drizzle throughout the day. Went to the State

Library, to look for some statistical facts as to the proportion of felonies committed by free negroes. Very unexpectedly I met with Gov. Wise. He returned my salutation so stiffly, that the next time we meet he shall speak first, or there will be no speaking between us. . . . A letter from Gov. Hammond, declining (as I feared he would,) to deliver the Anniversary Address to the Agr. Society. We find great difficulty to dispose of this honor.—I could not get ready to go home with Mr. [William H.] Harrison this afternoon when he went, but have promised to follow him tomorrow. I have long been wishing to pay him a visit—& now have time, when he also is at leisure, during the vacation of his school. . . .

*Sept. 17. . . .* Made an arrangement by which [740] my writing will first be published in the Southern Planter, & thence transferred to pamphlet form—so that I can have as many pamphlet copies as I shall want for distribution, at the cost of the latter printing only —or without any charge for composition. . . . At 4 P.M. I took the Danville train for Amelia. Mr. Harrison met me on the way, & we went to Lewis E. Harvie's & remained through the night. Much of our conversation on Gov. Wise's & his son's delinquencies.

*Sept. 19.* Wrote some additional notes to my free negro article. Spent the day in conversation mostly, either sitting or walking, with Mr. Harrison. . . . William Harrison is a singular & remarkable man, & also one of the most estimable. His father, Edmund Harrison (my father's first cousin,) had been possessor of a large estate, in Amelia, all his life, & had lived in suitable manner. By unfortunate purchase, & bad management, in the latter part of his life, his estate was so impaired, that after his death, it was found to be insolvent. He left a widow [741] & six children, of whom William, the oldest, was not grown. He had been, to that time, well educated. By the aid of a loan from that excellent man, Gen. John H. Cocke, (our kinsman,) he obtained means to complete his education at the University of Virginia. He then returned to Amelia, & opened a classical & mathematical school. He was thus enabled, & succeeded, in supporting first his mother, & his brothers & sisters—& also in giving excellent educations to most of the latter, qualifying them for teachers, which employment most of them afterwards undertook, & filled with honor & usefulness. Before this service was nearly gone through, he had married, & had a fast growing family of his own, of which the older children have been, or are being educated in the best manner. And while thus so long bearing these burdens of expense, & having nothing but what his own labor brought in, he has been able to accumulate enough to become the possessor of a large & valuable farm, well stocked, & is altogether in good circumstances, & his income now free from nearly all incumbrances, except the support of his own family.... Our families, though related, were so far separated, & had been for so long a time apart, that I did not know William Harrison until after I was 45, & he nearly 30 years of age. But no sooner was our acquaintance made than I learned to love him, & still more & more to esteem [742] him, as I gradually learned, from the report of others, the conduct that so much deserves esteem & admiration. He appears to be as happy in his family relations as any person can be—having an excellent, attractive, & agreeable wife, & eight children, all of sound body & mind.

*Sept. 20.* A steady rain, gradually increasing, & after dark, (& some intermission,) very heavy. We had arranged before we had parted in Richmond, to return there today—which Mr. Harrison was compelled to, by a business appointment made.... So we drove 10 miles through the (then slow) rain to the nearest station on the railroad, & before 4 P.M. set out on the train for Richmond. At the Exchange Hotel found Mr. De Yampert, & his son & daughter —& sundry other persons whom I had known at the Springs, & who have just arrived thence. Went to my room early, & wrote & read.

*Sept. 21....* Saw Mr. Williams, (who now is acting editor of the Southern Planter,) & the printer, & saw the beginning of the setting up of my article. Called on & saw Thomas Giles, to learn from him about some writings of his father, Gov. Wm. B. Giles, in support of the power of a state to impose discriminating license taxes. Obtained the loan of a volume of his writings, containing some incidental opinions to this effect—but not as much to the purpose as I had hoped for.... Went to the State Library, & found other statistical facts, suitable for proofs, to be used as notes....

*Sept. 22.* Began last night, & finished this forenoon, reading in part, & glancing over the remainder of [Hinton Rowan Helper's] "The Impending Crisis," an anti-slavery volume, which has been made much of at the North, because written by a North-Carolinian. He left home because guilty of, & detected in, stealing from his employer, & going to the North, sought & gained favor there by denouncing & calumniating his southern country & countrymen. It is an ultra violent assault on negro slavery—a collection of every such opinion uttered by distinguished characters, of every argument, &

every statement, true or false. Much the greater part is of false opinions or facts, & weak or foolish arguments. [744]—Saw Harvie. Pryor has been nominated for Congress, by a District Convention. He has gained great favor, but none with me.—Received a letter from Mildred, & answered it. She will be married to Mr. Burwell B. Sayre, on Oct. 4th. I had waited for this letter—& as there is nothing required for my daughter's service that I should now be at Marlbourne, I shall go tomorrow to Prince George Co. to stay until near the time to go to attend the marriage. It will be to me a very painful duty. . . .

*Sept. 23.* Left Richmond at 6 A.M. on the steamer. The river so high that the wharves were covered. Landed at Maycox, & hired a boat to carry me across the creek to Coggin's Point, whence I walked to the Beechwood house. . . .

*Sept. 26.* . . . The mail brought very concise telegraphic news of importance. The English & French squadron of steamers, on their way up the river [blank], carrying the ambassadors of these two countries to Pekin, were stopped by the Chinese, & a fight ensued in which the European forces were repelled, & 500 of the English killed. If true, this must bring on a renewal of the late war, & a much more serious contest, & important changes in the issue. It seems that the American minister, who went under the sanction of a treaty similar to those concluded between the Chinese government & England & France, had proceeded without molestation, & was [746] in Pekin. This will be very important for American interests. It is to be hoped that the result of all these difficulties, as well as of the amicable negotiations, will be soon to open the great Chinese empire to the commerce & intercourse of the civilized world, from both of which it has so long been self-excluded. The recently opened access to Japan will also, in a few years, begin to show great & beneficial results. Though our treaty with that power has authorized the first foreign commerce, some years ago, there has been scarcely any trade as yet. But the intercourse with our naval & civil officials, & the friendly & frequent visits of our ships of war, have served to allay previous jealousy & fears, & to impress the Japanese with the great value of the improvements of art & science, offered by America & Europe, & of which they are anxious & ready to avail themselves.—The great recent event, has been the actual departure from the Thames, & successful passage & performance of the gigantic iron steamer, the "Great Eastern," of some [blank] feet in length, & of 30,000 tons in capacity. This is but a trial & short voyage, to Portland in England, whence she will soon set out for this country. If the performance of this enormous steamer shall equal the confident expectations, it will produce a great & speedy revolution in ocean steam navigation. There is also in the course of preparation, in New York, a balloon, which in size exceeds all prior balloons, as much as the Great Eastern exceeds all prior ships, [747] in which the attempt will be made to cross the Atlantic ocean. But, even if successful, such aerial voyages will never become useful or common, owing to the enormous expense, & risk of life. . . .

*Sept. 27.* Finished reading Dr. [William Ellery] Channing's essay on the character of Napoleon Bonaparte. He seems to have truly appreciated this great bad man.—After dinner rode to Julian's, & missed his carriage bringing all the family to Beechwood. Awaited their return, & staid all night, as I had designed. Continuation of consultation as to Mildred's business matters, & the new complications in regard to the Marlbourne property.

*Sept. 29.* . . . After early breakfast, left Beechwood, & drove to Petersburg. . . . Saw & conferred with Charles Friend Chairman of the Ex. Com. of the Union Society, in reference to the arrangements for our joint Fair. At 5.30 P.M. left on the train, & reached Richmond by 7. . . .

When riding this morning from Beechwood, I read Dr. Channing's "Moral Argument against Calvinism." It was the first article of theology, or controversy, on this subject that I had ever read—& also the first theological writing of any kind by a Unitarian. This however, contains nothing of the views peculiar to that sect. Able as is the argument, it added nothing to the strength of my previous opinions of & objections to Calvinism, & which would not be & had not been before raised by the simple enunciation of the fundamental doctrines, (or the "five points" of Calvinism,) as adopted by the Synod of Dort, & universally recognized by Calvinistic divines & their followers. Before reading Dr. Channing's opposing argument, all the evidences, citations of passages of scripture, & reasoning & deductions therefrom, that could be adduced, would never make me believe that the all-beneficent & benevolent & merciful creator of mankind should have doomed the greater number, from & because of the first offence & fall of Adam, & irrespective of their acts in life, to misery & tortures from which the most cruel monsters among mankind would have shrunk from [750] inflicting (if possible to be inflicted,) on their worst & most hated enemies. If Nero, or Domitian, or a king of Ashantee or Dahomey, could execute on millions of millions the vengeance or torture to which they could & did subject a few thousands only of their subjects—if they could have increased those tortures to the utmost that human life could exist under for a few minutes, & then could have extended them to eternity—if, further, these tortured victims were selected without regard to their conduct, and it was impossible for them by any acts to avoid their fate—such extended, unlimited, & immeasurable injustice & cruelty would barely equal that which [is] ascribed by the Calvinistic creed to the all benevolent God of Christianity! And this God, made up of wrath against his unborn & innocent creatures, of injustice, of ferocious love of cruelty, is professed to be loved by his worshippers, with a devotion exceeding all other sentiments! I would as soon believe that the victims of the most bloody, unjust, & cruel persecutors could be loved & reverenced by their victims, in the moments of their greatest sufferings. There is nothing of iniquity ascribed to Satan, in my opinion, that is worse than the Calvinistic creed ascribes to the Almighty & all-merciful God—& nothing in Satan that would forbid his receiving all the amount of love & veneration professed to be given to God, provided that Satan was only believed to have become possessed [of] the supreme power of God.

*Sept. 30.* Left Richmond at 4 A.M. in the mail coach, & reached Old Church by 7, & walked the short distance to Marlbourne before any of the family or visitors were out of their beds. Found Charles there, & also Mr. Burwell Sayre & his daughter [751] Virginia, by his former marriage. The two Messrs. Sayre had returned last night from an unsuccessful trip up James River, to look at an estate for sale. . . . I try to put the best face on things—but I cannot help feeling wretchedly. This approaching marriage, in forming new & close connections for my daughter, will operate more or less to weaken hers before existing, because the two whole families cannot assimilate. This would be, even if her locality should be unchanged. But much more so, when this marriage is but the first step to the removal of both my daughters from their present residence at Marlbourne, & their probable future removal to some distant land in the southwest! Mr. Wm. Sayre, for himself, & brother, had before proposed to my sons, the other joint owners of the Marlbourne estate, to buy out their shares. And as they declined thus to sell, & divest themselves of their patrimony, he then offered to sell, & required them to buy—the alternative being necessarily the sale to a stranger buyer. In either case, it is understood that the brothers will seek a new & distant settlement. . . .

*October 1.* Mr. Williams had sent me the proofsheet of the first portion of my article on Free Negroes, in the Southern Planter— which I corrected this morning, & returned by mail. I ordered 2000 extra copies in pamphlet form, to [752] be printed for me.—Mr. B. Sayre left last evening on business preparatory to his marriage. All the five joint owners of Marlbourne discussing the proposed changes of their business relations, & the terms of the proposed sale of two-fifths of the property to others of the owners.—The parties came to an agreement as to valuation, much more readily than I had expected. The terms were settled, & Mildred's sale of her portion completed, the bonds for payment & the deed executed before night. Also the same bargain made with Mr. Wm. Sayre, for his selling to Julian, but of which the writings are yet to be executed, & for which there was not now time. The marriage settlement also executed— for which Mildred makes over her property in trust to William Sayre, the brother of her intended husband, as sole trustee. This has been a busy & laborious day to my sons—& a dismal one to me & to my daughters. . . .

*Oct. 4.* This the day for the marriage. A dismal time for me, & especially from the time that the invited guests began to arrive, to the last departure. The marriage took place at noon. After a collation, about 2 P.M. the married couple left for a tour to the north —& in half an hour more, Edmund, Julian, Nanny [754] & I also set out for Richmond—Nanny to stop & attend the ceremonies of the General Episcopal Convention for the U.S., which begins its sessions tomorrow, & the others to proceed to Prince George. The Hotels so full of strangers, that I could scarcely obtain a place at the Exchange. Met several acquaintances from remote places—among them Mr. Lawton of Charleston, & Gov. Winston & Mr. W. P. Bocock of Ala. . . . I heard Mildred last night play some of her beautiful anthems, which I so much love, on her Melodeon. Probably it will be the last time of my hearing her perform on that instrument, or in that house. If I had died five years ago, how much of unhappiness would have been escaped! [End of MS Volume 4—p. 755]

*Oct. 5.* We left Richmond very early, Julian through Petersburg for home, & Edmund & I by the steamer. A heavy fog delayed our setting out, & we reached Beechwood not much before 1 P.M. It seemed strange to enter this house, & find no one except the servants. . . . After 5 P.M. Edmund & I drove to Ruthven, to stay the night. . . . Julian has been unwell, & returns home still more so. He has been far from well for some time—& yet, having no overseer, is burdened with the labor & exposure required for superintending his farm.

*Oct. 9*. . . . Gloomy weather, & still more dull time. I have plenty of books, & read most of my time when not in bed. But I tire even of light reading, & I cannot resort to anything more agreeable. Charles came to dinner. He also has [757] determined & agreed to sell out his 5th share of the Marlbourne property, at the recent valuation, (for purchase from Mr. Sayre & from Mildred,) to Edmund & Julian, who will thus become possessors of the whole.

*Oct. 10*. . . . I had appointed (with Mr. Williams) & therefore must go today to Richmond, to correct the last proofs, & to finish the pamphlet on hand.—Left the shore at 12, & reached Richmond soon after 4 P.M. Saw Mr. Williams. No orator obtained. Wrote to ask the service of Willoughby Newton. Corrected last proofsheet of pamphlet. . . . My trip here has been useless as to business. I could as well have corrected the proof at home—& there is no prospect of the printing of the pamphlet being completed very soon.

*Oct. 11*. Almost nothing either to amuse or to occupy myself about —unless to attend the sitting of the Episcopal Convention, or the church services, for which I have no inclination. Saw Harvie & F. Ruffin, for very short times—and my good old friend Gen. John H. Cocke. . . .

*Oct. 13*. I returned to Beechwood. Read portions of Gov. Giles' writings from 1824 to '29. Much on the subjects of slavery & the Colonization Society. While there were numerous truths, [758] then scarcely known to any, perceived & uttered by this far-seeing statesman, even he then concurred in the almost universal opinion that negro slavery was an evil—& hoped & expected that Virginia would finally be cleared of that evil.—Looking over census tables in reference to slavery statistics.

*Oct. 17*. . . . The mail brought information that my early contemporary & associate, Judge John Y. Mason, minister to France, had died.[30] He was a man who had throughout his life the good fortune

---

[30] A native Virginian, John Young Mason served three terms in Congress in the 1830's and was then appointed successively to the positions of secretary of the navy, attorney general of the United States, and United States minister to France. He died in Paris on October 3, 1859.

always to be estimated for much more ability than he possessed, & to be raised to high official posts, & to retain them, more because of affable & pleasant manners than of talents necessary for any of his political stations.—50 copies of my pamphlet had been sent to me . . . , & I have mailed them to distinguished persons, mostly out of Va, & in different legislatures of southern states. Others were ordered to be sent to all the governors of slaveholding states, & to all the members of the Va. legislature.

*Oct. 18.* I have latterly felt more the want of occupation than since my giving up business. Since my last writing was completed, I [have] not undertaken, or designed to undertake any other, & have no object whatever to strive for. We three who only are here now seem to have exhausted all subjects for conversation—& fond of reading as I am, I cannot take pleasure in reading all day, & day after day. I fear that I am now about to enter that condition of idleness & wearisomeness which I always dreaded—& which I have until now kept off by keeping my mind occupied with some study or pursuit. I had promised to pay a visit to Alabama as soon as our State Fair is over, & my being released from my engagements [760] in that connection. But I already feel disinclined to make the necessary exertion. If I had not promised sundry friends that I would make this visit, I should abandon the intention. Already I feel it disagreeable to make any exertion to seek either pleasure or employment, though I know it to be more necessary than ever before. I have lived long enough—& a little more time of such unused & wearisome passage of time will make my life too long.

*Oct. 19.* A letter from Willoughby Newton stating his consent to deliver the Address—of which I am very glad.—The papers bring news of remarkable events, for our usually quiet & calm population in Va. An insurrection occurred at Harper's Ferry, on the night following last Sunday. The insurgents overawed the people of the village, compelled them to remain within their houses, if not made prisoners—took forcible possession of the U.S. Armory & public property, killed & wounded some of the functionaries, stopped the railroad trains, cut the telegraph wires, & made prisoners (as if for hostages,) of respectable neighbors, on their farms, several miles off. They were enlisting or forcing others, both white & black, into their ranks. The insurgents were reported to be 250 or 300—greatly exaggerated, I suppose. Who they were, or what their object, was only guessed at. Armed forces were ordered to move, as soon as the outbreak was heard of, by both the governor of Va, & the President of U.S. The neighboring militia & volunteers soon recaptured the village; & when reinforced, the [761]strong-hold of the insurgents, the U.S. Armory, was stormed, & all the insurgents killed, wounded, or taken prisoners. There were only about 20, of which 15 were killed, & of the remaining prisoners, 2 only were not wounded. Several of the assailants were killed & more wounded. Some few of the insurgents had previously gone northward, taking some negroes with them. But of all yet known of those engaged, their number & their means were as contemptible, as the effort was remarkable for boldness & temerity. All the actors are northerners & new-comers—even the few negroes. And incredible as it seemed at first naming, by rumor, it really seems now most probable that the outbreak was planned & instigated by northern abolitionists, & with the expectation of thus starting a general slave insurrection. I earnestly hope that such may be the truth of the case. Such a practical exercise of abolition principles is needed to stir the sluggish blood of the south. —Wrote some additional items of statistics for my before published article on "Slavery & Free Labor, defined & compared," in case there should be another publication.

*Oct. 21*. . . . The mail brought additional particulars of the late outbreak at Harper's Ferry, but no later occurrences after the suppression. There are evidences, with the confession of the leader, Brown, that the plan had long [762] [been] laid by Northern abolitionists. Arms, Sharps rifles, revolvers, & pikes (for slaves) were provided for several thousand men, & which were all found in Brown's house, in the neighborhood. Every one of the party, white or black, was from the northern & north-western states. . . .

*Oct. 22*. . . . Temp. this morning 27°.—Rode after breakfast to see Julian, in his field, as I knew that Lotty & her children had gone to visit her relatives in Petersburg. This had enabled Julian to add nearly all of his house force to the field laborers. I found him busily at work [763] with his negroes, in his shirt sleeves. After staying with him some time, I returned to dinner. . . .

*Oct. 23*. Sunday. . . . The recent outbreak at Harper's Ferry is subject for astonishment to every one—for the long continued & extensive preparation of means & especially of arms, the audacity & first success of the few insurgents, & their utter & sudden defeat. . . .

*Oct. 24*. . . . The mail brought nothing new in the great mass of details, repetitions & contradictory statements, in regard to the Harper's Ferry out-break. The so-called "republican" (or abolition) newspapers of the North, so far as heard from make no comments hostile to the actors & instigators. I trust that this diabolical attempt will arouse the southern people to use new & better means both for precaution, & resistance & punishment to abolition action. [764]—Political agitation & troubles seem not to be subsiding in Central Italy —but on the contrary, more threatening than before. I trust that there will be a speedy outbreak against the Austrian & Papal powers, & that Garibaldi will be the head of the movement.

*Oct. 26.* . . . The trials of the few of the insurgents who still remain alive, have already been commenced, in Jefferson county. Besides the outbreak in the general, there are several of its incidents that were very strange & remarkable. The leader is John Brown, who had before gained notoriety as the leader of the brigands, murderers & robbers, kept in arms in Kansas by the "Emigrant Aid Society" of the north, whose object & effect were, to put down slaveholding by force of arms & by murdering, if not expelling the slaveholders. His murderous feats in Kansas he afterwards proclaimed in the northern states, as a public lecturer. He is as thorough a fanatic as ever suffered martyrdom—& a very brave & able man, humble & obscure as has been all his life, except in his latter bloody operations [765] in support of the abolition of slavery. With seven grown sons he commenced his dangerous & bloody course in Kansas, of which, the last remaining two were shot by his side at Harper's Ferry. It is impossible for me not to respect his thorough devotion to his bad cause, & the undaunted courage with which he has sustained it, through all losses & hazards. Among the strange incidents is the entire mistake of so able a conspirator, of his support expected from the slaves. His 21 men (all coming from the north,) in darkness & secrecy took the unguarded U.S. arsenal, with all its supply of arms. But long before, Brown had received from the north 1500 pikes, & a large number of fire-arms, all new from the hands of the manufacturers in New England. He evidently had counted on a general rush to his aid of the slave population, so as to make him immediately stronger than any opposing force, & enable him to put down slavery, & even to revolutionize the federal government. This is evident from the circumstances, his papers, & his own very full statements. But, with all his claims of success & of strength, & his supremacy in & around Harper's Ferry for 30 hours, not a single slave, or any other resident of the slave-holding country, joined his ranks. In seizing as prisoners (& hostages) some of the neighboring proprietors, & plundering their valuable moveables, they forced some of their slaves to go with them. But every such slave used the earliest opportunity to escape, & return to their several homes—& [766] not one remained when the insurgent force were besieged in the arsenal. This entire failure, after months of preparation, of obtaining even one slave to join in the attempt at insurrection, must astonish the northerners, & remove much of their general & erroneous impression of the discontent of the slaves, & their readiness for revolt. Another remarkable exposition is of the extent of fanaticism of northern abolitionists. Among the papers & letters of Brown, some show the complicity in the bloody outbreak, of sundry persons who could not have expected success except through blood-shed & horrors beyond example. Among the writers who offer the expressions of their sympathy, & their encouragement, to this murderous & horrible service, are some delicate & well-educated women, & others of the peace-loving Quakers!

*Oct. 28.* . . . Learned, from Mr. Williams' letter, that the Fair of the Richmond Society had been successful. Also, that my series on "Slavery & Free Labor" would be republished in the next two Nos. (Dec. & Jan.) of Southern Planter. Of these also I will have printed a pamphlet edition, for more general & distant distribution, & mostly gratuitously.—The trial of the abolition conspirators has been commenced & is in progress. [767]

*Oct. 30.* Sunday. Went to church, with all the family. . . . Preparing to set off tomorrow to attend the Annual Meeting & Fair of the V.S.A. Society.

*Oct. 31.* Wrote rough draft of a form of petition to the Va. legislature on the trade &c. of the state. In the steamer by 1 P.M. at Maycox, & from City Point, by railroad to Petersburg. At Bollingbrook Hotel. Meeting of Ex. Com. that evening, & consideration, amendments, & final adoption of the Annual Report of the Ex. Com. to the Farmers' Assembly. It is written by Mr. Williams, as I had requested to be excused from the service. Many acquaintances among the newly arrived visitors.

*November 1.* The first day of the Fair, which is always mainly but preparatory. A thin attendance, even for the first day. Pretty fair exhibition of articles. At night the Annual Address to the Society was delivered by Willoughby Newton.

*Nov. 2.* Daniel H. London arrived—whom I had invited to deliver an address to the Society on the disadvantages to which the direct trade of Va. with Europe is subjected. Had my form of petition on that subject &c. [768] printed, & began to distribute it to obtain signatures.[31] Other forms have been before in circulation, which I did not like so well.—A large assemblage on the Fair ground. The Farmers' Assembly, which had not a quorum yesterday, was enabled to go to business today. My constitutional limit of service being reached by this year's service, my place was vacant, & John R. Edmunds was elected President—beating Newton, a much better man for the place, & who has rendered much greater service to the Society. All the other members of the Ex. Com. were re-elected. At night, Mr. London delivered his address. Then the Farmers' Assembly sat again, concluded its business & adjourned *sine die.*—There was a very great crowd on the Fair Ground today, & altogether a very creditable exhibition. I feel heartily rejoiced that my service is nearly terminated, & I shall give up the small remainder, (to the end of the year,) to the first Vice President, who also is to be my successor. I declined being elected to a place in the Executive Committee.

*Nov. 3.* I commenced a conversation this morning with my nephew & former son-in-law, Dr. J. Dupuy, designed to be on business, in relation to the pecuniary support of his daughter & my granddaughter. This subject brought in other points, & without either of us having sought or expected it, we finally went into full statements of our respective grounds of complaint of the conduct of the other party. I found that he had imagined affronts & injuries from my words, even [769] older than his marriage—& in things which I had never the slightest idea of giving offence. . . . I could only declare my entire innocence, of intended offence, attempt to remove mistaken impressions, & to assure him, that, even when I also had become offended by his coldness & evident alienation, if not dislike, that I had never entertained for him any other than sentiments of respect & esteem, & wishes for his best welfare. I do not know that our mutual explanations [770] will remove all the coldness—but I trust that it may—& that our early kind relations may be resumed. At least our interview

---

[31] Ruffin's petition called on the legislature to "make such enactments and establish such State policy as in your discretion and wisdom may be deemed constitutional and expedient, and useful to protect and defend the Commercial and Agricultural interests of Virginia, and the still more important proprietary and political rights and social welfare involved in the institution of Negro Slavery in the States in which that institution now exists."

closed in this amicable spirit, & in perfect kindness of manners.—On the Fair Ground for a very short time, (yesterday not at all,) merely for appearances. Saw there all the younger children of my daughter Agnes, (except Edmund,) & received them kindly—made a small present to each, & a larger one to the oldest of them, Thomas, who I believe is an industrious & fine boy, & promises well, but for his worthless father's direction. This meeting probably induced what was both disagreeable & painful to me, a visit in the afternoon of Agnes & her daughter Margaret, at my hotel. I had not met with either before for nearly two years. I endeavored to be courteous & kind in manner—but could not affect fondness, or gratification. The closest bonds, when broken as ours have been, may have the breaches covered by hypocrisy, but can never be completely re-united. . . . A meeting [771] of the Society was called for this evening, for conversational discussion on agricultural or other subjects—but so few attended that we soon adjourned. Arranged to leave in the morning.—After 10 at night, received a telegraphic dispatch from Mr. B. Sayre stating that he & Mildred were at Richmond, on their way to Beechwood, & inquiring whether I would meet them there. I am very unwilling to be away any part of their visit there. But having arranged everything to pay a short visit to Judge Ruffin, & hoping to be able to persuade one or both Jane & Patty to come back with me, I decided . . . that I would proceed, & return to Beechwood earlier, & by next Wednesday.

*Nov. 4.* Had yesterday turned over the business of President for the remainder of my term of service to the First Vice P., J. R. Edmunds, who is also elected my successor. Set out this morning on the R.R. after 7 A.M. & reached the Company's Shops at 6.30 P.M. Hired a conveyance there, & drove to Alamance by 8 P.M. Found both Jane & Patty were from home, to my great disappointment. . . . Judge Ruffin has been greatly reduced—but has been improving for two months, & has gained 8 or 9 pounds of his previously lost flesh— which is a good deal, for one always so thin. His cough is still very troublesome. . . . [772]

*Nov. 5.* . . . Judge R. this day sent to the Governor of the State his letter of resignation of his place on the Supreme Court, on account of his ill health, & consequent inability to perform the labors of the office. . . .

*Nov. 8.* Left Alamance, & on the rail-road at noon. As the trains do not pass over the more direct route by Gaston, I had to go to Goldsborough, to get to Weldon. At supper at Goldsborough saw Thomas Ruffin, M.C.—Immediately after on the Wilmington train going northward. Made acquaintance with the Rev. ———— Owen, & had much conversation with him on the recent out-break of Harper's Ferry, & the slavery subject, as incidental thereto. Afterwards, continued to converse on like subjects with two other neighboring passengers—a northerner who had long lived in Va, & a [773] German residing in New York. We all agreed very well in the general. Reached Petersburg, at 2 o'clock in the night, where I stopped for the remainder of the night.

*Nov. 9.* At 7 A.M. left on the RR. for City Point—& had to wait at that miserable place nearly three hours before the Steamer Schultz arrived, on which I proceeded, & was landed on Coggin's Point, & walked to the Beechwood house. . . .

*Nov. 10.* . . . Looking over accumulated newspapers. Brown & some others of his companions have been tried & condemned to death. The most important of the very remarkable circumstances of this conspiracy & outbreak, is the very general sympathy intimated for the criminals, either directly or indirectly, through many of the northern states. The thorough abolition papers & speakers justify & applaud the attempt, for everything except its rashness & imprudence—& would have rejoiced (as they plainly indicate,) at its success, even if ever so destructive to the whites. Even the papers [774] always opposed to the abolitionists, & desirous to do justice (as they deemed it,) to the south, as the "Journal of Commerce" of N.Y. is appealing to Virginia to *pardon* the convicts, on grounds of mercy, magnanimity, & *policy.* Other less friendly papers are proclaiming that the convicts will not be put to death, because Virginia dares not execute the sentence. All these shades of opinion concur in one general import—which is that the great mass of the people of the north, even embracing many who have been deemed most our friends, are more or less enemies of the south, as well as of negro slavery, & do not entirely condemn the attempt to excite insurrection of the slaves, with all the unspeakable atrocities & horrors which would attend even their partial success. Their complete success, in establishing their freedom, even with all the aid of our northern white *brethren,* is utterly impossible. But it is not impossible that renewed & extended attempts of this kind may produce a war of races, to be terminated only in the extermination of the blacks, & ruin, with their victory, to the whites.

*Nov. 11.* The mail. Gerritt [*sic*] Smith, the great sustainer of the abolition cause, & deeply implicated in aiding, by his money, the late attempt of Brown's, is said to be insane—& has been placed in an asylum for lunatics. . . .

*Nov. 12.* Finished looking over & partly reading the papers & periodicals received previously—including last numbers of De Bow's Review, Russell's Magazine, & Southern Planter. The last contains the latter portion of my free negro argument. In the pamphlet form I have been making an extensive gratuitous distribution, & shall continue to do so, as opportunities offer. One copy, by mail & post-paid, was sent to each member of the Va. legislature. I trust that the recent Abolition conspiracy & outbreak will operate to facilitate the carrying out my views on this & other connected subjects.—Went with all the family to dine at the Glebe. Dr. John J. Dupuy the only male there of my sister's family. . . . My granddaughter Jane well & in high glee, in meeting with little John. I wish that these & also my other young grandchildren at Ruthven could more frequently enjoy the great pleasure & also benefit of being together. . . .

*Nov. 13.* Sunday. A stormy day of rain & wind, at intervals, & dark & gloomy throughout. No one went to church. Dr. Dupuy & Charles came, bringing the bad news of a great loss to the latter. Last night, before 9 o'clock, fire was put to his stable, & that with his only three mules were burnt, together with another building containing all his saved fodder. Neither Charles nor his overseer were at home, but all his negroes were. There is every appearance that they were guilty of the designed burning—which is worse than the pecuniary loss by the fire. This is the continuation of a dreadful state of things. This is the fifth house-burning that has occurred to the properties of my different children, & four of them by design, within a few years. Yet in the 44 years in which I was head of a farm, there was not the slightest loss by house-burning, either accidental or other.

*Nov. 14.* Edmund . . . went to Charles' farm, where met Julian, Dr. Dupuy, & several others of the neighbors. They spent nearly all the day in investigating the circumstances of the fire. Each of the negroes was [777] questioned apart from the others—& nothing could be learned to indicate the actual perpetrator. It is certain that the burning must have been made by malicious intention—& scarcely possible to have been without the action or knowledge of some one or more of the negroes, all then at home & close by. Yet it is extremely improbable that either they, or any other person, designing the act, & wishing to escape all suspicion, would have chosen so early an hour, when almost everybody was awake, & many moving about.—The mails. All the apprehended conspirators & murderers at Harper's Ferry have been tried & condemned to death, except one, [Aaron D.] Stevens, who was badly wounded, & who has been turned over to the Federal Government, to be tried, so that the presence of the northern abettors, as Seward, may be summoned as witnesses, or compelled to come for trial. I predict that this criminal will not be hanged, even if he should be convicted in a federal court. . . .[32]

*Nov. 16.* The newspapers show more extension of the northern feeling favorable to Brown & his gang—the abolitionists justifying their attempt, & even the papers deemed conservative, & just to the south, are asking for their pardon, on the ground of *policy*—that is that the northern people & opinion may not be more exasperated, but conciliated & soothed!—More developments of northern conspirators in Tennessee. Every thing seems to indicate that, contemptible as were the overt acts of the conspirators, & easily & effectually as their outbreak was suppressed, the plan had long been laid, & had abettors throughout the northern states & Canada.—Wrote a petition to the Va. legislature, for new & stringent enactments to prevent illegal dealings with slaves, by native liquor dealers & receivers of stolen goods, & by northern abolitionists, inviting their desertion, or insurrection. I trust that the like opinions are becoming general through Virginia. The newspapers tell of various [779] occurrences of northern or other unknown vagrants being ordered away from the places in which they appeared.

*Nov. 18.* With some help from Nanny & my niece Eliza Cocke, wrote 4 more copies of the petition—& enclosed & directed 5 to different newspapers, with the request to have it published. If this can be done, & so an extensive circulation obtained, perhaps it may induce many remote persons to sign it, & so produce effect on the legislature. However, my hopes for this, as well as for the previously printed petition, are but faint—even with all the aid that the Harper's Ferry excitement may lend to both. . . . The mail brought telegraphic reports of sundry rumors & alarms about Harper's Ferry . . . . It is astonishing even to me, & also very gratifying to me, that

---

[32] The diarist was wrong in his prediction. Aaron Dwight Stevens, who first joined Brown in Kansas after escaping from Leavenworth Prison, was executed on March 16, 1860.

there should be so *general* an excitement & avowed sympathy among the people of the North for the late atrocious conspiracy & outbreak, & for the villains engaged therein. If there are not serious & even effective efforts to rescue the condemned criminals, [780] it will be for want of courage, & not want of sympathy. And in the south, as well as the north, the excitement has been increasing, & will be productive (I trust) of important results. We may now see that a great majority of the northern people are so much the enemies of negro slavery, that they sympathise even with treason, murder, & every accompanyment of insurrection, & with the worst criminals acting therein, to overthrow slavery. The northern friends of the south are so few, or so timid, that most of them remain silent, or join in the general claim for mercy & pardon to Brown & his associates. This must open the eyes of the people of the south who have heretofore trusted to the justice & forbearance of the majority of the northern people—& it will be evident to many who have most feared & abhorred disunion, that that will be the only safeguard from the insane hostility of the north to southern institutions & interests. ... [781]

*Nov. 19.* Julian was all day yesterday in Petersburg, & heard of no new telegraphic reports. So no doubt all these alarms were false ... & probably were fabricated by abolitionists, both to cause uneasiness & expense, or with the further view of so causing future alarms to be discredited, & then to make a real attempt to rescue the convicts.—Went to a neighborhood meeting, called to settle matters about the general enclosure system of this neighborhood. I used the occasion to offer both my petitions for signatures, & met with general approval. There were 24 men only present, & all signed the latest drawn petition, which I have designated as the "Harper's Ferry Memorial." I think this outbreak of abolition conspirators, & the consequent exasperation of feelings, both north & south, must have important consequences, in widening the breach, & forwarding the separation of the slaveholding states.—There has been much difficulty in this neighborhood about carrying into full effect the law I obtained in 1858 to sanction a general enclosure, owing to some supposed ambiguity in the law, but more from the obstinate resistance thereto of one person, whose lands are very extensive, & prevent the extension of the benefit. But [782] the meeting today resolved to remain content with the law as it is, & trust to time to remove existing prejudices & opposition—& I have no doubt that all will work rightly. Already the one general enclosure has been extended so as to include all the farms from the corporation line of Petersburg to the lands of J. B. Cocke (the pig-headed proprietor opposed,) & from Appomatox [*sic*] & James rivers to beyond the main rail road. . . .

*Nov. 21.* After breakfast, I drove with Mr. [Burwell] Sayre to show him something of the lands of this neighborhood. He used the opportunity to consult with me about his present position, & plans—and being thus invited, I stated my opinion, which fortunately concurred in the main with his. He had, until lately, yielded in every thing to the supposed better judgment of his brother William, in regard to their purchase of land, & future location. But Mr. W. S. has already changed his views more than once, & (in my opinion, & probably now also his brother's opinion,) he [783] has acted in this matter so injudiciously for his own interest, as well as improperly to others, that I presume B. S. deems it necessary that he shall no longer bind his position to his brother's, & be led by his choice, however changing. Mr. W. S.'s first scheme & offer, was for himself & brother to buy out all the other interests in the whole Marlbourne estate. Next, on my sons Edmund & Julian properly refusing to thus sell out their patrimony, (& with the necessary incident of very long & uncertain terms & amounts of payment—) the alternative was forced on them to buy, & with the intention by W. S. of his & his brother with their wives moving to Arkansas, or elsewhere far in the south-west cotton region. This was the understood plan before & after Mildred's marriage, & the privation of my daughters' neighborhood & association to which I had to look. While bad feelings & causes of offence were being planted thus between us, the new arrangements of business affairs caused a more open rupture between Mr. W. S. & myself, which he made just before the marriage ceremony of my daughter & his brother took place. Each of us deemed himself very badly treated by the other. I soon put an end to what was becoming on W. S.'s part a very angry as well as insulting course of complaint & remark—& as soon as I could, after the marriage, & the leaving of the married pair, I went away. . . . Since then, it seems that Mr. W. S.'s previous determination to go, & [784] carry the others to the far south-western new settlements, has been given up, & he has been in vain seeking land to purchase, & to settle on, in Virginia. Probably (as I then partly suspected,) it was but designed as a threat, to operate on my sons to sell, rather than to permit the far removal of their sisters. . . . Before Mr. B. S. spoke to me on the subject this morning, I had already come to the conclusion that, (looking merely to himself & to Mildred's interest & pleasure,) it would be best for him not to abandon his profession of teaching, in which he had reached very high reputation, & great profit, to embark all his capital & personal exertion in farming, in which business he is an entire novice, & would have to rely entirely, & be guided by his brother's judgment & experience—which I have learned to distrust greatly. They [785] have together made several journeys to examine lands offered for sale—in Cumberland, near Lynchburg, & lastly in Gloucester—& all in vain. Mr. B. S. has come to think that it will be best for him to return to Frankfort, Ky, & resume the charge of the large & profitable school which he had there, & which he so left, that he can resume charge of it, if so choosing, at the end of the year. I concur in this opinion. Even in reference to my own feelings, I prefer that Mildred should live in the refined & excellent society of Frankfort, with a good income, & she & her husband having a vacation of three months to visit us, & thus to be with her nearest relatives in Va. nearly every year, than to be even settled on a farm in Va. so remote & difficult of access as either of those heretofore in view—even if any desirable & suitable farm can be found & purchased on satisfactory terms. My conversation with Mr. B. S., as all our recent intercourse previously, was conducted in the most cordial manner. . . . The fire burnings, of barns &c., near Charlestown, were all of neighboring farmers who had served as jurors on the trial of Brown &c. This indicates pretty clearly that northern abolitionists are the movers. The other alarms, all false, have induced the assembling at Charleston of [786] more than 1000 volunteers, ordered there by the Governor—& who now will remain until after the executions. The great assemblage, & the excitement of the public mind, must make the occasion very interesting, & I have a strong inclination to go there—& certainly would, but for my suffering so much from exposure to cold.

*Nov. 22.* Mr. Sayre sought & had a private conversation with Edmund, in which he repeated his views expressed to me yesterday, & others. He went through a matter which Mildred had before begun to speak on to Edmund, but was interrupted. This, now renewed, is the proposition, coming thus indirectly, but fully authorised by Mr. W. Sayre, . . . that his contract of sale shall be annulled, &, so far as to him, that his joint ownership of Marlbourne, & his position there, to continue as before. This is surprising, after his before determined & apparently inflexible resolution *not* to remain—& also to sell, & to remove—& all stated upon different reasons which he deemed insuperable. . . . I am glad of this retraction & offer, & of its being readily accepted by my sons. But, in doing what was designed, there should be some guaranty to them against another speedy & as sudden a determination of Mr. S. to sell out & remove, so as again, & soon, to require all the difficulty & trouble of arranging terms, & values, which have been incurred for nothing. However, the sale of Mildred's share will stand—as both parties think that it will be better for Mr. B. S. to have together the whole of her & his capitals, & at his command. . . .

*Nov. 23.* The mail brought a notification of the Southern Rights [788] Association of Richmond being [called] to meet next Friday night. Hoping that the current events, & new & strengthened feelings prompted thereby, may make this meeting of some account, I determined to go earlier to Richmond, so as to learn something in advance, & to attend the meeting. In the evening, went to Julian's, & stayed all night.

*Nov. 24.* Returned to Beechwood to breakfast. Had barely time to arrange & pack my hand trunk, before setting out for the steamer —by which I reached Richmond before 4 P.M. . . . Saw in the paper of today that my trade petition had been adopted as the form for the county of Louisa, upon the occasion of D. H. London's delivering there one of his speeches—& that it will be largely signed in that county. Also the Examiner & Whig of 22nd. both printed my later petition, which I lately offered for signatures in Prince George. I trust that both petitions will be widely diffused, & have more effect than my writings or recommendations have yet had. The present juncture is especially favorable. Many persons, heretofore the most "conservative," or submissive to northern usurpations & aggressions, & clinging to the Union under all circumstances, are now saying that *something* must be done by the south—& separation is admitted by others as the coming result, if not the safeguard of slavery in the south, & of all valued by the south. . . . [789] Gov. Wise seems to be acting very foolishly in sending troops to & back. A new howitzer company, (& which, by the way, has not been provided with howitzers,) was among the number lately sent to Charlestown, on account of the late alarms, & soon remanded home. Again this company has been ordered to return to Charlestown, & is to set out tonight. The rail-road fare, alone, will make a heavy item of expense.

*Nov. 25.* Had but little to do or to amuse myself with. Saw D. H. London, & conversed with him about the business of tonight. Wrote some strongly worded resolutions, on the present political condition of things, north & south, to offer. . . . The large court-room of the City Hall was well filled, but the greater number were merely auditors, & only 70 names were entered as members of the Southern Rights Association. I offered & read . . . [my] resolutions, which I feared would be opposed, as too violent. But not a word of opposition or a negative vote was uttered, & they were adopted unanimously. There were but few of the upper class present—most being of the middle class. . . .

*Nov. 26.* At 6.30 A.M. on the cars & on my way to the "seat of war." . . . At Washington by 2.30 P.M. & reached the Relay House, not far short of Baltimore, after 4. There I took the Balt. & Ohio railroad, & reached Harper's Ferry before 8. . . .

*Nov. 27.* Sunday. . . . Walked to see the sublime scenery of this place—which however falls far below Mr. Jefferson's description, for which however he drew upon his imagination, as he had not seen it. The almost perpendicular & in some cases over-hanging cliffs of limestone on both sides of the river at the junction of the Shenandoah with the Potomac, are very grand, & the rivers beautiful. After breakfast, I called on Mr. A[lfred W.] Barbour, the Superintendent of the U.S. Arsenal, & had with him, & with others much interesting conversation on the incidents of the outbreak of the abolition invaders, & its suppression. Mr. Barbour was absent at the time. I saw, & heard the reports of, several who were actors in the fight, or prisoners to the outlaws. I saw the engine house, into which they retreated, with their prisoners held as hostages, & which remains just as it was left after its being stormed, & showing evidences of the dangerous situation of both the defenders [792] & their assailants. The doors pierced by rifle balls, & the one shattered as it was broken down by the U.S. Marines. But long before that time, the outlaws had really been defeated, & three-fourths of their whole number killed by the people of the village & the neighborhood—& who had the remaining 5 surrounded & entrapped in this engine house, without possibility of their escape. The more speedy assault was only prevented by the assailants knowing that there were twice as many of their neighbors & friends prisoners, & equally exposed to their fire, as the outlaws. Considering the total ignorance of who & what the foes were, & their number, exaggerated to hundreds, & the total want of preparation, of arms (at first) & of ammunition, & of military organization, I think that the inhabitants acted well & bravely. In fact Brown was defeated before he took refuge in the engine house —& nearly all of his men who were killed, did not reach that place of refuge.—The village full of troops. One company of volunteers stationed here. Two others arrived last night from Wheeling. One of this [*sic*] is composed entirely of Germans, & it seems strange to hear the men of a Virginia volunteer company talking with each other in a foreign language. There would have been no train today, on the Winchester Rail Road—but 80 of the cadets of our Military Institute arrived by a special train from Richmond, & were sent on to Charlestown at 1 P.M. I went on [793] this train. As soon as I left the train at Charlestown, I was accosted by Mr. Hawks, who introduced himself & invited me to go to his house & remain, in so cordial & hospitable a manner that I could not refuse—& especially as no vacant place could be obtained for a lodger at a public house. Mr. Hawks is entertaining others, & I met at his house & table, of my acquaintance, Col. August & Capt. Geo. Randolph of Richmond, Col. [Francis H.] Smith, commander of the Military Institute,[33] & to supper, Gen. [William B.] Taliaferro, who by the family favor of Gov. Wise, & his higher though recent rank, is commander in chief, over older & better officers.[34] I met in the streets, many others whom I knew—& many young men, I suppose of the Richmond & Petersburg companies, saluted me as we passed, though I did not know them. It is a stirring time. There was a dress parade in the afternoon, & there is very little indication of the day being Sunday. Rumors of alarms, & coming through persons in service, are still coming in. A telegram to Mr. Barbour, this forenoon, from Hagerstown, Md, sent by an employed agent, announced the appearances of "trouble ahead." At night, videttes reported seeing rockets thrown up on the neighboring mountains. I think that it is extremely improbable that any attempt to rescue Brown & the other prisoners

---

[33] A graduate of West Point, Colonel Smith was superintendent of Virginia Military Institute for half a century (1840–89). At this time he held the rank of colonel in the state militia and was the commanding officer at John Brown's execution.

[34] Only thirty-seven years old when he commanded the militia at Harpers Ferry following Brown's capture, William Booth Taliaferro later rose to the rank of major general in the Confederate Army.

[362]

will be made, in the face of the large force assembled. Still, with his great popularity at the north, & the violent fanatical hatred of the south & of negro slavery there prevailing, it is not [794] impossible that a large body of desperadoes may be sent to attempt a rescue. [With] the facility of approach to Harper's Ferry & Charlestown by railroads from three directions, & the thousands of persons who will come to witness the execution, it would not be difficult for 500 or even 1000 to come as rescuers, & to pass as innocent visitors from Virginia & Maryland. Some discreet men here think that there are unknown agents in this village, & that it is to communicate with them that the rockets are fired in the mountains, as signals. Col. Smith, in whose opinion I place more confidence than in any other, thinks that if any rescue is attempted, it will begin by setting fire to the town. The patrol duty, in the village, & through the surrounding country is strict, & very severe on the military, & also those not in military service. For my part, I wish that the abolitionists of the north may attempt a rescue. If it is done, & defeated, every one engaged will be put to death like wolves. And even the possible success of the attempt may be risked, & the killing of many good men on our side, for the benefit of the results. If an armed attempt to rescue is made, accompanied by blood-shed, whether successful or not, it will be a certain cause of separation of [795] the southern from the northern states. In ordinary cases, it would be too absurd a supposition for any one to entertain, that any persons would attempt to rescue from deserved punishment these atrocious villains—who even long before this last offence had been guilty of crimes deserving death. Yet such is the direction of the northern mind in their favor, so general, & so furious the zeal of many for their escape, that no doubt every thing possible would have been done for this end, if the strong military force, & other measures of prevention had not been used. The murderer & robber & fire-raiser so notorious for these crimes in his Kansas career, & now the attempter of the thousand-fold horrors in Virginia, is, for these reasons, the present popular idol of the north. In one of the many eulogies lately pronounced on Brown, & from the pulpit, the Rev. Mr. Wheelock declared, in a sermon, that Brown, if at large, could command the vote of the northern states for the Presidency, by a majority of [a] million votes. Any amount of money required could be raised to pay for his rescue, & doubtless thousands of desperadoes would be ready to enlist for the service, & the glory as well as the payment for the deed.—Col. August, the officer of the day, & my fellow lodger with Mr. Hawks, promised to let me go with him on the "grand rounds" tonight to visit the posted sentinels surrounding the town. To be ready for this, I remained alone in the parlor, sitting or reclining in a rocking chair before a good coalfire, & passed the time in writing & reading, & might have slept well, but did not feel so disposed. [796]

*Nov. 28.* The grand rounds were designed to be begun between 12 & 1. But some of the usual false alarms caused several sentinels on their posts to challenge & to fire at some supposed object—& these foolish alarms had required Col. August's attention, & delayed him until 3 in the morning before he called me. I accompanied him & the general, & other officers on their route & duty. It was only disagreeable on account of the very rough & stony ground, & the darkness which made it difficult to find good ground. At half after 4, I returned & got to bed, & slept until roused before 8, when I rose, entirely refreshed, & well. After breakfast, the Rev. Mr. North, the brother in law of Mr. Hawks came, & claimed me as his guest—& as he (being a resident of the upper margin of the town,) had no regular guest, & Mr. Hawks' table was filled, I readily agreed to go to Mr. North's, & to be there to dinner, as I did. Saw in the street, (where I & most other non-residents spend most of the day,) Col. Braxton Davenport,[35] the only former acquaintance I have in this county. Promised to go out to his farm (near town,) & spend tonight & tomorrow to dinner with him. In the course of the day, I saw & was introduced to sundry persons who had figured in the recent events. One was Col. [Lewis W.] Washington,[36] who was taken prisoner in his bed, & with all his negroes, carried by [John E.] Cook to Harper's Ferry, & detained for 40 hours in the Engine House, & until it was stormed: Lieut. [Israel] Green of the Marines, who headed [797] the storming party, & who captured Brown after dealing to him a last disabling cut with his sabre.[37] It had never been sharpened, & its

---

[35] Colonel Davenport was the presiding justice at the preliminary hearing accorded Brown and his surviving colleagues.

[36] A great-grandnephew of the first president, Colonel Washington had in his possession a sword purportedly presented to his illustrious ancestor by Frederick the Great. One of the first acts of the leader of the raiding party which captured Washington was to compel him to surrender this sword to a Negro member of the insurgent group.

[37] Although a native of Vermont, Green resigned his federal commission in May, 1861, to become a major in the Confederate Marine Corps. He died in 1909 at the age of eighty-six.

dull edge alone prevented the cut being fatal: Judge [Richard] Parker[38] who presided at the trial: Henry Davenport, son of Col. D., who as Lieutenant of the Jefferson volunteer company, shared in the battle. I also met with & made the personal acquaintance of [David H.] Strother, (Porte Crayon,) whose delineations with both pencil & pen I have seen with so much pleasure, & whom I have long desired to know personally.—Two companies arrived here yesterday, & five more (volunteer companies) came today. There must now be 1500 troops in Charlestown, & several more hundreds in adjacent quarters. Among the newly arrived private volunteers from Petersburg, I saw my old friend Hugh Nelson, who is 67, & has for this occasion put on uniform, & come to serve as a private soldier. I should like to assume a similar position, if my worse than useless left hand did not disable me from shouldering a musket, or supporting it to fire—or even grasping a bridle, if on horseback. Also met, among the new arrivals, my friend W. W. Gilmer of Albemarle, whose presence, as always, is very noisy & very amusing, & also, to those who know him well, very gratifying for better reasons than his power to produce merriment & laughter. In the evening, Col. Davenport came for me, & we drove to his residence. At night, there were added to us, Henry Davenport, Mr. Pennybacker, a member of the Senate of Va, & Mr. Smith, a lawyer of distinction, & all volunteers on duty. An animated conversation on the recent events, & especially the hostile disposition evinced by the northern people, [798] & this as a provocation of, & probable means for, the secession of the southern states. This I advocated strenuously, & seemingly with effect on my younger auditors. Col. D. was silent on this subject.

*Nov. 29.* After breakfast, Col. Davenport & I walked out to give me a view of his extensive, fertile & beautiful farm. I never saw more beautiful farming land. And though the Jefferson lands generally are far from equal to this farm in maintenance or improvement of fertility, yet the like general features, & high grade of natural fertility & value pervade the whole of this part of the great "Valley" of Virginia. Saw Col. D.'s flock of Cashmire [sic] goats—of which 5 are of full blood, & the remainder of some 20 in all, are different grades of mixed blood. He also has a few Nubian sheep, which having hair

---

[38] Son of Judge Richard E. Parker of the Virginia Court of Appeals, Parker (1809–93) became a circuit court judge in 1851 after serving a single term in Congress. After the war he opened a law school in his native Winchester and was one of the leading members of the Virginia bar until the time of his death.

instead of wool, are of no value except for the flesh, & as curiosities. After dinner we drove to Charlestown.—Within a few hours after I had written of the report of rockets, I heard the solution of the mystery. When we went on the grand rounds, Capt. Geo. Randolph, who commanded the patrol, had satisfied himself & others that the supposed rockets were merely sparks of distant chimneys, seen over intervening houses, which prevented their sources being seen. The imagination of the viewers placing these lights as far off as the mountains, of course enlarged the sizes in proportion to the distance. And with this "looming" [799] caused by imaginary distance, the resemblance was enough to deceive. . . . At night went back to Mr. North's to sup & lodge. My last petition appears today in one of the town papers, together with my late resolutions—& the latter in two of the Richmond papers also. I have placed copies of the petition in the hands of several zealous approvers, who I hope will do good service in obtaining signatures.

*Nov. 30.* Several more arrests today of suspicious characters—& one prisoner, arrested in Harrisonburg & sent here, is fully believed to be one of the outlaws. Others who are strangers, & can furnish no vouchers of good character, are ordered off, & put across the Potomac. The town is every day more crowded with military & visitors. Today were commenced more strict orders to exclude all unknown new-comers, & increased guards, & the whole body of troops kept ready for action, day & night. There seems to be almost a suspension of business in the town. The weather has been very fine—& it seems as if every man & boy was in the main street, which is crowded with people, military & others, all day—& the females looking on, especially during parade hours, from the houses & side-walks. Every day the interest & excitement are increased. I feel my youthful military fervor, which has been asleep for nearly 45 years, awakened & growing. Tried to make some arrangements for my serving in one of the companies on the 2nd Dec. when Brown is to be executed, if he does not escape, or be rescued earlier. [800] And there are persons, & some who are neither weak nor timid, who believe there is still danger of attempted rescue. This is because of the plans known to have been laid, & of the number (computed at 2000) of the desperadoes connected with Brown, & sworn to obey him, & to defend or avenge each other. Besides, there is all the influence of extended northern sympathy, & of the enormous amount of money that is doubtless offered for Brown's rescue. This robber & murderer, & villain of unmitigated turpitude, even before this last conspiracy & attempt, is now the idol of the abolitionists, & perhaps of a majority of all the northern people.—The number of troops in Charlestown has been exaggerated. I heard this afternoon that there were not more than 1300 in this town. Some 4 or 5 of the companies are well drilled. But all the others have been newly raised, & have had but little opportunity to acquire good training. But every company is composed of the best materials—& who would fight as well as any troops not much older in training & service.—Dined at Mr. Andrew Hunter's,[39] with Porte Crayon. Afternoon spent, as usual, in viewing the parade, & in street talk, & at night returned to Mr. North's. [801]

*December 1.* The sentries yesterday were placed for day as well as nights, & those on the routes ordered to arrest every person not known. The first effect of this order, was to stop, on the main entrance to town, many persons of all descriptions, including ladies & negro-women & children. I was invited to dine with Mr. Hunter, whose house is on the outskirt, & was among the first who were arrested, & marched through the mainstreet, under guard, to the guard-house, to be examined & released. This was but an amusing incident, of the foolishly executed order. But in design, & in the subsequent & corrected operation, it is the proper course, &, with the other new arrangements, will render any assemblage of dangerous strangers, for a rescue, impossible. Also the cars on the rail-roads are now examined, & no unknown or suspicious persons allowed to stop, or to come to this place. Any especially suspicious are turned back on their route, whether they came from north or west. Four members of congress from Ohio, on their way to Washington, wanted to come here from Harper's Ferry, but were not [802] permitted to stop. Still, however, another came today, & no northern or western man is prevented, if he brings satisfactory vouchers for his character & conduct. The governor has issued a proclamation recommending every body to stay at home—& it is understood that none except the military, & others in some official position will be allowed to come near the execution. To obtain the means of being near, & also of aiding, if any military action should be by possibility needed, I have obtained the leave & aid of Col. Smith, commanding the Cadets of the Military Institute, for me to join, for tomorrow, that admirable corps. I shall occupy the somewhat ludicrous position of being the

---

[39] Andrew Hunter (1804–88), a Charlestown lawyer and state legislator, was the special prosecutor appointed to prosecute Brown for the state of Virginia.

youngest member (or recruit,) of this company of boyish soldiers. I received today, on loan, the arms, & the uniform over-coat of a private, for my use tomorrow.—I wrote yesterday a label for the pike which I am to have, of the number captured from Brown, & today I pasted a copy, in large letters, on the handle of one in possession of Mr. Hawks, thus: "*Sample of the favors designed for us by our Northern Brethren.*" The pike, so labelled, was exhibited & attracted much attention. I hope that it will produce some effect. The people hereabout are much more unionists than in lower Virginia. I use every suitable occasion to express my disunion sentiments. Sometimes they are approved, but [803] more generally disapproved.— Dined at Mr. Hunter's. There I saw, with great pleasure, the portfolio of Mr. Strother, containing many of his unpublished drawings. —Brown's wife arrived last night at Harper's Ferry, & asked leave to visit her husband. It was permitted—& a carriage, with a guard of dragoons, (for her protection) was sent for her. She arrived here so escorted, & also a U.S. military officer rode in the carriage with her. Several hundred U.S. infantry arrived Harper's Ferry yesterday. It is a pity that 20 of them had not been kept there before Brown's seizing the arsenal, & its only 4 unarmed watchmen.—Arranged with Major Gilham, of the Military Institute, & Officer of the Day, to attend him on the grand rounds tonight—which I shall sit up to wait for, either awake, or partly sleeping in a rocking chair—& reading.

*Dec. 2.* After 2 A.M. Major Gilham called for me, & I walked the grand rounds with him. Returned after 4, & did not go to bed, but slept on a sofa, until roused by the beat of drums at day-break, when I arose to get ready for parade at 7.30. Went, in my borrowed uniform overcoat & arms of the Virginia Military Institute, to join the corps of Cadets for the day, & so to witness the execution of Brown. When I made my appearance, I could see, what was very natural & excusable, that my position was very amusing, & perhaps ludicrous, to the young men, & it required all the constraint of their good manners to hide their merriment. However, I entered into familiar chat with them, & soon made some acquaintance; & before half [804] the duty for the day was over, I think from their manner, that I had gained much on their favor, & perhaps on their respect. Luckily for me, the exercises for this occasion consisted mainly of marching, & with some wheeling, which I could perform well. I remembered enough of my youthful military service to march well, without music, or signal of any kind, and in the march of more than two miles to & from the ground, the keeping of time & step I could do as well as any one. So my awkwardness in other matters of the drill was not exposed, & my service was performed very creditably, & caused me to receive sundry compliments from spectators afterwards. Before 9 we marched to the execution ground, & as with all the companies, & also returning, without music, or even a tap of the drum. We stood on our ground for two hours before the prisoner Brown was brought from the jail, under a strong escort of troops. Except a few persons, having special claims of office, profession, &c. no spectator was allowed on the ground except the military on duty there. All others who obtained entrance, were under some pretence & assumption of military office, or duty. The gallows was erected in the middle of a field of more than 30 acres, surrounded by a straight rail or plank fence. All persons having no business had been, by the Governor's proclamation, earnestly advised to remain at home. The neighboring residents, of both town & country, were the more ready to obey this advice, because they feared the occasion would be used to burn the town, or other buildings. Even of the military large numbers were serving [805] on piquet ground, or as patrol parties (of cavalry) at different distances outside of the enclosure, to keep off all persons approaching who were not known as good citizens. So, except the troops on duty, infantry, cavalry & artillery, there were very few present, & there was good opportunity for all to see who were near enough. Our company was nearest, & about 50 yards from the gallows, & facing its later occupants. After 11, Brown was brought, in a light & open wagon, sitting on his coffin, & with the Sheriff, Jailor, & another assistant. As Brown came near to the gallows, I recognized him by his likeness to the published portraits. His arms were closely pinioned at the elbows, by a cord crossing his back. As he passed by the gallows, he looked at it intently. After being assisted to alight, which the confinement of his arms required, he ascended the steps of the scaffold, with his attendants, with readiness & seeming alacrity. There was a dead silence among the surrounding troops, (all the best drilled companies,) & all the spectators. Nothing was said by the criminal, or on the scaffold, except in such low tones that the high wind, blowing from our line, prevented our hearing a word. I learned afterwards that he said very little, & nothing that was not required, & in relation to the work in hand. His movements & manner gave no evidence of his being either terrified or concerned, & he went through what was required of him apparently with as little agitation as if he had been the willing assistant, instead of the victim. The halter was adjusted around [806] his neck, & fastened to the hook in the beam above. His ancles [*sic*] were put close together, & fastened around with a cord. A large hood of white linen was placed over his head, through an aperture in which the halter passed. The criminal stood erect, & must then have expected every moment to be his last. But all the troops which had formed his escort had not yet reached their assigned positions, & halted there, & waiting for this, the signal was still delayed. This delay seemed to me full five minutes, or longer—during all which time, Brown stood erect, & as motionless as if he had been a statue. Not the smallest movement, or shifting of position was visible to me, & no shrinking or failing of the body to the mind, because of the long continuance of this awful state of suspense. This (as it seemed to me) cruel & most trying infliction was not intended, for in every respect his treatment had been very indulgent & kind, notwithstanding his atrocious crimes, & worse intentions. At last however the signal was given, & the sheriff left the platform & it instantly dropped, leaving the criminal suspended by the halter. The fall was not more than 12 or 15 inches. I could not perceive the least movement of the body or limbs, for about a minute of time after the fall. But another spectator by my side thought that he saw the hands raised a little, as only the ligature allowed, the instant after the fall. But after about a minute, the hands were moved convulsively, but still only slightly, for a short time. Then again the whole frame seemed motionless. But [807] I might possibly have been deceived in this, as the wind caused the suspended body to swing like a pendulum during all the time. After some 5 minutes or more of real or apparent entire absence of motion, I perceived slight convulsive motions of the legs, which also soon ceased, & all was still, & so remained, except the swaying of the body to & fro by the wind. When about half an hour had passed, physicians examined to find whether life was extinct; & at nearly 45 minutes, the body was lifted, & placed in the coffin to be delivered (as had been requested,) to the care of his wife, to carry northward. She had returned to Harper's Ferry, where the body will be sent to her this evening, after some detention here in the jail, & further medical examination, to be sure of life being extinguished. The return of the corpse to the jail was accompanied by the same numerous escort, of several uniformed companies. This was the only part of the ceremonies & conduct which I think was decidedly objectionable. It seemed like offering evidences of respect & honorable attention to the atrocious criminal. The procedure throughout was orderly & solemn. During the execution, not the sound of any voice was heard in the large assemblage, all of whom heartily approved & rejoiced in the infliction of the punishment. And afterwards, after life seemed extinct, the interesting incidents, or other opinions, were conversed on by the spectators in voices so low as not to be heard except to those within a few feet of distance. As soon as the body was removed, the remaining troops marched back to their quarters in the [808] same stillness & decorum, as before. The fine band of music accompanied the march, but not a note was sounded before all the troops were again in quarters, & until the afternoon parade. The villain whose life has thus been forfeited, possessed but one virtue (if it should be so called,) or one quality that is more highly esteemed by the world than the most rare & perfect virtues. This is physical or animal courage, or the most complete fearlessness of & insensibility to danger & death. In this quality he seems to me to have had few equals.—The fatigue of the forenoon & my loss of sleep last night made me very tired & sleepy in the afternoon. After writing the foregoing notes of the day, I shall go to bed earlier than usual.

*Dec. 3.* The weather has been clear & latterly also warm, until to-day—when it was first drizzly, & afterwards fine hail & snow, & at night the earth covered with sleet.—Three of the volunteer companies discharged & sent home by this morning's train, & more soon to follow. All ought to be, except a guard of 100 men for the remaining criminals, to be hung on the 16th. For Brown, the idol of the northern abolitionists, any amount of effort to rescue might have been apprehended. But for the inferior villains, under sentence of death, or yet to be tried, it is not likely that any 20 men would risk their lives to save.—As I wish to stop in Washington during the heat of the expected contest for the election of speaker, which will commence with the session of Congress on the 5th, I shall wait a few days longer; & this will [give] [809] me time to accept some one of the sundry invitations that have been pressed on me to visit proprietors in the adjacent country. I fixed on John A. Thompson, a gentleman whom I became acquainted with some years ago, & whom I met in Charlestown. I left my kind host, Mr. North, & after waiting for the train to Winchester long after its due time, went on it 7 miles to Summit Point station, whence I walked a short distance

[371]

to Mr. Thompson's house.... Conversation almost entirely on subjects suggested or in connection with Brown & his attempt. Gov. Wise, in his speech at Richmond, after his return from Harper's Ferry, published to the world two great mistakes of his making, & in both he has given our northern traducers, & the worshippers of Brown, a great support & aid. For his first, though erroneous opinion, that the people of the vicinity were wanting in proper courage & conduct in not capturing all the insurgents much earlier, & without the aid of the marines, he was very excusable. But he might have learned his mistake on the spot—& not have published what was an unfounded calumny, if he had been truly informed. In his remarks on Brown, he has given him a high eulogy for truth & other noble qualities, of which he was perfectly [810] destitute—possessing only that of physical courage. And this false eulogy, coming from the lips of an enemy, & the governor of Virginia, will be used for his vindication & glorification by the northern abolitionists, with great force, & more effect than, to northern understandings, the full truth, or any opposing argument can ever overcome. I predict that when a monument shall be erected to Brown in the North, ( as it certainly will,) some of the extravagant & false eulogistic expressions of Wise will be there copied & inscribed, as the best possible evidence of his exalted merits & noble qualities. The whole south, in this great controversy & coming struggle, will suffer for this wretched blunder of Governor Wise. If any one man's testimony can establish the claim of this atrocious villain to be a man of "clear head, of courage, fortitude, & simple ingenuousness."... "humane to his prisoners ... & who inspired me [Gov. Wise] with great trust in his integrity as a man of truth."... that "He is firm, truthful & intelligent," it will be established by Gov. Wise. This eulogised miscreant indeed played his part well enough to deceive Gov. Wise. But his whole course was one of deception & falsehood except when it best served his purpose to be [811] "ingenuous." He was "humane to his prisoners" taken at Harper's Ferry, because he held them as hostages, & his own chances for escape, & for life, depended on preserving them. In Kansas he had in like manner taken prisoners from their beds—& had cut their throats, though unoffending & powerless, before the eyes of their wives or mothers.

Col. Smith of the V.M.I. was officer of the day on the 2nd, & doubtless to him were mainly due the excellent arrangements, & procedure. His corps of Cadets were not in their dress uniform—

which I objected to wearing, because it would have been too laughable on me—but in one equally striking, & more martial in appearance, & which I would have assumed if knowing it in time, so as not to be different from the others. All the privates & non-commissioned officers wore scarlet flannel shirts, bought for the occasion, with their uniform gray pantaloons, & with neither vest nor coat, but only the two whole shoulder belts crossing over the shirt.

*Dec. 4.* Sunday. This day continued cloudy, but the sleet is partially melted. Mr. Thompson is a well-read & intelligent man. He is a whig, but not a party man—or about as little a whig as I am a democrat. Though differing entirely on important political questions, we yet concurred in many of our views. His opinions in opposition to our seceding from the northern states are founded on conditions of this & the more western parts of Virginia which are new to me, & which he deems certain, & which if correctly understood by him are important. He thinks that if separation of the states was effected, & war ensued, or even without war, an army was required to [812] be kept, at the expense of Virginia, in this region, to protect our then northern frontier, that the non-slaveholders, who greatly surpass the slaveholders in number, would not concur; & that their jealousy of the richer, as well as self-interest, would cause them to side with the north, & to go for the abolition of slavery. He thinks that such would be the case with all Va. west of the Blue Ridge—& that there were already evidences of such feelings & opinions of non-slaveholders. The shock thus given the institution of slavery would endanger its existence, if not overturn it throughout Virginia & Maryland, if not through all the more southern states. With these views, he thinks that the dissolution of the union would be the death-sentence of southern negro slavery. He also informed me, in connection with this subject, that the greater number of the inhabitants of Harper's Ferry, who are northerners & foreigners, workmen in the armory works, did scarcely any thing to quell the late outbreak—the fighting men being nearly all from the adjacent country & neighboring towns, before the arrival of the marines. . . .

*Dec. 5.* Still misty & gloomy. After waiting to 11, & supposing some promise of clearing, we set out, as arranged yesterday, in a covered buggy to see the country, & to visit my acquaintance Hugh Nelson in Clarke. But the worse appearance of the weather forbade, & Mr. Thompson, instead, drove me to Mr. Wm. Turner's residence [813], who was a college companion of Edmund, & who had before invited me to visit him. His house is 5 miles from Mr. Thompson's, & as much from Charlestown. There we determined to stay through the night. We found there with Mr. Turner, Major Armistead of the U.S. Army,[40] & Lieut. Green of the U.S. Marines, who was the officer who led the storming party at Harper's Ferry, & finished the contest. Mr. Turner's elder brother, George, a man of high ability & education, & worth, was killed there by a shot from the engine house, as he advanced & was in the act of firing on the insurgents. I found all these gentlemen very intelligent & agreeable in conversation. We talked mostly about the present condition of the south, in reference to the hostile spirit shown by the north generally to the south, & the probable consequences of separation of the southern from the northern states. All were conservative, in different degrees, or for still adhering to the union, without further injuries being inflicted, except myself & Lieut. Green, whom I was gratified to find entirely with me. Yet he is a New Yorker by birth, & by residence, before entering the marine corps—but married in Virginia. He thinks that the large majority of the officers of both the army & navy would side with the south, in the event of separation. I inquired of Major Armistead as to the best lands for settlement of new immigrants, in the new states or teritories, of which he has seen much—& of which I wish to be informed, in the event that Virginia will not defend herself & the institution of slavery against the North. He thinks that the lands south of the Red River, in Texas, & within 60 miles of that river & [814] of Fort Towson in the Indian Territory, is the best land he has found in his extensive military wanderings—consisting of intermixed patches of wood-land & prairie, on a surface in broad undulations. He was quartered four years with troops at Fort Towson, & found it a healthy place.

*Dec. 6.* Still another misty & gloomy morning, & afterwards drizzly. Had intended to take the train this morning, but our breakfast was too late to permit it. So Mr. Thompson drove me to Charlestown, where I wished to make my last calls on the new friends made there—as I did on Mr. Hawks—& dined by invitation with Mr. Hunter, & called afterwards on Mr. North. At Mr. Hunter's, met with

---

[40] Presumably Lewis Addison Armistead (1817–63), who distinguished himself while serving with the Second United States Infantry in the Mexican War. During the Civil War he commanded the Fifty-seventh Virginia Infantry Brigade from the Peninsula to Gettysburg and fell mortally wounded at the head of his brigade in Pickett's charge against Cemetery Ridge.

Gen. Taliaferro, & his aid, the noted O. J. Wise, son of Gov. Wise, & his mouth-piece, as editor of the Enquirer. When introduced to him, I bowed, without offering to shake hands, & he did the same—& we approached no nearer in the subsequent general & animated conversation. I had stopped first at a hotel, & finding I could have a single room, had taken quarters—where I went at dark.—Though cut off from most of our intended excursion, I saw, through the thick atmosphere many of the fine farms of this beautiful & fertile country. The land was much as I had been previously taught to expect to see. But there were other features that were unexpected. There were no small properties—& almost every farm, generally of from 300 to 1000 acres, had spacious, costly, & handsome mansions. There are scarcely any very small & poor landholders, or such as are non-slaveholders. The latter class [815] reside in the sundry villages of this country, as mechanics or shop-keepers, & constitute the much larger number of the white inhabitants.—The newspapers full of the howlings of the northern abolitionists over Brown's execution, & their glorification of his character & deeds.—I had obtained the only N.Y. Herald which I had seen since leaving Richmond, (of 5th.) & thus accidentally found a passage relating to myself, which otherwise I might have been long before hearing of.[41] I proceeded at once to write a denial, to be sent by next mail to the Herald, & some copies for other papers. [816]

*Dec. 7.* Making hasty arrangements for departing for Harper's Ferry, as previously designed. Ordered the printing of my last night's writing here, & sent off other copies by the mail. After 10, left on the train, & reached Harper's Ferry at 12. This is the fifth successive day of continued very gloomy, & misty or drizzly weather, & this the worst of all, drizzling all day, & rain increasing in afternoon. I stopped here to give a day to viewing the scenery &c., but there is no chance even to go out, so far. If, instead of beautiful clear weather having continued through the execution day, this long & dismal spell had begun with that day, the northern fanatics would have seen in it an indication of God's anger with the execution, for which the Heaven was draped in mourning.—After dinner, saw Mr. Barbour, the Superintendent, & obtained one of the spears which Brown

---

[41] The *Herald* recounted an alleged encounter between Ruffin and one Col. Baylor. The latter reportedly was incensed by what he termed a "treasonable harangue" delivered by Ruffin to a crowd in the streets of Charlestown. According to the diarist, the entire affair was a complete fabrication.

had brought to arm the slaves whom he counted on joining him. I shall take it home with me, & farther south, if I should go.—The papers show that there is no present prospect of an election of speaker being effected soon in the House of Representatives—where the "Black Republicans" or Abolition party want but five votes of a majority, & the remainder are divided into the two parties of democrats & "opposition" embracing whigs & "Americans." This last party, though containing but 23 members, of different political creeds, holds the balance of power in their hands. In the mean time, the Harper's Ferry conspiracy has been taken up formally in the Senate, & the subject is informally agitated in the other house. There will be more & more of irritation & exasperation—& it is seriously feared by the lovers of the union that it may come to an end in the breaking up of this session of Congress. [817]—Dull company as well as gloomy weather. High & very cold wind, & fine hail freezing to sleet. There seems so little probability of weather good enough tomorrow for me to climb the mountains & view the scenery here from the most commanding points, that instead of waiting longer, as designed, I will go on by the first train, in the night, to Washington. My object there is to witness something of the present turmoil, & to see, if possible, to what early end it is tending.—There are some 300 U.S. troops assembled here, for the time embracing the two executions (2nd & 16th of Dec.) & then to return to Fortress Monroe. They are here to protect the U.S. armory & other property. It is a pity that 20 of the number had not been kept here before the seizure of the arsenal by Brown with less than 30 men.

*Dec. 8.* At 3 A.M. set out for Washington. Reached the Relay House (9 miles from Baltimore) at 6.30, where we had to wait two hours for the Washington train, where arrived at 10. At Brown's hotel—where there are many southern members of Congress. Among them, soon saw of my former acquaintance, Th. Ruffin & Senator [Thomas] Bragg[42] of N.C., [Henry A.] Edmundson of Va,[43] [John] McQueen of S.C. Also Elwood Fisher. My spear, in the public hall, attracted much notice. After dressing, went to the gallery of the H. of R., which was so full that I could scarcely squeeze in—& then

---

[42] Bragg (1810–72) was in his first year as United States senator after serving four years as governor of North Carolina. From 1861 to 1863 he was attorney general of the Confederacy.

[43] Edmundson was in his sixth consecutive term as a member of the Virginia congressional delegation. He commanded the Twenty-seventh Virginia Cavalry during the War Between the States.

could not hear anything of most of the speeches. . . . This house is still unable to elect a speaker, & the speeches are all upon the present enmities of North [818] & South. I trust that the differences & difficulties may increase, & that the state legislatures may stand up properly for the rights & dignity of the South, in reference to the outpouring of the hostility & malignity of the North, as shown in the sending out Brown's expedition, & also the general sympathy shown for him since his defeat. If precisely the same course had been pursued by any one independent nation against another, it would have been good cause for a declaration of war. Opinions of southern members seem much heated. I understand that they are not less so of the Virginia legislature, also assembled last Monday. I conversed last night with several members of Congress, from N & S Carolina & Alabama, who were ready for secession. I maintained that the conspiracy of the abolitionists, its outbreak in the invasion of Harper's Ferry, & the very general sympathy of the northern people with the murderers, afforded the best practical ground for dissolution that the South had ever had—& that it ought not to be passed over. We ought to agitate & exasperate the already highly excited indignation of the south. If we submitted to this, the northern fanatics would repeat these attempts, until they destroy the safety of the institution of slavery, & soon after, the institution itself.

*Dec. 9.* Went early to the gallery of the H. of R. & obtained a good seat by aid of an order for my entrance to the ladies' portion. Another ineffectual ballot, & no election. The remainder of the long session spent in violent & turbulent debates, on political quarrels & parties, & two members from Illinois, a Douglas man & an Abolitionist, were in touching distance for a fight, when they were separated by their respective friends. A few days ago, there was still more danger of a general row, which, if entered into would [819] have probably resulted in the deaths of sundry members. It is understood that many members then armed themselves, for defence. A ballot for speaker was tried, & the largest vote (for a black republican, or abolitionist, [John] Sherman [Republican, Ohio],) was still short of a majority by 6 votes. This state of disorganization will continue until one of the other small parties—the southern whigs or the Douglas democrats—will vote for a plurality to decide, & then of course the abolitionist will make that plurality.—About dark, fire broke out, from one of the furnace flues, in this hotel. It was an hour before it was completely extinguished, & much alarm was excited among many of the inmates. Afterwards called on Senator Clay of Ala., & his wife, who lodge here. Saw that the Tribune of N.Y. had published the false statement of the Herald concerning me—on which account I sent my previous denial to the N.Y. Day Book, with comments.

*Dec. 10.* . . . Went early to the H. of R. & stayed until nearly 4, when the ayes & noes were being called on a motion for adjournment. Turbulent debates as before—but closed by a regular & uninterrupted speech, of great force, by Curry of Ala, exposing & denouncing the acts & designs of the northern "republican" party, with much effect. . . . Richmond papers of today containing reports of sundry county meetings in reference to the abolition outbreak at Harper's Ferry, all of which passed strong resolutions. I hope that it is not all gas, which after effervescing & escaping will leave the body of the liquor flat, stale [820], & dead. Mr. Washington of this place, & Gen. [Sydenham] Moore, M.C. of Alabama called & sat with me.[44] Our conversation, as almost always of any southern men, on the present position of the north & the south. Wrote a short article for the Examiner on Brown's pikes, recommending that one shall be sent to every governor of the slaveholding states, to be placed in the legislative hall of each capitol.

*Dec. 11. Sunday.* . . . After breakfast, Mr. Curry & Gen. McQueen called & sat with me awhile. Subsequently I learned that Gen. Bonham of S.C. is (like the others) lodging close to me, & I visited him at night. In the crowd here, two acquaintances might not see each other for a week, & remain ignorant of being near each other.— Under a sudden thought & impulse, I began to write an article, urging on Virginia the reasons for early separation from the northern states, & leading in the movement for a southern confederacy. It extended to 10 pages, of which 7 were copied in more legible & corrected writing. At night, mailed the writing to the Richmond Examiner for publication. . . . A letter . . . from Mr. Wm. Sayre, expressing sorrow for his angry & disrespectful words & manner to me in our last interview, & asking to have our previous friendly intercourse restored. Of course I shall be glad to be again on terms of amity & intimate intercourse with the husband of my daughter—& shall so

---

[44] A veteran of the Mexican War and a former circuit judge, Moore (1817–62) was brigadier general of the Alabama militia and a second-term congressman. He was mortally wounded in the Battle of Seven Pines while commanding the Eleventh Alabama Regiment during the war.

write—& receive as sufficiently conciliatory Mr. Sayre's apology. But still I do not learn from his letter that there has been removed from his mind the erroneous impression of my conduct, which induced his anger & its expression. If he retains this impression, it is impossible that either he or I can return to our previous cordial & friendly feelings, though the outward appearance may be assumed because of our family relations. . . .

*Dec. 12.* In the Senate gallery today, expecting to hear C. C. Clay of Ala. deliver an appointed speech—but instead waited [822] there more than three tedious hours hearing other speeches which were of little interest. Wrote another short article, & sent it to the Examiner. It seems, from all I hear, that the best spirit prevails among the people of all middle & lower Va. The legislature is going on as well (apparently) as I could hope for, except that no direct proposition for secession, or a convention, has yet been proposed. . . . Heard that a speech very offensive to the south was today made by [John] Hickman [Democrat, Pennsylvania], a northern abolitionist, who claims to be a democrat.[45] No ballot taken today. Had a singular meeting last night, in the hall, with a man whom I had before observed opposite to [me] at dinner. He made himself known to me as Col. [J. Egbert] Farnham whom I met here & conversed with last winter, & stated his then communications on the matters of the slave ship Wanderer. As then stated, he was one of the officers of that vessel—& has been arrested in New York, a few days ago, on a requisition from Georgia, & is now going to Savannah to be tried as a pirate (or African slave trader,) for his life. He was waiting here, for the delay of the officers, & was at large on his parole, I suppose. He seemed in very good spirits, & expressed the very confident hope that they would not hang him in Savannah—in which I accorded.

*Dec. 13.* Went to the gallery of the H. of R. The notorious [Daniel E.] Sickles [Democrat, New York] spoke, & I soon was weary, & returned to my lodgings & wrote letters . . . . [823]

*Dec. 14.* The Examiner of yesterday contained my first communication.[46] I am to obtain the fulfilment of the measure proposed much earlier, though in a less imposing manner than I proposed. I told Col. Barbour (Superintendent of the Harper's Ferry Armory,)

---

[45] Hickman was later elected to the Thirty-seventh Congress as a Republican.

[46] In his letter to the *Examiner,* Ruffin proposed that the Virginia legislature present one of Brown's pikes to the governor of each slaveholding state so that it might be placed on public exhibition.

whom I saw here today, of what I had done & wished, & he offered to send the requisite number of pikes to me here, for me to supply one to each of the slave-holding states. I am much gratified by this. —Attended first in the gallery of the H. of R. & afterwards of the Senate. Heard our Senator Mason deliver an excellent speech on the conduct of the North & the "republican" party in regard to the Harper's Ferry affair. After an animated debate of more than a week & strong endeavors of the 22 abolitionists in the Senate indirectly to defeat, his resolution of inquiry into that affair was carried by a unanimous vote—the abolitionists not daring to vote directly against it, though wishing to do so. The notorious Sumner has resumed his seat. Seward still absent in Europe—by which he has escaped hearing the severe animadversions on his conduct which have been freely uttered. J. Letcher, our governor-elect, arrived. After dinner, I went with him to call on Senators Mason & Hunter. . . . No election of speaker yet, & no ballot today. [824]

*Dec. 15.* Heard in the H. of R. an excellent & sound speech from [Clement L.] Vallandigham [Democrat, Ohio]. Two ballots taken, & no change of the last results. 110 votes for Sherman the abolition candidate, & 85 for [Thomas S.] Bocock [of Virginia], the democratic. Some 30 or more votes scattering. . . . At my convenience, writing labels for the expected pikes—& letters to the Governors of the respective slave-holding states, to be sent before or with the pikes.

*Dec. 16.* . . . To the gallery of the H. of R. Two more ballots, without any material change of the two larger votes. Speeches from Bonham of S.C. & [William E.] Simms [Democrat, Kentucky] of Ga. [*sic*] The "republicans" or the Brown-Helper party, as it ought to be designated, have for some days remained mute, under the severe denunciations of the democrats & southerners. The spirit of disunion seems to be growing fast in Virginia especially, & the other heretofore luke-warm southern states. Except for the almost total want of arms & military preparation, everything would now seem ripe for striking the first blow for secession [825] of the Southern States. And I would prefer that Virginia should now begin, while the spirit of the people is up, than to let that spirit cool, & have six months of preparation.—The two condemned white prisoners, [John E.] Cooke [*sic*] & [Edwin] Coppie [*sic*] [47] last night escaped from their jail, but were discovered & shot at by the outer guard, before getting out of

---

[47] The prisoner's actual name was Edwin Coppoc.

the outer wall—& retaken. This is the day for the execution.—Had part in the private & confidential conversations of some five or six members of S.C., N.Ca, & Ala, in the room of Branch of N.Ca. At night, again visited & conversed with Mr. Letcher, with other friends of his present.

*Dec. 17.* After breakfast, I asked Mr. Letcher to my room, where we could be private. We had a conversation on the present state of affairs. First requesting him not to answer any question or remark of mine that he did not choose, or think it proper to express an opinion of, I asked what he thought of the present prospects of the Union. He answered promptly & plainly that he thought it must be dissolved, & at no distant time. I then stated that if he was correct in that opinion, the dissolution would occur during his administration, perhaps very early in his term of service—and that he would commence his administration (Jan 1. 1860) at a more important crisis, than any other Governor of Va. since Patrick Henry. He seemed to think that there was little that he could do in the remainder of this session of the legislature of Va. as the measures of reform or of preparation had already been marked out, & the [826] work was in progress. I stated my reasons why, notwithstanding this, he could do much, by recommending a convention for Va. and a general convention of the southern states, and also by his influence, more or less directing other measures that were in progress. I trust that he is a safe & useful man for the crisis, though certainly not a great man. He has a practical mind, is discreet & judicious, & is well acquainted with political events, & men. He is certainly for the dissolution of the Union, under present circumstances, & has no hope for its preservation, together with that of the rights of the people of Va, & of all the south.—Again disappointed in not receiving the pikes from Harper's Ferry, by Express. Finished writing the labels for them, & letters to all the 15 governors of slaveholding states—including one to Letcher, which is dated Jan. 1, 1860, & not to be considered as delivered until then. There is some verbal differences in the letters, caused by accidental variations or designed improvements, as writing them. But there is no difference of purport. The large label is like mine, "Sample of the favors designed for us by our Northern Brethren." Some of them have also in small letters added below, "The most precious benefit derived from the Northern States by the Southern, if, rightly using it, out of this nettle danger, we pluck the flower *safety.*" [827]

Washington D.C.   Dec. 16, 1859
To his Excellency W. H. Gist, Governor of South Carolina
  Sir
  Permit me to present to the State of South Carolina, through you
its Chief Magistrate, one of the pikes which were sent from the
North to arm the negro slaves, & to be imbrued in the blood of the
whites of the South, in the designed & expected general insurrection
which Northern Abolitionists had planned, & recently and fruitless-
ly attempted to excite, and to commence the practical execution of,
at Harper's Ferry. It is requested that this weapon may be placed in
some conspicuous position in the State House of South Carolina,
there to remain, & be preserved, as abiding & impressive evidence
of the fanatical hatred borne by the dominant northern party to the
institutions & the people of the Southern States, and of the unscrupulous & atrocious means resorted to for the attainment of the
objects sought by that party.

> Very respectfully
> Edmund Ruffin
> of Virginia [829]

Two more ballots in the House of Rep. today, & no change in the
main votes. The abolitionist candidate Sherman had 110, & still
needs 4 more votes to give him a majority—& the democratic candidate has no prospect of increasing his vote much above 85, and
no possibility of his being elected. There are enough scattering votes
to elect either of the two. The aspect & condition of the body is remarkable. The middle aisle is the separation of the two parties, of
democratic & mostly southern members on the right (of the speaker,)
and on the left, exclusively northern, & "republican" or abolition,
or Brown-Helper party men. The latter remain mute—neither latterly any one making a speech, nor even questioning or denying any
statement of the democratic speakers, who denounce them in no
measured terms of reproach. Probably the Brown-Helpers think that
they cannot defend themselves to any purpose, & so had better receive the censures without reply. It may be that they also fear that
conflict in words might bring on conflict in action. It is understood
that every member is armed—& any physical collision would probably cost several if not many lives to be lost on the floor of the hall.
There is very little intercourse of courtesy between any members
of these opposite parties—& as bodies, there is almost no contact or
intermingling.

*Dec. 18.* Sunday. Sent a telegraphic dispatch to Harper's Ferry to inquire about the expected pikes, for which I have been now waiting two days—& received no answer. I am almost hopeless now of getting them. I cannot wait longer than this night. So I have placed the prepared [830] letters (to the governors) & my instructions, in charge of Senator Clay—& the labels in charge of his charming wife, who is a true & ardent southerner, & who will affix them to the pikes should they arrive, & have them distributed.—Elwood Fisher in my room this forenoon, & we had a long conversation. At night, in Mr. Letcher's room, where there were sundry other visitors, & among them, part of the time, Senator Hunter.

*Dec. 19.* Left Washington early. In the steam boat, my pike with its labels attracted much attention. I made a very agreeable acquaintance with Ex-Governor [Charles J.] McDonald of Ga,[48] who hearing who I was sought me out, to be introduced to me, & then carried me to his wife. . . . Both the husband & wife very intelligent & agreeable. They gave me a hearty & earnest invitation to visit them at their residence in Georgia.—Arrived at Richmond at 2 P.M. . . . Saw Mr. Williams, & sundry former acquaintances in members of the legislature . . . . Read last portion of my series (Slavery & Free Labor compared,) in the course of publication in the Southern Planter, & to go into pamphlet form. Afterwards found it was too late for correction, as the pamphlet sheets were already printed.

*Dec. 20.* Was at the Capitol for a short time, & saw a few members of my acquaintance. Saw Col. A. W. Barbour, & was glad to hear from him that he would yet send the 15 pikes to Washington for me—though I do not feel confident of it. . . .

*Dec. 21.* . . . To the steamer, & at Beechwood before 12 M. Found no one at home but Mrs. Lorraine & my little grandson John. Edmund had gone to Petersburg, on his way to Richmond, & [832] Nanny with him as far as Petersburg. . . . Edmund has gone for his children, who are at school, to return with them.—From the little that I learned from members & otherwise, of the course of the legislature, there seems to be a will to put the state in good military condition. Also, to adopt measures of police &c. to restrain northern enemies & emissaries, & to restrict northern trade, & encourage our

---

[48] At this time a justice on the Georgia Supreme Court, Charles James McDonald was governor from 1839 to 1843 and later played an important role at the Nashville Convention of 1850.

own productions, & direct trade with Europe. This is well so far. But I fear that the warm & angry spirit now pervading the people of Va. will subside, & cool, before it is put to use for asserting our independence. It is true that we are unprepared, in regard to military organization & discipline, & as to arms & all other equipments for defence. But I would prefer that Va. should secede, unprepared as we are, but with this noble spirit of resistance prevailing, to having a year of preparation, & losing that spirit. If Virginia, the now especially aggrieved & endangered state, would now move in advance, but inviting the co-operation of all the other southern states, nearly all would follow immediately, & any few remaining, (as probably would Maryland & Tennessee, & perhaps a few others,) would find in a few months that to join [833] their southern brethren was the only guaranty of their political safety, if not existence. Unprepared as we are, in every slaveholding state except South Carolina, if so far united in secession, & determination to resist attack, we would be strong enough to repel & defeat attack & invasion if the northern states should be so ill-advised as to make the attempt.

*Dec. 22.* Read some old letters which had been forwarded to me from Marlbourne, & one of them from Dr. S. W. Barker, of Senate of S.C. which I regret much I did not receive in time. Answered it immediately, though too late—on the present state of the south—& sending my free-negro pamphlet, which he wanted. Wrote also to Senator Clay, Gen. McQueen, & sent latest & other pamphlets to them & to some other members of Congress. Then rode to Ruthven. . . . Stayed through the night. Conversation mostly on the recent events connected with Harper's Ferry—&, with Julian, our family affairs & difficulties. . . .

*Dec. 23.* Wrote some letters, one to Mr. Letcher & to members of the Va. legislature on northern affairs, affecting us. At noon returned to Beechwood. Edmund & his 4 children had just arrived, with 4 of Edward Lorraine's children. The others of his family will come tomorrow. . . . The papers brought news of an important occurrence, of which the uncertain rumors & [835] anticipation were heard some days before. 267 of the southern medical students at the two colleges in Philadelphia, have, by agreement, left those institutions, though they had paid their fees, & came on to the Medical College of Richmond on the 22nd. This is a notable & important evidence of the prevailing disposition of people of the south to separation of intercourse with the North.—The withdrawing of southern

custom[ers] from the north, already, & though the result of individual & separate action, has caused most important losses to many
northern commercial & manufacturing establishments, & caused
some large ones to fail, & close business. . . .

*Dec. 24.* . . . . All E. Lorraine's family now here, except his oldest
son. At night read Gov. Wise's Message in reference to the Harper's
Ferry affair. It is excellent in the general remarks, & far better than
anything I have yet seen of his writing or speaking.

*Dec. 25.* Christmas day & Sunday. The children in a tumult of delight with their presents from their parents. All of us to church, except old Mrs. Lorraine & the youngest children . . . . Mr. Hansburgh
was lately ordained, & this his first sermon. It was but 21 minutes
long—& yet I did not keep awake through the whole of it. . . . Our
conversation at night mainly [836] on the Harper's Ferry affairs, &
the present & partly consequent condition of state & federal affairs.

*Dec. 26.* . . . . The mail brought no news. Congress & the Va. legislature doing nothing during Christmas week.—Besides all the children of this house, & Mr. Lorraine's, Julian's son Meade stayed, &
four from Mrs. Cocke's came to enjoy the promised festivities of the
evening. They tried to dance, the first time for most of them, but
could not for the want of music. No one here could play dances on
the piano. Afterwards, all went into the basement to see the shades
of the Magic Lantern, which Edmund is exhibiting. The young children, & the negroes, are delighted—& all the grown persons, except myself, are there to enjoy the joy & pleasure of the children. A
few minutes of attendance were enough for me—as I have performed the part of the exhibitor so often myself.—I received by Mr.
Lorraine sheets enough to make 50 of my last pamphlets. Folded &
stitched them this forenoon, & began to send them by mail, to
members of Congress & others. . . .

*Dec. 31.* All of us had been invited to dine today at the Glebe.
The weather again raw, cloudy, & threatening worse. After the carriages (Edmund's & my sister's) had set out, the snow began to fall
very fast & heavy, & so continued until night. Mrs. Lorraine sen.
[838] Edmund & I, only of the grown people, did not go. The others
returned after dark—& reported that, notwithstanding the terrible
weather, they had passed a very cheerful & agreeable day.—I finished reading Dickens' last interesting but foolish book "A Tale of
Two Cities," which I began in Washington. . . .

This year closes with appearances of awful portent to the South-

[385]

ern States & to the whole union. The leading northern politicians have used the pretence of opposition to negro slavery solely for their own political gain, & selfish objects, until they have made fanatics of the majority of every northern state. Blind as all fanatics are, these see no danger, & no evil consequences, in executing the abolition of slavery in the southern states, in any manner, & by every available means. They do not believe that there is either courage or strength enough in the south to resist these efforts. And probably, some would be glad of resistance in arms, as it is fully believed that, in a struggle in arms between the northern & southern states, all the slaves of the latter would be the ready & zealous allies of the former. The total failure of the recent northern conspiracy, of which John Brown was the agent, has not served to open their eyes in this respect. Therefore, the conquest of the [839] resisting south is expected as certain—bringing with it the annihilation of negro slavery in these states. The southern states, & especially Virginia, have never before been so much aroused by northern aggressions. The people are in this respect in advance of their legislators & magistrates. Never has there been such an opportunity for secession. But I fear it will be allowed to pass unused—& that after the present fever of excitement & indignation, & spirit of resistance, there will succeed a general chill & collapse. The hypocricy [*sic*] of the pretended horror of slavery as actuating northern abolitionists is sufficiently manifest in this, that all their efforts are directed against these southern states, where, by universal admission, the condition of bondage is more humane, by far, than any where else. In or for Cuba & Brazil, where it is inhuman & horrible, we never hear of any act, and rarely even a word of censure, from northern abolitionists. If our secession & independence were once accomplished, & northern politicians could no longer command votes or power by denouncing slavery, we should be nearly as safe from their anti-slavery action, as are Brazil & Cuba now.

The difficulty of electing a speaker in the House of Representatives is not diminished. The "Brown-Helper" candidate still wants but four more votes for his election. Even if no election could be effected through the session, it might not be very injurious to federal & general political interests in ordinary times. But [840] this cause of constant irritation—the hostile attitude of the opposed parties in Congress, & the likelihood of hostile action & bloodshed—serve to foment & increase the general exasperations. In the mean time, though not one of the southern states yet expresses, or probably feels, a readiness to secede, in co-operation with others—except South Carolina, which has repeated its long avowed readiness— still, nearly all are arming & preparing to be ready. The legislature of Va. is especially zealous in this effort. Sundry measures are now under consideration, & I trust some of them will be carried out, most of which I have long urged in vain. Besides the general military preparation, the other measures I refer to are, taxing heavily or prohibiting the use of northern products & trade—cutting off the means for northern abolition emissaries—admitting negro testimony —preventing post-obituary emancipation of slaves—& banishing or enslaving the greater number of negroes now free. If even half of these measures, affecting northern emissaries & trade, are put in force, we may control the north, & save ourselves, even in the union. If none are adopted at this session of the legislature, the next & certain thing will be to submit to northern dictation, in emancipation & in every thing else. [841]

# January–June

*ᐧᐧᐧᐧᐧ*

# 1860

THE VIRGINIA LEGISLATURE IN SESSION ᐧᐧᐧ
VIEWING THE STATE PARTY CONVENTIONS
ᐧᐧᐧ "ANTICIPATIONS OF THE FUTURE" ᐧᐧᐧ A
VISIT TO JUDGE THOMAS RUFFIN ᐧᐧᐧ A GUEST
AT THE SOUTH CAROLINA DEMOCRATIC
CONVENTION ᐧᐧᐧ AT THE RICHMOND AND
BALTIMORE CONVENTIONS

*January 1.* Sunday. Snow lying six inches deep, & cloudy & very cold. Still the carriage full went to church—& reported that Mr. Hansburgh preached a very good sermon to a congregation of 16 persons. . . .

*Jan. 3.* This was the day appointed for me to leave, & also for Mr. Lorraine's family, & my grandsons for school. . . . Got to Richmond at 6.30 P.M. & I went to the Exchange Hotel. . . . I met with sundry acquaintants, members of the legislature & others. Sat in John Seddon's room, with some half dozen, conversing on the present state of political affairs. . . .

*Jan. 4.* Saw Gov. Letcher this morning. His term of service began on the 1st. I had before written to him, & also to some members of the legislature concerning the existing & great evil of northern vessels, manned by northern negro crews coming into our ports. A motion, founded on the evidence I had obtained was made in the Senate to inquire into the matter, & the propriety of prohibiting the dangerous abuse. I trust that at least this broad way of access & impunity for abolition agents may be closed.—Got from the printing office more of my last pamphlet, & mailed them to southern members of Congress. Nothing of interest before either house of the Assembly. Most of my time spent in conversing with members, either old or new acquaintance. Already getting tired of my stay . . . .

*Jan. 5.* . . . I believe that almost every measure which I have attempted to urge the adoption of in latter years has been brought up for consideration, & referred to committees. [843] They embrace the taxing by licences, or prohibiting the products and imports of the northern states—stringent precautions & remedies against abolition emissaries & agents—the legalizing of negro evidence—the enslaving or banishing of free negroes—the regulation of the discipline & management of hireling slaves in towns, in which gross abuses exist —the prohibition of post-obit. emancipations of slaves—& the allowing of free-negroes entering the state as hands on northern vessels. This last abuse I recently obtained proof of, & it was referred to committees of both houses yesterday. The only omitted abuse of this general character not yet questioned & assailed, & subjected to legislative inquiry, is the proffered bounty to the Colonization Society, of $50 for every free negro transported to Liberia, & the existing connexion with the Colonization Society—& this subject a member has promised me to bring up.—Nothing of interest before the legislature today. The Speaker of the House of Delegates, when he took his seat was evidently a little drunk—as he frequently is, & more than a little, when not on duty. . . . At the request of a member, I wrote the provisions which I deem proper for a law to forbid negro sailors coming on northern vessels . . . .

*Jan. 6.* Yesterday was my birthday—66 years of age. In the county of my birth & early residence, there are now living but two men who are older than myself, within my knowledge.—As usual here, much of the day consumed in reading newspapers & chatting with acquaintances (mostly members of the legislature) in the public halls. After dinner, by appointment, & request of Mr. Paxton of the Senate, he came to my room to read to me his bill for the taxing of oysters, & to have my advice as to its provisions. The general object & principle of the bill—aiming to exclude catchers of oysters from other states, & to obtain a revenue from our oysters, I entirely approve—& did not see any objection to the details of the bill. . . . From 8 to 10 hearing a speech from Daniel H. London, on the subject of the legal obstructions to the trade of Virginia. It was more full, & better, than the speech on the same which he delivered at our agricultural fair in Petersburg. . . . [845]

*Jan. 7.* . . . Gov. Letcher's inaugural message was received & read today, but I missed hearing it. I hear that it is a strong southern paper. No speaker elected yet in Congress, & there are now hopes that Sherman cannot gain the four more votes required for his election. I distrust, more & more, the future action of this Assembly of Va. It is true that all the proper subjects have been brought up for consideration, & referred to committees. But there is no general interest shown for their passage by members generally, nor even zeal by the particular members who moved the consideration. . . .

*Jan. 9.* Read the governor's message. A strong southern paper. At night, as appointed Edmund came, to take his daughters again to school, & also Julian. They both go to Marlbourne tomorrow morning, & I also, for a short visit. . . . Two out of the three pieces I sent from Washington to the Examiner had not been published, & when I came thence to Richmond, I wrote immediately to the editor to have them returned to me if there was any objection to their being inserted. I received, on my return to Richmond, at different times, different excuses for the neglect, & I again demanded the [846] manuscripts, whether they were approved or not. It was not until yesterday evening that I could have returned to me the longer of the two articles. The other, (a short & not important article,) was not returned, & I suppose has been lost, by still greater carelessness. There are too many managers of the Examiner. But though that may in part account for this neglectful & slighting treatment, I must suppose there is some additional reason. I fully recognize the right, & the propriety, of an editor admitting or rejecting communications entirely with reference to the interest of his publication. The editor of the Examiner knows this—& I should not have shown the least displeasure, nor have asked a reason, if these or any other of my offered writings had been promptly rejected. But the delay, (& as I believe, without their having been read or looked into,) & for weeks after I had asked for them to be returned to me, & had several times repeated the demand, I deem bad treatment, though I will not quarrel about it. But, whatever the cause, I shall deem the action as notice that my contributions are not wanted, & shall not again offer any to the Examiner. Perhaps I ought further to construe this conduct into such admonition as Gil Blas offered to the Archbishop of Grenada—of faculties too much impaired by age to enable the writer to instruct the public, or to maintain his previous reputation. However, not deterred by this suspicion, I offered the recovered piece to the Index, in which semi-weekly paper it will appear next Friday. [847]

*Jan. 10.* Julian & I left Richmond in the mail coach by 3.30, & reached Marlbourne . . . a little after 7. Mr. Sayre & Elizabeth alone at home. . . . Getting together my clothing, & other articles that

I need to have with me soon, & putting them in a trunk to carry away. It is a gloomy time. Mildred's absence, & her removal to a far remote residence—this being but a visit of mine, rarely to be repeated, to what had before been my home—& the causes of these changes—all rendered the occasion very painful to me—which feelings I endeavored to conceal. My reception, & intercourse with Mr. Sayre & Elizabeth, were kindly in manner, & no allusion has been made to any of recent painful passages. But of course he retains his former opinion of being wronged by me, & also by Julian, & of course his wife thinks as he does, & I hold not only that he received no wrong, but that he was much to be blamed. . . . I do not expect to be again [848] at Marlbourne, except rarely & for short visits, merely to preserve outward appearances of the affection, & respect, which no longer exist.

*Jan. 12.* . . . Mr. Sayre sought & had a conversation with me, in which he went further than in his letter to explain & apologise for his conduct to me—admitting that he was under mistake &c. I received his apology in amicable & proper manner; & trust that, at least to outward appearance, this difficulty has been removed. Still I believe that he still deems himself to have been the aggrieved party —& that, most unjustly he includes Julian in the offence to him. . . . At night, saw Jem. Sykes, my former black overseer here,[1] and [849] still the foreman—& had a long conversation with him on the attempt & fate of Brown & his companions, & on the abolitionists, negro slavery, & the manner of its establishment here &c. I aimed to give to him, & through him to his fellows, correct information on this general subject, & particularly as to the late attempt of Brown, his expectations, & the causes of his complete failure, & of which such must always operate.

*Jan. 13.* After breakfast, . . . left Marlbourne, with Mr. Sayre in his carriage. Reached Richmond by 12. Went to the Exchange Hotel, which is crowded. Last night arrived there Mr. [Christopher G.] Memminger, the distinguished Commissioner sent by the legislature of South Carolina to confer with Virginia, & to forward the movement of secession, if possible. I waited on him immediately, & was accompanied & introduced by John Seddon. I was most kindly received, & Mr. Memminger made many inquiries of me, & we conversed some time on the present state of affairs & of public opinion in

---

[1] See William K. Scarborough, *The Overseer: Plantation Management in the Old South* (Baton Rouge: Louisiana State University Press, 1966), 17–18.

Virginia, & until several other visitors had come in, when I took my leave. Mr. M. seemed disposed to pay so much respect to my opinions on these subjects, that I thought it proper to warn him that, while I was ready to speak frankly & fully, without reserve, yet I was a political outlaw, bound or directed by no party allegiance, & knowing very little of party tactics & movements—so that my opinions were worth but little.—Found that my article sent to the Index was printed in today's paper.[2] [852]—Among the strangers here, met with Lieut. Green, whom I became acquainted with at Charlestown. Also Col. A. W. Barbour, the Superintendent of Harper's Ferry, who again assured me that the promised pikes shall be sent for me to Senator Clay, & in the course of next week. . . . William H. Harrison of Amelia here, who sat with me in my room until 11 P.M. There is no one of my friends whose conversation I enjoy more than his, & no one whom I esteem more for his virtues & admirable & noble qualities.

*Jan. 14.* . . . Again called on Mr. Meminger [*sic*], & conversed with him some time. I fear that he will not find more than a small minority of the legislature that will be ready to come up to the sentiments & offered pledges of South Carolina. James A. Seddon, the former distinguished & able member of congress from this district, sat with me in my room [853] & conversed on this subject, & afterwards he had a conference with Mr. Meminger. Mr. S. is a strong partizan of Hunter, for the presidency—& like every other leading partizan of a presidential candidate, is fearful of weakening or breaking down the democratic party, on which his candidate depends for success. Mr. S. is as much for disunion, in itself, as I am. But he fears its being advocated, as being yet hopeless of being adopted, & its agitation being dangerous to the democratic party & to his candidate.—Also met with Col. Smith of the V.M.I., who with others sat with me. . . . Put in Col. Smith's hands duplicate copies of most of my writings, in volumes & pamphlets, (except the Farmers' Register,) to be presented to the Cadets of V.M.I. . . .

*Jan. 15.* Sunday. Went to church. Jeremiah Morton & Mr. Boulwane arrived. They & sundry others in my room at different times. At one time, a conversation with Mr. Boulwane, Col. Smith, & J. Baldwin of Staunton, on the present condition of the country, & of polit-

---

[2] In this article, entitled "Subversion of Negro Slavery, or the Dissolution of the Present Union, the Only Alternative for the South," Ruffin made a strong plea for secession, based largely on Brown's raid upon Harpers Ferry.

ical parties. All these very intelligent gentlemen, & Baldwin & Smith also whigs.—Dr. Thompson, who is on the Harper's Ferry committee, informed me, in confidence, that the Report had been presented to the committee, & printed, but not yet received. He allowed me to read it. It is quite too weak to suit my views—which might be expected, as it is written by [Alexander H. H.] Stuart, the chairman, who was the apologist for [854] the worst acts of President Fillmore, committed under abolition influence.[3]

*Jan. 16.* Some hours of the day in the State Library. Conversation in my room at night with several persons on the present state of affairs.—My former labors, & of others of the State Agricultural Society in opposition to the policy of legal inspections, have not been fruitless. Though no change of law has yet been obtained, there has been in opposition to abuses under the law. The flour inspector here has been sued, & finally cost, for his illegal perquisites, & one miller has obtained a judgment against him for some $2500 or more of damages, & other suits may amerce him for ten times as much, & much more than he will be able to pay. This triumph over fraud & peculation never would have been gained, or even sought, if our publications had not stimulated the cheated millers to resist.

*Jan. 17.* The bill for appropriating $500,000 to establishing an Armory, & arming the militia, passed the House of Delegates unanimously, excepting two votes, both from the extreme northern counties, which are infected by abolition sentiments. In the Senate, the bill was today opposed, not directly, which but few will dare to do, but by offering amendments to weaken or destroy it. The Whigs of that body are inimical to the bill.—Saw Mr. Memminger again. I fear that the great body of the members will not in any way respond to his views & propositions. His credentials were presented on Saturday to the legislature through the Governor. It is expected that he will speak before the legislature on the 19th. [855]

*Jan. 18.* In the State Library, finished reading two sermons of the Rev. ——— Hall, a clergyman of Dorchester near Boston,[4] one of them denouncing slavery, & the other glorifying John Brown.—At-

---

[3] A native of Staunton, Virginia, Alexander Hugh Holmes Stuart (1807–91) served as secretary of the interior under President Fillmore. He was later a member of the Virginia Secession Convention.

[4] Probably Robert Bernard Hall (1812–68), one of the original members of Garrison's New England Anti-Slavery Society and a founder of the American Anti-Slavery Society. Hall, an Episcopalian clergyman, served two terms in Congress during the late 1850's.

tended the session of the Senate, & heard the debate continued on the bill for establishing an armory & arming the militia. Alex. Rives, a whig, delivered a long & vehement speech in opposition, the argument of which, if sound, would have gone against even the smallest outlay for arming, or the least effort for state defence. He & his party evidently fear the measure as the indication & the means for defending the State against the federal power. The debate not closed.—Received from the Speaker (Crutchfield,) a letter of invitation, & card of admission, to the Hall tomorrow, when Mr. Memminger is to speak. . . .

*Jan. 19.* This day the whole legislature assembled in the Hall of the Delegates, to receive the Commissioner of South Carolina—which was done with all respect & due ceremony. Mr. Memminger delivered an eloquent & very impressive argument, [856] which occupied three & a half hours. It was listened to with great attention —& I now trust will have important influence & effect. While the commissioner drew a vivid picture of the early patriotic sacrifices of the southern states, & especially Virginia, to the Union, & their later wrongs, & final deprivation of all the great benefits proposed, & designed to be secured, by the federal constitution, he spoke calmly & temperately. He proposed no particular action for Virginia, except one measure, which seems so favorably received by all of the few members whom I have since conversed with, that I hope strongly it may be adopted. This is the sending of Commissioners to meet & confer with others deputed by each & all of the Southern States, to confer on their grievances, & to devise & agree upon such declaratory or other amendments, & strengthened guaranties of the federal constitution, as shall serve to defend the rights of the slaveholding states, as they ought to have been maintained under the existing provisions of the constitution. This is so reasonable, that it [can] scarcely be directly opposed even by the whigs who are not thorough submissionists. And if acted out, I think that the thus bringing together the southern mind, & considering grievances, wrongs & remedies, will bring about the only remedy that is effective—as I have no idea that the fanatical people of the North will *agree* to secure anything to the South. The hall was completely filled with the members & invited guests, with a few ladies. The two galleries were [857] filled with ladies. Hundreds came who failed to obtain entrance—& thousands of other persons would have been there, if they could have been admitted. The seat next to mine was occupied by Miss Memminger, whose acquaintance I had previously made, when meeting her in her father's apartment. She seems a very agreeable & attractive young lady.—At night, with Col. Knight, I went to the theatre, to see the dramatic spectacle or opera of "The Enchantress." Expecting but little, I was rather agreeably disappointed. But there was the general manner of ranting & mouthing which has so disgusted me with theatrical performances that I had given out all thought of ever going to another. Miss [Caroline] Richings, the principal female performer,[5] appears to me to have the best voice I ever heard—powerful, yet sweet—& the most highly cultivated by art—too much so for my taste. I was much gratified by her powers whenever she adhered to the air, & even when she executed perfectly & admirably passages which would have been impossible to any untaught singer. But her trills & cadences, introduced merely to show her wonderful power & command of voice, were not only not musical, but absolutely disagreeable to my ear. Yet these were precisely the parts which were applauded most by the audience. And, if the singer had introduced the most perfect imitation of the mewing of a cat, or the braying of an ass, the same applauding audience would have been as much gratified, & would have applauded as much—provided [858] they had been only assured that these imitations had been applauded by all preceding audiences, & persons of musical taste.

*Jan. 20.* The debate in the Senate on the Armament bill was resumed. The opposers of the entire measure, who aimed first to strike out the armory feature, were defeated, by a vote of 26 to 20. The amendment being offered to defeat the bill, I presume that all others will also be rejected, & the bill passed by at least as large a majority. . . . John Seddon offered a resolution to authorise the appointing of Commissioners to meet & confer with others from all the other southern states. It lies over for later consideration. . . . A very long letter from J. M. Botts appeared in the Whig yesterday, probably by design on the same day with the speech of Mr. Memminger, addressed to his followers, in his usual egotistic & arrogant style, condemning everything of recent & former southern resistance to the North, & urging the maintenance of the union, under all circumstances. It is easy to see in this letter the source of the opposition to

---

[5] An English-born pianist, opera singer, and composer, Miss Richings came to the United States as a child and made her operatic debut in 1852.

arming the state, which Rives, [Christopher Y.] Thomas, & other Bottsites have recently started in the Senate.

*Jan. 21.* Left Richmond in the Steamer, & landed on [859] Beechwood, & reached the house before 12. All at home & well. Conversing with Mrs. Lorraine & Nanny, . . . & with Edmund mostly on public affairs. The general ferment has in this county caused the getting up of a volunteer troop of cavalry, of which he was chosen captain. He would have preferred being a private—but could not resist the nearly unanimous preference & call for his service in command.

*Jan. 22.* Sunday. Went to church. . . . Wrote a letter to Gov. Letcher, suggesting the appointment of Prof. Holcombe as one of the Commissioners of Va, if to be chosen by the governor, & stating Mr. Holcombe's great & especial fitness for that high trust & service. But there will be but small chance for any one except a popular politician to obtain this honor. Had I the power of selection, I would choose Willoughby Newton & James A. Seddon for the other two commissioners, if three are to be appointed. . . .

*Jan. 23.* Had begun in Richmond, & completed this morning, the reading of the debate in the Va. Convention of 1851, & especially the speeches of Wise, & marking passages containing his heterodox opinions, and also the comments of other speakers on his opinions. Began to copy these passages, & to write a commentary thereon, as materials for future use. At this time, it is useless to attempt to show his errors to the public. He has gained greatly in popularity by the Harper's Ferry [860] affair—& the more foolish, or reprehensible his conduct, the more he has been applauded. But surely this folly of the public cannot be permanent. When the tide turns, truth & reason may be heard. . . . Wrote (mostly copying extracts,) 11 pages before late bed-time. . . .

*Jan. 24.* Finished copying the extracts, & then walked to Ruthven, without much fatigue. The distance is called 5 miles, but I do not think it is more than four. . . . Looking over & partially reading the back Numbers . . . of the Weekly N.Y. Day Book & Tribune. I take the latter vile abolition paper for the purpose of seeing the worst words & movements of our enemies. Read therein the full report of Wendell Phillips' speech in N.Y. in glorification of John Brown. In this, he very properly cites Wise's testimony to sustain the high qualities of his hero.

*Jan. 25.* Wrote 5 pages of additional comments on Wise's doctrines. Re-read Theodore Parker's long letter from Rome justifying

& eulogizing the conduct & objects of John Brown, & emancipation of negro slaves by the slaying of the whites. . . . [861]

*Jan. 27.* . . . The mail brought me a letter from my much valued friend the Rev. J. Bachman of S.C. on my last pamphlet, & on the present state of the Union. Also one from a committee of the Cadets of V.M.I., thanking me for copies of sundry of my published writings, lately presented to the corps, as "my comrades for a day," from me, as their "youngest recruit" on Dec. 2nd. at Charlestown.— No election of speaker for Congress, & less prospect of one than earlier. I hope that there will be none. The struggle will serve still more to widen the separation between North & South. . . .

*Jan. 30.* Finished & mailed my letter to Dr. Bachman—mostly on the present political state of Va, & filled nearly three sheets.— Young John Newton arrived before dinner. As this is his third visit to Nanny, & evidently as a designed suitor, I hope he will now state his business—which I think will also close his negotiation, as he does not seem likely to gain much favor. . . . The newspapers took my time in reading from before 2 to dark, & yet contained no news of any account. The last ballot for Speaker came within 3 votes of electing [William N. H.] Smith of N.C., by the democratic vote added to the few whigs, to which party Mr. S. belongs. I earnestly hope that he may gain the few additional [863] votes required for his election. His being a whig would be no objection to me; & I should rejoice to see all the democrats thus sacrifice party to the support of a worthy southern whig, to defeat the Brown-Helper abolition party.

*February 2.* Temp 1½° after sunrise. . . . After breakfast, despite of Julian's urging me to use his carriage, I set out to walk to Beechwood. Well defended in his heavy over-coat, gambadoes, & coarse woollen socks over my boots, I was quite comfortable, & even rather too warm. Reached Beechwood just as Mr. J. Newton was leaving. Poor fellow! He had received his dismissal, as I anticipated. . . . The attempt to elect Smith failed for want of two more votes. Sherman was then withdrawn, & [William] Pennington of N.J. was run by the abolition party. He, in one ballot, wanted one vote only to be elected. In the Va. legislature the indications are that the conference asked by S.Ca. will not be agreed to. Except arming the militia, I fear that nothing of any importance will be done to oppose northern aggression. [864]

*Feb. 3.* Very cold. . . . The mail brought information that at last a

Speaker had been elected—Pennington of N.J. He is one of the "republican," or Brown-Helper party—but he was not one of those who endorsed the doctrines of Helper's vile book, & aided in its circulation. Nothing else of news, except this close of the long struggle, & final victory of the abolitionists.

*Feb.* 5. Sunday—Milder. Went to church. A small congregation, on account of the weather. Mr. Hansburgh came back with us, & in the afternoon, performed the funeral services over a negro woman of Edmund's, who died yesterday—of consumption. . . .

*Feb.* 6. . . . Finished correcting & copying my late writing, showing Wise's opposition, in the last Va Convention, to the rights of the states & to the defensive power of the southern states. I think that it is a strong article, & would have [865] effect on unprejudiced minds, or in regard to any delinquent politician except Wise. But, open to reprehension as he is in many things, & blameable for most of his public conduct, he seems to gain popularity & strength from his errors & fooleries & their exposure. Before the Harper's Ferry affair, he had but little support in Va. (& none elsewhere,) for the presidency, which he was seeking so boldly & shamelessly. But his conduct in & since that affair, though very blameable for indiscretion, & foolish & useless & very expensive military parade, has given him more popularity than all he ever had acquired for his real worth & ability, or his praise-worthy public services. He seems likely now to be the candidate preferred by Virginia—& if the same madness rules elsewhere, he may have some chance for the nomination of the democratic party. It would be useless to bring any charges against him now, no matter how grave, or well sustained. His friends would not regard them—& probably he might be strengthened by the attack being deemed persecution of a meritorious patriot. I will therefore wait—& will publish my strictures when there seems some intermission of this popular delusion, or otherwise some better chance for a fair hearing.—The mail. . . . Congress now organized, under an abolition speaker, & the infamous scoundrel, private & political, [John W.] Forney [of Pennsylvania] as clerk. In the legislature of Va, numerous sets of resolutions offered by different members, both *pro* & *con* the S.C. mission—& I fear nothing likely to be done. [866]—Wrote . . . answers to three letters of compliment, lately received—two of them from the two literary societies of the Va. Military Institute, each having elected me as an honorary member. The third was a letter of thanks from the Appomattox Ring Fence Association of this county, for my services in obtaining the law authorizing general or joint enclosures of many farms under one surrounding fence.

*Feb. 8.* . . . Sundry newspapers, but little news. Ministers of the *Gospel* of Washington have throughout this session, as usual, officiated to deliver public prayers before each house of Congress. A Jewish rabbi, Raphael, served in this duty lately, & prayed before the House of Representatives. I take this as a very remarkable [867] [occurrence] as it is a novel indication of the growth of religious toleration. I have seen no censure of the proceeding in any newspaper, nor any other remark, except one of high commendation of the prayer delivered by the rabbi. The newspapers contained the speech of Mr. Memminger before the Va. legislature, & also Senator Hunter's on the slavery question, & Gov. Wise's at the complimentary dinner given to him in Richmond recently. Read the two latter—which, with the other matter of the papers, occupied me from 2 P.M. to 9. Reserved Memminger to be read later. Wise's dinner speech, (of which the delivery took up to two hours,) is of his usual strain—Wise-like—& with enough of bad taste & utter foolery in it to attract universal censure or ridicule if from any other speaker—but which, from him, is but a matter of course, & applauded by his "tail" of admirers, & passed over without remark or notice by all others. Hunter's is a good speech, and much bolder in its tone against northern abolition, than latterly has been usual with him, or indeed is to be expected of any candidate for the presidency, who, by his ambition & hopes, is bribed to curry favor with the north, for the purpose of gaining or saving northern votes, without which he cannot possibly be elected, even if the entire south was for him.

*Feb. 9.* With Edmund, drove to court, in the carriage. . . . On this court day, there were to be held two public meetings. One, of the volunteer troop of cavalry, lately raised, (& of which Edmund had been chosen captain,) was to organize, & adopt its uniform & by-laws. Another, of the Democratic party, to send members to both [868] the State & the District Conventions, for the Presidential election. At the latter, after the regular business, Edmund moved two series of resolutions, which he had prepared previously, on the relations of North & South, & which after an animated discussion, though opposed but by one person, were passed, & all unanimously, except one dissentient to one only of the resolutions. The opinions & expressions are strong—& I trust that they will not be without effect on the present doubtful condition of the feeble & wavering legislature. . . . After supper, we read aloud, in our family circle, the speech of Mr. Memminger, which I had heard delivered to the legislature. It commanded the high applause of all of us. The legislature had printed 10,000 copies, a number larger by 6000, than any document ever before. But I earnestly wish that there could be enough for every man in Virginia to see & read this admirable & persuasive exposition & argument. I have better hopes of the attainment of the first object of this speech, & the speaker's mission, the concurrence of the legislature in a Southern Conference, inasmuch as Governor Wise, union-saving as it is now his part to act, & of course his mouth-piece the Enquirer, strongly advocate the conference, & the concurrence of Virginia. The reading of this speech furnished to us subjects for agreeable conversation for the remainder of the evening.

*Feb. 10.* The mail brought but little news. Gov. Letcher had sent a requisition for another Coppic [*sic*], who was engaged at Harper's Ferry, & was one of the few who made their escape early in the affair—& who was in Iowa.[6] The governor of that state refused to obey the requisition [869] on the alleged ground that it was informal—but I doubt not to screen the felon. He received information, & doubtless by contrivance of the governor, & so escaped beyond present reach before he could be arrested. It is understood that there [are] several others still at large of these villains, all of whom must have fled from Harper's Ferry early, before the band was surrounded by assailants. After that, there was no possibility of escape. Of these one or two, besides this Coppic, are sheltered, & protected, in Ohio, some in Canada, & one in England—or at least one who there claims the honor of having been engaged in the attempt at Harper's Ferry, & therefore is receiving notice & support from the English. . . .

*Feb. 11.* . . . Wrote first part of some remarks on the late voluminous report of the committee on the Harper's Ferry outrage to the Va legislature, by Alex. H. Stuart, which is in the spirit of a thorough union-worshipper & submissionist, as he is, but so cunningly shaped as to deceive most readers, & the weak body for which he acted. . . .

*Feb. 13.* Wrote a continuation to the remarks begun lately—but

---

[6] Barclay Coppoc, younger brother of Edwin, fled to Iowa after his escape from Harpers Ferry. He later went to Kansas and in September, 1861, plunged to his death in the Platte River after Confederate forces burned the supports of a rail trestle.

the farther I proceeded, the less I liked my performance; [870] so that I shall wait to consider whether I shall finish & use it.—Reading (second time,) & looking over, "The White Slaves of England."— The mail—no news of any importance. Mr. Memminger has returned to S.Ca., & nothing yet done by the legislature in regard to his mission. The resolutions which my son Edmund wrote & offered to the democratic meeting on last court-day, were in the Petersburg paper. . . .[7] [871]

*Feb. 14.* By previous appointment, we all went to dine at Julian's, with the Glebe family. . . . At my instigation, all the younger ladies, after dinner, tried, (most of them for the first time,) firing a revolver at a target. I urged them to make up a "Ladies' Shooting Club," & to practice shooting both with gun & pistol, until acquiring readiness in the handling & use of the weapons. If this were done generally by our country females, it would insure their safety from all approach of thieves, or danger of insult, when necessarily left without male protectors. I have always been in favor of this plan—& would be very glad to forward its being made fashionable. . . .

*Feb. 15.* Finished the writing, & most of the copying, of an article commenting on & censuring the late report to the legislature on the Harper's Ferry Outrage. . . .

*Feb. 16.* Left Beechwood for Richmond, in the steamer. The state democratic convention began its session this forenoon. On my arrival, at 5 P.M. found the Exchange, & the two next most important hotels so full that there was not a room or a bed empty for me. But later, a room just vacated was obtained at the Exchange. At night, went as a spectator to the adjourned meeting of the convention. The largest church in town packed full—& much confusion. After 9, I left —& retired to my [872] room, to read the newspapers—as all my acquaintances were at the convention.

*Feb. 17.* . . . On an incidental vote, serving to test the strength of the parties in the Convention, it seemed that two-thirds of the members (or rather of the votes represented,) are for Wise for President. Yet before the Harper's Ferry affair, he did not appear to have the least chance for the vote of Virginia. The more foolishly & blameably he has acted, the more popularity & supporters he has gained. I attended the session of the convention, in the gallery, but part of its

---

[7] The strongly worded resolutions threatened secession if a Republican were elected President and called for a meeting of commissioners from the southern states to adopt a "concerted plan of action."

time today. In the forenoon I was wearied with long speeches, for & against the proposal to express by vote a [873] preference for Wise. The speeches were to close at 9 P.M. & the vote to be then taken, by ayes & noes. But such was the disorderly conduct of the meeting, the noise, & riotous confusion, that nothing could be heard or done for two hours. The calling the names & votes began only at 10.40 P.M., while still the noise scarcely permitted the names to be heard, or the votes.—Received today from the tailor, & put on, a full suit of cheap cloth clothes, manufactured in Virginia. This plan is spreading, & I trust will be extensively used in the southern states. Already, our factories of woollen & cotton cloth cannot supply the increased & new demand—& many branches of trade or production at the north have suffered greatly because of the diminution of the previous southern demand & consumption.—I had brought my Harper's Ferry pike with me, & placed it, labelled as it is, in the State Library, for exhibition.—My article on the "Report of the Harper's Ferry Outrage," put in the printer's hands.

*Feb. 18.* Heard that the convention sat last night until 1 A.M. & only had one vote, without yet having counted the results. The subject of recent discussion is a resolution offered, declaring that Wise is the choice of the convention (& of the State) & a substitute for it resolving that it is inexpedient to state any preference. The substitute is supported by the Hunter party—& as they are weakest, their object is to prevent final action. The session before dinner today another scene of noise & uproar. The afternoon session I did not attend. A compromise was at last made, that the vote on the substitute should be counted, & the report published [874], & that no vote should be taken on the original resolution, recommending Wise, as the preference of the Convention & of the State. The vote on the substitute (declaring it inexpedient to declare any preference,) was lost by votes representing about 1500 popular votes—or 40,000 & more for, & more than 41,000 against the substitute. This was nearly a drawn battle—claimed by the Wise men as a victory, & that claim denied by the Hunter men.—During the night session, an attempt was made to have a vote of the Convention in favor of the S.Ca. Conference. This was received with so much disapprobation, (as business for that body,) that it was speedily withdrawn, & at the same time notice given that as soon as the convention adjourned that night, the members, & all others present, would immediately form a mass meeting, to vote on the conference. This was done—at past 10. Some 5 or 6 animated speeches were delivered, all except one strongly urging the recommendation of the conference. Even my name, among others who spoke, was called for so loudly, & at several different times, that at last I responded to the call, in a very few sentences, expressing strongly my general opinion on the measure. I was surprised that I was able to speak, even this little, clearly, & without evidence of embarrassment & difficulty. I believe that what I said was to the point, & well received. Much the greater portion of the members must have remained & voted—& also many others from the galleries, & among these sundry whigs & Botts men of Richmond. The final vote, even with these added opposing, showed a very large majority in favor of the conference. Gen. Burwell Starke, Commissioner from [875] the legislature of Mississippi, sent to invite Va. to the Southern Conference, had arrived this afternoon. When the vote was decided, many members went, with the President of the meeting, to call on the Commissioners. One of them only was found (Mr. Starke,) & he in bed. Nevertheless, he dressed himself, & came down to the hall of the Hotel, & delivered a very good though short speech to his visitors, on the occasion. Much enthusiasm was exhibited in the meeting, & also at this after proceeding, which did not close before midnight. I trust that this demonstration of popular will, from all parts of the state, will have some effect in urging on the laggard movements of the legislature—of whose proper action I had entertained but little hope.

*Feb. 19.* Sunday. Conversation, generally in the hall of the hotel, where there is generally a crowd, most of the day. . . . Visited Gov. Letcher & his lady in the afternoon. They had permitted all their servants to go abroad, & the door was therefore opened, on my ringing the bell, by Mrs. Letcher, & afterwards, to other visitors, by the Governor. I was pleased to see this absence of all pretension, & simplicity of manners, induced as it was by kind indulgence to the servants.—At night went to the sitting room of James W. Cook, of Greenville, & sat an hour with him & Mrs. Cook. He is a very intelligent & true southern man, whose [876] company & conversation I value much.

*Feb. 20.* Went to the sittings of the houses, but neither doing anything of any interest. The Whig Convention is to commence here on the 22nd, & many members have already arrived. Another great crowd may be expected. Obtained some dozen copies of Memminger's speech in pamphlet form.—The prospect of the legislature supporting the scheme of a Southern Conference seems more & more faint. I aided, with Cook, Douglas of King Wm. & a few others in the drawing up a letter to Gen. Starke, the Miss. Commissioner, requesting him, after the business of his mission is done, to address a public meeting on the great southern question. If the object is approved, & enough signatures obtained from men of high standing of both parties, the letter will be delivered. Otherwise not.

*Feb. 21.* The 1st No. of my last piece appeared this morning, in the Index. The other two Nos. are to be printed in the next issue, of 24th. The subject will be under discussion, & possibly these pieces may throw some light on it, & the Report.[8]—Visitors arrived in great number, to attend the Whig State Convention tomorrow. Among them, found sundry of my old acquaintances. Obtained a few whig signatures to the letter to Gen. Starke, inviting him to speak. ... [881]

*Feb. 22.* A drizzly & gloomy day, until past 2 P.M. Bad for the designed military display, & for the Whig Convention. This assembled at 12. I obtained admittance, & was wearied in hearing three speeches from as many of their dignitaries—on nothing—except general remarks & declamation on the glorious union, & the sins of the democratic party. Did not go in the afternoon. The hotel is as full as it can be packed—& a great crowd attending the Convention. —Sent to the Charleston Mercury my paper against Wise. It ought to injure him greatly, with the southern & states-rights men—but I doubt whether it will do him any harm in Virginia. There are enough of his follies & misconduct, already exposed, to kill off half a dozen political leaders, if shared among them. But both his friends & enemies have been so long accustomed to such things from Wise, that they pay no regard to any new information of like offences. ...

*Feb. 23.* With much difficulty, I got into the gallery of the church in which the Whig Convention is sitting—& heard nothing except wearisome speeches on general subjects. But it was then voted that John M. Botts ( who was not a member, & had not appeared, ) should be invited to address the meeting at night. This I determined to at-

---

[8] In his piece, "Remarks on the Report of the Harper's Ferry Committee—Addressed to the Members of the General Assembly of Virginia," Ruffin denounced the report, written by Sen. A. H. H. Stuart, and demanded legislation to arm the state, restrict the movement of free Negroes and abolitionist agitators, and encourage the growth of southern manufactures.

tend, if possible.—Met [882] with Richard K. Crallé, the former private secretary & friend of Mr. Calhoun, who was entrusted to arrange & select his papers & writings for publication, since his death. In our conversation, I referred to the hatred always borne by Wise for state-right doctrines, & for Mr. Calhoun. C. said that I was mistaken as to the latter part of the life of Mr. Calhoun—for he had seen a letter of Wise's, addressed to Calhoun, while the former was minister in Brazil, & Calhoun was Secretary of State, expressing an entire change of opinion in that respect—& stating, that, while he had been long hostile, he would use the remainder of his life to render justice to Calhoun. Crallé said that the letter, (or letters,) of Wise to Calhoun had been, with the other papers, in his possession. But that, about three years ago, Wise had requested the loan of them, for him to make extracts—& that they had not been returned to him. I told him that I strongly suspected that it was not Wise's intention to return them, unless he could not avoid it, & urged him to require the return, without longer delay—which he said he would. I believe Wise to be a political liar of the first magnitude. And though he claims & boasts to be the very soul of chivalrous honor, he will go much farther than merely verbal falsehood, to effect his political purposes & ends.—At night, with great difficulty, got into the gallery to hear Botts. The house was completely filled—not only every [883] seat was occupied, but every aisle was filled with persons standing. He spoke for nearly two hours. I have rarely heard a speech with more gratification, much as I detest both his principles & himself. He is a great speaker. As I expected, & desired, he used this occasion to rejoin to Wise's late foolish & abusive reply, uttered at the public dinner—& it was well done. If Wise was not invulnerable to censure, & to ridicule, he would sink under such a well-deserved load of both. But he & Botts are much alike in sundry respects. They are both powerful public speakers, having more power over popular audiences than any men living in this country. They are both great egotists, of inordinate ambition, & candidates for the presidency. They both have, in their respective parties in Va., numerous unlimited admirers, & devoted friends & partizans, & yet large minorities of bitter enemies, holding them in scorn & contempt. Wise stands fair in his private character—but, as I think, as a politician he is a liar, a deceiver, a renegade, & totally untrustworthy, except that, in all his changes, he will ever seek his own personal & political advancement. Botts, in his private life, whether undeserved, (as his friends say,) or deserved, stands low. He is not even deemed respectable, except by his friends. But he has maintained his ultra political doctrines, even when most unpalatable to the public, &, in part, to his own party, with a consistency & boldness, & honesty, that I am compelled to admire, & readily testify to. He & Wise are in everything opposed, & bitterly hostile to each other. I trust that they will go on, & [884] continue to do, what they are so well qualified to do, expose & vilify each other, & enable posterity to see, even if not the living generation, how little they both deserve the admiration & worship of their respective followers. . . .

*Feb. 24.* . . . Went to the Capitol, &, by appointment, had a conversation with Mr. James Barbour, a prominent member, who is chairman of the "Harper's Ferry" Committee, & also of the committee of finance, & who has brought in the bill to tax licenses, so as to burden or prohibit the sale of sundry kinds of northern productions. I suggested the including of school-books, among the prohibited articles. He received my suggestions with much courtesy, & requested me to present any other views that may occur to me. I have, however, scarcely any hope that anything will be done, either by this bill, or any other new policy, to defend ourselves against the north—except the act, already passed, for arming the state. And, I believe, that if this had been delayed to this time, the opposition to it would be much stronger, & perhaps enabled, by indirect action, to defeat it. The Commissioner of Mississippi has made his communication to the Governor, & through him to the Legislature. He has been received with all courtesy, & made the guest of the state. But no favorable response will be made to him.—Attempted twice to get into the galleries of the Convention, [885] but could not penetrate near enough to the assembly for me to hear the debates.—The Index of this morning contained the Nos. II & III of my article on the Report of the Harper's Ferry committee.—In the afternoon, I went with Edmund to call upon & introduce him to the Governor. We had some pleasant & free conversation, mostly on Botts' speech of last night, & his showing up of Wise, & on the remissness of the legislature to do anything, when its expected final adjournment is now within a week. Yet within the last & the current week, six days of the session have been almost totally lost, by the members, as spectators, attending the two political conventions! The governor seemed to intimate that if the legislature adjourned before acting upon its important & essential business, under the expectation of a called session next winter, that he would make the call immediately, before the members had time to leave. At night, at the request of the Commissioner of Mi[ss]., I had a private conversation with him on the subject of his mission, its expected failure here—& the course & prospects of the South. I stated my reasons for being confident that neither Virginia, or any other border slave state, will take any efficient step in advance, but will be compelled to follow a movement of even a few of the more southern states—& my earnest advice, that whether for the proposed conference, or any more conclusive measure, that these states will no longer wait for Virginia, but act without her. For the reasons which I stated in [886] 1856, (in "Consequences of Abolition Agitation") for successful & peaceful secession, I think it would be even preferable that the movement should be first made by the more southern states alone. The border slave-holding states, with N.Ca. & Tennessee, remaining in the present federal union, would prevent the occurrence of bloodshed from border feuds along Mason & Dickson's [*sic*] line, & serve as an impregnable barrier of defence to the seceding states. And in a few months, after the new southern confederacy had organized its government & its power, then the more northern slave-holding states would follow the movement, & have no choice.

*Feb. 25.* Edmund went to Norfolk, by the York river route, & I went to Beechwood. Reaching there before 12, found that Mrs. Lorraine & Nanny had gone to Ruthven, where I followed them, on horseback. Spent a pleasant day. . . . We returned to Beechwood at night. . . . [887]

*Feb. 26.* Sunday. Went to church, where I met with most of my friends of the neighborhood. Heard that the Botts wing of the Whig convention had been out-voted by a very large majority—more than 3 to 1.—Finished reading "Wild Scenes of the South," a very foolish book, which I regret having bought, or spent the time in reading. But the subject promised something, & the idea might be carried out to good purpose. It is a *prospective* narrative of the supposed incidents & results of a separation of the Union. But the writer, I think, shows little sagacity in his conceptions of future political consequences & events, or of genius to contrive a natural & interesting narrative of fiction.

*Feb. 29.* . . . The very foolish "Wild Southern Scenes," which I have just read is a *prospective* account of the supposed consequences of disunion. The design (which is wretchedly carried out by the author,) suggested to my mind the idea of something on the same plan, which I began, & wrote 7 pages. My plan is to assume the position of an English correspondent of the London Times, residing in America, & whose letters of news & comments thereon will commence with Seward's second election to the presidency—& will show how extreme oppression may be inflicted on the southern states, & their virtual bondage to the north, without any [889] infraction of the federal constitution.[9] . . . After reading the newspapers received today, looking over Helper's book again.

*March 1.* Wrote 10 more pages. I like the subject & plan still more. The passages will consist mostly of separate (supposed) incidents, & comments thereon when needed—& may be extended or contracted, suspended or resumed as convenient. Stopped writing before 2 P.M. & soon after, Edmund returned from his visit to Norfolk. . . . Finished glancing over Helper's "Impending Crisis," for the second time. Besides the many other lies & exaggerations in this book, one of its main objects was to establish the position that there exists hostility between the non-slaveholders, & the slave-holders of the southern states. Of this, the people of the north are well convinced. The delusion in this respect, I doubt not, was one of the main inducements for the John Brown attempt. I trust that they may continue in this delusion, & the other of the general discontent & disloyalty of the slaves. If they knew the exact truth of the case, they would be more prudent, & more effective in their efforts to cause insurrection [890] & the abolition of slavery. The renegad[e] Helper had previously written another book "The Land of Gold," in which he had expressed strong (& true) pro-slavery sentiments, in reference to the value of negro slavery for California, & the absolute necessity for it in Central America. From his own personal experience, he knows to be false many of the statements which he makes in the "Impending Crisis," of the condition of slaves & the slaveholding states. But if his evidence is deemed sufficient (& the best possible) to convince the northern abolitionists that such falsehoods are true, & to induce them to act accordingly, he will have worked to do as much future good to the south, as he & his abettors designed harm. The endorsement of his book by Sherman & 67 other northern members of Congress, induced the defeat of Sherman, & great notoriety to the book, & a subsequent demand & circulation beyond all expectation. The cheap

---

[9] The work upon which the diarist is embarking is his political novel, *Anticipations of the Future.*

(endorsed) edition, of increased virulence & incendiary recommendations, of 100,000 copies, was exhausted, & others have since been printed & sold. If Helper's statements & arguments are taken as good authority, the fanatical hatred of negro slavery, & of the southern people will be greatly increased, & also the wish to use, & the faith in the effects, of such action as led to, & induced Brown's attempt. The greater the extent of their delusion, & madness in this respect, & the greater their perseverance, the better for us will be the result. [891]

*March 3.* I had procured through Julian, who went to Petersburg yesterday, some of largest sized wire, ( ¼ inch, or more in diameter,) which I carried with me this morning to the blacksmith's shop, & had it cut, bent & welded, so as to make three hoops for the boys to roll. Carried Meade, & the hoops, with me to the Glebe, where we met the family from Beechwood, to which place we returned by night. Taught John & Meade how to roll their hoops, & also Jane, whom I provided with one of smaller size. All of them delighted with their new hoops, which are of better kind than any of wood. . . .

*March 5.* . . . The mail. A letter from editor of the Charleston Mercury, asking, for reasons stated, some postponement of the publication of my article on Wise. Answered it—& added remarks of present affairs. A second & longer communication from the Miss. Commissioner to our Governor, published in the papers. It is a concise but strong argument, which he has very adroitly made out, almost entirely, by quoting the words & stated facts of the Report of the joint committee on the "Harper's Ferry Outrage," already received, & seemingly approved, by the legislature. This is the report, so brave in general & preliminary words, & so treacherous & feeble, & contemptible in conclusion, & in facts, which I had lately denounced in print.

*March 6.* . . . Continue writing—reached to 45 pp. in all. Read Seward's elaborate speech lately delivered to the Senate, on the slavery question. A deal of sounding verbiagge [*sic*], to conceal ideas & purposes. Read over ( in De Bow's Review, for 1857,) my disunion article, written in 1856, & first published in the Enquirer. My attention was attracted to it now by Rhett's asking for a copy of it in pamphlet—of which I have not one remaining. He referred to it with commendation, & wished to republish the latter portion in which the manner of secession was advised.

*March 7.* More interested in my present writing—to which I

added 15 pages today. The mail. The conference asked for by S.Ca. & Miss. has been rejected by the Senate of Va. by the very large majority vote of 31 to 11. The rejection I had counted upon—but the number of opponents I was not prepared for.

*March 9.* . . . Wrote a few pages, & read the newspapers. . . . The Southern Conference also rejected in the House of Delegates, by a vote of near three to one. . . . [895]

*March 10.* . . . Suspended the progress of my article in hand, & began to copy the first portion. As generally, the copying, with correcting, takes twice as long as the first writing of any portion. Copied only 6 pages. . . .

*March 16.* . . . The Charleston Mercury, with a long & excellent article of comment on the general subject, republishes a long extract from my disunion pamphlet, of 1856–7, advising as to the mode for the secession of the Southern states. Altered & copied my MS. to 103rd page. . . . The Governor of Va. has recently demanded the surrender of three of the criminals who were engaged in the attempted insurrection [896] at Harper's Ferry, & who escaped thence early in the fray. Of these, Coppoc, (whose brother was captured, tried & hung,) has gone to Iowa, & Owen Brown & [Francis J.] Merriam to Ohio. The legal requisitions made for their bodies, to be brought to Va. for trial, were severally refused by both Gov. [Samuel J.] Kirkwood of Iowa, & Gov. [William] Dennison of Ohio, on different empty pretexts of technical or formal objections. These are new & striking evidences of the sympathy felt by the greater number of the people of these states, & as may be inferred, of most of the northern states, for these atrocious villains, & for the work they attempted. For no governor would take such grounds for their protection, unless he were satisfied that his refusal to execute the law, & his duty & oath of office, would be approved by the majority of the people of his state.—This is the day for the execution of [Aaron D.] Stevens & [Albert] Hazlett, the last two convicted of the Harper's Ferry convicts, & which execution will close the legal & military operations & enormous expenses of this little war, carried up by the folly of Gov. Wise's extensive arrangements & by the subsequent foolish liberality of the Va. legislature to $225,000 already, & as is supposed, the whole expenses, (& not including any for arms, or any other objects of abiding use,) will reach $300,000.

*March 17.* Edmund went to the Court House, to Captain to muster the new troop of volunteer cavalry. The success of the effort to establish the troop is not yet past doubt.—Copied & corrected, with some new pages added, to 110th page, at which I must suspend the narrative, for want of topographical materials. Began to read over the whole copy regularly, for [897] correction, & to judge better of the general appearance, in connection.

*March 20.* . . . Before 12, set out for the Maycox wharf, to go on board the steamer for Richmond—which reached at 5 P.M. Saw a few acquaintances, & attended to some business, read the last newspapers, & then wrote in my room. The legislature now sits at night, which prevented my seeing any members at the hotel during the time of session.

*March 21.* Saw & conversed with several intelligent members of the [898] legislature from the North-western part of Va., & learned from them much concerning the topography, & the great routes of rail-roads & of the Ohio river. Also consulted guide books & maps, & bought a large map of Va (lately published) showing all the routes of railways. . . .

*March 23.* Returned, by steamer, to Beechwood. Arrived, from Maycox, where I hired a boat, by 11. A.M. . . . Continued my writing, which is so copious & long, that I must reject much of the latter parts. It will not do to be so extended in details.

*March 24.* . . . There have been late accounts of two Mexican war vessels, belonging to Miramon's (or the Church) party, being captured by an American man of war, & sent in as prizes. The whole affair is strange, & scarcely credible as to the causes stated. It may lead to war with Mexico, or at least with one of its two hostile factions. These steamers had just arrived from Havanna, where they had been bought, & manned & equipped for Miramon, & had arrived off Vera Cruz, to assist the contemplated siege. They were without any proper national character, or protection, & therefore pronounced to be piratical, inasmuch as when required by the Captain of the U.S. ship Saratoga, to explain their character, they fired on him, & after a short conflict, were captured & sent to the U.S. According to the reports, the U.S. officer was altogether right. But it seems to me incredible that this feeble force should have dared to fire first on a strong American vessel, & with other American war vessels in sight.

*March 29.* Writing. Reached to p. 158 of first draft, & mostly copied.

*March 30.* Copied to p. 146. Mail. The district elections of delegates to the Charleston Convention (to nominate a democratic can-

[411]

didate for the Presidency) from Va. so far as yet elected, show a decided majority for Hunter over Wise—& the prospect is that it will not be altered by the elections yet to occur.—The further explanations of the late fight with & capture of two Mexican (or Spanish) steam war vessels, do not clear up the difficulty. This, with the other previous subjects of dispute with one of the two factions of Mexico, & the total absence of order & regular or general government in that distracted & anarchical country, I fear may bring about war. A robber chief, Cortinas, has long ago, & repeatedly, crossed the line from Mexico, & invaded Texas, robbing, burning, & killing. At last, U.S. troops have driven him back, & have pursued his band across the border into Mexico. A foreign war would now be a good thing for cementing the Union, & fixing the submission of the southern states to the Northern—&, to my views, would be most calamitous for the South, & the maintenance of its rights.

*March 31.* Correcting first draught, & wrote 7 new pages.—Reading "The Rivals" a new book, a mongrel between a novel & a eulogistic biography of Aaron Burr.

*April 3.* Soon after daybreak, left Ruthven in Julian's carriage, for the station 9 miles distant on the Norfolk & Petersburg Railroad, for Suffolk, which I reached at 10.30. There hired a conveyance, & servant to bring it back, & drove to Redclyffe, the farm & residence of Bruce Gwynn, who married Judge Ruffin's youngest daughter, Sally. Found Patty there. My plan of our returning on next Thursday, & going first to Marlbourne, did not suit her, as she cannot stay but a week with us all. So to prevent her visit being too soon, I had to agree to stay here until next Monday—much longer than I desire. . . .

*April 6.* Mr. Gwynn drove me to Suffolk, where we went on the train going to Norfolk, & got out about 4 miles in the Dismal Swamp. My object was to examine the soils, farther on than I had done before, & the pine trees. I had but poor opportu[ni]ties for both. A broad ditch, deep in water, on both sides of the railroad, made it difficult to find passways across—& recent fires had burnt the fallen cones, & leaves, by which otherwise I could readily have identified the species of the pines. Moreover, the smutty remaining stems of reeds & bushes, made the walking over the burnt ground a dirty & disagreeable job. From the few cones I could obtain, & the distant view of those on the trees, I supposed, as I had anticipated, that most of them are *p. serotina*, or pond pine. But on the swamp soil I saw some *p. toeda*, & I believe some *p. variabilis*. After a walk of four miles along the railroad, we were overtaken by the returning train, & in it returned to Suffolk, & thence drove back to Mr. Gwynn's.—Finished reading "Peg Woffington," [10] which is amusing, & has two well-drawn characters—but is not commendable otherwise. . . .

*April 7.* . . . Reading 16th Chapter of Gibbon's Rome, with Milman's notes.—Have come to what seems a proper place for stopping my writing—& that source of amusement is therefore stopped for the present. My effort, & my main difficulty in conducting the narrative, & especially of the latter part, has been to shorten, & to pass over what might more easily have been extended to more length. This is the first time I ever attempted to write anything of the narrative form, or of imaginative plot & details. Vey likely it may be a failure, & even the most foolish thing that I ever wrote. But, from the beginning, it has afforded me more amusement, & has been the most pleasant labor of the kind that I have ever performed. In writing argumentative pieces, or any such as I have heretofore written, I never could compose anything, not even as much as a single sentence, in advance of the actual writing. Indeed it seemed as if I could not think, except with pen in hand & writing my thoughts as they occurred. . . . But with this article, it has been different. Being in the form of narrative, & the events being of the supposed future, & entirely imaginary, I could make them as I pleased, within the limits of probability, & of the connexion & influence of known causes upon unknown effects. I have passed many separate portions of what otherwise would have been wearisome time of solitude [904] or wakefulness, in imagining what would be the probable results of even improbable incidents & political causes, & planning suitable succeeding incidents & consequences. Every such fragmentary plan was found defective in some part of the structure, & had afterwards to be altered & remodelled—or rejected entirely. And this occurred often after the first writing, & for 10 or more pages together. But the first plan & the alterations, all were alike amusing to my mind, & all the time & labor so given were conducive to immediate pleasure. But this attempt has caused me, more than ever, to wonder at the facility of the composition of romance writers—& how, not only poor works of fiction, but also the best, could be dictated to an amanuensis, or even written by the author's hand, at a single sit-

---

[10] A novel by Charles Reade, published in 1853 and based on the life of a famous eighteenth-century Covent Garden actress.

ting, & sent off to the press, as a chapter of an extended work, with no delay for second consideration, & scarcely for verbal corrections. Thus were most of Scott's great romances composed & sent piecemeal, & immediately to the press, as is manifest from his biography by Lockhart. And G[eorge] P[ayne] R[ainsford] James, the very fertile though much inferior romance writer, told me that his works were dictated to a secretary, written thus from his lips, & that he did not even read them over for correction usually, for want of time, before they were sent to the press.[11] Now this is to me inconceivable. It seems to me that even that which we know to be true, (the procedure of Scott's,) is impossible. For with all the vividness of imagination, & power of thinking, & ready mastership of language, that Scott possessed, or that any man can possess, I would suppose that his first planned incidents would often need alterations to suit later occurring circumstances, & that his first writing, even of the main incidents & general plot, would therefore need revising & correcting. ... [905]

*April 8.* Easter Sunday. A cloudy & gloomy forenoon, with rain. Afterwards clear. Reading 5th vol. of Irving's "Life of Washington," which I had not seen before, since its publication.

*April 9.* As at first arranged, this forenoon, Patty & I left for Prince George. We left Mr. Gwynn's, for Suffolk, & there took the train at 1. P.M., reaching Disputanta in Prince George at 3, where Julian's carriage was waiting for us, & arrived at Ruthven at 5 P.M. ... Spent a pleasant time in conversation until nearly 11 before we separated to go to bed. ...

*April 10.* ... The Charleston Mercury at last contains my attack on the anti-state-rights course of Wise in the last Va. convention. ...

*April 11.* ... Before we rose from dinner at Ruthven, Edmund, with Nanny & John arrived from Beechwood—& after sitting some hours, Patty & I returned with them. ... A pleasant evening of conversation at Beechwood to a late hour. It is five years since Patty was here on her last visit, to attend the marriage of my daughter Jane, & remained some weeks after at Marlbourne & here. How happy we were then—& how many miserable occurrences since!

*April 12.* A letter from the editor of the Charleston Mercury, by

---

[11] The diarist doubtless became acquainted with James, an early imitator of Sir Walter Scott, while the novelist was serving as British consul at Norfolk from 1852 to 1858.

last mail, stated his wish to have my last writing for publication. I doubt whether he will be pleased with it. Revised it to page 85, which may be made a stopping place, if required, & will send that much by next mail. Continue, as convenient, the further revising & correcting of the remainder. . . .

*April 14.* Reading, altering & correcting the remaining portion of my last writing. Finished reading "The Rivals," a foolish & false book. . . . The legislature adjourned on the 2nd. having, after so many indications of such intended action, done almost nothing in the many subjects before them in reference to the wrongs inflicted or threatened by the north on the south. The bill for establishing the manufacture of arms, & for arming the militia, is the only important exception. And if that had been delayed to near the end of the session, I verily believe that even that measure would have failed to pass. The violent agitation & impulse caused by the Harper's Ferry affair seem to have completely subsided. . . .

*April 20.* Interpolated 15 pages of new writing, which completes the matter designed, & also the first rough draft—in all making 230 pages. Of this nearly 150 pages have been corrected & copied, but still my ideas of the best arrangements of incidents change so often, that no doubt changes will require to be made in this supposed finished portion. The first 85 pages had been sent to the Charleston [910] [Mercury], & that paper, of 18th, received today, contains the first letter. . . .

*April 22.* Sunday. All of us to church. . . . Finished looking over, & but partly reading Custis' "Recollections of Washington," a poor thing—foolish, & in many things manifestly false.—Copied a few pages of my manuscript. . . .

*April 25-27.* Continue to correct, & to copy. Have reached to page 250.—The papers full of the proceedings of the Charleston Democratic General Convention, for nominating a candidate for the Presidency. Much disorder. The balloting not begun to last reports. Opinions so conflicting that no conclusion can be reached as to who stands a good chance to be nominated.—My 2nd letter ( of "Glimpses of the Future,") appeared in the Charleston Mercury which came today. I subscribed lately for the Daily N.Y. Herald, of which the first received No. came today. We have now so many papers, that to get through them will occupy me for the half of every mail day. . . .

*April 30.* . . . Finished my writing, extended to 271 pages, & all corrected, though not all copied. The latter part is very unsatisfactory to me—the subject drags heavily, there are too many words for the matter, & repetitions of matter, which I have not been able to get rid of. I fear this writing of mine (if not also some previous) would offer to a capable judge, indications of a failing mind. On account of this suspicion, if the subject were different, I would be glad to hold it back for consideration. But its interest, & utility, if any, will depend on its early appearance—as the events of every passing day may serve to contradict my predicted or supposed incidents before their being first announced. Though the Charleston Mercury has begun, & is going on with the publication of the first portion of the series, I doubt whether the editor will choose to allow space for the whole of so long an article. But if the early portion, thus published, shall attract no attention, or induce any desire of the public for the continuation, it will be taken by me as notice to stop—& to intrude on the public with no more later writings. [913] ... The mail, & latest telegraphic reports from the Charleston Convention. Balloting for a candidate not begun, & still complete uncertainty as to the choice that will be made. . . . Gov. Wise, seeing that the majority of the Va. delegates lately elected, was opposed to him, wrote & published a letter withdrawing his name as a candidate, so as not to endanger the unanimity of the vote of Va. in the Charleston Convention. No doubt he thought this declining of what he had no chance to obtain, would appear as an act of noble disinterestedness & patriotism, & which might possibly cause his name to be taken up by the Convention, if failing to elect any of earlier favorites of strong minorities. But in this hope he will not less deceive himself. He never had any chance for support except in Va.; & his name has not even been mentioned at Charleston, among the dozen or more, spoken of as likely to be voted for.

*May 1.* Finished reading over & correcting the last written pages. And now my last labor is done, I shall feel the want of steady employment. I have scarcely ever written more steadily than for the [914] [two months?] [12] since I began this job, or with more sustained pleasure. Began to read Miss [Dinah M.] Mulock's novel "The Head of the Family." . . .

*May 2.* . . . Finished "The Head of the Family" by 11 A.M. The reading of the latter part caused my eyes to become moist—which

---

[12] A gradually widening tear in one of the upper corners of the diary causes some difficulty on the next seventy-six MS pages. Wherever possible, the illegible portion will either be deleted entirely or reconstructed by the editor.

is not easy for me, whether for fictitious or real pictures of sorrow.—
The newspapers—Stormy proceedings in the Charleston Convention. The delegates of 7 states (S.Ca. Ala. Fla. La. Miss. & Texas,)[13]
have withdrawn from the Convention, & those of other southern
states are expected to follow. The quarrel is upon the language of the
"platform," or declared political principles—these states requiring
such as will repudiate the doctrine of "squatter sovereignty," & its
great patron Douglas. It seems that this consummate intriguer & unblushing electioneer, either has a majority or very near it, of friends
in the Convention—& those states are utterly opposed to him & refuse to submit to his being nominated as the candidate for the presidency. I rejoice at this, not only to defeat Douglas, but as I hope it
may break up the present *national* democratic party. If it shall forward the election of Seward, or any other abolitionist, so much
the better. . . . [915]

*May 4.* . . . The newspapers.—More southern states seceded from
the Convention at Charleston—& the remainder of the Convention,
(of which I am sorry that the Va. delegates made part,) began to
ballot, but could not obtain the requisite two-thirds majority of the
whole to make a nomination. 152 votes for Douglas. Finally, the
Convention adjourned to meet in Baltimore on June 18th. This is a
trick to have pretended delegations renewed in place of all those
seceded, & to be made up of creatures of Douglas, as no others will
participate in the farce of election. I trust that all the intriguing talent of Douglas, & the subserviences [of] his numerous satellites &
devoted tools, will not be able to re-unite the broken threads of the
plot. I do not see from the newspaper report how many of the slave-
holding states seceded from the Convention—but enough to show
that all the South is against Douglas. The delegates of Va. did not
withdraw—but it was not because they were not as much opposed
to Douglas, but with the vain foolish hope of securing northern votes
for Hunter. Neither [916] [he] nor any other southern candidate has
the least chance [to obtain] enough northern votes to be nominated
or elected to the presidency. This I maintained & published long
ago. The balloting at Charleston has served to show that nearly all
the northern delegates are for Douglas (152, equal to 76 electoral
votes,) & that all the southern states are against him, & regard his
doctrine of "squatter sovereignty" as little better than Seward's
anti-slavery doctrine. This also indicates, what I have supposed, that

---

[13] The diarist should have included Georgia.

but few northern democrats are really sound on the slavery question, according to southern views—& that in that question most of them incline more to the views of the moderate abolitionists than to southern views. Therefore I rejoice in the belief that this disruption of the Convention, in reference to Douglas & his doctrines, is the initiatory act of the separation of the southern from the northern portion of the democratic party—or the arraying of a southern party so separated from the north, that no southern aspirant for the presidency can hereafter pander to northern heresies, & betray the principles & interests of the South, in the vain hope of thereby securing northern votes for himself.

*May 7.* The mail. The seceding delegates from the Charleston Con[vention] were either the whole, or large majorities of 9 states, & minorities from three others. Va. Ky. & Ten. only remained entirely to the rump of the Convention. The seceding delegations have adjourned to meet in Richmond on June 11th, inviting to join them those representatives from all the other states opposed to "squatter sovereignty"—& to its advocate Douglas.—The impression seems abroad that this secession from & disruption of the Convention is the first & effective measure of the disruption of the "national" democratic party. . . .

*May 8.* All from Beechwood went to dine at Ruthven—& I to stay all night, to be sent to Petersburg, on my way to Nottaway. I, with my sons, Edmund & Julian, & my nephew, J. J. Dupuy, have been invited to attend an agricultural meeting, & to make our headquarters with Mr. Freeman Epes, who married my niece Rebecca Dupuy.

*May 9.* Was called up soon after 2. A.M., & at 3, set out in Julian's carriage. He & Edmund could not go. At 7 A.M. on the Southside Rail-Road, (meeting there with Dr. Dupuy,) & reached Wellville station soon after 9. Mr. Epes' carriage waiting there for us, & took us to his house, 4 miles distant.

*May 10.* Attended the meeting, which opened at 11. It is a meeting of the long standing Farmers' Club of Nottaway, whose meetings I have attended before—together with many other farmers of this & neighboring counties, to the number of some 150. Four [918] [hours] were spent in the hearing of statements of facts & opinions [on] subjects of practical agriculture, which seemed to be interesting to most of the assemblage. A very plentiful & good but plain dinner was served, & eaten by the guests & their hosts (the Club,) in the time. . . . Plentiful & good as was the entertainment in all other respects, there was nothing to drink except lemonade & water. The omission of intoxicating liquors is highly commendable. Returned at night . . . in Mr. Epes' carriage, to his house.—Yesterday, heard of the death of Littleton W. Tazewell, at the age of 85. His was one of the greatest minds that any resident of Va. ever had—& I doubt whether it was not more powerful than would be the combined intellects of all the public men now in the public service of this state. But Mr. Tazewell's powers, great as they were, were put to but little use for his country. For a quarter of a century he has lived retired, & entirely withdrawn from all public affairs, & even from all society, except of such slight intercourse with either old friends who sought him in his seclusion, or others who might be less welcome. But of both, there were but few who rarely intruded on that seclusion which his own habits so clearly showed that he preferred. His life, in all this time, has been of no benefit to mankind, of gratification to his friends, nor, as I would suppose, of pleasure to himself. If it were my own case, I would rather have died, than to live even one year as he had done for 25, without employment, amusement, or any object of life.

*May 11.* . . .The mail brought the report of [919] the proceedings of the "National Opposition Convention" at B[altimore]. John Bell, of Tennessee, has received the nomination for Pre[sident &] Edward Everett for Vice President. Botts, who has worked so long & so hard for the honor, & who (with his tail of adorers,) was so hopeful of reaching it, did not receive but 9½ votes—or but little more than Va has of electoral votes—& less than I supposed his own tail could have given. I suppose that at this time, the most disappointed & mortified three men in the U.S. are Botts, Wise, & President Buchanan. The last, like Wise, was not even mentioned by anybody at Charleston, among all of the number who had some followers, in or out of the Convention, to present their claims to the Presidency, to the public.

*May 12.* At 8.30 A.M. left Mr. Epes' in his carriage, for the station at Wellville, & found soon after that I had a decided though slight chill. . . . I sat over a fire at Wellville, while waiting for the train, more than an hour, & the chilly sensation had ceased before I set out at 11. Still I felt badly, & through the subsequent drive to Ruthven, where I arrived at 5 P.M. in Julian's buggy, which had been sent to Petersburg to meet me. . . .

*May 14.* . . . Latterly there have appeared in the newspapers two remarkable publications of English opinions on the government of the U.S. & its working, & abuses, which I trust will command more attention than would be if they had been written by any of our own citizens. Indeed, no party man in this country would dare to utter such sentiments, true as they are. One of these pieces is a letter from Macaulay censuring the system of universal suffrage, & arguing that it must end in mobocracy & general destruction of the rights of property, if not prevented by the probable earlier establishment of the more acceptable rule of a single despot. The other is a recent speech of Earl Grey, in the House of Lords, commenting on & coinciding with Macaulay's [921] letter, & enlarging on the evils already produced [from] the virtual disfranchisement of all the more worthy & [torn] [por]tion of the people, & the scandalous & barefaced corruption practised by the U.S. administration. Of the latter, some facts were stated of President Buchanan, that ought to overwhelm him with shame, if he were not shameless. All these evidences of great deterioration & corruption, & of the virtual change of this formerly free government (& of most of the states also,) to a government of the *worst*, instead of the *best* of the people, are true—& sundry of them I have adverted to, in my poor way & to closed ears, for years past. But all who exercise, or hope to wield, this unrighteous power, would ignore, if they cannot crush any such assaults—& there are few men who would dare to utter any such opinions indicating disloyalty to the so-called democratic power. In my last written article, before I saw Macaulay's letter, I had stated similar opinions in different manner, as permitted by my subject. The power that has been conferred on demagogues, by the machinery of conventions, & founded on universal suffrage, will never be recovered by the sound & worthy portion of the people. Our political condition will gradually grow worse—until, to save ourselves from the worst of political evils, the rule of demagogues sustained by the mass of the most ignorant & vicious of the people, we will gladly succumb to the usurpation of a wise & patriotic Cromwell, a military Napoleon, or even a Louis Napoleon, able, unprincipled, & infamous. . . .

*May 15.* . . . Wrote to Dr. Bachman. Read the anniversary proceedings of the Anti-slavery & other societies in New York. The bitter hostility to the South, & the direct recommendations of negro insurrection, and approval of John Brown's attempt, as strong as ever.

*May 16.* . . . A slave ship, (fitted out in New York,) has been captured, near Cuba, by a U.S. vessel of war. The slaves, 520 then alive, were landed in Florida. This will be another supply to Liberia, at a cost of not less than $200,000 for the transmission, & the co[n]tracting for the support & "education" of the negroes, which will be but the enslaving these re-captured Africans, for long "apprenticeship" to the lazy negro colonists of Liberia.

*May 19....* Edmund attended the regimental parade of his troops—for the first time in uniform.—Finished Southey's Life of Wesley—a very interesting book, & in reference to a very remarkable & great man, & a very clear exposition of his greatness, piety & virtues, as well as of his weak points, & of the defects & evil operation of his system of religion & of church discipline. Began to read "Southern Wealth & Northern Profits."

*May 21.* This morning finished reading [Thomas P.] Kettell's "Southern Wealth & Northern Profits," a new statistical & argumentative work written & published in N.Y. by an able northern statistician, on the southern side of the great question of [924] [slavery &] the differences of the North & South. A clear & strong [argumen]t. ... The mail—confirmation of the report that the abolition convention at Chicago, had not nominated Seward, as expected, or Bates, Banks, or Chase, or Cameron, or Wade, who had been spoken of as the most probable alternative choices, but Lincoln of Illinois, inferior in ability & reputation to all—& whom no one had mentioned before. I am sorry they did not nominate their ablest man, Seward, & so made their success more probable.... Wrote to Gov. Hammond, enclosing some of my unpublished notes on African Colonization, & urging him to take up the subject in the U.S. Senate, in reference to the recent recapture of Africans, & the repetition of the extravagant folly of sending them to Liberia, at such enormous cost to the government, & to the effect only of making them slaves to the colonists.... [925]

*May 22.* Finished the newspapers. I have lately added [the New] York Herald to all of our previous supply, & there are so [many that] it takes me from 6 to 10 hours to look through all the papers [brought?] by each tri-weekly mail.... Besides the advent of the Japanese embassy,[14] which is to visit New York, there are two other arrivals expected there which will produce there the greatest ex-

---

[14] The first two diplomatic representatives from Japan to the United States had arrived in San Francisco in April, 1860.

citement—the Great Eastern steamer, which seems at last about to move, & is coming first to New York—& the Prince of Wales, who, with a suite of noblemen is to visit Canada & the U.S. in July. This visit, for this country, I very much regret. All the flunkeyism & snobbery, & especially of New York, will go mad with delight, & will not be able to humiliate itself low enough in prostration at the feet of a prince, & the heir of the British crown. . . .

*May 23.* . . . The mail. Another capture of a slaver (like the first, fitted out in New York,) with 550 slaves, which were landed at Key West. This will make another enormously costly job for the government, & fat bonus for the Colonization Society & Liberia. I trust that the repetition may induce Congress to do something to prevent the continuance of these great abuses.—Garibaldi has gone to join the Sicilian insurgents, & no doubt to lead them. This is a significant fact. Mazzini, the noted republican conspirator, & one of the most influential on the revolutionary feeling of Italy, has published his urgent advice to the Sicilians to annex themselves & Sicily to the dominions of the King of Sardinia, as the best means for attaining independence, freedom, & unity for Italy. This is certainly the best course —& which if concurred in by the republicans, & now acted upon in Sicily, will operate to extinguish the three remaining vile despotisms, & unite all Italy under the limited monarchical government of Victor Emmanuel—by which the Italians will have independence & unity, & as much of individual liberty as they, or any people of the continent of Europe are fitted to preserve. . . .

*May 24.* Edmund came to Ruthven for me, on his way [927] to the Court-House, whence I proceeded in his ca[rriage to] Petersburg. After dinner, went to see Mrs. Campbe[ll, & at] 4.45, set out in the train for Weldon. As there is [not any] night train over the Raleigh & Gaston road, went to Goldsborough, where arrived at 1. A.M. & slept a few hours.

*May 25.* Left Goldsborough at 5.30 A.M. At Hillsborough, R. Brown Ruffin & Alice, (Judge Ruffin's children) got in, & we proceeded together to Graham—where the carriage coming for Cousin Alice, afforded me a speedier passage to Alamance . . . . We reached Alamance by 1. All well there. . . . My reception, from all, the kindest, as usual, & most affectionate from Jane & Patty. Judge Ruffin much better, & has gone to Plymouth on indispensable business.

*May 26.* Began to read [John] Pickering's Vocabulary of Americanisms, which, though published in 1816, I never saw or heard of before. Before night, Judge Ruffin arrived, & with him, the Rev. M[oses] A. Curtis of Hillsborough. . . .

*May 27.* Sunday. We went to Graham, & heard Mr. Curtis [preach to] a very small congregation in the Court-House. . . . Finished reading "Vocabulary of Americanisms"—from which I learned much that I did not know before—& especially that sundry words that I use in writing are not good English. But the much greater number of the words which the author enumerates as being improperly used in the U.S. are merely Yankee provincialisms, or vulgarisms, never used in the southern states. . . . Judge Ruffin's health has improved much, but he is reduced in flesh below his always lean condition, when in good health, & his cough still continues, & is frequent & troublesome. Talking much makes him worse—& I am fearful of inducing him to be imprudent in this respect, by my conversation.

*May 29.* Rode out with Judge Ruffin, to see his crops. . . . [929] Afternoon left Alamance for the "Shops" Station, . . . & at 6.15 P.M. took the Express Train for Columbia, [S.C., to] which I go to attend the session of the state convent[ion whi]ch is to meet tomorrow, to choose delegates to the seceding convention, which is to meet at Richmond on June 11th. I wish to see what is the disposition as to secession of the cotton states ( or any of them) from the Union.

*May 30.* Travelled all night. Luckily, I can sleep very well sitting, & travelling, & do not lose much sleep by travelling all night, or longer continuously. Reached Columbia (the Station) at 4.45 A.M. & took quarters at the U.S. Hotel. . . . Went to the Carolinian Office, & made acquaintance with the editor, F. Gaillard, who very politely invited me to read his exchange newspapers, & as often as I desired. Among the delegates, renewed acquaintance with sundry gentlemen whom I had known formerly, & made acquaintance with others. Among the former, I met with R. B. Rhett, former U.S. Senator—his sons, R. B. jr. Editor of the Mercury, & Edmund Rhett of Beaufort —Ex. Gov. [John H.] Means, Gen. Howard, John [S.] Palmer,[15] Isaac Hayne, A[lfred] P. Aldrich, J[ohn] I. Middleton,[16] Dr. [John]

---

[15] A physician and rice planter, John Saunders Palmer ( 1804–81) was a member of the state legislature for twelve years and sat in the secession convention.

[16] A member of one of the most distinguished South Carolina families and a large slaveholder, John Izard Middleton ( 1800–77) was a member of the state legislature for two decades and was a delegate to the secession convention.

Douglas[s],[17] Dr. S[anford W.] Barker.—John [S.] Preston[18] I met with for the first time, & Gen. [Samuel] McAliley.[19] These, & many others, received me with much kindness & attention, & many asked my opinions of public matters, & especially of things in Va, as evincing for my opinions more respect than perhaps they deserve. The instruction I aimed to impress on all, was, that though neither Va. nor [930] [any other border] state would now or ever move first for [secession], or simultaneously with the more ardent cotton s[tates], yet whenever any portion of these declared their independence, Va. & all the other border states would be compelled to follow their lead —& would join the seceding southern states within a few months, after having served during that time as an impregnable barrier of defence against any attack from the north, or the federal government.—Attended the session of the Convention at night, for an hour, when I retired to bed. The proceedings were only for organization, & went no farther than the election of Gov. Means as permanent President.

*May 31.* This morning, after having *assumed* a seat among the members, (to which I had been invited by many individually,) I was surprised to hear a member move that I should be invited by the Convention to take a seat in the body. The resolution was adopted unanimously. Soon after, the President sent to me two of the Vice-Presidents to request me to take a seat with them on the elevated stage. This I respectfully declined, having no wish to be put in so conspicuous a position. Sorry to find elements of discord here also —& I fear that there are not many more avowed advocates for secession from the North than there are in Va. R. B. Rhett, the former senator & distinguished nullifier & seceder, was the first choice of one of the four state delegates to the Convention [931] at Richmond— thus indicating a major[ity] [torn] southern men. But the minority were much dissa[tisfied with him?]. Several able speeches were de-

---

[17] Dr. Douglass (1795–1870), who received his M.D. from the University of Pennsylvania, was a member of the Nullification Convention of 1832–33 and served in both the South Carolina House and Senate during the 1830's and 1840's.

[18] A strong advocate of southern rights, John Smith Preston amassed a great fortune as a sugar planter in Ascension Parish, Louisiana, and then returned to South Carolina, where he was a member of the state Senate from 1848 to 1856. During the Civil War, Preston was superintendent of the Bureau of Conscription in Richmond.

[19] A lawyer and planter from Chester District, McAliley (1799–1880) is probably most noteworthy for having cast the lone vote in the Senate against calling a secession convention.

livered in the aftern[oon to] produce conciliation—by Hayne, Aldrich, & Rhett. The other elections were afterwards made, & the Convention adjourned.

*June 1.* At 5 A.M. set out on the rail-road for Charleston—& arrived at Charleston Hotel after 1. P.M. Dressed & dined, & then went to see Dr. Bachman, whom I found at dinner. . . . After sitting an hour with Dr. B. he had to go to perform some of his appointed pastoral duties, & I rode with him in his carriage, to the Mercury Office. I there took my M.S. to make some corrections—returned to my lodging, read it over, & made the corrections. I shall not now add to the first quantity (84 pages) sent to Rhett for publication. Dr. Bachman had, at my request, conferred with some of the publishing booksellers here, & found no one disposed to publish the piece as a volume, except at my own entire cost & risk.—A third slave vessel has been captured by a U.S. war vessel, & its slaves, more than 400, sent into Key West.—Garibaldi has landed successfully in Sicily, & is expected soon to organize the existing insurrection, & to overthrow the Neapolitan vile despotism. [932]

*June 2.* [I re]turned the first part of my M.S. to Rhett. He [wish]es to continue its publication in the Mercury, but it [is conti]nued so slowly, that the object of present or early instruction will be lost, before one half can appear. Soon after breakfast, went to Dr. Bachman's, & stayed two or three hours. Found there Dr. James G. Rowe, of Marengo Ala., an intelligent & interesting talker. He is one of the few private individuals who is using, for agricultural labor, camels, which animals were first introduced in the U.S. a few years ago, by the government, for army transportation purposes in the western unsettled territory. Dr. R. speaks very highly of their valuable qualities for draught, & ploughing. They are strong, & docile, & will live on the coarsest food—as corn-shucks, top-fodder, & almost any weeds or shrubs for browsing. Grain is hurtful to their health, & none ought ever to be given them. One camel will plough as much as two mules, & will cost less than one for feeding. They live & breed well in this country, as has been tested on a large scale in the number used for the army in the west.—Talked with Judge [Wade] Key[e]s, of Ala.[20] (who introduced himself to me,) about the action of Ala. & the other southern states, in reference to secession, & the prospects of the approaching convention of the states

---

[20] Keyes served throughout the war as assistant attorney general of the Confederacy.

whose delegates seceded from the Charleston Convention.—Afternoon, went again to see Dr. Bachman, & stayed until after tea. Heard much from him of his recent visit to Florida, & of the beauties & advantages of that country. It seems to me to offer more advantages for [933] new settlers than any country I have heard of, [& I would] prefer it, if designing to emigrate. I have all my li[fe been stur]dily opposed to leaving the land of my birth. But [from] the present political prospects—of abolition supremacy in the federal government, & of the submission of Va, I feel a strong disposition that I & my children shall move southward, where resistance, & safety for slave property, may be hoped for—& which I fear are hopeless in Va.

*June 3.* Sunday. Left Charleston, on the train, at 8.30 A.M. & reached Charlotte, N.C. at 10.30 P.M. Thence proceeded without any delay, & on

*June 4.* at 4. A.M. got out at the "Company's Shops." No one at the hotel up except one servant to hand luggage. Left my trunk in his charge, & walked to Alamance, 5 miles, or more, in 2 hours & 5 minutes, without unpleasant fatigue . . . . Reading parts of the 1st. volume of Parton's "Life of Andrew Jackson," (a recent publication) [934] [& which] I had begun to look over when here before. [Talking wi]th Judge R. on the subject, I find that he, with all [consid]eration & discretion, thinks of Jackson's earlier career almost as badly as I do—though he thinks much more highly of his ability & worth in his position as President. . . .

*June 5.* . . . After dark, my son Edmund arrived, as much to the surprise as gratification of all of us. . . .

*June 7.* Got nearly through the first vol. of Life of Jackson. It is a much better work than I had expected from the author of the "Life of Aaron Burr," & seems truthful. The wrongful & the foolish or ridiculous acts are set forth plainly, as well as those the most lauded. —The illness of a young daughter of Brown Ruffin required that she should be sent to a Chalybeate Spring, & Jane has been called upon to accompany & stay with her. I & Edmund had also arranged to return to Va. tomorrow—& so we will go together. In the afternoon, we left Alamance, & drove to the station at the "Company's Shops," to stay the night at the hotel, & take the Express train tomorrow morning before daybreak. We three passed a pleasant evening together . . . . I think that Edmund & Jane seem to be much gratif[ied at] their meeting & conversation. I shall greatly rejoice if the growing attachment should lead to their mutual love & marriage.

[426]

While I have given no intimation to either of them, this has been the object of my earnest wish & prayers. With their excellent qualities, & points of attraction, I think they are eminently qualified to make each other happy in marriage—& therefore it is my earnest desire, notwithstanding all fears of trouble & difficulty caused by the children of a first marriage. May God grant the desired result—& prevent any of the evils feared from this cause!

*June 8.* We were called up at 3 A.M. to be ready for the Express train to pass at 3.45. . . . Ex. Gov. Morehead was on the train to Raleigh, & introduced me to Gov. [John W.] Ellis. Conversed with both about the swamp lands of lower N.C., & afterwards with Gov. Ellis on my writings on that & other agricultural subjects, & my difficulty to get them published, unless [936] [at my c]harge & entire loss. He at once offered to [have them] published by the state of N.C., & as parts of [torn] in connexion with the Geological Report of that state. I promised him to furnish to him the manuscripts for this purpose, should he find them suitable.—On the train there were some of the delegates from S.C. & Ala. on their way to the Convention in Richmond, which I also am on my way to attend as a spectator, & to meet & converse with such of the delegates as I already know, or may become acquainted with. We reached Richmond at 6.30 P.M. At the Exchange I met four or five other delegates from Ala. & more from S.C. & introduced them to each other.—There have been three slave-ships captured lately, & 1700 recaptured Africans are now at Key West. I wrote some weeks ago to Senator Hammond on the subject, & since to Ex. Gov. Wm. Smith, urging both to take measures to defeat the law before Congress, to pay the Colonization Society $100 for each of these, & all future recaptured Africans, & to send them to Liberia. Opposition has been made, & I saw that Gov. Smith had indicated taking a leading part therein. . . .

*June 9.* Wrote to Gov. Ellis, & sent to him my writings for his inspection. Attempting to arrange for a publication in book form of my last writing, on southern secession. . . . There came R. B. Rhett & J. I. Middleton of S.C. & sundry other delegates to the Convention. Had much conversation previously with the earlier arrivals. At night, attended a public speech by R[obert] G. Scott of Ala, which was followed by a few strong remarks by M. Fisher of Va.

*June 10.* Sunday. Sundry more delegates arrived—& some others of my acquaintance—among the former, A. P. Calhoun, & of the latter, James A. Seddon & Wm. Boulwane. Had a long conversation in my room with Seddon, consulting upon the present state of affairs. He deplores & condemns the refusal of the Va delegates to secede from the Convention at Charleston—& I trust his influence may do much to correct the error. With him, & Harvie (by my letter from Charleston,) & in conversation [938] [with s]undry of the delegates from the states of S.C. [& Ala., I have] been urging the policy of bringing Va into line [with the] more southern states, by the nomination of Hunter for President, on the assurance of entire fellow-feeling & cooperation of Va with the other southern states. This would bring N.C. & Md. in also—& with Gen. [Joseph] Lane of Oregon nominated as Vice-President, probably the ticket would have the support of Oregon & California. If we could not elect our southern candidate, his support would serve to unite the south. And if the northern democrats went off, so much the better. I would rejoice to be rid of them, & that there should be a southern party only, for all true southern men to act in.—Wrote to Mildred—announcing my intention of visiting her in Frankfort in Sept. & taking Nanny with me.—At night, in the public hall of the Hotel, conversing with many delegates & others—& among them Gov. Letcher.

*June 11.* W. L. Yancey arrived & many other delegates this morning. The Convention met at 12, & made only the temporary organization—& without anything else being done, except appointing a general committee, adjourned to tomorrow 10 o'clock. One delegate from Va, Fisher of the Accomac district, was in the body, as he had (alone) seceded at Charleston. Two delegates, elected from the Knoxville district, also came from Tennessee. . . . In the afternoon, most of the del[egates from] Florida arrived, & more from other of the 8 [states whose] delegates entirely seceded from the Charleston Con[vention.] Those of Arkansas only are still absent. At night, [the] public hall of the Exchange Hotel crowded, & all, in separate & varying little clusters talking of the business in hand. It is not expected that anything will be done now, except to adjourn, & wait for the action of the convention at Balt. next week. This, the members from Ala, Ga, & La. are instructed to attend—& that will compel an adjournment—to re-assemble here afterwards.

*June 12.* I made arrangements for the publication of two of my writings. The last article, partly issued through the Mercury, will be published in book form, by J. W. Randolph, on shares with me —two thirds of the cost & receipts to be mine, & one third his—I giving in the writing against his taking charge of the publication

& sale, & having all the trouble. As all the book-printers in Richmond are fully engaged for some time to come, & I want the earliest possible issue, Mr R. will send the job to Baltimore. This will prevent my revising the proof sheets. The other publication will be of my "Notes on the Cane-brake lands of Ala." This will appear in the Southern Planter, & from the same type-setting, a pamphlet edition, of which I am to have a few hundred copies. As I shall leave tomorrow, early, I had to read over & correct all the already printed portion of "Anticipations of the Future &c." & also enough of the other article for one number. [940] . . . The Con[vention] met at 10 A.M. & by 12, adjourned to the 21—when it is to meet again here. This is to allow time for the Baltimore Convention to act—& for those seceding delegations to act in it, as instructed by their constituents. The S.C. & Florida delegations were not so instructed, & will not offer to enter the Balt. Convention. . . .

*June 13.* . . . At 6.30 A.M. I set out for Washington—with most of the delegates from S.C., Ala, Ga & Miss. Reached Washington at 2.30 P.M. . . . Both houses of Congress sit in the evening, from 7 P.M. In going to the capitol, I met first Senator Mason of Va. & next Mr. Keitt of S.C. & both talked freely of the present crisis. Mr. Mason said we were approaching the [941] end of the government. Mr. Keitt says it is [certain that] Lincoln will be elected President—& he urg[es that S.C.,] even if alone, shall then forthwith secede from [the U]nion. I advocate the same—under the belief that S. [Car]olina would not be alone long. . . .

*June 14.* After breakfast, had a long conversation (on the street,) with W[illiam] H. Clark, of Halifax, one of the Va Delegates to the Convention, & I think to good effect, in inducing him to follow the example of the more southern delegates, in seceding from the convention when it re-assembles at Balt. on 18th. It is here generally supposed that the pretended & grossly fraudulent delegations, of Douglas men, sent by very small minorities from Ala. & Ga. will be admitted as rightful representatives of these states—& by that admission, or by direct rejection, the true delegations will be refused re-admittance, which they are instructed to seek, for further trial of the question of political principles on which the convention before was split at Charleston. If so, these delegations will again withdraw—& I & others are working to induce the Va delegation to withdraw with them, if this great outrage is committed. And if the Va. delegation shall so withdraw, we hope that those of all the other slaveholding states will do the same—&, the convention of seceders, at Richmond, will unite in nominating candidates who sustain southern rights. Besides Miers Fisher, who alone seceded at Charleston, there were several [942] [others in th]e Va delegation at Charleston strongly [torn]—& I trust that all will come to that [conclusi]on at Baltimore, except the few re[al Do]uglas men. These, & all others, are playing a desperate game to nominate & elect their favorite, if possible, & by any means. It is reported that Douglas, in his corrupt efforts to secure the presidency, has incurred debts to the amount of $400,000. All his chance to escape irretrievable ruin, & his creditors to be paid, depend on his election, & having the patronage & plunder of the treasury to bestow.—I have conversed with sundry delegates from S.C. & Ala. & heard from all of them—& infer the like opinion of all others of the cotton states—that they go for secession of their several states from the Union, as soon as a Black Republican shall be elected President—which we suppose, (& many of us hope,) will occur next November. But not one of these states will move in secession first & alone, unless S.C. will—& therefore I fear that all will continue to submit longer, if not indefinitely. I heard this policy, in this contingency, acquiesced in by James A. Seddon, who arrived here today.—There is a great crowd here, of southern delegates mostly, & almost all conversation is on the subject of the action of the conventions.—Called on Senator Hammond before 11. No action of Congress is now to be hoped for, to prevent the large [943] bounty of the U.S. government being paid [to the Colo]nization Society, for taking charge of the [re-captured] Africans. . . . Went to the galleries of Congress. The House of Representatives then, as always of late, a perfect scene of disorder, though not half the members were present. Few were attending to the business of the House, a general buzz of conversation, & other noises, prevented hearing the speakers, & very often two & sometimes more were speaking at once. Whenever one ceased, five or six others would rise together, & all bawling out "Mr. Speaker," & each claiming the right to the floor. It seemed to me impossible that the presiding officer could ever know which member had the right to speak, or that he or any other member could hear & understand the course of business under discussion. . . . The Japanese embassy left Washington some 8 or 10 days back, & visited Baltimore & Philadelphia on their route to New York, where they will embark to return home. Their presence has caused all sorts of foolish expense by the government, & the different city authorities

—& of ill-mannered & intrusive conduct of the people, both low & high in the social scale. I think that the Japanese will go home with as bad opinions of the social condition of this country, as of the good opinions of mechanical improvements & arts. . . . [944]

*June 15.* Last evening & this morning, the southern delegates still arriving. Met with R[obert R.] Bridgers & Bedford Brown of N.Ca.[21] Also, Elwood Fisher, & Major Ben. McCulloch.[22] A Mr. Crandall, who was introduced to me, I learned was "Eutaw" the Washington correspondent of the Charleston Mercury. . . . By accidental information, I learned that the 15 pikes had been received by Senator [Clement C.] Clay, & that they were now being labelled, ready to send to the governors of the southern states. I am very much gratified with this—as I had supposed all hope of the pikes being sent to me, as promised by Col. Barbour, was at an end.—Went to see Yancey, at the urgent request of his friend [James L.] Pugh of Ala.[23] with whom Yancey is lodging. He received me very politely—but he did not seem disposed to converse freely, & I inferred, as I had heard intimated, that he was fearful of saying something to commit himself. So I soon left him. . . .

*June 16.* Saw the pikes at the room of the Senate Committee of Commerce, (of which Mr. Clay is chairman,) & beautifully labelled, by the clerk, who was directed by Mrs. Clay, who has taken much interest in this matter. She is a most intelligent, & facsinating [*sic*] woman, & zealous & ardent in southern feeling. As Mr. Clay's serious & long indisposition must prevent his taking the trouble of distributing the pikes to proper persons to take charge of them, I ordered the box containing them to be sent to my apartment, where they were taken out, & were seen by many of the southern delegates.—Lewis E. Harvie, & other Va delegates arrived—& many

---

[21] At this time chairman of the Judiciary Committee of the North Carolina Assembly, Robert Rufus Bridgers (1819–88) later served in the Confederate Congress. For many years he was president and director of the Wilmington and Weldon Railroad. Brown (1795–1870), a state senator, opposed secession in the crisis of 1860–61.

[22] A veteran of the Mexican War, in which he commanded a mounted unit known as McCulloch's Texas Rangers, Major McCulloch was at this time marshal for the coastal district of Texas. He was a Confederate brigadier general during the Civil War and met his death at the Battle of Elkhorn Tavern in western Virginia in the spring of 1862.

[23] A freshman congressman at this time, James Lawrence Pugh (1820–1907) would later serve two terms in the Confederate Congress and nearly two decades in the United States Senate.

from the North-western states. Great interest about the issue of the Convention. The Douglas men very zealous, loud & defiant, & his opponents equally so. All is uncertain as to whether the delegations of the states which before seceded at Charleston, & who now will demand re-admission (to again test the principles of the body) will be admitted, or the *bogus* or fraudulent Douglas delegations sent by a few from Ala & Ga. The delegations of S.Ca. & Fla. will not go into the Convention. Then, it is doubtful whether, in any case, the whole body will act, & proceed to nominate a candidate, or whether the same southern states, & nearly all others that remained, will not [946] [join in a] general secession of southern states, to add [delegates to the] convention at Richmond, & there make a [separate] nomination. If the latter should be the result, [it would] have the good effect of uniting & banding together all the slave-holding states, & organizing them separately for different future action, & a much more important secession from the northern states. This consequence is now deemed probable by many, & looked to with hope by most of the far south, & with dread by others. For the purpose of best drawing Va to the more southern states, & all the southern states together in one great & exciting contest, I urge the nomination (at Richmond) of Hunter. And if the southern states & people can be brought to act together, & separately from the northern, in this object, I trust that by next November, & the election of an abolitionist, some one or more of the Southern states will promptly secede, & that all the others, including Va & Md, *must* soon follow in the movement. . . . Mr. [William T. S.] Barry of Miss.,[24] Harvie, & several other delegates, accidentally met in my room, to see the pikes, & sat & conversed a long time on the prospects of coming [947] events. The Miss delegates think that [their state] will secede, even if alone, when Lin[coln is elected.] And I, & many others, think that Douglas' elec[tion, &] his "squatter sovereignty" doctrine, will, for the [torn] administration, do as much harm to the south as the success of Lincoln & the Black Republican party.—Besides this all-important political objection to Douglas, his own conduct to reach the Presidency deserves the detestation & contempt of every honest man. He has not only been the first open & avowed seeker of the position by

---

[24] William Taylor Sullivan Barry (1821–68) was Speaker of the Mississippi House and leader of the secessionist wing of the state Democratic Party. He later presided over the Mississippi Secession Convention and was a member of the Confederate Provisional Congress.

systematic & widespread operations of personal electioneering, but bribery, in promises, & even the treating with liquor, & descending to the lowest & basest means to buy popular favor, have been used by him, personally & through his agents, to great extent. . . . President Buchanan seems to have sunk into well-deserved contempt. The democrats, under party discipline say nothing against him publickly—but there are few who will not condemn his acts privately. The opposition, Black Republican party, have been investigating the vile corrupt doings of the administration, & have lately passed [948] [a resolution in] the House of Representatives, of strong cen[sure of the administ]ration of the President—well deserved by [torn], though the act of the House may be illegal [& impro]per. —This morning, Gen. Duff Green, whom I had not seen for 18 years, accosted me, & renewed our acquaintance. He was formerly a noted character, & as a writer, & editor of the "Washington Telegraph" wielded a powerful influence over a large portion of the public— first as the supporter of Jackson, & afterwards in opposition to him, & his successor Van Buren. He was an able writer. Since then he has been entirely withdrawn from public life & notice.

*June 17.* Sunday. Many persons have left for Baltimore, but the crowd here is continually resupplied by new arrivals. The public hall is almost always full, & the conversation of every two or more men together is on the convention & its probable issue. Doubt increases, as the opening approaches. . . . At night, Elwood Fisher, A. P. Calhoun, & J. I. Middleton in my room until late—conversing on the present prospects & doubts—& discussing whether there is any chance for the secession of any of the southern states when the abolitionist Lincoln shall be known to be elected President. Fisher [949] thinks that there will be general acqui[escence & sub]mission —and if any (as S.C.) should s[ecede, & the] federal government should march troops [through Va.] & N.Ca. to attack the seceders, that neither of th[ose] states will oppose any armed resistance. I think otherwise. Much as Va has become degraded by submission, I cannot think yet that she is so low.—Called on Gov. [Andrew B.] Moore of Ala. who is here, confined with rheumatism—& delivered to him my letter, & the pike for the state of Ala. He received me very courteously & cordially. I had called on him some years ago at the State House in Montgomery. He conversed freely on the present crisis, & intimated very clearly that he thought the southern states ought to secede, before Lincoln is inaugurated as President.

*June 18.* This is the day for the Baltimore Convention. Went to the Senate gallery, & heard an interesting debate on the government measures for suppressing the slave trade. Heard two members use a little of "my thunder," furnished by my pamphlet on "African Colonization," but, of course, without any reference to the source. Afterwards, on the floor of the Hall of Representatives. This is contrary to the rule, & a great abuse. But as everybody else go in, invited by members, & there is a convenience in it, I increased the nuisance by my presence. I thus saw sundry members of my former acquaintance, & was introduced to others, whom otherwise I should have missed. . . .

*June 19.* [We]nt to Baltimore in the early train, (6.20 A.M.) [Returne]d by 6 P.M. An immense crowd there. On my arrival, I sought for Harvie, whom I could not find until later, but saw John Seddon, & several other of the Va. delegates. By great effort, & with the aid, at last, of a "complimentary ticket" obtained for me from the President, C[aleb] Cushing, I got into the theatre where the Convention assembled. In an hour, it adjourned, to allow the committee on credentials of members to deliberate. I believe (& fear) that the broken peace will be patched up, by the seceding delegations being admitted, & a nomination made. But it seems now that Douglas will not be the nominee for President. The delegations of S.C. & Fla. refuse to enter, or to seek admittance.—The main object of my going to Balt. was to seek out the printer whom Randolph had engaged to print my book—which I luckily effected, as I did not know either his name or residence. I had wished to make some change in the plan or plot of the narrative, & for this purpose was engaged for some hours in reading & altering the first portion which had been sent to the printer. . . . Messrs. Calhoun, Middleton, [951] & Elwood Fisher sat with me in my room [at night.] Afterwards, going into the hall, I found & c[onversed with] Senator Wigfall of Texas, & was much am[used at his] oddity of speech & opinions, & their extravagance of [express]ion. Sat up until 12, after rising this morning before 5, & having no sleep between.

*June 20.* The committee of credentials have not yet agreed upon a report to the Convention at Baltimore—& since yesterday morning, it has only met & adjourned to a later hour, to give time for the committee to act. The last action reported by telegraph was the adjournment this afternoon to tomorrow 10 A.M. But though nothing has been done, & but little spoken, in the Convention, there are reports of opinions which are believed, & are important—as well as numerous reports not credited. It is now understood that the archdemagogue & most corrupt & corrupting candidate, Douglas, has not the slightest chance for the nomination, should one be made. But it is also supposed that the united convention will come to no result of combined action, but will break up on the question of credentials of the southern delegations. . . . Read over & corrected for republication, (as an addition to the volume,) my pamphlet on the "Consequences [952] [of Abo]lition Agitation, published first in 1856–7. . . .

*June 21.* The morning Balt. Sun states, as a rumor, that there is a scheme to have the Richmond Convention forthwith adjourned (after the expected separation) to Baltimore, where all the seceding delegates will unite, & make a nomination. The President, Col. [John] Erwin,[25] & the S.C. delegates are now in Richmond. I trust that they will not consent to leave Richmond. As a Convention of the South, it will lose both dignity & *prestige* by coming to Baltimore —& moreover will be there exposed to a heavy northern outside pressure. I am very uneasy at this reported impediment to the otherwise good prospects of increased southern secession. Wrote a letter to this effect to Middleton & the other S.C. delegates now waiting in Richmond—& also sent a warning by telegraph dispatch.—Corrected & copied the preface for my book.—Every body in a fever of anxiety for the successive telegraphic dispatches from Baltimore. At 1. A.M. we thus learned that the committee on credentials had reported, & in favor of admitting the *bogus* (Douglas) delegates from [953] all the three [*sic*] southern states (Ala, Ga, Ark, & La) fr[om which] fraudulent delegations had been sent—exclu[ding those repre]sentatives who had seceded at Charleston, & [torn] to Baltimore as well as to Richmond. After several . . . false rumors, Gen. Lane received a dispatch, which he [show]ed to me, stating that before voting on the report, the N.Y. delegation had asked an adjournment to tomorrow 10 A.M. to allow them time to consult with each other—which was agreed to. This numerous delegation (35 electoral votes) holds the balance of power—& I have no doubt they will consider to which party they can sell the state vote to most

---

[25] Erwin's last public appearance was as president of the Richmond convention. A Greensboro, Alabama, lawyer, he had previously been a delegate to the Nashville Convention of 1850 and had presided over the Democratic National Convention which nominated Franklin Pierce for the presidency. Erwin died on December 10, 1860.

profit. I went to carry this news to [James A.] Seddon, & found Mr. Hunter still in his room, whom I had left there a few minutes before. On my stating my opinion of the views of the N.Y. delegates, he told me of a confirmatory opinion uttered by Senator Wigfall lately. Some one asked him if he did not suppose that the Convention would break up, without being able to agree on a nomination, he answered in the negative. When asked for the ground of his opinion, in which so few concurred, he answered, "Because I have unbounded confidence in the rascality of New York." Heard a good deal that was interesting from Mr. Hunter in this conversation, in which he spoke more freely than I had ever heard from him before.... [As] the great struggle, & the probable breaking up [of the c]onvention, (unless prevented as Wigfall supposes,) will probably occur tomorrow, I will again go to Baltimore, for the day. I would go to Richmond, if assured that there will be a re-assembling of the Convention there.

*June 22.* Went to Baltimore by the early train. Saw some of my acquaintance among the Va & other delegates, & was rejoiced to learn (privately) that the best spirit prevailed. That the exclusion of the seceding & admission of the *bogus* delegations would certainly be made, on which, Va leading, all the southern delegations would secede from the Convention, by large majorities of each, & also some minorities of northern states. Went to the theatre, where the convention sits, nearly half an hour before the time of meeting, 10 A.M. My "complimentary" ticket gained for me ready entrance to the lobbies, but there was no chance to squeeze in any where. Most of the lower tier of boxes were reserved for ladies, & already every seat was occupied, & the central aisle or staircase filled by ladies standing on the steps. However, I took my stand outside of the rear row of ladies who filled this entrance, & just before a police officer who had invited me to occupy that position. Afterwards, by some of the ladies before me leaving, I got more forward, but continued standing until near the adjournment, when a seat in a neighbor box was offered me. While standing I was pressed against [955] the ladies, & learned, by actual co[ntact, more about] hoops than I had known before.... [Th]e majority report of the committee of [credentials & the] minority report were read—the former [refused th]e before seceding delegates who had bogus [cont]estants, & admitted the latter. The minority report was the reverse. The latter was voted out by 150 to 100 votes. Then the resolutions of the majority were voted upon, separately, & by states—& all passed, except the last. The 35 votes of N.Y. had before been all given on every resolution to the Douglas side. But on the last resolution, (admitting both the claiming sets of delegates of Ga,) all the N.Y. delegates voted for admitting the seceders & refusing the bogus, so as to secure these ends. Then, before anything else could be done, they moved & forced an adjournment to 7 P.M. I would have waited for this, but for the fear that I might not again gain admittance, &, even if entering, that new causes of delay would prevent my witnessing the interesting expected action of secession by the southern delegates.— Returned to Washington by 6 P.M. . . . There was great interest & excitement, & the hall of this hotel crowded by persons who came to see the expected telegraphic dispatches, which began to arrive by 9 o'clock. I had been fearing that the rascally politicians from N.Y., after finding that the southern delegates designed to withdraw, would reverse the previous work of the Convention, by reconsideration, & pass the minority report, (rejecting all the *bogus* delegates,) & so heal the breach. But my anxiety was removed by the [957] first telegram, which announced [that the majority report] had been adopted, & that the Va de[legates had seceded.] The next, named North-Carolina, excepting [torn].[26] The next, that all California & Oregon, & half fr[om the Mary]land delegation had followed, & all of the more sou[thern] states—& that the delegations of Kentucky & Tennessee had gone out to consult, & were not expected to return. Laus Deo! . . .

*June 23.* Garabaldi [*sic*] has possession of all Sicily—& the King is in great danger of losing all his dominions. He has appealed to the five great powers to protect his throne, & they have refused to interfere. . . . Reports received successively by telegraph announced that Douglas had been nominated for the presidency in the rump convention, by 173 electoral votes—nearly the whole represented & the bogus delegations included, & he was declared the nominee of the democratic party. What a farce! And yet a most serious & expensive farce. The seceding delegates met in Convention at 12, & organized temporarily, & adjourned to meet again at 5 P.M. Since 7, all here have waited in feverish anxiety to hear [959] of further pr[oceedings, but no dispatch] has come. . . . I have [determined] to leave for Richmond in the morning.—The Charleston Mercury is now pub-

---

[26] Sixteen of North Carolina's twenty delegates withdrew from the convention.

lishing my article quite fast—& the 19th letter has reached me.—At 10.30, a telegram came, stating that [John C.] Breckenridge [*sic*] of Ky had been nominated, in the seceders' convention as the candidate for the presidency, & Lane of Oregon for vice-president—both with great unanimity. Though I would prefer Hunter, I do not object to this nomination. It is in fact a southern & sectional nomination, as Lincoln's & Douglas' are both northern nominations. There are indeed minorities of the delegations of some 6 or 8 northern states, & a majority of those of Mass. in the former convention. But they represent the democratic party in states which cannot possibly give a vote to any democrat. Therefore I regard these as nothing—& that it is really a southern convention, & representing only & all of the slaveholding states. This, I trust, is the breaking down of the national democratic party—or the cutting loose of the southern from the northern portion. Every southern democrat whose opinion I have heard expressed, approves the nomination.

*June 24.* Sunday. Left the hotel at 6 A.M. & the wharf in the steamer soon after.... Reached Richmond at 2 P.M.... Found, in the Mercury, & corrected, two more of the letters, reaching to the 20th. Had some instructive conversation with Gen. [William E.] Martin, of Charleston, about the forts of Charleston, which showed me that it would be necessary to write over again my account of their capture. Gen. M. promises to send to me some printed papers on the subject, as soon as he shall reach home.... All the S.C. delegates still here, meeting & adjourning from day to day, & waiting for the other southern delegates, of whom but few have come on yet from Baltimore, & some of these have not stopped in Richmond. Interesting conversation with the delegates & others concerning the recent nominations & connected incidents.

*June 25.* Saw & conversed with J. W. Randolph about the publication—& Mr. Williams. Went to the State Library, & there met with Gov. Letcher.—I had disposed of 13 of the 15 pikes designed to be presented to the slave-holding states, placing in the charge of different gentlemen, members of Congress or delegates to the Convention, who will deliver them to the governors of the several states. I withheld two. One of these, at first designed for Delaware, I withheld, because I doubted whether the gift [961] would be appreciated, & I gave it [instead to Mr. Clay, on ac]count of the interest which he [& Mrs. Clay had shown, &] the assistance they both gave to [torn] my object. The other, designed for [torn] [I could] not find any person to convey—& therefore I [presented] it to the city of Charleston, through its mayor. Le[tter] sent with it to him, as was done to each of the Governors. . . .

*June 26.* . . . At 2 P.M., many southern delegates arrived—& at 4 P.M., the Convention met, & unanimously concurred in the nomination of Breckinridge & Lane, & then adjourned.—A mass meeting of the citizens of Richmond had been called to ratify the nominations, & which met on the Capitol square at 8 P.M. I went, got tired of the speaking in half an hour, & returned to my apartment. All the delegates will leave tomorrow morning. I have found among them many agreeable acquaintances, old & new, & I believe that they appreciate my fellowship & sympathy with them highly.

*June 27.* Was called at 4 A.M. to get ready, & reached the steamer & soon after was on the passage down the river. . . . [Reached B]eechwood before 11. . . . Found an accumulation of more than half a bushel of unopened newspapers, received during my absence, besides all that Edmund chose to open, & were not worth preserving. Also two pamphlets on agriculture & the swamp lands of N.C. by the state geologist, sent to me by Gov. Ellis. I could take but a hasty glance at a few of the latest papers, before throwing all aside—to proceed to add to & alter some of the latter letters which have appeared (to XXI) in the Charleston Mercury. My recent information about the fortifications below Charleston will require me to make considerable alterations for the volume. Shall write to Gen. Martin for more particular information.

*June 29.* Continue my alterations & additions in the [remainder, though did] not complete even the first in order, for want of [particular] information about the forts & harbor of Charleston— w[hich I] hope to obtain from Gen. Martin. Lieut. Johnson has sent to me some military reports & maps, which I am reading with interest, & especially a long report by Lieut. [Matthew F.] Maury. From this, I learn to think much less of large & permanent fortifications for defence—& much more of small batteries of a few heavy cannon, behind temporary earth works, or walls built of bags of sand, to oppose attacking or passing ships of war. . . .

# July–December

⚜

# 1860

---

VACATIONING IN OLD POINT COMFORT AND
AT THE SPRINGS ⚜ A TRIP TO KENTUCKY
⚜ PUBLICATION OF "ANTICIPATIONS OF
THE FUTURE" ⚜ LINCOLN ELECTED ⚜
TAKING THE STUMP IN SOUTH CAROLINA
⚜ AGITATING IN GEORGIA AND FLORIDA
⚜ A GUEST AT THE SOUTH CAROLINA
SECESSION CONVENTION

*July 1.* Sunday. At church. . . . Correcting & added to my writing. Finished reading in part, & looking over the Military Reports of the U.S. Fortifications & system of coast & harbor defence. Began two Agrl. Reports of E[benezer] Emmons, Geologist of N.C. which [964] [Gov. Ellis had s]ent to me by mail. . . .

*July 2.* Julian . . . by appointment came to Beechwood for me, & after early dinner we went to Petersburg—where he stayed through the night, & I went, on the train, to Richmond. Had received by the mail today, the first printed sheet of my "Anticipations of the Future" —with so many errors of the printing, that I corrected it, on the trip on the rail-road, & at night mailed it to the printer in Baltimore— though I fear it is too late. . . .

*July 3.* Found at Randolph's more printed copy in a later Mercury, & a second proof sheet—both of which I corrected, & wrote again directions to the printer. Left these & all the M.S. copy to be sent on by next express to the printer.—Julian had come over early—& having failed to obtain a conveyance by either of the stage coaches, had to hire a conveyance. And I . . . determined to go on to Marlbourne with him, instead of later, as I had designed. . . . [We set] out at 11.30 A.M. . . . . It has been very dry generally, for some weeks, & also oppressively hot for the last week, although some hasty & heavy showers have fallen. Reading newspapers, & afterwards articles in the latest English Reviews.

*July 4.* Walked out on the farm . . . . The crops here are bad. The wheat perhaps is better than is general through lower Va, & on Beechwood & Ruthven, where it is very bad. The corn here, for the land, is much worse than is general—having suffered greatly from heavy rains & wetness of the ground, & latterly & now suffering excessively with drought. . . . [967]

*July 7.* According to our previous arrangement, Julian & I left for Richmond at 4 A.M., Mr. Sayre going also. . . . I found no proof-sheets to correct, as I had expected. . . . So, Julian & I went by the afternoon train to Petersburg, & thence, by his buggy, to Ruthven. . . .

*July 8.* . . . I finished reading Prof. Emmons' pamphlet on the Swamp Lands of N.Ca. (a poor affair,) & also "Lovel the Widower" the last work of [William M.] Thackaray [*sic*], & the last newspapers. . . .

*July 9.* Left Beechwood for Maycox wharf, where I took the steamer for Old Point. On the way, a gentleman who landed for Williamsburg, by mistake took my carpetbag instead of his own. Though I know who has it, & that it will be safely returned in two days, it will cause me no little inconvenience—as my books & papers, showing things, & my smaller articles of dress are all in this small & portable bag. My trunk had been taken by Edmund to Old Point Comfort—where I arrived before 4 P.M. Found Nanny & my niece Eliza Cocke—& Edmund after 9, as he had spent the day in Norfolk.

*July 11.* . . . After 8, went with Nanny to hear the military band in the Fortress play—but there was a cool breeze which I feared might be injurious to her, & we did not remain long. Recovered my lost carpet-bag—&, for the first time, having a book to read, I read in my room at night. This place is especially tiresome after dark, to those who, like myself, do not dance, or drink, or play cards. There is no public room for gentlemen to meet in at night for conversation, & so there is no meeting of that kind.

*July 12.* . . . There arrived here today, from Washington, a vessel with a new cannon of enormous size, which is to be mounted & tried here. I have no question that it will prove a failure, if it does not produce such disastrous results as the other great gun, which in bursting, killed [Abel P.] Upshur, [Thomas W.] Gilmer, & four other persons of less note.[1] This cannon would weigh lbs. 49,000, & its solid

---

[1] Reference is to the bursting of a new gun on the USS *Princeton* on February 28, 1844, which caused the deaths of Secretary of State Upshur and Secretary of the Navy Gilmer.

balls are 15 inches in diameter, & weigh lbs. 430. Its being landed was not attempted today, because of the rough weather.—An easterly cold wind, & slow rain. In such weather, this is a very dull place.

*July 13.* The vessel whose only & heavy lading is the big gun, drew up to the wharf, & nearly all day a strong force was raising the cannon, to prepare for landing it, without making much progress.— Walked to Hampton, to see Mr. Tyler, who has a summer residence on the near out-skirt, & who, as I had heard had arrived there two days before. But he was again away. . . . At night, in my room reading "The Lost Principle," by my friend John Scott, & am gratified & surprised to find so able & well written a book from so unpractised a writer, & one so little known to the public as a man of ability.

*July 14.* The great cannon was placed on the wharf by dark.— Finished reading "The Lost Principle"—with which I am much pleased. The author goes even farther than the opinion I have held for 35 years, that Madison was detestable for his political apostacies [*sic*] & infidelities to principle & to creed & to duty. The book is a strong argument against the principles & operation of the federal constitution, & for disruption of the present union of the northern & southern states, unless the equilibrium [972] [between North & South shall be re]stored & its maintenance secured.

*July 16.* This forenoon, together with Mr. Boulwane & Mr. R. Douthat, & my son, I drove to see Mr. Tyler, at his summer residence near Hampton—& spent with him two hours very pleasantly. After dinner, there arrived Frank Ruffin, with his new wife—& later, Mr. Paul Cameron, with his two daughters, & Jane Ruffin. As much gratified as I was to see her, I was as much sorry that our party had arranged to leave tomorrow morning. . . .

*July 17.* Left at 6 A.M. with Nanny, & Eliza Cocke, on the James river steamer. Edmund remained. . . . Reached [Maycox] . . . where the boat was waiting f[or us, & arrived at Beechwood by] 1 P.M. . . . Found a letter from Mr. B. B. [Sayre, in]forming me that his wife, my daughter Mildred had bee[n] delivered of a daughter on July 4th, & that both the mother & infant were doing well. . . . In the S.C. papers, appears a notice of my pike sent to the Governor of South Carolina, with a comment by the editor of the first publication.[2] The labels I had affixed to this & all the other pikes were alike, ( except for the name of the state,) & as follows:

---

[2] The Columbia ( S.C. ) *Guardian.*

## July 26, 1860

"To the State of South Carolina.

"SAMPLE OF THE FAVORS DESIGNED FOR US BY OUR NORTHERN BRETHREN.

"The most precious benefit derived from the Northern States, by the Southern, if, rightly using it, 'out of this nettle *danger*, we pluck the flower *safety*.' " [974]

*July 19.* . . . I sat some hours, reading, & finished last No. of De Bow's Review, in the woods on the river bank, & slept a short part of the time, lying on the ground.—Edmund came home at 1 P.M. Afternoon, a violent storm of wind & rain.—Began to read the "Debates in the Virginia Convention" of 1788, which accepted the Federal Constitution. This re-reading, after some 40 years since the first, was induced by my late reading of the "Lost Principle." . . .

*July 20.* . . . Began to copy, with alterations & additions, the omitted parts of my former manuscript "African Colonization Unveiled" —which parts were at first necessarily excluded, to bring the printing within the compass of one sheet of 32 pages. By mail, received another proof sheet, (reaching to page 120,) which I corrected, to return by next mail. . . . Continuing to read, at intervals, the Va. Debates of 1788. . . .

*July 21.* Continued & completed my copying & alterations—making "Addenda" to the formerly published pamphlet "African Col. Un." of 22 pages. Did not finish until after dark. Wrote to De Bow, offering it for his Review, & to know, if wishing it, how long its publication will have to be delayed. The long delays, & interruptions, of the publications of my writings heretofore, have offended me, & it is long since I sent anything to this Review, which is the only monthly periodical, or any other than newspapers, on the southern side, in this country. This is far from an able or well conducted work. But as it is the only one, it is used by the ablest men of the south, & it has an extensive list of readers. De Bow himself is a crafty & mean Yankee in conduct & principle, though a southerner by birth & residence, & in political [976] [philosophy]. . . .[3]

*July 26.* . . . There was to have been a children's dance last night at Beechwood, & I had stayed away long enough for it to be over in my absence. But on returning, I heard it had been postponed, & is still to come off tonight. However, to make amends for the delay,

---

[3] Unfortunately, a tear in the MS—now reaching very large proportions— renders illegible the diarist's remaining comments on De Bow. One may infer, however, that they were not complimentary.

[443]

the young people assembled, staying here, & some other guests who came by mistake, danced until midnight.—Finished reading [Charles] Campbell's "Hist. of Va"—by passing over some of the chapters which are not history, & others which I was well enough informed upon.—At night came the visitors—young grown people as well as children—with some older—& nearly all had a joyous time, dancing very badly to the music of the piano, until past midnight. I soon was tired of the dancing, though amused for a while by the great pleasure of the dancers, & I went to bed by 10.30.

*July 27.* Resumed the reading of "Debates of Va. Convention," in the morning, & when undisturbed, hoping then best to remember . . . . The mail brought . . . some articles, having some allusion to [me, whi]ch will be appended. To Yancey's letter to Slaugh[ter, intend]ed as private, there has latterly been given a most extensive circulation —being published in Douglas' speech, & in sundry newspapers.[4] In that, he justly ascribed to me the (then recent) originating of the plan of a "Southern League," to which so much importance is attached by the unknown writer who signs his communication to the Douglas paper (States & Union) "Alabama." [5] I receive his designed slighting mention of me as a compliment—& only wish that what he states as the progress & operations of the "Southern League" were true. Certainly I aimed at & hoped for such operations, (but without any aid or adoption of "oaths, secrecy, &c.," as alleged—) but if there have been any such operations or effects, I am entirely uninformed, & have no faith in this statement. [980]

*July 29.* Sunday. At church. Afternoon, walked alone to the site of my old residence on Coggin's Point.—Finished "The Problem of Free Society"—which the author does not solve—though his facts & views are very interesting & impressive. For the great evils, oppressions, & sufferings of free society, caused by the competition of the indigent for food, & by the supply of labor exceeding the demand, I cannot see but one means of prevention, & that means as yet seems

---

[4] The reference is to a letter from Yancey to James S. Slaughter of Alabama, dated June 15, 1860, in which the former counseled southern resistance through the League of United Southerners, rather than through a national or even a sectional party.

[5] The anonymous Alabamian to whom the diarist refers warned of the threat posed by the League of United Southerners and delivered a unionist diatribe against Yancey, with one slighting reference to Ruffin. Pointing to the alleged collaboration between Yancey and Ruffin, the writer charged that they were the leaders of a conspiracy working secretly for disunion.

unattainable. It would be found in any sufficient preventive check to the increase of population of the indigent class. But while the general proposition of Malthus on this subject has been received by political economists & statesmen, no important practical application of his doctrines has yet been made. If such proper application could be made, by affording a sufficient preventive (or prudential) check to the marriages, & too great increase of population of the most destitute & suffering class, a remedy to the evils of redundant labor, & its ruinous competition for employment, might be found—& not otherwise.

*July 31.* . . . By the carriage last night, I had brought to me a chart of Charleston harbor, & the surrounding lands, sent to me by Gen. Wm. E. Martin. This, as well as an earlier letter from him by mail, giving the topographical information I asked for, was too late—as *my* account of the military operations there was printed before this information arrived. . . . [982]

*August 1.* . . . Received a pamphlet of 64 pages, from the author, Gilbert J. Beebe, editor of the "Banner of Liberty," Middletown, N.Y. He was introduced to me in Washington. He utters such sound opinions concerning the southern question, & slavery, that they are surprising as coming from a N.York editor. His pamphlet is an answer, & a very complete one, to Helper's infamous & lying "Impending Crisis." Read it before night.—Afternoon, walked, & sat, reading, in the woods on the river side, or the "wilderness." . . . I think my present publication will be my last writing offered to the public, of any later time. And then, when not having that resource for pleasant occupation & excitement, I fear that I shall be very dull & spend my time unhappily for the remainder of my life—which I earnestly hope may not be extended longer than the failure of my faculties. It was to avoid the misery of idleness that I undertook, (after giving up my farm & business,) these labors of writing. And one of them, to keep up the habit of writing, was the keeping of this Diary. This, I have forced myself to continue, even when it was disagreeable, because receiving nothing but the entries of daily & unimportant circumstances, entirely useless for being either noted or afterwards recurred to. Still I was sensible that if I did not enter something every day, & waited for occurrences, or thoughts, worth being recorded, that the habit would soon cease, & all its designed benefits be lost to myself. . . . It has been to me an impressive & mortifying fact, that my children, & sons as well as daughters, have seemed to take but little interest in my writings & publications, & rarely express any opinions about them voluntarily—& of course I do not annoy them with inquiries, to draw out their opinions. Their usual silence in this respect, has served with me as the strongest indirect indication of the want of interest or worth of my writings—both the published & the unpublished, (which last they have not cared to read,) & more strong than any direct or indirect indications of disapproval from any other quarter. . . .

*Aug. 3.* Edmund, with his three boys, set out in the steamer for Old Point Comfort, to see the Great Eastern steam-ship.[6] The numbers who have visited the exhibition, at New York & Cape May, have been immense—from 7000 to 16000 a day. This will be the only profit of the voyage. . . . A letter from Mr. B. B. Sayre bringing the sorrowful news of the death of his & Mildred's infant. She lived but 21 days—& seemed very healthy to 15 hours before [989] [her death]. . . .

*Aug. 5.* Sunday. Edmund & his boys returned, all enraptured with their sight of the Great Eastern. The concourse of visitors was immense. No possibility of finding in-door lodging, & scarcely any chance to get a meal at the hotels. Edmund & his sons slept on straw under a tent. The great steamer anchored opposite to Fortress Monroe—& left, for Annapolis, this morning. . . . Finished "Adam Bede," a work of great interest, merit, & written with great power. It is difficult to conceive that the writer is a maiden lady.[7]—I have read, with the attempt of unusual attention, but truly in my usual glancing & inattentive manner, two of the three volumes of the Debates of the Va [990] [Convention of 1788] . . . . [Although the members were apprehensive about certain powers granted by the Constitution to the federal government, they apparently] had no suspicion of others which have served to . . . oppress the southern states. Thus, they feared & opposed the power of unlimited direct taxation by the federal government, & had no fears of indirect, through imposts. Yet, by the latter, the southern section has been subjected to the north, & the whole principle of the government altered. Direct taxes have not

---

[6] An iron steamer of nearly 19,000 deadweight tons, the British liner *Great Eastern* had docked in New York on June 28 after her maiden voyage across the Atlantic. During her first five days in New York almost 150,000 persons thronged to visit her.

[7] Published in 1859, *Adam Bede* was written by the English novelist Mary Ann Evans, who used the pseudonym George Eliot.

been resorted to through the much longer time of the existence of the government. If these *only* had been authorized by the constitution, & allowed to unlimited extent, the government would have remained economical, & comparatively pure, trade free, & the south free, & at least equal in wealth & power with the north—& the balance of power with the states, instead of with the federal government as has been produced by the corrupt & malign influence of indirect taxation serving to oppress & weaken the South, & to foster, enrich, & strengthen the northern states, by indirect bounties to manufacturing & commercial pursuits & investments. [End of MS Volume 5—p. 991]

*Aug. 7.* Completed my arrangements, & the packing my clothes, & usual travelling supply of pamphlets (for gratuitous distribution abroad), & before 11 set out for the wharf to take the steamer for Richmond. My necessary business there is to confer further with the publisher, & to be more convenient to receive & return the next proofsheets, from Baltimore. Edmund & Nanny will follow in two days, on their way to the Springs. My course may be the same, somewhat later—but is now uncertain. Reached Richmond before 5 P.M. Saw & [992] conversed with Mr. Williams, & then with Lewis E. Harvie. For want of something else to amuse myself, I went to the Democratic Meeting, called to elect delegates to the democratic state convention which is to be held at Charlottesville on the 16th. Heard part of a campaign speech from Dr. Wellford, & all of another from O. J. Wise, & neither worth hearing, & then left, to go to bed at the Exchange Hotel.

*Aug. 8.* . . . Conversed with Randolph about the publication of the book, & wrote again to hurry the printer, & to enclose to him a short additional letter, to be inserted, which I wrote this morning. At the State Library, &c. Nothing to occupy my time, & I am already very tired of staying here. . . .

*Aug. 9.* An excessively hot day. Lounging in Randolph's bookstore & elsewhere—nothing received by mail, & I am heartily tired of waiting. Afternoon, Edmund & Nanny arrived . . . . Determined to go on with them tomorrow to the White Sulphur Springs.

*Aug. 10.* We left Richmond at 6.30 A.M., reached the present terminus of the Railroad, on Jackson's river in about 12 hours, & then in stage coaches to Callaghan's at 11 P.M. I had taken my place in the mail coach—& went on without stopping to go to bed, but with a delay of 3 hours before proceeding.

*Aug. 11.* I reached the White Sulphur Springs by 7 A.M. First could only obtain a temporary place—& not before night permanent lodging. . . .

There is an immense crowd of visitors here—1600 in all, as is stated. Met many acquaintances—among them, Mr. Boulwane, Dr. [Sterling] Neblett, Jeremiah Morton, John Baldwin & Judge John Robertson of Va., Mr. [Alexander H.] Boykin,[8] & others of S.C., Thomas Ruffin (M.C.) & H. K. Burgwin [*sic*] of N.C., Mr. & Mrs. Hayden of La. & sundry others whom I knew before but slightly, or made acquaintance with for the first time. . . . [994]

*Aug. 12.* Senator [James] Chesnut of S.C.,[9] & Judge Perkins of La., P[atrick] H[enry] Aylett,[10] Judge [Thomas S.] Gholson, Daniel London of Va, Gov. [William] McWillie of Miss. among the visitors. Also L .Q. Washington of D.C. one of the most agreeable & well-informed. Had a long conversation with Mr. Chesnut, on secession. He is for it if . . . enough of the cotton states unite in it to make their supply of cotton essential to the markets of Europe—but not of S.C. or any one state alone. This is in the supposed event of Lincoln being elected President, which is deemed most probable. All others from the cotton states, with whom I have conversed here, are for secession, in the event of Lincoln's election.

*Aug. 13.* A rainy day, especially disagreeable at this place—but clear before sunset. 6 or 8 coaches filled with passengers arrive daily, & no room to receive any. However, by performing quarantine for a day or two at Dry Creek, they continue to get in here, as other lodgers leave for the other Springs. 1650 lodgers, of all kinds, now here.

*Aug. 15.* Jane M. Ruffin, with her nieces the Camerons, arrived last night, from the Rockbridge Alum Springs . . . . They make part of a pleasant party (of 8) too large to be united with ours. Among my former acquaintances, & new arrivals, Col. F[rancis] H. Smith, J[oseph] R[eid] Anderson,[11] Dr. Ro. Archer—& my nephew George

---

[8] Boykin was a state senator from Kershaw District, South Carolina.

[9] Lawyer, planter, and United States senator, James Chesnut, Jr. (1815–85) was one of the most prominent men in South Carolina. He was later a member of the state secession convention and an aide to General Beauregard at Fort Sumter and First Manassas. His wife, Mary Boykin Chesnut, wrote the well-known *A Diary from Dixie*.

[10] Editor of the Richmond *Examiner*.

[11] Anderson was owner of the famous Tredegar Iron Works in Richmond, Virginia.

Dupuy, & his two sisters, Mrs. Marshall & Juliana Dupuy. With all the many agreeable & intelligent acquaintances, & some valued friends, I find much of the time here to hang heavy on my hands.

*Aug. 16.* Col. N. Williams, of Darlington S.C., arrived with his large family. He is the first man I have conversed with from so far south who is an unionist *per se*—or despite of all existing & prospective grounds for disunion. There is however certainly one other, in Mr. [James L.] Pettigru [*sic*], the great lawyer of Charleston.

*Aug. 17.* This place still crowded to its utmost capacity. On that account there is much less of sociable & agreeable conversation in mixed company, or in groups brought accidentally together. I find much less pleasure here than formerly. Borrowed some periodicals of Judge Perkins, which will enable me to fill [996] the intervals of wearisome time. Johnson Barbour & Col. P. S. Cocke here.

*Aug. 18.* Dr. [William S.] Plumer, my old acquaintance, & celebrated Presbyterian preacher arrived today—Also Mr. Little of Fred[ericksbur]g, the editor of the "News" a Whig paper, & a very intelligent & agreeable companion. Professor [Albert T.] Bledsoe of the University also.[12]

*Aug. 20.* Alice Ruffin, the older sister of Jane, arrived late last evening. 150 guests left this morning, & their places immediately filled by persons who before were staying in hotels in the neighborhood. . . .

*Aug. 23.* Gen. Walker has organized another force to invade Central America. He sailed with 500 men. One of the vessels containing arms was stopped at Belize, & the boxes of arms seized by the British authorities. He landed with his men at Truxillo, & captured it with very little resistance or loss. That town is the nearest, on the main land of Honduras, to the island of Ruatan, which the British government has so long held illegally, & is now ready to surrender to Honduras. The inhabitants, British subjects, & mostly negroes from Jamaica or Belize, are much opposed to the transfer to Honduras, & are determined to resist it by arms. In the absence of the British power, & the resistance to that of Honduras, I think that Walker, (if he can maintain his present ground,) will soon be able to occupy Ruatan, & to turn the spirit of mutiny & resistance to Hon-

---

[12] At this time professor of mathematics at the University of Virginia, Bledsoe (1809–77) was a Confederate agent in London during the war. Upon his return to the United States he founded the *Southern Review* in Baltimore and utilized its editorial pages to preach against reconciliation with the North.

duras, which prevails there, to the service of his objects.—The Great Eastern steamer has set out for England, without taking any freight, & with only about 100 passengers. Except as a show, & for the receipts from visitors, the voyage has been a dead loss, without results—& I doubt whether the monster ship will ever again cross the ocean. Except that its speed has fallen short of the previous expectation, I know of no failure. Yet the omission to take freight, or of offering to take any, seems to indicate some causes of unfitness not yet known to the public. [998]

*Aug. 25.* The divisions & difficulties of parties in regard to the election of a President of U.S. seem to excite but little zeal. That subject, however, with the prospects & reasons for a dissolution of the union, furnish most of the subjects of conversation here among the men. There are many here from the more southern states—most of them contingent or conditional disunionists—on the condition that Lincoln shall be elected—& he is the only candidate who has any chance for election by the popular vote, & very much the best chance in the House of Representatives. I find myself alone, as an avowed disunionist *per se*, & I avow that opinion upon every occasion.

*Aug. 26.* Sunday. The mail brought me the 14th sheet of my book, which reaches nearly to the close of the manuscript & new portion. . . . Wrote to J. W. Randolph, & sent a check for $200 in part of my share of the expense of the publication.

*Aug. 27.* . . . 130 persons left this day, & 70 arrivals. At night, Prof. J. P. Holcombe arrived, with whom I had an interesting conversation on the prospects [999] of the South, & the faint hopes of resistance to the northern power & aggressions. He has to leave early tomorrow morning, much to my regret.

*Aug. 28.* . . . Dr. Plumer & I being together in the portico, fell into conversation on different subjects for a considerable time. We spoke of slavery, & the effects of the enslaving of Africans, & the African slave-trade. I stated my views of the inefficacy of preaching to convert savage Africans to Christianity, & referred for proof, to the missionary Livingstone having failed to convert even one, in his five years of travel, & continued teachings of his numerous escort of natives. I said that if he had, instead, asked & obtained of one of the chiefs, his friends, a grant of a large tract of land, & of enough negroes ( already slaves ) to cultivate it, & had settled & tilled the land, & held & governed the negroes as slaves, he would have rendered them a great service, in meliorating their condition, a service to the country, & [1000] in time, (it might take to the next generation,) such condition would make more christian converts than the mere preaching of 100 missionaries for as long a time. And that if enough of civilized white masters would thus cultivate lands in Africa by other negro slaves, it might be the means, & the only means, to greatly extend civilization & Christianity in the now savage Africa. I deemed enslavement to white & Christian masters, whether in or out of Africa, the only possible means for making them Christians. Mr. Plumer neither assented to or denied my views—though he deemed the best results of this kind insufficient to justify the re-opening or carrying on of the slave-trade. But he stated some facts stronger than I had before known to show the great superiority of the condition of slavery to freedom of negroes to aid their being christianized. Even of the negroes who had once been enslaved, & subsequently emancipated, he said that religious statistics & reports showed a great falling off after the change. In Surinam, the Moravians had withdrawn their missionary labors & establishments, because of latter failure & complete discouragement. In Jamaica Christianity was dying out. And as a remarkable contrast, he said that among the negro slaves of the southern states, there were now thrice as many Christians, as there were converts to Christianity, or older Christians, among the heathen & savage nations of the whole world.—Among later visitors here, there are Alex. Little, whom I value highly—Col. Prince of Ala., a very intelligent gentleman, ex-Gov. R[obert F. W.] Alston of S.C., ex-Gov. [Hardin R.] Runnels of Texas,[13] Mr. Spratt of Charleston, [1001] L. Q. Washington.—I did not exactly understand Mr. Plumer. He meant that the whole black population, (& not the slaves only,) in this country furnished thrice the number of Christians that are elsewhere converts in all heathen lands. But he added, when I asked for his explanation, that the free negroes were but a few compared to the slaves, that all of the former, or their parents, had been trained in slavery, & that most of them had obtained their emancipation through their superior merit & worth. Of course the first generation would not show the falling off from religion which occurs in their progeny.

---

[13] Runnels migrated to Texas from Mississippi in 1841 and became a cotton planter on the Red River. After serving as Speaker of the House in the state legislature, Runnels defeated Sam Houston in the gubernatorial election of 1857. However, two years later, in a second contest between Runnels and Houston, the result was reversed.

*Aug. 29.* This morning, after very early breakfast, Alice & Jane Ruffin, with the Camerons & the Messrs. Brodnax, (all one party,) set out for N.C., & my son Edmund for his home, leaving Nanny in my care, until I shall [return from] Frankfort. The routes of both will be the same to Richmond. I have refrained, even in this secret writing, to say anything of a matter of daily & intense interest to me, because of the uncertainty of the circumstances & result, & the delicacy of the subject. I still have not the slightest information from the chief agents—& indirectly have heard what I may now venture & rejoice to say. Edmund had loved Jane from his meeting with her at Alamance. When they again met at Old Point Comfort, & were some days together, he had distinctly preferred his suit for her affections & hand, & had repeatedly urged it. She rejected him, positively. But still, as always, she felt & acknowledged so much esteem, high consideration & friendly regard for him, that he was encouraged to persevere. . . . He knew she was coming here, & took advantage of Nanny's necessary visit, to be here also. . . . His renewed, & scarcely remitting courtship has latterly been successful—as I was very sure of from its beginning. I was confident that such regard & esteem, as I knew Jane felt, would not fail to ripen into love. But even after reaching & confessing this position, she would not engage to marry him, until existing & strong objections should be removed. First, her mother & older sister (Alice) were strongly opposed to her marrying the father of so many children. But others of her family . . . are favorable—& with these friends in the citadel, I have no fear of Jane's not gaining over the opposers. But a much more serious difficulty was the expectation of much stronger objections on the part of Edmund's children. Jane declared that she would not, by marrying, bring unhappiness into a man's family—& particularly that the consent of Nanny, as the oldest & only grown child, & that consent to be offered in kind & affectionate manner, would be indispensable to her (Jane's) consent to marry her father, even if all other difficulties were removed. Nanny did not suspect the state of her father's affections & wishes before we were all here together—or if suspecting, she had uttered no indication of it. Of course, & naturally, the idea of her father's second marriage is very painful to her. But whatever she may feel, she has acted well & admirably. She has, as much as possible, put restraint upon her feelings, & has tried to act courteously & kindly towards Jane, & has sent to her, through her father, kind messages suited to the occasion. May God grant that all such prejudices & fears may be removed! This is the only cause for dread. [1004] The two parties are eminently gifted to attract love, & to make each other happy as husband & wife. If effected, as I now feel sure of, it will be a result I have ardently desired long before they met . . . . I have been conferring with Judge Perkins for some time about a scheme of his, which we put in operation at a meeting of the parties. He & I, with Dr. Tabb, Col. Philip St. G. Cocke (both [1005] of these whigs,) James Lyons[14] & Henry Burgwyn, have formed a "Publication Society," & bound ourselves to furnish $100 each annually, for three years, unless choosing to withdraw earlier. The object is to publish books & pamphlets the best calculated to sustain the rights of the southern states. We hope & expect to add sundry other persons to the association—but still do not wish it to be much larger, & therefore unmanageable.—Today saw Mackintosh, the former Liberian judge, & now the bath attendant here, whose statements I took notes of & Little published last year. I urged him to have his life in Liberia written & published in a pamphlet, & to offer it for sale at the bath house especially. I think that it would sell well & yield a good profit—& also work admirably against the Colonization Society.—Besides declaring my disunion doctrines to all proper persons, I have given away nearly all of many copies of my pro-slavery pamphlets which I brought for that purpose.

*Aug. 30.* A letter from Mildred at last, to Edmund, & saying that she cannot leave home. So we will go to her, by the next coach, to-morrow morning. Wrote letters to . . . Prof. Holcombe, & to J. W. Randolph. From the last received the last sheet but one of my book —so that I hope it will be published in another week. A busy day for me. At night attended another meeting of our "Publication Society," increased now to 9, by the addition of three more members —& nearly completed the arrangements. . . .

*Aug. 31.* Nanny & I left in the stage at 7.30 A.M. . . . We dined at Salt Sulphur Springs, & only reached Red Sulphur Springs by dark, where we slept.

*September 1.* Reached Newbern, on the Va. & Tenn R.R. at sunset —having taken two full days' travel by mail stage coach to make 80 to 83 miles. Supped, & waited at the tavern, until 10.46 P.M. when the train came by going west, & we set out on our long & circuitous route.—The stage-route was through Greenbrier, Monroe, Giles &

---

[14] A prominent Richmond lawyer, James Lyons later served in the Confederate Congress.

Pulaski. Most of the country seen is mountainous & rugged—the latter part, in Pulaski, more level, & rich, & under fine grass generally, & the tilled land under fine corn. Some very fine scenery, more sublime than beautiful, along New River, which we crossed on a ferry scow, & along the borders of which the road extended, for some 4 or 5 miles. At the village of Pearisburg, in Giles, was surprised to hear that a large proportion of the people of the village & of the close surrounding country were then sick, three different epidemics prevailing—typhoid fever, dysentery, & the new throat disease called *diptheria* [*sic*]. The latter is especially dangerous, producing death by suffocation, & with long protracted torture. . . . Yet, because of being but [1007] little subject to diseases of malaria, or bilious disorders, this mountain region is held to be remarkably healthy, as its inhabitants deem our tide-water country to be very sickly. We may well submit to our few & slight bilious fevers & chills, in lieu of the terrible diseases (however few,) & the epidemics of the hilly & mountainous & (so-called) healthy region.

*Sept. 2.* After travelling all night, reached the Tennessee line about daybreak—& proceeded on to Knoxville, which reached & left by noon. Thence on for Nashville. The country less hilly than I had expected to see.

*Sept. 3.* Reached Nashville before 9 A.M., & to my great disappointment found that the train did not proceed to Louisville until late in the afternoon. Went to a hotel, where some rest was agreeable to Nanny—but otherwise the detention will be without any gratification, or benefit. The southward & circuitous course of my route passed into Alabama for a short distance, during last night. The Cumberland river, at Nashville, is now low, & the water is still, muddy, & greenish—an ugly river. Saw nothing in the city worth notice, except the suspension bridge over the river, one private residence, Mrs. Polk's, & the new State House, which is a noble structure. At Chatanooga [*sic*], the town was not visible from the rail-road, except the adjacent great hotel. The mosquitoes there invaded our cars, & were troublesome during the night.—At Nashville saw J. D. B. De Bow, like myself a transient visitor, & the only person whom I knew or had any conversation with, except [1008] a Mr. Holt of Ga, who introduced himself to me, & with whom I had some agreeable political conversation. Some of the most respectable gentlemen of the city, sat & conversed with each other in the afternoon outside of the Hotel entrance, near to myself & other guests. But not one addressed a word of welcome to me. Mr. De Bow wished to introduce me to them—but I declined, on the ground that as they (knowing who I was, or if only that I was a respectable stranger,) did not seek, in their own city, to make my acquaintance, I certainly should not seek theirs. Left Nashville, at 6 P.M. on the train for Louisville. The cars filled, & with a large proportion of ladies.

*Sept. 4.* While taking such uncomfortable sleep as we could sitting, & crowded two on every double seat, the engine & forward cars ran off the track. Some villain had placed logs across the track. The engine & forward car were much damaged, & the engine was pushed nearly up the side of the cut (about 6 feet ascent) in which the stoppage occurred. A brakesman was much hurt, if not dangerously injured. None of the passengers suffered more than from heavy thumps. We were in the rear car, & I was barely awakened by the sudden stoppage, & Nanny struck her head against the adjoining seat, so as to cause a slight bruise only. There we remained through the night, trusting that the Conductor's telegraphic despatch to Louisville would bring a train in time to make us lose the morning train to Frankfort only, & enable us [1009] to connect with the afternoon train. But by shameful neglect, or rather design, none was sent until the regular train from Nashville, which reached us between 11 & 12, & was so slow that it did not reach Louisville until about 4 P.M., after the last train was gone. So we have again to stay another night—having [lost] in the three detentions full 38 hours. Stopped in Louisville at the Galt House. . . . I walked out to see something of the city. Though my view was limited, it seems very superior to Nashville, & to have very fine private buildings. The City Hall, or Court House, is a noble edifice. This was my first view of the Ohio river—as this is my first visit to any western state—or sight of any river flowing to the Mississippi, except some of the affluent rivers in western Virginia.

*Sept. 5.* The train for Frankfort left at 5 P.M. with us on board. One of my fellow passengers was Mr. J[ohnson] J. Hooper,[15] with whom I became acquainted yesterday during our detention on the track. He is one of the editors of the "Mail" newspaper of Montgomery, Ala, a whig & an "American" or "Know Nothing," but a

---

[15] A native of Wilmington, North Carolina, Johnson Jones Hooper (1815–62) was a member of the well-known school of southern humorists. He is probably best remembered for *Some Adventures of Captain Simon Suggs, Late Captain of the Tallapoosa Volunteers,* published in 1846.

strong advocate for southern rights, & for secession, as well as for the election of Breckinridge in this contest for the presidency, & is going on now (with many others,) to hear a public speech from Breckinridge to be delivered this day in Lexington. We had much political conversation, & agreed well in our general views. He told me of much [1010] that has not entered the newspapers, in which indeed there has been very little said, either of statement or comment, of the abolition & incendiary doings in the south.[16] . . . No doubt there are gross exaggerations of the facts, & probably many innocent negroes may suffer for the guilty. Among the statements was that as many as 100 vials of strychnine had been taken from slaves, supplied by the white inciters to murder, arson & insurrection. Mr. Hooper tells me that like discoveries have been made in different parts of Alabama—& that the infuriated inhabitants have in sundry cases executed summary vengeance (or justice, if not mistaken,) on the detected culprits, white & black. The white instigators are generally known to be northerners, & probably are always such.—On arriving at the station in Frankfort, I found Mr. Sayre & Mildred there awaiting our arrival—I had notified it by telegraph yesterday. I need not mention the delight evidenced by [1011] Mildred in our meeting, & the full return on our part. We soon went on to Mr. Sayre's house, which is in a thinly settled outskirt, across the river from the city proper, & from which it is distinguished by the common name of South Frankfort. Mr. Sayre received us with the greatest cordiality & kindness of manner. Mildred looks as if her usual good health was restored, & also her good spirits. Mr. Sayre's daughter Virginia, by his former marriage, 13 years old, & taller than Nanny, at home—& also her venerable grandfather, Dr. Theobald of Miss., is now here on a visit. . . .

*Sept. 6.* The country through which I have passed, both in Ten. & Ky., [1012] very generally of limestone formation & soil, & so far as I had daylight to observe it, is more fertile in east Tennessee, & more free from stone on the surface, & far more level, thoughout the whole route, than I had expected to see. From Bristol to Chattanooga, our first day's travel in daylight, mountains were seen only at a distance except at & near the Cumberland mountain, where we crossed a spur through a long tunnel. In western Ten. & Ky. I was prepared by previous information to see rich lands generally—&

---

[16] The diarist refers here to alleged, abolitionist-inspired slave uprisings in Texas.

therefore, perhaps, they did not seem to me as rich as I had expected. But I was surprised to see the general surface so level, & so little encumbered by stone generally. Much the greater portion of all the country seen by me in Ten. & Ky. (the portion of Ala. passed through was in the night,) is more level than the lower half of the Piedmont region of Va, or of the counties of Nottaway & Amelia &c., & incomparably more level than any of the limestone lands I have seen in Va, not including river bottoms or flats. There was also a peculiar disposition of the limestone seen for 50 miles south of Nashville, & north of it into Ky., which is doubtless connected in effect with the remarkable comparatively level or slightly undulating surface of the earth. In our limestone (& all other elevated) region, the strata of rocks are generally & greatly inclined, & of course broken—the dip being from 30 to 40 degrees with the horizon, or more. But of all the country here observed, (say 50 miles on both sides of Nashville,) the limestone lies almost perfectly horizontally. When [1013] it is exposed on the surface, it shows like level pavement of very large flat stones, of irregular outlines, each separated from the surrounding stones by narrow fissures. When a mass of such rock is cut through perpendicularly, as in graduating roads or streets, the strata of limestone, separated by horizontal seams, & parted at every few feet of the length by perpendicular fissures, look more like a wall of artificial masonry than a work of nature. . . . At night, I was drawn, against my will & previous intention, into a discussion with Dr. Theobald on the present condition of the slave-holding states, & the institution of negro slavery, under the unceasing assaults of the northern people, & the probable consequences. I had been somewhat prepared by Mr. Sayre's previous statements of the almost universal disposition in Ky to submission to every & to the utmost final wrongs in this respect. But I had not conceived the extent of this disposition until hearing what was now said. Mr. Sayre himself is what in Va would be termed a "conservative" or "union" man— willing, for the preservation of the union, to submit to so much wrong from the North, that *I* would deem him almost a "submissionist." But he would not submit to every oppression, or to the manifest attempt for the extinction of slavery. And for avowing such opinions, he is considered here almost a disunionist. He mentioned the opinions & open declarations of very wealthy slave-holders, not only in Ky, but in Miss., who avowed their preference to sacrifice their slaves, & give up the institution of slavery, & incur all the evils to the southern states of that measure, rather than to lose the present union. Even Dr. Theobald, intelligent & moderate as he is, & a wealthy Mississippi planter, concurs in these views. He only hopes [1015] & trusts that the good sense & forbearance of the northern people will prevent their urging on this certain ultimate end precipitately, & with the then necessary disastrous consequences of ruin to the country. But he counts upon, & is content, that slavery shall be driven from the now border slave-holding states by the pressure of northern abolition action, causing the discontent & aiding the escape of slaves from their owners, & thereby compelling the gradual removal or sale of all the others to more southern localities—so that the present border states, Md, Va, Ky & Mo will first be deprived of slaves, & rendered free states—& next another tier of the states most exposed to abolition action, & so on to the end. Dr. T. hopes that in this gradual process, free white labor may be substituted for the present slave labor, & without great loss to individuals, or utter ruin (as I maintain) to the southern states thus operated on. In this conversation I restrained myself from entering upon the general discussion, or expressing my own extreme views—but which are not at all concealed, & already understood here—but confined my argument to maintaining the perfect ability of the southern states, when disunited from the North, to resist effectually any warlike invasion or assaults from the latter. This Dr. T. has no hope for, & mainly because of the supposed power of a northern hostile or invading army to encourage & produce general negro insurrection in the south.—In the forenoon Mr. Scott an [1016] intelligent gentleman & wealthy farmer of the neighborhood called on me, & paid me much attention. ... He had heard the whole of Breckinridge's speech yesterday— & told me enough (in answer to my cautious inquiries, without expressing any opinion of my own,) that B. had made a union-saving speech, & had refused to answer the two questions which Douglas explicitly & boldly answered in his late speeches in Va., on the right of state secession, & the proper mode of the treatment of state secession by the federal government. By the general union-lauding tenor of Breckinridge's speech, & his declining to answer these questions, I consider that he has placed himself with Douglas in that respect, but wants the boldness to avow that position. Douglas utterly denied the legal right of peaceable secession—& declared as the proper remedy for such act of a state, its prompt suppression as was intended by Pres. Jackson for S.C. in 1833. I used the information as grounds for a letter which I wrote before dinner to the Charleston Mercury, & sent to the post. The two questions put to Douglas, (by a written memorandum sent by the editor of the Norfolk Argus,) with his answers, were as follows: 1st. "If Abraham Lincoln be elected President of the United States, will the Southern States be justified in seceding from [1017] the Union?" *Douglas.* "To this I answer emphatically, no. The election of a man to the presidency by the American people, in conformity with the constitution of the United States, would not justify any attempt at dissolving the Union." 2nd. "If the Southern States secede from the Union upon the inauguration of Lincoln, before he commits an overt act against their constitutional rights, will you advise or vindicate resistance by force to their secession?" *Douglas.* "I answer emphatically that it is the duty of the President of the U.S., & all others in authority under him, to enforce the laws of the U.S. as passed by Congress & as the Court expound them. And I, as in duty bound by my oath of fidelity to the constitution, would do all in my power to aid the Government of the U.S. in maintaining the supremacy of the laws against all resistance to them, come from what quarter it might. In other words, I think the President of the U.S., whoever he may be, should treat all attempts to break up the Union, by resistance to its laws, as Old Hickory treated the nullifiers in 1832." That is, as Jackson wished & intended to treat them, with repression by the bayonet, & punishment by the halter. These same questons were sent to Mr. Breckinridge, & I presume by Mr. Hooper, of Ala, who designed to do so, & which Mr. B. did not notice, nor reply to in any other manner. This induced my letter written to the Charleston Mercury . . . . [1020]

*Sept. 7.* . . . . Frankfort, though containing only some 3500 inhabitants, yet being the seat of the state government, has many residents of high position, & very select society. . . . And already, the calls on me, & cordial & kind attentions paid to me have been remarkable, especially when considering that the reputation of my very odious opinions as a disunionist had preceded me, & were notorious—& among these thorough [1021] unionists & submissionists, I must be deemed a sort of speculative Benedict Arnold—a traitor & enemy of the country in wishes & design, though not yet in action. This forenoon I received, through Mr. Sayre, a message from Senator [John J.] Crittenden, saying that he & Mrs. Crittenden had been prevented coming to see me &c. this forenoon, but that he would come in the afternoon & hoped to have our company at his house at night. Also Col. Charles S. Todd, now staying here on a visit, hearing of my being here, immediately recalled our former acquaintance at Wm. & Mary College, & stated his intention of calling on me—& on Mr. Sayre's invitation, came & partook of our family dinner. We had never been intimate, or very well acquainted, owing to my being then a boy of 16, & he an advanced student three years older. It had been a little more than 50 years since we last saw each other, & have since occupied far remote & very different fields of action. He has served in diplomatic positions in Russia & in South America, & once as full minister to one of the South American republics. Afterwards came Mr. Thomas Theobald, the younger brother of Dr. T. & a very near neighbor of this family, & later, Senator Crittenden with Col. Carneale, a very wealthy & highly respected citizen.... All these visitors with Dr. Theobald (who is here generally,) remained from one to two hours together in pleasant conversation. It was remarkable that of the six guests assembled, I was the youngest by [1022] two years—Dr. T. being over 70, & Mr. Crittenden nearly 80 —& it was a further coincidence that all of us had served in the war of 1812, all as officers except myself, who only had served my six-months tour of volunteer duty as a private militia soldier. Senator Crittenden is the first man in this state for high political position & talent, & in the consideration of his countrymen & the public at large, not excepting his recent successful competitor for the seat in the U.S. Senate (which Mr. C. had so long filled,) Breckinridge, & the latter being more recently the prominent candidate of the democratic party for the Presidency. The change of political power from the whig party, of which Mr. C. was the head in this state, to democratic supremacy, has thus deprived Mr. C. of his former political eminence & office, but without lowering him in the least otherwise, or less[en]ing his high position in the estimation of his countrymen, including his political opponents. Because of his advanced age, as well as his eminent position, & also his abhorrence of my political opinions & course, I had no right to expect any advances or attentions from Mr. C. Yet they have been offered most promptly & earnestly. His wife, who is his junior by 25 or 30 years, married him a few years ago. She, as the widow of Gen. [William H.] Ashley of Mo. was worth $1,500,000, (Mr. C. was & is in very moderate circumstances otherwise,) & had been long, in Washington, among the leaders of fashionable society.[17] She had called on my daughter but a few days before [1023] my arrival—which, with her intended & frustrated call this forenoon, . . . was accepted by our ladies as sufficient attention to them—& so the renewed invitation of Mr. Crittenden was accepted by us all, & after 8.30 P.M. we walked to his residence. He had only notified us of having invited a few persons—but his modest parlor was crowded with guests, mostly ladies, & we old gentlemen were very willing after a short time to sit together in the passage. Ex-Gov. [Robert P.] Letcher was one—now aged & very infirm, & almost crippled by rheumatism.[18] He was especially cordial & frank in his manner to me, & before we parted, he declared that he knew me as thoroughly as if we had been acquainted 20 years instead of but a few hours. He very soon led our conversation to party topics, the speech of Breckinridge, the prospects of the several candidates for the presidency, &c. in which all the others then present joined, & all in asking (directly or otherwise) my views, while not one, except Gov. L. stated his own—& I should not have learned from anything said what was the party or the preference of either speaker. (Mr. Crittenden was not then with us, & I heard not a word from him on politics.) I had a difficult part to play, & to avoid (as I had previously determined while here,) all political discussion, or the voluntary & uncalled for expression of my very unpopular opinions—but without attempting to disguise or disavow them. When it was necessary in my remarks to give any indication of my own opinions, in the present party contest, or otherwise [1024], which I knew to be different from, & unpalatable to all my other auditors, I did so in jocular manner, & sometimes with exaggerated expressions, which prevented any invasion of the good temper & kind feeling of the party. Thus, without any approach to saying what was offensive or unpleasant, I permitted, by tacit admission, my most odious doctrines to be inferred & understood, & expressed my strong objections, & even contempt, for past political occurrences, & their chief agents or most prominent puppets, of which

---

[17] Mrs. Elizabeth Wilcox, in 1832, became the third wife of William Henry Ashley (1778–1838), Missouri explorer and congressman. Some twenty years later she married Senator Crittenden, who also had had two previous spouses.

[18] Not to be confused with Virginia Governor John Letcher, Robert Perkins Letcher (1788–1861) was governor of Kentucky from 1840 to 1844. Previously, he had served six terms in the United States House of Representatives.

these persons held opinions exactly the reverse of mine. Thus, I do not think that I lost ground in any one's favor—& seemed to gain the heart of Gov. Letcher, the most violent, open, & strongly prejudiced whig & unionist, & submissionist. . . . Mr. Crittenden told me that the population of all this part of Kentucky was derived from Virginia, & that scarcely a name could be mentioned of any family which was not Virginian. He supposed that the population was more purely or unmixed of the Virginia stock, than in any part of Va. This I denied, as the whole rural population of Eastern Va, with very few exceptions, is of the [1026] old stock, & that was very generally of English blood, though to a small extent of French Huguenot ancestry. But I readily admitted what was not claimed by Mr. C., that the Kentuckian descendants had a more worthy & noble ancestry than the whole body of Virginians of this day. The Virginian emigrants to Ky were (as Mr. C. said,) mostly men who had lost their property in the disasters & sacrifices of the revolutionary war, & who subsequently, as impoverished men, came to Ky, as their only resource, to settle upon the then wild lands which were their only recompense for military services, either as soldiers or officers in that war. Thus these pioneers, the fathers of the present generation, & especially of the better classes, were men who had devoted years of their lives, & most or all of their properties, to the patriotic defence of their country's cause in the field—& who further, had the courage & resolution & energy to seek to rebuild their fortunes by the then dangerous & arduous enterprise of settling in & subduing the almost untrodden savage western wilderness. There could not well be supplied, in our land & times, a more noble ancestry. But how wofully [*sic*] have the descendants degenerated in political worth, in being now entirely ready to submit to wrongs & oppressions a hundred-fold greater than those [1027] formerly inflicted by the mother country, & against which their brave ancestors rebelled, & resisted at every hazard to property, & to life itself!

*Sept. 9. Sunday.* . . . Went to the Episcopal church. Thence went by invitation to take early family dinner with Major Carneale, a very wealthy & kind-hearted man, but somewhat peculiar, & often rough in his manners, & who though entirely opposed to me in political opinions, seems to have taken a fancy to me. Dr. Theobald was with me—& there we joined Mr. [J. M.] Lancaster, a Catholic priest officiating here regularly, Mr. Flagg, a Connecticut man residing in Cincinnati, & his wife, the daughter of the millionaire [Nicholas] Longworth of Cin., & who is the niece of Major Carneale's deceased wife. . . . Our little party embraced several different sects of religion & politics—& I knew no man's opinions, of either kind, except that Dr. Theobald is a Methodist, & Mr. Lancaster a Catholic. We conversed pleasantly, & with apparent freedom, & even grazed sundry subjects on which we differed, but without going at all too far. I found Mr. Flagg intelligent & agreeable. Dr. Theobald & I returned early. . . . [1028]

*Sept. 10.* The mail brought me a letter from Elizabeth, . . . & one from Edmund to Nanny. All well. Also there came to me the expected two copies of "Anticipations of the Future," which makes a very neat 12 mo volume (with the Appendix) of 426 pages. There are however numerous errors of the printer, mostly in letters & punctuation—& the binding is inferior. I am much gratified that the publication is made at last. And though in fear of deserved censure for literary demerit, (if the work is treated as one of imagination—) I cannot help sanguinely hoping that the book, as an argument & incentive to defence & resistance by the South, & for disunion, will have noted & good effect. If noticed at all by northern or submission critics, of course it will be denounced & vilified. But the more so the better, if the [1029] censure be directed against its design & operation—& not to its defects as a literary performance.—With Mildred, I went to return some visits—& among them, we called on Mr. & Mrs. Crittenden, & on Major Carneale, & on the Rev. Mr. & Mrs. [John N.] Norton.[19] Received by all with the utmost courtesy & kindness of manner. This is universal with all whom I have met in society here . . . . Mr. Norton is a literary man, & a pastor deservedly honored. Though he has become, by marriage, wealthy, he continues to devote the greater portion of his present means to works of true charity, as he did before of all he then had, his time & his labor.

*Sept. 11.* Finished writing a short article begun yesterday, in the rough sketch. Reading a volume of Simms' tales. Walking in the afternoon, with Mildred & Nanny over some of the beautiful grass covered hills which surround Frankfort—& conversation.

Some days ago there appeared in a northern paper (the N.Y. Express,) & from a northern correspondent in Texas, a statement of the late atrocities attempted & planned by northern abolitionists, [1030] in Texas, full as strong as the article before annexed [to this diary]

---

[19] A native of New York, John Nicholas Norton (1820–81) was rector of the Episcopal Church of Ascension in Frankfort from 1847 to 1870.

from a southern writer & witness. But the northern letter-writer adds the important conclusion, that at that time almost every resident was a disunionist, & made so by these unheard of incendiary & murderous plots & attempts. This is the proper operating of such physic—& such as I would have expected. It is deplorable that such horrors should exist, or be attempted. But if any more are brought about, & to even such great extent of design or completion, I earnestly hope that it may be in Georgia. If the dull spirit & lethargic body of that great central southern state could be thus thoroughly aroused to self-defence against the north, & would take the step of secession, every adjoining state (except N.C.) would immediately follow, & the movement would be secure & effective—& necessarily soon to be followed by all the more northern slaveholding states. In the meantime, sundry other of the northern incendiary agents (or those so charged by the negroes, or by circumstances,) have been hung, in Texas & in Ala, which is the best result. The farther this course extends, if to the guilty in the slightest degree, so much the better. I trust that it may come to this that no northerner will dare to come upon southern ground, without being known as of good character, & conduct, or bringing unquestionable evidence of his deserving such recommendation. [1031]

*Sept. 12.* . . . I had intended to go this morning to the Show & Fair of the Agricultural Society, now holding in Lexington. But yesterday I received a message from ex-Gov. Letcher asking me to accompany him there tomorrow—to which delay & arrangement I readily acceded. . . .

*Sept. 13.* . . . Mr. Sayre & I had early breakfast & hastened to go on an early extra train, at 7 A.M. Gov. Letcher soon joine[d] us in the car. We sat together, & had much pleasant [1032] chat, notwithstanding that the noise of the moving train makes it difficult for me to hear, & disagreeable to speak—so that, generally, I prefer not to converse when moving on a railway. Gov. Letcher had been resident minister for the U.S. government in Mexico, in Taylor & Fillmore's administrations—& he told much that was curious & amusing of the occurrences, & habits of the people. He thinks that the present intestine war there, as of most of their civil wars, is simply a contest between the upper & the lower classes—of those who have property to lose, against those who have none, & who are aiming to seize it by force. Thus he supposes that the party of Miramon embraces nearly all of the little virtue, education, & the wealth of Mexico, & that of

Juarez (which our government has acknowledged,) as the needy & desperate, & the soldiers to be robbers whenever opportunity serves. At the Fair, there was a numerous assemblage. Gov. Letcher, whom, by chance, I again met with there as soon as I reached the great enclosing building, introduced me immediately to Judge [George] Robertson,[20] by whom I was invited to the Judges' Stand, the most eligible place for seeing. . . . Among the many today introduced to me . . . were sundry of Mr. Sayre's former pupils, & warm friends—& among the dignitaries, Vice-President Breckinridge, (who resides in Lexington,) & sundry of the other most respectable gentlemen among the visitors. Before going to the Fair, & after leaving it, Mr. S. & I walked (during the day,) five miles or more, mostly over the environs of Lexington. At 5 P.M. we left on the returning extra train. Mr. [Beriah] Magoffin, the present governor of the state, was in a distant part of the car, which I did not know until afterwards. Mr. Sayre came to me & asked me to go with him & be introduced to some gentlemen at the other end of the car, who wished to converse with me. I was about to rise to accompany him, when one came up to me, & was introduced to me as Gov. Magoffin. He sat down by me, & after a little of general conversation, he glided into politics, in reference to the disputes between the north & south growing out of the institution of slavery, on which he discoursed earnestly & sometimes vehemently for more than an hour. I took care, in [1034] respect to his official position, to ask no questions, & not even by suggestion to endeavor to lead the conversation to these points. But I was glad to encourage its continuance by my few remarks. Gov. Dennison of Ohio has added to his course of violation of the constitution & his duty, & to his perjury, which he exhibited in refusing to deliver the murderer Owen Brown to the requisition of the Governor of Va, a like refusal to surrender an abductor of slaves to the Governor of Kentucky—& did not even signify his refusal, or any answer, until four months after the application. Gov. Magoffin enlarged on this subject, & declared that he meant to bring the delinquency of the Governor of Ohio before the Supreme Court of the U.S., & before Congress. Subsequently he referred to the questions

---

[20] Judge Robertson (1790–1874) was chief justice of the Kentucky Court of Appeals from 1829 to 1834. For the next two decades he was on the faculty of the Transylvania University Law School. He supported the Union during the war and, in 1864, was named court of appeals judge for the Second District of Kentucky.

asked of Douglas, & answered by him in Va. He declared that though Breckinridge had declined to notice them, he (M.) was ready to reply to the second—& to this purport: that if, in the event of Lincoln's election, any portion of the more southern states chose to secede from the Union, & the northern power (or U.S. government,) sent an army to conquer the seceding states, if that army attempted to march through Kentucky while he was still governor, every night's encampment should be made a grave-yard. I took care not to lessen the merit of this good resolution by citing old Governor [John] Floyd's[21] like determination to oppose President Jackson's design to march troops to crush S.C. in 1833. There was but one point in which I thought Gov. M. deficient. He is one of those who deems it [1035] necessary, after the election of an abolitionist president, by a sectional majority, to wait for him to commit an "overt act," of unconstitutional wrong to the South, before resisting his government. However, I let this pass, without any discussion, or named objection. And even with it, I found Gov. Magoffin to be decidedly the most southern man in his avowed opinions, of all the Kentuckians or residents of whom I have heard—unless Mr. Sayre furnishes the only exception. . . .[22]

*Sept. 15.* Wrote the rough draft of a second letter on Kentucky politics to the Mercury. . . . Mr. Blackburn, a young man whom I met with on our way to the Fair, & was introduced to me by Mr. Sayre, as his friend & former pupil, came to dine with us today. He is the first Kentuckian I have met with who is an avowed disunionist. He has resided, as a lawyer, most of his adult life, in Chicago, & left it for a slave-holding home, heartily disgusted with Chicago, & its people & their political opinions & actions. He is an intelligent & pleasant converser—& I think that he & I were well pleased with each other. . . .

*Sept. 16.* Sunday. . . . Copied, & enlarged my letter for the Mercury to nearly 8 pages. Gratified by hearing Mildred play on her Melodeon, (the same she had at Marlbourne,) most of the fine anthems & other pieces of church music which so often & so long ago, I have heard from her on the same instrument. . . .

---

[21] Governor of Virginia, 1830–34.

[22] Governor Magoffin's pronounced Confederate sympathies precipitated conflict between the executive and the unionist legislature following the outbreak of war. Finally, in 1862, Magoffin resigned his office after the legislature demanded (over his veto) the removal of all Confederate troops from Kentucky.

*Sept. 18.* Walked to the town (across the river) & read the news-papers at the office of the "Yeoman," whose editor, Mr. S. Major, was introduced to me by Mr. Sayre, & who was one of his old pupils, & is one of his particular friends. Afternoon, as usual we walked, & to one of the sundry beautiful hill-tops which surround Frankfort. . . .

*Sept. 19.* Read Calhoun's "Disquisition on Government" which I had read before, when it first appeared, & again with instruction & pleasure. For, as in regard to everything else read in latter years, but a faint & general idea of its purport remained on my memory. Afterwards began (also a second reading,) of Maury's "Physical Geography of the Sea." Went as usual to see the newspapers at the Yeoman Office. . . .

*Sept. 21.* Dr. Theobald, at his own invitation, drove me about 12 miles out of Frankfort on the turnpike towards Lexington (by the Versailles route,) into Woodford county, to see samples of the most fertile & beautiful lands [1039] of the "blue grass country." . . . After a very pleasant drive of 26 miles, over excellent roads & a beautiful & fertile country, we returned to Mr. Sayre's to dinner, after 3 P.M.

*Sept. 22.* Garibaldi is said, at last accounts, to be within 30 miles of Naples, & marching without opposition, from Calabria, to that city. The King of Naples had for some time had his valuables on board a steamer, ready for his flight at the first alarm. The King of Sardinia had 8 vessels of war in the harbor of Naples, & has ordered the march to the city of 30,000 men, "to prevent disturbances," as al-leged, but of course to take possession of the fruits of Garibaldi's deeds. If this is done, doubtless the Roman territory will next be oc-cupied, & then Venetia, making all of Italy.—Walker was compelled to evacuate Truxillo by the order of the captain of the British ship of war Icarus, with about 75 men, carrying only their arms & the clothing on their persons—& next, all were compelled to surrender as prisoners to a detachment from the same ship. It is reported that the prisoners (except the wounded) were transferred to the au-thorities of Honduras, & that Walker, if not more, will be shot.— The Prince of Wales having completed his appointed progress through Canada, landed, at Detroit, with his suite of noblemen, but in the character of a private traveller, Baron Renfrew, on the 20th, & afterwards proceeded to Chicago. As I had feared, the sycophantic & boot-licking propensities [1041] of many of the Ameri-can people, & especially of the northern states, are already fully ex-posed, & far greater crowds assemble to see, & to offer adulation to this youth, who is of no note or merit, apart from his being heir to the crown of Britain, than would unite to do honor to the greatest of American patriots & benefactors, or to any untitled foreigners of the greatest worth or talent. The prince is to be in Cincinnati on the 28th & 29th. We shall pass through that city on the 24th—& I shall be glad to miss meeting the flood of sycophancy & servility that will prevail there a few days later. . . .

*Sept. 23.* Sunday. All of us at church. Afternoon, walked to the nearest hill-top. Mildred played for me on the melodeon all the favorite anthems which we have both loved so much always, & which when before death had entered our household, & my three unmarried daughters were with me at Marlbourne, we made a family choir of four parts, with the aid [1042] [of] this same instrument, played on so sweetly by Mildred. How lonely & desolate now, in comparison! . . .

*Sept. 24.* All ready for our early departure, & fortunately the weather good. We had an earlier breakfast than usual, & left for the station, & set out on the train at 8 A.M. Reached Lexington by 10, & had to wait there until 12 M., when set out on the train for Covington, & the Ohio, & reached Cincinnati at 6 P.M. There had to wait, (at the Burnett House) until 11 P.M., without occupation, acquaintance or amusement, when we again set out on the R Road by Columbus & Zanesville, to Bellaire, on the Ohio, which we reached by 10 A.M.

*Sept. 25.* From light, I observed the lands & farming through which the road passed, & compared them with those of Kentucky, & found both inferior to the latter. I saw no neat, or apparently good farming in Ohio. Especially was the drainage deficient. Scarcely were any ditches seen that deserved the name—but instead, mostly natural gutters, with but rare & insufficient attempts either to straighten or deepen them. Yet the denouncers of slavery have boldly claimed [1043] greatly superior industry & good farming for Ohio over Kentucky, & ascribed these falsely claimed results to the system of free labor in Ohio, & of slavery in Kentucky. In Cincinnati last night we were greatly annoyed by the numerous mosquitoes—& the cars were so full of them that they disturbed us all night, & accompanied us far into the interior. I was much disappointed in the size of the river Ohio both at Cincinnati & Bellaire & Berwood, (just below Wheeling). It was low water indeed—but the margins covered at high water were obvious, & when they were covered, the river would not have been half a mile wide at Cincinnati & still less at Berwood. I have been still more disappointed in the want of beauty in the western rivers. The Cumberland at Nashville, the Kentucky at Frankfort, the Licking, which ran near to our road for 50 miles yesterday, & the Ohio, all were muddy—& the three former even had a greenish stagnant appearance. But this is not always the case. To these, a marked appearance of cleanness & beauty was shown today by both the Mongahela [*sic*], & its affluent the Tygart. There were striking features in the grand scenery of the route, on the Ohio & Baltimore R.R. to Cumberland, east of the Allegheny summit, in Md. The natural difficulties of this route were immense, & they have been admirably & effectively overcome. There are sundry tunnels, through which the road & trains pass—the largest nearly a mile in length. In crossing the deep gorge by Cheat river, which I had made so important a scene of my book, I found that I had been misinformed in the features which I supposed to be correct—as well as being entirely out in others (as expected) of which I had no particular reports, & made the local features & scenery to suit my story.[23] However, I do not care much for such variances. They could scarcely have been [1044] much less, as of all scenes for military & other operations assumed, I had not seen one, except in part Charleston Harbor, & that very slightly, & Washington & Harper's Ferry. New York I had not seen in 30 years, & had not even a map of any mentioned locality, except of Charleston, & that not a good or recent one. But the difficulties of the north-west for an invading army, as seen from the train, are even worse than I had imagined. Nearly the whole way for 50 miles or more from the Ohio is along the bottom of very narrow valleys, or defiles, bordered on both sides by steep hills, sometimes almost precipitous. After passing the Allegheny summit, we reached Cumberland at 8.30. . . .

*Sept. 26.* Left at 8 A.M. Bea[u]tiful scenery along the borders of the Potomac river & the canal—then through the good land of Berkley & Jefferson in Va, (but not to compare to Kentucky,) to Harper's Ferry, where we stopped for some 20 minutes—& gave Nannie some opportunity to see the sublime natural scenery, & the beautiful structures of the Armory &c., & also to see the remaining mementoes of the battle with John Brown's marauding & murdering party. Pursuing our route we reached the Junction of the Washing-

---

[23] The diarist refers here to his recently published political novel, *Anticipations of the Future.*

ton R.R. before 5 P.M., & the Steamer on the Potomac river after dark. Thence down the river to Aquia Creek, & on the Fredericksburg R.R. to Richmond by 4 A.M., & to Petersburg—[1045] where we arrived by 6 A.M. on

*Sept. 27....* Hired a carriage, & as soon as we had eaten an early breakfast, we set out & reached Beechwood by 9 A.M. Found all the family at home, & all well.... The family of my sister, at the Glebe, are preparing for breaking up. The land is to be sold. The slaves were divided yesterday among the heirs. My sister Dupuy will go to Mobile with her daughter Mrs. Marshall—her daughter Juliana will live in Richmond with her brother Montgomery, Anna will be married & live in New Orleans—& John will seek for a purchase & settlement in Texas or Florida.—At night, I had a long & full conversation with Edmund in reference to his family & love affairs. His uncertainty has not yet been decided—& he has heard nothing, in answer to his letters, for four weeks. Of course he is extremely anxious & uneasy, & fearful of the result.

*Sept. 28....* The Charleston Mercury contained my last letter from Frankfort.... [24] I have not yet seen anything of the earlier letter. Probably it was excluded, because likely to be injurious in the South to the success of Breckenridge.—The abolition plots, & consequent troubles, & acts of lawless justice, or doubtless in some cases misplaced vengeance, have not ceased in Texas—though but little of the details have been published.... If but one-tenth of these plots & attempts be true, added to the attempt made through John Brown, it would be alone sufficient for a separation of the Union, to exclude northern emissaries & incendiaries from southern territory. Until that is done, ten northern emissaries, or even one, may at any time incite discontent & rebellion—while, after separation, we may more securely defy the whole power of northern abolitionism. [1049]

*Sept. 29....* Yesterday & this morning looking over the latter of the accumulated newspapers, & at other times reading [Anthony] Trollope's "West Indies & the Spanish Main," a new work.—It had been announced in the newspapers that, contrary to the previous arrangement, by which the Prince of Wales & his suite were to come no farther south than Washington, that they were to come to Richmond, & to make an excursion down James river. Mr. [Hill] Carter

---

[24] In this letter Ruffin decried the ascendancy of submissionism in Kentucky and denied that free labor was cheaper and more profitable than slave labor. There were, asserted the diarist, no "natural limits" to the expansion of slavery.

[of Shirley] tells us that it is understood that the party will call at Westover, Mr. Selden's farm, nearly opposite to this Point—& Mr. S. himself considers the call as having been arranged. [1050]

*October 1....* I finished reading Trollope's "West- [1051] Indies." The book is written in a lively & amusing manner, & contains much information about Jamaica & the degradation of the negro population. The author furnishes plenty of facts to show, & admits the manifest conclusions, that the improvement of the negroes is hopeless. Yet he is so foolish as to rely upon the future amalgamation of the white & black races to produce a mixed breed capable of self-support & industry. He is also an advocate (rather cold indeed) of the act of emancipation—though his book is full of evidence of its ruinous effects. He states but one British tropical colony to have laborious negroes, or to make proper agricultural returns—Barbados—& he explains the cause in its dense population, & there being no vacant ground. There, as of white laborers in England, the destitute negro must work unremittingly, or go without food for his daily sustenance. And however lazy & improvident he may be, hunger & the close approaching danger of starvation, must drive the negro as well as the white laborer to work.—The mail, at last, brought the long expected answer from J[ane] R[uffin] (it was dated the 13th ult.) & her final & fixed decision, the rejection of E[dmund]'s suit. The long delay (though accidental, & of the mail,) had taught us to fear such an answer. Nevertheless, it came upon me as an unlooked-for & grievous blow. But it is now proper to dismiss the subject, & forever.... Walker, after retreating from Truxillo, (whence he was ordered off by the commander of the British ship of war Icarus,) was captured by, or surrendered to the same British officer. Walker & his [1052] second in command, Col. Rudler, were delivered to the authorities of Honduras, & by them, it is said, that Gen. Walker was shot. The privates were sent to New Orleans by the British captain, where they have arrived in wretched condition.—I received a letter from the Governor of N.Ca. highly complimenting the writings I had placed in his hands (at his request,) & accepting them to be published as public documents for the state.... Received from J. W. Randolph his bills for printing & binding my book, (total $469.56 for 1000 copies,) & sent him a check for $113.04, that being [t]he balance due for my two-thirds of the expenses.

*Oct. 4.* A day of slow rain, or drizzle. Finished reading our last supply of newspapers. Began the Report (a volume,) to the Senate of U.S. & testimony before the Committee of the John Brown affair.

*Oct. 7.* Received a long letter from Willoughby Newton on southern politics, which I answered forthwith.—Went to church with the others of the family. . . .

*Oct. 8.* Edmund returned home from Marlbourne & Richmond. The Prince of Wales came to Richmond from Washington after dark on Saturday evening, & instead of coming down the river today, as was designed, he & his party returned to Washington by the same route today. He went to St. Paul's church on Sunday, where it happened that my son & his two daughters attended & saw him. Edmund describes him as being small, & his face rather homely, & not intellectual, & his head narrow. He seemed modest & gentlemanly, attended very closely to the religious services, & behaved with great propriety in every respect.

*Oct. 10.* . . . Before the Prince of Wales had reached Washington, it had been arranged, & so published in the newspapers, that one of the chief parts of his entertainment there would be taking him & his suite, on an excursion to Mount Vernon, accompanied by the President & a select company, made up of government officers &c. To this was devoted most of the only entire day he gave to Washington & the President. This pilgrimage to the tomb of the great hero of our country, & deemed (though erroneously as I think,) the chief if not sole founder of its independence, if it had been proposed by or for the heir of the English crown, would have been a most graceful compliment to this country, & marked homage to the merits of Washington. But if, as I infer, it was proposed & arranged by the President of the U.S., & of course forced upon the Prince, (as he could not possibly have declined or objected,) [1056] the matter was entirely changed, & was in extremely bad taste. . . . If [Benedict] Arnold's private character, & the motives for his treason to the United States, had been as pure as Washington's, & his motives for the treason of the latter to the government of England, it would have been not in worse taste, to invite the American ambassador in England, or the American President, to make a respectful visit to the tomb of Arnold. . . .

*Oct. 11.* . . . Finished reading the "Woman in White." [25] Interesting, which is indeed the main object & merit of a mere work of fiction

---

[25] A new novel by William Wilkie Collins (1824–89), who is considered by some critics to be the first English writer of bona fide detective and mystery novels.

& amusement. But the great improbability of many of the incidents, essential to working out the plot, are [*sic*] disagreeable. In works of imagination & fictitious narrative, I do not object to the most marvellous incidents & results, provided they are made to appear as the not very improbable consequences of the premises. But consequences which are altogether improbable, & illegitimate [1057] from the premises, or for the stated characters & conditions of the actors, always offend or disgust me. . . .

*Oct. 12.* . . . Important political news. The Pennsylvania election for governor occurred on the 9th. As it would show the strength of the abolition candidate, [Andrew G.] Curtin, in comparison with all the opposing popular vote, united for [Henry D.] Foster, this election was looked for with general anxiety. The issue is that the abolitionist is elected certainly, though by what majority is not yet known. It is variously computed at from 20,000 to 32,000. This result shows that the great state of Pennsylvania, with her thirty odd electoral votes will go for Lincoln for President. Nothing now but New York going against him, can prevent his election by the popular voice. I heartily rejoice for this increased probability. I wish the southern states to be forced to choose between secession & submission to abolition domination, though I greatly fear that, even if Lincoln shall be elected, not one state will thereupon secede.

*Oct. 13.* . . . A letter from Governor Ellis, received last mail, informing that my manuscripts had been sent, as I requested, to Richmond, for my last revision—& which has been done too late for my purpose—will compel me to go to Richmond, & thence to Raleigh, to arrange with Governor Ellis, & with the printer, about the printing & correction of the sheets. I also do not exactly understand whether any of the articles which have already been published, as well as the unpublished manuscript articles, are desired to be printed in this collection of documents for the State of N.Ca. . . .

*Oct. 15.* Took passage on the steam-boat, & reached Richmond at 15 minutes after 3 P.M. Saw J. W. Randolph—heard that the demand for my book has been but small—much less than I should have supposed that curiosity would have induced. . . . Got my manuscripts, sent, as I had requested, by Gov. Ellis. Shall set out for Raleigh tomorrow morning. Read & corrected manuscripts until 10 P.M.

*Oct. 16.* Left Richmond at 4 A.M. & reached Raleigh at about 4 P.M. Did not know until on the way, that the Agricultural Fair of the State Society meets today. Could not get in at Yarborough's Hotel, because every bed was occupied. Stopped at the Guyon House, but only as one of 3 or 4 to a room, even if not to share a bed with some stranger. So after shaving [1059] & washing, I went to seek better accommodations, & found them (where recommended by an acquaintance,) at the private house of Mrs. Primrose, a widow lady who has consented to take some gentlemen as boarders during the Fair. Heard that Judge Ruffin was in town—& afterwards sought & found him at the meeting of the Agr. Society, in the Capitol, at night. There also saw several other of my former acquaintances, & among them Mr. Kenneth Raynor [*sic*], with whom Judge Ruffin is staying . . . .26

*Oct. 17.* Went early to see Gov. Ellis. He approves of & wishes to include in the series every one of the articles submitted to him, those which have already been printed, as well as the four which remain in manuscript. They will be printed as a series, & will make a thin octavo volume, uniform in page & letter with the other reports which have been or will be hereafter published, by authority of the state of N.C. Conferred also with the printer, & placed in his hands the revised & earlier portions of the series.—Saw Senators Clingman & Bragg, & Th. Ruffin, M.C. on the Fair Ground. Conversed with them & others on the probability (now almost certainty,) of Lincoln being elected, & what is to be done. All fear that the southern states will *all* submit. I hope that *one*, at least, may secede—& if one only takes [1060] that step, others will follow—& soon all other slave-holding states, or those which do not, must yield & submit implicitly to abolition rule. Gov. Ellis told me that he had received a letter from Gov. Gist of S.C. stating his opinion that a convention will be called by that state, if Lincoln is elected—& that if no other state will secede, & lead in the movement, that S.C. will secede alone.—Saw in the Mercury of 13th. the annexed letter.27 Corrected & sent another short letter. I think of keeping up such a fire, in very short & carelessly written letters. These may be read—as I am sure my long & elaborate articles have not been, except by very few.—At night attended the meeting of the Agricultural Society, & joined a

---

26 Kenneth Rayner (1808–84), a former Whig congressman and state senator, was appointed to the *Alabama* Claims Commission by President Grant after the war.

27 A letter by Ruffin criticizing the friendly reception accorded to Dr. Martin R. Delany, a Canadian Negro and conspirator in the John Brown affair, at the Statistical Congress in London.

little in the discussion of some facts in regard to under-draining, & the use of tile pipes. [1061]

*Oct. 18.* Again on the Fair Ground. Saw the drill or exercises of the company of Cadets of the Hillsborough Military Academy. Their discipline does great credit to their commander, & principal of the Academy, Col. C[harles] C. Tew, who began & established the institution at his own private expense & risk. He himself was a beneficiary pupil of one of the state Military Academies of South Carolina. I sought an introduction to him.—At night again at the meeting of the Agricultural Society.—Finished reading & giving last corrections to most of the articles to be published for the State, & as much as required re-examination—& directed to the printer all that had not been previously put in his hands.

*Oct. 19.* At 9. A.M.,with Judge Ruffin, left Raleigh for Graham, on my way to his house, where we arrived at 2 P.M. . . . . Mr. Hamilton, who married Fanny Roulhac, & who is a teacher & officer of the Hillsborough Military Academy, came with us. . . . Judge Ruffin always avoids talking on politics, or holding any argument. Therefore we rarely discuss points, as on union & secession, [1062] in regard to which we differ widely. Still, in a light & jocular manner, a good deal of our talk in the family circle was on these now exciting subjects, in which the ladies, all unionists, took their part. In William Ruffin's room, to which his lameness confines him mostly, we, with Sterling & Mr. Hamilton, agreeing with each other in the main, talked on these subjects more freely. W. R. had read "Anticipations of the Future"—& from him I heard almost the first high approbation of the book, both for its manner & argument. He gave to it the credit of having removed his lingering devotion to the union, & hopes of preserving it—& that he now concurred in the necessity for secession. There are few minds better qualified than his to judge of the merit of an argumentative or literary work, & I hold his opinion & applause in high estimation.—Judge Ruffin told me that last night, after I had left the meeting, a resolution was offered by Mr. Battle, (with whom I have no personal acquaintance,) & unanimously adopted by the Society, testifying to its high appreciation of my services to agriculture, & especially to the agricultural interests of N.Ca.

*Oct. 21.* . . . . Political conversation, with William & Thomas Ruffin especially, on the probability of secession of some southern state following the expected election of Lincoln. Fears are entertained

[475]

that, in the event of separation of the Union, N.Ca. may choose to remain attached to the north rather than to follow the secession movement & go with the more southern states. But this I deem impossible, as an ultimate decision. For if Va or N.C. were so to do, after most, or indeed any, of the more southern states had seceded, it would be ruinous to such remaining slave-holding state. Its then connection with the abolition states would compel the speedy extinction of slavery—& the separation from the South would cause the seceding states to refuse to buy or receive the slaves of states which had become foreign & hostile to them—unless receiving masters as well as slaves, by immigration & settlement. The extinction of the institution of negro slavery, no matter how effected, would be a deadly blow to the prosperity of N.C. or Va., even if every slave were paid for. If their money value also was lost, the injury would be more than doubled. And if individual proprietors, to avoid either or both of these evils, should expatriate themselves, & move with their slaves & all other property to the seceded states, they might thus save their own interests, but their removal would still more injure the state they left.—Read Yancey's speech, lately delivered in the city of New York. It is an able [1064] speech, & showing great tact in the speaker, in adapting his argument to suit a northern audience.

*Oct. 23.* As before designed, I left for home, going to Graham to take the mail train at 12. Not an allusion has been made, on either side, . . . of the recent courtship & its termination. We all seemed to have determined to ignore the whole affair.—Set off from Graham at 12 M. & reached Goldsborough at 6.30 P.M. (there being no evening train over the Raleigh & Gaston road—) then, from 7 to 11 P.M. reached Weldon, & from 11.30 P.M. to 3 A.M. travelled to Petersburg.

*Oct. 24.* Had, in bed, rather more than one hour's sleep before I was roused at 5 A.M. to get ready for the train to City Point, which, after all the hurry, & cutting very short both my morning's sleep & breakfast, did not set out until 8 A.M. On arriving at City Point, found there Edmund's boat & servant, sent there for some freight articles, by which conveyance I proceeded, & reached Beechwood at 11.30. Edmund alone at home—the others went yesterday to Richmond to the Agricultural Fair, & to stay two weeks.—The Prince of Wales has embarked (from Portland,) for England. I am heartily glad he has left this country. I am tired of so much of the newspapers being filled with reports of his movements, & still more tired & disgusted with the sycophancy. [1065]

Mr. R B Rhett jr., the editor of the Charleston Mercury, has inserted one of my late short communications as if editorial....[28] I am very willing he shall use this liberty—as editorials are much more apt to be read, & to have influence, than if the same words appeared as communicated from any other, & especially an anonymous source. Received also a private letter from Mr. Rhett, in which he states that he will in the same manner use two communications which I sent him from Raleigh.... I have avoided going to this Fair of the State Agrl. Society for several reasons. One is the coalition between the State Society & the Central (or Richmond) Agr. Society, which [1066] had shown so jealous & hostile a spirit to the State Society, & which now has the chief control of the united Fair. Further, my efforts for the benefit of the State Society, & especially the protecting it (but partially,) from the host of extortionate bloodsuckers who robbed it by extortion of every kind of $1500 to $2000 a year, served to offend them & to bring all their lies & influence to bear against me—& this was doubled by the removal of the fairs, for two years, from Richmond, being ascribed by common understanding exclusively to my action. All these influences, combined, have operated to make my presidency & myself unpopular with the greater number, & odious to not a few. Thus, for my best acts I have gained most blame. If I had allowed the swindling to go on, without any effort to check it, as did my predecessor, & almost all in the Ex. Committee, I should have continued to be as popular a president, as when thrice before elected unanimously. Under these circumstances, I could not go to the present Fair, & to appear by my presence to ask for attentions to me because of my former position in & my services to the Society—whether such attention should be accorded, or slightingly withheld. Edmund will go to the Fair tomorrow, & I will stay at Ruthven until next Monday, or until Edmund shall return. [1067] ... The appearances in the newspapers seem to indicate more probability of some secession movement as soon as Lincoln is elected—if by no other state leading, I think that South Carolina will move. [1069]

*Oct. 26.* ... Wrote first sketch of another short article for the Mercury. In that paper received today, the editor has inserted, as

---

[28] In this communication, entitled "The Sinews of War," the diarist deplored the lack of concerted action in the South to resist northern encroachments and called for the formation of civil and military associations to promote the southern cause.

editorial, another of these communications[29]—so I suppose that he approves them, & thinks them likely to have effect, as he adopts them himself. . . . The N.Y. Herald contains sundry articles selected from southern newspapers, & also communications written from the South, with comments thereon, all going to show the strong feeling for resistance & secession in the impending event of Lincoln's election to the Presidency. It is the great object of the Herald now to alarm the North, & so prevent this election, by showing the danger & the consequences to the north of a disruption of the Union. I trust that these truths will be, as heretofore, preached to deafness. The insanity of the Northern people, their entire disregard of the possibility of the Southern states seceding, or the southern people being able to maintain secession & independence, is astonishing. I trust they will still remain thus self-deluded & demented, & perpetuate [1071] by this election, the crowning act of avowed threatening of ruin, & speedy destruction, of every thing precious & necessary for the salvation of the South. Much as the states of the South have already submitted to, & seemed ready to continue to submit to any such gradually imposed wrongs, this great danger, accompanied by open threats of its evil consequences, will scarcely be endured quietly by *all* the southern states, though certainly most of them are prepared still to submit. But my trust is that a few, or at least one, will submit no longer, but secede as soon as Lincoln's election is known, (or even his having a plurality of votes, & all of abolition states,)—& if but one secedes, that must draw more very soon—& before long even the now submissionist border states of Va. Md. & Ky.

*Oct. 27.* Corrected & copied the short communication to the Mercury, & carried it to the Post Office to be mailed. Also, the papers prepared for the printer in Raleigh.—Discoveries (real or supposed) of northern plots, & plotters, for incendiary or murderous action of slaves in the south, continue to be made in various places, besides the most notable & numerous in Texas. Not one such attempt reached being put in execution, except the burning of many homes & sundry small towns in Texas. Some few of the northern instigators have been hung—among them a Methodist preacher. Although nearly all the trials of such persons have been made by popular & unauthorized judgment, & the executions without any sanction or

---

[29] Ruffin, in this noteworthy article, accused the Republicans of working toward general emancipation and argued for secession as the only means of preserving slavery and preventing slave insurrection.

form of law, it seems that they have been conducted with deliberation, & every regard to justice. Indeed, it is wonderful that so many
of persons, of whose guilt, to more or less extent, [1072] there seemed
(from the newspaper reports,) to be no doubt, should have been acquitted, or subjected to no greater penalty than an order for immediate departure from the state. The most remarkable case is reported in the last papers, of such discharge of two emissaries, in S.C.
whose papers showed the purchase or ordering of $1200 worth of
arms, to be sent from the North to places in North & South Carolina,
& of which the purpose could have been nothing else but to start &
aid servile insurrection. These men, Hitchings, were father & son,
& the father an Englishman—formerly settled in N.Y. & latterly in
N.C., where the older had been whipped for illegal dealing with
slaves. I thought that these men certainly ought to be & would have
been hung. Yet, upon full trial before a "vigilance committee" of 70,
only 11 voices were for hanging them, & they were only sent northward, & so passed out of S.C.—Picked up a newly published little
book, by the Rev. P. Slaughter, "Man & Woman," which I read
through, (in my ordinary cursory manner,) in a few hours. It is a good
argument, & also good instruction. The object of the writer is to
account for the notorious fact that so many more of professing &
also of worthy Christians should be of the female sex. He endeavors,
& with much effect, to show that it is owing to the more religious, &
moral training of young girls than of boys, & the consequent greater
purity of their youthful lives.

*Oct. 28. Sunday*. . . . Julian & I went to the Glebe. He stayed until
near bed-time, [1073] & I remained longer. Much of our conversation on the expected election of Lincoln, & the prospects & con-
tingencies of secession of one or more of the more southern states.
Dr. John Dupuy is a strong whig, & is going to vote for Bell. But he
is also a good southerner, & ready to go for secession as soon as
Lincoln's election shall inaugurate abolition rule.

*Oct. 29*. While lying awake last night, a thought occurred to me,
which I carried out this forenoon. This was to write to Yancey, &
urge him as strongly as I could, to assume the position in regard to
secession that Patrick Henry did for the rights of the colonies in the
time of the stamp-act. A corrected & somewhat extended copy of the
rough draft, making above 5 pages, was finished & sent to the mail.[30]

---

[30] See Appendix E for the rough draft of this remarkable letter.

—The northern & other newspapers, opposed to disunion & to Lincoln, are filled with alarms for his expected election. The N.Y. Herald which has so zealously combatted on this side, seems now hopeless in regard to the election—& publishes from southern papers many arguments, threats & pledges for secession, as soon as the abolition candidate succeeds. My own wishes are more sanguine, as to both of these results. . . . After dinner I . . . went to Beechwood, where I found Edmund returned from Richmond. . . .

*Oct. 30.* A steady rain throughout the day—partly heavy.—Wrote [1074] two short communications (on secession) for the Mercury. Finished reading yesterday's newspapers & the Nov. No. of De Bow's Review, & by 7 P.M. was out of employment, & wishing for the arrival of bed-time. . . .

*Oct. 31.* Copied my pieces—8 pages.—The mail. The alarm & prospect of disruption of the Union are growing rapidly—& the northern people & abolitionists are now alarmed. A declaration of one of Lincoln's chief friends, stating a much moderated policy for his presidency, has been published to appease the South—& I very much fear that it may offend his most fanatical supporters, so as to make them quit Lincoln, & vote for Gerrit Smith, so as by this division of their party, to defeat the election of the former. This result would not show the abolition party to be weaker, or less dangerous to the South. But it would postpone the complete triumph of that party for four years. This would prevent all chance for secession at this time. Yet if Lincoln is elected, [1075] which is now admitted to be almost certain (if having his full party vote,) I have but little question but that at least South Carolina will secede, & others must soon follow—& finally all the states that choose to continue the institution of slavery, & to save their property in slaves.—The late victory of Garibaldi, at Capua, over the king's army of regular troops (mostly German mercenaries,) was so complete, though after a very long & bloody contest, that the king's cause cannot be much longer maintained. The annexation of the Neapolitan dominions to those of Piedmont, all making the "Kingdom of Italy," now seems certain. But a new & important & also mysterious element is put into the political medley, by Napoleon increasing his army of occupation in Rome to 60,000 men, & placing strong garrisons in all the outer towns of the former papal dominion (or "Patrimony of St. Peter.") This may be an indication that he means to secure the pope in the possession & government of all that extent of territory. Or, as there is no truth or honesty in the imperial knave & villain, possibly he means to use the pretence to have a strong army in Italy, for some other & entirely selfish objects. Austria is threatened with the loss of Venetia. Russia & Prussia seem disposed to intervene for the protection of Austria. Extended warfare may be expected in Europe, & also, by European troops & policy, in Asia. The combined French & British forces were approaching Pekin, & the French troops in Syria, had marched into the interior, to punish the Druses for their renewed massacres of Maronites or other Christians. The most rigorous & bloody measures of the Turkish general have not [1076] served to quell the fanatical & rebellious spirit of the Druses —& it seems necessary, as well as probable, that France shall compel & maintain obedience, & occupy Syria, & so begin the partition & overthrow of the dying Turkish empire.[31] It is very desirable, for the world's good, that it should be so. Also, if these United States are about to be separated, & war should ensue between the northern & southern portions, (which latter I do not believe in as a consequence of separation,) it is very desirable, for us of the South, that France & England shall be well occupied with their own affairs, & have no opportunity to intermeddle with ours.

*November 1....* I determined some 10 days ago, contrary to my previous intention, to vote in the coming election. Breckinridge does not come up to my standard of what a southern candidate should be, or a true & bold maintainer of the rights of the South. But as nearly all of the true southerners will vote for him, & as I wish to avert the disgrace of Va giving a plurality vote to Bell, I determined to add my voice to Breckinridge. For this object only I have latterly been waiting at home. I shall vote on the 6th, & on the 7th proceed to South Carolina, where I hope that even my feeble aid may be worth something to forward the secession of that state, & consequently of the whole South.

*Nov. 2.* The newspapers all full of alarms for the prospect of Lincoln's election, & the consequent expected movements for secession. I earnestly hope for both—& with increased expectation—but still fear being disappointed in on[e] or the other. . . . There [were] sent to me today by mail 200 copies of (secession) pamphlets to distribute. They are the Tracts No 1 & 2, published by the "Association

---

[31] The French expeditionary force, sent in at the behest of the major European powers after some 12,000 Christians had been slaughtered by the Moslem Druses, was evacuated from Syria in June, 1861.

of 1860" of Charleston S.C. of which the object is [1078] to publish & circulate in this manner pamphlets containing the best articles for operating on the popular mind. Virginia is as yet a bad soil on which to sow such seeds. However I must do the best I can with them—& began this afternoon to give out some for the neighborhood, through the post-office.

*Nov. 3.* . . . At night Julian came, & also Edmund, who had been attending to his duty as captain of the troop of cavalry, at the Court House. Our conversation mostly on the impending presidential election & its probable consequences. My sons differ from me in one respect. They earnestly wish Lincoln to be defeated, because they do not believe that any of the southern states will secede in the event of his election. I have much fear that they may be right. Still, I most earnestly & anxiously desire Lincoln to be elected—because I have hope that at least one state S.C. will secede, & that others will follow—& even if otherwise, I wish the question tested & settled now. If there is general submission now, there never will be future maintenance of our rights—& the end of negro slavery may be considered as settled. I can think of little else than this momentous crisis of our institutions & [1079] our fate. I regret that my obligation to give my vote prevents my going earlier to S.C. to confer with the most zealous for secession.

*Nov. 5.* . . . No news—but the roaring of the approaching storm is heard from every part of the southern states. Yet after all, I fear that not one, unless South Carolina, will be ready to declare for secession as soon as the election of Lincoln is certain. Also the alarm in the northern states, of southern secession & its consequences to the north, is still increasing. I hope earnestly that it may not so increase as to cause Lincoln to be defeated.

*Nov. 6.* This is the day for the election of electors—the momentous election which, if showing the subsequent election of Lincoln to be certain, will serve to show whether these southern states are to remain free, or to be politically enslaved—whether the institution of negro slavery, on which the social & political existence of the south rests, is to be secured by our resistance, or to be abolished in a short time, as the certain result of our present submission to northern domination.—We went to the Court House, where we gave our vote for Breckinridge & Lane, & thence the carriage took me to Petersburg. . . . Heard from the latest reports, that the elections in Richmond & Petersburg were going for Bell & Everett far beyond my previous expectations. Took my place on the train for the

South, which started at 5 P.M. I had sent about half of the pamphlets (received from Charleston) by Edmund to Richmond, to F. G. Ruffin & D. H. London, for them to distribute. The remaining supply, I carried with me, & distributed them to best advantage, some to fellow passengers, but mainly by throwing out a few at the office of every station on the route through Va & N.Ca. There were very few passengers. One, a resident of Florida, gave strong assurances for the readiness of that state for secession. Travelled all night.

*Nov. 7.* Reached Wilmington N.Ca. after 5 A.M. The awkward & slow shiftings of baggage, on negroes' heads & shoulders, from one train to the ferry steamer, & then to the Manchester rail train, caused a delay of nearly two hours, to cross the river of less than half a mile distance. At Wilmington heard the first telegraphic dispatch stating that the city of New York had voted against Lincoln by 30,000 majority only. This is much less than expected, & Lincoln will therefore certainly gain the state—& New York going for him, will secure his election. It is good news for me. At every station there were collected some of the neighboring people, anxious to hear the news. Through the remaining portion of N.C. the sentiment of "conservatism" or union was visible. But in S.C., universal secession feeling appeared, so far as I [1081] elicited opinions in answer to my remarks to any of the people. Before reaching Kingsville, our small number of passengers was much increased, several gentlemen wearing the blue cockade which is the distinguishing mark of the "minute men." Among the passengers was Col. [Simeon] Fair,[32] whom I formerly knew. With him & others had some earnest conversation, all for early secession of S.C. Heard, & also saw in the papers of the day that last night there had been strong exhibition of public feeling in Columbia. A serenade & calls from the people had called upon sundry of the public men, there on the legislature assembled yesterday, or visitors there, & they had answered by zealous & excited speeches, on the policy of the state in the expected event of Lincoln's election. Senator Chesnut, Mr. [William W.] Boyce[33] & Gen. Bonham, members of Congress, &

---

[32] A veteran of the Seminole War and colonel in the state militia, Simeon Fair (1801–73) was solicitor of Newberry for twenty years, vice president of the Columbia and Greenville Railroad, and one of the founders of Newberry College. He was also a member of the South Carolina Secession Convention.

[33] Currently serving his fourth consecutive term in the United States House of Representatives, William Waters Boyce (1818–90) would soon represent his state in the Provisional Confederate Congress and in the First and Second Confederate congresses.

R. B. Rhett were among the speakers. No division of opinion. All for immediate secession. Those who hold opposing opinions are cautious in expressing them.—Arrived at Columbia about 4 P.M. & went to the principal hotel, the Congaree House. Soon accosted by some old acquaintances, among them the three Rhetts, [Olin M.] Dantzler,[34] Bonham, Boyce, Edw[ard G.] Palmer,[35] Yeadon, & sundry others, & was introduced to more than I can remember. My reception by both former acquaintances & strangers very cordial & gratifying. My opinions as to matters in hand, & especially as to Va, were continually asked, & I was thus kept continually in conversation in the public rooms, which were crowded. One of the former (slight) acquaintances thus renewed was with Bishop [Patrick N.] Lynch, Roman Catholic Bishop of Charleston, & a man of great ability & high character.[36] He was in the public hall of the hotel, like any other visitor. We soon got upon the all-absorbing topic. He feared the consequences of S.C. seceding alone, & remaining alone, & the U.S. [1083] government refraining from any hostile attack, but keeping strong garrisons in the forts, a squadron of armed ships in the harbor & merely compelling all vessels entering to pay duties to the U.S. This he maintained would drive off the trade of Charleston to Savannah, & greatly damage S.C. without her having any remedy. I opposed his views, & our argument soon drew a dense crowd around us, which made me anxious to get out of it—especially as the bishop reasoned fluently & forcibly, & I felt him to be an able antagonist—greatly my superior in the manner of argument. But I happened to utter some expression, to the purport that even if all the dangers & losses he feared were to be certain, it would still be proper to meet them, rather than the greater alternative dangers of submission, or even delay. The surrounding crowd, in which there were many students of the College & the Military Academy, before perfectly silent, broke out in a storm of applause, under cover of which I retired from the contest. I aimed to do so with all respect to my opponent, by saying to him that if he had the best of

---

[34] Dantzler, an Orangeburg District planter, was a member of the South Carolina Senate. He was killed at the Battle of Bermuda Hundred in June, 1864, while serving as colonel of the Twenty-second Regiment, South Carolina Volunteers.

[35] A Fairfield District planter and railroad executive, Palmer was also a state senator at this time.

[36] Patrick Neeson Lynch (1817–82), a native of Ireland, came to America in 1819 and was bishop at Charleston from 1858 to 1882.

the argument, it seemed that I had the different advantage of having the sympathies of the hearers.—Soon after another serenade began before the door, the music being but an apology for calling out speakers. I was the first called for, & as unused to such service, & incapable as I was, made some remarks which were well received. My self-possession was much better than I could [1084] have anticipated. But no doubt I was strengthened by the manifest kind feeling & approval of all who heard me. My coming here as I have done, added to all that I have before tried to do in cooperation with S.C. & for the South, seem to be highly appreciated & applauded. I said but little more than to earnestly urge the immediate action of S.C. for secession even if she should be alone—but also affirming that others would soon follow, & finally Va & all others of the South. Sundry other speakers were vociferously called for, & delivered speeches. The scene had not closed when I went to bed at 11.30 P.M.—Saw Mr. Boykin, Richard Yeadon, Senator Chesnut, & several . . . other of my former acquaintances.—The Mercury for 6th & 7th contained the two last pieces which I had sent, designed for this particular juncture.[37]—Judge [Andrew G.] Magrath, of the Federal District Court,[38] U.S. Attorney [James] Conner,[39] & Collector [William F.] Colcock,[40] all of Charleston, have today resigned their offices, on account of Lincoln's election—also two holders of inferior offices.

---

[37] In the first of these articles, "What Would a Seceding Southern State Suffer from Northern Invasion and Open Warfare?" Ruffin concluded that the application of military force against even a single state, such as South Carolina, would be unfeasible because other Southerners would rally to the defense of their threatened compatriots. In his second piece, entitled "The Consequences of the Blockade of a Seceded State," he contended that no effective blockade of South Carolina would be possible because of the nature of the coastline and also because of outlets in North Carolina and Georgia. Furthermore, he predicted incorrectly that "neither England nor France would submit for a single month" to a "Paper Blockade."

[38] Magrath, a native Charlestonian, was a delegate to the state secession convention and served as governor of South Carolina during the last two years of the war.

[39] Appointed United States attorney for the district of South Carolina in 1856, James Conner (1829–83) attracted national attention through his vigorous prosecution of the owners of the slave-ship *Echo*. He rose to the rank of brigadier general during the war and saw extensive service in the eastern theater of operations. In 1876 he was elected attorney general of South Carolina.

[40] After two terms in Congress, William Ferguson Colcock (1804–89) was appointed collector of the Port of Charleston in 1853 and served in that capacity for the next twelve years, under both the United States and Confederate governments.

*Nov.* 8. Sought Gen. Jones, the chief of the organization of "Minute Men" of S.C. & after learning from him that the obligations of a member were general, & not special, I enrolled myself as a member. I had before seen Mr. Bachman, the son of my old friend Dr. B., who informed me that his sister Catherine was at his house. I sent her a request to make a cockade for me, & meeting the family afterwards, she sewed it on my hat.—This forenoon, a deputation of three students of the senior class of the College of S.C. waited on me, & requested in the name of all their fellow students that I would visit them & make them an address, & permit them to escort me from the College to the State House. I thanked them but promptly declined such formality & parade, & promised, instead, [1087] to visit them informally, & without ceremony at the College, tomorrow at noon. I owe this compliment to the favorable report of the students who heard me speak last night.—After 1 o'clock, I went into the gallery of the House of Representatives. Col. [W. S.] Mullins, a member, soon came to me, & informed me that both the Senate & lower House had, by unanimous votes, offered to me the privilege of a seat in their respective halls, during their session. On his invitation, I proceeded to use my privilege, & also his own chair.—A bill to call a Convention, with the view to secession, was introduced yesterday, & will go through its stages as fast as the rules allow. The only avowed ground of division of opinion in either house, is the question of time. But a very large majority are for the earliest time. Also a resolution was introduced, & referred to a committee, to appropriate [1088] $1,000,000 (or as much as deemed requisite,) to buy arms & ammunition for the state. Everything seems to indicate that the state will secede, & speedily—& singly, if no other state shall join in the movement.—A telegraphic dispatch from Richmond today says that the indications are that Breckinridge had the vote of Va. by a small majority—& not Bell, as I had supposed almost certain. I still fear that the last report is too good to be true.

*Nov.* 9. Last night, having nothing to occupy me, went to bed soon after 9, & did not know until this morning that there had been last night another assemblage (the name of "serenade" is used, but not suitable,) & more speeches from sundry gentlemen called upon. All are of precisely the same general purport—for the secession of the state, alone, if not aided & accompanied by others. The Charleston papers of yesterday morning contained sketches of my remarks made the night before, & which were sent by telegraph the same

night, & printed for the morning's publication. I did not know that
this was intended. Before I was aware of such intention, the editor
of the Southern Guardian, about 11 yesterday, asked me to give him
notes of my speech. I doubted my ability to do it, as my expressions
were off-hand, & I could not be sure of what I had said. I only
promised to *attempt* to write a short sketch of the substance—&
would send it in only if satisfactory to myself. This I did, in great
haste, for the issue of this morning. . . . [1090]—A dismal rainy day.
Still, at 12 M. I went to the S.C. College to meet my appointment.
Mr. Warren & Mr. Leitner[41] accompanied me. I was received by
the students with great enthusiasm, conducted to the Chapel & on
the platform, with the Palmetto flag hoisted & waving over me. The
students seated themselves as an audience, & after cheering uproar-
iously, came to order. Our relative positions showed, clearly enough,
that notwithstanding my declining yesterday, they expected an address. Therefore, I proceeded to speak as well as I could, but in plain
manner & concisely. They then called upon my companions, each of
whom gave them a much longer speech, strongly political, & for the
crisis. Afterwards I was introduced to many of them, & among them
found sons of some of my old friends. Thence, I went to the State
House & called upon Gov. Gist, in his office. He showed me the
pike, with its labels, which I had formerly sent to him, & which is
kept in full view in the Governor's Office. Next went into the Senate
Chamber, occupying the chair offered to me by the clerk, Gen.
W[illiam] E. Martin, who met me to lead me to my seat. The debate
on the bill for calling [1091] a Convention was on its passage. I had
the great gratification of witnessing its enactment, by a vote of 44
to 1. The only dissentient was not opposed to the main object of the
bill, but to its details. The bill requires a convention to be elected on
Jan 8th, & to assemble on Jan. 15th. All but 8 who voted for it would
have greatly preferred much earlier action. But to conciliate & secure these 8 votes, & for harmony, this later time was agreed upon.
The disposition of both houses is almost unanimously for the Convention, & for its expected result of declaring the secession of the
State—alone, if no other joins in the movement, as is generally
feared. However, the last reports from Georgia (especially, & the
most doubted state,) & Ala. indicate strong secession feeling there, as

---

[41] Probably William Zachariah Leitner (1829–88), an 1849 graduate of South
Carolina College, who served in the Army of Northern Virginia during the war
and lost a leg at Gettysburg.

soon as the news of Lincoln's election was received. In S.C. the popular feeling is very strong, especially in Charleston. Yesterday, a vessel coming in, from Philadelphia, was not permitted, by the boys of the city, to come to the wharf with the U.S. flag flying, & until the captain had it pulled down. Today, as learned by telegraph, a beginning was made, by order of the U.S. commander of Fort Moultrie, to remove from the U.S. Arsenal in Charleston the arms belonging to the federal government. Volunteer companies were called out, & required the operation to be stopped, & it was acceded to. I am very sorry for this occurrence—& fear that the people will run ahead of the government & the Convention, & make a disruption of the Union by revolutionary & illegal action, instead of by deliberate & legal secession.

*Nov. 10.* Nothing yet certain as to the vote of Va, which, at any rate, will be very nearly equal between Breckinridge & Bell. All the other southern [1092] states, from which certain reports have been received, voted for Breckinridge, except Kentucky. Some not yet reported. Saw & was introduced to Gen. Owens of Florida, who says that that state is ready for secession, and will speedily follow the leading of S.C. When at the "South Carolinian" Office, (as usual every morning, to read the papers from Va. & elsewhere,) I found the proprietor, my friend Dr. [Robert W.] Gibbes, & the editor Mr. Gaillard, in consultation about having made a flag, & hoisting it. Dr. Gibbes had already ordered the making of the Palmetto flag, of the state of S.C. I recommended instead that the original flag of S.C., which was flying over Fort Moultrie during its defence, should be used, as more suitable to the occasion, & to the South generally, & significant of the expected increase of states & of strength. While I held the palmetto flag in the highest respect, it belonged peculiarly to S.C. & would not be appropriate to the expected Southern Confederacy. No flag had such noble historical grounds for preference as that which waved over the defenders of Fort Moultrie, & its emblem & motto were both suitable to our cause. My reasons were readily concurred in—& as soon as possible a flag was prepared, & hoisted before the office of the S. Carolinian, with the crescent, & motto of "Crescit eundo." The only departure from the old flag was inserting a single star, to represent S.Ca., to which will be added others for other states as they shall secede & unite in the cause.—Went to the hall of representatives, & witnessed the whole proceedings. The convention bill of the Senate had been referred to a committee, & its adoption recommended with the amendments of forwarding the times of electing & assembling the Convention respectively to the 6th & 7th of Decbr. After an able [1093] debate, & opposition of two of the members from the upper districts, (all of whom want longer time,) the bill was passed, unanimously. As the names of the members were called, & answered, the interest was intense, for fear that some "noes" might mar the unanimity. But the objecting members (to the early time,) all voted with the more ardent. The Senate will meet tonight, & no doubt adopt the amendments.—By invitation, dined with Dr. Gibbes & some 9 or 10 guests, all except myself members of the legislature. Pleasant conversation, almost entirely upon the present state of political affairs. A[t] 7 P.M. went to attend the session of the Senate. In that body also the Convention bill, as amended, passed unanimously. It is now substantially the law of the state—though, as a matter of form, it will have to go to the House of Representatives for its third & last reading, & the final vote. Thus this great & important measure, which I have so long anxiously desired, is adopted —& on this hereafter glorious day, the 10th of November, is inaugurated the revolution which will tear the slave-holding states from their connection with the northern section, & establish their separate independence.—Last night there had been a great popular meeting in Charleston, & Judge Magrath, & Messrs Conner & Colcock, (the three principal resigning U.S. officers,) were sent as a deputation, & arrived here this afternoon, to urge on the Charleston delegates (& indirectly on the legislature,) to adopt the earliest time for assembling the Convention. The usual serenading was begun unusually early, & with display of military parade & fireworks. A large crowd (for this small town) was assembled soon after 8 P.M. before the door of this hotel, & the deputies called [1094] for to speak.... I squeezed into the throng, & heard the greater portion of the first speech by Conner, & all from Magrath & Colcock who followed. All three able & eloquent speakers. Cunningham & [Henry W.] Garlington[42] followed these. Then I retired, to warm myself before going to bed, & so missed, among others, R. B. Rhett, whom I should have liked to hear. He is deemed the head of the extreme secession party —& his views, though adopted by all now, have previously rendered him very unpopular with all who were more "conservative," and

---

[42] A Laurens District planter, Garlington would shortly be elected to the secession convention.

more patient under the oppressions & wrongs of the North & the federal government.—Before I left home, I had thought of a plan for the military defence of Charleston, & since being here, & inquiring as to the particulars of topography, & of legal proprietorship, I have become still more assured of its feasibility. The property of the U.S. does not extend but to a very small & narrow border around Fort Moultrie, & the adjacent land, & all of Sullivan's Island belongs to the State of S.C. Before knowing these latter facts, I inferred, from merely inspecting the chart of the harbor, that if fortifications of earthwork were thrown up below Fort Moultrie, (say 400 to 1000 yards distant,) & a few guns of a very large calibre & long range were there mounted, the garrison might command both Fort Moultrie & the channel, & prevent any reinforcements being brought to either of the three forts—with the aid of troops also [1095] stationed elsewhere. The state has the unquestionable legal right, while still under the U.S. government, to construct fortifications, & arm them, anywhere on her own soil—& also to assemble any of her militia force there to drill, & to guard the works. Not only would the U.S. garrisons, or the U.S. government have no legal right to disturb or assail these preparations—but there are houses of individuals on the intervening ground, which must be destroyed by any firing from the fort to the site of the proposed earth works. The establishment & maintenance of this new position, should war be begun by the federal government, would insure the speedy surrender of the three forts (Moultrie, Sumter, & Castle Pinckney,) if only by their being shut out from supplies & reinforcements. I stated my scheme to three different members of the Military Committee, who seemed to think favorably of its efficiency. But it is not deemed as necessary as I supposed, because these gentlemen, & most others whom I have heard opinions from, make very light of Fort Moultrie & Castle Pinckney, & think that they could easily be taken by the militia, in the event of war being made by the federal government. Fort Sumter, (on the opposite side,) being surrounded by water, would be less accessible. But the danger of war seems to grow less, with every successive report brought from Washington, at least during the remainder of the administration of Buchanan. And this expectation of peace, & having peaceable possession of the forts, more than any other reasons, will prevent much attention being paid to my plan of a new & commanding fortification.

*Nov. 11.* Sunday. . . . A. P. Calhoun came yesterday & came to my room this forenoon. When not in my room, writing letters, or this diary, I am nearly all day talking with different individuals, & on the same topics—remarking on the recent events here, & the probable future elsewhere. Especially I have frequently to answer questions as to what Virginia will do. I am at a loss as to the cause of the calm & silence in Va. so different from other states. The only newspapers I see here from Va, the Enquirer (democratic) & the Dispatch, (neutral) say nothing to indicate whether they approve or disapprove of the proceedings of S.C.—either by the editors or others. Even N.Ca. is said to be moved, & somewhat disposed to resist, since Lincoln's election, & not only Ga, but Florida & Ala. are said to be ready to follow the example of S.C. I hope that the quiet of Va. is but the lull which precedes a storm.—Saw Gen. Wm. Owens, of Florida, & had a long conversation with him in regard to the lands of that state, & political affairs. He thinks that Florida is ripe for secession, & will soon follow S.C. The legislature of Florida will meet tomorrow.—Senator Chesnut sent in his resignation to the legislature of S.C. yesterday. Senator Toombs of Ga has also resigned his seat in the Senate of U.S.—and the legislature of Ga refused to go into an election to fill the previous vacancy caused by the [1097] expiration of the term of service of the other U.S. Senator, [Alfred] Iverson. These are significant facts. From all the indications afforded by these, by the demonstrations of public feeling in Savannah & Augusta, & by the letters received here from citizens of Ga., it seems almost certain that that state will soon declare for secession—& then the course of events is inevitable to the like action of every southern state. Even in Md., it is reported that there is great ferment of the people in different localities. Yet in Va. there seems universal calm, or lethargy, except in Wise's speeches, & resolutions to get up minute men, & committees of safety. I have studied his resolutions, . . . & cannot determine what he means—& doubt whether he did not design so to envelope the subject in fog, as not to be understood, or to hereafter construe his resolutions as he may please, according to future events. If we construe his resolutions freely [&] liberally, they may mean complete revolution—throwing off the State government as well as the federal, & by popular will & action. On the other hand, if construing strictly, all this cumbrous & difficult system & complicated machinery leads to merely the "lame & impotent conclusion" of asking the legislature to defend the state—which might be done as well without any such machinery of committees of safety &c. All that [1098] I can infer is, that Wise is in the process of throwing another summerset, & means to take the side of secession & southern rights & independence—& is embarrassed by his previous boisterous advocacy of "Union," & his denunciations of disunionists. Still, his aid is valuable, because of his astonishing power as a stump speaker, & over the ignorant masses. He is totally unreliable for his political consistency or principles, & still more for loyalty to state & southern rights. But he is sure to support his own political interests & advancement, to the best of his knowledge. Therefore in his recent veering around to urge vehemently the maintenance of southern rights, he shows his opinion as to which side is about to be the strongest—& in that respect, he is as reliable as is a weathercock to indicate when the wind has changed, & the direction in which it blows.

*Nov. 12.* The northern people, as I judge from the newspapers received this morning are not yet startled from their delusion, by the recent movements here. They continue to believe that there is no danger of the southern people resisting northern outrages & now established domination, & they ascribe all demonstrations to the contrary as mere bluster & boasting, which will quickly subside, in entire submission. May their astonishing delusion & blindness continue. No movement in Va. except of a public meeting in Rockbridge Co. to resolve for holding to the Union! Even in N.C. & Md. there are indications of a disposition to resist—& in Va., as in Ky., there are none!—At 11 A.M. went to call on Miss Catherine Bachman, & afterwards visited Mrs. [Louisa] McCord, the widow of Col. David [1099) McCord,[43] & the daughter of Langdon Cheves. To her & to her husband, at their residence & elsewhere, & also to her distinguished father, I had been indebted for much kind attention. . . . She is a lady of fine mind & manners, & of no small note as an author. She received me with much cordiality & apparent gratification. Her carriage was ready to convey her to the State House, to hear the debates, in which I accompanied her, with her daughter & another young lady.—The Convention Act, as a matter of form, was sent from the Senate to the House of Rep. for its third reading there, & its final passage—which was done, as before, unanimously. But substantially, the act was passed, & the measure completed on the 10th, which may be deemed the inauguration of the revolution of

---

[43] David James McCord, former editor of the Columbia *Telescope* and a South Carolina legislator and bank executive, died in May, 1855.

1860. The legislature engaged in other subsidiary measures for strengthening the military & financial position of the State.—Tomorrow the State Agricultural Society will meet here, & the Fair open. Thousands of visitors are arriving, & the hotels filled completely. From before 2 P.M. to my retiring for bed, the office & the public halls here crowded, & almost every thing uttered was on the secession movements. Every opinion is favorable to the action of the legislature. Since I have been here, I have not heard of a dissenting opinion, either from or of man or woman in S.C. Among the new visitors was Capt. Stroman of Orangeburg, whose residence I visited in 1843, on my then service as Agricultural Surveyor of S.C. He seemed delighted to meet me again. After 9 P.M. music of the band, & public speaking, as before, from the piazza of this house, [1100] & to a crowd twice as large as heretofore. Hon. L. Keitt, M.C. was first called for. He delivered, in his usual fiery manner, a strong & telling speech, denouncing the northern section & party, & their outrages & designs on the South, in the strongest terms. When he had occasion to speak of the existing union of the states, he termed it "the accursed union," the expression drawing forth shouts of applause from the crowd. He was followed by A. P. Aldrich, & Ex. Gov. [John P.] Richardson (just arrived) & sundry others. I retired before the close of the speaking.—The telegraphic dispatches bring more good news. Reliable authorities state that the legislature of Ga. (in session now,) will certainly call a convention, with a view to secession. The Gov. of Ala. has publickly announced his intention to call a Convention within 30 days. There seems good reason to believe that the movement of S.C. will be speedily sustained & the example followed by both these states & also Fla. & Mississippi. Nothing has been yet heard from Texas. But it is supposed that that state is among the most ready to act. The difficulty there will [be] in that old scoundrel, & traitor to the South, Houston being governor, who will do all that his official position allows to retard & obstruct the assertion of southern rights, by disruption of the Union. The Governor of Miss. has called the legislature. The other U.S. Senator of S.C., Hammond, has also resigned. Two obscure newspapers in Va (The Lynchburg Republican & the Clarke Journal,) have come out for secession.—Prayer is offered every day before the two houses in succession. I have never witnessed this service for a legislative body so respectfully observed [1101] by the auditors. The first prayer of the session was by the Rev. Mr. Barnwell . . . . The Rev. A[ugustus] B[aldwin] Longstreet D.D. formerly Judge in Georgia, & author of the humorous "Georgia Scenes," prayed today. His prayer was uttered as if extempore, though no doubt prepared, & well suited to the occasion. . . . Wrote a short communication to the Richmond Dispatch.

*Nov. 13.* Wrote a letter to the Richmond Enquirer, which from its strong secession character, I doubt whether they will publish.—Read newspapers in the editors' offices, & then went to the Agricultural Fair. . . . The legislature adjourned early today, to meet again in the last week of this month.—Yesterday, for the first time, I had leisure & opportunity to go into & examine the structure now in progress for the new State House. The exterior of three storeys of the main building is completed. It will be a magnificent building, & yet simple & chaste in its design. The chief material for the outer walls is of very white & good granite, obtained from neighboring quarries. This is polished to a smoother surface than I have ever seen before of granite. The columns are beautifully carved. One part only of the outer part, of the front entrance, is cased with marble, sculptured in Italy. The ornamental portion of this represents oak foliage & acorns, in high relief. It is beautiful—but so liable to be broken & injured, that it is a pity that such fragile ornament has been adopted. This building is on an enormous [1102] scale of cost, for this small commonwealth. It is supposed that it will cost, when complete, between two & three millions of dollars. It will suit much better for the Capitol of the future Southern Confederacy, should this beautiful little city be chosen for the seat of the federal government.—At night, went to the meeting of the Agricultural Society, & heard the annual address of the President, A. P. Calhoun. A long & very good composition—but entirely applicable to the present political crisis, & situation of the Southern states.—This hotel is crowded with visitors, & the public rooms, & the piazza, & the street before the door, generally crowded with persons standing & conversing. The other principal hotel, close by, is as full. Great numbers, who could get no lodgings at the public houses, are received into the private houses of residents.—At night, more speaking to the crowd assembled in the street, from the piazza of this hotel, as usual.

*Nov. 14.* I had waited for this afternoon to set out for Charleston, & previously to make a visit to the Fair, in compliment to the Society & its president, & to see acquaintances among the numerous visitors.

But this forenoon, I was accosted by Mr. [John N.] Frierson,[44] & informed that he & Mr. [John S.] Richardson,[45] (who also met me afterwards,) had been deputed by a public meeting at Sumterville,[46] to come & request me to visit the village (& county seat,) & to deliver an address to them at another public meeting appointed for tomorrow. At first I declined the service. But upon farther learning the extent of the compliment, & also that Mr. [1103] Frierson had come by the last train, & would return by the next back train, upon his urgency, I agreed to go with him this afternoon. Set out from Columbia at 2 P.M. & arrived at Sumterville a little after 5 P.M. . . . . Soon after my arrival, I was called upon by Col. [James D.] Blanding, captain of the Minute Men, with two others of the corps, to pay their respects to me, & to inform me that the corps (which numbers about 150,) would come to serenade me before 9. Of course here is required another speech. They came, with music & firing of a cannon, & assembled in the great hall of the hotel, where a short address was made to me by the captain, & which I answered. I confined myself mostly to military matters, so as not to have to repeat any part tomorrow.

*Nov. 15.* . . . At 11, Capt. Blanding with a number of the Minute men came & escorted me to the Court House, a very large hall, which was soon filled with citizens including some ladies. The business of the meeting, independent of my being present, was to select candidates for the Convention. But first, the Senator & three representatives were called upon for their views, [1104] & all delivered strong speeches for immediate secession, & even if S.C. should be alone. A resolution subsequently was adopted unanimously requiring that all candidates for the Convention should pledge themselves to the same policy. After these speeches, I was called upon. I spoke, & without embarrassment, after the beginning, for about three-quarters of an hour—& then stopped, having forgotten to bring in some of my main points. I referred to no notes. I was greatly applauded, &

---

[44] A large planter and former state legislator, John Napoleon Frierson (1818–87) served in the Confederate Army during the war and was a member of the state Senate in 1866–67.

[45] John Smythe Richardson (1828–94) was a prominent lawyer in Sumter. He too saw military service during the Civil War and was a member of the South Carolina House of Representatives from 1865 to 1867. After the end of Reconstruction he served two terms in Congress.

[46] The name of the village was changed officially to Sumter in 1855, but obviously the old name was still much in vogue at the time of Ruffin's visit.

I believe, from what I was told afterwards that my remarks, & my plain manner of delivering them, gave much satisfaction. Indeed some have so far complimented me, both here & at Columbia, as to declare that they thought my presence in this state had operated to strengthen & forward the action of secession. But though the compliment is gratifying to my self-love, I cannot accept it as conveying truth. . . . The Charleston Courier of today contains some telegraphic dispatches, which indicate the beginning already of the serious troubles of the northern people, in consequence of the probability of southern secession. This slight foretaste of what is to come, is earlier than I had anticipated. Before, no abolition paper seemed to attach any importance to the southern movement, treating it with derision & sneers. They seem now to be [1105] beginning to discover that it is of awfully serious importance. The financial crisis threatened at the North[47] is no doubt hastened by an act passed by the late session in S.C. to permit the banks of this state to suspend specie payments. This was to guard against the heavy drafts already making from the North, & which were expected to increase. The banks of S.C. have not as yet availed themselves of the privilege.

*Nov. 16.* Left Sumpterville [*sic*], on the railroad, by Kingsville, at 4 A.M. & reached Charleston Hotel at 1.30 P.M. After dressing & washing, dined, & immediately after, went to the Mercury office. Did not see the editor, but read the last Va. newspapers. Even yet, it is not known whether Breckinridge or Bell had the majority vote of the State. I have however the vote for Lincoln, so far as heard from, which must be nearly all of the disgraceful number. They are, Fairfax 24, Fauquier 1, Portsmouth 4, Shenandoah 13—& Brooke 173, Marion 1, Ohio (including Wheeling,) 771, Marshall, 195. The last 4 counties constitute the "Pan-Handle." Early in afternoon walked to see Dr. Bachman & family, & staid to past 7. . . . While writing the foregoing items, some gentlemen called on me, of whom the spokesman was Mr. Carlisle, one of the editors of the Courier, & informed me that a serenade was about to be given in compliment to me, & of course I would be expected to reply in a speech. As they remained with me for the short time until it arrived, & the music had been played, I had no opportunity to collect my ideas, before I had to begin my speech. I did not please myself as well as in my previous trials—& do not know whether I pleased my hearers. There was in-

---

[47] Latest reports indicated that banks in New York and elsewhere might soon have to suspend specie payments.

deed plenty of applause—but that I suppose would have been bestowed on me, even if my performance had been much worse. Though I am much gratified by the compliment, I wish it had not been shown in compelling me to speak tonight. For there will be a great display tomorrow, when of course I shall be expected to be present, & again to speak—& I cannot then say what would be necessary [1107], without repeating part of what I said tonight.[48] There has just been erected a secession pole, or flag-staff 90 feet high, from which tomorrow the Palmetto flag is to be unfurled—with much ceremony, including no doubt many speeches. On my arrival today, I heard the shouts which welcomed the erecting of the pole, then just raised.

*Nov. 17.* This morning I was surprised to see in the Mercury, printed last night, so full a report of my speech delivered but a few hours earlier. I counted upon being again called upon to speak, today [1108], on the ceremony of raising the Palmetto flag on the newly erected pole, which is not 50 feet from the window of my lodging room. Therefore, as I had been taken by surprise last night, I endeavored to prepare myself better for this occasion. But, whether it was because of unwillingness to press so much upon me, or for other reasons, I was not called upon. It was well. For there was a strong wind blowing, & I would have been physically unable to make my voice audible to one-half of the immense assembled crowd —& I should not have attempted it, except to utter a few compliments to the flag, & to the occasion, & to beg to be excused.—Dr. Bachman was with me when the ceremonies commenced. Cannon were fired, & music from a fine military band, (which was used last night). The crowd opposite this Hotel & about the flag staff filled the street. A high stand was raised in the middle of the street, from which, after a prayer from a clergyman, there were delivered sundry speeches, all much too long to be in good taste for the occasion. Received visits from several gentlemen—& went to the Offices of Courier & Mercury, to read Va. newspapers. After dinner was invited by Mr. Carlisle, & rode with him & others in a carriage 4 miles into the country, to see a trial of improved fire-arms. Before went to Russell & Jones' bookstore. Began to read a new work, "The Ebony

---

[48] In his impromptu remarks, Ruffin expressed the hope that Virginia would stand ultimately with South Carolina and stated emphatically, "If Virginia will not act as South Carolina, I have no longer a home, and I am a banished man."

Idol." [49] At night, another impromptu assemblage around the [1109] flag, (which is kept raised,) & some dozen or more speeches have already been spoken, accompanied by vociferous shouts, & having after each very fine music from the band. I would have been glad to witness at least a part of this popular demonstration, as one of the audience. But I knew, in such an irregular procedure, if I showed myself there, that I would have been called out, & so I kept in my room, where the sound of the speakers' voices is quite audible, through my closed window, but without my hearing a word of what is said. It is now 9.40, & the noise louder than before. The crowd dispersed soon after.—I place on the next page an editorial article from the Chicago Democrat, as a sample of abolition language at this time.[50] The northern people generally, & all the abolitionists, seemed to have no conception that the South would resist, or even any one state would secede, until very lately. Now, however, they begin to be seriously alarmed. I fear they will offer conciliation, or even guarantees. They may even yet, by directing part of their electors' votes from Lincoln, defeat & yield his election, & elect Breckinridge, as a propitiation of the South, & to prevent what they will soon know to be inevitable, a disruption of the Union. Should they adopt this policy, before any other states besides S.C. are fully committed to secession, I fear it would draw them back.

*Nov. 18.* Sunday. Finished the "Ebony Idol." It is a northern satire on abolition fanaticism, & so far is very well written. But beyond that, as a novel, is a poor plot, & some of its negro incidents are very disgusting to a southerner.—Went [1110] to the public services at St. Philip's church. The chime of bells furnishes fine music for half an hour before the service is begun. It is played by a negro. After church, went to the Mercury Office, where I had been invited by the sub-editor, to obtain newspapers from Va, which, as well as others he supplied me with. The Governor of Va. has forwarded the time for the called session of the legislature, to Jan 7th, on account of the present political state of the country. Several county meetings are summoned, to petition for a convention—& also the articles in the newspapers indicate that the public mind in Va. is ripening for secession, much faster than I had hoped, & predicted. I had sent,

---

[49] Written by Mrs. G. M. Flanders and published in New York by D. Appleton & Company, this novel satirized an abolitionist organization.

[50] The writer of this inflammatory editorial, entitled "The Southern Braggarts," dared the South to secede.

from Columbia, a short piece to the Dispatch, & a letter to the Enquirer, & doubted whether either paper would publish its missive.
But I see both inserted in the last numbers of these respective
papers . . . .[51] [1112]

*Nov. 19.* Called to see Wm. M. Lawton & Gen. Wm. E. Martin, &
conversed with both on the present state of affairs, & my designed
visit to Milledgeville. I had received an application from . . . [the]
editor of the Bulletin of Petersburg, for a number of copies of
secession pamphlets for distribution. Obtained 300, to be sent to him,
& by paying $5, made myself a member of the "Association of 1860,"
which prints & circulates pamphlets maintaining southern rights, &
urging resistance to northern wrongs. . . . After dinner, went to Dr.
Bachman's, & took leave. Next, went to the Citadel, which is the
quarters of the Cadets of the Military Academy (a state institution,)
& saw the afternoon drilling & parade of that fine & well trained
corps. I was introduced to some of the officers & professors, & also
some of the Cadets. I was standing, with the superior officers on one
of the upper galleries over the enclosed area of the Citadel, looking
at the closing of the parade, when the companies were discharged.
Immediately three cheers were given by them, which I had to be informed that it was in compliment to me, & learnt it barely in time, to
take off my hat & bow. I had arrived after the parade was commenced, & did not suppose [1113] that but few, if any of the young
men knew who I was. Their complimentary notice did not stop
there. At night, two of them, deputed by the corps, waited on me in
my room, & requested that I would go tomorrow, & make an address
to the Cadets. My engagement to leave tomorrow morning luckily
served to excuse me from this additional trial of speech-making.
They wanted me to promise it when I returned, but I declined on account of the remoteness & uncertainty of the time. Later came Mr.
Lawton who brought to me a ticket for my free passage on the steam
boats of the Florida line, of which he is president, & Gen. Martin
had offered me one for the railroad to Savannah, in case I should use
either of these routes, in my intention to visit the capitals of Fla.
& Ga. . . .

*Nov. 20.* At 4.30 A.M. called up, & at 6, off on the train for Milledgeville. Left Augusta about 2 P.M. At the junction of the Waynes-

---

[51] In these communications, Ruffin reported the rising tide of secession sentiment in the Deep South states—particularly in South Carolina—and sought to
generate a similar spirit in Virginia and the other border states.

boro with the Savannah rail-road, R. B. Rhett esq. met me, also on a visit of observation to Milledgeville—which place we reached at 12.30. Could not get a single bedded room, at the principal hotel, & had to sleep in a large room with three other white men, all strangers to me, & two negro men servants.

*Nov. 21.* Rose very early, to secure enough water for washing, & the [1114] clean towels. After breakfast, went to deliver some letters of introduction. The first delivered was to Mr. Lewis, representative of Hancock, & son-in-law of Dr. Whitten. He enabled me to obtain a room in his boarding house, where I shall be comfortably fixed. Next called on Alex[ander R.] Lawton, member of the Senate, to whom I had two letters of introduction.[52] Two other members were with him, & soon after Mr. Rhett also came in, & we had together free conversation about the political state of Ga. Next, . . . I went to the State House, where I joined Mr. Lawton & Mr. Rhett, & was introduced by the former to more of the members of the Senate (we were in the Lobby,) than I will be able to remember one-half of either the faces or names. Mr. Lawton afterwards carried us to the apartment of the Governor ( [Joseph E.] Brown,) & introduced us, & with whom we had a long & apparently frank conversation. He & all the members whom I have yet conversed with seem to be fully up to the mark of secession & independence for Ga. But all state that there are strong elements of opposition in the state, & that division & opposition are much to be feared. Gov. Brown invited us to take tea with him this evening, & when we excused ourselves, as being previously engaged, to dinner with him tomorrow. On returning to the Senate Lobby for a few minutes, & also to that of the House of Representatives, we were told that the Senate had invited Mr. Rhett & myself to occupy seats in their hall. Waiving the acceptance of the compliment for the present, I returned to my lodgings to bring up my diary for yesterday [1115] & this morning. For the present, & until better informed, I will postpone my impressions of the state of public opinion. The legislature has passed the act appropriating a million of dollars for arming the militia—& also the act for calling a Conven-

---

[52] A graduate of West Point, Alexander Robert Lawton (1818–96) had a long and illustrious career as railroad executive, army officer, lawyer, and diplomat. During the 1850's he was a leading advocate of secession in the Georgia legislature. Following the outbreak of war he was first a brigadier general in the Army of Northern Virginia and, after 1863, quartermaster general of the Confederacy. Some years after the war, in 1882, he was elected president of the American Bar Association, and during the first Cleveland administration he was appointed United States Minister to Austria.

tion on Jan. 16th, 1861, on the grounds, as stated in the preamble, that "the present crisis in our national affairs, in the judgment of this General Assembly demands *resistance;*" & that it is the privilege & right of the people to determine upon the mode, measure, & time of such *resistance*—& both of these acts were passed unanimously in both houses. Still, though these acts would seem to indicate as much unanimity as existed in the legislature of S.C., it is far from being the case, either in the legislature, or among the people. In fact, Ga. cannot be induced to secede in advance of any other state—& the strong advocates for secession fear that even the example of S.C., alone, may not be sufficient to induce Ga. to follow.—After tea, went, by previous invitation & agreement, to the quarters of Mr. McGee, a prominent member of the Senate, where I met with Mr. Rhett, Judge [Henry L.] Benning,[53] Gen. Williams the Speaker of the H. of Rep, Mr. Lawton, Col. [William J.] Hardee,[54] a Georgian & also now of U.S.A. (& just from Richmond, where he was instructing the volunteer cavalry during their encampment—) & several other gentlemen. Nearly all the conversation, which was free & animated, on the present crisis of the Southern states, the probability of the secession of Ga, & of other states, & incidental matters. Some bottles of Champagne were drunk, in great moderation, & I committed the unusual excess of drinking half a glass, to the most speedy secession of Ga. Returned home & to bed at half-past 10. . . . Read A[lexander H.] Stephens' late union speech. He & B[enjamin H.] Hill are the [1116] most able & influential opposers, in Ga, of immediate secession. Yet even they profess to advocate *resistance* to the North—but will try to break the force of resistance, & prevent secession, by proposing other measures, & thereby inducing delay of action.

*Nov. 22.* . . . My travelling trunk was a miserable Yankee cheat,

---

[53] A Columbus lawyer, Henry Lewis Benning (1814-75) was an associate justice on the Georgia Supreme Court from 1853 to 1859. In the year of crisis he was a delegate to the Democratic conventions in both Charleston and Baltimore, serving as vice president of the latter, and he was elected to the Georgia Secession Convention. As a brigadier general, Confederate States of America, he saw action at Antietam, Gettysburg, Chickamauga, and the Wilderness during the War Between the States. One of the nation's largest army posts, Fort Benning, Georgia, was named for him.

[54] Born in Camden County, Georgia, Hardee (1815–73) saw service in the Mexican War and became a corps commander for the Confederacy in the western theater of operations. He is probably best known for his textbook, *Rifle and Light Infantry Tactics*, published in 1855. See Nathaniel C. Hughes, *General William J. Hardee, Old Reliable* (Baton Rouge: Louisiana State University Press, 1965).

& has so completely failed, that I was last evening compelled to buy a new one, at the cost of $25, & which may prove to be also an imposition.—Went to each of the Houses of the legislature for a short time, in acceptance & acknowledgement of the compliment paid to me (as was also to Mr. Rhett,) yesterday, in resolutions passed inviting me to seats in both halls. Dined with the Governor, in his usual very plain manner. A few others were invited, & among them Mr. Rhett, Mr. Lawton, & Col. Hardee. The dinner was early, to suit the usual early hour of adjournment of the legislature, which generally sits again in the afternoon, & we left immediately after dinner.—As all the business relating to the Convention, or to the expected secession, is done, & the ordinary course of legislation is now resumed, there is nothing more for me to wait for, & I determined to leave tonight, & to return home for a few weeks.—The banks of Richmond & Petersburg, Baltimore & Philadelphia, have all suspended specie payments. Nearly all others will soon follow. This is a result of the expected troubles of secession—& a part of the general interruption of the ordinary [1117] course of business, & of the beginning of general distress in the northern cities.—Left Milledgeville on the Railway train, for Va, at 8 P.M.

*Nov. 23.* About 3.30 A.M. the train from Macon to Savannah, reached Miller station, where [the] road joins with the one for Augusta, by which route I intended to go & for which my trunk was checked. The Conductor called out "Passengers for Augusta change cars!" He, with shameful neglect, for strangers, omitted to say that there were two trains waiting, besides the one we had come in, or to indicate the direction of the one for Augusta. I hurried out, & seeing but one train, & not suspecting there being another, went into that, following other passengers whom I saw entering it. The train soon started with me. Soon the Conductor came along to collect the passage money. When I asked him what I should pay to Augusta, he told me that I was not on the way to Augusta, but going back towards Macon. It was too late for any remedy. I was carried to the next station, Herndon, 11 miles back, which we reached long before daybreak, & in rain. There, by the kindness of a fellow passenger, who stopped there, I found a shelter, & fire to sit by. At 6 A.M. a train of freight cars was to proceed to Savannah, & on it I obtained a passage back to Miller, where there is a tolerable public house. There I had to remain, without amusement or occupation, until 3 P.M. when the next train for Augusta came on, & on which I took passage. Still slowly raining. Reached Augusta before 7 P.M. & found my trunk. Soon took passage on the route to Charlestown [*sic*]. Reached Branchville at midnight, where I took another train to Kingsville, & there another proceeding to Wilmington.

*Nov. 24.* Took breakfast at Florence. . . . Reached Wilmington at 1 P.M. There heard that the secession feeling was very warm, & entertained [1118] by a large majority. The old party distinctions were no longer observed. A town meeting had been held in Wilmington in which the whigs & Bell men of a few weeks past, took the lead, & by which resolutions indicating resistance to the federal government, in some shape, were passed almost unanimously. An intelligent passenger, who resides in the neighborhood, told me that the secession sentiment was stronger in the neighboring country than in the town. —Reached Goldsborough about dark. Heard there that nearly everybody in that neighborhood was for secession. The inhabitants of Goldsborough had just raised a liberty (or secession) pole & flag. Mr. Ro[bert R.] Bridgers, a prominent member of the N.C. legislature there came on the train, & gave me his impressions of the sentiment of the legislature. And first, the Governor, in concurrence with the prominent men of the democratic party, had prepared & inserted in his Message, (just delivered) a strong *resistance* passage, claiming redress from the Northern States, & indemnity & security for the South for the future, & manifestly looking to secession as the alternative, on their refusal to do & secure justice. Mr. Bridgers thinks that this course will be supported by a large majority of the legislature & people—& though none may demand secession as the first measure, all will go for it in the almost certain contingency of the demanded security being refused by the northern states which have already nullified the law & constitution in reference to the restitution of fugitive slaves from the southern states.—Reached Weldon at 11 P.M. & proceeded onward.—N.Ca. is ahead of Va. in the secession feeling.

*Nov. 25.* Sunday. Reached Richmond at 5.30 A.M. Did [1119] not lie down, nor feel the need of it, though I had travelled three whole nights in succession, & had not lain down during the whole time. . . . In snatches, & by day as well as by night, I believe that I sleep nearly as long when travelling by rail, as when at home, or elsewhere in a comfortable bed. Stopped at the American Hotel. . . . After breakfast wrote letters, & read newspapers. . . . Afterwards called for a short time on Governor Letcher, to inform him, in general, of the state of political affairs, as I have learned in S.Ca., N.Ca.,

& Ga. He did not seem disposed to inquire much, & still less to express any opinions of his own on political affairs, so I soon dropped the subject. I heard from him a better account of the military preparation of the state than I had supposed existed. Returning to my lodgings, I found D. H. London, & soon after came also to my room, Mr. Wylie of Amelia, Jeremiah Morton, & two other gentlemen. We talked on southern questions for some hours, before they left me.

*Nov. 26.* Attended to sundry small matters of business .... At 5 P.M., by appointment, Mr. [1120] John Howard, a young lawyer of distinction, came to my room to converse with me, & afterwards W. Old, editor of the Examiner, James Cooke of Greensville, Col. Wylie, & Dr. Cheatham of Amelia, & J. Morton of Orange—all anxious to hear my news & my views of S.C. & Ga. We conversed continually on this subject, & the course for Va. & the results of the present matters in progress, until nearly 10 P.M. From all that I can learn, there has already been a great change of opinion in Va. in favor of measures of resistance of some kind, or of secession. My anticipations of this kind, as expressed in S.C. seem to be like to be more than realized.—Another insurrection of abolitionist outlaws, from 300 to 500 in number, under [James] Montgomery,[55] a former leader in actions of like atrocity, has broken out in Kansas, which threatens to invade Missouri, & to emancipate the slaves there. It is another John Brown raid, on a much larger scale, & carried on by like desperate villains & [1121] fanatics, robbers & cut-throats. This will operate to excite still more the people of the South, against northern abolitionists, & to encourage the disposition in the South to secede.—So many banks have already suspended payment, that the suspension will very soon be general. Great distress already reported as begun in the great northern cities, the consequence of the decrease or suspension of business, & the discharge of thousands of laborers. The "Journal of Commerce" of New York, which I think is the most truthful & honest paper I know, thinks that 25,000 persons in that city have been discharged from employment since the day of the presidential election.

*Nov. 27.* Left Richmond before day-break for the steamer, on which, reached Maycox wharf by 10 A.M. .... Reaching Beechwood,

---

[55] James Montgomery (1814–71), a native of Ohio, moved to Kansas in 1852 and became the leader of the "Jayhawker" element there. He conducted destructive forays into Missouri in 1857 and during the Civil War, as a regimental commander, was noted for his ruthless plundering of captured communities in Missouri and elsewhere in the South.

found all at home . . . . In my absence, Nanny has (as before intended,) fitted up a room specially for me, in the old house in the yard—in which everything will be much more convenient.—Plenty of subjects for conversation, in reference to my late observations in S.C. & Ga. & since.

The time which I have spent in South Carolina (especially,) & elsewhere since I left home on the 6th inst. has been to me the most gratifying of my life, both on personal & general grounds. In addition to the exciting & important, & most gratifying political events, of the progress of secession, I have myself been made the subject of kind feeling & favor, & of general appreciation, [1122] such as I had never before experienced, & never expected to receive. Yet even this was accompanied by the powerful & mortifying reflection, that at home, in my own country, in which I had long lived & labored, & had so much served & benefited, not only would have been withheld from me every such reward of public applause & appreciation, but there are far more enemies to depreciate, & to censure me, & many to calumniate, than there are friends & approvers to applaud. Some of these different effects are doubtless owing to the truth that "a prophet is not without honor, except in his own country." But I fear that much more of the enmity or ill-will that I have gained, among those with whom I have lived, & by whom I ought to be best known, has been produced by my own faulty manners.

*Nov. 28.* Another rainy day.—Corrected & copied a preamble & resolutions which I had before written, in favor of secession, (as a form suitable for any public meeting,) & sent them, with a letter inviting their being used, to C. J. Fox, of Charlotte, in Mecklenburg Co. N.Ca. I think that place, on account of its early patriotic & bold movement for independence in 1775, would be most appropriate for a like movement now.—The mail. It is at last known that Va. has given a plurality of votes to Bell, by 200 to 300 only. California & Oregon, which had been counted on to be opposed to Lincoln, have both voted for him. . . . Various extracts of letters from all of the southern states show the fast growing spirit of resistance, & disposition to join heartily in the secession movement. Among these are Arkansas, Louisiana & Texas, from which little had been heard before. Delaware is silent—& can scarcely now be deemed a slaveholding state. Missouri was doubtful. But that state will now be infuriated by this late outbreak of practical abolition under Montgomery in Kansas, with the avowed design to invade Missouri. This movement is like to essentially aid the secession movement in all the south. 600 volunteers, well provided, have left [1124] St. Louis, to guard the border of Missouri, & if it should be invaded, to repel & pursue the abolitionists to wherever they may retire, & exact bloody & ample vengeance. The U.S. government has also ordered regular troops, under Gen. [William S.] Harney, to Kansas. Yet such is the imbecility of this administration, as evinced before in Kansas, & later against the Mormons in Utah, that I expect Montgomery & all his men, as in the other cases, will merely be quieted, & not one of them killed in battle, or punished by law. . . .

*Nov. 29.* Soon after breakfast, rode to the Glebe. . . . The preparations going on for the sale tomorrow of the land & all the moveables, except the slaves—to be followed by the dispersion of the family. . . .

*Nov. 30.* Julian & I rode to the Glebe, to attend the sale. Found the few persons with whom I conversed on the subject inclined for secession. I think that that sentiment is fast gaining ground in Va. . . . The Governor of S.C. has taken more notice of the presentation of my pike to that state than the case required—& I regret that he went so far as to ask for me the thanks of the legislature, which is entirely uncalled for, by so small a service.—The spirit & disposition of the North, or of the fanaticism which influences or directs the whole North, is illustrated by the annexed circular letter of invitation, to persons of distinction to celebrate, by a great anti-slavery meeting,[56] the day of martyrdom of the holy St. John Brown. I most earnestly hope that they may draw together a meeting as large & respectable, & as zealous & open in speech & act, as the North & the abolition sect can produce.—Since my trip to the South, & here since my return, I have been more the object of notice than ever before, & especially of political [1126] enemies. Before my getting back, some person ( unknown to the hearer,) had said in conversation in the office of the Enquirer, while I was in S.C., that if I came back to Richmond soon, I would incur the risk of being "rode upon a rail," by popular indignation & violence, which proceeding the speaker evidently was favorable to, & no opposition was uttered by any of his several hearers. Some of my remarks there, in conversation, ( such as I have uttered for 10 years back, & before the world,)

---

[56] To be held at Tremont Temple in Boston.

were deemed worthy of being included in a letter from the Richmond reporter of the N.Y. Herald . . . .[57]

*December 2. Sunday.* . . . From the conversations held with neighbors, I infer that already there has taken place great & general change of opinion. Very few, before the election of Lincoln, or rather before the action of S.Ca., would have avowed their preference for secession, to being ruled by an abolition administration. But now, almost every man heard from, whether before a unionist or otherwise, believes that the union is about to be broken, & that, in that event, Va ought to go with the southern fragment. I do not question that this is or soon will be the general sentiment of all Va, unless of the North-West section—even of that I believe all will be true to the South, with perhaps the exception of Wheeling & the other "pan-handle" counties, in the narrow strip of Va, stretching northward, between Pa. & Ohio.

*Dec. 3.* . . . The mail brought nothing new—but additional evidences of southern disposition for secession, & progress of distress in the northern commercial & manufacturing cities.—Snowing at night.—The king of Italy (as he may now be termed,) has entered the city of Naples, & he & Garibaldi met with all the evidences of respect & kindness which ought to exist between the bestower & the receiver of a kingdom. Garibaldi forthwith resigned his dictatorship of the kingdom which he had conquered—& despite of the repeated remonstrances & entreaties of the king, has also resigned his military rank, & has withdrawn to his humble home in the little island of Caprera—also refusing all other rewards & offered favors, he has gone to obscurity & poverty. As he is on the best terms with the king, I can only infer that this retirement of Garibaldi is but for a time, & to prevent the rising of jealousies & enmities between his especial partizans & those of the king, in case he had retained his power & rank. When war is recommenced, & his aid shall be needed, the noblest of modern patriots & heroes will doubtless be ready again to seek & direct the contest for consummating the independence of all Italy, under free institutions of government. [1129]

*Dec. 5.* The mail. The assembling of Congress. Less appearance of hostility between northern & southern members than expected. The

---

[57] The *Herald* reporter simply asserted that Ruffin, upon his return to Richmond from South Carolina, had stated that he was for disunion no matter who was elected President.

President's Message—denies the right of S.C. to secede, yet opposes any attempt to coerce her into the union. Indications from every quarter of the southern states of the progress of the disunion sentiment—& from the north, that nothing will be attempted of warlike action to prevent. Still, many threats are still uttered, & even in the South many still believe that it will be impossible to separate peaceably. In Va. as yet very few openly advocate disunion—but there are scarcely any expressed opinions which do not admit the necessity for this State going with the South, if separation takes place, & that result but few doubt now. . . .

*Dec. 8.* My daughter, Mrs. Elizabeth Sayre, died, at her residence Marlbourne, in consequence of having given birth to a child on the 4th. This fatal result of her pregnancy, in her diseased condition (having a large internal tumor, latterly growing fast,) had been feared by all. But her otherwise good health had served to moderate these fears, & we waited with anxiety to hear of her delivery, of which the expected time was very uncertain. No notice was sent to us of its occurrence, or of her situation & increased danger, until at mid-day on the 7th. when the danger was very great. The messenger did not cross the river, from Evelynton, & reach Beechwood until nearly 11 in the night of the 7th. & after I was in bed. As early as could be effected next morning, Edmund & I crossed the river—& obtaining the only available conveyance, (belonging to the overseer at Evelynton,) & that a poor & frail one, in both horse & carriage, we could not reach Marlbourne until 4.30 P.M.—to hear that my daughter's death had taken place at 9 in the morning. Next forenoon, 9th., Julian & Lotty, & Charles, . . . arrived, by way of Petersburg & Richmond. On the 10th. the burial & funeral services took place, the neighbors attending. On the 11th., Edmund & I returned to Beechwood—& the others to Petersburg, on their way to home. My daughter's infant, a son, is living, & seems healthy, though of very small size. [1132]

*Dec. 13.* . . . The newspapers full of interesting political reports, but nothing new. Everything indicates the increase of the spirit of resistance & separation of the southern states—& also the inability, (& indisposition of the present administration) of the Federal government to attempt coercion on any seceding state. The federal treasury is empty, & unable to answer the demands for current & ordinary expenses, & drafts on it have been dishonored. There is no prospect of conciliation of the North & South. The President's Message conveys no clear meaning—or rather every opinion on the crisis is in conflict with some other declaration in another part. He disclaims any intention (or legal power) to use force against S.C. or any seceding state—yet declares that he will continue to collect revenue in their ports. If he does this, it will be war, just as much as would be armed invasion for conquest. I have trust in the President's imbecility, that he will not invite, & certainly bring on war in this one useless attempt, when he carefully will avoid war in every other mode. . . . This is Court day. It had been designed by some that a meeting of the people [1133] would have been called, & resolutions, as strong as the public sentiment would admit, be passed. But, owing to our absence, & the cause of it, Edmund & I did not advertise notice, & none was given, in the papers or otherwise. Therefore, we supposed there would be no meeting, & we did not go to Court. But, from Dr. Dupuy, who went, & returned at night, I learn that there was a meeting, & a full one, without distinction of former parties, or party divisions of any kind, & resolutions passed almost unanimously. From his remembrance of their form, I infer that they are not near as strong as I would have proposed, & do not name *secession* as the proper policy. But they ask for a Convention of the state, & the only use of that must be to make resistance to the northern domination, & the only available means will be secession. Such is the general form & character of the resolutions which have passed at nearly all the county meetings yet held in Va. I believe that if the leaders dared to offer much stronger propositions, the mass of the people are prepared to support them. If there was only time enough for action, after the legislature of Va will meet, on Jan. 7th., I am persuaded that both Va. & Md, (which *must* go with Va.,) would secede before the 4th of March. This is especially desirable, inasmuch as the District of Columbia, being included in the territory of Md, would then of necessity fall to the Southern Confederacy. . . .

*Dec. 14.* . . . No change of importance in our political affairs. In action, in the cotton states, everything in progress towards early conventions & to separation from the North: but in these southern & in the border states, & also the northern, every element of opposition to the secession movement is urging delay, & the common object of all these is to prevent action, & induce final accommodation with, if not submission to the North. I maintain, & shall contend for the proposition that *Delay is Submission.* It is therefore all-important that not a day's postponement of action shall be allowed to the urgent arguments of friends (real or pretended) in favor of delay of secession.—Preparing to leave home tomorrow, to go to Columbia, as I had arranged for & promised, to be present at the first meeting of the S.C. Convention, & at its expected speedy declaration of independence. If I possess the slightest influence, it will be zealously executed in opposition to delay—for which appeals will be made from various friendly quarters.

*Dec. 15.* This morning the ground covered with snow, & snowing fast until night, when it seemed to be 9 inches deep. This storm made it difficult & even dangerous for me to go to take the steamer, as I had intended, to get to Petersburg, & even if I had reached that place, the railroad would be impassable for 24 hours after the snow ceased to fall. And [1135] it is now so cold, that there is every prospect that ice on the bay will prevent our boat going to the wharf by the next day of passage (17th.). I am very much disappointed in being thus prevented reaching Columbia on the 17th—& fear that my journey may be prevented much longer. . . .

*Dec. 17.* After an early breakfast, my sister, her daughter Anna, Dr. J. J. Dupuy & I set out in the carriage, & our luggage in a four-mule wagon, for Maycox wharf. . . . When we reached the wharf, we were relieved of one previous fear, as there was no fixed ice outside of the wharf. But we had forgot to fear the difficulty of our steamer setting out from high up the narrow Chickahominy river, where it was certainly frozen across this morning. The steamer which usually reaches Maycox by 11 to 11.30 A.M. did not arrive until [1136] 1.30 P.M. & the steamer from Richmond was still longer behind its time. We reached City Point, & there heard of another cause of delay, the train having run off the track, & three hours detention being counted on in consequence. . . . I quickly determined to go on to Richmond, to take thence the morning train. I had no business, & arrived after dark, & did nothing whatever by going there, except to go to the Reading Room, & read the late papers. Gen. Cass, the superannuated Secretary of State has resigned, because the President declines to reinforce the Charleston forts. [Howell] Cobb, of Ga, the Secretary of the Treasury, had still earlier resigned, because the President's Message declared against the right of a state to secede from the Union. The conciliation committee of Congress, of one member from each state, has done nothing, & cannot do anything. The Abolition party maintains its ground stiffly, & will yield nothing. There are sundry schemes for conciliation of various kinds, & from various quarters—but none of which will come to anything—unless, which is all that I fear, inducing some delay of action in the states now willing to secede. I regret very much my not being able to reach Columbia (as designed) before this day—& that it will now be the morning of the 19th before I can reach there. The smallpox is there, & the alarm may cause both the Convention & the [1137] Legislature to adjourn to Charleston. I shall regret this, as necessarily causing at least one day's delay.—The legislature has elected F[rancis] W. Pickens Governor of S.C. I would have preferred any of the other persons named. I think he is an empty boaster. S.C. needs at this time one of her best men to fill the place of Governor.

*Dec. 18.* Left Richmond on the southern train at 4 A.M. & reached Wilmington N.C. at 7 P.M. Proceeded on the Wilmington & Manchester Rail Road. Heard that both legislature & Convention had adjourned on the evening of the 17th to Charleston, on account of the small-pox at Columbia—which caused me also to make the same change in my direction. Took the North-Eastern R.R. at Florence, & reached Charleston next morning, 8.30 A.M. on

*Dec. 19.* Went to Charleston Hotel—where I could obtain only a very small room, without a fire-place. Luckily it has become so much warmer, that fire is scarcely needed, & there is none even in the public rooms of the hotel. Saw many acquaintances among the members. By favor of Gen. [David F.] Jamison, President of the Convention,[58] I got a seat in the hall, which is so small that but few others than the members could find places to stand. Heard several interesting discussions on subjects incidental & preliminary to the act of secession, which is not yet prepared. Still the act of secession is virtually, though not formally enacted. For on the first day of the session, it was unanimously resolved "that it is the opinion of this Convention that the State of South [1138] Carolina should forthwith secede from the Federal Union, known as the United States of America."—A rainy afternoon. . . .

*Dec. 20.* In conversation with various individuals, met by chance. Among them, the only Virginian was old Col. Burwell. Another was the former Professor [George] Tucker of the University of Va, but

---

[58] A native of Orangeburg District, David Flavel Jamison (1810–64) was a prominent South Carolina lawyer and planter and a close friend of William Gilmore Simms. During the war he presided over the military court of General Beauregard's corps. Jamison died of yellow fever in September, 1864.

since, & for a long time, a resident of Phila., & a thorough northerner in opinion.[59] He was very guarded in his expression of opinion on the current events here. At 12, attended the session of the Convention. The Committee who had been charged with the preparation of the Ordinance of Secession reported the same, in very concise form. Not the slightest amendment was proposed, or objection made, nor was there a word of debate. The question was put, the ayes & nays required. Every member was in the meeting, (about 170) & every one voted for the passage. Such remarkable unanimity is unprecedented. This vote was taken at 1 P.M. When the Convention adjourned, it was to meet again at 7 P.M. at Secession Hall, a very large room, to sign & ratify the act of secession & independence. I was taken in by Ex-Gov. [John L.] Manning, among the members of the Convention, in the centre of the hall. On one side was the Senate, & on the other the House of Representatives. In the rear & on the sides of the hall, & in very spacious galleries above, there were places for an immense audience—& every seat was filled. The crowd was as enthusiastic as it was numerous. The session was opened by prayer—& I was gratified [1139] to see that the officiating clergyman was my old friend Dr. Bachman, who is a great man, as well as one of the best of all the good men whom I have known. The signing occupied more than two hours, during which time there was nothing to entertain the spectators except their enthusiasm & joy. Yet no one was weary, & no one left. Demonstrations of approbation, in clapping & cheers were frequent—& when all the signatures had been affixed, & the President, holding up the parchment, proclaimed South Carolina to be a free & independent community, the cheers of the whole assembly continued for some minutes, while every man waved or threw up his hat, & every lady waved her handkerchief. The Convention then adjourned, & the meeting separated. In the streets there had been going on other popular demonstrations of joy, from early in the afternoon. Some military companies paraded, salutes were fired, & as night came on, bonfires, made of barrels of rosin, were lighted in the principal streets, rockets discharged, & innumerable crackers fired by the boys. As I now write,

---

[59] After serving three consecutive terms in Congress, Tucker in 1825 was appointed professor of moral philosophy at the University of Virginia. He resigned that position in 1845 and moved to Philadelphia, where he continued to write on economic and historical subjects. He died on April 10, 1861—just two days before the attack on Fort Sumter.

after 10 P.M., I hear the distant sounds of rejoicing, with music of a military band, as if there was no thought of ceasing.—Caleb Cushing of Massachusetts arrived here this afternoon from Washington, on a mission from the President to the Governor (who is here,) & no doubt to urge delay. But finding that the ordinance of secession had passed, he was to return by the next train, & in a few hours after his arrival.—I obtained one of the pens used [1140] by the members to sign their names to the ordinance of dissolution, which I will keep as a valued memento of the occasion.—But with all the unanimity prevailing, there are still troublesome incidental questions to settle, about which opinions will be greatly divided. These were discussed, but not decided, this afternoon. The difficulty is what to do about superseding the U.S. authority in directing the post-office, & the custom house, so as to prevent an intermission of these important public services. Some of the ablest men in the Convention are for permitting these services (by request to the officers) to go on as before, until otherwise ordered by the legislature or the governor. Many others strongly oppose this course, as a continuing submission of the State to the U.S. government, & consenting to pay it tribute. The difficulty is increased in one aspect, & lessened in another, by the fact that the receipts of the customs, & of the Post Office, in South Carolina, do not pay the respective expenses of these services in the State.

*Dec. 21.* Telegraphic dispatches from various towns in the Southern States, report great excitement & joy, in consequence of the hearing yesterday (by telegraph) of the Secession of S.C. In Augusta, Savannah, & Columbus, Ga, Montgomery & Mobile, Ala, & Pensacola, Fla. there were salutes fired, & manifestations of great joy. In Washington City, as great panic & despondency produced. Called on Com. Hunter . . . at his office. He is a Virginian, & Inspector of Light Houses, in this & adjacent states. In addition to other conversation, he communicated to me the request [1141] of Mr. [Jesse] Bolles, an artist of highest reputation, that I would permit him to take my photographic likeness. I readily agreed to accept the compliment, & afterwards, accompanied by Capt. Hunter, went & sat for the portrait. Next went to the sitting of the Convention, as heretofore under the charge of the President. But a motion was soon made to sit with closed doors, excluding all but members, & I immediately went out, without waiting for the vote. This order was very proper, considering the difficult subject of discussion, before adverted to. Understood afterwards that the session had been private, & continued to a late hour. . . .

*Dec. 22.* . . . At 12, went to the Convention. But again, as expected, that body went into secret session, so that I did not hear much of interesting business. Yesterday the convention appointed three commissioners to go to Washington, to negotiate terms of settlement & separation with the Federal Government. The Commissioners chosen were Robert Barnwell, Ex-Gov. [James H.] Adams,[60] & James Orr. It is understood that they will set out on Monday 24th inst. This evening the legislature adjourned, to meet again early in January.— I begin to find lack of occupation, & this a very dull evening. . . .

*Dec. 23.* Sunday. Attended the Lutheran, Dr. Bachman's church, & heard him preach. Allusion was made to the recent political change in S.C. both in his prayer & his sermon, & the heretofore regular & formal prayer for the President of the U.S. & Congress was omitted. After dinner went, with some members of the legislature to Sullivan's Island, to inspect the outside of Fort Moultrie—no visitors being now allowed to go inside. The garrison is said to consist of 65 men only—but there are many laborers employed, & much has been lately done, or is now in progress, for strengthening the fortification. Strong efforts have been made to induce the president of the U.S. to reinforce the forts, but he has declined. It seems to be the understanding that the forts are not to be reinforced; & if not reinforced, they [1143] will not be attacked, until their surrender to S.C. is finally refused, or until Lincoln's administration is about to commence. But it is also determined here, that if the forts are reinforced, or are not surrendered before the 4th of March, they will be assaulted & taken at any cost. The steamer carried us close by Castle Pinckney & Fort Sumter. The former, though dangerous because of its close vicinity to Charleston, is a weak fortification, & with a weak garrison. Fort Sumter is very strong, & well armed with cannon—but has only a guard of 12 men. If this should be well manned, it would be extremely difficult to be taken.—At night, I was introduced, at his request, to Gov. [Madison S.] Perry of Florida, who arrived here today from Washington, where he went to purchase arms for that State. He was in Washington when the news was received of the secession of S.C. He says that it evidently had a very solemnizing effect on the abolition members of Congress, &

---

[60] A wealthy Richland District planter, James Hopkins Adams (1812–61) was elected governor of South Carolina in 1854.

seemed to be the first thing to convince them that S.C. would secede. He represents every thing in Florida as very favorable to secession, & has no doubt of its being promptly ordained by the Convention which has been called to meet on Jan. 3rd. I had some intention
of going to attend this session—& may do so, if nothing more
interesting occurs.

*Dec. 24.* Went to see Dr. Bachman, & he wrote for me a letter of
introduction to his friends in Florida. I determined to go on in the
steamer tonight to Fernandina. . . . Went to the session of the Convention. The [1144] whole first session (to past 4 P.M.) occupied in
discussing & amending the two addresses, before reported, one by
Mr. Memminger, to the world, setting forth the immediate causes of
the secession of S.C., & the other to the slaveholding states, stating more fully our common wrongs, & inviting their cooperation.
Both papers finally adopted. After the recess a later session will be
secret. I have heard that its business will be to determine the present
policy of customs & trade—& that the policy probably will be what
I have advocated; viz: free import trade of the states south of the
non-slaveholding, & with all European nations that make commercial treaties with S.C. & so acknowledge her independence—& the
former duties to be imposed on the imported commodities of all
other states & nations, including the northern states.—At 6 P.M. left
the hotel for the steamer, which moved off at 8. Before 9, I retired to
my berth, merely taking of[f] coat & boots, & lay down to guard
against sea-sickness, to which I am subject, & which was threatened
by the motion of the steamer. At 10.30 P.M. I heard the steam discharging, & on inquiring heard that the main shaft was broken, next
to one of the paddle wheels. The situation was very dangerous, &
I heard afterwards that it was much more so than I had supposed.
After some time of delay, the machinery was fixed so that one wheel
[1145] could be worked, & the steamer was put back for Charleston.
Reached the wharf at 4 A.M. on

*Dec. 25.* Waited until 8 A.M. in vain to learn whether the other
steamer will go this afternoon or not, & whether to take away my
trunk or not. I had been offered, & furnished with, a free passage
ticket on this line to Fernandina, by Mr. Lawton, the President,
which makes it a matter of some importance for me to go by this
route rather than by Savannah. After going to the Charleston Hotel,
returned to the wharf, and heard that a steamer would set out this
evening for Fernandina. Went to dine with Dr. Bachman—who, at 6

P.M. drove me to the steamer, only to learn that its starting was put off to tomorrow, the regular day. So returned to stay the intervening time with Dr. Bachman. The Convention sat today, & after an hour, with closed doors. . . .

*Dec. 26.* A letter from Julian, with the information, not unexpected, that the infant of Mr. Sayre had died.—As usual, went to the opening of the session of the Convention, but it went into secret session as soon as the roll had been called. A 6 P.M. went to the steamer, which set out for Fernandina at 7.10 P.M. After we had passed Fort Moultrie about 4 miles, I was on the upper deck looking out on the water, when I heard two loud discharges of cannon from that fort, in quick succession. It was an unusual occurrence, as everything there latterly has been conducted so as to be as quiet as possible. There has not even been the firing of a gun at sunset, as is the general practice of all fortresses. I supposed this firing, [1146] at so unusual an hour must have been a signal for something. . . .[61]

*Dec. 27.* Saw a beautiful sunrise on the ocean. Soon after, the low coast of Georgia visible, in one point only. Reached the St. Mary's river about 9 A.M. & Fernandina soon after. This is a new & fast growing town, on that river & in Amelia Island, which was a noted place some 45 years ago, when, under the Spanish government, it was captured by the freebooters or "flibustiers" under Gen. Gregor McGregor, & from them taken by the U.S. forces, in advance of the purchase of Florida.—The train left about 1 P.M. During my stay at Fernandina, I had been introduced to sundry of the residents, & among them to young Mr. Ashe, the son of my acquaintance W[illiam] S. Ashe of Wilmington, & President of the Railroad there.[62] This young man is Agent of Transportation on the Florida R.R., as I afterwards learned by his voluntarily procuring for me tickets for my free passage on that road for my present excursion. I found that Gainesville, about 100 miles on, was my nearest place to Gen. Owens' residence in Marion, where I design to go, to see something of the lands of his neighborhood while waiting for the session

---

[61] On the night of December 26, 1860, Major Robert Anderson moved the federal garrison in Charleston from Fort Moultrie to the more formidable Fort Sumter. It seems probable that the guns heard by Ruffin were associated in some way with this movement.

[62] After serving three terms in Congress, Ashe (1814–62) was elected in 1858 to the North Carolina Senate. During the war he was a colonel in the Confederate Army.

of the Florida Convention. On the route, we were astounded by seeing a telegraphic dispatch which stated that the garrison had blown up Fort Moultrie, & passed over to Sumter. When the train reached Baldwin (the junction of the two crossing railroads,) we used the short time of detention to telegraph to Savannah, [1147] to the operator, to obtain either the contradiction or confirmation of this strange & incredible report. This was more than an hour after the first dispatch had been received through that office from Charleston. The return dispatch repeated the same general statement, with the addition, that the cannon at Fort Moultrie had been spiked, & the carriages burnt, by the retreating garrison. If true, this is an awful event, indicating the determination of the federal government on hostile & warlike coercion to be attempted on S.C. The event must put Charleston in a fever of excitement & rage. I regretted much that I should have left just before the beginning of such interesting events, & was much inclined to go back by the next returning train & steamer (by Savannah,) by which I could reach Charleston on the 29th. Some still remaining doubt of the truth of the statement alone prevented my returning. If it is true, the authorities & other principal friends of S.C. have been egregiously deceived by the President & Secretary of War. For I heard from sundry sources, including Gov. Perry & Gov. Pickens, that there was not the least ground for apprehension on account of the U.S. forces holding the forts—& intimations from them that assurances had been given to that effect, though confidentially. I heard this expressed strongly & confidently by Gov. Perry—& the same was said yesterday by Gov. Pickens to Dr. Bachman, who immediately repeated the assurance to me. At the same time he delivered to me two messages from Gov. Pickens, sent on hearing that I was going to Tallahassee. One was to request me to telegraph to him immediately the occurrence of the Convention declaring the independence of Florida. The other was that if Va. would secede before the 4th of March, there would not be a [1148] drop of blood shed to secure the independence of the southern states, & that moreover the northern party & organization of states would be utterly broken up.—Dr. Hume was sent for by Dr. Bachman, & came to see me yesterday. He was one of the Commissioners who directed the construction of the first deep sewers through Charleston, & I was anxious to learn how they had operated for drainage, & if as I had predicted, when I saw them in their unfinished state some years past. He told me that their drainage effect had been very extensive, & altogether satisfactory. Since then, some miles more of similar sewers had been constructed. He mentioned as one certain fact in proof, that a grave had been lately dug, 7 feet deep, & dry to the bottom, in a graveyard where formerly water was reached within two feet, or less. This particular grave was within 50 feet of one of the deep draining sewers.—Reached Gainesville at 6.30 P.M., & there took a carriage to Micanopy, 12 miles, where I arrived at 8.45, & slept at a hotel.

*Dec. 28.* Had last night directed the hiring a conveyance to Gen. Owens,' & an early start—but did not get off until nearly 10 A.M. & then with a weak & slow horse, hired at an extortionate price to draw the buggy to Col. S. Owens,' 10 miles. When arriving there, he was not at home, but Mrs. Owens received me most hospitably, & when I declined staying, sent me on to Gen. Owens' residence, 7 miles farther on. He was at home, & soon after came his brother Samuel. After dinner, we walked out, & I examined some of the soils & stones, [1149] as to the presence or absence of carbonate of lime. Found very pure lime-rock, in the lower stratum exposed in sinks, & all the stone & gravel on the surface destitute of lime, though some had evidently been of marine origin, & formerly of lime more or less. . . .

*Dec. 29.* Immediately after breakfast, Gen. Owen[s] drove me to his brother Samuel's, & thence to their large Fort Drane plantation, 3 miles beyond. Gen. & Col. Owens being officers of a newly raised troop of volunteer cavalry, had to go to Flemington to their first muster. I was left under the care of Mr. Ransom, their manager, who conducted me to various points deemed worthy of being observed, especially for my object of learning how far the prevailing opinion was correct, of the stone & soil being generally & highly calcareous. Examining, & testing with muriatic acid, only a few soils deemed by the residents the most certainly & likely calcareous, & by me as most likely to be so, I found not one that showed the slightest effervescence with acid—& not one specimen of stone, even when full of shells, or their casts, & appearing most like marl-rock, of all found at or near the general surface—or even in a well 40 feet deep, & 20 into the soft white rock. But in the sink-holes, where the rock is visible, it is always calcareous. . . . In regard to news, this is more out of the world than any place I was ever in before. None of the persons seen have yet received any later papers than the Charleston papers of 20th, & Tallahassee of 22nd—& the report which I heard on my way, of Fort Moultrie being blown up, though circulated generally, has neither been confirmed nor contradicted.

*Dec. 30. Sunday.* . . . Saw still more remarkable examples, in stone collected for masonry, of what has every indication of being nearly entirely composed of carbonate of lime, & yet is not calcareous. These indications are texture, white color, lightness, & presence of shells, or thin casts, in quantity. The stone appears very like the hard marl rock of Ala, S.C. & southern N.C. & is in some cases almost a conglomerate of shells.—Saw here growing (until stopped by frost,) sugar cane (over large spaces,) & the arrow-root plant, & the banana. The latter bears in perfection, but requires to be protected by some covering in the winter. . . . A letter arrived directed to Mr. J[ames] Owens, from Savannah, which his brother opened. It was from a near neighbor, dated 28th, & confirmed the transfer of the U.S. garrison of Fort Moultrie to Fort Sumter, & incidentally mentioned the spiking of the cannon, but said nothing of the mining & blowing up the walls of Fort Moultrie. The letter added that volunteers of Savannah, in consequence, were going to take Fort Pulaski. I earnestly wish that this may be so, & that it may be successful. It is a necessary step, to prevent the fort being reinforced; & also the execution will serve to precipitate the secession of Georgia.

*Dec. 31.* After breakfast drove to Col. S. Owens' house, whence he went with me to see Orange Lake, about 3 miles distant, & the beautiful orange grove on its nearest border. The whole space formerly covered by a thick undergrowth of orange trees, of natural growth, was some hundreds of acres. The growth was . . . in the course of being cut down for cultivation, & to prevent the complete destruction, the Messrs. Owens & other neighbors bought 5 acres on the lake, which was the place we visited. It is hammock land, & the larger trees of the kinds usual on the hammocks—sweet gum, magnolia, live-oak & water-oak, ash, hackberry &c. Under this, is a thick & continuous cover of orange trees, not exceeding 20 feet high. This has been a bad bearing year, & much the greater number of the trees in the woods have no fruit now. But a small proportion of the trees, here & there, are full of ripe oranges, with some younger & yet green. In the adjoining cleared [1152] field, where scattering orange trees had been left, they were loaded with fruit. These, & also the dense grove, open at bottom, & clear of all shrubbery, but shaded thickly by evergreen leaves, were beautiful objects. The wild oranges here are not the sweet, but of two different kinds, the sour

& the "bitter-sweet." Both have the interior white membrane, which covers the pulp, & also is interposed between the lobes or sections of the fruit, [&] is bitter. But if this membrane is carefully removed, the pulp & juice of the "bitter-sweet," is quite sweet, & the other entirely sour, as a lemon. The fruit here is free for public use, & it is surprising that so little has been removed. The oranges do not drop when fully ripe, but will hang for months, or even a year, unless pulled off, or shaken down by violent wind.—Returned to dinner to Col. Owens,' & to stay to next morning, when Mr. James Owens, who is a delegate to the Convention, will come by to take me in his carriage to the rail-road.

# January–April

е∽о

# 1861

ADDRESSING THE FLORIDA CONVENTION
е∽о INSPECTING THE FORTIFICATIONS IN
CHARLESTON HARBOR е∽о AT THE VIRGINIA
CONVENTION е∽о LINCOLN INAUGURATED
е∽о AN EXILE IN SOUTH CAROLINA е∽о A
VOLUNTEER WITH THE PALMETTO GUARD
е∽о THE BOMBARDMENT OF FORT SUMTER—
WAR BEGINS!

*January 1.*... Mr. James Owens, with his daughter came about 10, & soon after we proceeded on our journey.... Returned on the same road I came, to Gainesville, 24 miles. So much of the road of deep sand, that, though in a light carriage with good horses, & our trunks sent separately, we did not reach Gainesville until nearly sunset— where we stopped at a very plain tavern, the best in the place....

*Jan 2.*... At 8 A.M. left on the train, & reached the junction of the two crossing roads, at Baldwin by 11.30 A.M., where had to wait 5 or more hours for the train to Tallahassee. Here found a printed telegraphic despatch from Savannah, which though still very uncertain, indicates important events in progress at Charleston—& that coercion is about to be attempted by the federal government. A war vessel is to enter the harbor today & will be opposed by the batteries manned by the S.C. troops, & war is expected to begin forthwith. If I could have known of such exciting events, I would have remained at Charleston, & I wish I had, both for my health & my pleasure. But having come so far on the way to Tallahassee, I deem it best to go on. Probably this news, & the beginning of war, with some bloodshed, will serve to determine quicker the position of the Convention which was for waiting for co-operation from other states, or for delay on other grounds. This is no time to advocate delay. Hostilities at Charleston will require the Convention of Florida, & the others soon to follow, to go quickly either for secession, &

co-operating with the already seceded state or states, or submission to the federal & northern power. So I trust that matters will be hastened by this new phase of the contest. . . . Later, while waiting at Baldwin for the train (to 3.30), more telegraphic despatches were received from Washington [1155], & Charleston, as late as today—& I saw also an intelligent gentleman lately from Charleston, who informed me of arrangements which I have not seen in any paper. A *Mercury* of 1st. also was seen, & from all these sources I will repeat the existing facts. The action of the U.S. commander of Fort Moultrie in occupying Fort Sumter was not authorised by the administration, but since approved. The President has changed his previous policy for coercion. On account of this infidelity to his previous understanding with the authorities of S.C. [John B.] Floyd, Sec. of War has resigned, & [Joseph] Holt is the nominal successor, but Gen. Scott supposed to be really directing the department. Troops of S.C. have been called into service, have occupied both Forts Moultrie & Pinckney, & also raised earth-work batteries on Cummings' Point, Morris Island, below & on the opposite side to Fort Moultrie, & some other points, where large cannon can prevent the passage of ships. The harbor buoys are removed, & the light of the Lighthouse extinguished. A U.S. revenue cutter, an armed steamer, was expected to enter the harbor today. It had been warned off, & if persisting, would be fired on from the batteries, which probably would precipitate the collision with the federal troops expected every day. In Washington, it is understood that the policy of the abolition administration is to be coercive & warlike, & pushed to every extremity needed for such policy. Reports from the border slave-holding states show that the secession feeling is fast growing—& it is said that the coercion feeling is gaining strength among the northern people. Collisions & war must soon ensue. Their occurrence, with bloodshed of the South Carolinians [1156] defending their soil & their rights, or maintaining the possession of their harbor & its defending fortifications, will stir doubly fast the sluggish blood of the more backward southerners, & must soon draw all the southern states to secession, & to intimate alliance, in advance of a confederacy.—Reached Lake City, only 40 miles from Baldwin, where we have to stop through the night, for want of a continuous train. The delay is very vexatious to me. Most of the passengers are members either of the Convention or Legislature, both to open tomorrow. . . . By latest accounts, it appears that thirteen only of the cannon on Fort Moultrie, those which bore on Fort Sumter, were spiked, & their carriages burnt. The spiking was done so imperfectly as to be easy to be drilled out, & the wood-work of the carriages will soon be replaced.

*Jan. 3.* . . . Set out on the train at 5. A number of delegates to the Convention or legislature along, to sundry of whom I was introduced. Also, Mr. [Edward C.] Bullock, the Commissioner sent by Ala. to Fla.[1]—Reached Tallahassee at 12 M. Met Gov. Perry as soon as reaching the hotel, & soon after was shown by him a telegraphic dispatch from Gov. Brown of Ga, stating that, in consequence of the seizure of Fort Sumter by the federal troops, [1157] he had ordered the U.S. forts at the mouth of the Savannah river, which are without garrisons, to be occupied by Ga. militia. This will be an important move, which I trust will serve to commit Ga to secession. The Convention met here, & adjourned previous to permanent organization, to the 5th. The reasons—some 15 members not arrived, & tomorrow is the appointed fast day. The delay was also deemed requisite to better know the real strength of the two parties who respectively go for immediate & separate secession, & for delay & co-operation with the other southern states. It is feared that the former party is not certainly the strongest at present.—There was such a crowd at the hotel that I could not there (nor at any other,) get a comfortable room. So at night I accepted an invitation . . . from Mr. Beard, a former slight acquaintance, to take my quarters at his house, & went there by dark.—I was very sorry that there should be any need for the adjournment of the Convention—& in addition was displeased with one of the reasons being respect for the religious services of tomorrow. The keeping of this day for fasting & humiliation, is by a recommendatory proclamation of the President of the U.S., on account of the political dangers & disasters now impending, & to be produced, not by northern abolitionism, but by the spirit of resistance & disunion of the southern states. The very appointment of the day & service is a rebuke & censure of the seceding states, & of their cause, & of the very action which this Convention is assembled to consummate. And yet, the first & immediate action of the Convention is to adjourn over the fast day, in respect to [1158] its objects.

---

[1] A native of Charleston, Bullock moved to Alabama in 1843 and entered the practice of law in Eufaula. From 1857 to 1861 he was a member of the Alabama Senate. While serving as colonel of the Eighteenth Alabama Regiment, he contracted typhoid fever in Mobile and died on December 23, 1861.

*Jan. 4.* I would not attend the religious services of the day—though I heard from some who did, that the minister of the Episcopal Church preached a strong disunion sermon, in favor of the immediate secession of this state. I afterwards heard that the bishop of that church, who resides here, would not attend the service, because viewing the matter somewhat as I did.—Mr. [Leonidas W.] Spratt, commissioner of S.C. to Fla. arrived today from Charleston. He informed me that Fort Sumter was blockaded by the several batteries of S.C., & guarded on the water, so that no supplies could be introduced except by force.—A telegram from the war department at Washington to Pensacola was intercepted, or its contents made known, yesterday at Atlanta Ga., & made known this morning to the Governor of Fla. It directed the reinforcement of the previous garrisons of the two forts at Pensacola, & the destruction of lbs. 5000 of gunpowder which was unprotected by any garrison in the U.S. Arsenal on the Apalachicola. There was an informal & confidential meeting of the members of the Convention with the Governor on this subject—& I have reason to believe that he was indirectly authorized to occupy the other fort at St. Augustine, & arsenal that are not garrisoned. The forts at Pensacola are garrisoned.—From after breakfast to dark I was generally at the principal hotel, talking with various members of the Convention & [1159] others on the current events, & on secession. Many seem to attach value to my presence, & pay much respect to my arguments. . . . After tea, Bishop Rutledge came in to visit the family. I was very much pleased with the venerable old minister, & with his ardent & active patriotic sentiments. He is a native of S.Ca., & said he had himself already seceded, with his native state, & in advance of Florida. We had agreeable conversation on this & various subjects until he left at 9 o'clock, & I retired to my apartment to write these entries, & to read the N.Y. Tribune, the chief abolition newspaper.—I have learned that, when the Convention met yesterday, it was estimated that there was barely a majority of one of those who had been elected as immediate & separate secessionists—all the others being for delayed secession, or for waiting for the previous action, or co-operation, of the adjoining stronger states. It was supposed that a little delay (by the adjournment,) & conference among the members would serve to increase the majority greatly. The subsequent action of the Governor of Ga, in occupying Fort Pulaski, by committing that state, will further strengthen the party & the feeling here for immediate secession.

*Jan. 5.* My birth-day—67 years old. The Convention met at 12 M. After the organization, & election of all the officers, on motion I was invited to occupy a seat in the hall, & after the recess, I was conducted to the chair assigned for me [1160] by two members deputed for the purpose. I would have preferred a less ceremoneous [*sic*] introduction, but could not avoid it. . . . The proceedings of the evening session gave indications of discord, & there was great want of the exercise & knowledge of parliamentary law, & much violation of order & decorum by the audience. After the adjournment, was invited & went to sup at Col. Williams' house. Spent there a pleasant evening with several other guests, & especially with Judge [Jesse J.] Finley, a very intelligent & agreeable gentleman, a member of the Convention.[2] After returning, heard from Mr. Beard that the fort at Mobile had been occupied by order of the Governor of Ala. I heard it whispered that similar orders had been issued here, as to the U.S. arsenal on the Apalachicola. As we have not yet heard that the powder there is destroyed, as ordered by the telegram from Washington, I trust that the orders were not only examined at Atlanta, but their farther passage stopped.

*Jan. 6.* Sunday. No mail, & no telegraphic news, though, as frequently, false rumors of reports of hostilities at Charleston. . . . Afternoon, went to visit (& to return the call of) my old [1161] acquaintance Col. Ro[bert] Gamble, who resides here, & who is now more than 80 years old.[3] Returned to Mr. Beard's to tea. Read newspapers, & as part of one, a sermon lately preached in Brooklyn by the Rev. Mr. [Henry J.] Vandyke,[4] which is an admirable argument against & exposition of the errors & evils of abolitionism.

*Jan. 7.* The Convention met at 10 A.M. & I took my assigned seat. The commissioners of Ala. & S.C. Messrs. Bullock & Spratt, were first introduced, & invited to address the Convention. Mr. Bullock spoke for about three-quarters of an hour, & delivered a most

[2] Jesse Johnson Finley (1812–1904) was born in Tennessee and served briefly as mayor of Memphis before moving to Florida in 1846. Judge of the western circuit of Florida from 1853 to 1861, Finley rose to the rank of brigadier general, Confederate States of America, during the war and, in the late 1870's, was elected to Congress.

[3] A native of Virginia, Gamble moved to Florida in the 1830's and became prominent in various enterprises.

[4] Henry Jackson Van Dyke (1822–91), a native of Pennsylvania and graduate of Princeton Theological Seminary, was pastor of the First Presbyterian Church of Brooklyn from 1853 until the time of his death.

eloquent speech, in favor of immediate & separate secession, & of the union of the southern states. Mr. Spratt followed, reading the documents of S.C. sent by him to this Convention, & following with a logical & able argument. When he had closed, to my great astonishment, (when I understood it,) Mr. Pelot, a member of ability,[5] moved that I should be invited to address the Convention—which was carried, without dissent. I was not attending to what was said, deeming it the routine business, & with my deafness, did not know what motion was made, or voted upon, until informed by the President of the wish of the Convention. I immediately rose, & though greatly embarrassed by the novel & unlooked-for requisition, I proceeded to speak—disclaiming all authority or right to speak for Va —but declaring the great importance of the early action of Fla. to hasten the secession of Va. & all the border states, which (excepting of Missouri & Delaware,) I predicted would be accomplished by the [1162] 4th of March, provided Fla. & the adjoining states moved as soon as their severally meeting in Conventions permitted. I spoke earnestly, & but for a short time, & seemed to have pleased my auditors. Next, the resolution introduced on the 5th. was taken up & discussed, & before 1 P.M. was passed with but 5 dissenting votes —as follows: "*Whereas,* all hope of the preservation of the Federal Union, upon terms consistent with the safety & honor of the slave-holding states, has been finally dissipated by the recent indications of the strength of the anti-slavery sentiment of the free states— Therefore, *Be it resolved by the people of Florida in Convention assembled,* That, as it is the undoubted right of the several states of the Federal Union, known as the United States of America, to withdraw from the said Union at such time & for such cause or causes as in the opinion of the people of each state, acting in their sovereign capacity, may be just & proper, in the opinion of this convention, the existing causes are such as to compel the State of Florida to proceed to exercise this right." The passage of this resolution was followed by another to appoint a committee to draw up a form of Ordinance of Secession. These two measures are equivalent to a declaration of secession, but at [1161a][6] an uncertain though early time. This pledge being secured, the enactment of independence *may* be postponed until Ala & Miss. (whose conventions meet today,) or even

---

[5] Pelot, of Alachua County, had occupied the position of temporary chairman when the convention convened on January 3.

[6] Misnumbered by diarist. Should be page 1163.

Ga, next week, shall act. Still many are for speedy definitive decision. Supposing that I shall witness nothing more, for some days to come, I now think of leaving tomorrow, to go to witness the session of the Ala. Convention at Montgomery. If not going so soon, I shall probably be too late to be present at the act of secession there. I sent on the report of the action of the Convention, by magnetic telegraph, to the Examiner, Richmond—& trust that the annunciation was published there in an hour after the action of the Convention. This is the day for the called meeting of the legislature—so that I trust my communication will have the more effect.—Heard from the Governor that he had received a dispatch stating that the elections in Ga so far gave 170 immediate secessionists to 80 co-operationists. The remaining counties will not probably materially alter this proportion—& even if all were to go against immediate secession, they cannot reverse the majority. So Ga is certain for secession.—A confidential telegraphic dispatch received today by the Governor from the U.S. Senators of Fla., & communicated in secret session to the Convention, informed that body that the policy of the federal administration was military coercion on S.C. & urged the Convention to secede forthwith.—In the evening, [1162b] with Dr. G[eorge] T. Maxwell of Savannah, who introduced himself to me.[7] I had been desirous of meeting & knowing him, to learn from himself, as I now sought & effected, the account of a late daring and also amusing adventure in which he had been one of the principal actors, the capturing of the U.S. armed revenue cutter in the Savannah river, as a prelude to the occupation of Fort Pulaski. With Dr. Maxwell's consent, I took notes of the affair, & wrote an account of it before going to bed. The act however was unauthorized, & went beyond the Governor's designed policy of occupying & retaining the forts. So as soon as the captors offered to him the charge of the vessel, he ordered it to be restored to the previous U.S. commander.

*Jan. 8.* The celebration of the battle of New Orleans interrupted the proceedings of the Convention after 12 M. Sundry speeches, from distinguished members or strangers, & among them one from Mr. Bullock, which I would like to have heard, but did not go to

---

[7] At this time professor of obstetrics at Oglethorpe Medical College in Savannah, George Troup Maxwell ( 1827–97 ) had formerly practiced medicine in Tallahassee and Key West. During the Civil War he was a colonel in the Confederate Army but was captured and spent the last three years of the conflict in a northern prison.

the hall, for fear that I should be called upon, & I would especially object to speak before ladies, who made up a large part of the audience. The telegraphic wires out of order all day.

*Jan. 9.* Telegrams made public, & announced to the Convention at different times of its session, announced that the "Star of the West," a California sea steamer, had brought troops for the Federal Government to Charleston harbor, & attempted to reinforce Fort Sumter, but had been repulsed & driven back by cannonading from the Carolinian [1163] batteries. This sent by Gov. Pickens. No other details. Another dispatch from New Orleans stated that troops had been embarked at Boston to reinforce the federal forts on the coast of Florida, & especially that at Key West. I was informed confidentially that Gov. Perry had yesterday given authority to Major [William H.] Chase, of Pensacola, to capture the forts there, if he could attempt it with assurance of success. These forts have military garrisons, though not strong ones, & might be reinforced by men from two ships of war lying in the harbor. As nothing has been since heard, I fear that the attempt has been frustrated, or judged to be hopeless. . . . A long & earnest debate today, & the opposition members, (for delay, or co-operative secession—none being avowed for submission, or union—) tried every scheme to prevent the victory of the separate & immediate secessionists. It was nearly dark when the final vote on the main question was about to be put, when the majority yielded to the wishes of the minority, & adjourned to tomorrow 10 A.M. when the question will be decided. [1164] It is certain now that immediate secession will be enacted—& it is hoped that this postponement will serve to much increase the already sure majority. I have arranged to set out tomorrow afternoon for Charleston, S.C. . . . The fort at St. Augustine is in possession of a volunteer garrison, under Capt. Gibbs, of that town, who requested & obtained the authority of Gov. Perry to occupy it.

*Jan. 10.* Telegram that the Convention of Miss. declared secession yesterday. The Convention here met at 11, & after hearing four or five tedious speeches from members who had steadily opposed, but now designed to vote for the action which they still argued against, the vote was taken, & resulted in the enactment of secession & independence of Florida, by 62 ayes to 7 noes. I immediately telegraphed the result to Gov. Pickens at Charleston, & to the Editors of the Enquirer at Richmond. The charge most extortionate. The message was of minimum length (three words each, though counted as much as ten—) & for the two, I paid $6.30, for transmission. . . . My departure had been arranged for 4 P.M., by taking leave of my hospitable & very agreeable [1165] host & family this morning. Set out on the train for Monticello, & there (after 6 P.M.) took a stage coach to Quitman, 27 miles, which is the present terminus of the Albany Rail Road to Savannah. . . . The coach reached the terminus two hours before the time for the train to set out, & I was put down by side of the road, with my trunk, some 50 yards from the standing train. I went to this, with difficulty through the dark, & over the inequalities of the ground & of the structure of the railroad—once falling, & hurting my shin over a log—& could find no fire, nor even an unoccupied seat in the cold passenger car—all having been made use of for beds for the sleeping conductor & other employe's [*sic*]. I should have had to sit on my trunk . . . for two hours, & my feet suffering with cold, but for the circumstance that a number of Irish laborers were standing or sitting around two fires of large pine logs, close by, waiting as they had been all the night to go on the train to Savannah. . . . To be enabled to stand up by a good fire, for the two hours of waiting, was a great benefit. And chatting with the good-humored Irishmen, & hearing their remarks in their rich brogue, furnished some amusement.

*Jan. 11.* At last, at 3.30 A.M. the train started—after which, I got some hours sleep, & for the first time. Reached Savannah about 1 P.M. & stopped at the principal hotel, the Pulaski House. . . . Telegram that Ala. had seceded, on 11th. This will remove every doubt of the like speedy action of Ga, whose convention will meet on 17th. —Reports that men had gone from Ala to aid in taking the U.S. Forts at Pensacola, & from New Orleans (whether with or without the governor's authority,) to take the forts & arsenal in La. Also Fort Caswell on the Cape Fear River has been taken by unauthorised persons. Thus, the bad faith of the President, in justifying the garrisoning of Fort Sumter, has speedily led to the occupying, by the southern states, all the ungarrisoned forts & arsenals in Fla, all without exception in Ga, Ala, & La, & one [1167] very important fort in N.C. If Fort Sumter had not been treacherously garrisoned, no state would have seized a fort, or at least not in advance of actual secession—& every one might & would have been quietly supplied with a garrison of U.S. soldiers, which, even if small, with the aid of artillery, & behind strong walls, would have been very difficult, & destructive of life, for militia volunteers to conquer. [1168] Hon. R.

Barnwell Rhett arrived here today. I had sent him my card, failing
to find him, & at night he came to visit me in my room, & we had a
long & interesting conversation about matters in Charleston, of
which I was before imperfectly informed by the newspapers. He
drew for my instruction a rough chart of the channels, & the points
on which sand-works have been or will be thrown up. He thinks
that the approaches into the harbor through the main ship channel, & Maffitt's channel along & below Sullivan's Island, may be severally & perfectly commanded by two of the new sand-batteries,
even before being aided by Fort Moultrie—& that no supplies or reinforcements can be thrown into Fort Sumter. If not choosing to
wait for the slow operation of blockade, without firing on either side,
he thinks that the rear & weaker part of the walls may be breached
by batteries from Morris,' & another higher point, still nearer to Fort
Sumter, & for which heavy cannon are not yet in hand. When the
unarmed steamer (Star of the West,) with supplies, & 250 soldiers,
was sent in, the government must have relied on terror, & dread of
federal vengeance, preventing the Carolinians firing a gun. There
were but three guns (24 pounders) at the sand battery on Morris's
Island, & only one instrument for taking aim, which caused slow
firing. But 7 shots were fired, of which 3 struck, as supposed—& the
vessel then turned, & steamed off to sea, before it had gone so high
as opposite or nearest to the battery. Two other shots were fired at
the steamer from [1169] Fort Moultrie—but too distant to do any
damage, & only serving to insult Fort Sumter. No attempt yet made
by the latter to interrupt the passage of vessels—though it is
threatened, if U.S. vessels bound for Fort Sumter shall be again
fired upon. Mr. Rhett thinks that every thing promises well for the
success of South Carolina but secured by a heavy military expense,
for 7000 men now under arms. . . .

*Jan. 12.* At 7 A.M. left Savannah, & reached Charleston by
1 P.M. Went immediately to the printing offices to see the papers
from Va. & elsewhere. The proceedings of the legislature of Va. indicate a much stronger tone for southern defence than I had expected from such a mean body. I trust, with increased confidence, that
Va & Md, & thirteen states will secede before March 4th. The northern papers (not abolition) are just beginning to realize the probability of the secession movement being effectual—& are foolishly
urging the repeal of the northern unconstitutional anti-slavery laws,
& amendments of the federal constitution, as guaranties for southern

rights & interests, & expecting the steps already taken by southern states then to be retraced! Vain hope! No state which shall have seceded will desire to return to its previous connection with the north—& not one will trust again to any pledges or guaranties offered by the north & the abolition party, even if the latter would offer any of importance, which they certainly will not.—Went to see Dr. Bachman in the afternoon. Later, met & conversed with many acquaintances, [1170] members of the legislature, now in session, & others, in the hall of the Charleston Hotel, where I am again lodged.

*Jan. 13.* Sunday. Had applied by note last night to Gen. Jamison (who is now Secretary of War for S.C.) for a permit to visit the fortifications. This morning went to his lodgings for it. Learned from him that an order had been issued to prohibit all permits to visitors —but that he was going around this morning on visits of inspection to all the fortifications, & he invited me to accompany him, in the steamer prepared for the purpose. We embarked, together with Col. [James H.] Trapier, of the state engineers,[8] & some other gentlemen, sundry volunteers, & 100 negro slaves, sent by their owners gratuitously, to work on the fortifications. There are near 1000 of these, in all, now thus afforded by the patriotism & liberality of private planters. We first stopped at Castle Pinckney—& next at Fort Moultrie, after passing by the frowning but silent & inactive Fort Sumter, which is surrounded by water. At Fort Moultrie, all was activity & gayety. The volunteers, many the sons of the men of high position & wealth, and the negroes, were alike busily engaged in shovelling & wheeling sand, to fill barrels & bags on the ramparts. The negro laborers were employed in bringing sand from below, & outside of the fort, to a pile within, & on the walls, whence it was continually removed by the volunteer soldiers, in wheel-barrows, to the ramparts, & used there to construct "traverses" of sand-bags &c. While I was standing by the pile of sand where the work of the two gangs of laborers met, & observing the operations & the different classes of laborers, I asked one of the soldiers, who was employed in loading, to let me take his place for a few minutes, "so as to allow me to commit a little treason to the northern government." He handed me his

[8] A graduate of West Point, Colonel Trapier (1815–66) was engineer-in-chief of Morris Island and constructed the batteries at that site which were used to bombard Fort Sumter. During most of the war he commanded the Fourth District of South Carolina, holding the rank of brigadier general, Confederate States of America.

[531]

shovel, & I filled the wheel-barrow then waiting. I intended then to give back the shovel—but before I had done so, the next arriving laborer called out to ask me to fill his barrow also, which I did. He had at the same time accosted me by name, & offered his hand, which I shook, but without recognizing him, or suspecting that I had before & recently known him under very different guise & conditions. The soldier, like the others, had stripped off his coat & vest for labor, & seemed like an ordinary laborer as he was a private volunteer. He, seeing that I did not remember him, told me his name as he hurried off with his load, & the occasion on which we had before met. He was Alex[ande]r Haskell, who had been the most prominent of the students of the University of S.C. at Columbia, in lately inviting & receiving me, & bestowing on me complimentary attentions. Very soon after, he graduated in the highest class, left college for his home, & entered & went into service in a newly raised company of volunteers. He is the son of Charles Haskell, one of the wealthy & most respected gentlemen of S.C.—& also grandson of Langdon Cheves . . . . Leaving this fort, we passed below & in rear of Fort Sumter to Cummings' Point, the nearest land to it, 1230 yards, or thereabout. Here was just commenced the work for a new sand-battery, to have mounted some heavy cannon & mortars, to batter & shell Fort Sumter from the rear, where the walls & defences are comparatively weak. Col. Trapier, formerly a U.S. engineer, who has charge of this structure, does not doubt the feasibility [1171] of its being used to compel the fort to surrender. We next walked along the sea beach to Fort Morris, where such good service was lately done in striking & turning back the "Star of the West." The only artillery force on that occasion (& the infantry could not act at all,) consisted of 40 cadets of the Military Academy, commanded by their officer & professor, Major [P. F.] Stevens, who is now a student of divinity, & intended soon to resign his military professorship, & be ordained to preach the gospel. He pointed all the seven guns which were fired. Two struck, & one of them passed through the steamer & the engine room. This little battery is so small & inconspicuous, that it is not distinguishable from the water side, unless by observing the muzzles of the three cannon—and I walked across the area, in the rear, & might not have known that I had been over a battery, if not noticing the cannon & the plank platform on which they stood on the carriages, & which is level with the sand bottom. There is no bank, except towards the sea. There is confidence entertained that this battery can prevent the passage of large vessels, along the neighboring main ship channel. But this channel can be closed (by sinking hulks,) & has been partly, so as to force all vessels to enter the port by Maffitt's channel, which passes close under the eastern shore of Sullivan's Island, & which passage can be perfectly commanded by a sand-battery which is about to be constructed, & which will be out of danger from the fire of Fort Sumter. The great risk of Fort Sumter being supplied & reinforced, is not by large vessels, but by boats sent from them in dark [1172] nights, when they may escape the vigilance of the guard boats of the Carolinians. We would next have called at old Fort Johnson, where there is another newly constructed sand-battery—but the high wind prevented. . . . The U.S. war steamer Brooklyn had entered the outer harbor yesterday, & was in sight of the garrison of Fort Morris. Its object, as inferred, was to aid the "Star of the West"—& learning that that vessel was not in the harbor, the Brooklyn drew off. It was seen, stationary yesterday afternoon off Cape Romain, 40 miles northeast of Charleston harbor. I incline to believe that there will be no further attempt to force the way to Fort Sumter, & no more firing, or war. Such was the infatuation of the northern people that all (both our foes & friends,) expected that the "Star of the West" would be permitted to reinforce Fort Sumter, without the least resistance. All the North, & the Federal administration, are astonished at the very different result. The determined resistance of S.C. & the rapid secession of other states, will teach all our enemies, if they can learn anything, that they can effect nothing by hostility. The Journal of Commerce, & other northern papers have already begun to advocate the yielding to the inevitable separation of the southern states.—Major Stevens, the commander of the Citadel boys in the late brush, & Capt. [J. P.] Thomas, second in command, & both professors of the Academy, returned with us in the steamer, [1173] from Fort Morris. . . .

*Jan. 14.* . . . Learned . . . that the Va legislature, much quicker than I had expected, had already called a Convention—but with the very bad provision of referring its action back to be ratified or rejected by the votes of the people. This will cause some weeks of additional delay. . . .

*Jan. 15.* The morning very foggy & damp. Left Charleston at 8 A.M. Passed by Kingstree, to go as much of the way as could be where I had free tickets of passage. . . . Crossed the Cape Fear river to Wilmington at 1.45 A.M.

*Jan. 16.* Reached Goldsboro at 6 A.M. (then raining,) & Weldon by 10.30 A.M. where had to wait to 1 P.M. for the regular time of the train to Petersburg. Had concluded that I was too sick to go to Richmond; & though much better this afternoon, stopped at Petersburg, (at 5 P.M.) for the night, & to get home as well as I can tomorrow. Also, I wish to consult with my son Edmund.

*Jan. 17.* . . . I went on the morning train of the Norfolk Rail Road to Disputanta, & there hired a buggy & driver to Beechwood. I arrived there by 10.30 A.M. . . . Edmund had gone to Ruthven to dine. So I followed him as soon as I could have a horse saddled. Found Julian's family all well. After telling & hearing the more interesting news on both sides, I proceeded to propose & discuss with Edmund, & with the aid of Julian's judgment, what I had in view. I proposed, & urged upon Edmund, that he should forthwith offer himself to his election district, (composed of [1175] the counties of Prince George & Surry,) as a candidate to represent them in the approaching convention, & as an avowed advocate to the secession of Va. I stated my reasons why a fit candidate, competent for the service, & of sound political principles, should be offered to the people, whether likely to succeed or not. I greatly preferred that Edmund should be the candidate—but [1176] that if he should finally refuse, as he was inclined to do at first, that *I* would assume the place, & incur what would be to me, the more serious & also more probable chances for defeat. Indeed the prospect of success is very small for either of us, but much less for me than for him, as both Julian & I thought. Edmund, like myself, has never sought nor cultivated general popularity, & his acquaintance is very limited even in his own county, & he is scarcely known personally by any in Surry. But, while his opinions favoring disunion, & in other political questions, are like mine, & never concealed, he has not made himself personally odious as I have done by having been notorious for the most unguarded & violent expressions of opinions, & the most unpopular, until recently, & which are only now growing into favor. There are hundreds, perhaps thousands, both of my personal acquaintances & those with whom I have never conversed personally, who while themselves blind worshippers of the Union, came to hate my opposite doctrine, & also to dislike me as the actual promulgator. Most of these persons have latterly come over to my disunion views, & perhaps, in many cases, have been (unknowingly) aided by my teachings. But while thus coming to concur with my opinions, they have not changed their former hostility to the teacher, to personal favor. In addition to the grounds for want of personal favor of [1177] both my son & myself, the county of Prince George, owing to its intimate connection with Petersburg, & the long established political ascendancy of certain demagogues (especially Tim[othy] Rives & F[rancis] E. Rives,)[9] there was here a stronger Douglas & Union support in the recent presidential election, & more prevalence of blind unionism, than perhaps in any other county of the lower country. It is doubtful whether even now there are not a majority opposed to the policy of secession—& all of whom of course would now oppose any secession candidate. Add[ed] to all these discouragements, there has been already announced in the newspapers a candidate for this district, in Matthew Rainey of this county, a popular, though ordinary man; & who is a secessionist, yet recommended to the public by his friends as being "conservative." Still, I urged the necessity for there being presented for the votes of the district a candidate of sound principles, & of ability for the place. After full discussion, & viewing the question in every known light, Edmund agreed to announce himself as a candidate, & will send the notice to the newspapers tomorrow. Saw, in the last Enquirer (15th,) that some friend or friends of mine in Hanover county, had recommended me to the people of that county, as their representative in the Convention. . . . Heard from Edmund some unexpected & very gratifying news. His intercourse, by writing, with Jane Ruffin had been renewed—or rather, had never been entirely ended—he had renewed his suit, &, on a visit to her, had been accepted. . . . May God grant that . . . this marriage may produce as much happiness to all parties, as ought to be the results of the good qualities & mutual regard of the two to be united.

*Jan. 18.* Another continued rainy day. My books, book-cases, harmonicon &c. had been sent for & brought from Marlbourne to Evelynton before I left home, & since, have been brought over the river, & put into my room. . . . Played on the harmonicon, the first time I think for 9 months for [1179] the least trial—& for nearly two years for any extent worth consideration. Found my performance very defective . . . . Wrote a letter to L. Q. Washington, of Washing-

---

[9] A planter, developer of internal improvements, and veteran state legislator, Francis Everod Rives (1792–1861) by this time had left the political wars behind him. He achieved his greatest prominence in the 1830's and 1840's as a two-term congressman and as mayor of Petersburg in 1847–48.

ton city, applauding his late resolutions, & procedure to maintain there southern principles, & urging co-operative action of the people of Washington with Va & Md, when seceding. . . .

*Jan. 19.* . . . Wrote an article of 6 pages, for the Southern Planter, on some of the peculiarities of the soils of Florida. Read in De Bow's Review for Jan. He has at last thought proper to quote a long passage from "Anticipations of the Future." Also in the last No. of Literary Messenger, the new editor, Dr. [George W.] Bagby, has given of that work a favorable notice, at some length. These are almost the first indications I have had that my book had not fallen dead from the press—neither denounced by enemies nor noticed by friends, if not unknown to all.

*Jan. 21.* Left home. Took the steamer off the Point. At City Pt., received the newspapers, from which I learned that Georgia had seceded on 19th. Vote of the Convention, for immediate secession, 208 to 89. This consummates & rounds the southern operation. Ga., as a key-stone, fills up, completes, & makes impregnable, the glorious southern arch, now extending from the Atlantic to the Mississippi. . . . Arrived at Richmond after 6 P.M. Went to the American Hotel. After tea, went to the Exchange, where saw & conversed with W. B. Newton, & some other acquaintances of the Legislature, & others. To bed early.

*Jan. 22.* Furnished my last written article (on Florida) to the Southern Planter. Offered another to the new editor (Dr. Bagby,) of the Literary Messenger. Subscribed for the latter work, because of the strong ground recently taken in it for the South. . . . After tea, went to the Exchange, & saw & conversed with many persons. Among them, Ex. President Tyler, who had just arrived. He is on his way to Washington, to act as Commissioner of Va, to confer with the President.

*Jan. 23.* Left Richmond at 6 A.M. to take passage by the steamer. Landed on Coggin's Point, after a slow passage, [1182] before noon. . . . I came home heartily disgusted with the dilatory & unreliable procedure of the Va. legislature, in regard to the great question before us. Except the calling a Convention, every thing else is calculated to cause delay of action, & distrust of the southern sentiment of the legislature, & of the state.

*Jan. 24.* . . . A very dull day. . . . Played on the harmonicon, as I do now every night, to recover something of my former skill, lost or impaired for want of practice. Read part of Senator Benjamin's late & excellent speech, & the Rev. Dr. [Benjamin M.] Palmer's admirable & eloquent sermon, delivered at N.O. on the Fast Day, & in reference to the southern question & movement.[10]

*Jan. 25.* . . . Edmund . . . went to Cabin Point to attend a called meeting of the two counties, Surry & Prince George, to nominate a candidate for the Convention. [1183] Late at night, Thomas Cocke came by, from the meeting, to inform us of the proceedings. First, all divided into two separate meetings, more than 70 for immediate secession, & the others . . . for union. The former gave a majority of votes for Edmund Ruffin jr., in which nomination all the minority of that portion concurred. The smaller union meeting nominated Tim. Rives, the thorough demagogue & long-established popular leader in this county. So the contest will be between these two, the one representing the opinions of those for immediate secession, & the other of those for submission, & of all shades of opinion in favor of delay of secession.—A dull day. No news, & nothing to read. Finished another communication on Florida (No. II,) for Southern Planter.

*Jan. 28.* The mail brought the joyful news that Louisiana had seceded . . . . No report yet, which I have anxiously been looking for, of the taking of Fort Sumter, or Fort Pickens, from the Federal troops holding them. An address from the two U.S. Senators from Va, & eight of the Representatives, appears today, which ought to forward and strengthen the secession party in this state.[11] The called public meeting in Hanover, on 22nd, nominated, by a majority of votes, as the secession candidate for the Convention, Col. G. W. Richardson, whig & union advocate until recently, & now for immediate secession. The strongest union or submission candidate opposed, & voted for by all for submission or delay, was Nelson, the late representative of the county, & a bigotted [*sic*] democrat. This state of things, & the choice made, is to me gratifying indication of the present disregard of the old party names & divisions.—Mr. Edward [1185] A. Marks called in the afternoon, & gave us more full

---

[10] Born in Charleston, Benjamin Morgan Palmer (1818–1902) graduated from Columbia Theological Seminary in South Carolina and became one of the most prominent Presbyterian clergymen in the South. In 1856 he assumed the pastorate of the First Presbyterian Church in New Orleans.

[11] Charging that because of Republican intransigence there was no hope for compromise in Congress, the Virginia representatives urged "prompt and decided action" by the state convention to avert civil war and to preserve "the hope of reconstructing a Union already dissolved."

accounts of the late meeting in Cabin Point. Though a whig, & until lately a unionist, he is now hearty for secession, & for Edmund's election. However, he thinks the issue doubtful, fearing that the union sentiment prevails in Surry, as Tim. Rives' popularity does in Prince George.

*Jan. 29.* . . . At night, Edmund returned from his electioneering trip, having attended & spoken at public meetings on three several days. . . . The last Enquirer contained one of the articles I wrote from Tallahassee . . . . The other was not received from the mail. Also two out of three telegraphic dispatches which I sent from Tallahassee, & paid for at rates of incredible extortion, failed to be received. I regret the loss of this communication. It was a zealous appeal to Va not to delay following the example of the more southern seceding states until after March 4th.

*Jan. 30.* . . . The mail. No special reports of actual operations, but all general reports encouraging for the secession movement. Favorable reports from N.W. Va, from Texas, Tennessee & Kentucky. I have been anxiously hoping & somewhat expecting, for several mails, to [1186] hear of the conquest of Fort Pickens at Pensacola, or Fort Sumter, or both. The former, with more than 200 soldiers has been for some time blockaded by more than 2000 volunteers of Florida & Alabama, & reinforcements on their march. Also, the U.S. war steamer Brooklyn is on its voyage there, with two companies of artillery to reinforce Fort Pickens. On its arrival, fighting must take place. The last commissioner [1187] (Col. I. Hayne) sent by S.C. to Washington, has returned, & his mission has been fruitless, unless it was designed to postpone active hostilities, & gain time for better preparation to attack Fort Sumter. The possession of these two forts, garrisoned by the soldiers of the federal power, is all-important to the South.

*Jan. 31.* . . . The present political condition of this country, in regard to the secession of some of the States, is very strange, & very different from all anticipations of such events, including my own, though I had so long thought & argued in advance on the subject. I had not expected war between the old government & the seceded states, as a necessary or even probable result, provided all the southern states should secede at once, or even 6 or 8 of the more southern states, with the early sympathy & final concurrence of the remaining & more northern slaveholding states. But I had certainly also expected, in the other contingency, of one only, or a few states

[538]

seceding, that the first & immediate action of the federal government (denying the right of secession,) would be to [1188] attempt the coercion & conquest of the seceded portion by prompt & vigorous military attack. Instead of this, no such attempt has yet been made, & nothing beyond the very partial & insufficient reinforcing or strengthening three only of the many forts in the seceded & other southern states. The only acts of military hostility, on both sides, have been the seizures or holding possession of these forts. And the only one of all these acts of the federal government which improved its condition, was the occupation of Fort Sumter, effected by a gross & shameful breach of faith, truth, & honor, by President Buchanan. The imbecility of the executive department, added to the want of funds & means by the federal government, have prevented any thing being done to coerce the seceded states. This impunity from military attack must now continue to the southern states until the 4th of March, when the new abolition administration, of the northern sectional party will begin, & by which, if before in power, the attempt to coerce the first seceded states would certainly have been made. But the actual inter-regnum of federal power, continuing from Nov. 6th, the day of the election of Lincoln, to the 4th of next March, when he will be inaugurated President, has given four months [1189] of unforeseen & almost undisturbed time for action for the seceding states. Thus, there has been avoided, what I certainly counted upon, the interregnum of lawful power, or transition state of disorder, or illegal rule & perhaps of revolutionary anarchy, expected to attend the change of government of every separately seceding state, & of all, from the rule of the old to that of the new confederacy. On the contrary there has been nothing of this kind. Neither of the seceding states has had to resort to any revolutionary or even hasty action. . . . Each of the six seceded states by its legally called legislature, called a convention, & that convention deliberately & formally declared the secession of the state. The general convention of the seceded states, composed of members appointed by the several state conventions, will meet at Montgomery, on Feby 4th, & there [1190] without hindrance, adopt a provisional constitution for the new Southern Confederacy. This provisional constitution, as now seems indicated, will be the existing federal constitution, with as few changes as will serve for the changed circumstances.

The governors of Texas & Maryland both refused to call their legislatures. Therefore it was done by the popular will, & general agreement, in Texas—& the like course may be taken in Maryland. In Va, as elsewhere, the policy of the submissionists was to induce delay of action, by every pretext, in the hope of thus preventing all action for secession. Their success in this policy, though conventions are called in Va & in N.C. & some other states, may make the consummation of the consequent acts of secession too late for March 4th. If so, I trust that the conventions will throw off the shackles intended to cripple or confine their proper power, & disregard forms to secure substance, & the known will of their constituents. If these delays could prevent any other states seceding before the abolition administration shall possess & wield all the power of the present federal government, there is no doubt of that government, in its madness, making war on the 6 seceded states, & attempting, however hopelessly, to crush them by force of arms. But if Va would, soon enough for the later secession of Md. & other remaining states, secede from the present union, all the other border slaveholding [1191] states, (except Delaware perhaps,) would speedily follow. And when the 4th of March arrived, the new northern administration would find 13 or 14, or possibly 15 states seceded, & united in a new Southern Confederacy, with regular federal government everywhere established & in operation. Under such circumstances, it would be a degree of folly or infatuation altogether inconceivable, for the northern section to attempt the coercion & conquest of [the] south by war. No offensive war would then be attempted. Even if collisions should have previously occurred in capturing Fort Sumter & Fort Pickens, & hundreds of men had been slain, this would not bring war, if these forts were so taken, or subsequently surrendered to the southern states. Thus, it is of vital importance to the maintenance of peace, that the secession of Va. shall be as early as can be. If Va. (as of any other adjacent or border slaveholding states,) could remain attached to & governed by the Northern section & party, after 6 or 8 or more southern states had withdrawn their aid in the Federal Union & Congress, the consequences would be most disastrous to such remaining states. The abolition states would then be numerous enough in the diminished northern confederacy, to make up three-fourths of the whole—& so could abolish slavery by altering the federal constitution according to its own required conditions. Can any submissionist of good sense among us, doubt that this would be done? That this party would not destroy the institution of negro slavery, & property in slaves, when [1192] able to do so legally & constitutionally, when it has been striving to effect these objects for forty years, in disregard of law & constitution? Thus, by the emancipation of its slaves, (after their being previously excluded from sale in the seceded states, of course,) Va would be impoverished, & degraded socially & politically. But in addition to fully sharing in all the economical, social, & political evils & dangers of Va., Md, if remaining to the North, when all the states south had seceded, would suffer ruin to its commerce. A large portion of the back-country, supplying trade to Baltimore, is in Va. Further, no trade of Md, either to east or west, can pass out of Md, except through the territory of Va—which passages would of course be shut, if these states severally made portions of hostile confederacies. Therefore, the conforming of Md to the course of Va. is absolutely certain. If Va shall secede by Feby 20th, Md, whether with or without legal forms, must speedily follow. And if both these acts of secession occur before March, the District of Columbia will go with these states, & remain an integral portion of the slaveholding states & the Southern Confederacy. Lincoln, in that case, would not dare to hold his government in Washington, even if not opposed, [1193] & no war existing. And if he did, every functionary of the northern government, thus surrounded by southern territory, would be a hostage virtually given to the southern power, & the northern government, while so located, would be effectually bound to keep the peace, & to its good behavior. But if even a nominal state of hostilities then existed (as now,) or if the occurrence of actual war was merely feared, & deemed probable, the northern government would not be maintained for a week in Washington. Though the delay recently to attack Fort Sumter, & [1194] still longer delay to storm Fort Pickens, have seemed to me at first unaccountable, there is now sufficient reason for such policy of inactivity in the near approaching election (on the 4th inst.) of the Va Convention, & its assembling, (on the 13th.) If the elections, even in advance of the meeting of the Convention, shall clearly indicate that a decided majority of the members are for secession, as is most probable, then the other border states will begin to move to secede with Va—and there will be no war, nor attempt of the northern section to coerce the already seceded states. This is a sufficient reason, operating lately & now, for the southern authorities to continue inactive, & to avoid shedding blood, unless attempts are made to strengthen or reinforce the garrisons in the besieged forts. But should the election of members show that Va will refuse to secede, or leave its course very doubtful, then it will be good policy in that respect, as well as demanded by general considerations, that the continued possession of these forts by a hostile power shall no longer be submitted to. The shedding of blood then, in defence of the undoubted right of the Southern states to their soil & waters, will serve to change many voters in the hesitating states, [1195] from the submission or procrastinating ranks, to the zealous for immediate secession. If I could direct the course of things, I would, on these grounds, have no fighting, unless necessary to prevent reinforcing the forts, until the character of the Va Convention shall be ascertained—nor then, if its action will be certainly for secession. But to attack these forts as vigorously as possible, as soon as it may be known that the disposition of this Convention is for submission or delay. The commencement of open war between the federal or northern power & the seceded states will quickly bring the remaining southern states to side with the seceded & attacked states.

*February 1.* . . . No news of importance of the secession movement. Nothing yet heard of the attempt to reinforce Forts Sumter & Pickens, nor of the Brooklyn sent with reinforcements. . . . The S.Ca. commissioner has *not* returned from Washington. I cannot conceive any good reason for his being sent, or remaining there—unless it was desired to gain time for preparing to attack Fort Sumter.

*Feb. 3.* Sunday. Steady slow rain until 2 P.M. Afterwards ceased, & Edmund set out for the outer part of the county, to attend tomorrow morning the meeting for a precinct election. . . . Tomorrow, the election day for the Va Convention, will be a momentous epoch. On the choice of the majority of voters, either for candidates who will go for submission (or delay, which is equivalent,) or for secession, will depend not only the policy in these respects of Va, but of all the neighboring slave-holding states—and, consequently, whether there will be peace or war between the northern & southern sections of the former United States of America. [1196]

*Feb. 4.* This morning snowing fast, & the earth soon well covered. I should have gone to the election even in this worst condition of weather—but the snowing ceased before we set out, in the carriage, at 10 A.M. Did not remain longer than to give my vote, at the polls of the precinct, & returned home. Early in the afternoon, Edmund returned. From the partial returns from two precincts, & the full vote of one other, out of the six, we have little doubt of Edmund being defeated, & by a larger majority than even he had expected. Thus demagogueism & submission triumph. But it is probable that an auxiliary cause of his failure is my son's inheriting from me some of the popular aversion, or dislike, which I have always succeeded in acquiring wherever I have resided, & especially of the lower & meaner class of those who by our miserable constitution have the right of suffrage, & who are numerous enough, being led & arrayed by some demagogue, to carry elections in almost every county. As to myself, while I have received evidences of very high appreciation, respect, & applause, from strangers, & far from my home, at home, & in my own state, & more especially in my own neighborhood, I have met with, from [1197] much the greater number, slight, neglect, if not actual enmity. If some of my imputed sins were not visited on my son, all the arts of the demagogue in his opponent, could scarcely have so greatly overcome his superior moral & intellectual worth, and also his better cause.—This day has been elected the Convention, which I trust will be compelled by political events & prospects, even if not inclined, to withdraw Va from the existing union with the North—& in so doing cause to follow all the other remaining slaveholding states. On this day also was to assemble at Montgomery the Congress of delegates from all the seceding states, to adopt a provisional government for the Southern Confederacy. And also on this day was to meet the "Peace Congress" at Washington, invited by Va. to be formed of delegates from all the states that will send. This will be a miserable failure of a hopeless effort for compromise—as its authors well knew, & only advocated the measure to cause delay of secession action, as the best means to induce submission to the North.

*Feb. 5.* Our friend & neighbor, E. A. Marks, came in the forenoon, & gave such reports already learned of the election as to make it certain that Edmund has been defeated, & by a much larger majority than even he had expected. . . . Began to read (second time,) [Louis Adolphe] Thiers' "History of the French Revolution."

*Feb. 6.* . . . The mail brought no news, except the reports, either partial or complete, of many of the elections of the nearest towns & counties. So far, there appears to be a large majority of Union candidates elected.—Today Edmund sets out for Alamance—to be absent a week.

*Feb. 8.* Very cold, but clear.—The mail. Returns of the elections for the Va Convention as yet mostly incomplete. But enough is certain to show that the open & avowed immediate secessionists have been successful in but few cases. One paper says that there have not been 30 of such candidates elected, & another says not 12. Even Willoughby Newton, on that ground, has been beaten by a very ordinary union or delay competitor, & by a large majority. My son has been beaten by nearly 400 majority. But this county, for its devotion to its long ruling demagogue well deserves to be called "Tim. Rives' Tail." Still, the result is by no means so bad, or so ominous of defeat to the secession cause, as these elections would intimate. For even the submissionists, & the heretofore union-worshippers, (with a few exceptions, like [John M.] Botts & his "tail"—which by the way could not prevent his defeat—) have some limit to the extent of their forbearance. And if there shall be no yielding, or giving of new guaranties, by the black republican party, there will be but few of the members of the convention, though elected as "union men," "conservatives," or professing to try & wait for every remedy before breaking the union, who will not either be ready, or otherwise be forced, to resort to secession. The great cause for fear is the delay, in waiting for conciliatory action of the North, which will not come from the majorities, though already clamorously urged by the minorities of sundry northern states. No abolition [1201] party, or prominent leader, in any state, has yet offered to abate anything of their previous demands, or to offer any security to the south. They will view the elections of Va. as declaring for the union without conditions, & as a declaration of submission to the abolition power, by Va. & all the remaining states that will certainly stand or move with Va. In this view, the Governor of Pennsylvania very properly ordered a salute of 34 guns to be fired, in rejoicing for the result of the elections in Va. I trust that an indirect & great benefit of these elections will be to confirm the resolution & "harden the hearts" of the abolition leaders, so that they will persevere in their policy of yielding nothing to the South. And for the quicker & more evident showing of this fixed policy, this otherwise useless & ridiculous "Peace Convention," now in session at Washington, may be of great service to forward the completion of secession by the remaining border states. To this convention proposed by the Va legislature, & to which all the states were invited to send members, to confer about terms of compromise & security, only 6 or 7 northern states have as yet sent delegates. If all were to send them, nothing would be done to secure southern rights. If this issue is made evident, & the convention breaks up without effecting anything, (which I deem almost certain,) then Va will be forced, & is already pledged by the declaration of her legislature, to unite with the South. If this can only be done early enough, or for Va & Md. to secede before March 4th.! But I now fear that that is impossible. Even without any expectation of this event, the [1202] abolitionists have suspected that there was a plot on foot to oppose the inauguration of Lincoln by armed force. Acting under this impression & influence, Lieut. Gen. Scott, who now acts as a military dictator, has brought regular troops to garrison Washington, & to defend the abolition administration. He already has there about 1000 regulars, including artillery & cavalry, and volunteer militia of the city are embodied, drilled, & their loyalty strengthened by a new & special oath of obedience. In the mean time the madness of the abolition leaders & the blind obedience of their followers indicate the doomed destruction of the party. In this time of disruption of the union, of states following each other rapidly in secession, & with the prospect of nearly half the states being thus taken away, & much more than half of all the revenue of the former union, Congress is using the withdrawal of the southern representatives & their opposition, to pass through measures which will rouse new opposition & enmity of the remaining southern states, & also of England & France, whom it should now be especially desirable to conciliate. A bill has passed both houses of Congress to construct not only one, but three railroads to the Pacific ocean—which scheme will probably require two or three hundred millions to complete, & which cannot be completed before the Pacific states will have seceded, & the great object [1203] of the connection by rail-roads will have been frustrated. Another measure is the authorising another loan, for $25,000,000, required immediately for the incoming administration. Another is the greatly increasing the protecting duties, & the stringency & burden of the tariff law, which will equally offend or exasperate European commercial powers, & any southern states if remaining in union with the North. And all these measures are begun when the federal treasury is almost bankrupt, & there is not either land or naval force at command of the federal government to protect its forts in the southern states, or to enforce its threats, or protect itself from insult! This madness of the dominant party is precisely what I would wish for its destruction. —The Convention of Texas also has declared for secession, by a nearly unanimous vote. But as that body was assembled informally, (because Gov. Houston refused to concur,) its decision has been referred to the popular vote for ratification—which no doubt will be accorded.—The English papers afford evidence of a strong "cotton fright" having been produced in that country, by the secession movement here. They foolishly suppose that the South will be afflicted with civil war, & servile insurrection, to such extent as seriously to lessen cultivation, & the production of cotton, & so deprive England of the indispensable supply for her manufacturing operations. This fear is groundless & absurd. But it serves a good purpose, in indicating clearly that there is no danger of the anti-slavery fanaticism of England inducing the government or people to favor the North, when its great interest is inseparably connected [1204] with & dependent upon the production & unobstructed transportation of cotton, & which the seceded states only can supply for England's great demand. It has been counted on by the abolitionists, & also by many timid southerners, that in the event of separation of the northern & southern states, the anti-slavery fanaticism of England would induce its government to side with the North, & use the opportunity to destroy negro slavery in the South. I have never believed that there was any danger of England's fanaticism going so far, when the necessary means would crush England's greatest interest. But besides this general ground of self-interest—or even if it did not have half its actual operation—the northern manufacturing interest, always in rivalship & opposed to that of England, is now about to put the latter under still greater difficulties than before, & to shut out English commodities, as much as possible, by additional protective or prohibitory duties. If this prohibitory policy shall be met by the Southern Confederacy adopting the policy of either very low duties on imports, & solely for revenue, or entirely free trade with friendly nations which would reciprocate such favors, this will complete the making of every European commercial [1205] country deeply interested in the commercial [wel]fare, (& of course political & general welfare,) of the [South]ern Confederacy; & removing all such interest in [the] welfare of the northern states. Therefore I earnestly wish for the passage of the most oppressive tariff law by the Northern party—& also for the keeping up the "cotton fright" in Europe, on its absurd & impossible grounds, which could only be supposed in the most perfect ignorance of the conditions of the southern states. But this utter ignorance is the result of Europeans deriving all their information of the whole United States, from northern newspapers, books, or persons. Seen through such false mediums, foreigners have good reason to suppose that the south is as unable to maintain, as to justify its quarrel with the North.

*Feb. 9.* . . . About sunset, there arrived in a buggy, with two horses & a servant, a young man who, on entering, introduced himself as Mr. Chamliss, & soon asked for Miss Eliza Cocke. I afterwards learned that he was but slightly acquainted with her, & with no member of this family—&, as we judged, used that acquaintance as a pretext to gain access to this house. He is a noted sponger, or given to making long visits where his company is not wanted, & also for [1206] [his ef]forts to marry advantageously, & his successively an[noy]ing different young ladies with his attentions or ad[d]resses. He has before attempted in vain to be introduced to Nanny, & now he makes this move for that purpose, & to get another comfortable house to make long visits to. I, in place of the absent master, shall be merely coldly polite to him, & only as a guest myself. . . .

*Feb. 10.* Sunday. All went to Church. We had Mr. Chamliss' trunk put on his buggy, as if supposing it a matter of course. Yet, after the service, he drove on after the carriage, & I have no question designed to return with the family. But if so, I prevented it, very politely. I returned on horseback, & managed to be just ahead of his buggy before our private road turned off from the public road. After our carriage had turned off, & as I was about turning off, I looked back to Mr. Chamliss, without altering my gait, & made a bow to him. He continued on, & I fear that in getting rid of him, I inflicted his company on our poor parson. From what I heard today of Mr. Chamliss' conduct, he must have a touch either [1207] of insanity or idiotcy [*sic*].

*Feb. 11.* . . . The mail brought me two letters from Mildred—the last one written merely to enclose a wood-engraved likeness of me, from the photograph taken in Charleston—which it seems was published in a Northern illustrated paper.[12] It is a coarse & bad portrait.—The news. The "Peace Congress" has done nothing as yet, but to appoint a Committee. The Congress at Montgomery has adopted the Constitution of the U.S., with a few necessary changes only, as the form of provisional government of the Southern Confederacy. . . . The U.S. Arsenal at Little Rock (the state capital,) has been taken possession of by authority of the governor of Arkansas. This

---

[12] *Frank Leslie's Illustrated Newspaper.*

sufficiently indicates the disposition of that state for secession.—The S.C. Commissioner at Washington has returned home. A portion of the southern volunteer force investing Fort Pickens has been sent home. Major Anderson, though blockaded in Fort Sumter, &, as supposed, to be starved into surrender, has latterly been allowed to contract for, & receive regularly from Charleston, fresh meats & vegetables, for the [1208] garrison, at discretion. I cannot understand these things, unless there is another secret understanding with President Buchanan. He ought not to be again trusted. . . .

*Feb. 12.* . . . The abolition governor of Pennsylvania had a national salute, thirty four guns, fired in *honor* of the elections for the Convention in Va.—& the like was done in several different parts of the state of New York. This marked applause offered by the abolitionists & the north, ought to cover with shame the union savers & majority in the recent election by the state.—Read the able speech of Jefferson Davis, on the present crisis, delivered in the Senate of U.S. on Jan 10, 1861. [End of MS Volume 6—p. 1209]

*Feb. 13.* . . . The mail brought much interesting information. The provisional constitution & acting government of the "Confederated States of North America," have been established, & are in operation. . . . The constitution of the United States has been adopted for the provisional government, (whose power is limited to one year,) with only a few changes or additions, such as are required by the changes of subjects & locality. Among these changes, are, the recognition of the right of state secession & the constitutional prohibition of the African slave trade. The Congress next elected (unanimously,) Jefferson Davis of Miss. provisional President of the "Confederated States," & Alexander H. Stephens of Ga. Vice-President. It may be inferred that every department of the new government will next & speedily be supplied with officers & functionaries, & that the provisional government will very soon be in full operation. The expected assaults on the blockaded Forts Sumter & Pickens, not having been made previously, will of course now be delayed for [1210] the direction of the federal administration, to whose authority the conduct of war operations belong. The negotiation of S.C. with President Buchanan, for the surrender of Fort Sumter had failed, & the Commissioner, [Isaac] Hayne, had just returned to Charleston. Actual operations at Fort Pickens had been previously suspended, & part of the blockading volunteer force had been discharged. At Charleston, everything seems to be ready, (or very nearly so,) for the assault of Fort Sumter, should it be necessary.—The "Peace Congress" has done nothing as yet, except to refer their business to a Committee. 20 states only are represented by deputies, & those of one other state only looked for. It is reported that a plan of adjustment will be agreed to by the Convention, & recommended as an amendment to the Constitution. I do not believe that such discordant parties can agree to any plan satisfactory to both. But even if this can be, & the Convention even nearly unanimous, there can be no possibility of its being adopted by two-thirds of Congress & three-fourths of the states, both of which are required to amend the federal constitution. The representatives of 6 states have already left the Congress—(& those of two more must soon follow—) but these states are still claimed by the northern & federal power to belong to the Union, & their representatives therefore must be counted in fixing the quorum of Congress. To have two-thirds of both houses, counting all these absentees [1211] as members, will require nearly the unanimous votes of all the still remaining members. And, in like manner, if counting as states of the federal Union, (as the ruling powers will insist upon,) the seceded states, it will require nearly all the still united states to make up the necessary votes of three-fourths of all. Therefore, it is absurd to expect, (if any of the contrivers were so foolish as to expect,) any possible results to save the Union by constitutional amendments, on the recommendation of this "Peace Congress." Its time spent in discussions will serve however to cause delay of action, & to afford excuses for delay for all other southern public men who desire to preserve the Union by submission to the North.—Recent occurrences have served to place the government & dominant party of New York, in a collision with the South, in as contemptible a position as was the federal administration in the vain attempt to reinforce Fort Sumter. 28 cases, containing 950 muskets &c. had been ordered from the north by private individuals in Ga. & Ala. & were shipped at New York for Savannah. The city police, under orders from Governor [Edwin D.] Morgan, (as it now appears,) seized & retained these arms, as contraband of war. As soon as the facts were learned, Gov. Brown of Ga. sent by telegraphic dispatch to the Governor of N.Y. to demand the delivery of the arms so seized. Gov. Morgan answered that he had ordered the seizure & detention [1212] of the arms because Ga. was making war on the U.S., & that he was bound by his oath to support the constitution of the U.S. to do so. Gov. Brown immediately ordered, as reprisal, the seizing of all the N.Y. vessels then in the port of Savannah, which was done, to be held as security for the restoration of the arms. This seizure (of 5 vessels,) was immediately communicated by the commanders to their employers, & by them to Gov. Morgan, who then, without an hour's delay, ordered the delivery of the arms to the agent, before authorized by Ga. to receive & transmit them. Upon this prompt restoration being communicated to the Governor of Ga. he forthwith ordered the release of the N.Y. vessels. There never was a negotiation between different governments, on a disputed & difficult question of right, so speedily carried through & settled. . . . The bill has been enacted to borrow $25,000,000 for the northern federal government—if capitalists will lend, which is doubtful, unless at enormous discount. The credit of the government now stands lower than at any time since 1814. The treasury being almost bankrupt adds another & an unexpected difficulty to any attempt to conquer the seceded states.

*Feb. 14.* The newspapers, of yesterday's mail, were not all read, or looked through, before 11. Afterwards, a dull time, with other reading of books for the second or third time. Such time I am latterly dividing between Thiers, & the attractive articles of the "Living Age." As soon as finishing the reading of the newspapers of one mail, I begin to long for the arrival of another supply. The interest I feel for political affairs, & the Southern Confederation, absorbs every other.

*Feb. 15.* Nothing more heard of expected political events. The Convention of Va has spent its first two days in but partially organizing—taking as much time to elect door-keepers (for their individual emolument,) as the Convention of S.C. used to dissolve the Union. . . . The debates of the Convention of the "Confederated States," are secret, & nothing heard except final decisions. The construction of a permanent constitution has been referred to a Committee. It is understood that it will be the policy to adopt a tariff of low duties, say of 10 percent, on imports. This I highly approve. While this low rate, in times of peace, will supply abundant revenue for the new federal government, it will also serve to enlist the interest of European governments in favor of the seceded states, to apply both persuasive & coercive pressure on the remaining slaveholding states to unite with the seceded—& to greatly damage the commercial, manufacturing, & navigation interests of the abolition [1215] states. This last will occur, even if they refrain from actual hostile action, & are treated as all other friendly nations. But if making war, & so ex-

cluded from all benefits of southern trade, & the northern shipping
exposed to the depredations of hundreds of privateers authorised by
the Southern Confederate States, which have almost no ships on the
ocean, & therefore cannot be much hurt by hostile privateers, the
ruin of the North will be very probable. Read a long & forcible letter
of Mr. Spratt's, addressed to Judge J. Perkins (in the Mercury,) on
the impolicy of the recent act of the Southern Convention, in making the prohibition of the African slave trade a *constitutional* provision of the new government.—The Southern Convention without
any previous electioneering, or much prior deliberation, & without
difficulty or opposition, elected a President & Vice-President, who,
for intellectual ability & moral worth are superior to any President
& Vice-President, elected together, of the United States since Madison's administration. Yet, in latter times, it has put the whole people
of the U.S. in turmoil for a year or more, & has cost millions of dollars expended, directly or indirectly, & mostly corruptly, to select
persons for those offices, & the choice always made of corrupt or incapable men. Would that this experience, of both sides, could induce
the so altering the mode of election by the Southern Confederacy as
to get rid of the baleful [1216] influence of universal suffrage &
popular election in these high offices!

*Feb. 18.* The mail brought but few papers, & none from Richmond
or New York. The "Peace Congress" at Washington has for some
days been doing nothing, waiting for its committee to prepare &
report a plan of compromise & adjustment. The Va. Convention, at
Richmond, has been, since its meeting, doing nothing, waiting for
the action of the "Peace Congress," & to know whether the North
will grant such terms as even the union & submission men of Va will
accept. The Congress of the Southern Confederacy, at Montgomery,
has been [1217] doing many & most important things, in adopting a
federal constitution & fixing on the policy of the new government.
Still, it has been held back from acting, & from publishing its discussions on the relations with the "United States," because also
waiting for the action of the Va Convention, & from that to infer
what will be the action as to secession or otherwise, of Va & all the
other border slaveholding states. But I now trust that all these delays, especially so injurious to our cause & objects at this time, so
near to March 4th, will now soon end, as their first cause is at an
end. It is understood that the committee has agreed upon, & reported, a plan which is substantially the same with that offered in

the resolutions of Crittenden. This, even if adopted, & made part of the Constitution, is of but little worth for reparation or security to the slaveholding states, &, as such, scarcely worth their acceptance, & still less as compensation for remaining in the Union, & subject to all other assaults from the antislavery party, & northern states, now doubled in relative strength, by the secession of 7 southern states. But, delusive & nugatory as would be these proposed amendments, for securing & conciliating the south, it is probable that they cannot pass in the "Peace Convention," as the representatives of antislavery states therein have a large majority—(of 12 states, to 8 only from slaveholding states.) If however, the Convention *should* sanction the plan, & recommend it for adoption in the constitution, there [1218] can be no possible chance for a ratification by the votes of two-thirds of the members of both houses of Congress, . . . & three-fourths of all the states . . . . The adoption of *any* plan of adjustment, which will be yielded by the fanatical & dominant North, & accepted as satisfactory even by the most submissive sentiment of the border South, is clearly impossible. But it is not more impossible than must have been foreseen at first by the advocates & constructors of this "Peace Convention," whose only expected & designed effect was to cause delay, & in the time of delay, to permit Lincoln's administration to be inaugurated quietly, before more secessions of states could be in progress, & while all military & other hostile operations of the seceded states would be held in abeyance, for the playing out of this political farce. Now, there certainly will be no time for the action of the "Peace Convention," of the Congress of the United States, & subsequently of the Va Convention, before the 4th of March—& so will be lost the great measure of general secession of the border states before that time, & the consequent perfect security & peace of the South. This is greatly to be deplored. But, on the other hand, this triumph of the unionists & submissionists will doubtless operate to encourage the North [1219] to carry out its previously designed plan of policy, dictated by anti-slavery fanaticism, & the avowal of that policy, indicated in the rejection of the plan for adjustment, will serve as well, though later, to compel the remaining southern states to follow in the act of secession. If the apparent submission of the border states shall be understood in their agreeing to receive this pitiful & delusive plan of adjustment, then the North will try war against the seceded states. The attempt at military invasion or naval coercion of the seceded states, with the first bloodshed, will serve to make other states secede, & soon the whole south to be arrayed together under the new Confederated States Government. Or, even if possible without resorting to war, the North, now all powerful in Congress, will so abuse its power & show its designed operation on the remaining southern states, as to drive them to seek their proper confederates. And we already have affor[d]ed in Lincoln's recent public declarations, that the incoming administration will abate nothing of the previous plan & policy of the party, to conciliate the South, or to avoid the attempt of military coercion. Lincoln has set out on his leisurely triumphal progress to Washington, delivering speeches in every town the trains pass through. These speeches indicate no depth of thought, or statesmanlike knowledge —but enough of party feeling, & of northern blindness & fanaticism, to show clearly that *he* means to yield nothing of the principles [1217][13] or the previous policy of his party. Among sundry other as narrow & objectionable views thus exhibited, he has declared that the South had nothing to complain of—that the majority ought & must always rule the minority—& that, as President, he must "enforce the laws," in enforcing the collection of revenue in the seceded states, which he stupidly considers, with President Buchanan, *not* to be offensive hostility, or military coercion. Of course, if he & his party act up to these views, they will bring about complete secession within a few months. But, even should it be so, & the new organization be effected safely, & maintained in peace, it will still be ever to be lamented that any of the southern states should have remained even for a day under the rule of Lincoln & his abolition party.—The people of Tennessee are so generally disposed to submission, that in the recent elections for a state convention, there were only two secessionists elected in the state, & the majority of votes against secession amounted to 50,000—& a smaller but large majority against assembling a convention—that question having been referred to the popular vote.

*Feb. 19. . . .* In the forenoon, I began to arrange my letters received since the last job of the kind, & to the end of 1860, so as to stitch them together for reference & preservation—keeping separate [1218], as always heretofore, the letters of members of my family, from others. . . . I did not begin to preserve my letters, (except very few, & for special reason,) until in latter years. I regret much that I had not pursued my present course of preserving & thus ar-

---

[13] Misnumbered by diarist. Should be page 1220.

ranging most that have since been addressed to me. But even now, as formerly, I do not preserve copies of my own letters, & very rarely have made a copy of any, unless when necessary to retain one for business or other reasons. Thus, I suppose there are very few of my own letters in existence . . . .

*Feb. 20.* Continued to arrange letters for some hours, & to prepare them for being stitched & covered. Reading as before until the mail arrived—which though unusually full, (in delayed papers,) contained but little news. The President of the Southern Confederacy was inaugurated on the 18th., & the Provisional government is now in power & operation. The Committee of the Peace Conference has reported to it a plan, which is nearly that of Crittenden's, but worse for the South. In the committee, three members only voted against it—Judge Thos. Ruffin, J. A. Seddon, & Gen. [Alexander W.] Doniphan,[14] representing respectively the delegations of N.C., Va, & Mo. Nothing done by the Conference, except to continue delay of action, which is the object of the southern union-worshippers & submissionists, as well as of the Northern abolitionists.—Read papers, & in last No. of De Bow's Review, until 9 P.M.—when, as usual, I retired to my own room to kill another hour, or longer, in writing, or reading, & music. [1222]

*Feb. 21.* I was surprised today to find . . . [a favorable review of *Anticipations of the Future*] in a long & well written letter of a Richmond correspondent of the N.Y. Herald. I am obliged to the unknown writer for his favorable opinion, as expressed, of my book, & its estimation.[15] The only objection is that I fear there is not the least foundation for its having been so applauded, or even noticed by any portion of the southern public. It is to me a mortifying truth, that, instead of being thus welcomed, my book has been scarcely noticed, & its very existence seems to be ignored by the public, even in the more southern states, where, if no where else, I expected notice & approval. . . . [1223]

*Feb. 22.* . . . The mail—still nothing done by the Peace Conference —not even to consider the report by its committee. It seems plain to

---

[14] A veteran of the Mexican War and at this time a major general in command of the Missouri militia, Alexander William Doniphan (1808–87) was one of the leading criminal lawyers in his state.

[15] "This book," commented the reviewer, "bids fair to create a furor in the South, similar to that caused at the North by the notorious Helper book. The work displays considerable ability, and its predictions are not at all inconsistent with the principles of the black republican party."

me that the northern abolitionists & the southern submissionists, who together make the much larger number of that body, do not mean to do anything, but to drag out the session until the inauguration of Lincoln. And the Va. Convention continues to do nothing, & the worthless legislature of Va, which now has nothing to do, continues in session, so as to be spectators of the Convention. The election in Va, indicating such prevalence of union sentiment, has encouraged the north & discouraged opposition in all the remaining states—& there has been since shown the first falling back in the previous steady progress of the secession movement. Md. & N.C. have become much more quiet—& the example of Ten. seems about to be followed [1224] by Ark. & Mo. in voting against the assembling of Conventions in those states. Thus, owing to the predominance of union & submission feeling in Va, & its Convention, there is no longer any hope for the secession of this state before March 4th. But it is not the less certain to come, at a later time. When the northern people shall refuse all substantial guaranties to the remaining Southern states, as I deem certain, Va will be forced to secede—& even this Convention, in which there are not 40 members elected as avowed secessionists, will have to vote for the further disruption of the Union. A still earlier mode of reaching the same end. Va., N.C., & even Kentucky, are all solemnly pledged by their legislatures, to resist any attempt to invade or make offensive war on the seceded states. Lincoln's administration will doubtless attempt coercion of the Southern Confederacy—& if so, the secession of Va, & consequently of the other border states will be more speedily brought about. I trust that proper occasion will not long be wanting. . . .

*Feb. 25.* . . . Lincoln, after a progress of triumph, popular adulation, & glorification by hundreds of thousands of citizens & sycophants on the route—of more honors & respect than were even offered to Washington—has reached the federal city. But he was so much afraid of assassination in Maryland, that he passed through that state in the night, & in disguise, so that none but his special attendants, in the same rail-way car, knew he was present. A later hour of setting off, from Harrisburg, Pa, & a day journey, had been published, with a stoppage in Baltimore. But he took an earlier train, secretly, & reached Washington before day. Even there, & with Gen. Scott & 1000 regular soldiers for his guard, I suppose Lincoln will be in a tremor of terror until after his inauguration.—There are three very important measures before the U.S. Congress, & partly through, but neither yet completed—all of which will either damage or threaten the South. These are the higher tariff—a law for building screw war steamers of shallow draft, designed to enter & navigate southern rivers—& the "force bill," which is to authorise the president to call out the militia of any states, to attack or crush the seceded states. All these will probably be passed by both houses. But it is doubtful whether Buchanan will sign the force bill, if the others. In addition to his general imbecility, & especially on this subject, he seems to [1226] most desire to *do nothing*—& to leave to his successor the whole business of either coercing the seceded states, or of yielding to the acts of secession. . . . The President & Congress of the Confederate States are arranging & establishing the policy of the new government, but no important measures have yet been completed—except fixing the new tariff of duties on imports, which will now speedily go into effect. The rates are much lower than those of the U.S. tariff (without the proposed increase,) & they will be levied on the ships & goods of the northern (or United) States, as on other *foreign* countries. I am very anxious to see how this physic will work.

*Feb. 26.* . . . Since my last return to Beechwood, I have again read (partially, using only the attractive articles,) the 7 vols. of the last series of Littell's Living Age, which is my third time of thus going over them. The 19 vols., of the earlier series, will be my next resort, which have in like manner been gone through three times. Thiers' "French Revolution" I read only in the morning, when my mind can give something more of attention to what I am reading—& in this, I have barely entered the 2nd. volume.—I have been well fixed in my new lodging room, in the east end of the old house, with my furniture, books &c. . . . The door of my room opens on the porch, or open passage which connects this with the larger part of the house. My door, when I am here, is never locked at night, but merely fastened by the bolt which is turned from the outside as well as within. The windows, though closed, are almost as accessible to any intruder, or thief, as the door. My son's boys, when at home, sleep in the same unsuspicious & exposed manner, in another room of this old house. And there is but little more of security, or of care to guard against either violence or thieving, in any country house in this slave-holding region. For, though doors & windows may usually be fastened, the negro servants always keep the keys of the doors, or have [1228] otherwise the most ready access into the house at night, if not to every separate lodging room. Therefore, whether there be more or less care to guard against thieves, or other intruders, it may be truly said that every house & family is every night perfectly exposed to any attempt of our slaves to commit robbery or murder. Yet we all feel so secure, & are so free from all suspicion of such danger, that no care is taken for self-protection—& in many cases, as in mine, not even the outer door is locked. This state of things would seem incredible to northerners, who have to use every precaution to guard their houses from robberies, & who suppose that every slave in the South wants nothing but the safe opportunity to kill his master. . . . I keep no available arms for defence. For if ever so well armed, any designed murderer could shoot me, as lying in bed, from & through the window & its frail shutter, or otherwise overpower me before I was roused from sleep. Such attempts are possible. But the chance is so remote, & such occurrences so rare, that neither I nor any one else thinks of using any safeguard [1229] from such dangers, other than to lock the doors of lodging rooms, which is usually done only when the lodgers are females. We all know, that if our slaves so choose, they could kill every white person on any farm, or even through a neighborhood, in any night. Yet so little ground is there to suppose the occurrence of such attempts, that no fear is entertained by the most timid of the whites—& there is consequently a blameable & general neglect of all proper police regulations, & of means for defence against such possible violence.

*Feb. 27.* I had designed to go to Richmond as soon as the Convention got to work. That has not occurred yet. But I will wait no longer. Tomorrow I will go there to learn the state & prospect of matters. But I do not expect to stay in Richmond longer than March 3rd, & then to set out for the Confederate States. I will be out of Va before Lincoln's inauguration, & so will avoid being, as a Virginian, under his government even for an hour. I, at least, will become a citizen of the seceded Confederate States, & will not again reside in my native state, nor enter it except to make visits to my children, until Va shall also secede, & become a member of the Southern Confederacy. This result, though now postponed by the trick & fraud of assembling the "Peace Congress," cannot be delayed long— probably not a year—when, as a citizen of the "Confederate States," I shall resume my citizenship of & in Va, then one of them. [1230] . . . Contrary to the first known facts & indications in Arkansas, the elections to the Convention have gone in favor of the secessionists, so that its accession to the Confederate States may be counted upon to follow soon.—The papers are full of comments, far from complimentary to the President-elect, on his secret flight through Maryland to Washington, for fear of popular violence, or attempted assassination. . . .

*Feb. 28.* Left home, . . . taking the steamer off Coggin's Point. . . . Reached Richmond before 5 P.M. Took lodgings at the Exchange Hotel. . . . Found many persons at the hall of the Hotel, & elsewhere, & soon began to meet with acquaintances. Ex-President Tyler & J. A. Seddon, two of the Commissioners of Va to the late "Peace Conference," among them. Mr. Tyler was, in conversation with a surrounding circle, giving an account of the procedure & close of that body. The report finally agreed to is still worse for the South than the "Crittenden Resolutions."—At night, a military band, attended by a great crowd of people came into the street in front of the hotel, to call out speakers. Mr. Tyler was first [1231] called for & next Seddon. Both spoke on the report of the "Peace Conference," (which they & Judge [John W.] Brockenbrough[16] had voted against, & [William C.] Rives & [George W.] Summers[17] had voted for—) & both denounced it in the strongest terms. Next Lieut. Gov. [Robert L.] Montague spoke, & next I was called for, & spoke for a short time. I denounced the scheme of the "Peace Conference" & the result of its labors—urged the necessity of the secession of Va, & eulogised in strong expressions the noble conduct of South Carolina —closing with the declaration that as Athens was to the other cities of Greece in the time of the war with Persia, so was South Carolina to the other states of the South recently & now. Several other persons followed, & all in favor of resistance by Va, & all sentiments in favor of secession were strongly applauded by the crowd.

*March 1.* Continue to meet & to converse with many acquaintances. One was Ex. Gov. Wise. The last time I saw him, & accosted him, he was so cold & distant in his manner, that I resolved that

---

[16] Long judge of the United States Circuit Court for the Western District of Virginia, Brockenbrough was one of five Virginia representatives sent to the Provisional Confederate Congress after the state seceded. Following the war Judge Brockenbrough was a key figure in persuading General Robert E. Lee to accept the presidency of Washington College in Lexington.

[17] A former two-term Whig congressman, George William Summers ( 1804–68 ) served as judge of the Eighteenth Judicial Circuit of Virginia from 1852 to 1858. In addition to attending the Peace Conference, he was a member of the Virginia Secession Convention.

whenever we met again, he should speak first, if we spoke at all. I acted on this resolution & when we met, I made no movement of recognition. But he immediately spoke to me, very courteously, & with some & sufficient approach to cordiality, which I returned. We however had no conversation further than exchanging salutations. At 12, went to the hall of the Convention, & by favor of a ticket, obtained a good seat on the floor of the hall, near the President's chair. Nothing [1232] done, except sundry speeches, for union & submission, or the contrary. The majority of this Convention is more basely submissive than I had supposed possible. No official report has yet been received from the delegates to the "Peace Conference," & of course no opinion of the body expressed thereupon. But it is supposed that the general committee (on Federal Relations,) will approve & recommend the published report of the Peace Conference, . . . & that the Convention will adopt it for reference to the popular vote.—Judge Ruffin arrived from Washington & stopped here today. He seems to be worse, & no doubt has suffered in fatigue of both body & mind in his recent service. I regret that he voted for the report, though he did so without deeming it satisfactory. . . . At night another crowd with music, & which seemed to be a union demonstration, as voices, at first & for a long time, clamorously called for W. C. Rives, Gov. Morehead (of N.C.) & other union men. But they would not appear, & soon other names, on the opposite side were intermingled with those of union men. Two short speeches only were thus called forth, & both were strongly for secession, & warmly applauded, without any dissent. The incidents of both nights indicate a great change of popular opinion in Richmond. . . .

*March 2.* Found that to avoid detention of 12 hours on the route, I must set out today at 3 P.M., which I prepared for, & did. . . . There went with me, seeking southern military or other employment, three other Virginians, one of whom is my old acquaintance Capt. John Scott of Fauquier, whom I have noticed, as a cavalry officer, in "Anticipations of the Future."

*March 3.* Sunday. Reached Wilmington at or before day-break. Found that there was no train today on the North-Eastern R.R. (from Florence,) so had to use the longer route by Kingsville. . . . Reached Charleston at 10.30 P.M., & went to the Charleston Hotel.

*March 4.* Most of the forenoon seeing & conversing with chance-met acquaintances. Went to the offices of Mercury & Courier, to read the papers. Went to Charleston College to see Prof. [Francis S.]

Holmes, but he was absent. Afternoon, went to see Dr. Bachman. Next to the Mercury office to learn the telegraphic dispatches. Lincoln's inaugural speech thus received. It settles the question that there must be war. He renounces & declares against any invasion, or forcible coercion [1235] of the seceded states. But at the same time, as absurd as Buchanan, contends that the revenue from duties & imports must be collected from the seceded states, for the benefit of the former government & the non-seceded states, & that this will not be aggression or a war measure!—Gen. Beauregard, an excellent officer, formerly in the U.S. service, & lately appointed a general of the regular army of the Confederate States, today took command of all the forces & military posts near Charleston. As previously a stranger to his new command, of course he will need some short time to become better acquainted. But very soon I expect he will attack Fort Sumter. Perhaps hostilities may be begun still earlier, by the attempt to reinforce Fort Sumter, by the forcible entry of armed ships. I earnestly hope that this may be the beginning, & if war is to occur, that such attempt to reinforce may be made before another week passes.—Lincoln, in his message, denies any possible right of a state to secede—claims that the union of the former U.S. is still unbroken—& that it will be his sworn duty to execute the laws, so far as practicable in all the 34 states. This involves the necessity for recapturing the former U.S. forts now occupied by the C.S. just as much as to maintain the continued possession of Forts Sumter & Pickens.—Great interest & excitement, & crowds of people at the bulletin board, on which the telegrams were affixed as they arrived. But although the tenor of the President's speech was understood to indicate war speedily to be begun here, I heard [1236] not a single expression of regret or of apprehension, but on the contrary, many of gratification that things would now be brought to an issue.

*March 5.* Went to see the newspapers at the reading rooms of the Merchants, & of the Club—to both of which I was invited yesterday. This will be a great resource for me. I already find the passage of time heavy, for want of some employment. . . . I find opinions much opposed as to the results expected from the indications of the President's message. Gen. Jamison (Secretary of War) told me that he expected nothing of more active hostility & attack than a continuation of Buchanan's policy, for some time to come. Another public officer, not so high in grade, & not in the Council, but having excellent opportunity to learn opinions, told me that we shall soon have flagrant war—perhaps in three days.—The abolition party has rejected the "Peace Conference" reported plan in both houses of Congress of U.S.—for which I heartily rejoice.—Called on Prof. Holmes, & also Major [Walter] Gwynn, now acting as chief of the engineer corps of S.Ca. Also went in the afternoon to the Citadel, & saw the drill of the Cadets. Among the many acquaintances whom I have met with here, besides those mentioned, are Lieut. Gov. [1237] [William W.] Harlee [*sic*],[18] Ex. Governors Allston & Means, & John Preston.

*March 6.* Having obtained a permit, (which now is a difficult matter, & rarely conferred,) I went in the steamer, at 10 A.M. to Fort Moultrie, calling by the batteries at old Fort Johnson, without landing there, as the stop was not long enough. On the passage, I was introduced to two officers of the S.Ca. regular army, one of whom, Major [William H. C.] Whiting,[19] offered me a letter of introduction to Col. [Roswell S.] Ripley, now in command at Fort Moultrie.[20] Landed & admitted into the fort, I was very courteously received by Col. Ripley, & received much attention from him & other officers. The defences are greatly strengthened since my previous visit. Next I went to the 5 gun battery ¾ of a mile farther east along the shore, which commands Maffitt's Channel. . . . Returning to the wharf, had to wait there for the regular time of the steamer, 5 P.M., when I returned to Charleston. Col. Trapier on board, & some other gentlemen, with whom there was agreeable conversation on the state of political affairs. . . . [1238] Arranged with Major Gwynn to visit the

---

[18] A veteran South Carolina militia officer, William Wallace Harllee (1812–97) was a member of the secession convention and occupied the office of lieutenant governor from 1860 to 1862. Later, as a Confederate brigadier general, he commanded the Harllee Legion.

[19] After graduating from West Point at the head of his class, W. H. C. Whiting served with the United States Corps of Engineers until his resignation on February 20, 1861. At the time of his encounter with Ruffin, he was planning new defenses for Charleston Harbor and Morris Island. Later he fought at First Manassas, commanded a division under "Stonewall" Jackson in the Valley and in the Peninsular Campaign, and, after receiving a promotion to major general, commanded the military district of Wilmington, North Carolina. He was mortally wounded in the defense of Fort Fisher, North Carolina, in January, 1865.

[20] Roswell Sabine Ripley (1823–87), a native of Ohio and veteran of the Mexican and Seminole wars, settled in South Carolina in the 1850's and cast his lot with the Confederacy when war threatened. He was promoted to brigadier general in August, 1861, and spent most of the war in South Carolina. The cantankerous Ripley was perhaps most distinguished by his inability to get along with superiors.

batteries at Morris Island & Cummings' Point tomorrow. No news of importance today except that the first reports of the elections for the Convention in N.C., which showed a strong majority, in the first reported counties, opposed to secession, are changed in the later stated elections. It would be a most glorious event, & too good to be expected after the recent course of Va, if N.C. should go for secession now. But I fear the news is too good to be true.—The Pacific rail-road act has been lost, for want of the President's signature. The force bill was defeated in Congress. The tariff bill, increasing the rates of duty & protection, is a law—which will be beneficial for the C.S. & injurious to the U.S.

*March 7.* Went in the government steamer to visit the new batteries at Cummings' Point. Two are complete & heavy cannon & mortars mounted, & another nearly finished, & already armed. Several more batteries are begun elsewhere—& two or three weeks will still be required to get all ready for the best service. From late information, I have come to believe more in the ability of defending Fort Sumter—& also of war steamers of light draught being able to force their passage to Fort Sumter. The trial of one or both will probably be made within two weeks. Returned to Charleston to dinner. ... Afternoon, went to see Dr. Bachman, & afterwards drove with him to examine the floating battery which is nearly finished, & designed to aid in the assault of Fort Sumter. It is 80 feet long, & 40 wide. It is to be armed on its front side (of 80 feet) only, with 2 guns of 32 lbs. & two of 42 lbs., to fire through small embrasures. The rear is raised with bags of sand, appearing as a rampart. But it is not for defence, but to balance the enormous weight of the front. The two ends are unprotected. The front side, through embrasures in which the cannons are to be pointed, is about 4½ feet thick—3 feet of which is made up of squared palmetto logs. Outside of them is solid pine, 1½ feet, covered with an outer close covering of iron bars, half an inch thick. The roof is also to be covered with like iron bars. It is supposed that the diverging slopes of both wall & roof will cause the striking balls to glance, & to do much [1240] less damage than if striking at right-angles. The great difficulty will be to place the battery in the desired position near to Fort Sumter. ...

*March 8.* Yesterday saw the new flag of the C.S. waving from the mast-head of a ship in the harbor. Some smaller ones had been raised in the city the day before.—In the afternoon, went to the Citadel to see the weekly dress parade of the Cadets. A great many ladies among the spectators, in the galleries around the enclosed area, in which the companies formed.—Lincoln has appointed all strong abolitionists to the seven places in his cabinet—& all of them from the non-slaveholding states, except [Edward] Bates of Missouri, & M[ontgomery] Blair of Md. Seward is the most able & Chase the most virulent of them, & enemies of the South, & of slavery.—It will be some two or three weeks before the last begun earth batteries will be completed, & not before, if then, will any attack be made on Fort Sumter. And from what I hear from those who have good opportunities for information, it is not believed that the northern government will immediately, if at all, make an attempt to reinforce Fort Sumter [1241] or to attack Fort Moultrie. Being tired of waiting here, I will use the expected interval of quiet to go away for some days & visit some old acquaintances, & will set out tomorrow, unless some thing occurs sooner to prevent. I received yesterday a kind & urgent invitation from Col. James Ferguson, to visit him . . . . This day, the dismantling of Castle Pinckney was begun—& the removal of the guns & garrison to other batteries, where they are much more needed. Castle Pinckney is of little use for defence of the city—& if seized by a hostile power, with naval superiority, might be the means of destroying the city.

*March 9.* . . . Left Charleston at 2 P.M., on the N.E. Rail-road, & at 24 miles distance stopped at Strawberry station. From thence, Dr. Moultrie (a neighbor & my former acquaintance,) took me in his carriage to Col. Ferguson's residence, between 1 & 2 miles distant. Found there, of the family, Col. F. & wife & one son, (two others in military service near Charleston,) & Mr. P. Gourdin, their friend. Conversation & the last newspapers occupied us until late bed-time. —Col. F. is a well preserved [1242] & hale old man, 77 years of age. He & his wife are both well educated & well informed, & very intelligent & agreeable. This neighborhood I visited in 1843, when I commenced my labors on the Agricultural Survey of S.C. & then became acquainted with Col. F. & sundry of his then & now neighbors. I have also met him & his family several times since, in Charleston & at the Va. Springs.

*March 10.* Sunday. With Col. F. drove about part of the neighboring lands, & to the residence of Mr. P. Gourdin, whom we found awaiting us. Returned to dinner, & found another old acquaintance of 1843, Dr. Sanford Barker,[21] brother of Mrs. Ferguson. . . .

---

[21] A prominent planter, physician, and botanist, Barker (1807–91) resided at South Mulberry plantation, St. John's Parish, Berkeley District. He was a state senator from 1850 to 1865.

*March 11.* After breakfast, drove with Col. F. & Dr. Barker ... to the plantation of Dr. St. Julien Ravenel, & a locality near Steep Bluff, a very high exposure of the rich marl-stone, which I had examined, among many others in this neighborhood, when I was Agricultural Surveyor of S.C. in 1843. Dr. Ravenel has here erected an excellent perpetual kiln, for burning the marl to lime, & the machinery, propelled by a steam engine, to make barrels in which to put the lime for sale. The operations are very interesting.[22] The neighboring planters, whom I urged, in vain, formerly to use the rich marl which underlies & is easily accessible on almost every plantation, are beginning to use [1243] lime as manure, when they can buy it at 15 cents the bushel, unslaked. It is astonishing, & would seem incredible, that highly intelligent men, as are many of these proprietors, should not have used this manure, in its crude state as marl, & over all their land. ... We drove to the station to get the papers, & to hear any later news. The indications, from Washington, are of the U.S. government being unyielding, & of course its action tending to war. The popular vote in N.Ca. has been against calling a state convention, by 1000 majority—& much more strongly against secession —two to one, as reported. The Committee on Federal Relations of Va. Convention have reported, & only to recommend the calling of a Convention of the border slave states, to consider what they should do in reference to attempted coercion of the seceded states by the U.S. government. Several minority reports were also made—& one of them, of 3 members only, (out of 21,) recommended the immediate secession of Va.

*March 12.* Dr. Moultrie called to visit me. Also came, on his way to Charleston, Alfred Huger esq. P[ost] M[aster], an old gentleman of deservedly high character & estimation.[23] We came up together from the city, & he sought me out on the train to introduce himself, & make my acquaintance.—Yesterday, we heard it stated (correctly,) that a telegram had been received, & published [1244] in Charleston stating that Fort Sumter was ordered to be surrendered to the south-

---

[22] This apparatus, established on Cooper River in 1857, was the first of its kind in the state. Ravenel (1819–82), a noted physician and agricultural chemist, was a surgeon in charge of the Confederate hospital in Columbia, South Carolina, during the war. It was he who proposed the artesian well system for Charleston, described earlier by the diarist.

[23] Postmaster of Charleston since 1834, Alfred Huger (1788–1872), also a prominent planter and railroad director, had previously sat in the state Senate and in the Nullification Convention of 1832–33.

ern forces. But I placed no confidence in the dispatch, which was contradictory to all other information & indications. But by various accounts in the papers received today, it would seem that the report was true. On this account, I will go tomorrow morning to Charleston. —In the forenoon, Col. Ferguson & I walked about 5 miles, over his plantation, & viewing his extensive rice fields, & his barn & steam thrashing & other machinery.... The Convention of the Confederate States have agreed upon a plan of the permanent constitution—which will be submitted to the several states for their separate ratification. It varies but slightly, yet is improved upon, the former federal constitution.

*March 13.* Took the train at 7 A.M..... Went to the Charleston Hotel. Heard that there was no truth in the expected surrender, or immediately. It is only understood, by reports from Washington, that the provisions &c. will not last more than two weeks longer, & that it would require 10,000 men to force a passage for reinforcements & supplies. Therefore the surrender must occur soon. Telegraphic dispatches received [1245] later state that the Commissioners of the C.S. at Washington have been refused a hearing by the Northern administration. I trust that this refusal will be taken as a declaration of intended hostilities, & prevent all further delay in attacking the forts here & at Pensacola. Another dispatch ( unofficial, ) reported that a messenger is on his way from Washington, to order the surrender of Fort Sumter. No vigilance will be intermitted here, on account of these rumors & expectations. This evening, Gen. [Robert G. M.] Dunovant introduced Gen. Beauregard to me.[24] From them, as from others, I learned that the preparations are not all ready yet, but will be in a few days. Gen. Jamison will make his round of visiting all the defences next Saturday, & has invited me to go again with him —which I shall be glad to do. I went this forenoon in the daily steamer to Cummings' Point batteries, but did not stay long, & returned by the steamer. A company of volunteer artillery went in it to relieve another, which returned. Among sundry other gentlemen who were passengers, was the Rev. H. G. Van Dyke of N.Y. whose very able sermon in Brooklyn, in defence of slavery, I read when in Tallahassee. I asked for an introduction, & was pleased to become acquainted & to converse with him.... Went again to see the floating

---

[24] Robert Gill Mills Dunovant ( 1821–98 ), veteran of the Mexican War and an Edgefield District planter, was brigadier general of state troops and the senior officer in Charleston before the arrival of Beauregard.

battery, which seems but little nearer being quite finished, than a week ago. . . . [1246]

*March 14.* Called on Mr. Van dyke, to carry to him some of my pamphlets, and had a conversation with him on the subject of negro slavery. . . . Walked on the beautiful promenade called the Battery. —In addition to the exciting rumors of the surrendering of Fort Sumter which start here, or from telegrams received here, the newspapers of Washington & New York have sundry reports to the same purport. So I suppose that it must take place in a week or two, even if not attacked. Another report is that several ships of war, with soldiers, have set off for the south, &, as supposed, to reinforce Fort Sumter. I do not believe in such an attempt. However, I wish most heartily it may be made, & with a strong force. The conflict which would ensue would certainly serve to bring Virginia, Md. & N.Ca. to unite with the Confederate States. . . .

*March 15.* . . . Went again to the floating battery, which has its guns on board, & was said to require but a few hours' work to be ready for service. . . . Drove in the omnibus to the newspaper offices [1247] to inquire for news by telegraph—& heard none, except a reported more authoritative dispatch from Mr. [John] Forsythe, one of the Commissioners at Washington,[25] to Gov. Pickens, stating that Fort Sumter will be surrendered very soon. *Per contra*, Dr. Gibbes told me that Major Anderson had been hard at work all last night mounting more large cannon, Columbiads. If the steamers, with soldiers & supplies, were ordered to this place, (which nobody here seems to believe,) they will be due by daybreak tomorrow morning.

*March 16.* After reading the morning papers, went on board the steamer, as before invited by Gen. Jamison, (Sec. of War of S.C.) to accompany him around to visit the forts. Found on board a large party of ladies as well as gentlemen. Among the company were Judge Magrath, (Sec. of State,) Ex. Governors Allston & Means, Gen. Jones, Isaac Hayne, late Commissioner to Washington. We landed first at old Fort Johnson. There are three batteries, one of which will be abandoned, being badly placed, & will be substituted by one of the others not yet finished. Next passing (on the ordinary track) almost encircling Fort Sumter, & within half a mile of it, we went to

---

[25] John Forsyth, son of the Georgia statesman of the same name, was editor of the Mobile *Register* and a strong Douglas supporter in the election of 1860. The other two Confederate commissioners were Martin J. Crawford of Georgia and A. B. Roman of Louisiana.

Morris' Island, landing at Cummings' Point, where there are three new batteries. Thence we walked as low as the Lighthouse, about a mile distance, the greater part of which there is a connected covered way, secured by embankments from balls. Three or four more batteries are at different points along this distance. The companies of regular artillery, that man the batteries, & of more numerous volunteer infantry [1248] & riflemen, are quartered mostly in tents. Here serving as common soldiers are many young men of high position of wealth & family connections. The batteries have either mortars or heavy cannon, & some Columbiads for throwing either shells or solid balls of great weight. After remaining here more than two hours, & witnessing some very accurate firing of cannon from all the gun-batteries on this island, we steamed across to Sullivan's Island, & walked to Fort Moultrie. Another battery for two heavy mortars, a little higher than the fort, has been completed since my previous visit. I did not again walk to the 5-gun battery below, which commands Maffitt's Channel—nor did we visit another battery still lower, commanding the deep inlet between Sullivan's & Long Island —nor the battery on the Mount Pleasant shore. Every completed battery seems well prepared for an enemy's approach. Most of the guns & all the mortar batteries bear on Fort Sumter. But all the lower batteries, & part of the guns of Moultrie are to fire on vessels if attempting to force an entrance. Returning, the steamer reached the wharf after sunset. . . .

*March 17.* Sunday. . . . Went to St. Philip's church—which I prefer, because of the sacred music played on the chime of bells before the service, & the fine music with the organ in the service. I sat in the pew with Major Trapier, & afterwards we walked together, & conversed on the state of military affairs. He is in the engineer service, formerly of the same in the U.S. army, & is one of the two contrivers of the floating battery. He is of opinion that there will be no assault on Fort Sumter, but [1250] the besiegers will prefer to wait for the inevitable necessity for the garrison to surrender, for want [of] food & other necessaries—even if the Northern government shall not (as reported) order an earlier surrender. Major Trapier intimated a reason for the forbearance of the officers of the besieging army, who had recently resigned commissions under the U.S. government, because of their reluctance to take the initiative in firing upon the flag under which they so long & zealously served—& upon men who were before their fellow officers & friends.—Taken altogether, this is a most singular state of war—as war it is—between the U.S. government & the seceded states, now making the C.S. When secession was in prospect, or threatened, it was expected by all the North, & by nearly all of the South, that the first act of secession, & declaration of independence of any state or states would induce immediate hostile or coercive action by the federal government, & that war would be begun. It was the opinion of all unionists, & of most of even strong disunionists, that disruption of the union could not occur without war, & immediate war. Yet it is now almost three months since the first act of independence by S.C. & more than four months since that act was in certain & near prospect—& to this time not a hostile shot has been fired, except those which repelled & drove off the "Star of [1251] the West," when attempting to reinforce Fort Sumter, & not a drop of blood has been shed in any conflict. Fort Sumter is surrounded by batteries prepared to batter or shell it—& a strict blockade maintained to prevent its receiving supplies or reinforcements—and any hostile or war vessels, if attempting to enter the harbor would be fired upon, & resisted to the last extremity. Nearly the like state of things exists as to Fort Pickens near Pensacola. There, in addition, a squadron of 3 or 4 U.S. armed vessels are anchored off the harbor, having reinforcements of soldiers on board, & one other armed vessel, the Wyandot, has heretofore been permitted to pass daily, under a flag of truce, between the ships & the besieged fort. The officers of the fort & the besieging C.S. army even exchange friendly visits, & dine at each other's quarters. And here, though such intimacy has not existed, every courtesy has been extended to the commander of Fort Sumter, not serving to counteract seriously its ultimate capture. Fresh meat, vegetables, & other such comforts are received every day from the city by Major Anderson, & upon his unlimited orders to his agents. His correspondence has not been obstructed or restricted—& even his near relatives allowed to visit him. Two different governments are now existing, & the new one completely organized & established in safety & quietude—while the most violent threats of hostile intentions have been expressed by the northern people & the U.S. government. These however are becoming confined to fewer & fewer. Most reasonable men of the North are beginning to see the utter impossibility [1252] of the seceded states being conquered or coerced by the remaining U.S. power. Still, on the part of the latter, impotent as it has been in action, there has been no intermission of threats of coercion, or any intimation of agreeing to peaceable arrangements with the Confederate States. While war has thus been in formal existence & operation between the government of the U.S. & the seceded states, peaceful relations have continued between the two peoples, despite of the violent animosity of the communities, & still more of individuals of the two sections. While every participation in & aid to secession in the South is denounced in the North as treason to the U.S. government, & even so declared judicially, southern & northern men freely visit & travel any where in the other section, without being interfered with by any legal restraint or penalty. Vessels continue to come from the north & without hindrance obtain (if they can) cargoes in southern ports. Southern merchants (in advance of the operation of the new tariffs, of both North & South,) have lately gone to make purchases of goods in the northern cities. The mails are uninterrupted, & the railway trains, express transportation & telegraph lines, through both sections, now politically separated. It is true that northerners travelling or sojourning in the south, when convicted of incendiary or other violations of our laws, have been in some cases legally punished. In many more cases, when others were certainly guilty or strongly suspected of abolition action, they have been either merely driven off, or otherwise punished besides, by popular & illegal action. Also, southern secessionists, openly expressing their opinions & so affronting [1253] public opinion, have been insulted or maltreated in northern states. This perhaps might happen to me, if I were to express my opinions even in Kentucky, or North-Western Va, at this time. But all such cases, south or north, would be founded either on previously existing laws, or upon popular & illegal violence—& would not be the necessary consequence of the actual state of war between the Northern & Southern Confederacies.

*March 18.* . . . No news of importance. Still continued rumors from Washington of the intended evacuation of Fort Sumter. But I will wait no longer merely to witness it, & I have now not the least expectation of the occurrence of any fighting here. . . . I shall attend a Convention of the state of N.C. which is called to assemble at Goldsborough, on 22nd inst. to consider the political condition of affairs.

*March 19.* . . . Saw Mr. John Preston, of Columbia, & had a conversation with him on the character of the Va Convention, & the causes of its so misrepresenting the people—in regard to which our views perfectly accorded. I urged him (unsuccessfully [1254] so far,) to go

[569]

to the N.C. Convention at Goldsborough, as I also did Gen. Garlington. Afterwards I wrote to Hon. W. S. Ashe, Wilmington, & to Hon. Thomas Ruffin, Goldsborough, suggesting the inviting of these gentlemen, and also Judge Magrath of Charleston, & Prof. Holcombe & such views are sustained by the New York Herald & other northern books, & but little conversation.

*March 20. . . .* Had a conversation yesterday & another today with Collector Colcock on the working of the two different tariffs, of South & North. Already, as I learned from him & from others, northern products, which ought to pay duties in the South, are imported in quantity through the Express agency on the railways, & so are smuggled in without paying any duties. On the other hand, I expect, & such views are sustained by the New York Herald & other northern commercial authorities, that many of the commodities of Europe, imported for consumption in the northern states, as well as all for the southern, will be imported through southern ports, & the former thence be conveyed over interior routes to the northern states. Mr. Colcock [1255] & I agree, that low as our tariff is (the existing U.S. tariff of 1857) compared to the new U.S. tariff, just enacted, & going into operation on April 1st., it would be much better policy if ours was still lower—say laying only 10 percent. duties on all commodities, or on none more than 15 percent. In this case, the inducement to import European goods for northern consumption, through southern ports, paying there the low duty, & thence the northern owners smuggling them into the U.S., would be far more operative. And even if there were no interior custom houses, on the border lines, it would scarcely pay any profit to smuggle northern products into the south, to avoid duties of merely 10 percent. I have long maintained that by tariff regulations, & low duties in general & for friendly nations, (if not entire free trade,) & higher discriminating duties on unfriendly nations, the Southern Confederacy would use the most effective weapons to secure its rights, & perfectly effective against the hostile northern states.

*March 21.* At 2 P.M. left Charleston by the N.E. Railroad. Reached Wilmington before 2 A.M. next morning, & had to sit up in the public room until the train set out northward, which was at 5 A.M.

*March 22.* Reached Goldsborough after 9 A.M. . . . The question of calling a Convention has recently been decided in the negative, by merely 194 majority [1256] of the popular vote of the state. Some

300 or more attendants on this meeting. Many intelligent men, & good speakers. At 1 P.M. the meeting was organized. A committee was sent to invite Mr. [Franklin I.] Moses of S.C. (who had come on with me,) & myself to attend & address the meeting. Mr. M. is a member of the Senate of S.C. & a good speaker.[26] He spoke more than an hour, defending the procedure of S.C. & urging secession for N.C. I was called on next, & made a shorter & plain address, on such points only as my predecessor had omitted or barely touched. We were both warmly welcomed & with enthusiasm. Part of my remarks were to the same general purport as I wrote more particularly upon yesterday in a letter to Gov. Ellis, showing the great danger of the forts in N.C. being garrisoned, & combatting the governor's opinion that his oath forbids them being occupied by his authority.[27] Several other speakers of N.C. followed, then, or at night, & spoke well. Having had but little sleep last night I had to retire before 10 P.M. & before the adjournment. The meeting will continue through tomorrow, when many additional attendants are expected. But I regret that I cannot stay, as, if doing so, by the train stopping the following day (Sunday) I shall be delayed in getting to Judge Ruffin's.

*March 23.* After very early breakfast, left Goldsboro' at 6.30 A.M. At Hillsborough, the Rev. M. A. Curtis entered the car, on his way to Alamance also, & to preach [1257] tomorrow. At Graham, we got out, & found there waiting for him, Judge Ruffin's buggy, by which I obtained for myself & trunk a more ready conveyance. . . . Judge Ruffin, after his return from Washington, & doubtless because of his service & exposure there, was much worse, & confined to his bed. He is again better, & going about the house & yard—but still very feeble. I fear he will never be much better in strength or health. . . .

*March 24.* . . . Before night, Jane & I had a long walk, &, for the first time, we had reference [1258] in conversation, to her engagement to my son . . . . I learned that she had consented to fix the time, & that their marriage is to take place on the 25th of next month. May God bless her in this marriage, & grant that it may promote the

---

[26] A Sumter lawyer and planter, Franklin Israel Moses was a member of the state Senate from 1841 to 1865. Unlike Ruffin, Moses accommodated easily to the postwar situation; he was elected to a district judgeship in 1865, and served as chief justice of the South Carolina Supreme Court from 1868 until his death nine years later.

[27] See Appendix F for the full text of this letter.

happiness of all the parties & relations!—When I was here before, in last October, Judge Ruffin was still strongly opposed to secession, & all of his family residing here except his sons, William & Sterling. He continued so until the Union was broken, & no hope left to his mind that the northern people would render justice to the south by any new & necessary guaranties, or that (for want of them,) the former union could be reconstructed. Since, he has become a secessionist, & so is every member of his family. Judge Ruffin has been so long a portion of his life in a high judicial station, in which he deemed it his duty to avoid expressing his political opinions of men, & every thing like partizan feeling, that he has trained his conduct to caution & silence in regard to political questions. Therefore, from long habit, he still preserves much of this cautious reserve, & rarely permits himself to express freely the ill opinions he may entertain of public men or their acts. But his late stay in Washington, as a member of the "Peace Conference" & his necessary communication in that body with noted abolitionists, & his then opportunity of observing their [1259] conduct in the government, have excited his indignation & contempt so that he speaks of them as harshly as I would. He pronounces them to be the greatest scoundrels that ever formed a great party, & controlled the policy of a constitutional government. This I have long thought. And it is now, & lately, especially manifest. According to the general & earnest opinions of all of this abolition (or "republican") party, the ruin of the government of the U.S. & of the country is in progress in the disruption of the Union. Yet they make not the slightest effort to save it—& profit by their late undisputed supremacy in Congress, caused by the withdrawal of members of the seven seceded states, to glut themselves with plunder of the treasury, in offices & jobs. Since Lincoln's inauguration, the Senate has been in session, & the whole action & care of the administration has been to appoint members of the successful party to lucrative offices. And every prominent member of the party, in or out of Congress, & thousands of the more obscure, are eager & ravenous seekers of public office, or public plunder in some other shape. This great army of robbers, are all so busily employed in seising [*sic*] & sharing the enormous booty which has suddenly fallen to them, & in quarrelling about the claimed shares, that they take but little care of the progress of secession, & scarcely now impede the work of disruption of the Union. [1260]

*March 25....* No important news or changes of political affairs.

Everything seems to indicate that the abolition government has not power or strength to attempt open hostilities against the C.S. & therefore its present (or ostensible) policy will be peaceable. The approach of the time (April 1.,) when the new tariff for the U.S. will go into operation, & its contrast with the much lower existing southern tariff, causes increasing apprehensions in the minds of all men of prudence & good judgment in the North. There is a clamor for the calling of an extra session of Congress, to repeal, or greatly modify, this tariff just enacted by the wisdom & zeal of the ruling party. I trust that there can be no speedy bringing together of Congress, or of change of the high tariff, until it shall have worked its effect on northern commerce & the U.S. finances for a few months at least. It will do more to defend & strengthen the cause of the C.S., & to promote their objects & prosperity, than would their having both an army & navy stronger than any the U.S. can put in service. ... [1261]

*March 27.* ... The mail brought plenty of newspapers, but no news of importance. No surrender or evacuation of Fort Sumter yet. The administration at Washington busily engaged in distributing offices to abolitionists. The Convention at Richmond continuing to discuss & speechify about the several schemes for saving the union. The secessionists, with all their accessions, are still in a minority in that body—but are more numerous than the advocates of any other one plan of measures & policy.

*March 28.* Left Alamance, & at Graham, took the train for Charlotte—which I reached by 8 P.M. Met sundry gentlemen who urgently invited me to stop, first at Salisbury, & afterwards at Charlotte. They counted more upon my influence in forwarding secession than it deserves. At Charlotte, had political conversation in the public hall of the hotel until bed-time.

*March 29.* Left at 5 A.M. & reached Charleston at 10.30 P.M. & the Charleston Hotel at 11. Saw several acquaintances in the hall.

*March 30.* When leaving the breakfast room, Gen. Beauregard, who was seated at another table, & whom I had not seen, sent his Aid after me, to invite me to go with him & a large party around to visit the batteries today. I accept[ed] his invitation, not to see the forts again, but for the company. [1262] Before 10 A.M. we embarked on two steamers, as one would not have held the passengers. The members of the Convention were invited, & most of them were present, the body having adjourned yesterday for the purpose. There were also present several officers of the Executive, Gen. Harlee [*sic*], Lieut. Governor, Gen. Jamison, Ex. Governors Allston, Means, & Gist, & sundry other persons of less note. . . . The steamers went first to Fort Moultrie—& when leaving passed down by the fort & several sand batteries through Maffitt's channel, & then crossed over to the landing at Cummings' Point, on Morris' Island. As we were about passing by Fort Moultrie, its cannon were fired, with blank cartridge, in succession, & more than once, & rapidly one after another, so that the smoke from the discharges scarcely was blown off on one side before the last guns were fired on the other. On reaching Morris' Island, & part of the company having gone to visit the more remote batteries, (which I did not, having been twice before,) all the cannon & bombs, from all the batteries were fired several times each, with balls or shells, at different floating targets (buoys,) in the harbor, & both above & below Fort Sumter, exhibiting much accuracy of aim. On returning in the afternoon, the larger steamer, the [1263] Carolina, in which I was, was steered so as to pass within 200 yards of Fort Sumter, our band then playing, & all our large company assembled on the decks. Previously, all passing steamers had kept at half a mile distance. Many of the garrison gathered on the ramparts, to see the passing steamer, & among them was Major Anderson, (who was known to some of our party,) who walked to & fro, as if impatient at so near an approach of forbidden visitors.—The delay of the surrender still continues, & seems no nearer its termination than two weeks ago. Every day there is a new report of statements which would indicate that the surrender could not be more than one or two days distant. Two different persons have been sent by Lincoln to confer with Anderson, & were permitted to visit him. Both of them verbally stated to him that he was free to evacuate the fort—but both declined giving him the authority in writing—without which he is very properly unwilling to act. It is believed by Gen. Beauregard that the President & cabinet wish the surrender to be made, but on the commander's responsibility—& then will throw the blame on him, & so try to escape the odium & shame, & the displeasure of their abolition party. Major Anderson is unwilling to be so victimized, & so requires written orders. In addition, the garrison cannot get out, or have conveyance by a vessel, without formal leave of our general, asked & granted. This cannot be done, without an indirect or implied acknowledgment [1264] by Lincoln of the separate nationality of the Confederate States, & the rightful authority of their officers in command here. This would be a galling humiliation. Thus, though the northern government has so long admitted the necessity for the surrender, & that it would be made—& latterly has wished it done—still it is delayed. Major Gwinn [*sic*] thinks, as he told me, & he is alone in the opinion, that the fort will not be surrendered peaceably, & must be attacked & forced to surrender.... Among the company on board the steamers today I met with my old acquaintance Wm. Elliott.[28] I know few men who are better informed, & no one more agreeable in conversation.... Chancellor [James P.] Carroll [29] was there, with his wife & daughters. This lady & her two daughters arrived with me yesterday. I was struck by the uncommon beauty of all three, as members [1265] of one family. The mother subsequently accosted me, to renew a former slight acquaintance (at the Va. Springs,) which I could not recollect. She is daughter of the late & distinguished J. Macpherson Berrien of Ga. Her husband, a member of the Convention, I had before become acquainted with here....

*March 31.* Sunday (Easter.)... Afternoon, at Dr. Bachman's church.... Gen. Jamison told me, in confidence, that the Governor had received a telegram from Mr. [Martin J.] Crawford, one of the commissioners of C.S. at Washington, stating that Lincoln's cabinet had certainly decided for the surrender of Fort Sumter—but that it would not be avowed until after the elections in Connecticut & Rhode Island, which will take place tomorrow & next Wednesday, for fear of the ill effects on the votes. The government will lose character abroad, & gain censure & disgrace even among its friends at home, by this surrender.

*April 1.* Attended (having a ticket of admittance from President,) the opening of the session of the Convention today. But as the main business, the question of ratification of the new constitution for the C.S., is with closed doors, I had to leave before anything of interest was discussed. [1266] R. B. Rhett, Middleton, Spratt, & some other prominent members are so much opposed to some of the features of the new constitution, that they are for requiring amendments as conditional to ratification by S.Ca. But though perhaps a large ma-

---

[28] A graduate of Harvard, Elliott (1788–1863) was a highly cultured Beaufort District planter and political pamphleteer.

[29] Elected to the secession convention from Edgefield District, James Parsons Carroll (1809–83) was chancellor of the court of equity from 1859 until his office was abolished by the Constitution of 1868.

jority object to these or other features, it is understood to be the general disposition to waive minor objections, & adopt the constitution without conditions. Five of the states have already done so, & by majorities so great as to approach unanimity in each convention. S.Ca. & Florida only now have to act. There is no doubt of the ratification by both. . . .

*April 2.* . . . Heard (confidentially) from Ex-Gov. Richardson, a member of the Convention, that it was certain, (as communicated privately by members of each delegation to the General Convention at Montgomery,) that it was supposed by the delegates that the majority of the people of every state except S.Ca. was indisposed to the disruption of the Union—and that if the question of reconstruction of the former union was referred to the popular vote, that there was probability of its being approved. This is the first authoritative statement which I have heard of such disposition. It is alarming—& ought to silence the objections of members of this convention to the federal constitution, & hasten the ratification. I am sure that any extensive popular objections to secession & independence must be founded, not on reason & judgment, but [1267] on sentiment, prejudice, & in some cases the first pressure of increased taxation & expectation of greater privations. It is but necessary for the new political machine to be put fully in operation, & the different effects on the South & the North to be made manifest, for the superiority of southern independence & separate nationality to be evident to all.

*April 3.* Reading, or glancing over, books in or brought from the adjacent book-store of McCarter & Davison—in addition to the daily & large reading of newspapers.—Afternoon, visited Dr. Bachman & family.—On returning, heard a startling rumor that there had been firing from one of the lower batteries on a vessel entering under the U.S. flag, & which did not stop for the warning shot fired ahead, but returned after being fired at. I went with others to the city battery (the promenade) to see what was going on at Fort Sumter—but could see nothing more before the speedy approach of twilight. It is reported that communications are now going on between Gen. Beauregard & Major Anderson on the subject of the firing.

*April 4.* The vessel which was fired at & turned back, sailed away before night, & today nothing more certain has been heard. The last battery was completed night before last, & it is said that all supplies for Fort Sumter are to be cut off tomorrow. Partly read & glanced over Dr. Van Evrie's new work "Negroes & Negro slavery."—The news from Virginia indicates continued changes going on of the popular [1268] mind in favor of secession—but not reaching a majority yet of the people, & still less of the Convention.—Two of the most distinguished men of Charleston, both in private life & now very old, lately left their cards for me, & today I went to return their calls—Mr. [James L.] Pettigru [*sic*] & Judge Mitchell King. . . . The city is full of rumors. The stopping of the supplies of fresh provision to Fort Sumter, (which is certainly to begin tomorrow,) it is conjectured may cause Major Anderson to cut off the communication between the city & batteries &c. If so, it will bring on hostilities. In one way or other (& not by voluntary or uncoerced surrender,) the high authorities here expect to have possession of the fort within a week. This afternoon, all of the officers & soldiers belonging to any of the batteries or camps, & absent by leave, were ordered to join their companies immediately.—Reports confirming previous rumors state that a strong Spanish force has seized & assumed the re-annexation of the Dominican territory—& it is thence inferred that the same course will be pursued by France, with aid of Spain, to re-conquer & subdue Hayti. I trust that both may be done. For bad as is Spanish domination, it is of the white race—& it will be a great benefit to civilization, to the world, & especially [1269] to the slave-holding interests of these C. States, that the mongrel race of Dominica shall be overcome, & finally eradicated, by the intrusion of white conquerors & colonists. Still better will it be for the like results to be produced in the barbarous negro government & territory of Hayti. But while these events & prospects are, as I deem, very desirable for us, they are very offensive & grievous to the northern & abolition confederacy. The government are offended at such conquest being made by a European monarchy so close to this country. And besides this political objection, the dominant abolition sect will be still more outraged of this conquest & repression of free-negroism, & the strong probability of negro slavery being re-established in this great & fertile territory. Spain would not have dared to attempt this conquest if the U.S. power had remained entire & as strong as before the disruption. Perhaps even the rump U.S. government may deem it necessary to interfere. If so, so much the better for the C.S. being left unassailed & quiet. So also, the previous national dispute with Great Britain as to the right to St. Juan island in Vancouver's strait,[30] & the unended insubordination of Mormondom, (Utah,) will remain as legacies to the northern rump government. Its struggling

---

[30] This dispute was not finally resolved until 1872, when an international arbitrator awarded the entire San Juan archipelago to the United States.

& contending for these claims of right will occupy the resources of the North—& whether it shall be successful or defeated will be of no interest to the South.—Though the injunction of secrecy on the late proceedings of the S.C. Convention has not yet been removed, [1270] it is well understood that that body yesterday ratified the new federal constitution by a very large majority. There were several strong objections to its features, in many minds, & probably every man has some—as I certainly have. But the chief ground of objection, & the only one which induced nearly all of the opposing votes, was the absence of an absolute prohibition of any non-slaveholding state being hereafter admitted as a member of the southern Confederacy. No one would object to such admission more than myself. But I trust that the constitutional & other obstacles to such admissions will be enough to prevent their possibility. The dissentient votes against ratifying the constitution were 16.

*April 5.* There are sundry reports of movements of naval forces of U.S. & indications of warlike intentions, without the objects being stated. There has been set forth from sundry N.Y. & Washington papers & letter writing, the suggestion that the Lincoln government intends to repel the aggression of Spain on Dominica, by naval forces & arms—& some even intimate that war with Spain will be begun within 20 days. I believe that these reports are put out to blind the C.S. to a real intention of attacking the South, by reinforcing occupied forts, or otherwise, & to delude the authorities into false security. It is perfectly ridiculous to suppose that the Lincoln government, powerless & poor as it is, & utterly unable to assert what it claims of the obedience of the seceded states, should, letting alone these dangerous enemies at home, go abroad to make offensive war on a strong European [1271] power—& that merely for the preference of the domination of the mongrel population of Dominica, to the white race of Spain! No doubt the sympathies of the abolition party & its administration are with free-negroism everywhere. But that sympathy & preference will scarcely lead them to attempt foreign & aggressive war in support, & much less when there is so much demand for all the energies & efforts & means of the government to conduct safely the present contest with the C.S.—In the Va Convention, a direct vote has been taken for immediate secession, & obtained only 48 voices against 98. This is worse than I supposed possible even of that submissive & mean body. In the meantime, there are daily indications of continued popular changes to secession. One of the most recent, & strongest, is that the "Whig" newspaper of Richmond, the able & influential & main organ of the Unionists & Submissionists, has changed editors & sentiments, & is about to come out for immediate secession.—Afternoon, went to see Dr. Bachman, & then to the parade of the cadets of the Military Academy.—As usual, most of the day & evening consumed in reading or looking over newspapers, or in talking, in transient meetings, about the current political events & military rumors. Indeed there is scarcely any conversation heard, anywhere, or between any parties, of which the sole subject, remotely or immediately, is not the present political or military or commercial condition of the country. —The Literary [1272] Messenger for April, received today, presents as the leading article, my "Reminiscence of the time of Nullification." This was placed in the hands of the Editor before I determined to withdraw from the public press—but I have tried to keep its authorship entirely secret, except to the editor.

*April 6.* It had been rumored & believed generally, as for each of some days earlier, that this day the supplies of provisions, & all communications of Major Anderson & Fort Sumter were to be cut off. But provisions were again allowed to be received this morning, as usual, & the suspension is again said to be certain to be made tomorrow. I trust it may be so. There were reasons for delay until recently. The batteries were not completed until two or three days ago. Then, the troops were to be well supplied with provisions, lest Anderson should also cut off their communications. Besides these particular reasons for delay, there was & is the greatest reluctance to take the first step in real hostilities, & which would subject the South to the charge abroad of beginning or provoking war & blood-shed. But it is now generally thought by the people & the troops that there has been enough of delay & forbearance for every purpose, & that the mere occupation of Fort Sumter by a foreign force is an obvious act of offensive war that should no longer be permitted. The volunteers who compose nearly all the army in service, privates as well as officers, are men of respectable positions, who have left, in the greater number of cases, either good property or good business employment, comfortable homes, & families, [1273] to undergo, & cheerfully they have done it, all the hardships & privations of camp duties. There are many among the private soldiers who possess great wealth, or high position, & every desired luxury at home—& numerous sons of such fathers. In one case, the owner of numerous slaves has had a large number of them employed in constructing the earth-works, at his entire expense, & he not only directing their labors, but laboring himself as diligently as any of his slaves. In another case, a general of volunteer cavalry (at home) is serving as a private volunteer of infantry, because there was no call for his command, or for his own branch of the service. Such men, & all who are in service, came to defend S.C. & to fight—& while such service was in near prospect, they disregarded all hardships or personal considerations. But as it has latterly seemed the enduring policy of the government at Montgomery to wait, & to make no attempt to coerce the surrender of the hostile garrison of Fort Sumter, & that the suspense may yet continue for weeks, or until the malaria season begins, (which will be on Morris Island in May,) the troops & the citizens are becoming feverishly impatient for the reduction of Fort Sumter, & for the end of the present necessity of retaining the besieging forces.—The papers today present continued statements or rumors of the busy fitting out of war vessels, & preparing troops for warlike operations in the northern ports. Everything seems to indicate some new & serious attempt to strike an unlooked-for blow on the C.S.—either reinforcing the blockaded [1274] forts, or (as also rumored) to blockade the Missi[ssi]ppi river. I wish with all my heart, (but do not have any such expectation,) that Lincoln would send a strong squadron to force the passage & attack the defences of Charleston. I think that any such attack would be repelled, & the making it, & the immediate consequences, would soon bring Va & other delaying states into the southern confederacy.—I am wearied, pained & mortified, by having to answer questions asked of me every day & almost every hour, by acquaintances & even strangers, as to the condition & designed action of Va, & the causes of her failure to unite with the South in defence of her own as well as the common rights, against the wrongs & insults from the North. The people of S.Ca. have been schooled & in training for 30 years in their political doctrines—& they cannot realize, or conceive, the true state of public sentiment in Va, (& which was general until of late,) of blind veneration for the "Union," & of as blind enthrallment of the people to their leading politicians & demagogues, who were nearly all seeking for office from the Federal Government, & therefore were its corrupt tools.

*April 7.* Sunday. The seventh cloudy & cold & the second rainy day. . . . Telegraphic reports that war steamers have been dispatched from Boston & New York, with 1800 soldiers, [1275] to the South, but destination unknown. Some suppose to blockade the mouth of the Mississippi, others to make war in Texas, in aid of its late (deposed) governor, S. Houston the traitor—& I think, it more probable, to reinforce Fort Pickens. I wish the squadron, even if twice as strong, would attempt to reinforce Fort Sumter. But that is very unlikely. But upon other grounds, fighting may still sooner occur here—& every preparation has been made, & orders given, for all the troops & also the city companies now at home, to be ready under arms in the shortest possible time after hearing the alarm & call to arms sounded by the great bell of St. Michael's church. The ground is, that the previous supplies of provisions allowed to be sent to Fort Sumter, have been at last stopped, & also all other communications between the fort & the outer world. Of this Major Anderson was notified this forenoon. It remains to be seen whether he will submit to the restriction, without retaliation, or that he will also, by his cannon, interrupt all communication between the beseiging [sic] fortifications & the city, & the passage of vessels to & from sea. If he takes the former course, he will soon be starved out. If the latter, he will begin open war, before tomorrow night, & draw upon Fort Sumter the fire of the batteries around. It is very generally the wish of the citizens, & universally of the troops in service, that he may so choose, & thus begin open hostilities. [1276]

*April 8.* The eighth cloudy & cold day, & for all the afternoon & part of the morning, also the third rainy day. I went early after breakfast to the Citadel, & obtained from the commander the loan of a light musket, used by the cadets, with all the appertenent accoutrements, & ammunition—which I had placed at Lawton's counting house near the wharf, where I could obtain it in case of need— which however I have no expectation of. The regular passage steamer was to make its daily visit to the Forts, to carry supplies, munitions, & military passengers, at 10 A.M. It would be the earliest vessel passing near to Fort Sumter—& I supposed would be certainly fired at, to compel its stopping, if such course is designed by Major Anderson. On this account, I was desirous to be on board, & went, though not expecting to be permitted to leave the vessel at any of the batteries, as all previous passes & permission had been revoked. Capt. [J.] Jones, of the regular army was the only officer on board [31]—with some dozen privates, & a few civilians. I suggested

---

[31] Captain Jones was assistant commandant of batteries on Morris Island during the Sumter engagement.

to Capt. J. that the steamer ought not to stop, if fired at, whether with powder only, or with balls—& that he ought to assume the direction. He readily concurred, after ascertaining that the captain of the steamer had no orders how to act, in case of being fired upon. He also, (the captain of the steamer,) was very willing to push on, & not regard any firing on the steamer, unless it should be disabled from proceding [*sic*]. [1277] After leaving the wharf at Fort Johnson, the first stopping place, our steamer had to run around three-fourths of the circuit of Fort Sumter. When approaching within half a mile, of the outer angle, where the distance would be least, we saw through glasses that men on the rampart at that point were loading a cannon. Our course was within 500 to 600 yards of that point, (& returning, within 300 to 400,) but there was no further hostile exhibition. On this trial, I am confident that Anderson will not attempt to interrupt our communications. I wish that he would, & that he would have made the first attempt on this steamer. For I do not think that there would have been much danger to the passengers—& if one had been killed, or wounded, the act would have been the best possible for the cause of secession, & the bringing in Va & other waiting states. I greatly coveted the distinction & *eclat* which I might have acquired if the steamer had been fired upon, & we had refused to yield, & I deemed the danger to be incurred as very trifling. Learned that the mail communications of the garrison of Fort Sumter have not been interrupted. A boat, with flag of truce, left the fort for Fort Johnson, when the mail was left, as we returned from the latter.— At night arrived, from Washington, Capt. [Theodore] Talbot, who was in service at Fort Sumter until recently, when he was permitted, very improperly as I think, to leave, & go on to Washington, on the pretence that he was ordered to Oregon. His now coming back, & [1278] desiring to visit Anderson, proves that he left & has returned to convey secret information in both cases. He saw the Governor, who lodges here, & also Talbot stopped here. After his interviews with the governor & the general, sundry citizens, viewing Talbot as a privileged spy, determined that he should be politely ordered to return northward tonight, at 11 o'clock. Subsequently, I learned that the same order had been previously given by the governor. After I had returned to my room, Ex-Gov. J. P. Richardson came there to inform me of the latest reports just learned from the Governor, which are so important that I will note them, though partly uncertain. First—Capt. Talbot brought a message from Lincoln's government, that supplies had been sent for Fort Sumter, which if there landed without opposition, would be all. But if resisted by force, hostile measures would be used to take the batteries & defeat the southern besieging army. Other reports have also reached the Governor tonight, & which he relies upon in the main, that a squadron of U.S. vessels, (said to be as many as 20) were tonight in or off Bull's Bay, on the way to the harbor of Charleston. As, of course, every resistance will be made by our forces, an attack on our fortifications, by sea & land forces is looked for tomorrow. It is supposed that the land forces will land on Morris' Island, & assail the batteries in the rear. I will endeavor to get there early tomorrow. On account of the warlike preparations [1279] in northern ports, as stated lately in the newspapers, three more regiments had been called into service. One, of this city, will pass over to Morris Island tonight. Two others, from the upper country, will be here late tomorrow, or next day. I feel great confidence in the batteries repelling any vessels of war that may enter the harbor, even with Fort Sumter to aid them. But the attack, by land forces, of our raw though brave volunteers, in the rear of the works, is much more dangerous. The people of the city greatly excited. After 11 P.M. & when a previous long & very heavy rain had just slackened, seven cannon reports were fired in the city, to call immediately to parade, for embarkation, the 17th regiment of city volunteers. This was done, & the main shipment made in the night.

*April 9.* I rose at daybreak, & soon after, paid my bill, & with a small carpet bag only, I went to the wharf, but found the first steamer had gone, & the second, for Morris Island would not leave before the regular hour of 10 A.M. No appearance or report of the enemy's threatened invasion, nor of assault on Fort Sumter, which I think ought not now to be delayed another hour. If anything was before wanting, the intention of Lincoln, as explicitly notified through Talbot, is declared to be of forcible reinforcement—& the forces for the purpose are on the way. We ought to settle with Fort Sumter before another enemy shall be endeavoring to force the passage of the harbor, & to destroy our batteries, or, by troops being landed below, to assail them in the rear.—Obtained my musket & accoutrements, & at 10 embarked, with many volunteers who could not go by the previous night's passage. My going on this occasion was made so much of, & I was accosted by so [1280] many individuals, mostly unknown to me, with words of high praise & compliment, that I felt ashamed of such exaggerated commendation for my very small effort or sacrifice. The like general course was continued after my landing. Owing to the surf running high, the disembarkation was protracted, & a great crowd of previously resident volunteers was assembled at the landing. When I reached the shore, Capt. [George B.] Cuthbert (of the Palmetto Guard & the Iron Battery,) called out for "three cheers for Mr. Ruffin," which were given loudly, & which I acknowledged by taking off my hat, & bowing in silence. I was immediately accosted by Capt. Cuthbert, Major [P. F.] Stevens & Capt. [J. P.] Thomas of the Mil. Acad., & sundry other officers, & invited by several to attach myself more particularly to their respective companies. Capt. Cuthbert also invited me to dine with him, which I did with his mess, a pleasant party. For the companionship & association, I would be glad to remain with the Palmetto Guard, who have charge of the Iron Battery & the adjoining Point Battery, under the command of Major Stevens, who formerly pointed the cannon that were fired on the "Star of the West." But if fighting should occur, I could do nothing with an artillery force—as only with a musket—& moreover, if even so usefully employed in one of these batteries, I could see no more of the engagement outside, than if I was in a cellar in Charleston. So I will make no engagement of connexion—but wait for developments, should any attack be made. . . . Col. Maxcy Gregg, the commander of this post, invited me to pass the night at his quarters, which I accepted. Slept in a small tent close by (in preference to the Colonel's offer of his own bed, in the house,) on a pallet . . . where I slept soundly, open as the tent was, at the door, to the cold outer air.

*April 10.* As nothing has been heard of the arrival of any attacking force, to this morning, the latest report must have been false, as to a squadron of 7 ships being off the harbor. The strong adverse wind, & low tides, would have forbidden an attempt of hostile vessels to force a passage. But the guard steamers, (which every day go out to sea, & return to the lower harbor at night,) would have seen the hostile vessels if any where near. Either they were not there, or they have gone on to Pensacola or Texas, both of which are better points for attack than this. I now believe that even Lincoln's late declaration that he would either supply or forcibly reinforce Fort Sumter, was but another of the government lies for systematic deception.—
As before invited, I today took my quarters in the tent occupied by Major Stevens, Capt. Thomas, Lieut. [N.] Armstrong, (all officers of the Citadel Academy,) & Commissary (private) Holmes, & Clement

Stevens esq. Also, as there was no infantry force near Cummings' Point, & our tent, I concluded to accept the invitation of Capt. Cuthbert, urged on me as soon as I landed yesterday, to join his rifle company, acting as artillery, the "Palmetto Guard" of Charleston. I wrote my offer, to avoid [1282] any mistake. My letter to the Captain, & conditions, were referred to the company, & I was admitted with great enthusiasm. I offer to serve merely in actual military operations, & to join infantry forces, if such are engaged, & also to leave when the present danger of attack on us is over, or the expectation of our assailing Fort Sumter. Previously (last night) I had been elected an honorary member of the "Marion Artillery," another company from Charleston, whose tents are close by ours.—High tide makes today at 7 A.M. & near 8 P.M. With the still adverse wind, no hostile fleet can attempt to come in except at near high water.—Reports still coming from N.Y. indicating great activity & efficiency in fitting out & sending out armed vessels & troops (with sealed orders,)—& in Charleston an attack on our fortifications is generally believed to be close at hand. The officers here were warned by Gen. Beauregard, this evening, that he thought it very probable that an attacking force would reach us during the coming night. Still I am incredulous. Among the measures of precaution, three old vessels were anchored at intervals along the channel below Fort Sumter. These were filled with combustibles, & men left to guard them. Bright lights were kept on them, & if the enemy's vessels should attempt to pass, the illuminating materials, & the vessels, were to be set on fire, to light up the neighboring water.

*April 11.* Excitement increases hourly. To myself & others not in authority, or in the secrets of the high authorities, [1283] every hour passed before attacking Fort Sumter seems a loss of precious time & opportunity. If, as is threatened strongly, armed ships & soldiers are on their way to reinforce Fort Sumter, & as necessary means to attack these troops, it seems that we ought certainly to assail the fort, & take it first, if possible, before we have to meet another enemy, of armed vessels forcing their way up the harbor, & perhaps land forces also landed & assailing our entrenchments & their garrisons in the rear—& we having at the same time to engage Fort Sumter. I had thought that the assault of this Fort ought to have been begun the morning after Lincoln's intended forcible reinforcement was declared by his messenger Lieut. Talbot, & as early as a peremptory summons for surrender could have been sent to Major Anderson, & his negative answer received. So confident was I of the necessity of this course, & its being pursued, that I *tried* to set out for Morris Island before sunrise on the 9th, fearing that the assault would be made, & the communication cut off, before the passage of the regular steamer at 10 A.M. But though disappointed before, it seemed today that the thing would be done. A boat with a messenger bearing a flag of truce was sent by Gen. Beauregard to Major Anderson, demanding his surrender—to which demand a refusal was returned. It was announced on the return of the officer to Charleston, & soon reached us here, that the cannonading of Fort Sumter was to be begun that night at 8 o'clock. Our company, the Palmetto Guard, which has charge of both the Point Battery, & the Iron Battery, [1284] at Cummings' Point nearest (from 1250 to 1300 yards) to Fort Sumter, were paraded at 6, & marched from our tents to these batteries, about one-third of a mile, & within 50 to 100 yards of high water mark. I went with them with my musket & accoutrements. The regular members, though acting as artillery, have also rifles. The iron battery has 3 Columbiads to throw 64 lb. solid shot, or shells. The Point Battery has three mortars, for 10 inch shells, 2 cannon, 42 pounders, & a new rifle cannon, just received & placed tonight which will carry 12 lb. elongated shot, with great accuracy. We had our duties assigned, & arranged, (mine being voluntary,) & we remained at the guns until 8 P.M. Our captain fully expected that the fight would then begin. But at that time, when all our men were in anxious expectation & great excitement, we were discharged to return to our quarters. Still, later orders received, indicated as almost certain that the fight would be begun next morning before daybreak. With such expectation, I prepared for a very hasty movement, & took off (as the previous night,) only my coat & shoes, to go to bed. . . . The Palmetto Guard is composed of very select members—no one being admitted who is not perfectly respectable. Among the privates now in service is Henry Buist, the chairman of the Charleston delegation in the last legislature, & who was the member who moved the call of the Convention to take the state out of the United States. He was Paymaster General of the state militia, which position he resigned to take his place in service as a private of the Palmetto Guard.[32] . . . Capt. Cuthbert is an excellent officer, &

---

[32] A member of the South Carolina House of Representatives, 1858–62 and 1864–65, Henry Buist served in Virginia during the war with the Twenty-seventh South Carolina Regiment. He was captured at Petersburg and imprisoned until the end of the conflict. In 1865 Buist was elected to the state Senate and served until the Radicals seized power two years later.

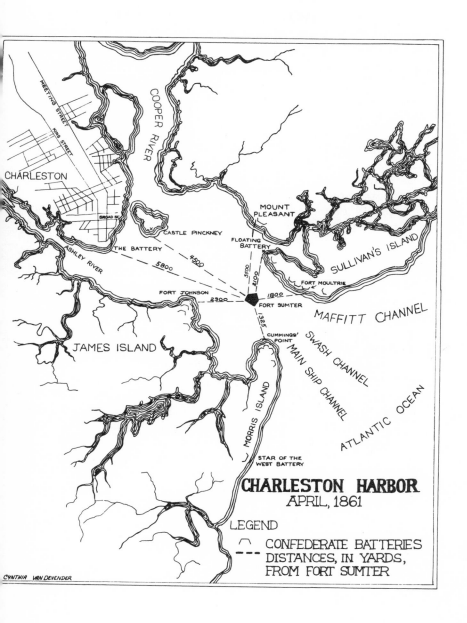

CHARLESTON

COOPER RIVER

MEETING STREET

KING STREET

BROAD ST.

CASTLE PINCKNEY

THE BATTERY

ASHLEY RIVER

FORT JOHNSON

2300

5800

4500

3700

2100

MOUNT PLEASANT

FLOATING BATTERY

1800

FORT SUMTER

1325

CUMMINGS' POINT

FORT MOULTRIE

SULLIVAN'S ISLAND

MAFFITT CHANNEL

SWASH CHANNEL

MAIN SHIP CHANNEL

ATLANTIC OCEAN

JAMES ISLAND

MORRIS ISLAND

STAR OF THE
WEST BATTERY

## CHARLESTON HARBOR
### APRIL, 1861

LEGEND

⌒ CONFEDERATE BATTERIES
--- DISTANCES, IN YARDS,
FROM FORT SUMTER

CYNTHIA VAN DEVENDER

[587]

had charge of the Iron battery—he & his gunners pointing all the guns of that battery. At the Point Battery, Lieut. Armstrong of the Military Academy, directed the firing of the three mortars, & Lieut. [T. Sumter] Brownfield the two 42 pound cannon. Capt. Thomas, of Military Academy, not in regular command here, had the particular charge of the rifle cannon. Major Stevens, commander of the Mil. Academy, (& who pointed the cannon which fired on the "Star of the West,") had the general superintendence & direction of the firing of both the Iron & Point batteries & also the next adjacent Trapier mortar battery, which was one of two batteries manned by the Marion Artillery. The other was the Howitzer battery, close by, but bearing only on the channel.

*April 12.* Before 4 A.M. the drums beat for parade, & our company was speedily on the march to the batteries which they were to man. At 4.30, a signal shell was thrown from a mortar battery at Fort Johnson, which had been before ordered to [1285] be taken as the command for immediate attack—& the firing from all the batteries bearing on Fort Sumter next began in the order arranged—which was that the discharges should be two minutes apart, & the round of all the pieces & batteries to be completed in 32 minutes, & then to begin again. The night before, when expecting to engage, Capt. Cuthbert had notified me that his company requested of me to discharge the first cannon to be fired, which was their 64 lb. Columbiad, loaded with shell. By order of Gen. Beauregard, made known the afternoon of the 11th, the attack was to be commenced by the first shot at the fort being fired by the Palmetto Guard, & from the Iron Battery. In accepting & acting upon this highly appreciated compliment, that company had made me its instrument. . . . Of course I was highly gratified by the compliment, & delighted to perform the service—which I did. The shell struck the fort, at the north-east angle of the parapet. The firing then proceeded, as stated, from 14 different batteries, including Fort Moultrie & the floating battery, which had been placed for this purpose in the cove, back of Sullivan's Island. Most of both shot & shells, at first, missed the fort. But many struck, & the proportion of effective balls & shells increased with the practice. To all this firing, not a gun was fired in return, for two hours or more—& I was fearful that Major Anderson, relying on the security of his men in the covered casemates, proof against shells, & in the strength of the walls against breaching by balls—& in the impossibility of successful storming of the strong fortress, surrounded by water, did not intend to fire at all. It would have cheapened our conquest of the fort, if effected, if no hostile defence had been made—& still more increased the disgrace of failure. So it was gratifying to all of us when Major Anderson opened his [1286] fire. He seemed to distribute his shot mostly between our two batteries, Fort Moultrie & the floating battery. Through the forenoon he fired mostly at our two batteries, & especially at the Point—& with 42 lb. round shot, if all were like a few that we then recovered. But later in the day, (about noon,) he directed most of his fire on Fort Moultrie—& for an hour before closing his firing at night, he did not send a shot to our side. A battery (the Trapier) of three large mortars, next below or eastward of our iron battery, fired regularly & well, but received but few of Anderson's balls, compared to others.[33]

There were more balls fired than I supposed at the Trapier Mortar Battery, & also into our camp of tents in the rear, (where the Palmetto & Marion Guards' tents were,) & completely open to the enemy's shot as well as shells. Some 12 or 15 balls were thus aimed, & several [which] struck the ground passed close by the encampment. I saw from our battery, some 8 or 10 men, (who were idle spectators of the scene, from distant posts,) running at their utmost speed in the direction from the fort. If judging merely from what appeared to my eyes, I might have supposed that they were running from the balls thrown just then from Fort Sumter. But the fact of the case was that they were running after spent balls, to secure them as memorials or trophies. This hunt was eagerly pursued by the men throughout the seige [sic], whenever a ball from the fort stopped near enough to be noticed & recovered. Four of the balls, at least, thus thrown near our camp, as I learned from Capt. Gadsden King, the commander of the Marion Guard, & of the Trapier & Howitzer batteries, were fired at individuals who were exposed, singly or in groups. Two of these balls, in succession were fired at Capt. King, while he was exposed in fixing the haulyard of his flag, which had got out of order. It was understood afterwards that Capt. [Abner] Doubleday, a Yankee abolitionist, directed all these shots at exposed individuals, & that it was contrary to Anderson's order.[34] More than

[33] The next paragraph is one of several addenda inserted by the diarist after writing his original account of the engagement.

[34] Doubleday, who is generally credited with inventing and naming the sport of baseball, fired the first shot from the fort against the besieging Confederates. He went on to achieve a distinguished war record, seeing action in the major eastern battles from Second Manassas to Gettysburg, and attaining the rank of major general.

one (three as believed,) of the early discharges from Fort Sumter, in this direction, were of shells. Of these, one exploded much too soon in its career, & another did not explode at all, & was dug out of the sand bank into which it fell. Of course, these shells must have been thrown from the only Columbiad in the fort, which was on the angle of the parapet nearest to these of our batteries, & which must have been soon after dismounted. Though in advance of the narrative, I will here state that Capt. King from the Trapier battery threw 170 shells, very many of which he thinks were well directed, & exploded over or within the fort.

By noon, it was reported that the expected war steamers & transports from the North had arrived below the bar. Three steamers could then be seen there from our batteries. Two of these were supposed to be recognized as the war steamers Pawnee & Harriet Lane. The other, a large steamer, provided with very large boats, was supposed to be for transporting & landing soldiers. Their position was about 6 miles from our channel batteries. I saw the flag at Fort Sumter lowered about half way, & then raised again—which probably was a signal of recognition, if not something more, of the war steamers, which were in sight of the fort. His being attacked, [1287] & in immediate peril, offered the strongest inducement for the steamers to attempt to reach & succor Fort Sumter immediately—or if unable then, certainly the next night—or to land troops in our rear. One or the other we thought very probable, & every man looked for such results. In comparing the effects of the opposite firing, so far as known, the advantage was much in our favor. It was thought that two, if not three, of the *barbette* guns of Fort Sumter had been dismounted by our balls. Some 5 or 6 chimneys of the houses in the fort had been knocked down. What damage had been done by our shells which fell within the walls, or exploded over the fort, we had no means for knowing. But though many of our balls had struck the fort, & in every case penetrated the walls far enough to dislodge a quantity of bricks or smaller fragments, & to throw off clouds of dust, & though these spots were sprinkled thickly over the walls, there was no break made, & the garrison might perhaps resist such cannonading for a week. On our side, the enemy's balls had done scarcely any damage. Though most of them were in good direction, & missed our parapet (of the Point battery) by very little— striking in the marsh in our rear at distances from 300 to less than 50 yards from the rear of the battery—still much the greater number did so pass over the parapet of sand bags, & none struck the defences until late in the day. These balls buried in the sand, without the least damage. More balls struck the iron battery—some 9 or 10. But they [1288] glanced off from the greatly inclined iron roof, in most cases without doing any harm, & without making much mark. One only, which struck the cover of a port hole, & which, to be lifted & closed, was necessarily made of much thinner iron than the doubled rail-road iron bars of the solid roof, was considerably indented, & the hinges of the trap-door broken. This damage was subsequently repaired, so as to resume the use of that port-hole & cannon. Not a man has yet been killed or struck. The discharges of cannon directed against our batteries could always be seen by the flame of the explosion, & the notice being given by one on the watch, all the garrison of the sand works could stoop low enough, or otherwise get behind defences, so as to be perfectly safe. The men working the cannon, & in the line of the open embrasures, only were necessarily exposed for a short time. After seeing the flash of the discharge, some 4 to 6 seconds of time were required for the balls to reach our positions, which, with notice called out, was ample time for the men to occupy safe postures or positions. After my firing the first gun in the iron battery, it was my assumed duty, with consent of Capt. Cuthbert & Lieut. Armstrong, to perform this service, of looking over the parapet of the Point Battery, [1289] to watch the striking of the balls & shells sent from it, & to call out the accuracy or defect of direction & effect—& to give notice of the coming balls. This was service essential to be performed by some one. But there were others of the unemployed soldiers (for the time,) who afterwards stood with me to indulge their curiosity, which caused Col. [Wilmot G.] De Saussure,[35] about 1 o'clock, to order all of us down, lest we should attract the notice & fire of Major Anderson. So I lost my post for the remainder of the day—& soon after, (as it was necessary to be performed) found another person, Mr. Buist, had been requested by an officer, & was acting in that capacity. So, for the remainder of the afternoon, I merely endeavored, in other places than looking over the parapet, to watch the effect of the balls & shells fired at Fort Sumter. Also, by invitation of the officers, or of the gunners, I fired off several other guns & mortars after they had been pointed. The last this day were the three 10 inch mortars in the Trapier battery next below our iron battery . . . . The day was cloudy, & with several

---

[35] Commandant of batteries on Morris Island.

transient slow rains. Soon after dark, there was a very heavy rain, which ceased in half an hour. After midday, the order had been given to reduce by half the previous quickness of firing, or to 4 minutes between every two discharges. The firing from Fort Sumter was entirely suspended an hour before dark. The mortars [1290] only continued to fire throughout the night, but so slowly that there was only one discharge from the whole once in 20 minutes. After dark, I went out of our tent to observe the appearance of the shells, in their luminous course, as seen in the night. A line of light shows along the whole curve of the course, preceded by the brilliant explosion of the discharge of the shell from the mortar, & another made by the final bursting of the shell. Before this, I had gone to bed (in our tent on the camp ground,) at 7 P.M. in the hope of getting some sleep early—but could not sleep, & arose & went out. Met sundry other persons also looking out, & trying, in vain, by aid of the transient illuminations by the faint sheet lightning to see the positions & movements of the enemy's war steamers. After again getting to bed, & to sleep, I was roused by hearing the irregular firing of cannon, quite near, & of small arms in quick succession. I hastily struck a light, & putting on the few articles of clothing I had thrown off, & my arms, I went out, thinking that the enemy from the ships had certainly landed, or were trying in the great darkness to pass in boats up the channel. On reaching the water's edge, a shell from the 64 lb. howi[t]zer battery, passed not far off, making a straight streak of light down the channel. But [1291] I soon learned that it was a false alarm, caused by some drunken Irishmen in a boat, who, when hailed, would neither stop nor reply properly. So the boat was supposed to be one of those expected from the steamers, & was fired upon not only by numerous muskets, but caused the heavy howitzers to throw their shells at random down the supposed track of the passage of the boats. Whether the boat with its drunken crew was struck, or not, no one then knew. The wind was high, & the night very dark, & the tide, which had risen unusually high, was falling after 9 or 10 P.M. so that no steamers could have ventured in. And the very heavy surf would have made landing from boats very difficult, though not hazardous to life.

. . . Nearly all our men of the engaged companies remained all night in their respective batteries, even the portions not required for duty at the time. To each of most of the batteries there was attached a close apartment, deeply covered, over the strong timber roof, with sand, & securely protected against both balls & shells. In these it was designed that the men off of duty should retire, & remain for safety. But very few resorted to these places, & at no time, unless by any disposed to sleep. As I could render no service at night, & very little was done by any, I designed to get as much sleep as possible. For this purpose, I went to our tent, & was the only lodger therein for that night. . . .

*April 13.* At daybreak, I arose, & hurried, with our company, to man our batteries, & resume the slow cannonade & bombarding, as during yesterday—which was done, from every battery. As on yesterday, there was no return from Fort Sumter, until nearly 7 A.M., when Anderson recommenced his fire, but directed it exclusively to Sullivan's Island & thence to Fort Moultrie & the Floating Battery. I had resumed, with consent of Lieut. Armstrong, my previous service of watching from the parapet the effect of our balls & shells, & to give notice of firing on us, if there had been any. It had been a disputed question whether Major Anderson had or had not a mortar —or shells, which even if having no mortar, he could throw from his one 10 inch Columbiad. It was supposed that he had shells, & the means for using them, but reserved them for more important [1292] service, when the war steamers should attempt to force their passage to reinforce or otherwise assist him. So we derived no assurance on this head from his having so far omitted (as then generally supposed,) to fire shells. We had some hope that his only Columbiad had been dismounted. He had fired some guns from the ramparts (placed *en barbette,*) yesterday forenoon, but having ceased to do so, we supposed that he found that service too great an exposure for his weak garrison of some 70 soldiers. On acount of their small number, it was not only important to prevent any being killed or disabled, but also to save them as much as possible from fatigue. For opposite reasons, we were trying to wear them down by want of opportunity for sleep & rest, as they were safe from cannon balls behind their thick walls, & from exploding shells, when under their bomb-proof case-mates. If he could not hurt us, (unless by shells, which, if used, would be most destructive in our perfectly open earth-work batteries,) his men were equally safe from us, so long as protected by the walls & casemates.—As no more balls were fired on our batteries, from the three lower (or casemate) cannon used for that purpose yesterday, we began to hope that all three of these guns had been dismounted, or otherwise that the men, when engaged there in firing, were [1293] too much exposed to our shot. Two of the three port holes looked as if enlarged by entering balls.—The fire of Major Anderson was continued, as on yesterday, but confined entirely to Fort Moultrie & the floating battery, & principally on the Fort. This preference was interpreted in different ways. Capt. Stephen D. Lee,[36] formerly in the U.S.A. & well acquainted with the places, thought that Anderson was trying to fire into & blow up the powder magazine, which formerly was very much exposed, & especially to the fire from Fort Sumter. Our commander, Major Stevens, thought that A. was aiming to cripple Fort Moultrie so that it could not prevent the passage of the war vessels now ready to reinforce Fort Sumter.[37]

Our breakfast had been brought from the kitchen at the camp, & I ate some crackers & drank a tin-cup of coffee. My meal being soon over, & having nothing to occupy me just then, I took a seat on a block, & leaned my back against the wall of the mortar battery—which inside was kept upright by being faced with squared logs. Without intending it, I fell asleep, & remained so until the first 10 inch mortar was fired. This was the one not far from my seat, & of which I was obliquely in front. Thus placed, the sound & concussion were unusually powerful, & I was roused not only by the loud & close report, but by a great shock to my ears & sense of hearing. My previous slight deafness was greatly increased. My hearing has remained greatly impaired, though with some gradual improvement, to this time, 10 days after the damage, & I fear will never be restored to the previous better condition. . . . It was after this that I fired off the greater number of the 27 discharges which, in all, I let off, of cannon & mortars, but took care not again to be in front of the mouths of the mortars when fired off.

Things so continued, & our shots & shells being more & more accurately aimed, until about 8 A.M. when a new incident occurred. A shell from one of the mortars (No 3) of the Point battery was seen to fall into the fort, near its western extremity. The smoke that suc-

---

[36] No relation to the Virginia Lees, Stephen Dill Lee (1833–1908) was born in South Carolina and graduated from West Point in 1854. He served as aide-de-camp to General Beauregard during the Sumter engagement and later saw extensive service in both the eastern and western theaters, rising by war's end to the rank of lieutenant general. Following the close of hostilities he settled in Mississippi, where he became the first president of what is now Mississippi State University.

[37] The following paragraph was written ten days after the incident recounted therein and inserted at this point in the narrative by the diarist.

ceeded continued longer than usual from the mere bursting of a shell, & afterwards increased. Some time after, flame was seen, & we knew that a roof was on fire. But all the houses were of brick, with slate roofs, & we feared that the progress of burning would be slow, & easily checked. To prevent this, every battery, without any order from abroad, & as from one impulse, abandoned the prescribed & very slow rate of firing, & began to throw shot or shells as fast as the pieces of artillery could be worked & well aimed—& ours, [1294] if not others, were especially directed, at first, to the flames of the burning house. The cannonade became rapid & of tremendous effect for the object in view. The wind blew strong from the west, where the fire broke out, & a volume of dense black smoke spread across the fort, through which the lurid flames could at first be but partly & irregularly visible. The spectacle, & especially with the increase of the rising flames, was of intense interest. In the impending consequences it was of still more interest & importance. Never did I feel such anxiety for a doubtful effect, or such excitement—in which all on our side fully participated. The hail of balls & shells kept pouring upon or within the fort, would have prevented the exertions which might have been otherwise made to put out the flames. The fire rose more & more, until the general destruction of the buildings was almost certain. At the first showing of the flame, & our men being notified of the fact that the fort was on fire, a general shout was made—& in like manner were indicated their joy & exultation at each successive renewal & violent increase of the work of destruction. The fire gradually passed across the whole breadth of the fort, from west to east, along the row of barracks, & at right angles to our position. But as the first part subsided, for want of more fuel, it was seen that the burning had been only of the row of houses of one (the southern) side of [1295] the area, & that buildings on the other side (as I supposed) had escaped, & might still escape. Presently, we heard sounds like the successive & irregular firing of numerous muskets, & also of cannon—& saw jets of white smoke, manifest[ly] the result of burning gunpowder, shooting out of & strongly contrasting with the black smoke of burning wood, & especially of resinous pine timbers. Sometimes, bright flames shot up above the smoke, the evident results of explosions of confined gunpowder. It was manifest that the flames, or heat, had reached a magazine of loaded shells & hand grenades. This settled the before disputed question as to whether the fort contained shells, & also settled all dread of their being used against us, by their present destruction. Some time after,

[595]

the flames, or heat, fired another small magazine (probably of cartridges,) from which a high & broad sheet of flame shot up from the eastern side of the interior of the fort, followed by much white smoke. The very rapid firing by the beseigers [*sic*] was kept up for an hour or more, & until the flames had swept over so much of the buildings . . . that their general destruction was inevitable. Then the firing was slackened to its previous rate, or nearly so. From time to time however, all the pieces of our two batteries were fired, & in volleys of each set. Thus, the three Columbiads (& now loaded with shell every time,) were discharged in quick succession—at another time in like manner the three 10 inch mortars of the Point, & the two 42 pounders at another time. The rifle cannon has been silent since yesterday afternoon, for want [1296] of more of its peculiar ammunition. After the conflagration had swept over the range of building on the near side of the fort, fire again rose seemingly where it had first begun, & flames soon after burst out of the roof of the western building which had remained unhurt before, & later, spread to the detached one on the east. The only remaining buildings were consumed, & it seemed, to our outside view & inferences, that the whole area of the fort must have been so hot, & full of suffocating smoke, as to be intolerable to the garrison. And there was another danger imminent, of far more awful character. The principal powder magazine was known to be under the angle of the fort nearest to us. It was certainly well supplied with powder, & however well secured from the approach of fire, it could scarcely escape when flames were passing over, besides all the explosions of shells. I looked on, with my feelings of joy & exultation at our now certain prospect of speedy success mixed with awe & horror at the danger of this terrible calamity, & pity for the men exposed to the consequences—& with high admiration for the indomitable spirit of the brave commander —who seemed determined to hold his position to the last extremity. During the conflagration, which lasted some 4 or 5 hours, Anderson continued to fire, though at more distant intervals, & always at Fort Moultrie. All of our men who were not engaged for the time at the guns & mortars, were intently looking on the scene at the fort. [1297] As no more firing on us was to be expected (there having been not a shot in all the day,) & no danger of the display of heads drawing fire on them, the previous prohibition was practically withdrawn, & very many soldiers & officers, not only of our own command, but some from the distant posts, were looking out, over the parapets, or

[596]

from the outside sand-banks. Whenever a new outburst of the conflagration was seen, or an explosion, a shout would be made by all
the spectators, which would be echoed by the men engaged in the
batteries. So far, the flag-staff & flag of the fort had remained unhurt, though, to our eyes, rising just out of dense smoke & flame. But
in the latter & closing passage of the conflagration, the flag-staff
suddenly fell, as if burnt at bottom, or cut off by cannon balls, & the
flag was no longer to be seen. Then arose the loudest & longest shout
of joy—as if this downfall of the flag, with its cause, was the representation of our victory. The accidental fall of the flag in itself was
nothing, as it could be forthwith replaced, & was, after some 15 minutes, by one on the parapet farthest from our position, & out of sight
from it, though visible to other places, & especially plain to Fort
Moultrie. As soon as the flag fell, all of our batteries ceased firing, &
in our three Morris Island batteries, the cessation was final. But after
some length of time, when (as we afterwards learned,) the substituted flag had been placed, & was seen by the more distant posts,
Fort Moultrie & the Mount Pleasant battery, the fire was resumed
slowly, & returned [1298] by Anderson, during his then situation, by
one discharge only that was visible to us. His long delay of replacing
his flag, & still longer delay as it appeared to our anxiety, induced
our commander to send off an officer, with a flag of truce, to repeat
the demand for surrender. L[ouis] T. Wigfall of Texas, acting aid to
Gen. Beauregard, was the bearer of the message. While the boat was
nearing the fort, some of the discharges of shells from our distant
batteries fell in rather dangerous proximity to our unseen flag of
truce. Soon after the boat reached the fort, a flag of truce was raised
there, together with the substituted U.S. flag, & all firing ceased.
After an anxious delay, on our side, the boat was seen returning, the
white flag still floating on the fort. When approaching the beach,
where numerous expectant spectators were waiting, Col. Wigfall
stood up & waved his hat, & gave three cheers, which were responded to by all on the shore. When he landed, & could be heard,
he announced that Major Anderson had yielded unconditionally, &
that it remained only to execute the formalities of capitulation.[38]

---

[38] Wigfall, who had spent more time surveying the bars of Charleston than
in aiding Beauregard, was not authorized to offer terms to the Union commander. For an amusing account of the comedy of errors which marked Anderson's efforts to surrender on the afternoon of April 13, see T. Harry Williams,
*P. G. T. Beauregard: Napoleon in Gray* (Baton Rouge: Louisiana State University Press, 1955), 59–61.

This was about 2 P.M. It was supposed by us that the honor of garrisoning the captured fort would be given to the Palmetto Guard, for more important reasons than the sufficient one that its men were all who were then at the nearest position. And expecting the order for occupation would be soon made, & no time for preparation, we remained there for two hours before going to the camp for refreshment. Still the arrangements were dragging on, & [1299] to our great disappointment & disgust, remained unfinished, & with the U.S. flag still flying on the fort, at night.—About 5 P.M. a boat with a strong crew of rowers, brought an officer with a flag of truce from the fleet to the beach, & the officer in command saw & communicated, at the Cummings' Point landing, with our commander. He stated (another most transparent lie,) that the squadron of war steamers, still anchored below in our sight, came to take away Major Anderson & his command—& proposed that they should be allowed still to do so. No consent was given, of course, or intimated—but a final communication, in answer, was promised at 9 A.M. tomorrow. Now this is the meanest, basest, & most enormous lie, & useless deception attempted, by this lying administration, of all yet perpetrated. These ships are filled with troops, & certainly came with hostile intention—either to reinforce Anderson, or to attack our forts, as previously indicated by everything, including the communication made from Lincoln through Capt. Talbot, sent after these vessels had been started. They were off our port on the 11th. Before 1 P.M. on the 12th (perhaps by 12,) when the bombardment was begun, four of these war steamers and a transport steamer were at their present anchorage below the bar, & only 6 miles distant from Fort Sumter & our channel batteries—& were seen by Major Anderson, & signals exchanged. Then there was full time to aid & save him, if deemed possible—& there were great facilities in very high tides, & a very dark & stormy night. They neither attempted to aid him, nor to communicate the now pretended business of peaceably removing the garrison. And now after Anderson's brave & desperate defence has [1300] been closed, & his surrender compelled, two or three hours after they must have seen that he had surrendered, this ridiculous tale is brought to be put off for the truth.

*April 14.* Sunday. A clear & warm day. The Palmetto Guard were complimented with being among the detachments, (& the only entire company ordered,) to take possession of Fort Sumter, as soon as it should be vacated by the U.S. troops. We paraded at 10, &, on motion of Capt. Cuthbert, I was chosen to carry the company flag—which I did. We embarked on board a steamer at 11, & dropped anchor at some 150 yards from Fort Sumter. The Isabel steamer lay near, which was to take away the garrison. Though the surrender had been unconditional, the most honorable terms, & every courtesy & indulgence had been awarded to the brave commander, as he well deserved. The fixing for & the final removal occupied several hours. But the time of waiting was not tedious, being occupied by viewing the scene before us, & in animated conversation on the recent occurrences. We now first heard from all the remote batteries, & learned that they, like ours, had not had a man killed or wounded. It was more remarkable that the garrison had been almost equally exempt, there having been only a few slight wounds from flying splinters or fragments. The neighboring water was covered with vessels of every discription [*sic*], from large steamers to small rowboats, filled with anxious spectators, who were content to look on for hours, though not to be permitted, even after the surrender, to enter the fort, or to land on its narrow margin outside of the walls. It was between 2 [1301] & 3 P.M. when the preparations for leaving had been completed, & Major Anderson proceeded to the last service, to fire a salute to his flag, before pulling it down. The cannon on the ramparts were discharged for this purpose, & I learned thereby that 11 pieces of artillery in that upper range were still ready for service, by as many separate guns being discharged. There were 50 discharges. When some 47 had been made, an additional explosion was heard, on the south-east side, which was opposite to the place of our vessel. It was some time before we heard the sad cause, by a boat coming for surgical aid. Some cannon cartridges which had been left when the rampart guns were abandoned, had subsequently been covered & concealed by the fallen rubbish. In firing the cannon near, a spark had exploded the gunpowder, & severely injured 6 of the U.S. soldiers. This disaster delayed the evacuation for two hours more, while the wounded men could receive necessary attention. One soon died, & was immediately burried [*sic*] in the area, by order of General Beauregard, (who, with sundry other dignitaries, was then in the fort,) with the honors of war. Two others seemed to be dying. Three others were dangerously hurt, but two of them were put on board the Isabel. The others, not too far gone, were afterwards sent to the hospital at Charleston. After 4 P.M. the last of the previous garrison had left, & our troops entered the fort—the steamer having some time before drawn close. It was not until the evacuation was complete, that the Confederate States flag & the Palmetto flag were hoisted simultaneously, on [1302] temporary & low flagstaffs. Our company then was permitted to enter the fort. A detachment of regulars, from Fort Moultrie, had just preceded us. We found there the Governor, & all the high authorities then in Charleston. We were immediately discharged, for the time, & I hastened to look over & around the fort. The walls outside were thickly sprinkled with marks of cannon balls, which had not penetrated more than from 6 to 18 inches, & had nowhere made a breach. Three-fourths of the numerous chimneys of the barracks were knocked down, or much shattered & weakened. Four of the cannon on the rampart (about the angle next to the Point batteries,) had been dismounted, & disabled. One of these was the 10 inch Columbiad, the only piece suited to throw shells. I presume that these guns had been either dismounted early in the cannonade, or the ramparts rendered altogether too dangerous for any guns to be served there. We did not go into the gun casemates (lower tier,) & therefore I did not then learn whether these also had been disabled, (as they did not so appear from outside the port-holes—) or whether these places also had been made too dangerous by the fire from our two batteries. But around each of the three adjacent port-holes, at the flattened south angle, (or *pancoupé*,) which only had been open, & from which all the balls were thrown towards the Morris Island side, (after the early cessation of firing from the parapet,) there were marks of several different balls, which struck so close to the edges of the port-holes, that they must have gone into them. The fire had been more destructive to the walls of the buildings than the shot & shells. And the fire was still going on, finding [1303] fuel in the timbers covered by fallen bricks & smaller rubbish. A fire engine was then vigorously worked, but was not enough to prevent the fire increasing, so that more firemen & another engine were sent for, after dark, to Charleston. It was said that the fire was then within 10 feet or less of the smaller of the two permanent magazines, both having quantities of gunpowder, & which could not then be removed, or rendered harmless by being wetted. These were not the only dangers of this kind. Broken cartridges, & loose powder were seen scattered about. Also, as Major Anderson notified one of our officers, the platform, or only landing place, in front of the sally-port, or south side, was mined, & filled with gunpowder & other combustibles, ready to be exploded if a storming force had landed. Further, many loaded shells had been buried under the closely laid pavement of very thick & broad stone, under the outer side of the wall on the south side (that of the Sally-port,) with strings attached to the friction fuses, which strings could be pulled by persons within the fort, & made to explode beneath the feet of assailants aiming to enter by storming the fort. All these things rendered the first occupancy of the fort hazardous.—Our captain informed us that, by order of the General, but one half of our company would remain, & the other half be sent back to Morris Island. All my baggage, & the provisions of our mess, . . . had been left on the beach, waiting for conveyance. Under these circumstances, I requested leave to be of the half to return, which was readily granted. It was [1304] some time after dark that I went out for this purpose, & on board a steamer lying alongside the fort . . . . I had designed to secure my bedding & baggage, & with them to go in the same steamer to Charleston. But I had scarcely got on the upper deck before the steamer set off, & my return was cut off before I learned that I was in the wrong steamer, & that this was going to Charleston for fire-engines & fire-men. . . . I went to the Charleston Hotel, & there got a late supper, which was the first food since my breakfast. As soon as I entered the hall, which as usual at night was crowded, I was surrounded by those who saw me, strangers as well as previous acquaintances, & I was beset with inquiries, & kept occupied in giving the required information of the siege & surrender until after 11, when I went to bed.

*April 15.* . . . Saw several late comers from Petersburg & the neighboring country, & among them Roger A. Pryor, who came lately & has taken service as Aid to the Governor. My greeting of him was much more cordial than any previous, since our difference some years ago. However unfaithful he then was to the defence of the south, & opposed to secession, he is now fully embarked in the cause. Therefore I am willing to forget former differences & their causes, & to receive him [1305] as an able & efficient auxiliary.—After 10. A.M. I again left in the regular steamer for Morris Island. There I found my luggage, & returned with it to Fort Sumter, where I expected to find my company, & after spending the day there, to again go to Charleston at night. None of the company, as I now learned, had returned last night to Morris Island. When the steamer went to the Fort, after leaving the island, I found that the Palmetto Guard had already gone there by another steamer, & without my seeing them on the passage..There was no way to get to them, & indeed it was unimportant, being now past noon. So I had to remain on the steamer—having no pass to enter the fort, or reason for it when my company had left—until the business for the vessel was done. I reached the hotel but a little before sunset.—When we first passed by the fort this forenoon, the fire engines were still at work, &, as heard, the covered fire not extinguished. But the engines were doing also the service of putting water to the gunpowder in the mine. Heard that more than 100 kegs of powder from one of the magazines, had been thrown out into the water, as the readiest mode of removing the danger of their possible explosion.—Since my first coming into S.C. in last November, I have been received & treated by all persons with whom I have come in contact, with great kindness & attention, as if I was really a public benefactor of rare merit. From entire strangers, & in many cases persons of humble position as well as the higher classes, in numerous cases I have received manifestations of great respect & high appreciation. [1306] But since the beginning of my recent military service, & still more since the surrender of Fort Sumter, the evidences of general popular favor & expressions of individual consideration & applause have increased ten-fold, & make me ashamed of such great distinction.—The Governor of N.Ca. has ordered bodies of volunteer militia to occupy the U.S. forts & arsenal in that state. This is a strong indication of the progress of public sentiment there in changes favorable to secession. Reports of great excitement in Richmond, & great changes in the state, especially hastened by the conflict of Fort Sumter, & Lincoln's recent proclamation calling on the states for 75,000 volunteers to subdue the South. Of these, portions are required from Va, & all the other southern states not yet seceded. A telegram sent to me & R. A. Pryor this afternoon from R[ichmon]d, 15th. from Thomas Branch, (a *union* member of the Convention, from Petersburg, but lately *instructed* by his changed constituents to vote for secession,) says that "an ordinance of secession will pass (The Convention) in sixty hours." This change, in so vile a submission body, is too great to be credible. . . . The indulgence of our authorities to the enemy, or neglect of all proper safeguards to prevent dangerous communication, has been remarkable & inexcusable. Not only were all mail communications allowed to Major Anderson & all of his garrison, throughout their occupancy of Fort Sumter, to two days before the bombardment, but spies & secret messengers were allowed repeatedly to visit the fort, or to leave it for Washington & then return. Indeed there was no refusal, in some 4 or more cases, until the last attempt of Talbot, returning from Washington. But the worst case occurred yesterday—& which seems to have been known or noticed by very few. I heard it early today, with astonishment, but have been more particularly informed by Pryor, who came late into my room, & conversed with me on this & kindred subjects. He is acting as Aid de Camp to the Governor—& as such, went down to the U.S. squadron, early on the morning of the 14th, in one of our government steamers, commanded by Capt. [Henry J.] Hartstein [*sic*],³⁹ to arrange the sending & receiving of the garrison. When returning, Com. Gillis, the commander of this hostile squadron—which certainly came to attack our batteries, & from which we have still every reason (except the remarkable [1308] omission heretofore,) to suppose they still threaten such attack—asked & obtained leave of Capt. Hartstein to come up in his company to Fort Sumter, & to return with Major Anderson. He did so, without even the formality, & notification to the public, of having a flag of truce. He came up the harbor, between & in full view of all our defences, freely using the great facilities afforded of looking over the whole adjacent & exposed country, & asking questions & having them answered in most cases, as if he had been a friendly visitor. He entered the fort by 9 A.M., remained there, & in the Isabel at anchor close by, until the final evacuation, after 4 P.M., & then returned in the Isabel, still more free to view with a good glass all the defences & the back country. A military or naval commander could scarcely have devised a better or more full general reconnaissance of the country & defensive fortifications & camps, which he designed to attack by surprise, by either or both land & water.—Major Ripley, the commandant of Fort Moultrie, was at Fort Sumter on the evening after the surrender. He told me that the buildings there were very much damaged by Anderson's shot. The earth-works were scarcely injured in the least—which is in evidence of their great superiority for defence.—Gov. Pickens was among the visitors to Fort Sumter, immediately after the surrender. ... He received & [1309] accosted me very politely, regretting that he had not been able to see me much earlier, & repeated the in-

---

³⁹ Formerly an officer in the United States Navy, Captain Hartstene was a voluntary aide-de-camp to General Beauregard and had charge of the harbor defenses at Charleston during the Sumter crisis. He was one of three aides sent to the fort to offer surrender terms following Wigfall's unauthorized visit on the afternoon of April 13.

vitation for me to call & visit him. He had previously, some time back, sent to me the like invitation in two special messages . . . . On each occasion I politely returned my thanks, but did not promise to accept the invitation, nor did I intend to do so. The Governor's polite attention came too late. When I first came to Charleston, I deemed it proper to call on the Governor at his office, & sent in my card. He was then engaged in business & excused himself—which I deemed entirely right. Afterwards, when he heard from Dr. Bachman that I was about to set out for Tallahassee, he sent a message to request me to report to him by telegraph the earliest news of the Secession of Florida. This I did, at a cost to myself of nearly $3—but I have never heard whether he received the telegram, as it has never been acknowledged. When I returned to Charleston, he had moved to this hotel. In consequence of his message & request to me, I thought it proper again to send my card to his parlor. He was not in—& I never heard anything from him, until the messages of invitation sent to me some 6 or 7 weeks afterwards. Now I certainly did not expect a governor to return my intended visit, or even to send his card. . . . But I at least expected, & waited for, some early acknowledgment of my [1310] attempted visit, & a verbal & general invitation for me to repeat it. As it was not so done, early, I will not accept any so long deferred civilities, if I can manage to evade them without rudeness, & obvious design to refuse.

*April 16.* Pryor is going to Montgomery—& by him I sent to President Davis a fragment of one of our bursted bomb-shells, which fell within Fort Sumter.—The U.S. squadron which had been anchored in the outer harbor since the 12th inst., this morning had disappeared—& a vessel which came in from sea later, reported seeing some of the steamers going northward. If they have returned, it is indeed a most pitiful & disgraceful affair. The squadron certainly was sent to reinforce Anderson, & by force. It was well provided & prepared in equipments, both for forcing a passage by water, or for landing the troops in the night, & attacking our batteries in the rear, which was entirely unprotected by cannon. Besides the 2000 or 2500 land troops reported to be on board, there were numerous boats, with all the oars muffled, as if for landing troops for an attack in the night & by surprise. And the squadron was in place, within 6 miles, & in full view of Fort Sumter 26 hours before it ceased its gallant defence—& when it would have been a most efficient auxiliary to an invading force. The refusal to aid Anderson, & the subsequent retreat

without attempting anything, seem to make a most contemptible admission of either weakness or timidity.—Two later telegrams from
Richmond indicate so great increase of the secession feeling, that an
act of secession is now counted upon by this Convention. [1311] Gov.
Wise reports that there was today a majority of the Convention
ready to vote for secession—but it was deemed politic not to press
for the vote today, because a larger majority may be expected soon.
Good news also from N.Ca. Gov. Ellis has ordered the occupation of
forts Macon & Caswell by volunteers—which was done yesterday—&
the arsenal at Fayetteville, which is guarded by 60 U.S. soldiers
was to be summoned today. But there are no cannon or ammunition
in these forts, & they were written for here, & will be supplied by
Gov. Pickens.—In the recent great crisis of the political condition
of S.Ca., when the most able citizens were needed to direct the state
—& when there were ready for the service of the state so many citizens of high talent & ability, (as was shown in a large proportion of
the members of the Convention—) it was very strange that at the
very time the legislature should have elected as the chief magistrate
so ordinary a man as Pickens, whose claims on the scores of talent,
patriotic services to the state, or fitness for the then great occasion,
were inferior to hundreds of other citizens. He was, when in Congress, more distinguished as an inflated bag of wind than for high
talent or services. In addition, he has become intemperate, & I have
heard is more or less elevated with his drinking almost every afternoon. This however was not his condition at the only time of my
meeting with him, at Fort Sumter.

*April 17.* . . . Extracts from the N.Y. Tribune & other papers of that
stamp, just seen, will confirm & extend what previously we could
only guess at, in regard to the [1313] strength & the objects of the
naval force lately off the harbor—& which left, & went to the northward on Monday evening. The strength, especially in land forces,
was greater than we supposed. If an attempt had been made on the
day or night of the 12th. to force the steamers by our batteries, & also
to land the troops to attack our rear, while Fort Sumter would be engaging Fort Moultrie, it might have been an ugly business for our
brave yet raw soldiers. But [1314] [as it] was then declined, when
high tides, rain-storm & darkness & Anderson's fighting, all favored
the attempt, it was hardly to be expected after the surrender of the
fort. Still, we did not expect the fleet to flee so soon, without attempting anything. . . . Telegraphic dispatches continue reports fa-

vorable to the progress of secession in Va, & also in other border states. The governors of Va, N.Ca. & Ky. have all in terms of indignation refused to comply with the requisition of Lincoln for volunteers to assail the C.S. There are secession movements reported at Memphis, Ten. & at Louisville, Ky. Duncan McRae[40] was sent here from N.C. to obtain cannon & ammunition to arm Fort Macon, which Gov. Pickens has supplied.—Telegraphic dispatch from R[ichmon]d that Gov. Letcher had ordered vessels to be sunk in the channel of the river below Norfolk, to prevent the passage of large vessels, either from sea, or out from the Navy Yard above. It is said that [1315] there are three U.S. warships at the Navy Yard, which, if this obstruction is maintained, will be prevented from escaping, if the Navy Yard should be taken. This measure of Letcher's is a strong indication of the public feeling for secession, considering that he has been very far from so disposed himself. Also there came last night, & were repeated today, telegrams from Ex-Gov. Wise, *seemingly* concurred in by Gov. Letcher, asking urgently of Gov. Pickens to send forthwith a body of some thousand of S.C. soldiers in aid of Va. & to seize on the Portsmouth Navy Yard. I cannot understand the need of, or any propriety for any such movement, even if Va is now ready for such extreme policy. Surely the state can furnish 5000 volunteers, without foreign aid. At any rate, I hope (& have so advised, through Pryor,) that Gov. Pickens shall take no such step on the suggestions of Wise, or any one but the Governor of the State, authorised to act for the State. At 5 P.M. the Va. Convention still in secret session, & no farther progress made in the work of secession so far as made known.

*April 18....* I was informed, confidentially, that the Va Convention had passed an ordinance of secession on yesterday,... but continued in secret session to prevent the northern government knowing the fact, & so prevent the early designs of the State. But the secret leaked out, & was communicated by telegraph to Augusta, Ga, & thence sent here by 2 P.M. I was immediately sent for at the hotel, & proceeded to the Courier [1316] office, to fire the "secession cannon," as a salute. This I did—as has been done by the same cannon for each of the 7 preceding states—one discharge for each act of

---

[40] Formerly United States consul at Paris, Duncan Kirkland McRae (1820–88) later served as colonel of the Fifth North Carolina Regiment before being wounded at Antietam in the fall of 1862. He performed diplomatic and editorial services for the balance of the war.

secession. In the afternoon, other dispatches reported that the Harper's Ferry Arsenal had been occupied by troops under orders of the Governor of Va—& confirmed the previous report that the channel below Norfolk had been obstructed, under state authority, by the sinking of old vessels.—Went to obtain more copies of the card photographs by Quinby, & could not be fully supplied. He informed me that he cannot supply the demand of purchasers, & that besides purchasers in person, he has now orders by mail for 50 copies. This brisk trade of his is some evidence of my recent celebrity. [George S.] Cook also had requested my sitting, & has finished large & good portraits in two different views, as well as three different card photographs.[41] Though he is the superior artist, I do not think his card photographs, at 50 cents, of which I bought a few, are as good pictures as Quinby's at 25. ... Went at 3, upon previous written invitation [1317] of Judge Mitchell King to dine with him & a family gathering of a portion of his sons & their wives. Was very kindly & respectfully received by all, & spent a pleasant time before & during dinner. The secession of Va had been just before announced, & I departed from my usual abstinence so far as to drink a glass of ale, & another of wine, on the occasion. Mrs. King (wife of an absent son of Judge K.,) the daughter of Mr. Pettigru [*sic*], whom I had known some 6 or 7 years ago, was one of the family party. She is a very talented, agreeable, & *fast* woman, & an authoress of ability & some distinction. . . .

*April 19.* Went to Quinby's, & sat for some 5 or 6 different portraits, as he desired, most of them in my military array.[42] After 10 A.M. went in the steamer to Morris Island, to see my comrades of the Palmetto Guard. . . . The paper of this morning contains three unquestionable dispatches to Gov. Pickens (severally from J. M. Mason, Judge John Robertson & Ex-Pres. Tyler,) that the Convention ordained the secession of Va. on the 17th. No details stated. Great rejoicings on that account at most of the southern cities, (as reported by telegraph,) but there is no display of joy here, though of course every one feels it. Afternoon, went to pay my farewell visit to Dr. Bachman's family—having determined to return to Va. tomorrow. The formal act of secession, & withdrawal from Lincoln's govern-

---

[41] Usually regarded as the Mathew B. Brady of Charleston, Cook is perhaps best remembered for his daring photographs taken from Fort Sumter during the federal bombardment of that installation in September, 1863.

[42] One of these portraits appears as the frontispiece of this volume.

ment, terminates my voluntary exile.—Strange events, or reports of, [1318] press on us fast—& it is difficult for me, in this record to distinguish at first the false from the true, & to avoid occupying half my writing with false rumors. Tonight, I met Gov. Pickens in the passage, & he immediately & of his own accord informed me of two important facts, one of which I had supposed a false rumor, & the other was new. Northern volunteers had been called for, & sent by rail, to Washington, which is now a great military encampment, to protect the city & the government. Bodies, either from N.Y. or Mass., passing through Baltimore were assailed by the people, with bricks & stones thrown at the cars, & the troops fired in return. A general conflict ensued, & more than 100 men had been killed, & the fighting still going on, when the dispatch was sent. The other communication was that a requisition had been made by the Gov. of Va. on Pres. Davis, & by him on Gov. Pickens, for 2000 volunteers to proceed immediately to Norfolk—& that they are to set out as early as possible, & perhaps by daybreak tomorrow. I had intended to go at 2 P.M. tomorrow, but I now concluded to go, if possible, with these troops. Paid my bill, & made necessary arrangements. After 9 P.M. went to see Gen. Beauregard at his office, & learned from him that the troops cannot be ready to set out before tomorrow night.—This afternoon, at the Mills House, Ex.-Gov. Manning introduced me to a Baron Sternberg, a Russian, who is supposed to be sent here by the Russian government, to see & know the true condition of things. He is a very well-informed man, & speaks English plainly & very correctly for a foreigner, though with a foreign [1319] accent & manner. As soon as my name was called, he evinced with much earnestness & apparent pleasure that he had heard of me, & was glad to meet with me. He spoke of my recent military position & my age—& requesting to know the manner of spelling my name, I wrote it on a card & gave it to him. He then gave me his card, on which, in copper-plate engraving was "Le Baron Ungern Sternberg, Chambellain de S.M. l'Empereur de Russie."

*April 20.* Report of the conflict in Baltimore corrected. Massachusetts troops fired, & killed 7 of the crowd, & had 2 only of their own body killed. Some wounded on both sides. The S.C. troops cannot be ready as soon as expected. I arranged to go by the 2 o'clock train, but afterwards learned that I should have to stop 12 hours, for Sunday, on the route. So determined to wait for the next train that will go straight on. Judge King called again to see me, & while sitting with him in the parlor, Senator Clingman of N.C. joined us. Judge King asked us both to take dinner with him, with his second weekly relay of his numerous children, with the husbands or wives of the married. We did so, & passed a pleasant time. Judge King is one of the first men of S.C. for his intellect & his virtues, though now very old, & withdrawn from all public matters. . . .

*April 21.* . . . Sent telegram to Ex. Pres. Tyler, urging the construction of earth-work batteries on the Va. heights overlooking & commanding Washington—to be defended from assault by musketry, until heavy artillery can be mounted. Heard various rumors of telegraphic reports, & went to the Courier bulletin board to read them. . . . The city is in feverish excitement on account of these reports, which, if true yield in importance to nothing yet done in the war, unless the capture of Fort Sumter. Crowds are at the bulletin boards —& nothing done anywhere, (out of the churches,) except to ask for & hear the late news.—Later reports, with additional particulars, seem to confirm the earlier. The U.S. Navy Yard at Gosport, near Portsmouth, a most important establishment, where were accumulated great quantities of munitions of naval war—three first-rate ships of war, several others on the stocks, &c. &c. was beleaguered by the neighboring Va. Volunteer companies, who had no artillery larger than 6 pounders. Yet the safety of the position & the ships of war was so endangered, & desperate, that the Commander, Com. [Charles S.] Macauley,[43] scuttled & sunk two (or all [1321] three) of the ships, spiked the cannon (of the Navy Yard,) destroyed other property of the Government, & burnt all the buildings, ships unfinished &c. The Pawnee, one of the war steamers lately off this port, came in previously, & escaped together with one other vessel, they being of shallow draft, so that they could go over the obstructions placed in the channel near Craney Island. It is reported that 2500 Northern troops had been brought to reinforce Fortress Monroe. One regiment of [S.C.] volunteers is to go on tonight to Va. to be soon followed by another. Other southern states it is understood will also furnish troops, to be concentrated in Va, & to attack Washington City, under immediate command of Pres. Davis. It is certain that the enemy have reinforced Fort Pickens. It is deemed certain that

---

[43] A native of Philadelphia, Captain Charles Stewart McCauley (1793-1869) had commanded the Pacific Squadron and the South Atlantic Squadron before being appointed commandant of the Norfolk Navy Yard in 1860. He retired from the naval service in 1862.

the "Star of the West," laden with provisions for U.S. troops, has been taken by Texas volunteers—and the "Yankee" steamer, which lately (& too late) came to this offing with provisions for Fort Sumter, has been seized at Wilmington, N.C. where it was compelled to go in for coal, & because of damages at sea. These are astounding incidents. My arrangements made to set out for Va at 11 P.M. which is the earliest time for any train to go through, without stopping.

# Appendices

❦

# Index

# Appendix A

೧~ಿ

Washington, June 29, 1841

Dear Sir

Immediately after your accession to presidential power, I presented to you, & to the public, my views, briefly but strongly stated, of your new position, & the glorious course opened to you—the course which you had no choice but to pursue, unless indeed you should also depart from every profession of a states-rights republican, & the general pledge furnished by your whole previous political life. After having thus spoken to you, I had no expectation or intention of saying more; & certainly would not have taken advantage of your hospitable attentions to address you personally on this subject. But when I called on you last night, with many others, & more distinguished visitors, you at once recurred to the subject, & stated your views, & we interchanged opinions as much at length as was permitted for *private* conversation under such circumstances. Your having thus invited discussion, induces me to depart further from my designed course of silent observation, &, trusting that it may not be displeasing or unacceptable to you, I shall here extend my remarks something beyond what was permitted by our short & hurried conversation of last night. . . . If I am neither a wise nor a judicious counsellor, you will at least believe me to be candid & disinterested.

You stated to me your intended firm & noble stand in maintenance of state-rights principles, "even if you should be left *alone.*" This is precisely what is demanded by patriotism, & devotion to your principles. But no such injurious result to yourself will occur—but the reverse. By taking that course, so avowedly & fully as to leave no ground for doubt or mistake, to either friend or foe, you will *strengthen* your position ten-fold, instead of losing anything personally. But it is not enough that you should *intend*, & even hereafter *act* fully up to your principles. There must be no room for doubt; & by permitting doubts to exist, some ground has already been lost, which ought to be speedily reoccupied. I must say to you frankly that your course as president, so far, has been observed with anxious fears by the state-rights republicans who voted for you—& with

---

Copied by the diarist from the original letter, still in the possession of Mr. Tyler, in November, 1857, and inserted in the diary following page 132 (MS page 220).

still more of doubt, & less of hope & trust, (as was most natural,) by those who voted against you, because of the men, & the anticipated objectionable measures connected with your election. But none entertain any other ground of opposition to *you*, & all of those will hasten to give to your administration their hearty support, so soon as your measures shall clearly show that you truly & fully wield your rightful authority, & direct your influence to maintain, in their integrity & purity, state-rights & republican principles & policy. Since *your* elevation to the chief magistracy, (& supposing your course to be designed as above stated,) there remains no longer any ground for difference between any true republicans, no matter how much divided & opposed before in regard to personal preferences, or other by-gone subjects of controversy. They will not, & ought not to look back to any such past divisions; but will all be ready to concur in sustaining our common principles & objects, by sustaining you in the chief magistracy. And this will be done, (if on the grounds stated,) not only for your present term of service, but also for the next. There are very strong & proper grounds of objection to such exended service—& I *had* thought that nothing could reconcile me to the *second* term of service of *any* individual. But yours is a peculiar case. The second term would be needed to prevent our losing what may be gained for our principles in the first term. And you may safely trust to state-rights republicans to support your election for a second term, because the same reasons & inducements would continue to operate, & with increased force. These reasons are, that by your fortunate position, you can do for our cause more than any other individual; & that *pledge of interest* is more strong than could be any of *mere words*. But the verbal pledge would not be wanting. I fully believe that all would be as ready to promise their support, on the grounds stated, as I do for myself; & that they will willingly postpone all personal preferences to this mode of attaining what all would deem the greatest of public benefits.

In thus drawing to your support (because supporting their professed principles,) the powerful minority now in opposition, or ready for opposition because of your supposed counsels, you would not lose any of your present supporters, except those, (& a very large number, I admit,) who, as thorough partizans of Clay or Webster, are already, in truth, your greatest enemies; & who lend to you a reluctant & hypocritical semblance of support, merely because deeming you the unavoidable & convenient *locum tenens* for their leader & idol. You would retain & invigorate the support of every whig who is also a republican—& also the numerous mercenaries of that party, no matter what their preferences, as such will always cling to power, & follow him who wields it. With the hearty support of all who are now ready to oppose you, & of half the whig party, which now yields to you so cold & reluctant a support, you would at once have more adherents than any other man can possibly draw together, & very far more authority than you can acquire by any other procedure.

And now permit me to expose what must be your position, if under oposite circumstances. You now receive such support & favor from the "centralists," (I use your own well-applied designation,) reluctant & almost contemptuous as it is, as they give solely upon the supposed ground of *your subserving their ends,* & tamely submitting to the dictation of their political chiefs. So long as they vainly flatter themselves with the belief that you will stoop to act this part, they will pay to you that kind of outward & seeming respect which in the ancient time of the French monarchy fell to the share of a *"roi faineant,"* as the price of his continuing to be the mere tool & slave of the mayor of the palace, & real ruler. But as soon as you shall show that you submit to no such guardianship & dictation, you will be denounced & opposed by all the partizans of Clay & Webster. Nothing now restrains them to their shallow seeming of supporting you, but their knowing that to quarrel with you *so soon* would overthrow their leaders, & ruin their prospects of the succession to your place. Yet even if you could & would stoop to the submission which they expect of you, you would not thereby gain from them the least increase of favor—but would only earn still more of their dislike—nay, even have their contempt added to dislike. Already it is said by them, & I have heard it uttered here in public, & with the seeming assent of the hearers, that "if Mr. Tyler had a proper view of the great difficulty & delicacy of his position, he would forthwith resign his station"—and thus give way to the full & undisputed sway of centralist leaders, & the perpetuation of centralist principles.

If then, by any *even supposed* (& not designed or real) departure from a true republican course, you should continue to repel the support of the republicans who have been in the opposite party ranks, you will not thereby strengthen your popularity with their antagonists. The seeming increased approbation of the latter party would be but evidence of increased secret dislike; & if, indeed, you *could* be induced to *do their work,* the more faithfully & efficiently you might labor in their cause, the more speedily they would be thereby enabled to throw you aside, as a thing used & worn out, & rendered worthless by its service.

I write almost immediately upon the close of our interrupted conversation, & in continuation of it. It will be the last time that I shall take such a liberty—or of offering to your notice any *private* expression of my opinions, unless again invited thereto by yourself. Should my frank & unvarnished exposition offend you, it will be to me a matter of great regret—but because of our heretofore private & friendly relations, & not because of your present exalted station. Of the *President of the United States* I have nothing to ask, to expect, or to fear.

With earnest wishes for the attainment of our great common objects, & for your utmost success as connected with their maintenance, I am, very respectfully,

Yours &c.

Edmund Ruffin

# Appendix B

❦

From my conversations with Ex-President Tyler, during my visit to him in Nov. 1857.

In reference to the stoppage of specie payments by the banks, & the consequent general money pressure & distress of the country:

Ruffin. What do you think will be the course of things? Tyler. Why I suppose they will run the same course, & for years, as after the bank suspension in 1837. Nor do I see any better remedy than my "Exchequer Bank" scheme which I formerly proposed to Congress. This would prevent the present enormous difference of value of the currency in different parts of the country, & break up the brokers' profits & trade. R—Though I formerly examined your scheme, when it was before Congress, I confess that I have forgotten it. What was it? T.—It was that every person who deposited in any one of the different sub-treasuries of the U.S. government, any amount of money in gold or silver, should receive therefor a certificate of the deposit, payable to him in any other city desired by the depositor, & where the government had surplus funds in its sub-treasury there. If no funds were there, then the certificate might be made payable at any other place, or if no other, at the place of deposit. Such a certificate would be as valuable as gold or silver, because payable therein, wherever it was made payable; & even at other points, it would sell at a very small discount. If such certificates could be had now, the holder could use them at par, or very nearly, at any city in the U.S.; & it would be impossible for the price of exchange on N.Y. at Richmond should be 12 to 15 percent, as lately, or even 6 percent, as now. The certificates would always be safe, because the precise amount of each, in specie, would lie where deposited, & be held sacred for redeeming the certificate. R.—Unless the administrators of the government, or their sub-agents, should prove faithless & fraudulent depositories, which would not be an impossible case. Suppose 30 millions to be so deposited on certificates issued, & the country, or a desperate administration, ready to go to destruction for want of funds—would not the deposits be "borrowed" for use of government, & then the "Exchequer Bank" stop payment? T.—Possibly—but that would be a very improbable contingency. And unless this occurred, this would

---

Inserted in the MS diary immediately following the letter printed in Appendix A.

be the safest of banks, holding a dollar in specie to answer every dollar of paper in circulation, & not liable to produce any injury. R.—Admitted— there could be no better or safer bank of deposit; & it would serve every purpose that *ought* to be served, or can be served, in *honest* banking, in supplying a currency. But it would not serve for discounting bills on time, which is the most important commercial function of legitimate & honest banking, if there was any such among what are called banks in this coun- try. But banks are established not for any legitimate & proper end, but mainly & almost exclusively to serve the purposes of those who want to *borrow*, & who deem the system best under which they can borrow most extensively. Your scheme would do nothing to aid this object—& there- fore it would be rejected by the great borrowing interest, who are most clamorous for banks & emissions of paper money. Admitting its working & perfect effect to equalize exchange, or reduce the prices to fair & proper rates, it would be a costly & cumbrous, & perhaps dangerous ma- chine to effect what could be as well done by private capital & enter- prise. If all the state governments would, as the U.S. government has done, adopt the independent treasury system, or receive & disburse specie only—or in any other mode compel all banks to pay specie at all times, exchange would be kept very nearly equal at all times. The transmitting funds by means of bills of exchange was in use (introduced by the Jews) in Europe, centuries before any bank existed there—& it exists in Asia now, in countries where there never has been either bank or paper currency. It is not a function of legitimate or proper banking—& still less does it need to be conducted gratuitously by government, for the con- venience of the people. The occasional exorbitant price of exchange, like the scarcity of money, the fictitious fluctuations of prices, &c. &c. are all the effects of our general system of paper-money banking, which is one of authorized scoundling & (whenever profitable) of legalized refusal to pay all obligations. If this fraudulent system were put down, & banks re- strained to their legitimate & good uses of receiving & transferring depos- its, & discounting *bona-fide* bills (at short times of payment,) & for actual sales of property, we need not restrain their number, nor the extent of their operations, any more than of any other commercial business. The harm they do is in being permitted to *manufacture money*, (& that too irrideemable [*sic*]—) & in lending this fictitious money to any amount to borrowers in long standing loans, under the false pretence & shallow dis- guise of discounting bills known to be for fictitious transactions.

---

Mr. Tyler pointed out to me my engraved portrait, hanging as a match to that of Webster. Both had been framed alike, & set around with em- broidered ornaments, by Mrs. Tyler's lately deceased sister. He said "I have placed you thus with Daniel Webster as I regard him as among the first of Americans in the political theatre, & you the first in agriculture." R.—You could not compliment my obscure merits more highly, & for which I could be more sensible, either in your own words, or in thus placing me with Webster. But while I rate him intellectually as high as do his best friends, I hold him very low in his moral qualities. T.—However that may be, he served his country well, & me also, as my Secretary of State. R.—Even there, I think he would have preferred to overthrow you, as much as Clay & his followers openly showed their wish to do so, if Webster could have seen how to profit by betraying your trust. T.—At first, he did seem to join, quiescently, in the general but disguised whig conspiracy against me. But he soon saw that I would not come into their measures, or be governed by any influence—& then he yielded to my views, & ably & in good faith, aided me to carry them out. After I had in vain tried to administer the government through whig members of the cabinet (except himself,) Webster said to me that he thought I had done enough in that attempt, &, inasmuch as it was impossible for a president to get on except by support of one of the two great parties, after I had vainly & fully tried & failed to obtain the aid of the whigs, he thought that I ought to throw myself upon the democratic party. And, to do that, there should be no divided counsels—& he was ready to resign his place as soon as I desired it. I answered that I did not admit the absolute necessity of the president's ruling by party support—& at all events I should try to do without—& that I wished him to remain in the Cabinet not only to conclude the negotiation of the Ashburton treaty with England, but as much longer as things would require. However, at a later time, he determined to retire, & did so of his own motion.

---

. . . T.—You, like me & almost all Virginia boys, first turned your attention to politics. But you soon gave up the pursuit, & devoted yourself to agriculture—& in that pursuit you have done more good to the country than all our political great men put together. Your little book on Calcareous Manures, in its valuable consequences, will be worth more to the country than all the state papers that have been the most celebrated in our time. How much better was it for you to have seen at first, & to refuse to pursue, the empty rewards of political life!—R.—I perceive that you, like many other friends who have known me more intimately, have mistaken me in this respect. It was not because I was devoid of ambition, or of the desire to wield political power, that I have not sought political stations. On the contrary, few persons would have been more gratified by being so placed—& very few young men read more, or felt more interest, in the subjects of government & political economy. But, in the first place, I felt sure that I had no talent for oratory, or to influence popular assemblies, & I was too proud to be willing to be deemed below any station in which I might be placed. Next, & mainly—even if I could have obtained popular favor (which I never possessed, or sought to gain,) & political eminence as its reward, I never knew the time that I would have been willing to purchase the honor, at the cost of paying the necessary price for popularity.

---

R.—I had never doubted that the deplorable act of Capt. [Alexander S.] Mackenzie, in having young [Philip] Spencer & two seamen hung at sea, for alleged mutiny, was a righteous though illegal punishment, justified only by the stern necessity of the case.[1] But I have since read [Thomas Hart] Benton's chapter on that subject—& if he is to be trusted for his facts (which I do not believe in any case,) there was no more evidence of guilt, than necessity for the summary execution. What did you think of it at the time?—T.—No doubt young Spencer had been guilty of great imprudence of speech, which probably brought his conduct within the definition of mutinous. But it was difficult to believe that an officer in the navy, the son of the actual Secretary of War, & a member of a family of high standing, could have conspired (as charged) to seize the ship of war, &, as a necessary condition, to murder its commander & the loyal portion of the crew, & to become a pirate. But for this he was tried, though without authority, condemned, & hung, because, as was alleged, it was only at great hazard to the safety of the ship & crew that the prisoners could be kept alive in confinement. When Capt. Mackenzie arrived & reported the case, a naval court was ordered for his trial, & a thorough investigation of the whole case. There never was assembled in this country a more dignified or able naval court. Its sentence acquitted Capt. Mackenzie, & I could do nothing but approve the sentence. If it had ordered Mackenzie to be shot, I would not have interposed to save him. Spencer, then still Secretary of War, was very urgent with me to set aside the trial, & to order another for the slayer of his son. But I answered that it would be contrary to the general rule of law, that when a man had been once fairly tried, & acquitted, he should not be tried again upon the same charges & evidence. But I determined that so long as my power should last, Capt. Mackenzie should never be entrusted with another command. . . .

---

[1] The alleged mutiny was uncovered aboard the USS *Somers* on November 26, 1842, and the three suspected leaders, including Midshipman Philip Spencer, son of Secretary of War John C. Spencer, were executed five days later. For a popularized account of this remarkable incident, see Frederic F. Van de Water, *The Captain Called It Mutiny* (New York: Ives Washburn, 1954).

# Appendix C

❧

*The Free Negro Nuisance and How to Abate It*

The great and growing evil of the existence of an inferior class in the free negroes of Virginia, is a subject that ought to cause anxious consideration to every thinking and patriotic citizen of the Commonwealth. Some few of those persons who have entered on the discussion, have denied that the existence of this class in our midst is an evil; or at least, they have maintained that the removal of the class, even if costing nothing else, would be a loss of value to the Commonwealth. Others, while admitting the evil, and its fullest claimed extent, have relied, and some few are even now so uninformed by all the lights of experience, as still to rely, on the scheme of colonization in Liberia, as a proper and effective mode of removing the free negroes from Virginia.

It is scarcely possible to remove or abate any long existing and widely extended evil in any community, without producing some other evil, or considerable inconvenience. But this is no reason to prevent action in the case, unless the effects of the remedy will be worse than those of the disease. In some counties, where free negroes are so numerous that their labor is important to the employers of labor in their neighborhood, the sudden and complete removal of the industrious of the class would, indeed, be a temporary inconvenience and evil. But this loss would probably, in every case, be more than compensated by the advantages of removing the idle, profligate and dishonest members of the class, whose depredations on property, and corrupting influence on slaves, would cause more loss than all their labor would replace, with the addition of that of the few who are really worthy and industrious.

Further: it may be admitted that the entire or partial removal of this class would be so much reduction of the population of Virginia, and that 60,000, (their supposed present number,) being lost, would have an important political bearing in regard to our representation in Congress. This, too, would be a serious evil, if permanent, and if not compensated by equal or greater advantages. But, in no possible case can the presence of a class that is generally lazy, improvident, degraded in every respect,

---

Printed in *The South,* July 2, 1858. Clipping appended to diary on pages 207–208 (MS pages 383–85).

vicious, incorrigible and shameless, be of more benefit than disadvantage and loss to the country and community in which such class resides and subsists. It would be as sound a proposition that the gipsies and professional beggars and thieves of England are elements of value and strength to that country, as that any clear benefit is produced to Virginia by the whole body of resident free negroes—and still less by the destitute, idle, and vicious portion of that body. It is to this latter portion of the class that I shall confine my recommendation of measures of reform. The industrious, thrifty, and virtuous free negroes are useful members of the community; and, on considerations of policy, as well as of justice and humanity, should not be oppressed or aggrieved, because of the vices of the greater number of their class.

As to the plan of removing the free negroes by colonization in Liberia, its futility has been so clearly exposed by [Thomas R.] DEW and others, and the vain attempts and continued failures of 40 years, have so strongly condemned it, that it does not now deserve the respect of being again refuted. If any answer is required, it is enough to say that the free negroes of Virginia *will not voluntarily go to Africa*; and unless the advocates of this scheme design to recommend adding coercion to persuasion and the State bounty, to all such emigrants, it is in vain to look to colonization as even a partial remedy of any appreciable utility. For years back there has been in operation the present State policy, by which $50 is offered and paid from the treasury of Virginia for every free negro that will go to Liberia, and with so little effect that both the advocates and the dupes of the policy pronounce the bounty to be of no material effect for this, the avowed object, and are demanding its being increased. And all other operations of and in aid of the Colonization Society have served to induce the emancipation, and to remove from Virginia more than twice as many of the useful and much-needed slaves, as they have taken away of the previously free negroes. Ignorant as are the free negroes in the general, they are too well informed of the fate they might expect to meet with in Liberia, to exchange for it their present degraded position, under the protection, even if often oppressive, of white men and of a superior and ruling race.

Passing by the scheme of voluntary emigration and colonization as unworthy of serious consideration, the only other remedies that have been proposed and discussed in the Legislature and in the newspapers though many and various, have been all of one general character. Disregarding the minor differences, these plans concur in proposing the banishment and forcible deportation of the whole body of free negroes—either in a longer or shorter space of time—to Liberia, or generally, at the expense of the treasury or otherwise, and with the offered option of remaining as slaves if not choosing to go free into exile.

[622]

## Appendix C

There is no question that it would have been beneficial to the free negroes generally, and for the whole class, if they had remained slaves; and that it would be advantageous to the much greater number, and still more to their posterity, for them to be now reduced to slavery. But public sentiment will not approve this procedure in reference to the innocent and worthy, and therefore every proposition of general banishment has failed. It would have been more politic, as well as more just and humane, to have taken a milder course, such as I will here advocate, and which policy would serve to effect all the benefit of gradually removing, or otherwise reducing to slavery, all free negroes who, as such, are nuisances in their neighborhood and a detriment to the Commonwealth, without the measures causing any important injury, or committing any unjust oppression.

The first object of any law designed to carry out this policy should be to draw a line of discrimination between the industrious, provident and honest free negroes, and those certainly deficient in these qualifications. It would be no hardship on any of the former class, in common with all others, to be required to show to the proper lawful authority that they possessed in property, or exercised in honest labor, the means of support for themselves and families. This being shown, from time to time, as required by law the free negroes should have every existing protection of law to their persons and property. But all who could not give evidence of living honestly on their own means, of labor, or of income from other sources, should be included in the general class of the idle, destitute and vicious, and to be dealt with as follows:

1. For every crime of a free negro that heretofore has been subject to be punished by confinement in the Penitentiary for the maximum time of not less than five years, the punishment should be changed into perpetual slavery. Murderers, or other criminals, who have heretofore been subject to suffer death, would still be subject to that penalty, unless when that punishment was commuted, in which case the commutation should be to perpetual slavery. This procedure would at once relieve the treasury of much expense in the present mode of punishing free negro criminals, and would further enrich it by their full price, obtained from the purchasers, and also would convert them to useful laborers for the public gain, serving to add to the supply of labor that is so much wanting in agriculture, and which the Colonization Society has done so much to lessen, in procuring the emancipation of slaves.

2. All free negroes convicted of minor criminal offences, which would previously have subjected them to shorter terms of confinement in the Penitentiary or other prisons, or to stripes, should be sold as slaves for limited times, of 5 years or longer, according to the degrees of crime.

3. All other free negroes, not convicted as violators of criminal law, but

[623]

of proved bad character and habits—as being habitually idle or drunken, or not having honest and sufficient means of support—should be hired out to the highest bidder, as slaves are hired and for two years' time, the money obtained for such hires to be used for the support of any helpless members of the offender's family, or, if not so required, to be paid into either the county or State treasury. After so serving his time, the free negro should be liberated. But in every case of continuing or resuming his previous vicious course, he should be sold into perpetual slavery.

4. Stringent legal measures should be adopted to compel the fulfilment of the obligations to their masters of these new hirelings or temporary slaves, and to leave no means of escape from these obligations—except by escaping also from the territory of Virginia into the Northern States. When this should occur, there would be no great individual loss in the due service of a criminal or worthless hireling, and it would be gaining more than one public benefit, in transferring such persons to become residents and citizens of the free and slave-stealing States. If any such idle free negroes, or others, before coming under the action of the new laws, should choose to emigrate, they should have free egress, and every proper facility for their departure; and if the Legislature of Virginia should choose to offer the bounty to such voluntary emigrants to the North, that is now so improperly offered and paid to the Colonization Society, the bounty would at least be much better bestowed for the public good.

Such legal policy as is here proposed would serve as the most effectual measure of reform for the idle and vicious of this class. Every such effect would be of great benefit to the particular individual, and of no small benefit to the community. And like benefits, greater or less, and both to the offender and to the Commonwealth, would result from the penalties imposed on the more obstinate cases of idleness and vice, or of still greater extent of criminality. Many a felonious as well as worthless free negro would be made a laborious, profitable and submissive slave. And if, when of worse character, he should abscond to the free States, his departure would be a great [benefit] compared to the present system, either of the full penitentiary punishment or the mitigation, by the superabounding and culpable measure of Executive clemency—and in either case, the hardened criminal remaining amongst us and free to resume and continue his offences.

If, as I verily believe, not more than one-fourth of the present free negroes would very long remain free from all operation of the proposed laws, it would be because no more now earn their living by honest labor, and live as useful and worthy members of society. Then the greater number of the able bodied males at least (according to this estimate) would soon be put to labor, either as hirelings or slaves, if not leaving the State to avoid the threatened penalties. The worthy members of the class would understand the tenure of their own exemption and safety; and, if not deaf and blind to all admonition and warning, their children would be thus induced to follow the worthy example of their parents. But, if any should take to the opposite courses, the law would still remain to control, punish, or banish all such evil-doers, and all of this class that should become, as the large majority now are, nuisances to good society, and depredators on the industry of the community.

But there would be going on at the same time, another process by which the destitute and helpless of the free negroes, and the idle who were not among the most immoral, would become slaves by choice, and greatly to their advantage. Even now, except for the existing facilities for gaining a support by pilfering, or dealing with pilfering slaves, a very large number of free negroes, and especially the mothers and children, would suffer the extremity of want. And such would be the case with great numbers, when the new measures of police had cut off their dishonest resources from the husbands and fathers. Also, if the choice were now presented to any number of free negroes either to leave the State, or to become slaves, great numbers would choose the latter alternative. And even if the place of exile were Liberia, with all its boasted advantages, and they were to be conveyed there at the cost of the State, a large proportion of strong men, as well as of feeble women, (for themselves and their children,) would prefer to become slaves to some kind and just white neighbor, to being free citizens in Africa. From the operation of these two causes, when the pressure of the proposed law was felt, and its future bearing anticipated, there would be thousands of cases of voluntary enslavement, instead of the few which now occur in Virginia, but which even now, are in sufficient numbers to require (as has been done,) a general law to be enacted to sanction such acts of voluntary enslavement.

The proposed policy would pay all respect to the virtuous and industrious of the class of free negroes. Where individuals of this character are found, whether bond or free, they deserve such respect and justice and humane treatment, according to their condition. But it is not usual for a free negro to be industrious or provident. Still less frequent is it for these rare qualities to extend to a second generation. And if the second or a later generation of the most industrious and thrifty free negro became idlers and prodigals, they would soon require to be made either exiles or slaves. Thus in a few generations, there would probably remain in Virginia no negroes except such as were in their proper and only suitable condition—that of being slaves to white masters.

If the Legislature of Virginia will adopt and carry out the general policy here recommended, it will render more benefit to the Commonwealth than has been done by all the legislation of the last ten years—or than will be done, as I fear, by all other legislative proceedings for ten years to come. The other and more Southern States as yet suffer less than Virginia under the great evil of a free negro population. But there is not one of them in which this policy is not needed and would be highly beneficial. And if all the slaveholding States would so act, the benefits that would result, in increasing the value of slave labor and the security of slave property, would be almost as great as would be another and the greatest benefit, the entire exclusion or effectual punishment of all incendiary agents of the Abolitionists of the North, operating within our borders.

R.

# Appendix D

ᕬᖇᕠ

## "CASSANDRA—WARNINGS"

When the admission of Missouri to the Union, as a slaveholding State, was first proposed in Congress, and the measure was resisted by the great body of the representatives of the northern States, there was first made obvious the before more silent policy of restricting, crippling, and finally extinguishing the institution of slavery and slaveholding interests, in the States where they then existed. Though the first attempt—to the extent of the entire prohibition of slavery in Missouri, and, as a consequence, in all future new States—was warded off, it was done only by the southern States submitting disgracefully to the prohibition of the subsequent extension of negro slavery, and removal of the property with the owners to all of the common territory of the United States lying north of latitude 36°30′, which limitation was fixed by the terms of the act since known as the "Missouri Compromise." The policy of extinguishing negro slavery did not cease to occupy and to influence the northern mind. But after the enactment of this so-called "compromise," the previous state of comparative quietude, or inactivity and silence of the abolitionists, again prevailed. Nevertheless, the hostile spirit and purpose were neither disclaimed nor concealed. Notwithstanding the previous compromise, the subsequent admission of each of the few later slaveholding States— Florida, Arkansas and Texas—was resisted by very many, if not always the majority, of the northern votes in Congress, and on the general ground of naked opposition to the admission of any and all slaveholding States. Finally, on the admission of California as a State (which was altogether an unconstitutional, fraudulent and iniquitous outrage and usurpation, perpetrated by the North on the rights of the South), the spirit of the Missouri Compromise was entirely disregarded; and the newly acquired Mexican territory south of 36°30′ was deprived of even the poor protection which the carrying out of the spirit of that compromise would have afforded to southern interests.

About 1833 the abolition feeling of the North became much more active, and incendiary and dangerous in its action in the southern States. Anti-slavery associations, or others with like views, were established throughout the northern States; public discussions were held (if discus-

Printed in the Charleston *Mercury*, July 21, 1859. Clipping annexed to diary on page 326 (MS pages 705–707).

sion could be where no voice was permitted to be raised but on one side of the argument); and numerous periodical or other publications were issued, all to oppose the institution and existence of negro slavery in the southern States. The great facilities offered by the mails and post offices were used to flood the South with incendiary publications; and other more effective means were used to reach and operate upon the minds or feelings of the ignorant negroes. Secret incendiary agents, under the guise of various business characters—as workmen and traders, drummers for northern dealers of all kinds, solicitors of subscriptions to northern publications, or of money for pious uses, teachers, preachers, invalids seeking health, &c., &c.—were sent from the North or voluntarily acted as voluntary amateur agents, to visit every accessible and available locality of the South, to secretly infuse their doctrines, and to excite discontent and insubordination among the slaves—who had then and thus, for the first time, to learn from these pretended friends that they were an injured, suffering, and miserable class—and to invite them to flee, and aid their fleeing from the service in which they had been before contented, comfortable and happy. These northern assaults on the most vital of southern interests, have been continued with increasing force and effect to this time.

The enactment by Congress (carried against a large majority of all the northern votes) of the law to enable the recovery of fugitive slaves, was the only one of the five measures of the new "compromise" of 1850, which promised, in the least, to defend or promote southern interests—or, indeed, that was not entirely and greatly inimical to them. But this very law, in its seeming to render something of tardy justice to the South, has, more than anything else, excited the abolition zeal of the North, and given to it increased venom, force and efficiency. This law, in aiming (or professing) to enable the recovery and rendition of absconded slaves from the northern States, in which they had found refuge, simply required the performance of what the Federal Constitution had engaged for, and what previous legislation had attempted in vain to secure. But when efforts were made to arrest and obtain the rendition of fugitive slaves under this new and (as supposed) more efficient law, it was found to be entirely worthless as a remedy. Wherever its execution was attempted, the all-powerful popular influence and force were brought in action to oppose and effectually nullify the law of Congress. This has, in effect, been done in every northern State in which the recovery of a fugitive slave has been attempted. And in the very few exceptional cases (out of thousands of such losses existing) of fugitive slaves being recovered by their owners, it was effected at a pecuniary loss and personal risk to the owners far exceeding the value of the property, besides twenty times as much expense to the Federal Government. Many fugitives, legally arrested, have

[628]

been violently rescued, and aided to escape, by armed and lawless mobs. Owners of the fugitive negros [*sic*], or their agents, and officers of the law acting to enforce its execution, in several cases have been murdered outright by popular violence. Even worse than this, for any future hope of redress by aid of the Federal Government, federal officers, marshals and judicial commissioners, whose sworn duty it was to execute this law, have openly and shamelessly violated their oaths, and notoriously failed to perform their plain and imperative duties, and have not been, therefore, dismissed from office, or censured, so far as known to the public, by the authorities that appointed and retained in office these perjured officials. . . . Further: sundry of the northern States have passed laws making it a penal offence for any of its State officers or citizens, in any way to aid the recovery of a fugitive slave. Thus every attempt is rendered manifestly futile, as well as extremely costly and dangerous. Under all these circumstances, it may be safely pronounced that the fugitive slave law is dead, and that there is not now offered the slightest redress or protection to any owner of an abducted or fugitive slave. And yet, this law is all the measure of benefit which is the portion of the southern States, to balance the enormous wrongs suffered by them, and of benefits bestowed on the northern States and their interests, by the operation of the "Compromise" of 1850! In the meantime, abolition has been steadily gaining strength in every non-slaveholding State, and is as triumphant in success as it is fanatical in spirit, in most of the northern States. It may be true that the opinion of the wisest and best portion of the people of every northern State is on our side, and is daily becoming more convinced of the great value and necessity, for all interests, of the institution of negro slavery. But the wise and the worthy in all communities are few, compared to the foolish and fanatical, or those deluded and led by vile and interested demagogues. Every year the anti-slavery majority in every northern State is increased, and every year there is, and will be, one or more new non-slaveholding, and, therefore, future abolition States, added to the Union. It is true that all these new States have not yet arrayed themselves, in all respects, against the South. Such is the case, as yet, with California and Oregon; and several other northwestern new States have not yet discarded their Senators who have respected the rights of the South. But this change must be made, and completely. The lines of party division are rapidly becoming geographical, and sooner or later must be identical with those which separate the slave-holding from the more northern States.

Therefore, however forbearing, or even friendly as yet, and identified with us in political action, may be a few of the new and non-slaveholding States, common sense and discretion ought to teach us even of these as being in transition, and about to be entirely arrayed against the South in the great and final struggle for the maintenance or existence of slavery in the States w[h]ere it exists. There are now thirty-three States in the Union, of which fifteen only, if including Delaware, are slaveholding; or but fourteen, if excluding Delaware, which holds very few slaves, and is already, in sentiment and political action, almost identified with the more northern States. Every new territory which will hereafter be opened for settlement, will necessarily be mostly filled by emigrants from the northern States, and newly arrived Europeans, still more ignorant dupes and fanatics than the ignorant natives of New England. The fact of there being always a very much larger proportion of needy or destitute persons in the North than in the South, will alone be enough always to secure the much earlier and larger emigration from the former to any new territory. And if this general and still increasing condition of poverty and destitution is not sufficient to effect the result of a predominant colonization of northern or anti-slavery settlers at first, in every case, that end could easily and would be secured by the associated and combined efforts of people of the northern States. The people of the North are accustomed to effect their common, or popular political objects, by these powerful means, while the people of the South are too careless or indolent to adopt and put in operation, even for the defence of their most vital and most endangered interests, which, by these means, are continually and successfully assailed. After the restriction of the Missouri Compromise had operated to prevent any other new slaveholding State being established north of latitude 36°30′, the recent repeal of the law, with the ambiguous and deceptious terms of the repealing law (the Nebraska Act), has operated to open all the remaining territory south of that line to invasion and conquest by abolitionism. The next ensuing session of Congress will admit Kansas as a non-slaveholding State. And in all the vast extent of unsettled territory north of Texas, of which twenty new States may be made—or it may be twice that number, by using the perfectly available policy of dividing existing large States—there is not the least probability that there will be even one such new State which will not be both non-slaveholding and northern in sentiment and action, in regard to the institution of slavery and the southern States. Texas, which is not included in the above estimate may, indeed, be divided into from three to five States. But such future division is dependent on the will of the people and government of Texas, both of which are entirely opposed to any division of its territory. And even if it were otherwise, and a division were soon to be effected, it is questionable whether at least one abolition State would not be carved out of the northern portion of Texas.

Thus, the present number and power of States are fourteen slaveholding to nineteen non-slaveholding. It will require but the further admission of nine more new States to raise the number of the abolition States to twenty-eight, while the slaveholding States will remain, as now, fourteen—even if Maryland and Missouri shall not sooner be compelled to follow the example of Delaware, still more to swell the anti-slavery power. But without this contingency (which every incendiary effort of abolitionism is now striving to bring about), and without the division of California, Oregon, Minnesota, or any other large non-slaveholding State (which abolition majorities, both in Congress and in the State to be divided, can effect at any time), the mere addition of nine more new States will make the non-slaveholding States three-fourths of the whole number (42) then in the Confederation;[1] and so will furnish the majority required by the Federal Constitution to make binding any alteration in its terms in regard to slavery that three-fourths of the States will approve and ratify. How long, or rather how short, a time can be expected to pass before nine more States will be added to this Union, and thereby establish the unlimited power to regulate, or restrict, or to utterly abolish the institution of slavery, and that power to be exercised legally and constitutionally by the northern or abolition States? Can any one suppose that this increase of the number of States and of power to abolition fanaticism, will not occur within the next fifteen years? And can any southern statesman and patriot be so credulous as to believe that, when this power shall be legally possessed, it will not be exercised and fully enforced by those who have heretofore steadily worked for the same end of general emancipation, while directly in opposition to the laws and constitution of the United States?

But there will, more probably, be no need for the abolition party to wait so long as fifteen years for this consummation. That party (which now impudently assumes and defiles the once deservedly venerated party designation of "republican") has but to elect a northern abolitionist to be President of the United States—or, still worse for us, a traitor from the South, who will better serve their purpose—and to elect a majority of both Houses of Congress, to precipitate this end. All the required and now deficient additional States could be admitted to the Union in a single session—and within a year thereafter, while duly respecting all the forms

---

[1] Ruffin's arithmetic is faulty here. The addition of nine more free states would have given the antislavery party only a *two-thirds'* majority in the Union. It would have required the addition of twenty-three non-slaveholding states to give antislavery forces the requisite *three-fourths'* majority needed to abolish slavery by constitutional amendment. However, Ruffin's argument is not entirely destroyed by his arithmetical error. Census statistics indicate that slavery was on the decline in the border states. For example, in Maryland the slave population declined 61 percent between 1850 and 1860. If only three of those states—say, Maryland, Kentucky, and Missouri—had shifted to the antislavery camp, it would have required the admission of only eleven more free states to provide the North with the necessary three-fourths' majority.

of law, and in strict literal conformity to all constitutional requirements, that instrument can and will be altered, so as to abolish slavery by general emancipation—without even a pretence of compensation to the owners of slaves, or of any partial safeguards of the before slaveholding States from the complete ruin to which they will thus be doomed. The people of the South may (as, unfortunately, many do) shut their eyes to these threatened and approaching calamities, and take comfort from the asserted improbability of their occurrence. But it should be enough to arouse their fears and vigilance, and to excite the spirit of resistance and defence in every bosom, that the effecting these results will be perfectly in the power of our enemies, who have every disposition to use illegal means to reach the same end. Will they hesitate to use means which will be perfectly legal and constitutional, as well as perfectly effective? Let those southerners who can feel secure under such circumstances continue to sleep and to dream of fraternity and union, and of the patriotism and sense of justice of their southern [*sic*—northern?] brethren. But all who perceive the approaching danger, and who admit its existence to even half the extent here asserted to be impending, ought to lose no more time before preparing for their earnest defence—unless indeed they are content to yield everything valuable to freemen, and to submit to utter ruin of their country and degradation and misery to its citizens.

R.

Hanover Co., Va., July 16th, 1859.

# Appendix E

❧

Hon. W. L. Yancey

Beechwood Va. Oct. 29, 1860

Dear Sir

Within a few days after this letter can reach you, the popular vote will have been given in the presidential election—& the result will be known to you. According to all present indications, that result (whether by a majority or plurality of votes,) will give the victory to the avowed abolitionist candidate, & by the unmixed support of the northern section & abolition party of these United States. I cannot doubt that you will view this result as I do—of the clear & unmistakeable indication of future & fixed domination of the northern section & its abolition policy over the southern states & people & their institutions, & the beginning of a sure & speedy progress to the extermination of negro slavery, & the consequent utter ruin of the prosperity of the south. I cannot doubt that you will see but one passage for escape from these impending & awful dangers & calamities—by secession of some, (if all are not then ready) of the southern states from the union with the northern, which has been changed from the former bond of fraternal love, & of mutual defence & support, to a yoke & manacles on the South, & the effective instrument for our oppression & destruction in the hands of our northern enemies & prospective masters.

The great talent & power which many men of the South possessed, & might have exerted—as Patrick Henry did successfully, for far less wrong inflicted or designed, & against a far more powerful oppressor, (as well as a much more loved & valued *union* to a mother country—) has been heretofore wasted—if not prostituted—to the minor & immeasurably inferior object, of making some one or other person president of the United States, & dispenser of the patronage of the government. It is true, that an incidental benefit of success, in such efforts of southern politicians, would be the partial staying the conquering progress & growing power of abolition for a short time. But any such success, even when heretofore achieved in past times, served for but a temporary check to the continually growing power of the zealous & indefatigable assailants. Pardon me for saying that even in your recent & brilliant campaign of political warfare & defence of

---

Rough draft entered in diary following page 479 (MS page 1072).

[633]

the claims of the South, striking as were your displays of the power of eloquence & zeal, & ardent patriotism, your utmost success would have served but to postpone the day of the death-sentence on southern institutions & welfare, & even political & social existence, for but one term of presidential service.

If instead of pursuing the miserable & even despicable political warfare & defence, in striving to make a president—& which attempt latterly has been, & will be certainly hereafter, a hopeless, & even an absurd pursuit —our able advocates & orators had maintained fully & properly the rights & interests of the Southern States, as did Patrick Henry & his noble compatriots & co-workers maintain the rights of the colonies against the oppression of & union with their mother country, our defence against the enmity, malignity & oppression of our northern co-states would long before this time have been as successful & complete as was the resistance of our noble & true fathers to the wrongs inflicted by the mother country.

All that we now need, for the like glorious result is another Patrick Henry. Doubtless we have many men in the South, who, (when they shall have once taken the right direction & means of effort,) may compare with that great defender of freedom & his country's rights, in patriotism & zeal & self-devotion. I fully believe you to be one of these. But you also are gifted, & in a remarkable & rare degree, with the power of eloquence, & through it, with power to sway the popular will, which enables one man to exercise as much influence as thousands could without this means & power for putting their intellect & patriotism to public use. You are the man for this great work. Will you undertake it? Will you be the Henry for this now impending contest? Move in it, & at once, & I would stake my life on the venture, that your success will not be less complete & glorious than that of your great exemplar. I earnestly desire that you may have assigned to you the best & most honored positions in the public councils, in which you may best exert your powers in our country's cause. But do not wait for that—or for anything, even for a single day, after you know that Lincoln has received the popular vote. Immediately after such notification I entreat you to assemble & address your fellow citizens of Montgomery in the terms & manner suited to the great crisis, & for which you need no preparation. Call upon Alabama to act forthwith, through her convention, & to lead, in the movement of secession. Devote your time, your labor, & your great power as a popular orator, to speaking to assemblages of the people, in every southern state. Your example will be followed by hundreds & thousands, to the extent of their ability—& long before the day for Lincoln's inauguration as President, southern states, or enough of them for perfect safety for the movement, (& to bring in all others within a short time,) will have seceded, declared their independence, & inaugurated, in peace & security, a new confederacy of southern states. *Peacefully,* if as many as five or six states shall concur in the early secession—because the northern power could not possibly harm so strong a confederacy. Nor would the northern people attempt hostile attack, unless utterly demented by their abolition fanaticism. Even one state, Ala. Mis[s]. Ga. or S.C., if seceding alone, & at first unsupported by any others, though subject to be annoyed & damaged for a time by northern hostility, would soon be joined, aided & defended, & rendered impregnable by other co-operating & soon confederated states—& their defence would be made, if not as peaceful & bloodless, at least as successful & triumphant as in the other supposed case.

I do not urge on you what I would not attempt myself, if endowed with your peculiar power as a public speaker—or even with a far less share—instead of being, as I am, entirely destitute of all such talent, or even usage. Already, & for years past, in a different & far less effective mode, I have labored, (by writing & publishing my views,) to influence the public mind in favor of this great object—but with such small success as might have been expected from my obscure name & position, & limited powers. I have had no aid in the work, & but little evidence afforded of either approval or effect. Nevertheless, I shall persevere while any ground for hope remains, & to such extent as my poor abilities & means will enable, I will gladly devote the best efforts of my mind & body, for the very short remainder of my life. But all that I can do is as nothing to what you can do—& with the sure prospect of earning imperishable fame for yourself, while leading in the successful pursuit of the far greater & nobler object of establishing the rights & freedom & security of the South.

I do not now see what more I can do for the southern cause in the fast approaching crisis, zealous & anxious as I am to render any such service. Clearly I can do nothing now in Virginia. Therefore, as soon as I shall give in my vote (for Breckinridge,) on Nov. 6th, I shall proceed immediately to Charleston, & soon after to Columbia, where I hope that something may be done soon, & to render any aid I can to the defence & the independence of the South. Your state, (by the enactment of the last legislature,) is in a position to act still earlier, if so disposed—as I trust it will be. Should such action be earlier indicated there, I shall hasten on to Montgomery—& there, (or elsewhere should another state take precedence of Ala.) offer what remains of my life & abilities, for any possible service to the great cause.

To me, individually, this letter will not need an answer, nor do I expect any. I trust that your time will be fully occupied with far more important duties. But, if for any reason, you should desire to communicate with me, I expect to be in Charleston from the 7th to 9th of Nov. & afterwards in Columbia for some days.

Respectfully<br>Edmund Ruffin

# Appendix F

ॐ✦०

EDMUND RUFFIN TO GOVERNOR JOHN W. ELLIS

*Private*

Charleston S.C.    March 20th 1861

His Excellency J. W. Ellis, Governor of N. Ca.

Dear Sir

Last summer you did me the honor to request my opinions on the political condition of the country. Although then, & afterwards, I furnished some of my views, in answer to your written request, I trust that it may still serve to excuse me, & acquit me of being intrusive & presumptuous, in my now again taking up the subject as to later & *present* occurrences—though in regard to your own action as governor of North Carolina, & as to measures about which I fear that our respective opinions stand opposed.

It seems from recent reports, as well as from the other like measures & attempts of the administration of the U.S. government, that one or all the three forts in N.C. may soon be garrisoned & armed. If this is done, as it can be quickly & effectually done, it will be, not to *protect* N.C. from foreign attack, (the only designed & constitutional object of the construction & possession of these forts by the U.S. government,) but to assail & control & to subjugate the state, or compel its submission to illegal northern & abolition rule & wrongs. If the arming & manning these forts shall be permitted, & effected, all the military force of N.C. when seceded, or even if aided by the Confederate States, will not be able to take them, or at least not without an enormous cost of valuable lives.

When some of these forts (being then without garrisons,) were taken possession of by unauthorized citizens of N.Ca., you immediately ordered their being restored to the federal government. The condition of affairs was then different from what it is now, & the peril to N.C. less imminent. But even if alike, respecting you as I do, I should respect your scruples, & your views of constitutional obligations, which directed your conduct. But there may be cases—& it seems to me that this *now* is one—when the strict observance of & obedience to the *letter* of the constitution would operate to violate & destroy the *spirit* & the substance.

The right of the federal government to occupy, arm, & strengthen these forts, under the constitution, rests only on the design to use them for their

Copied in diary after page 580 (MS page 1274).

constitutional purpose—which is exclusively to protect the coast & the state from the attacks of foreign enemies. It is self-evident that no such purpose can be now in view, any more than during the many past years when these forts have been left without garrisons, & almost untenanted. If garrisoned now, it can only be for the purpose of over-awing & subduing the people & government of the state, instead of defending it. If used for this purpose, clearly it is in violation of the intention of the constitution, & of the constitution itself. And if this be admitted, it follows irresistably [*sic*] that the preventing such procedure, even if by previous occupation of the forts by authority of the state government, will operate to prevent the most flagrant violation of the federal constitution by the federal authorities, as well as to ward off the most dangerous blow that can possibly be aimed at or inflicted on your state—which, as to all other modes of assault from abroad, is rendered impregnable by her topographical position.

I need not enlarge upon the proposition. It is sufficient thus to enunciate it—& leave the reasoning & application to be carried out by your mind.[1]

Very respectfully
Edmund Ruffin

---

[1] Governor Ellis finally ordered state troops to occupy the forts on April 15, after the surrender of Sumter and after receiving Lincoln's request for troops to put down the rebellion.

# Index

❧

*Index*

Canada: condition of free blacks in, 332; harbors escapees from Harpers Ferry, 400; Prince of Wales visits, 422, 467

Carey, Henry C., 152–54, 284, 285–86

Carolina City, N.C., 320

Carroll, James Parsons, 575 and *n*

Carter, Hill, 470–71

Carter, Williams, 166, 228, 338

Caskie, John S., 299 and *n*

Cass, Lewis, 38, 40, 234, 510

"Cassandra—Warnings": printed in Charleston *Mercury*, 319, 326, 627 *n*; text of, 627–32

Castle Pinckney, 490, 514, 522, 531, 563

Catholicism, 290

Cazneau, William L., 177 and *n*

Central Agricultural Society of Virginia: 1858 fair of, 199, 238, 240, 241, 247–48; and negotiations with Va. State Agricultural Society, 305, 310, 318, 325; 1859 fair of, 351; coalesces with state society, 477

Central America: racial composition of population in, 39, 73, 176; ER urges U.S. conquest of, 96; Walker's campaigns in, 133, 265, 449; syphilis in, 181; slavery in, 408. *See also* Honduras; Nicaragua

Channing, William Ellery, 344

Charles II, King of England, 48

Charleston, S.C.: drainage system in, 64, 65–66, 112, 517–18; artesian well system in, 64 *n*, 69, 184, 564 *n*; orphanage in, 66–67; political climate in, 67, 73; water supplies of, 69–71; synagogue in, 71–72; 1860 Democratic convention meets in, 415–18 *passim*; ER presents Brown pike to, 439; reaction to Lincoln's election in, 488, 489; ER addresses public meeting in, 496–97; popular demonstrations in, 497, 498, 512–13; secession convention meets in, 511–15 *passim*; pre-Sumter atmosphere in, 560, 576–83 *passim*; post-Sumter excitement in, 609

Charleston *Courier*, 72, 606

Charleston Harbor: ER seeks data on forts in, 438, 439, 445; feasibility of attacking forts in, 490; controversy over forts in, 514, 517, 521, 522; ER tours forts in, 531–33, 561,

562, 566–67, 573–74. *See also* Fort Johnson; Fort Moultrie; Fort Sumter; Morris Island; Sullivan's Island

Charleston *Mercury*: as outlet for political writings of ER, 65, 66, 225, 229, 230, 236, 240, 409, 410, 459, 466, 470, 474, 480, 485 *n*; prints "Cassandra—Warnings," 319, 326, 627 *n*; ER attacks Wises in, 328, 331, 404, 414; serializes *Anticipations of the Future*, 415, 416, 425, 437, 438, 439; Washington correspondent of, 431; runs ER's articles as editorials, 477 and *n*, 478 and *n*; prints ER's Charleston speech, 497

Charlestown, Va.: volunteers ordered to, 359, 360; ER recounts activities in, 362–71; John Brown executed in, 369–71

Chase, Salmon P., 160, 421, 563

Chase, William H., 528

Chesnut, James, 448 and *n*, 483, 485, 491

Chester District, S.C., 77

Cheves, Langdon, 339, 492, 532

China: ER favors European conquest of, 29, 96; U.S.S. *Minnesota* sails for, 86; civil war in, 181; European relations with, 226, 343

Chinese sorghum cane, 74, 76–77, 104, 107–108

Chowan County, N.C., 57–58

Cincinnati, Ohio, 164, 181, 468, 469

Citadel, The: cadets of, salute ER, 499; cadets of, man batteries at Fort Morris, 532, 533; ER views drill of cadets at, 561, 562, 579; ER borrows musket from, 581

City Point, Va., 354

Clark, George Rogers, 162

Clark, William H., 429

Clay, Clement C.: opposes subsidy for Colonization Society, 282, 284, 292; and John Brown pikes, 383, 392, 431, 438; mentioned, 150, 378, 379, 384

Clay, Henry, 126, 130, 232, 267

Clemson, Thomas Green, 265 and *n*

Clingman, Thomas L., 146, 474, 609

Cloud, Noah B., 184, 186, 220

Coates, Benjamin, 277, 283, 307

Cobb, Howell, 38, 214, 510

Cobb, Thomas R. R., 237

# Index

Lynch, Patrick N., 484 and *n*
Lynch, William Francis, 253 and *n*
Lyndhurst, Lord, 323
Lyon, Francis S., 330 and *n*
Lyons, James, 318–19, 453 and *n*

McAliley, Samuel, 424 and *n*
Macaulay, Thomas B., 420
McCauley, Charles Stewart, 609 and *n*
McCord, David James, 492 and *n*
McCulloch, Benjamin, 431 and *n*
McDonald, Charles J., 383 and *n*
McGee, Ga. state senator, 501
Mackay, Charles, 335 and *n*
Mackenzie, Alexander S., 620
Mackintosh, Joseph, 332–33, 453
McQueen, John, 256 and *n*, 376, 378, 384
McRae, Duncan, 101, 606 and *n*
McWillie, William, 448
Madison, James, 442
Magoffin, Beriah, 465, 466 and *n*
Magrath, Andrew G., 485 and *n*, 489, 566, 570
Malthus, Thomas, 308, 445
Mann, Ambrose Dudley, 34 and *n*, 35, 40, 84, 146, 148
Manning, John Lawrence: identified, 68 *n*; opposes reopening of African slave trade, 325, 332; at S.C. Secession Convention, 512; mentioned, 68, 73, 330, 608
Marengo County, Ala., 193, 201, 425
Marion Artillery (Charleston): ER elected honorary member of, 585; in Sumter engagement, 588–90 *passim*
Marl: on Cape Fear River, N.C., 52; in Alabama, 190–93 *passim*, 201; on Cooper River, S.C., 564
Marlbourne plantation: ownership of, 5–6, 345, 346, 347, 358, 359–60; drainage system on, 47, 62, 80, 81, 95, 99, 118, 171–73; increased productivity of, 86–88; arson on, 111–12, 169–70, 249–50; corn production on, 152, 169; illness of slaves on, 204, 215, 216, 219; analysis of soil on, 226; christening of slaves on, 284
Marshall, John, 161
Martin, William E., 438, 439, 445, 487, 499

Maryland: ER denounces governor of, 294; free Negroes in, 327; prospects for secession of, 384, 432, 478, 491, 492, 509, 530, 540, 541, 545, 555; and 1860 Democratic conventions, 437; scenery in, 469; Lincoln's flight through, 555, 558; slave population in, 631 *n*
Mason, George, 162
Mason, James M.: on Kans. question, 149; franks political pamphlets for ER, 180, 181; delivers Senate speech on Harpers Ferry incident, 380; on political crisis of 1860, p. 429; reports secession of Va., 607; mentioned, 37, 150, 158, 265
Mason, John Young, 347 and *n*, 348
Maury, Matthew Fontaine: praised by ER, 36, 148; biographical sketch of, 36 *n*; writings of, 439, 467; mentioned, 90, 146, 174, 236, 258
Maxwell, George Troup, 527 and *n*
Maxwell, William (president of Hampden Sydney College), 29
Maxwell, William Hamilton (Irish novelist), 172 and *n*
Mayo, Joseph, Jr., 233
Meade, William, 120, 121, 278
Means, John H., 423, 424, 561, 566, 574
Mecklenburg County, N.C., 505
Melville, Herman, 133
Memminger, Christopher G., 391–94, 400, 401, 515
Memphis, Tenn., 606
Merriam, Francis J., 410
Methodist Church, 338–39
Mexican War, 106, 107
Mexico: mixed population of, 176; Pratt discusses conditions in, 180–81; civil war in, 182, 464–65; ER favors transcontinental railroad across, 272; ancient civilization in, 282; ER fears war with, 411, 412
Middleton, John Izard, 423 and *n*, 427, 433, 434, 435, 575
Mill, John Stuart, 308–309
Milledgeville, Ga.: poor accommodations in, 500; ER confers with state officials in, 500–502
Miller, Hugh, 316 and *n*, 317–18
Millson, John S., 214 and *n*
Minge, George, 194, 340

## Index

troversy over Charleston forts, 517, 529, 533, 539, 574–75; on Va. politics during secession crisis, 536, 540–45 *passim*, 548, 580; on Peace Congress, 543–58 *passim*; on prospect of foreign intervention, 546; on Va. Secession Convention, 550, 551, 555, 559, 569, 578, 602; on intentions of Lincoln, 553, 555, 560, 578, 583, 584, 633; on security of southern whites against violence from blacks, 556–57; on Sumter crisis, 560, 566, 579–86; on Confederate tariff policy, 570; denounces Republicans, 572; on U.S. naval squadron off Charleston, 604–605; counsels Tyler upon accession to presidency, 614–17; on banking and currency, 619
—*Travels and observations*: visits Tyler, 122–33, 617–20; attends Montgomery Commercial Convention, 183, 186–88; recounts meeting with Walker, 189; tours Albemarle and Chesapeake Canal, 210–13; describes scene at Harpers Ferry, 361–62; describes events in Charlestown, Va., 362–71; witnesses execution of John Brown, 369–71; attends 1860 Va. Democratic convention, 401–402; attends 1860 S.C. Democratic convention, 424–25; views 1860 National Democratic Convention in Baltimore, 434, 436–37; visits Ky., 455–68; confers with Ga. political leaders, 500–502; gratified by reception in S.C., 505, 602; attends S.C. Secession Convention, 511–12, 515; attends Fla. Secession Convention, 525–28; tours forts in Charleston Harbor, 531–33, 561, 562, 566–67, 573–74; exiles self from Va., 557, 607–608; describes pre-Sumter atmosphere in Charleston, 560, 576–85 *passim*; describes bombardment of Sumter, 587–97; visits Sumter after surrender, 600–601
Ruffin, Edmund, Jr.: becomes co-owner of Marlbourne, 6; submits report on fence law, 116; attends 1858 Va. Democratic convention, 252; and romance with Jane Ruffin, 277, 426–27, 452, 453, 470, 471, 476, 535, 571; vacations at Virginia

Springs, 337–40, 448–51; captains volunteer troops of cavalry, 396, 399, 410, 421, 482; political views of, 399, 401 *n*, 482; vacations at Old Point Comfort, 441–42; views *Great Eastern*, 446; describes Prince of Wales, 472; as candidate for Va. Secession Convention, 534–38 *passim*, 542–44
Ruffin, Ella (daughter of ER), 8, 78, 216, 231
Ruffin, Frank G.: and death of wife, 95; as member of executive committee of Va. State Agricultural Society, 134, 242, 275; distributes secession pamphlets, 483; mentioned, 63, 86, 258, 293, 305, 310, 329, 347, 442
Ruffin, Jane M. (daughter of Judge Ruffin): ER's affection for, 197, 422; romance between Edmund, Jr., and, 277, 426–27, 453; Edmund, Jr.'s courtship of, 452, 470, 471, 476, 535, 571; mentioned, 53, 442, 448, 452
Ruffin, Julian C. (son of ER): and management of Marlbourne, 5, 6; estranged from William Sayre, 391; on secession crisis, 482
Ruffin, Lotty Meade (wife of Julian), 303
Ruffin, Mary (daughter-in-law of ER): illness of, 18, 62, 78, 81, 82, 88, 92, 93; death and funeral of, 94–95; ER mourns absence of, 109
Ruffin, Nanny (granddaughter of ER): confirmed by Bishop Meade, 120; health of, 218, 226, 227; attends Episcopal conventions, 303, 346; accompanies ER to Virginia Springs, 329–40, 448–53; vacations at Old Point Comfort, 441–42; accompanies ER to Ky., 454–70; and father's second marriage, 452
Ruffin, Patty (daughter of Judge Ruffin), 53, 197, 414, 422
Ruffin, P. B. (son of Judge Ruffin), 108, 114
Ruffin, R. Brown, 53, 318, 422
Ruffin, Rebecca (daughter of ER), 8
Ruffin, Sterling (son of Judge Ruffin): favors secession, 572
Ruffin, Thomas (judge); biographical sketch of, 53 *n*; lauded by ER, 53–54; recalls youth of Winfield Scott,

# Index

Smith, William N. H. (M.C., N.C.), 397

Smithsonian Institution, 172, 265

*Somers*, U.S.S.: mutiny on, 620 *n*

*South, The*: commences publication, 48; advocates legalization of African slave trade, 67; as outlet for ER's political writings, 160, 164, 199, 200, 206, 207, 621 *n*; prints Willoughby Newton's disunion speech, 215; attacks League of United Southerners, 220–21, 223; boycotted by ER, 225; amalgamated with *The States*, 247

South Carolina: agricultural observations by ER in, 63–64, 73–74, 77; sentiment for reopening African slave trade in, 139, 172, 325; ER cordial to persons from, 230; ER accorded rail free passage in, 319, 499, 533; sentiment for secession in, 387, 429, 430, 483–88 *passim*, 493, 495, 576; solicits Virginia's support for Southern Conference, 391–403 *passim*, 410; and 1860 Democratic conventions, 417, 429–35 *passim*, 438; unionists in, 449; prospects for secession of, 474, 477, 480–82, 486; abolitionists plot slave uprisings in, 479; legislature votes to call secession convention, 486, 487, 489, 492; ER's reception in, 505; secession convention of, 511–15; reaction to secession of, 513–15; policy toward Fort Sumter of, 524, 548; and ratification of Confederate constitution, 575–76, 578

South Carolina Association. *See* Association of 1860

South Carolina College, 486, 487

South Carolina State Agricultural Society, fair of, 494

Southern commercial conventions: at Montgomery, 186–88, 191; at Vicksburg, 301 *n*, 304

*Southern Literary Messenger*, 251, 255, 536, 579

*Southern Planter*: publishes agricultural writings by ER, 120, 122, 236, 429, 536, 537; publishes political writings by ER, 341, 346, 351, 355, 383; C. B. Williams named acting editor of, 342

*Southern Press*, 267

Southern Rights Association, 360, 361

Southey, Robert, 133 and *n*, 134, 421

Spain: Cuban policy of, 269, 290, 291; camels introduced into, 311; and relations with Dominican Republic, 577, 578

Spencer, John C., 620 and *n*

Spencer, Philip, 620 and *n*

*Spindle City Idea,* 175, 181

Spratt, Leonidas W.: defends crew of *Echo*, 285; biographical sketch of, 285 *n*; as S.C. commissioner to Fla., 524, 526; opposes Confederate ban on slave trade, 551, 575; mentioned, 451

Starke, Burwell, 403–409 *passim*

*Star of the West*, 528, 530, 532, 610

Steamboats: difficulties of travel by, 195, 510, 515

Stephens, Alexander H., 149, 501, 548

Sternberg, Baron Ungern, 608

Stevens, Aaron Dwight, 356 and *n*, 410

Stevens, Major P. F., 532, 533, 584, 588, 594

Stevenson, Andrew, 29, 30 and *n*

Stiles, Joseph C., 148

Stone, George W., 196 and *n*

Stone Mountain, Ga., 76

Stowe, Harriet Beecher, 120

Stringfellow, Thornton, 327 and *n*

Strother, David Hunter, 155, 156 and *n*, 365, 367, 368

Stuart, Alexander H. H., 393 and *n*, 400

Stuart, James, 201 and *n*, 202

Sugar. *See* Chinese sorghum cane; Imphee sorghum cane

Sullivan's Island, S.C.: ER inspects fortifications on, 514, 561, 567; floating battery behind, 562, 566; Major Anderson directs fire toward, 593. *See also* Fort Moultrie

Summer Hill plantation, 63

Summers, George William, 12, 558 and *n*

Sumner, Charles, 380

Sumterville, S.C., 495 and *n*

Surry County, Va., 538

Sykes, Jem, 86–87, 391

Syria: rebellion of Druses in, 481

Talbot, Theodore: mission to Charleston of, 582, 583, 585, 598, 603

denounces, 294–95, 329–33 *passim*, 362, 372, 396, 398, 399, 404, 405, 414; orders troops to Charlestown, 360; ER lauds Harpers Ferry message of, 385; popularity increased by Harpers Ferry affair, 396, 398, 401; favors southern conference, 400; ER compares with Botts, 405–406; moves toward secession, 491–92; reports Va. secession imminent, 605; requests S.C. volunteers, 606; mentioned, 123, 136, 151, 230, 310, 341, 558–59

Wise, O. Jennings: and fight with Ridgway, 151; opposes nomination of Letcher for governor, 252; and duel with Old, 329, 333; ER terms bully, 330, 333; mentioned, 375, 447

Witcher, Vincent, 10

Withers, Thomas Jefferson, 230 and *n*

Wood, Fernando, 83 *n*, 124

Woodford County, Ky., 467

Wragg, Dr., of Charleston, S.C., 65–66

Wray, Leonard: supervises operations on Hammond plantations, 74, 103–105, 119; on decline of Jamaica, 75; addresses U.S. Agricultural Society, 146; mentioned, 145

Yancey, William Lowndes: at Montgomery Commercial Convention, 185–89 *passim*; and League of United Southerners, 195–96, 200, 220–21, 228, 444; attends 1860 Democratic convention in Richmond, 428; reserved toward ER, 431; N.Y. speech of, 476; urged by ER to rouse South, 479, 634–35; mentioned, 205, 219

Yeadon, Richard, 72–73, 162, 184, 484, 485

Young, Brigham: and Mormon rebellion in Utah, 133 *n*, 140, 160, 198, 200, 249